Communications
in Computer and Information Science

1714

More information about this series at https://link.springer.com/bookseries/7899

Lin Zhang · Wensheng Yu · Haijun Jiang · Yuanjun Laili (Eds.)

Intelligent Networked Things

5th China Conference, CINT 2022
Urumqi, China, August 7–8, 2022
Revised Selected Papers

Editors
Lin Zhang
Beihang University
Beijing, China

Haijun Jiang
Xinjiang University
Xinjiang, China

Wensheng Yu
Beijing University of Posts
and Telecommunications
Beijing, China

Yuanjun Laili
Beihang University
Beijing, China

ISSN 1865-0929   ISSN 1865-0937 (electronic)
Communications in Computer and Information Science
ISBN 978-981-19-8914-8   ISBN 978-981-19-8915-5 (eBook)
https://doi.org/10.1007/978-981-19-8915-5

This Springer imprint is published by the registered company Springer Nature Singapore Pte Ltd.
The registered company address is: 152 Beach Road, #21-01/04 Gateway East, Singapore 189721, Singapore

Preface

This volume contains the papers from the 5th Conference on Intelligent Networked Things (CINT 2022). The conference was sponsored by the Committee of Intelligent Networked Things, China Simulation Federation (CSF CINT). It was organized by Xinjiang University and CSF CINT and co-organized by Peking University, Beihang University, the University of Science and Technology of China, the China People's Liberation Army National Defense University, Beijing University of Posts and Telecommunications, the University of Science and Technology Beijing, and the Institute of Automation, Chinese Academy of Sciences. The CSF CINT devotes to providing an opportunity for academic exchange among experts, scholars, students, and engineers in the field of intelligent Internet-of-Things (IoT) systems and Modeling & Simulation (M&S). It aims at promoting the research and application of state-of-the-art intelligent IoT theories, M&S methods, and related technologies.

CINT 2022 was held online on August 7–8, 2022. The conference invited leading experts in the field of intelligent IoT systems and M&S to make keynote speeches. Extensive academic seminars about popular topics and technologies were also included. From the perception of heterogenous devices to the intelligent collaboration of multidisciplinary knowledge and services, there are thousands of studies out there tackling multiple areas of interest, through various channels of communication. CINT 2022 tried to cluster some of the latest trends in these areas. The audience from industry to academia gave us the opportunity to achieve a good level of understanding of the mutual needs, requirements, and technical means available in this field of research.

The main topics of this conference include the following fields: the architecture of IoT, smart sensors, information fusion of multiple sensors, virtual reality and augmented reality, wearable devices, big data and artificial intelligence for IoT, cyber-physical system, high performance computing and simulation for IoT, embedded control systems, model-based system engineering, intelligent control and intelligent robotics, resource sharing and collaboration in IoT, multi-agent systems, intelligent optimization method for IoT management, intelligent manufacturing system, intelligent transportation systems, smart grids, networked control systems, intelligent information processing, smart homes, and so on.

The proceedings editors wish to thank the Advisory Committee of CINT 2022, Prof. Bohu Li from the Chinese Academy of Engineering, Prof. Huashu Qin from the Chinese Academy of Sciences, Prof. Long Wang from Peking University, and all authors, reviewers and committee chairs for their contributions. We also thank Springer for their trust and for publishing the proceedings of CINT 2022.

December 2022

Lin Zhang
Wensheng Yu
Haijun Jiang
Yuanjun Laili

Organization

Conference Chairs

Lin Zhang	Beihang University, China
Haijun Jiang	Xinjiang University, China

Scientific Committee

Wensheng Yu	Beijing University of Posts and Telecommunications, China
Yingmian Wu	Beijing Information Science and Technology University, China
Zhijian Ji	Qingdao University, China
Lei Ren	Beihang University, China
Feng Xiao	North China Electric Power University, China
Jinling Liang	Southeast University, China
Rongmin Cao	Beijing Information Science and Technology University, China
Xiaoyuan He	China People's Liberation Army National Defence University, China
Jiahu Qin	University of Science and Technology of China, China
Kehu Yang	China University of Mining & Technology, Beijing, China
Qiang Guan	Institute of Automation, Chinese Academy of Sciences, China

Organizing Committee

Yuanjun Laili	Beihang University, China
Yongnan Jia	University of Science and Technology Beijing, China
Zhiyong Yu	Xinjiang University, China
Cheng Hu	Xinjiang University, China
Fei Liu	Jiangnan University, China
Guoli Wang	Sun Yat-sen University, China
Xingwen Liu	Southwest Minzu University, China
Wendong Xiao	University of Science and Technology Beijing, China
Xinyan Feng	Xiangyang Zhongxin Electric, China

Local Committee

Jiarong Li   Xinjiang University, China
Shanshan Chen   Xinjiang University, China

Contents

Control of Intelligent Networked Things

Modeling, Simulation and Optimization of Intelligent Networked Things

Access, Perception, and Prediction in Intelligent Networked Things

Prediction of the Melt Pool Size in Single-Layer Single-Channel Selective Laser Melting Based on Neural Network

Yingyu Cao, Zhicheng Huang, Yuda Cao[✉], Kai Guo, and Lihong Qiao

Department of Industrial and Manufacturing Systems Engineering, Beihang University, Beijing 100191, China
yuda_cao@163.com

Abstract. The unstable forming quality of parts formed by selective laser melting (3LM) process has been one of the obstacles of its development and application, and the thermal process directly influences the forming quality in SLM process, such as the melt pool geometry. For the sake of studying the influence of different process parameters on the melt pool size in SLM forming process, a finite element model by ANSYS was established and single-layer single-channel temperature field imitation of the SLM 316 L stainless steel part under the combination of different laser power, scanning speed, focusing spot diameter and layer thickness was conducted in this paper. Since the neural network (NN) can fully approximate the complex nonlinear relationship, the melt pool size obtained by simulation is used as the training samples, and the NN model is trained to establish the mapping relation model between the SLM process parameters and the melt pool size, which provides the reference for the SLM process parameter optimization. The experimental results indicate that the deviation between the predicted results and the measured results is less, which indicates that the model has high prediction accuracy. A good mapping relation between the studied process parameters and the melt pool size is established.

Keywords: Selective laser melting · Melt pool size · Finite element modelling · Neural network predictive model

1 Introduction

Unlike the traditional machining process, Additive Manufacturing (AM) produces parts by the layer-upon-layer method, which is almost unrestricted by the complexity of the part model. Selective Laser Melting (SLM) is a kind of essential technology in AM, which applies a high-energy laser beam as an energy source and can directly form metal parts with high density and good mechanical properties [1]. Therefore, SLM has outstanding technical advantages in aerospace, biomedical, automobile and mold making applications.

However, SLM has a complex, dynamic and non-equilibrium forming process [2], which leads to many part quality issues. When the high-energy laser beam scans the

© The Author(s), under exclusive license to Springer Nature Singapore Pte Ltd. 2022
L. Zhang et al. (Eds.): CINT 2022, CCIS 1714, pp. 3–14, 2022.
https://doi.org/10.1007/978-981-19-8915-5_1

powder bed at a high speed, the selected metal powder melts instantaneously and shapes a micro melt pool, then rapidly cools and solidifies. This process results in considerable temperature variation within milliseconds, which is easy to cause the unstable structure of the melt pool and affects the temperature field spread. Therefore, balling, porosity, cracks and other quality defects easily occur in the forming process and hinder the further development and application of SLM. The process parameters are the main factors affecting the melt pool size. Therefore, exploring the impact of different process parameters on the melt pool size in SLM forming process is unusual meaningful to improve the quality stability of parts.

Due to the small size and terse reaction time of the melt pool in the forming process, it is difficult to observe the melt pool directly. Numerical simulation of the melt pool shape and dimensions using finite element analysis software is an effective research method.

Erdem et al.[3] established a 3D thermal model based on an adjustable finite element to simulate the thermal spread and melt pool geometry during the SLM manufacturing process, and verified its effectiveness through experiments on Inconel 625 alloy. Combined with finite element simulation and experiments, Song et al.[4] systematically studied the effects of laser power and scanning speed on the melt pool size in the process of SLM forming GH3536 alloy and concluded that the line energy density and melt pool size exhibit linear growth relationships in the range of the study parameters. Peng [5] established the finite element model of SLM TI-6Al-4V alloy parts. The results indicated that the melt pool size and the time in liquid phase would increase along with the raise of laser power and the reduce of scanning speed. Moreover, the larger hatch spacing would weaken the heat accumulation and reduce the remelting phenomenon.

However, the numerical simulation based on physical model still has certain limitations, and it is difficult to efficiently obtain the prediction of melt pool size in SLM process [6]. Neural Network (NN) is a complicated network system consisting of generous of simple processing units that are diffusely connected. NN can establish a complex and highly nonlinear relationship model between input and output features. It has strong evaluation and prediction ability, which can effectively realize SLM process parameter optimization. Its strong evaluation and prediction ability can effectively realize the SLM process parameter optimization.

Amir et al. [7] put forward a prediction model for the tensile strength of SLM TI-6Al-4V alloy parts using multilayer perceptron (MLP) and analyzed the impact of laser power, scanning speed and hatch spacing on the results. Yang et al. [8] used SLM to form 18Ni300 alloy parts and used NN to analyze and predict the importance of process parameters and mechanical behaviour. The results indicated that the order of importance were listed as: laser power, scanning speed, and hatch spacing. The error between the predicted value of tensile strength and the actual value was less.

In the present work, the single-layer single-channel transient temperature model of SLM 316 L stainless steel parts is established by ANSYS. The geometric size of the melt pool under the combination of different laser power, scanning speed, focusing spot diameter and layer thickness is studied, including melt pool length, width and depth. Based on the simulation results, the NN prediction model of melt pool size is established, which can provide a reference for SLM process parameter optimization and improve the stability of the melt pool size in SLM forming process.

2 Finite Element Simulation of SLM Single-Layer Single-Channel Melt Pool Forming Process

The SLM process has many influencing factors, and the thermophysical mechanism is very complex. Basic assumptions are usually presented in numerical simulation to simplify the model, and some secondary factors are ignored. The model established in this study follows the following assumptions:

- The substrate and the metal powder bed are isotropic continuous uniform medium.
- The metal fluid in the melt pool is laminar and incompressible Newtonian fluid.
- The vaporization reaction and flow effect of melt pool are ignored.
- The influence of laser pressure on melt pool surface is ignored and the free surface of the forming area is planar.
- The powder bed and substrate exchange energy in the form of natural convection.
- In SLM forming process, the laser beam is perpendicular to the processing area and its performance remains stable.
- Except thermal conductivity, specific heat capacity, and other thermal physical parameters of metal materials are independent of temperature.

2.1 Governing Equations and Boundary Conditions

The heat transfer process of SLM follows the Fourier Heat Conduction Theory [9]:

$$k(\frac{\partial^2 T}{\partial x^2} + \frac{\partial^2 T}{\partial y^2} + \frac{\partial^2 T}{\partial z^2}) + Q_0 = \rho C \frac{\partial T}{\partial t} \tag{1}$$

where k is the thermal conductivity; T is the temperature of metal powder; t is the action time of laser on powder bed; Q_0 is the internal heat; ρ is the density; C is the specific heat capacity.

Three forms of heat exchange, namely heat conduction, convection and radiation, always occur in SLM forming process. The initial and boundary conditions are as shown [10]:

$$T(x, y, z, 0) = T_0 \tag{2}$$

$$k\frac{\partial T}{\partial n} + \varepsilon\sigma(T^4 - T_0^4) + h_c(T - T_0) - q = 0 \tag{3}$$

where T_0 is the ambient temperature, set to 295 K; n is the normals of the model surfaces; ε is the emissivity of thermal radiation; σ is Stefan-Boltzmann constant; h_c is the natural convective heat transfer coefficient; q is the heat input of laser to the model.

In SLM process, the metal powder continues to undergo phase transition cycles of melting and solidification under the laser heat source. The role of latent heat of phase transformation cannot be ignored. In this study, the equivalent specific heat capacity method is adopted to solve the latent heat of phase transformation in simulation calculation, and the expression is as follow:

$$C_e = C + \frac{L}{T_L - T_S} \tag{4}$$

where C is the specific heat capacity in the liquid phase; L is the latent heat value; T_L is the liquidus temperature; T_S is the solidus temperature.

2.2 Moving Gauss Heat Source

In SLM process, it is assumed that the laser energy is subject to Gaussian distribution, and the effect of laser beam in the depth direction should be considered, so the Gauss heat source model with exponential attenuation in height is selected [11]:

$$q(x, y, z, t) = \frac{2AP}{\eta \pi r^2} \exp(-2\frac{(x - vt)^2 + y^2}{r^2}) \exp(-\frac{|z|}{\delta}) \tag{5}$$

where A is the absorption rate of metal powder to laser; P is laser power; r is focusing spot radius; δ is the laser penetration depth, set to the layer thickness.

2.3 Finite Element Model

Figure 1 shows the single-layer single-channel finite element model of SLM 316 L stainless steel parts in ANSYS Workbench.

In order to conform to the actual forming process, the size of the substrate is greater than that of the powder bed. The dimensions of substrate are 1.70 mm × 1.00 mm × 0.60 mm. And based on the different layer thickness, the dimensions of powder bed are 1.5 mm × 0.10 mm × 0.03 mm or 1.5 mm × 0.10 mm × 0.04 mm. The process of metal powder melting and forming in SLM process is simulated using birth-and-death method.

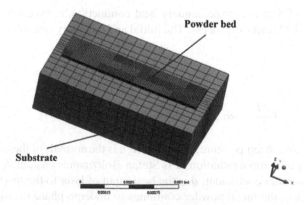

Fig. 1. The finite element model.

2.4 Experiment Design and Simulation Calculation

There are many process parameters that affect the quality of SLM parts. Laser power, scanning speed, focusing spot diameter and layer thickness all have significant influence [12]. In this study, laser power, scanning speed, focusing spot diameter and layer thickness are selected as the main process parameters, and various values are set for simulation. According to the simulation results, the size data of melt pool, namely the melt pool length, width and depth is obtained, as shown in Fig. 2. The laser power P is set to 100–450 W, the scanning speed v is set to 600–1200 mm/s, the focusing spot diameter d is set to 70 or 100 μm, and the layer thickness δ is set to 40 or 30 μm. The specific values of each parameter are indicated in Table 1.

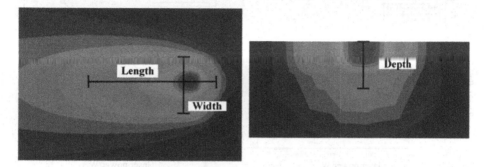

Fig. 2. Melt pool size.

Table 1. The value of SLM process parameters.

	Laser power (W)	Scanning speed (mm·s^{-1})	Focusing spot diameter (μm)	Layer thickness (μm)
1	100	600	70	30
2	150	700	100	40
3	200	800		
4	250	900		
5	300	1000		
6	350	1100		
7	400	1200		
8	450			

Because of the number of values set by laser power and scanning speed, it is not suitable to adopt an all-factor experiment or orthogonal experiment. Therefore, the laser power of 150 W, 250 W, 350 W and 450 W, scanning speed of 600 mm/s, 800 mm/s, 1000 mm/s, and 1200 mm/s follow the orthogonal array L16, and the remaining values are adopted all-factor experiment. A total of 64 groups of sample data are obtained.

According to the process parameters and the melt pool dimensions obtained, the variation of the melt pool length, width and depth with laser power and scanning speed is generated. Figure 3 and Fig. 4 show that within the range of parameters, the melt pool length, width and depth generally increase with the raise of laser power or the reduce of scanning speed. The main reason is that increasing the laser power will bring more energy, and reducing the scanning speed will make the laser beam stay in the forming area longer, both of which will increase the maximum temperature. With the increase in maximum temperature, the melting time is lengthened, and the ability of powder particles to transfer energy becomes more robust, eventually leading to a larger melting area.

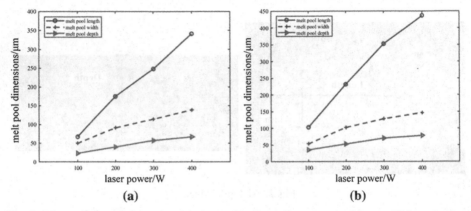

Fig. 3. The variation of the melt pool size under diverse laser power: (a) $v = 700$ mm/s, $d = 70$ μm, $\delta = 30$ μm; (b) $v = 700$ mm/s, $d = 70$ μm, $\delta = 40$ μm.

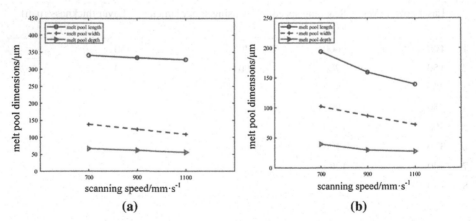

Fig. 4. The variation of the melt pool size under different scanning speed: (a) $P = 400$W, $d = 70$ μm, $\delta = 30$ μm; (b) $P = 200$ W, $d = 100$ μm, $\delta = 30$ μm.

3 Neural Network Prediction Model for Process Parameters and Melt Pool Size

3.1 Establishment of Neural Network Prediction Model

BP neural network is a feedforward NN trained on the basis of the error back propagation algorithm [13]. It has strong nonlinear mapping ability and fault tolerance, and is one of the most extensively applied NN models [14]. BP neural network contains input layer, hidden layer and output layer. The relevance between layers is established by weights and thresholds [15]. When the signal propagates forward, the original data is imported to the input layer, and then handled through each hidden layer. Finally, the calculated values are output by the output layer. If the error between the actual output value and the anticipated output value exceeds the set range and the number of iterations does not exceed the maximum, the error signal is transmitted back to the input layer through the hidden layer to obtain the error learning signal of each layer. Then the weights of neurons in each layer are modified based on the gradient descent method. The specific flow of BP neural network is shown in Fig. 5.

In this study, the NN prediction model is composed of four layers and its structure is 4-6-5-3, as shown in Fig. 6. The input layer contains 4 neurons: laser power, scanning speed, focusing spot diameter, and layer thickness. The first and second hidden layers contain 6 and 5 neurons. The output layer has 3 neurons: melt pool length, melt pool width, and melt pool depth. The network learning rate is 0.01, the maximum number of

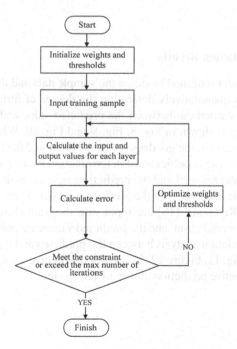

Fig. 5. The flow process of BP neural network algorithm.

iterations is 400, and the convergence error is 0.05. The activation function is set to the Relu function. In the 64 groups of sample data, 44 groups are selected as the training set, 10 as the test set, and 10 as the validation set for the prediction model.

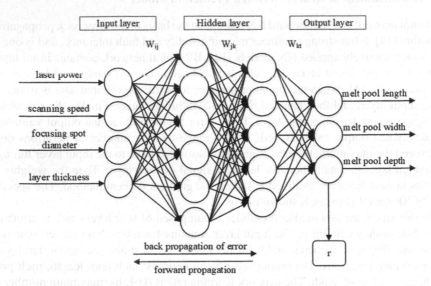

Fig. 6. The structure of BP neural network.

3.2 Analysis of Prediction Results

The NN prediction model is trained based on the sample data and the training loss value is shown in Fig. 7. To quantitatively determine the degree of fitting of the model, the correlation analysis is carried out between the predicted value and the measured value of each melt pool size, as shown in Fig. 8, Fig. 9 and Fig. 10. When the coefficient of determination R is closer to 1, the goodness of fit is higher and the fitting effect is better. As shown in the figures, each coefficient of determination is more significant than 0.95, indicating that the model fits well and the prediction error is small.

To further verify the availability of the prediction model, 5 groups of process parameter combinations in Reference [16] are input into the trained model as independent verification samples for prediction, and the predicted values are compared with the measured values. The correlation analysis between the predicted and the measured values of samples is shown in Fig. 11. Figure 12 shows that the relative errors are all within 20%, which verifies the effective prediction ability of the model.

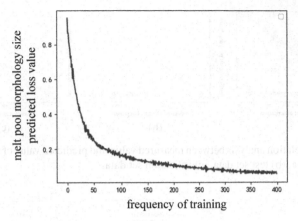

Fig. 7. The BP neural network training loss value.

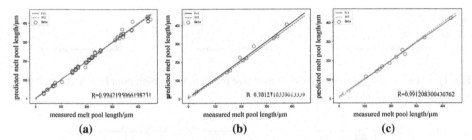

Fig. 8. The correlation analysis between measured value and predicted value of melt pool length: (a) training set data, (b) test set data, (c) validation set data.

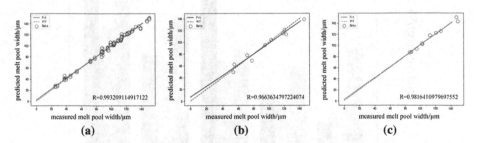

Fig. 9. The correlation analysis between measured value and predicted value of melt pool width: (a) training set data, (b) test set data, (c) validation set data.

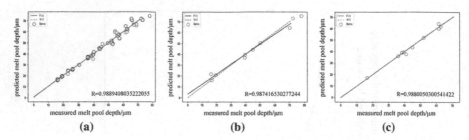

Fig. 10. The correlation analysis between measured value and predicted value of melt pool depth: (a) training set data, (b) test set data, (c) validation set data.

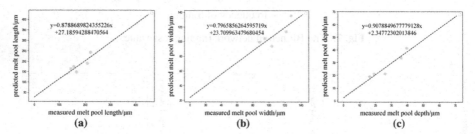

Fig. 11. The correlation analysis of melt pool size prediction: (a) melt pool length, (b) melt pool width, (c) melt pool depth.

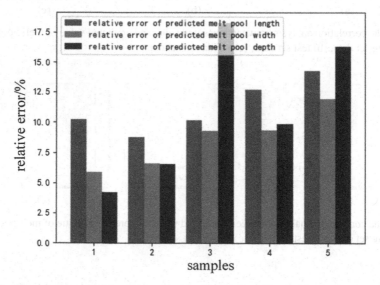

Fig. 12. The relative error between measured values and predicted values of melt pool size.

4 Conclusions

The finite element method is selected to simulate the melt pool size of 316 L stainless steel in the single-layer single-channel SLM process under different process parameters, and based on the simulation results, the prediction model of melt pool size is constructed by using BP neural network. The main conclusions are as follows:

- The melt pool size and temperature spread in SLM are closely related to laser power, scanning speed, focusing spot diameter, and layer thickness. In the range of 100–400 W laser power and 700–1000 mm/s scanning speed, the melt pool length, width and depth generally increase when the laser power increases or the scanning speed decreases.
- Using laser power, scanning speed, focusing spot diameter and layer thickness as input characteristics, the BP neural network model is established to predict and analyze the melt pool size in SLM forming process. The error between the predicted value and the measured value is small, and each coefficient of determination is more significant than 0.95. The relative error of independent verification samples are all within the range of 20%, which verifies the model's effectiveness. The results show that the prediction model has high prediction accuracy, the overall prediction effect is ideal, and a good mapping relationship is established between the studied process parameters and the melt pool size in SLM. An extended training set can be used for subsequent training, which can further improve the prediction model's accuracy and extend the model's applicable process range.

Acknowledgments. This work is supported by the National Natural Science Foundation (NNSF) of China (Grant 52005021).

References

1. Gong, G., Ye, J., Chi, Y., et al.: Research status of laser additive manufacturing for metal: a review. J. Market. Res. **15**, 855–884 (2021)
2. Cao, L., Zhou, Q., Han, Y., et al.: Review on intelligent monitoring of defects and process control of selective laser melting additive manufacturing. Acta Aeronautica ET Astronautica Sinica **42**(10), 199–233 (2021)
3. Kundakcıoğlu, E., Lazoglu, I., Poyraz, Ö., Yasa, E., Cizicioğlu, N.: Thermal and molten pool model in selective laser melting process of Inconel 625. Int. J. Adv. Manuf. Technol. **95**(9–12), 3977–3984 (2018). https://doi.org/10.1007/s00170-017-1489-1
4. Song, J., Wu, W., He, B., et al.: Effect of processing parameters on the size of molten pool in GH3536 alloy during selective laser melting. IOP Conf. Ser. Mater. Sci. Eng. **423**(1), 1 (2018)
5. Peng, G.: Numerical simulation on temperature field and stress field during selective laser melting of Titanium alloy. Huazhong University of Science and Technology, Wuhan, Hubei (2018)
6. Guo, S., Agarwal, M., Cooper, C., et al.: Machine learning for metal additive manufacturing: towards a physics-informed data-driven paradigm. J. Manuf. Syst. **62**, 145–163 (2022)

7. Khorasani, A.M., Gibson, I., Ghaderi, A., Mohammed, M.I.: Investigation on the effect of heat treatment and process parameters on the tensile behaviour of SLM Ti-6Al-4V parts. Int. J. Adv. Manuf. Technol. **101**(9–12), 3183–3197 (2018). https://doi.org/10.1007/s00170-018-3162-8

8. Yang, T., Zhang, P., Yin, Y., et al.: Microstructure based on selective laser melting and mechanical properties prediction through artificial neural net. Trans. China Weld. Inst. **40**(06), 100–106 (2019)

9. Li, Y., Zhou, K., Tan, P., et al.: Modeling temperature and residual stress fields in selective laser melting. Int. J. Mech. Sci. **136**, 24–35 (2018)

10. Xiao, D., He, K., Wang, D., et al.: Transient temperature evolution of Selective Laser Melting process based on multilayer finite element model. Infrared Laser Eng. **44**(9), 2672–2678 (2015)

11. Yin, J., et al.: A finite element model of thermal evolution in laser micro sintering. Int. J. Adv. Manuf. Technol. **83**(9–12), 1847–1859 (2015). https://doi.org/10.1007/s00170-015-7609-x

12. Mugwagwa, L., Dimitrov, D., Matope, S., et al.: Influence of process parameters on residual stress related distortions in selective laser melting. Procedia Manuf. **21**, 92–99 (2018)

13. Mu, W., Chen, X., Zhang, Y., et al.: Surface morphology analysis and roughness prediction of 316 L stainless steel by selective laser melting. Laser Optoelectron. Prog. **59**(07), 255–262 (2022)

14. Jing, Y., Li, J., Shi, W., et al.: Prediction of residual stress in selective laser melting based on neural network. High Power Laser Part. Beams **33**(10), 144–151 (2021)

15. Akbari, M., Saedodin, S., Panjehpour, A., et al.: Numerical simulation and designing artificial neural network for estimating melt pool geometry and temperature distribution in laser welding of Ti6Al4V alloy. Optik – Int. J. Light Electron Opt. **127**(23), 11161–11172 (2016)

16. He, K., Zhou, L., Yang, L.: A study of selective laser melting 316 L stainless steel: the temperature field simulation. Microstructure and Mechanical Properties, Laser & Optoelectronics Progress, pp. 1–18 (2019). http://kns.cnki.net/kcms/detail/31.1690.TN.20190923.1406.018.html

Implementation of Underwater Vehicle Pipeline Inspection Based on Machine Vision

Yujian Li[1,2], Ying Liu[1], Qianyi Wan[1], Lei Bi[3], and Xinyan Yin[1(✉)]

[1] Beijing Institute of Technology, Zhuhai, People's Republic of China
xiaowen122@yeah.net
[2] Shenzhen University, Shenzhen, People's Republic of China
[3] 93199 Troops of the PLA, Harbin, People's Republic of China

Abstract. Underwater oil pipeline inspection is an important field in the application of underwater robot. In the experimental environment, different shapes of attachments are used to represent different oil leakage points. Different shapes of oil leakage points are identified by underwater robots, and alarms are given by acousto-optic signals. In this paper, a semi open frame KAPI underwater robot is used. The robot realizes visual recognition and motion control of pipeline inspection based on Raspberry Pi and STM32. In image preprocessing, the binary processing of the collected image is used to avoid the interference of ambient light and shadow on the circle and square, the denoising, smoothing and transformation are carried out before pattern recognition. And, the image is denoised by the erosion-dilation algorithm. The number of sides of the shape of the pipe attachment is obtained by polygon fitting based on Douglas-Pucker algorithm to judge the shape of the attachment. The feasibility of the method based on machine vision is verified by experiments.

Keywords: Machine vision · Underwater robot · Pipeline inspection · Polygon fitting · KAPI

1 Introduction

With the development of science and technology and the need of industrial production, more and more underwater robots appear in the market. Underwater robot, also known as submersible, especially the extreme working robot, which can dive into the water to complete some operations instead of people. The underwater robots have been widely used in marine engineering, port construction, scientific research, naval defense and other fields to complete underwater search and rescue, exploration and salvage, deep-sea resource investigation,

Supported by the Characteristic Innovation Project of Colleges and Universities in Guangdong Province (Grant 2020 KTSCX186), the Special projects in Key Areas of Guangdong Province (Grant 2021 ZDZX4050) and the Educational Science Planning Project of Guangdong Province (Grant 2021GXJK179).

L. Zhang et al. (Eds.): CINT 2022, CCIS 1714, pp. 15–24, 2022.
https://doi.org/10.1007/978-981-19-8915-5_2

submarine pipeline laying, inspection and maintenance, underwater archaeology, power station and dam detection and other works. At present, underwater robots on the market are divided into observation and detection type and operation type. The observation type is equipped with underwater camera equipment, which can carry out regular observation and inspection for specific underwater targets. According to different requirements, the operation type can also be equipped with forward-looking sonar, side scan sonar, seabed mapping, seabed profile and other equipment and various manipulators for simple underwater operations [1–4]. With the theme of the real scene and future development of underwater pipeline intelligent detection, an underwater robot that completes underwater pipeline detection according to a given task is independently designed by using intelligent technology [5–7]. Intelligent underwater robot technology is a hot field in the research of underwater autonomous vehicles [8, 9]. The design of the motion control system of underwater inspection tubing robot is to realize the underwater pipeline detection of underwater autonomous vehicles in a harsh and complex environment [10–12].

A KAPI underwater robot is used to complete the simulated underwater oil pipeline inspection and oil leak detection based on machine vision in the laboratory environment.

2   Underwater Vehicle

The underwater vehicle is driven by four adaptive propellers. As shown in Table 1, the robot consists of five parts. The core cabin is a hexahedral sealed cabin with 24 interfaces on the outside, containing the main control board, propeller drive board, power board and battery inside. The frame is the structure of the robot, and the buoyancy block adjusts the buoyancy and the center of gravity of this underwater vehicle. The four adaptive propellers adjust the attitude of the underwater vehicle. In order to improve the stability of the underwater vehicle in water, parts with high density, such as battery compartment, control cabin and counterweight block, are installed at the lower end of the main frame. And, the buoyant materials with low density are installed at the upper end of the main frame. The reduced center of gravity and the raised center of buoyancy increase the righting moment of the underwater vehicle itself.

2.1   Hardware Design

The underwater robot for pipeline inspection uses STM32 as the main control board to control the propeller and infrared obstacle avoidance sensor. And, it uses the waterproof camera to collect image information, and uses the Raspberry Pi for image processing. Finally, the connection between Raspberry Pi and the main control board carries out by serial communication. Although the body of the underwater machine is small, it has a variety of functions, and can realize the functions of automatic tracking, object recognition and alarm (see Fig. 1).

Table 1. Parameters of autonomous underwater vehicle

Part	Parameter	Value
Core cabin	Main control board	STM32F427VI
	Propeller control board	STM32F103CBT6
	Auxiliary connection board	A/B/C/E/F Board
	Power board (battery)	11.1V
Raspberry Pi	Raspberry Pi	3B+
Propeller	KAPI propeller	DC brushless motor
Frame	Size	45 * 40 * 35 cm
	Weight	3kg
Other	Communication module	433M
	Waterproof camera	Kingcent (KS2A543)

The underwater robot is mainly composed of core cabin, Raspberry Pi, propeller, camera and fixed frame. The core cabin is composed of KAPI main control board, KAPI propeller drive board, auxiliary connection board (A/B/C/E/F board), power board and battery. The MCU of Kapi main control board is STM32F427VI, and the MCU of propeller drive board is STM32F103CBT6. The motor type of KAPI propeller is DC brushless motor, which is controlled by PWM. The core cabin is directly connected with the underwater propeller, light alarm module and waterproof infrared obstacle avoidance sensor. Raspberry Pi is connected with the camera and the core cabin through serial port communication.

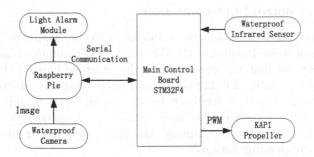

Fig. 1. Block diagram of the underwater robot

2.2 Mechanical Design

The frame of the underwater robot is used to install and protect all kinds of underwater equipments. And, the open frame structure is used to improve the stability of the body. This structure is convenient to add auxiliary equipment, and the water flow can also pass through the body smoothly. Furthermore, this structure reduces the buoyancy of the robot. As shown in Fig. 2, the mechanical structure of the underwater robot is mainly designed as a 45 * 40 * 35 cm rectangular structure. Considering that the center of gravity of the cuboid is located at the intersection of the diagonal of the vertex. The core cabin is designed at the center of gravity of the machine to increase the balance of the machine. Because of the open frame structure, buoyancy blocks made of materials with a density lower than that of water are used to make the machine float in the water. On the other hand, adding buoyancy blocks can increase the balance of the machine in the water. The propellers are installed on the tail end of the machine. The infrared sensor modules are installed at the front end, left and right sides of the machine.

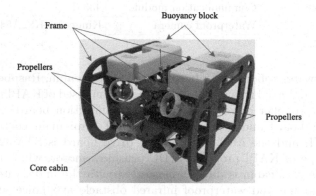

Fig. 2. Configuration of the underwater vehicle

2.3   Motion Control Implementation

The underwater robot control logic is shown as Fig. 3. Start the robot, enter the initialization state. Raspberry Pi 3B+ starts WiFi communication with the computer client, so that the operation of the machine can be shown on the PC. The lower computer, STM32 single chip microcomputer, starts to run the program. Through the data feedback by the six underwater infrared sensors connected to the underwater robot under different circumstances, through the program setting of the lower computer, the four propellers of the underwater robot make corresponding actions.

For example, No. 1 and No. 2, No. 3 and No. 4, No. 5 and No. 6 infrared sensors are symmetrically installed on the machine. The control priority gradually increases to the right, When No. 1 or No. 2 infrared sensor detects the pipeline, it sends a signal to the lower computer, which controls the action of the left or right forward propeller according to the set program, so as to correct the position offset of the machine on the pipeline. Similarly, No. 3 or No. 4 infrared sensor immediately feeds back data to the lower computer when the machine has a large offset on the pipeline, so that the propeller action can correct the offset. When the underwater robot needs to turn when it encounters a right angle bend

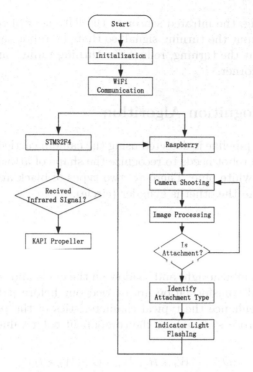

Fig. 3. Procedure flow chart

during inspection, No. 5 or No. 6 infrared sensor detects the right angle of the right pipe, and uses the opposite transformation of two forward propellers to realize the turning of the robot.

While inspecting the pipeline of the machine, the underwater robot also takes pictures of the pipeline surface. When the camera detects an attachment, the camera immediately takes pictures and retains the original image. After the attachment type is determined by analyzing the attachment data of the raspberry party on the upper computer, the corresponding LED light will flash briefly and the attachment identification information will be transmitted to the PC through WiFi, indicating that there is an attachment on the pipeline. After a round of inspection process, the camera continues to detect and identify pipeline attachments. When the underwater robot completes the one round inspection of the pipeline, the machine will automatically stop moving forward and keep the waiting state.

In the process of right angle turning in water, the turning radius is often too large, causing the robot to deviate from the water pipe. Try to modifying the program, but the problem can not be effectively solved. Then, try to change the position of the infrared sensors. The sensors are placed on both sides in the front of the robot. Finally, it can turn perfectly, realizing the function of automatic tracking. Because the position of the sensor is placed at the front end of the robot, when turning, the infrared sensor at the left end will recognize the pipe in advance and output the turning signal, so that the robot can make a turning action in advance at the turning, reduce the turning radius, and finally achieve a perfect straight corner.

3   Image Recognition Algorithm

In this project, the pipeline is detected using the camera carried by the underwater robot. And, the robot needs to recognize the shape of attachments randomly distributed on the white pipe. There are two types of black attachments, one is cube (rectangle) and the other is cylinder (circle).

3.1   Binary Processing

In image preprocessing, regional graphics inevitably have noise. In order to avoid the interference of ambient light and shadow on the circle and square, the denoising, smoothing and transformation are carried out before pattern recognition. It is necessary to enhance the typical characteristics of the pattern. Grayscale processing is the process of making the component color values of R, G and B to be equal.

$$D = \frac{1}{3}(W_r * R + W_g * G + W_b * B) \tag{1}$$

where, $W_r = 0.299$, $W_g = 0.587$, $W_b = 0.114$.

The gray value of the image is compared with the threshold value. To realize the binary processing, it is necessary to obtain the binary image from the gray image. This process enhances the whole image to show a more obvious black-and-white effect, and greatly reduce the amount of data.

Binarization thresholding, which is shown in the following formula,

$$dst(x,y) = \begin{cases} Val_{max} & if \quad src(x,y) > thresh \\ 0 & otherwise \end{cases} \tag{2}$$

where, $thresh$ indicates the threshold, $src(x,y)$ refers to the pixel gray of the original image.

3.2   Erosion and Dilation Operations

The binary image will contain noise, which can be removed by background erosion and expansion algorithm. Erosion and expansion are elementary morphological operations of gray image. The realization of erosion is based on the concept of filling structural elements. It uses a certain structural element to detect the image to find the area where the structural element can be placed in the image. And the expansion is the dual operation of erosion, which can be defined as the erosion operation on the complement of the image.

Set A is corroded by set B, expressed as $A \ominus B$. It is defined as,

$$A \ominus B = \{x : B + x \subset A\} \tag{3}$$

where A is the input image, B is the structure element.

Set A is expanded by set B, expressed as $A \oplus B$. It is defined as,

$$A \oplus B = [A^c \ominus (-B)]^c \tag{4}$$

where A^c is the complementary set of set A.

Structure element B has different types, as shown in Fig. 4. Choosing different structural element B, corroded or expanded A will have different effects.

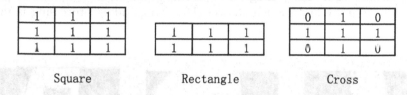

Square   Rectangle   Cross

Fig. 4. Common structure elements

Erosion operation: if all black points in the structural element are exactly the same as their corresponding large pixel points, then the point is black, otherwise it is white.

Dilation operation: as long as there is one or more black points in the structural element that are the same as its corresponding large image pixel points, the point is black, otherwise it is white.

3.3   Polygon Fitting Based on Douglas-Pucker Algorithm

The algorithm is described as follows,

*Step*1: Connect a straight line AB between the two points A and B at the beginning and end of the curve, which is the chord of the curve.

*Step*2: Calculate the distance D_i from other points in the line segment to the straight line AB.

*Step*3: Compare the distance with the preset threshold. If the maximum D_{max} of the vertical distance from these points to the straight line is less than the set threshold, all these points are rounded off. If not, turn to Step 4.

*Step*4: If the maximum distance D_{max} is greater than the set threshold, this point is retained. And the line segment is divided into two segments at this point AC and CB. Repeatedly calculate for these two segments to check whether the maximum vertical distance is greater than the set threshold. Repeat the Step 2 and Step 3.

*Step*5: Repeat this process until no extra points need to be rounded off.

Set a threshold N for the number of edges. If the number of edges (vertices) of the recognized image is greater than the threshold N, the shape is a circular(cylinder). Then, the warning light is red. On the contrary, it is a rectangular(cube), the warning light is green.

4   Experiments

After edge detection of the image captured by the underwater robot camera, some target features in the image need to be more prominent. Here, corrosion, expansion and binarization algorithms are used for operation.

For the corrosion and expansion of the binary image in this paper, the structure elements (small binary image, designed as $3 * 3$) are moved point by point on the whole image and compared, and the corresponding processing is made according to the comparison results.

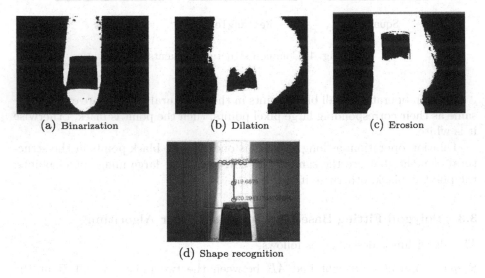

(a) Binarization   (b) Dilation   (c) Erosion

(d) Shape recognition

Fig. 5. Recognition of rectangular attachments

In this paper, infrared sensors are used as the main way of pipeline tracking. And, the information identified by infrared is fed back to the main control cabin to control the movement of the motor. The results show that in the pipeline tracking, the infrared sensor module can accurately judge and the motor can perform the corresponding action to achieve the desired effect.

In the shape recognition of attachments, the programming algorithm is mainly based on OpenCV. After a series of algorithms used for processing, the final test shows that due to the influence of the camera's own factors (the existence of halo will affect the integrity of the identified object), the recognition

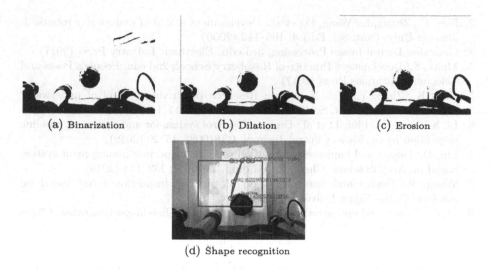

(a) Binarization   (b) Dilation   (c) Erosion

(d) Shape recognition

Fig. 6. Recognition of circle attachments

success rate is as high as 90%. So it can be considered that the object recognition can be carried out under normal circumstances

The process window of underwater robot processing the adsorbate identified by raspberry party mainly includes four windows: binarization, erosion, dilation and shape recognition, as shown in Fig. 5 and Fig. 6.

5   Conclusion

In summary, this method can obtain effective information from underwater images, and the shape information of pipe attachments can be obtained by analyzing the images. The experimental results show that the underwater pipeline inspection robot realizes the automatic inspection of underwater pipelines and the recognition of the shape of attachments on pipelines, and can realize the alarm prompt. It provides an effective method for the inspection of underwater oil pipelines. But this method is seriously affected by external light, especially the incandescent lamp causes local highlight, which leads to a serious decline in the recognition rate of attachments. The direct reason is that it affects the selection of image binarization threshold. In the future work, adaptive threshold algorithm will be used to further improve the intelligence of machine vision recognition.

References

1. Wang, X.: Brushless DC motor control system based on PWM. Nanjing University of Technology (2008)

2. Ren, F., Zhang, L., Wang, D., et al.: Development status of underwater robots. J. Jiamusi Univ. (Nat. Sci. Ed.) **4**, 105–112 (2000)
3. Gonzales: Digital Image Processing, 3rd edn. Electronic Industry Press (2017)
4. Monk, S.: Development Practice of Raspberry School, 2nd edn. People's Posts and Telecommunications Press (2017)
5. Guo, K., Zhao, Y., Yin, X., et al.: Research on driving control of underwater pipeline dredging robot. Sci. Technol. Innov. Appl. **11**(14), 42–44 (2021)
6. Li, X., Yang, D., Liui, J., et al.: Design of control system for underwater oil pipeline inspection robot. Meas. Control Technol. **038**(008), 15–20 (2019)
7. Liu, B.: Design and implementation of oil pipeline inspection management system based on ArcGIS server. Chem. Eng. Equip. **268**(05), 132–133 (2019)
8. Wang, P.: Design and implementation of pipeline inspection robot based on machine vision. Xijing University (2020)
9. Li, C.: Design and optimization of an underwater pipeline inspection robot. China Sci. Technol. Inf. **1**, 73–74 (2020)
10. Chen, S.: Research on key technologies of pipeline inspection robot vision system. China University of Mining and Technology (2019)
11. Song, L., Sun, X.: Target recognition and location detection technology of pipeline inspection robot. J. Jishou Univ. (Nat. Sci. Ed.) **42**(5), 38–43 (2021)
12. Liu, T., Qin, F., Zhu, X., et al.: Underwater autonomous robot navigation system. Ordnance Industr. Autom. **31**(11), 66–72 (2012)

Underwater Target Tracking Algorithm Based on Optical Flow

Xinyan Yin[1]($\boxtimes$), Song Wu[2], Ying Liu[1], Zihang Qin[1], Lei Bi[3], and Ruifeng Fan[4]

[1] Beijing Institute of Technology, Zhuhai, People's Republic of China
xiaowen122@yeah.net
[2] Aviation University Air Force, Harbin, People's Republic of China
[3] 93199 Troops of the PLA, Harbin, People's Republic of China
[4] Peking University, Beijing, People's Republic of China

Abstract. Because of uneven underwater light and high contrast and background noise, the underwater target detection and location need higher requirements. In this paper, the optical flow target tracking algorithm based on Kanade-Lucas-Tomasi (KLT) algorithm is implemented on OpenCV platform, and the algorithm is verified in the water pipeline intelligent inspection competition environment. Aiming at underwater target detection and location, this algorithm uses optical flow method to achieve high detection certainty and fast operation speed of image frame difference method. Using the incremental PID control, the closed-loop control of underwater vehicle underwater motion is realized with a more stable control error.

Keywords: Optical flow method · Location · Underwater robot · Lucas-Kanade optical flow

1 Introduction

With the further development of the science and technology, the application of underwater vehicle is gradually applied in the field of underwater survey, dam detection, pier detection, etc. It is difficult to keep the stability of robot in underwater environment. By studying the fish side line system, the artificial side line system is used to help the robot perceiving the surrounding water environment to improve the stability of the underwater robot in Peking University [1]. In the paper [2], a series of underwater positioning methods are summarized, such as underwater acoustic positioning system [3–5], underwater positioning system based on GPS [6], and probability positioning method [7–10]. In order to survey the target, the underwater vehicle needs to maintain stability in the water. But

Supported by the Characteristic Innovation Project of Colleges and Universities in Guangdong Province (Grant 2020 KTSCX186), the Special projects in Key Areas of Guangdong Province (Grant 2021 ZDZX4050) and the Educational Science Planning Project of Guangdong Province (Grant 2021GXJK179).

the above methods are difficult to achieve the hovering stability of underwater robot for the characteristics of sensors.

In this paper, an optical flow method based on machine vision is proposed to realize the location on the autonomous underwater vehicle. Optical flow method is a simple and practical expression of image motion. By detecting the change of image feature points with time, the detection of moving targets is achieved by inferring the moving speed and direction of the object [11]. In this research, the camera of the robot is moving and the target is static. And, combined with the robot motion control algorithm based on PID algorithm, it realizes the hovering stability of the autonomous underwater robot in the water by the improved optical flow algorithm based on the feature points.

2   Autonomous Underwater Vehicle

The autonomous underwater vehicle consists of four parts, as shown in Fig. 1 and Table 1. The core cabin is a hexahedral sealed cabin, with 24 interfaces on the outside, and the main control board, propeller drive board, power board and battery on the inside. The frame is the structure of the robot, and the buoyancy block adjusts the buoyancy and the center of gravity of this underwater vehicle. The four adaptive propellers adjust the attitude of the autonomous underwater vehicle. And, the autonomous underwater vehicle is driven by four adaptive propellers. In order to improve the stability of the underwater vehicle in water, parts with high density, such as battery compartment, control cabin and counterweight block, are installed at the lower end of the main frame. And, the buoyant materials with low density are installed at the upper end of the main frame. The reduced center of gravity and the raised center of buoyancy increase the righting moment of the autonomous underwater vehicle itself.

Table 1. Parameters of autonomous underwater vehicle

Parameter	Value
Main control MCU	STM32F427VI
Propeller control MCU	STM32F103CBT6
Propeller	KAPI propeller
Communication module	433 M
Camera	Kingcent (KS2A543)
Size	45 * 40 * 35 cm
Battery	11.1 V
Weight	3 kg

The electrical system of the autonomous underwater vehicle is divided into three layers: the upper layer, the main control layer and the executive layer. The

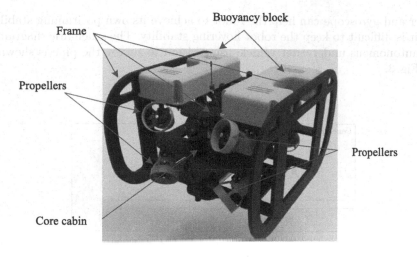

Fig. 1. Configuration of the underwater vehicle

upper layer contains the PC. It receives the data from the main control layer through TCP/IP and displays the information through the graphical interface. The main control layer contains the Raspberry and the accessory circuit components. It is the control center of the underwater vehicle. Its camera is used for observation. The motion control command is issued to the execution layer through the KLT algorithm and the incremental PID algorithm operated in the main control layer. The executive layer contains the four propellers and the infrared sensors. It receives the signals from the main control layer by the serial ports. And, it controls the autonomous underwater vehicle movement through the four propellers. The electrical system frame of the underwater vehicle is shown in the Fig. 2.

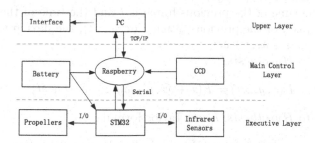

Fig. 2. Electrical system frame

Underwater oil pipe inspection needs line inspection and oil leakage point identification. During the survey, the autonomous underwater vehicle needs to keep trace the line and observe the defect in detail. The sensors such as depth meter and gyroscope can help the robot to achieve its own positioning stability, but it is difficult to keep the robot hovering stability. The schematic diagram of the autonomous underwater vehicle using vision to survey the pipe is shown in the Fig. 3.

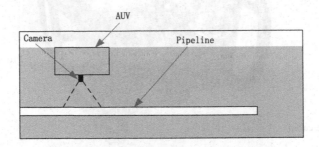

Fig. 3. Visual inspection of oil pipeline schematic diagram

3   Optical Flow Method

3.1   Lucas-Kanade Optical Flow Method

Lucas-Kanade optical flow algorithm is a two frame differential optical flow estimation algorithm. This algorithm is based on three assumptions.

HypothesisI: A pixel's brightness value (pixel gray value) is constant as it changes with time, constant brightness.

HypothesisII: The change of time will not cause the drastic change of position, small moving.

HypothesisIII: Adjacent pixels in the previous frame are also adjacent in the next frame, spatial consistency.

Suppose the time of the previous frame is t and the time of the next frame is $t + \delta t$. The pixel of the previous frame $F(x, y, z, t)$, the next frame's pixel is $F(x + \delta x, y + \delta y, z + \delta z, t + \delta t)$.

According to *HypothesisI*:

$$F(x, y, z, t) = F(x + \delta x, y + \delta y, z + \delta z, t + \delta t) \tag{1}$$

According to *HypothesisII* and Taylor formula:

$$
\begin{aligned}
F(x + \delta x, &y + \delta y, z + \delta z, t + \delta t)\\
&= F(x, y, z, t) + \frac{\partial F}{\partial x}\delta x + \frac{\partial F}{\partial y}\delta y + \frac{\partial F}{\partial z}\delta z\\
&+ \frac{\partial F}{\partial t}\delta t + H.O.T.
\end{aligned}
\tag{2}
$$

where $H.O.T. \approx 0$.

According to above two equations:

$$\frac{\partial F}{\partial x}\delta x + \frac{\partial F}{\partial y}\delta y + \frac{\partial F}{\partial z}\delta z + \frac{\partial F}{\partial t}\delta t = 0 \tag{3}$$

Then the optical flow equation is,

$$(F_x, F_v)(u, v) + F_t = 0 \tag{4}$$

where (u, v) indicates the velocity vector of a pixel. And, the pixel velocity vectors of all feature points constitute the optical flow field of image movement. The motion direction of the images is opposite to the actual motion of the robot.

3.2 Kanade-Lucas-Tomasi Optical Flow Algorithm

KLT (Kanade-Lucas-Tomasi) algorithm is efficient and fast to match two adjacent frames of video image. The matching of feature points between frames is realized by using the information of feature points between frames and the best estimation method.

In the image window, the feature pixel point(x, y) move in any direction (dx, dy), then the new position is $(x + dx, y + dy)$. The pixels in this window are filtered by Gaussian filtering formula,

$$\kappa(x, y) = exp(-(x^2 + y^2)/\sigma^2) \tag{5}$$

then, the gray value is,

$$E(m, l) = \sum_{x,y} \kappa(x, y)[F(x + m, x + l) - F(x, y)]^2 \tag{6}$$

where, m indicates the image windows motion in the x direction, l indicates the image windows motion in the y direction. $F(x + m, y + l)$ indicates the image windows gray value after moving, and $F(x, y)$ indicates the image windows gray value before moving.

Then,

$$E(m, l) = \sum_{x,y} \kappa(x, y)(F_x m + F_y l)^2$$
$$= \sum_{x,y} \kappa(x, y)[m, l] \begin{bmatrix} F_x^2 & F_x I_y \\ F_x I_y & F_y^2 \end{bmatrix} \begin{bmatrix} m \\ l \end{bmatrix} \tag{7}$$

$$Q = \sum_{x,y} \kappa(x, y) \begin{bmatrix} F_x^2 & I_x I_y \\ F_x I_y & F_y^2 \end{bmatrix} \tag{8}$$

When the two eigenvalues of the matrix Q are greater than the preset threshold, the point is considered to be an effective feature point.

If at the time t, the image window is $G(X) = \kappa(x, y)$, and at the time $t + \delta t$ is

$$H(x) = \kappa(x + \delta x, y + \delta y) \tag{9}$$

where $X = (x, y)$ is the image window coordinate, then

$$H(X) = G(X + d) + n(X) \tag{10}$$

where, $n(X)$ is the noise caused by the change of light condition in time δt. The sum of squares of gray difference of the image window is

$$\epsilon = \iint_v [G(X) - H(x)]^2 \kappa(x) dX \tag{11}$$

where, $d = (dx, dy)$. For a image window, when these two eigenvalues of its matrix Q satisfy $\lambda_1 > \lambda_2 > \lambda_{max}$, this image window will have good tracking effect. Then,

$$\begin{bmatrix} F_{xx} & F_{xy} \\ F_{yx} & F_{yy} \end{bmatrix} \begin{bmatrix} \Delta x \\ \Delta y \end{bmatrix} = - \begin{bmatrix} F_{xt} \\ F_{yt} \end{bmatrix} \tag{12}$$

So, each feature point is substituted into the algorithm and the displacement is calculated. Then, the best matching feature point can be found, so as to realize the target tracking.

4　Incremental PID Control Algorithm

The motion of the underwater vehicle in water is nonlinear, time-varying, and the KAPI propellers of the underwater vehicle are coupled with each other. It is difficult to build an accurate hydrodynamic model. PID control algorithm is mature and stable. It does not need to establish an accurate hydrodynamic model of the object, and can well solve the nonlinear problem of the system. The PID algorithm expression of continuous system is

$$u(t) = K_p [\epsilon(t) + \frac{1}{T_I} \int_0^t \epsilon(t) dt + T_D \frac{d\epsilon(t)}{dt}] \tag{13}$$

where, $u(t)$ is the output of the controller, $\epsilon(t)$ is the input of the controller, the deviation between the target value and the actual value. K_p, T_I and T_D are proportional amplification factor, integral time constant and differential time constant of the controller.

The expression of incremental PID control algorithm is as follows,

$$u(k) = K_p \epsilon(t) + K_I \sum_{j=0}^{k} \epsilon(j) + K_D [\epsilon(k) - \epsilon(k - 1)] \tag{14}$$

The sampling period is T, and

$$K_I = K_p \frac{T}{T_I}, K_D = K_p \frac{T_D}{T} \tag{15}$$

Then, the increment of control value $\Delta u(k)$ is

$$\begin{aligned}\Delta u(k) &=u(k) - u(k-1)\\&=A_1\epsilon(k) + A_2\epsilon(k-1) + A_3\epsilon(k-2)\end{aligned} \tag{16}$$

where, $A_1 = K_p + K_I + K_D$, $A_2 = -(K_p + 2K_D)$, $A_3 = K_D$.

Incremental PID control algorithm only needs the increment of output control value. This algorithm is suitable for single chip microcomputer because of the small amount of calculation. And the change of the actuator is small, which makes the operation error of the controlled object have little influence on the action. This algorithm is conducive to improve the stability of the control system, as shown in Fig. 4.

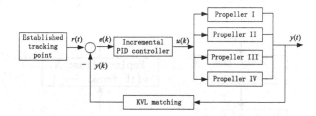

Fig. 4. Structure of incremental PID control system

5   Experimental Researches

The video image is captured through the camera carried by the underwater robot under the laboratory pool environment. The KLT algorithm is used to detect underwater video image feature points. Then, using accurate tracking of underwater video image feature points, the control system controls the hovering stability control of the underwater vehicle. The KVL algorithm flow is as follow.

   Step 1: Read the current frame image of the video, if it is the first frame, go to step 2, otherwise go to step 3.

   Step 2: Extracting feature points.

   Step 3: According to the state value of the target in the previous frame, the predicted value of the current position is obtained.

   Step 4: Based on KLT optical flow method, the observation position of the target in the current frame is obtained. If the difference between the coordinate position of the target and the previous frame is greater than a certain threshold, it belongs to the mismatching point and is deleted.

   Step 5: Combined with the predicted position and the observed position, the current modified position is obtained.

   Step 6: If tracking continues, go to step 1, otherwise end (Fig. 5).

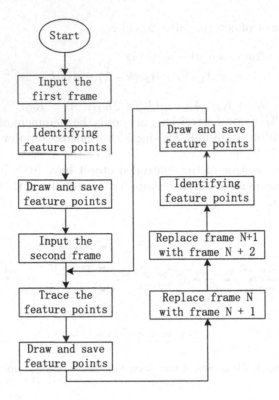

Fig. 5. KVL algorithm flow

The experiment pool is 3000 * 2000 * 600 mm. The depth of the water is 500 mm. The pipe is 75 mm in diameter white PVC. The attachment is a black 30 mm cube, indicating the oil leakage point. As shown in the Fig. 6, the feature points of the pipeline at the bottom of the pool are extracted, and different color marks are used to extract the feature points to generate the motion trajectory of the feature points. The circle points represent the feature points.

As shown in Fig. 6, the actual motion of the robot is opposite to the movement of the image feature points. And the displacement of the feature points is used for the deviation of PID control. The experiments are conducted for the station keeping of the underwater vehicle. According to experimental results, the error represents the distance between the robot and the desired target point reaches 4 cm, as shown in the Fig. 7. The control system of autonomous underwater vehicle is nonlinearity and coupling. It is difficult to control accurately in the floating state. The stability of hovering motion control of underwater robot is difficult because the driving force of the driver in the water is nonlinear.

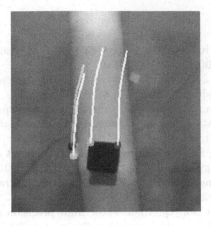

Fig. 6. Results of KVL algorithm

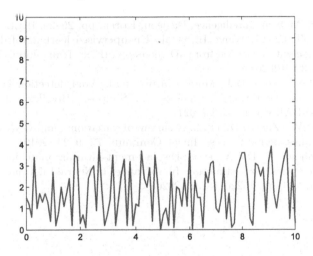

Fig. 7. Results of KVL & PID method

6   Conclusions

Through the research of KLT optical flow algorithm, the underwater target tracking and recognition is realized by using the displacement of the same feature point between each adjacent of two frames. The algorithm has the advantages of fast calculation speed and good robustness in target recognition and tracking. The algorithm can effectively solve the problem that underwater target recognition depends on color block methods. But in the experiments, the illumination affects the algorithm results and the hover control accuracy is not high. In the next work, the research of underwater image enhancement algorithm will be carried out to eliminate the problems caused by uneven illumination. The stability of motion control needs to be further improved. Then, it can further expand the fixed-point positioning application of underwater robot.

References

1. Wang, W., Zhong, K., Xie, G.: Review of man-made siding system. Ordnance Industr. Autom. **000**(012), 42–45 (2013)
2. Shang, C., Wang, W., Xie, G., et al.: Survey of localization methods for underwater robots. Ordnance Industr. Autom. **12**, 46–50 (2013)
3. Lv, C., Shen, B., Tian, C., et al.: Performance of spread spectrum communication for underwater acoustic positioning system. In: Electronic and Automation Control Conference (ITNEC), vol. 1, pp. 1033–1037. IEEE (2020)
4. Li, S., Bao, G., Wu, S.: Development status and prospect of underwater acoustic positioning technology. Mar. Technol. **24**(1), 131–135 (2005)
5. Feng, S., Wu, Y., Tang, Q.: Principle and application of ultrashort baseline acoustic positioning. Coast. Eng. **21**(4), 13–18 (2002)
6. Wang, Z., Luo, J., Chen, Q.: Underwater high precision stereo positioning and navigation system. Acoust. Electron. Eng. **78**(2), 1–3 (2005)
7. Ko, N., Kim, T.: Comparison of Kalman filter and particle filter used for localization of an underwater vehicle. In: The 9th International Conference on Ubiquitous Robots and Ambient Intelligence, Daejeon, Korea, pp. 26–29. IEEE (2012)
8. Wang, G., Zhang, C., Wang, H., et al.: Unsupervised learning of depth, optical flow and pose with occlusion from 3D geometry. IEEE Trans. Intell. Transp. Syst. **23**(1), 308–320 (2020)
9. Oliveira, D.N., Sousa, D.J., Morais, M.R., et al.: Void detection for UAV based on optical flow and vanishing points. In: Simposio Brasileiro de Automacao Inteligente-SBAI, vol. 1, no. 1 (2021)
10. Tu, Z., Xie, W., Zhang, D., et al.: A survey of variational and CNN-based optical flow techniques. Signal Process. Image Commun. **72**, 9–24 (2019)
11. Wang, J., Zhong, Y., Dai, Y., et al.: Displacement-invariant matching cost learning for accurate optical flow estimation. In: Advances in Neural Information Processing Systems, vol. 33, pp. 15220–15231 (2020)

Risk Monitoring Data Upload System for Safety Production of Hazardous Chemicals

Hong Yang$^{(\boxtimes)}$, Ningning Zhang, Yuxiao Zhai, and Yue Liu

Xinjiang Institute of Engineering, Urumqi, Xinjiang, China
18756500@qq.com

Abstract. In view of the harmfulness and severity of the consequences of hazardous chemical accidents, the state attaches great importance to the supervision of the safe production of hazardous chemicals in enterprises. Based on the complexity of the internal network architecture of large enterprises and the safety of industrial control network, given consideration to security and data interaction, this thesis uses TCP protocol, OPC protocol and other protocols to upload the relevant data of enterprise production to the government's monitoring and early warning platform to realize seamless and efficient data sharing.

Keywords: Hazardous chemicals · Safety production · Data upload

1 Introduction

According to the emergency management committee office of the State Council about accelerate the dangerous chemicals safety risk monitoring and early warning system of the construction of the guiding opinions "(EMC [2019] No. 11)," about "autonomous regions accelerate the dangerous chemicals safety risk monitoring and early warning system construction > notice (xin EMO [2019] No. 27) and other documents related to the requirements of Baowu Group Xinjiang Bayi Iron and Steel Co., Ltd. to meet the requirements of hazardous chemicals production data access early warning system. In order to save cost, realize data sharing. The data transmission of the system includes structured data and unstructured data (mainly video data). This thesis mainly discusses the transmission of structured data due to the multiple sources, communication protocols and complexity of network environment. Because of the high safety requirements of industrial production, especially in the production of dangerous chemicals, the safety requirements are particularly important.

In view of the above problems, this system adopts the method of network security grid architecture, uses Firewall, VLAN technology and C# language to develop software, and solves the security problems of data interconnection and network mixing of different communication protocols.

1. Energy Saving and Emission Reduction and Intelligent Electromechanical Technology Service Group of Toksun County.
2. Artificial Intelligence and Intelligent Mine Engineering Technology Center of Xinjiang Institute of Engineering.

© The Author(s), under exclusive license to Springer Nature Singapore Pte Ltd. 2022
L. Zhang et al. (Eds.): CINT 2022, CCIS 1714, pp. 35–45, 2022.
https://doi.org/10.1007/978-981-19-8915-5_4

2   Data Upload Scheme Design

Because the PLC manufacturer of each station is different, there are different data communication methods for different stations. On the premise of safe and controllable, without changing the original production system network structure and data transmission mode, coke chemical industry service station, produced oxygen service stations, dispatch of Power service station and CO online detection system of dangerous chemicals production data in the local data collection. Using various techniques, such as OPC, DCOM, ETL technology) to upload the production data on the server, software was developed on the data upload server in accordance with the data communication regulations of the autonomous region and uploaded to the risk monitoring and early warning system database of the autonomous region.

2.1   System Architecture

This system makes full use of the original network foundation, the original database, firewall and other hardware equipment as well as the existing industrial control network and PLC program and configuration software data communication and data storage, the new equipment integrated into the system. The data of all service stations are transmitted to the database of the autonomous Region dangerous chemical safety risk monitoring and early warning system through the data server of Xinjiang Bayi Iron and Steel Co., Ltd. The system architecture block diagram is shown in Fig. 1.

2.2   Network Design

The data collection of this system is characterized by wide data distribution and little site data. Each site only has more than 10 important data to be uploaded. Therefore, the network structure needs to rely on the office information network of Xinjiang Bayi Iron and Steel Co., Ltd for data transmission, and there are risks of virus transmission and misoperation in the office information. The network structure of the system is complex, including office network, energy metering network, industrial Internet and other multi-level networks mixed together. If not handled properly, network storm, IP conflict and other unpredictable risks will be caused. The dangerous chemical safety risk monitoring and early warning system from Xinjiang Bayi Iron and Steel Co., Ltd to Autonomous Region is connected by special line, so network security planning is the premise to ensure the safety, stability and reliability of the system.

Aiming at the above problems, CyberSecurity Mesh Architecture (CSMA) is adopted in network security Architecture. Firewall technology and VLAN technology are used as means to isolate the network according to the specific situation of the network environment. Dedicated lines are used to physically isolate the network from other networks to ensure the security of the network. The network topology is shown in Fig. 2.

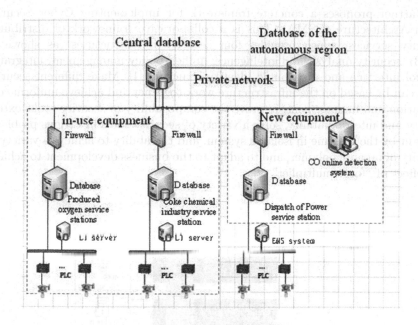

Fig. 1. System architecture block diagram.

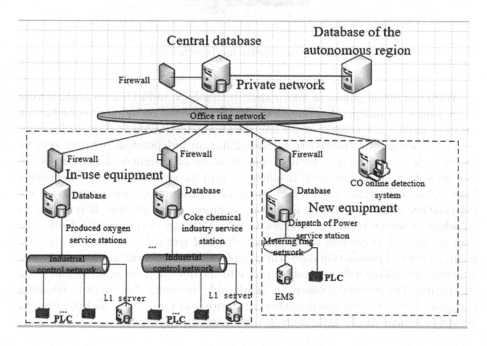

Fig. 2. Network topology.

Gartner proposes a concrete framework for implementing Cyber Security Mesh Architecture (CSMA). This is a collaborative framework of distributed security services, which provides four security infrastructures (as shown in Fig. 3): security analysis and intelligence, unified policy management, integrated control interface and distributed identity structure [1]. Make different security tools can be based on the infrastructure work together and achieve uniform configuration and management, improve the composability of security tools, extensibility and interoperability, solve a variety of security tools in various problems brought by the runtime in isolated system, and the ability to achieve a variety of security of organic polymer, and to adapt to the business development to achieve the effect of "force multiplier" [2].

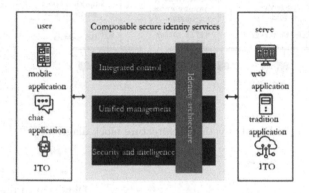

Fig. 3. Cyber security mesh architecture.

With the development of information technology, industrial control network is no longer an independent kingdom. Real-time data of industrial production provide basic data guarantee for the development of information technology. The traditional industrial control network has an independent network system, so network security is not the first consideration of designers. The corresponding network security design is insufficient, and its security is weak. Especially large group enterprises with a certain history, production line automation and information level vary widely. From the economic point of view, it is necessary to adopt different technical schemes to adapt to the development of information technology according to different industrial control networks. In the new form, industrial production data will be uploaded to different platforms for data supervision and big data analysis to promote the development of intelligent manufacturing. The industrial control network and the external network to establish the probability of data communication is more and more high, and the ensuing security threats and security risks are also significantly improved.

According to the guidance of industrial Control System Information Security Protection Guide in the network level, the industrial control firewall, industrial control intrusion detection and defense and leakage system, industrial control security audit system are used to divide and isolate the security area as well as data analysis and processing [3]. Combined with the actual situation of the enterprise, the following schemes can be adopted for industrial control network security protection: (1) Because the industrial control network and office network are not in the same network, the data acquisition server in the enterprise industrial control network adopts the dual network card mode to achieve, a network card and industrial control network in the same network off, through Tcp/IP, Modbus, OPC and other mainstream industrial protocols and protocols for data communication, the collected data stored in the regional database. The other network card connects to the office information network. (2) The area between the database server and office network, through a firewall between districts of safety logic isolation security protection, firewall should be able to provide for industrial protocol data depth filtration, realize the mainstream industrial Internet protocols and specifications of fine-grained check and filtering, blocking the spread of the virus and hacker attacks from network behavior, limit the illegal operation, avoid its influence on the control network and damage to the production process.

2.3 Database Design

Structured data refers to the data logically expressed and realized by two-dimensional table structure, which is the most important data model in information system and is mainly stored and managed by centralized relational database [4].

This system uses the relational database to access the data, according to the field signal type and quantity of the database design, field name using the field number, so that it is convenient for developers to communicate and maintenance personnel to facilitate the database. The database of this system is divided into two types. One is the central database, whose function is to write the non-alarm data of the database in all areas for 5 min and write the alarm data into the database in real time, as shown in Fig. 4. The other is the regional database, which records the non-alarm data of PLC or other real-time databases in 1min and writes the alarm data into the database in real time, as shown in Fig. 5. Database data is archived once a year to improve database performance. The database dynamically generates a data table at 00:00:00 on the first day of each month. The table name is XX year XX month and the data of the current month is stored in the table.

CLOCK	LI7005	TI7005	LI7006	TI7006	LI6008	LI6009	LI6010	LI6011	G6010	G7002
2022/4/10 11:26:15	2.49	10.8	3.31	21.2	0.473	1.042	0.09	0.148	0	0
2022/4/10 11:21:15	2.49	10.5	3.31	21.2	0.473	1.023	0.09	0.146	0	0
2022/4/10 11:16:15	2.49	10.6	3.31	21.2	0.473	1.007	0.09	0.237	0	0
2022/4/10 11:11:15	2.49	10.5	3.291	21.2	0.472	0.992	0.09	0.509	0	0
2022/4/10 11:06:15	2.49	10.6	3.269	21.1	0.472	0.977	0.09	0.783	0	0
2022/4/10 11:01:15	2.49	10.7	3.239	21.1	0.472	0.958	0.09	1.059	0	0
2022/4/10 10:56:15	2.49	10.4	3.22	21.1	0.472	0.942	0.09	1.338	0	0
2022/4/10 10:51:15	2.49	10.5	3.186	21.1	0.472	0.926	0.088	1.616	0	0
2022/4/10 10:46:09	2.49	10.4	3.16	21	0.472	0.91	0.088	1.901	0	0
2022/4/10 10:41:09	2.49	10.3	3.137	21	0.472	0.893	0.09	2.183	0	0
2022/4/10 10:36:09	2.49	10.4	3.111	21	0.472	0.877	0.088	2.462	0	0
2022/4/10 10:31:09	2.49	10.4	3.088	21	0.472	0.856	0.088	2.745	0	0
2022/4/10 10:26:09	2.49	10.5	3.062	21	0.472	0.841	0.088	3.03	0	0
2022/4/10 10:21:09	2.49	10.5	3.036	21.1	0.472	0.826	0.09	3.315	0	0
2022/4/10 10:16:09	2.49	10.5	3.009	21.1	0.472	0.81	0.088	3.597	0	0
2022/4/10 10:11:09	2.49	10.3	3.009	21.1	0.472	0.794	0.09	3.597	0	0
2022/4/10 10:06:09	2.49	10.3	3.005	21.1	0.473	0.775	0.09	3.598	0	0
2022/4/10 10:01:09	2.49	10.2	3.009	21.1	0.472	0.76	0.09	3.598	0	0
2022/4/10 9:56:09	2.49	10.1	3.009	21.1	0.473	0.744	0.09	3.598	0	0
2022/4/10 9:51:09	2.49	10.3	3.009	21.2	0.473	0.725	0.09	3.598	0	0
2022/4/10 9:46:09	2.49	10.3	3.005	21.2	0.472	0.707	0.09	3.597	0	0
2022/4/10 9:41:09	2.49	10.4	3.009	21.2	0.473	0.69	0.093	3.598	0	0
2022/4/10 9:36:04	2.49	10.4	3.009	21.2	0.473	0.676	0.093	3.597	0	0
2022/4/10 9:31:03	2.49	10.3	3.005	21.2	0.473	0.661	0.093	3.598	0	0
2022/4/10 9:26:03	2.49	10.4	3.009	21.2	0.473	0.644	0.093	3.598	0	0
2022/4/10 9:21:03	2.49	10.3	3.005	21.3	0.472	0.629	0.093	3.598	0	0
2022/4/10 9:16:04	2.49	10.2	3.005	21.3	0.473	0.611	0.093	3.597	0	0

Fig. 4. Central database record table.

CLOCK	T1_1_PICAS1741A_PV	T1_1_PICAS1741B_PV	T1_1_V1742A_PV	T1_1_V1742B_PV	T1_1_TI1742A_PV	T1_1_TI1742B_PV
2022/4/5 20:03:24	8.5	8.64	316.119995	828.190002	-172.119995	-179.5
2022/4/5 20:02:22	8.5	8.63	314.01001	828.380005	-172.119995	-179.5
2022/4/5 20:01:21	8.49	8.56	316.209991	828.23999	-172.119995	-179.5
2022/4/5 20:00:20	8.5	8.55	305.170013	828.570007	-172.119995	-179.5
2022/4/5 19:59:19	8.5	8.55	314.970001	827.619995	-172.119995	-179.5
2022/4/5 19:58:15	8.5	8.48	316.209991	828.719971	-172.119995	-179.490005
2022/4/5 19:57:14	8.49	8.42	311.480001	827.859985	-172.119995	-179.5
2022/4/5 19:56:12	8.5	8.45	316.209991	828	-172.119995	-179.490005
2022/4/5 19:55:08	8.5	8.46	306.649994	827.619995	-172.119995	-179.5
2022/4/5 19:54:08	8.51	8.45	315.829987	828.049988	-172.119995	-179.5
2022/4/5 19:53:04	8.5	8.46	304.309998	827.900024	-172.119995	-179.5
2022/4/5 19:52:03	8.51	8.44	315.299988	827.76001	-172.119995	-179.5
2022/4/5 19:51:02	8.51	8.43	315.779999	827.190002	-172.119995	-179.5
2022/4/5 19:50:01	8.51	8.45	313.529999	827.570007	-172.119995	-179.5
2022/4/5 19:48:59	8.51	8.43	316.5	827.330017	-172.139999	-179.5
2022/4/5 19:47:58	8.51	8.42	305.459991	827.090027	-172.139999	-179.5
2022/4/5 19:46:57	8.51	8.43	314.970001	827	-172.139999	-179.5
2022/4/5 19:45:56	8.51	8.49	315.829987	827.330017	-172.139999	-179.5
2022/4/5 19:44:55	8.51	8.55	309.619995	826.950012	-172.139999	-179.5
2022/4/5 19:43:54	8.51	8.57	315.26001	827.22998	-172.160004	-179.5
2022/4/5 19:42:52	8.51	8.57	315.920013	826.849976	-172.139999	-179.5
2022/4/5 19:41:52	8.51	8.54	307.230011	827.140015	-172.139999	-179.520004
2022/4/5 19:40:51	8.51	8.53	314.869995	827.22998	-172.160004	-179.5
2022/4/5 19:39:50	8.52	8.53	315.640015	827	-172.160004	-179.5
2022/4/5 19:38:48	8.51	8.52	312.529999	826.419983	-172.139999	-179.5
2022/4/5 19:37:48	8.51	8.56	315.399994	826.52002	-172.160004	-179.5
2022/4/5 19:36:47	8.51	8.58	315.540009	826.799988	-172.160004	-179.5

Fig. 5. Regional database record table.

Database design has two purposes: First, data storage tiering. If all data should be centralized in one database, the data throughput of the database would be too large. Second, to ensure data security, the central database and regional data backup.   .

2.4   Software Design

The software design of the system is divided into three parts: The first part is the regional database part, which is related data in the industrial control network to write regional database; The second part of the central database is the data center server to the regional server data extraction; The third part is the data uploading part, which is the latest data on the server of the center and sends data according to the interface requirements of the dangerous chemical safety risk monitoring and early warning system of autonomous Region.

Regional database part: The system is mainly to collect the field data to the database. Data collection is the basic work of structured data. It is also the most time-consuming work and the most difficult to connect with different interfaces, because there are many data sources and protocols. Field measurement of the instrument signal into PLC, PLC instrument signal data into non-professional people can read the data. There are three types of data sources: The first type is the coke, chemical industrial control network can be read and written with the PLC CPU by sending messages. The second type is the produced oxygen production industrial control network can be in the configuration software through OPC technology + DCOM technology to obtain data. OPC data access provides a means of reading and writing specific data from data sources [5]; DCOM is a seamless extension of COM that supports communication between component objects and clients on different computers or between components [6]. The third type is the energy metering ring network through the real-time database of EMS system data timing data extraction. The three most core steps of data ETL are extraction, transformation and loading, and each step can be expanded according to different application scenarios and specific requirements [7]. The data extraction function is mainly used to process and implement the extraction tasks conveyed by the background to ensure the efficiency and effect of core data processing [8]. Different data sources, using C# with different means of communication to implement the program (shown in Fig. 6).

The alarm conditions in the flow chart of the regional database (shown in Fig. 7) set the alarm range according to the requirements of the on-site process. Meeting the condition range refers to whether the time difference between meeting the requirement and the last record is 1min within the non-alarm range, and whether the requirement is written into the record.

Central database part: if the program judges that the latest record of the regional central database contains the record with alarm mark, it will extract

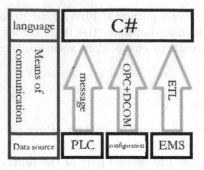

Fig. 6. Different means of communication.

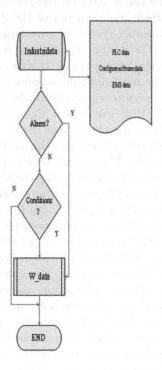

Fig. 7. Regional database flowchart.

this record in real time. In order to ensure the integrity of data, it will also extract data from other databases and write it into the central database. Otherwise, the latest data of all regional central databases will be extracted and written to the central database after 5 min. The central database program flow chart is shown in Fig. 8.

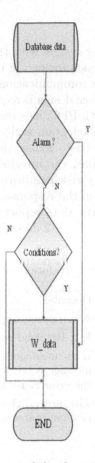

Fig. 8. Regional database flowchart.

Data uploading: If a third-party system reports data to the risk prevention and early warning platform, it is required to submit ClientKey, enterprise code, gateway code, data reporting frequency and index code table to the autonomous region's dangerous chemical safety risk monitoring and early warning system to ensure the validity of the message and index data. The data to be reported must be defined in the indicator code table. Packets are encrypted in AES mode and reported in Socket mode with ClientKey as the key.

Real-time indicator data will be reported according to data reporting frequency, and alarm data will be reported when the alarm status changes. If cached data exists, it is reported in the cached order after the network recovers.

The client must upload data packets in chronological order. The client can transmit the next packet only after receiving the response message that the previous packet is received successfully.

2.5   Interface Design

As the system is a data uploading system with the function of data transmission and sorting, the data sources of each region are inconsistent, and it is impossible to use the same method for data communication and data formats vary greatly. Therefore, communication interface design is required for data communication in each region. To communicate with PLC, it is necessary for PLC and the system to agree on message header and telegram style. In the OPC +DCOM technology for data communication, need to follow the OPC protocol and Microsoft DCOM specification; In particular, the interface design with the autonomous region dangerous chemical safety risk monitoring and early warning system is particularly important, otherwise, the response message cannot be carried out. Packets are divided into two parts: data report and response. Table 1 describes the format of data reporting and Table 2 describes the format of data response.

Table 1. Describes the format of data reporting.

Name	Type	Null	Describes
transactionId	UUID	No	When processing succeeds, the ID is empty
success	Bool	No	Is it Received success?
message	String	No	If the message is received successfully, the message is received successfully. If receivingfails, the error cause is displayed
	Space mark	No	The interval character of the response is a newline character

Example:
```
{
"enterpriseId": "abc123456",
"report": "xxxxxxxxxxxxxxxxxxxx"
}@@
```

Table 2. Describes the format of data response.

Name	Type	Null	Describes
enterpriseId	String	No	The enterprise code is delivered by the system
report	String	No	To encrypt a message
	Space mark	No	SockeSpace mar:@@

Example:
Received successfully:
"transactionId":"mnga161eb35c03f71cf80bccf8ed893cd78", "success": true, "message": "Received successfully"(newline character)
Received failure:
"transactionId":"mnga161eb35c03f71cf80bccf8ed893cd78", "success": false, "message": "Failed to receive, failure reason: XXXXXXXXXX"(newline)

3 Conclusion

Using C# language and the system of different manufacturers of PLC and configuration software, different network environment, the practice in the database data extraction, data through unified communication protocol in the autonomous regulations and the encryption technology, uploaded to the autonomous region of dangerous chemicals production safety risk monitoring platform, realizes the effective regulation hazards data of the enterprise by the government, promoted the enterprise to the hazard source effective management. After more than one year of operation by Baowu Group Xinjiang Bayi Iron and Steel Co., Ltd., the system's safety, stability and reliability having verified. It has laid a foundation for the future system development of data source diversity and network structure complexity.

References

1. Gartner Top Strategic Technology Trends for 2022: Cybersecurity Mesh [EB/OL]. https://www.gartner.com/en/doc/756665-cybersecurity-mesh. Accessed 18 Oct 2021
2. Zeng, H.: The concept of network security grid and its influence. Inf. Secur. Commun. Secur. (11), 55 (2022)
3. Qian, H.: Unit overall network security enhancement scheme. Inf. Secur. (09), 12 (2019)
4. Yu, B., Li, X., Zhao, H.: Structured data management method based on block chain storage extension. Trans. Beijing Inst. Technol. (11), 1160 (2019)
5. Yang, H., Liang, L., Wei, X.: Application of OPC technology in monitoring system. Metall. Industr. Autom. (S2), 747 (2009)
6. Zhou, X., Wu, J., Zhou, W.: Design of distributed cable test system based on DCOM. Inf. Secur. Commun. Secur. (01), 79 (2007)
7. Bao, G., Luo, X.: Analysis of automatic deployment method and implementation of DATA ETL. J. Radio Telev. Netw. (04), 70 (2022)
8. Li, J., Ma, Y., Fan, X.: Design of information management database based on computer technology. Inf. Comput. (03), 160 (2022)

Joint Feature Fusion Approach to Human Pose Estimation Using mmWave Radar

Jianxiong Zhang[1,2] , Zhongping Cao[2,3] , Wen Ding[2,3] , Rihui Chen[2,3] ,
Xuemei Guo[2,3] , and Guoli Wang[2,3(✉)]

[1] School of Artificial Intelligence, Sun-Yat-Sen University, Zhuhai 519000,
People's Republic of China
[2] Key Laboratory of Machine Intelligence and Advanced Computing,
Ministry of Education, Beijing, People's Republic of China
[3] School of Computer Science and Engineering, Sun-Yat-Sen University,
Guangzhou 510006, People's Republic of China
isswgl@mail.sysu.edu.cn

Abstract. This paper mainly studies the use of millimeter wave
(mmWave) radar for 3D human pose estimation. Although pioneering
works have achieved remarkable success, the lack of stability of continuous data acquisition by mmWave radar is still an intractable problem in
pose capturing. To mitigate this problem, a joint feature fusion method
is proposed, which is based on the assumption that human pose in a
motion sequence is domained by bone connection and specific motion
cooperation mechanism. Specifically, we introduce a forget gate to suppress error features extracted due to the loss of information, and a select
gate to select the most reasonable joint characteristics. Outputs of the
two gates are fused to form an anti distortion mechanism of human pose
estimation. Experiments show the effectiveness of our method.

Keywords: Human pose estimation · Millimeter radar · Feature fusion

1 Introduction

Human pose estimation has been a fundamental research interest with numerous applications in human-machine interaction, motion recognition, monitoring,
etc. Currently, with data from optical sensors, great progress has been made in
human pose estimation. However, optical sensors suffer from light sensitivity,
visual obstruction and privacy concerns. As opposed to optical sensors, these
problems can be avoided by using radio frequency (RF) sensors [1–3], which
have weak environment sensitivity, but strong penetrability and privacy protection. Moreover, mmWave radars have the advantages of small size, low energy
consumption and portability, making human pose estimation using mmWave
radar a hot topic.

However, because signals are traveling all directions, some reflected signals
can not be reflected back to radar. Not only that, the multipath effect during

L. Zhang et al. (Eds.): CINT 2022, CCIS 1714, pp. 46–57, 2022.
https://doi.org/10.1007/978-981-19-8915-5_5

signal traveling also leads to part of the reflected signals of human body lost [4]. An effective way to address this problem is to explore temporal features of human joints [4–6]. The underlying motivation is that the lost information of a joint in a frame can be predicted with information of the same joint in adjacent frames. But when information of the same joint is lost in a short sequence, only using temporal features may predict inaccuracy information.

To mitigate this problem, a joint feature fusion method is proposed under the condition that only a small part of joints is lost. Based on the assumption that human pose in a motion sequence is domained by bone connection and specific motion cooperation mechanism, the information of one joint can be inferred by the information of other joints in the same frame. For example, if the information of left hand is lost, the information of left elbow can help predict the approximate position of left hand. While under certain motions that require simultaneous movement of multi limbs, like stepping, the information of right hand can also help infer the information of left hand. Because they move together at the same speed in the opposite direction, generally. The correlation between joints without bone directly connection is found out through temporal features.

Thus, in our joint fusion method, firstly, temporal features are extracted in order to determine which joints have the strongest correlation. Then, a forget gate and a select gate are used to suppress error features extracted due to the loss of information and select the most relevant features for predicting the lost information, separately. Finally, fusing the features from the two gates to mitigate the influence from the loss of joints information. Experiments prove our method is effective.

The rest of the paper is organized as follows. In Sect. 2, the related work of human pose estimation will be introduced. Data acquisition unit, data pre-processing and the overview of our method will be introduced in Sect. 3. We elaborate our method in Sect. 4. Radar configuration, dataset and experimental results will be shown in Sect. 5. Conclusion is provided in Sect. 6.

2   Related Work

2.1   Human Pose Estimation Based on Radar

Because the data collected by radar is not limited by the environment, how to use radar to achieve tasks in the field of computer vision, such as human pose estimation, has gradually become a hot topic in recent years.

In [6], the authors propose a teacher-student model to solve the problem that it is hard to annotate human pose from radar data. Using both camera data and radar data, the authors first obtain the 3D skeleton coordinates from the camera data, and take the coordinates as the ground truth of the target 3D skeleton. The network that obtains camera data features is the teacher network, and the network that obtains radar data features is the student network. By calculating the difference between the output of the teacher network and the student network, the teacher network can guide the student network to predict skeleton coordinates. In [3], by projecting the 3D radar data onto two orthogonal planes, the computational complexity of feature extraction is reduced. After a series of convolution operations on the two 2D data, the obtained features are fused. Finally, the fused features are mapped to 3D skeleton coordinates through multi-layer perceptron. In [5], temporal features are considered. This paper proposes a multi persons pose estimation method using 4D radar data. 4D data consists of 3D spatial data and 1D temporal data. In order to reduce the computational complexity, the authors project 4D data into two 3D data. Each 3D data consists of 2D spatial data and 1D temporal data. For single person pose estimation, the position of each joint is obtained by convolution network (CNN) using those two 3D data. On the basis of single person estimation, a region proposal network is added to transform the multi person estimation problem into multiple single person estimation problems.

3   mmWave Radar Sensing System

This section will describe the data acquisition equipment, data processing and the proposed method framework.

3.1   Data Acquisition Unit

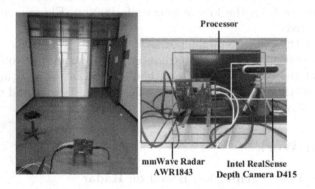

Fig. 1. The data collection environment is shown on the left. The data acquisition unit is shown on the right.

We use a commercial radar (AWR1843 by Texas Instruments Corp, Dallas, USA), which has four transmitting antennas and three receiving antennas, together with an adapter (DCA1000 by Texas Instruments Corp, Dallas, USA) to obtain raw data. After data processing, the final input data can be obtained. In addition, we use a camera (d415 by Intel) and the radar to collect data at the same time. The image data obtained by the camera will provide the ground truth of the target 3D skeleton as [6] did. The data collection environment and unit are shown in Fig. 1.

3.2   Data Processing

Because it is difficult to directly find the useful features for human pose estimation from the raw data, data processing is required. Firstly, multiple input multiple output (MIMO) technology is used to increase the radar received signal strength and throughput. Next, two-dimensional fast fourier transform (FFT) is adopted to convert raw data into Range-Doppler Map (RDM). An example of RDM is shown in Fig. 2. This spectrum indicates the distance and velocity of the human body relative to the radar at a certain time, of which the column values represent the distance and the row values represent the velocity. Finally we use constant false alarm rate (CFAR) to suppress the noise in the data. By extracting the distance and velocity features of human body parts relative to the radar, the human body pose can be constructed.

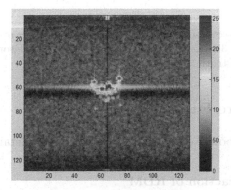

Fig. 2. This figure is an example of RDM, of which the column values represent the distance of the human body relative to the radar, and the row values represent the velocity of the human body relative to the radar. The color values represent the strength of the received signal at a certain frequency of distance and velocity.

3.3   Overview of Our Method

The framework of our human pose estimation method is shown in Fig. 3. The purpose of this method is to reconstruct 3D skeleton from RDM. The distance, velocity and signal intensity characteristics of the human body at a certain time are closely related to the shape and color values of RDM, so CNN is used to extract those features. Fully connected network (FC) is used to align features to each joint. Long short-term memory (LSTM) is further used to explore the relationship between each joint in a motion sequence. Based on the assumption that human pose in a motion sequence is domained by bone connection and specific motion cooperation mechanism, our joint feature fusion method is used to mitigate the problem that part of the reflected signals of human body are lost. The details of our method will be described in Sect. 4.

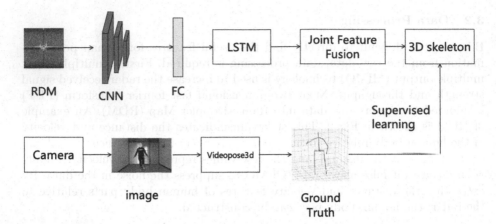

Fig. 3. This figure is the overview of our method. CNN is used to extract region features of RDM. FC is adopted to extract features of each joint. LSTM is used to find out the temporal relation between each joint. And videoposed3d is the method proposed in [7], which is used to map 3D skeleton from image data. 3D skeleton from image data is used to be the ground truth as [6] did.

4   Joint Feature Fusion Method

This section will elaborate our joint feature method in details.

4.1   Feature Extraction of RDM

RDM indicates the distance, velocity and reflected signal strength of human body relative to the radar at a certain time, which is represented by the distribution of color values. Thus CNN is used to extract features of RDM.

Firstly, 2D-CNN is adopted for feature extraction, followed by 2D max pooling layer and batch normalization to prevent over fitting. Finally, we realize nonlinear mapping of features by rectified linear unit (ReLU). We formulate those as follows:

$$F_{s1} = f_{mp}(W_c * X_{spectrum} + b_c). \tag{1}$$

$$F_{s2} = f_{bn}(\sigma(F_{s1})). \tag{2}$$

where F_{s1} represents features extracted from CNN. f_{mp} is max pooling function. W_c is the convolution core parameters and $*$ means convolution. The input of CNN is represented by $X_{spectrum}$. b_c is the bias parameters of CNN. F_{s2} is the features obtained through ReLU. f_{bn} means the batch normalization function and σ is ReLU function.

Then, in order to explore the relationship between each joint, we use LSTM to extract temporal features. That is because the relationship is implicitly expressed in a motion sequence. Especially, we first use FC to align features extracted from

CNN to each joint, then features aligned is regarded as the input of LSTM, which is formulated as follows:

$$F_{s3} = tanh(W_{f1} \cdot F_{s2} + b_{f1}). \tag{3}$$

$$F_t = f_{LSTM}(F_{s3}; \Theta). \tag{4}$$

where F_{s3} is the aligned features. $tanh$ is the hyperbolic tangent function (Tanh). W_{f1} means parameters of hidden layers of FC. b_{f1} represents bias parameters of FC. F_t is temporal features extracted from LSTM. f_{LSTM} is the LSTM function and Θ means the parameters of LSTM.

Once we get the relationship of each joint, joint feature fusion method is applied to predict the lost information.

4.2 Joint Feature Fusion Module

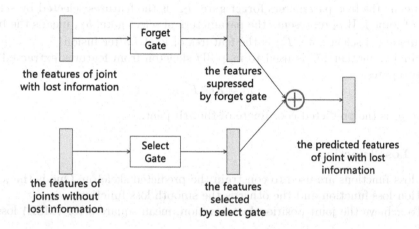

Fig. 4. This figure shows how joint feature fusion method works. Features of joint with lost information are passed through the forget gate to suppress the wrong features extracted due to the loss of information. Features of other joints that relative to lost joint are passed through the select gate to obtain the most relevant features for fusion. Fusion is achieved by element-wise addition.

Based on the assumption that human pose in a motion sequence is domaned by bone connection and specific motion cooperation mechanism, for a lost joint, the features of other joints can be used to predict its features through feature fusion. The flow path of feature fusion is shown in Fig. 4. Especially, the features of joint with lost information are passed through the forget gate, which is responsible for suppressing the wrong features. Other joints features are passed through the select gate, which is responsible for selecting the most relevant features used for fusion. Both of the forget gate and the select gate are composed of FC. The forget gate uses the activation function sigmoid to output the weights of the features, and the features are multiplied by the weights to obtain the retained features. The select gate uses the activation function tanh to output the features used for fusion. Finally, the fusion is completed by element-wise addition. We formulate joint fusion method as follows:

$$F'_{t_i} = F_{t_i} \odot sigmoid(W_{f2} \cdot F_{t_i} + b_{f2}). \tag{5}$$

$$F'_{t_j} = LeakyReLU(W_{f3} \cdot F_{t_j} + b_{f3}). \tag{6}$$

$$F''_{t_i} = F'_{t_i} \oplus F'_{t_j}, \quad j \neq i. \tag{7}$$

where F'_{t_i} is the features suppressed of joint i, and $\odot$ is element-wise multiplication. F_{t_i} is the features of joint i. $sigmoid$ is the sigmoid function. $LeakyReLU$ is the LeakyReLU function, and W_{f2} represents the parameters of forget gate. b_{f2} means the bias parameters forget gate. F'_{t_j} is the features selected by select gate of joint j. W_{f3} represents the parameters of select gate. b_{f3} means the bias parameters of select gate. F''_{t_i} is the features of joint i after fusion.

Finally, another FC is used to map 3D skeleton from features extracted by the two gates:

$$y'_i = FC(F''_{t_i}) \tag{8}$$

where y'_i is the predicted coordinate of the ith joint.

4.3   Loss Function

Two loss functions are used to constrain the predicted skeleton. One is the joint position loss function and the other is the smooth loss function.

To achieve the joint position loss function, mean square error (MSE) loss is used:

$$loss_{MSE} = \frac{1}{T} \sum_{t=1}^{T} \frac{1}{N} \sum_{k=1}^{N} \left(y_k - y'_k \right)^2. \tag{9}$$

where $loss_{MSE}$ is the values of MSE. T is the total number of frames. N represents the number of joints. y_k is the ground truth of the kth joint and y'_k is the predicted result of the kth joint.

We define the smooth as the position change of joints in two adjacent frames, and the smooth loss is the difference between ground truth smooth and predicted smooth:

$$loss_{smooth} = \frac{1}{T-1} \sum_{t=2}^{T} \frac{1}{N} \sum_{k=1}^{N} y''_k. \tag{10}$$

$$y''_k = \begin{cases} 0.5 \left(y_k - y'_k \right)^2, \left| y_k - y'_k \right| < 1 \\ \left| y_k - y'_k \right| - 0.5, \left| y_k - y'_k \right| \geq 1 \end{cases}. \tag{11}$$

where $loss_{smooth}$ is the values of smooth loss.

The total loss function is formulated as follows:

$$Loss = loss_{MSE} + loss_{smooth}. \tag{12}$$

5 Experimental Studies

Firstly, this section will describe the radar configuration, the data sets used in the experiment, and the model parameter settings in details. Then we will show the experimental results of the proposed method. Finally, we demonstrate the effectiveness of each component of our method through ablation studies.

5.1 Radar Configuration and Dataset

When collecting data, the software mmWave studio is used to set radar parameters. We set the starting frequency of the radar as 77 GHz, the frequency slope as 60.012 mHz/μs, the number of samples of the digital to analog converter as 128, the sampling rate as 2500KSPS, the frame rate as 20FPS, the bandwidth as 3.6 GHz, and the spectrum size after data processing as 128 × 128.

The layout of data collection environment is shown in Fig. 5. We have four action collectors and five types of actions, including boxing, hand raising, leg lifting, arm swinging and stepping, as shown in Fig. 6. A total of 75620 frames of radar data were collected, of which 60420 frames were used for training, and the remaining 15200 frames were used for testing. The ratio of training data size to test data size is 79.9% and 20.1%.

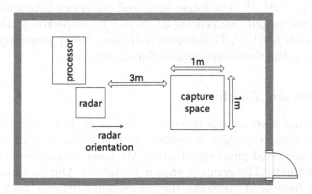

Fig. 5. The layout of data collection environment. Radar is placed directly in front of the capture space.

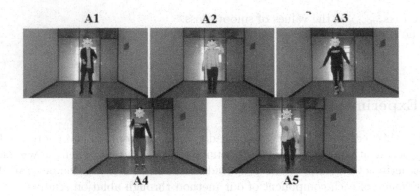

Fig. 6. An example of 5 motions. A1 to A5 are boxing, hand raising, leg lifting, arm swinging and stepping respectively [8].

5.2 Details of Our Model

Our model runs on Linux, with the graphics card Titan X, and the pytorch framework is used. The learning rate of the model is set to 0.001, which is divided by 2 every 10 epochs. The decay rate of the parameters is set to $1e - 5$. There are seven CNN's used to extract RDM features. The first CNN's kernel size is 7, and the rest are 3. The first two CNN's step sizes are 2, and the rest are 1. The number of channels ranges from 1024 to 8. The number of channels for each CNN is half of the previous one. The FC used is composed of five linear layers, and their output channels are 512, 256, 256, 256, 256, respectively. LSTM we choose to use is bidirectional LSTM, and the feature dimension of joints obtained is $R^{17 \times 10}$. The forget gate and the select gate are composed of three FC, and the output channels are 32, 16 and 10, respectively. The dimension of joint coordinate is $R^{17 \times 3}$, 17 indicates that there are 17 joints, and 3 indicates that joints are in the three-dimensional European space.

5.3 Experimental Results

Evaluation metric used in experiments is the Mean Per Joint Position Error (MPJPE) in millimeter, which is defined as the distance between the ground truth and the predicted joints coordinates. We compare our method with other well-known methods. The result is shown in Table 1. Our method reaches the best accuracy because it considers the relationship between each joint in the same frame. Information of the same joint may be lost during a short sequence so that only using temporal features is not enough to predict the lost information. Our method mitigates this problem by exploring the relationship of each joint during this sequence, and it is proved that other joints without lost information can help predict the lost information, according to our assumption. We show the visualization of our predicted results and ground truth from Fig. 7 to Fig. 8.

Table 1. MPJPE (mm): The comparison between our method and other well-known radar-based human pose estimation methods. All the methods were trained on the same dataset we collected.

	mmpose [3]	mpose [9]	Ours
Boxing	65.3	36.1	32.2
Hand raising	78.7	41.2	33.3
Leg lifting	61.9	43.4	44.0
Arm swinging	71.1	32.7	28.3
Stepping	52.5	47.5	40.0
Average	65.9	40.2	35.5

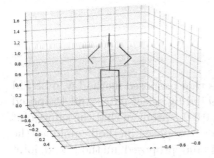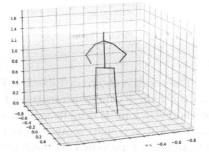

Fig. 7. Constructed 3D pose (left) and the corresponding ground truth (right) of boxing action.

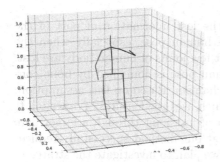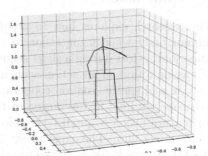

Fig. 8. Constructed 3D pose (left) and the corresponding ground truth (right) of hand raising action.

5.4   Ablation Study

To validate the necessary of each component in our method, we further set up an ablation study. Two ablated models are designed for comparison:

- Proposed method w/o LSTM: LSTM is not included in this method, as to say the relationship between each joint is not explored.

– Proposed method w/o joint feature fusion: This method reconstructs 3D skeleton after LSTM. Joint feature fusion is not included.

Table 2. MPJPE (mm): The ablation study of our method. Compared methods are proposed method w/o LSTM (w/o LSTM) and proposed method w/o joint feature fusion (w/o JFF).

	w/o LSTM	w/o JFF	Proposed method
Boxing	34.2	37.3	32.2
Hand raising	58.4	51.4	33.3
Leg lifting	45.7	50.3	44.0
Arm swinging	48.3	28.4	28.3
Stepping	42.3	45.4	40.0
Average	45.8	42.5	35.5

The result is shown in Table 2. It is obvious that proposed method w/o LSTM can not help decide which features to be selected by select gate. And Proposed method w/o joint feature fusion can not mitigate the problem that the same joint may be lost in a short sequence. As a result, our proposed method combines the advantages of proposed method w/o LSTM and proposed method w/o joint feature fusion, achieving the best accuracy.

6   Conclusion

This research explores how to predict for the lost information of part of the human body when using radar to estimate human pose, especially when the same joint is lost during a short sequence but few joints of human body are lost. We assume that in an action sequence, human pose is domained by bone connection and specific motion cooperation mechanism. Based on this assumption, we propose a joint feature fusion method, which uses the features of other joints for feature fusion to predict the information of lost joint through a forget gate and a select gate. The experiment shows that our method successfully reduces the MPJPE to 35.5 mm. In the future work, we plan to investigate the strategies against the loss of joint information in a long sequence.

Acknowledgements. This work was supported in part by the Natural Science Foundation of China under Grant 61772574 and 62171482 and in part by the Basic and Applied Basic Research of Guangdong Province, China, under Grant 2021A1515011758.

References

1. Wang, F., Zhou, S., Panev, S., Han, J., Huang, D.: Person-in-WiFi: fine-grained person perception using WiFi. In: Proceedings of the IEEE/CVF International Conference on Computer Vision (ICCV), October 2019

2. Jiang, W., et al.: Towards 3D human pose construction using WiFi. In: Proceedings of the 26th Annual International Conference on Mobile Computing and Networking, pp. 1–14 (2020). 35(8): 830–839, 2005
3. Sengupta, A., Jin, F., Zhang, R., Cao, S.: mm-Pose: real-time human skeletal posture estimation using mmWave radars and CNNs. IEEE Sens. J. **20**(17), 10032–10044 (2020)
4. Adib, F., Hsu, C.Y., Mao, H., et al.: Capturing the human figure through a wall. ACM Trans. Graph. (TOG) **34**(6), 1–13 (2015)
5. Zhao, M., et al.: Through-wall human pose estimation using radio signals. In: 2018 IEEE Conference on Computer Vision and Pattern Recognition, CVPR 2018, Salt Lake City, UT, USA, 18–22 June 2018, pp. 7356–7365. IEEE Computer Society (2018)
6. Zhao, M., et al.: RF-based 3D skeletons. In: Gorinsky, S., Tapolcai, J. (eds.) Proceedings of the 2018 Conference of the ACM Special Interest Group on Data Communication, SIGCOMM 2018, Budapest, Hungary, 20–25 August 2018, pp. 267–281, ACM (2018)
7 Pavllo, D., Feichtenhofer, C., Grangier, D., Auli, M.: 3D human pose estimation in video with temporal convolutions and semi supervised training. In: IEEE Conference on Computer Vision and Pattern Recognition, CVPR 2019, Long Beach, CA, USA, 16–20 June 2019, pp. 7753–7762. Computer Vision Foundation/IEEE (2019)
8. Ding, W., Cao, Z., Zhang, J., et al.: Radar-based 3D human skeleton estimation by kinematic constrained learning. IEEE Sens. J. **21**(20), 23174–23184 (2021)
9. Shi, C., Lu, L., Liu, J., et al.: mPose: environment-and subject-agnostic 3D skeleton posture reconstruction leveraging a single mmWave device. emphSmart Health **23**, 100228 (2022)

Question Answering Based on Entity-Aware Self-attention

Jiesong Chen[1], Honghui Fan[2(✉)], Hang Wu[1], Hongjin Zhu[2], and Changyu Yang[1]

[1] School of Mechanical Engineering, Jiangsu University of Technology, Changzhou 213001, China
[2] School of Computer Engineering, Jiangsu University of Technology, Changzhou 213001, China
fanhonghui@jsut.edu.cn

Abstract. With the advent of the Big Data era, computers and mobile networks are growing rapidly. We have ushered in the 5g network, more and more people have access to information, and hundreds of millions of information remains on the Internet every day. The wealth of information resources on the Internet has built a huge knowledge base and satisfied people's thirst for unknown information. The huge amount of information makes it difficult for people to obtain valuable information from it, and how to quickly filter this valuable information is the key to the intelligent question and answer system. In recent years, BERT [1] pre-trained models have shone on major natural language processing tasks with their huge semantic expressiveness. The model in this paper is based on the BERT model pre-trained using a large corpus of entity annotations obtained from Wikipedia, using an entity-aware self-attention mechanism, which is an extension of the self-attention mechanism. This model obtains desirable results on intelligent question and answer systems.

Keywords: BERT · Pre-training · Self-attention

1 Introduction

Smart question answering was widely used in today's work, study and life. Examples include the common Siri in Apple phones and other applications or devices. By domain, intelligent question answering systems can be divided into "domain-specific" intelligent question answering, such as those for education, law, sports, medicine and other professional fields. For reading comprehension, it continues to be subdivided into extractive smart question answering and generative smart question answering. By the source of the answer, intelligent question answering systems can be classified as intelligent quiz based on reading comprehension. This paper is an intelligent question answering built on reading comprehension, using the Stanford questions and answers training set SQuAD2.0, which adds 50,000 adversarial questions to the original SQuAD1.0 making it difficult for humans to answer, and adds a task to decision if the question is answerable built on the current text. The SQuAD2.0 dataset makes it necessary for the system to answer correctly when it can and to avoid answering when it cannot.

The task of an intelligent questions and answers system involves entities, and when identifying entities that do not exist in the knowledge base, traditional entity representation methods are incapable to do so, and traditional deep learning methods cannot output cross-level representations of entities, and secondly, although the transformer [2] is able to obtain complex relationships between words, it cannot capture complex relationships between words and entities, and between entities, as many entities are divided in the model into multiple tokens.

This paper uses a large corpus of entity annotations obtained from Wikipedia to predict masked words and entities, and uses the entity-aware self-attention mechanism. The Bert model using the self-attention mechanism does not capture the complex relationships between entities. Traditional deep learning methods for NLP tasks, such as word2vec [3], cannot handle the problem of multiple expressions of words, do not take into account contextual information, and do not take into account word order, which is limited by the window size. Therefore, the pre-training task in this paper is to apply the BERT model, and to fine-tune it in the question answering system task in order to obtain the desired results.

2 Brief Introduction to Transformer and BERT

2.1 Introduction to Transformer

The transformer model was published in 2018. It is important to note that transformer is not a pre-trained model, but is the core and foundation of many important pre-trained models.

Position Embedding. Since the transformer model does not have an order operation as recurrent neural network naturally have, we had to provide the transformer model with word order information of the sentences in order to reinforce the connections between words. The dimension of position embedding is [max_sequence_length, embedding_dimension], which is the same as that of word vector. [max_sequence_length] is a hyperparameter that refers to the maximal single sentence length, and the sin and cos functions are used to calculate information about the position of the words in each sentence for the model, i.e. a set of odd and even numbered dimensions corresponding to the *embedding_dimension* dimension. For example, a set of 0,1 and a set of 2,3, respectively, are processed using the sin and cos functions above, resulting in different periodic variations, while the location embedding in the *embedding_dimension* becomes slower and slower as the dimension number increases. The periodicity of the position embedding gets slower and slower as the dimension number increases, resulting in a texture with position information. The use of sin and cos functions enables the model to learn relative positions, where "*pos*" stands for position and "*i*" stands for the dimension.

$$PE_{(pos,2i)} = \sin\left(pos/10000^{2i/d}\right) \tag{1}$$

$$PE_{(pos\ 2i+1)} = \cos\left(pos/10000^{2i/d}\right) \tag{2}$$

Encoders and Decoders. The encoder side is made up of six identical modules linked together, each of which in turn consists of two modules, a multi-headed self-attention module, i.e. many self-attention connected together by linear transformations, and a FFN module, and the FFN module is composed of two linear transformations, one of which is the RELU activation function. It should be noted that each large module on the Encoder side receives different inputs, the input of the first large module is the embedding of the received input sequence, and the input information for the other large modules is the output information from the preceding large module, but in the last module the output information is used as the output information for the whole encoder side. The decoder side is also stitched together from six modules, each consisting of three smaller modules, namely a multi-headed self-attention module, a multi-headed encoder-decoder attention interaction module, and a FFN module, which differs from the Encoder side in that the multi-head Encoder-Decoder attention interaction module is consistent with the multi-head self-attentive module. The only difference is that the matrix is derived from the output of the preceding submodule and the output information of the encoded submodule, and that the input received by each of the Decoder modules is different. The transformer structure diagram is shown below (Fig. 1).

Self-attention Layer. For the input sentence X, word vector information for each word in the sentence is obtained by the word embedding algorithm, while the position vectors of all words are obtained by Position Embedding, which are summed to come the true vector representation of the word. Then three matrices WQ, WK, and WV need to be defined, using each of these three matrices to perform three times for all word vectors linear transformations of all the word vectors, so that the three matrices Q(Query), K(key) and V(value) are obtained, respectively. A dot product is then performed using Q and the transpose of K. The result of the dot product can be very large, so it is restricted by dividing it by d, which denotes the dimension of the Q and K vectors. This result is then normalized by the soft-max layer to obtain its probability distribution. The probability values obtained are then multiplied by a vector of V. Finally, these weighted values are vector-summed, which gives a representation with weights. Its calculation formula is as below.

$$Attention(Q, K, V) = softmax\left(\frac{QK^T}{\sqrt{d_k}}\right)V \tag{3}$$

Multi-head Attention. Multiattention means splitting Q, K, V into multiple representations, then doing self-attention, repeating the process several times, and finally combining the results and feeding it into a fully connected layer. Similar to the multi-channel mechanism employed in convolutional neural networks in order to obtain feature selection. Different heads can learn different semantic features.

2.2 Introduction to Bert

Bert Model Structure. The Bert model is made up of three parts: the input layer, the encoding layer and the output layer. The input layer is obtained by summing the three feature embedding representations. The coding layer is the encoder of the transformer and the output layer is mainly the MLM and the NSP.

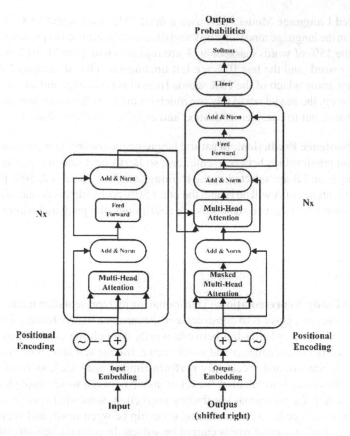

Fig. 1. Transformer structure.

Bert Input. The tokenizer is used to acquire embedding representation information for each phrase in the input sentence, followed by the segment encoding representation and the position encoding representation. The segment and location encodings are learned by the model. The *CLS* in the position of the start of the sentence and is the classifier, while *SEP* is placed between two sentences and is the separator. This is shown in Fig. 2 below.

Input	[CLS]	my	name	is	jingxin	[SEP]	i	like	study	##ing	[SEP]
Token Embeddings	$E_{[CLS]}$	E_{my}	E_{name}	E_{is}	$E_{jingxin}$	$E_{[SEP]}$	E_i	E_{like}	E_{study}	$E_{\#\#ing}$	$E_{[SEP]}$
	+	+	+	+	+	+	+	+	+	+	+
Segment Embeddings	E_A	E_A	E_A	E_A	E_A	E_A	E_B	E_B	E_B	E_B	E_B
	+	+	+	+	+	+	+	+	+	+	+
Position Embeddings	E_0	E_1	E_2	E_3	E_4	E_5	E_6	E_7	E_8	E_9	E_{10}

Fig. 2. Token embedding.

Bert Masked Language Model. Bert uses a mask. This means that 15% of the words are masked in the language modelling task and the model is allowed to predict the masked words. Of the 15% of words masked, 80% are replaced with [mask], 10% are replaced with another word, and the last 10% are left unchanged. The advantage of this is that Bert does not know which of the 15% words [mask] is replacing, and any word can be replaced, forcing the model not to rely too much on the current word when encoding the current moment, but to consider its context and even 'correct' the context.

Bert Next Sentence Prediction. In natural language processing, language models need to understand relationships between sentences, so Bert's next sentence prediction is for that purpose. A and B are selected as the training samples. There is A 50% probability that the next sentence of A will be B, and the other 50% probability is A sentence selected by random swiping. If the two sentences are continuous, the predicted output will be 1, and if they are not continuous, the predicted output will be 0. The model was trained to predict whether A's next sentence would be B. When combined with the MLM task, this model can more accurately portray semantic information at the sentence level and even at the text level.

Traditional Entity Representation. Traditional entity representation methods include glove, word2vec, etc. glove is to construct a co-occurrence matrix based on the corpus, and then calculate the relationship between words through the approximate relations between the co-occurrence matrix and word vector. But the semantic information of the word vector is limited, and it can only perform limited tasks such as word similarity calculation. Word2vec is to calculate the relationship between words through CBOW or skip-gram method for contextual vocabulary prediction, somewhat similar to MLM of bert task, but word2vec has a one-to-one relationship between words and vectors, so the problem of multiple meaning words cannot be solved. In contrast, self-attention mechanism can richly express the semantic information of words. In addition, Word2vec is a static approach, which is general but cannot do dynamic optimization for specific tasks, while pre-training tasks of bert can be dynamically optimized for different downstream tasks.

3   Improvements Based on Bert

3.1   Entity-Aware Self-attention

Self Attention directly links the association of any two words in a sentence through a single computational step, so the distance between distantly dependent features is greatly reduced, facilitating the effective use of these features. However, in the intelligent question answering task of this paper, the answers to the questions are often related to entities, so more attention to the entities is required, so this paper uses entity-aware Self Attention instead of the self attention in Bert. Enter a sequence of input vectors $x_1, x_2, \ldots, x_k$, each of the output vectors $y_1, y_2, \ldots, y_k$, is computed based on the weighted sum of the transformed input vectors. Here, each input and output vector corresponds to a token (a word or an entity) in our model; therefore, $k = m + n$. The $i - th$ output vector y_i is computed as:

$$y_i = \sum_{j=1}^{k} \alpha_{ij} \mathbf{V} \mathbf{x}_j \tag{4}$$

$$e_{ij} = \frac{\mathbf{K} \mathbf{x}_j^T \mathbf{Q} \mathbf{x}_i}{\sqrt{L}} \tag{5}$$

$$\alpha_{ij} = softmax(e_{ij}) \tag{6}$$

where $Q \in R^{L \times D}$, $K \in R^{L \times D}$, and $V \in R^{L \times D}$ denote the query, key, and value matrices, respectively.

This paper strengthens this entity-aware query by using a different query matrix for each pair of possible token types for x_i and x_j, that is, the attention score e_{ij} is computed as below.

$$e_{ij} = \begin{cases} \mathbf{K} \mathbf{x}_j^T \mathbf{Q} \mathbf{x}_i, & \text{if both } x_i \text{ and } x_j \text{ are words} \\ \mathbf{K} \mathbf{x}_j^T \mathbf{Q}_{w2e} \mathbf{x}_i, & \text{if } x_i \text{ is word and } x_j \text{ is entity} \\ \mathbf{K} \mathbf{x}_j^T \mathbf{Q}_{e2w} \mathbf{x}_i, & \text{if } x_i \text{ is entity and } x_j \text{ is word} \\ \mathbf{K} \mathbf{x}_j^T \mathbf{Q}_{e2e} \mathbf{x}_i, & \text{if both } x_i \text{ and } x_j \text{ are entities} \end{cases} \tag{7}$$

where Q, Q_{w2e}, Q_{e2w}, Q_{e2e} denote the word-to-word query matrix, the word-to-entity query matrix, the entity-to-word query matrix, and the entity-to-entity query matrix, respectively. In addition, the computational cost of entity-aware self-attention proposed in this paper is the same as that of self-attention, although additional costs are required for computing the gradient and updating the query matrix parameters during training.

3.2 Pre-training Task

We use an MLM task, which is a traditional task, and we still use a new pre-training task which is an extension of MLM for learning entity representations. In this paper, the pre-training task is based on the BERT model pre-trained using a large corpus of entity annotations obtained from Wikipedia. This paper does an MLM task, which means that the [mask] entity is used to randomly mask 15% of the words in the sentence. The traditional pre-training task of Bert also has an NSP task, which is the task of determining whether the second clause follows the first sentence, but according to experiments, the presence or absence of the NSP task has little effect on the experimental results, so the NSP task is not used in this paper. Another new pre-training task is that we use [mask] entities to replace a certain percentage of entities in the sentence. Formally, we use the soft-max function for all entities of the vocabulary to predict the original entities of the masked entities:

$$\hat{y} = softmax(BTm + b_o) \tag{8}$$

$$m = layer\_norm(gelu(W_h h_e + b_h)) \tag{9}$$

where h_e is the representation corresponding to the masked entity, $T \in R^{H \times D}$ and $W_h \in R^{D \times D}$ are weight matrices, $b_o \in R^{Ve}$ and $b_h \in R^D$ are bias vectors, GELU $(\cdot)$ [4] is the activation function, and layer norm $(\cdot)$ [5] is the layer normalization function. Our final loss function is the sum of the MLM loss and the cross-entropy loss of the predicted masked entities, where the latter is calculated in the same way as the former.

4 Experimental Results and Analysis

To verify the availability of applying entity-aware self-attention and prediction of masked entity tasks. This paper uses Pytorch to do it. The environment is as follows: Pytorch 1.2.0 and Python 3.6, 22 G memory, Intel core i5-10400 processor, Win10 Professional 64-bit OS, Nvidia GeForce RTX 2080 ti SUPER, CUDA version 10.4.

4.1 SQuAD2.0 DataSet

The SQuAD dataset is a public dataset provided by Stanford University's Department of Computer Science in 2016, in which Stanford University randomly selected over 500 files from Wikipedia and further subdivided them into more than 20,000 paragraphs. Using a crowdsourcing approach, a group of people read these files, asked five questions for each paragraph, and marked the answers in the paragraphs. The final result is SQuAD, a reading comprehension dataset with over 100,000 questions, but SQuAD 1.1 has the following shortcomings: it is limited by the number of questions that can be answered by selecting span, the need to find answers within a given passage, and the preservation of answers within a passage. In response to these shortcomings, SQuAD 2.0 was proposed as an improvement on the original SQuAD 1.0 by adding adversarial questions and a new task: determining whether a question can be answered based on the provided reading text. Stanford NLP officials say that compared to the 100,000 questions and answers in SQuAD 1.1, SQuAD 2.0 adds another 50,000 human-authored questions, and the questions don't necessarily have corresponding answers. The model performing the SQuAD 2.0 reading comprehension task must not only be able to give answers to questions that can be answered when encountered, but also determine which questions are not supported by the material in the read text and refuse to answer those questions.

4.2 Parameter Settings

The BERT model is Google's open-source pre-training model. In this paper, we use BERT-large for experiments. The size of the learning rate is 15e-6, the size of the iteration epoch is 5, the batch size is 128, and the train-batch-size is 2. The longest sentence length is 384, and 24 network layers are used, 64 attention dimensions, and 12 self-attention consisting of multi-head self-attention. The total parameters is about 468M, of which 340M are for BERT and 128M for word embedding. The input text is split by a word splitter with $V_w = 50K$ words for BERT. For reasons of computational efficiency, the entity dictionary does not include all entities, but only the entities with $V_w = 500K$ that appear frequently in the entity annotation. The entity dictionary also contains two special entities, namely [UNK] and [MASK].

4.3 Results

This paper scores the training and prediction of the model on the SQuAD 2.0 dataset using the F1-score evaluation metric and exact match (EM). F1-score summarizes and reflects both precision and recall, with precision representing the proportion of all examples that are actually really positive out of all those that are predicted to be positive. Recall represents the proportion of predictions that are actually correct out of all examples that are actually positive. Precision and recall are calculated by calculating the proportion of True positive (Correctly predicting a positive sample), true negative (Correctly predicting a negative sample), false positive (error predicting a positive sample), and false negative (error predicting a negative sample). The formulae for recall and precision and the F1-score are as below.

$$Precision = \frac{TP}{TP + FP} \tag{10}$$

$$Recall = \frac{TP}{TP + FN} \tag{11}$$

$$F - score = \frac{2Precision * Recall}{Precision + Recall} \tag{12}$$

The results are shown in Table 1, where we used the Bert model of entity-aware self-attention with an F1-score of 94.9 and an EM of 89.8 on the validation set and an F1-score of 95.0 and an EM of 90.1 on the test set.

Table 1. Experimental results

	Dev F1-score	Dev EM	Test F1-score	Test EM
Bert entity input	94.9	89.8	95.0	90.1
Bert	92.4	89.1	94.5	89.4

4.4 Analyses

Influences of Entity Representations. We looked at the performance of the test task with and without entity representation. We performed the extractive quizzing task with the SQuAD2.0 dataset without any input entities. In this case, our model uses only word sequences to calculate the expression of each word. We can see in the table above that there is a significant reduction in the F1-score and EM scores of the model on the validation and test sets in the absence of entity input, and we used the dataset with entity inputs for validation and testing, and the entity characterization capability was significantly improved. The main reason is because a dataset with entity inputs enables the model to learn more information about entity representations during training, allowing the model to more accurately identify and assign information when it encounters entities during validation and testing. In addition, during the training process, the model cannot correctly identify the information of entities when it encounters entities that do not exist in the corpus, but since the Wikipedia corpus already covers almost all entities, the probability that the training process encounters entities that do not exist is extremely low and does not affect the superiority of the model.

Influence of Entity-Aware Self-attention. We investigated the extent to which our entity-aware self-attention mechanism influenced the model by comparing whether or not it was used. As shown in the table, we can see that entity-aware self-attentive outperformed the primitive attention mechanism on both the validation set and the test set in the question-and-answer task. The main reason is because the question-and-answer task in this paper involves reasoning based on the relations between entities, and the entity-aware self-attention enhances the representation of entities. We argue that our entity-aware self-attention enables the model (i.e., the attention head) to focus more on the relationships between entities, but also on the complex relationships between entities and words (Table 2).

Table 2. Experimental analyses

	Dev F1-score	Dev EM	Test F1-score	Test EM
Original attention	93.1	88.2	93.6	88.4
Entity-aware attention	94.9	89.8	95.0	90.1

5 Conclusions

In this paper we use an entity-aware self-attentive to replace Bert's original self-attention mechanism, using a new pre-training task to enhance the representation of entities in sentences. His effectiveness on a question answering task is demonstrated in the experimental results. The present experiments are not currently applied to domain-specific work, and in the future the improved Bert model could be applied to domain-specific assignments, for instance in medicine and law.

References

1. Devlin, J., Chang, M.W., Lee, K., Toutanova, K.: BERT: pre-training of deep bidirectional transformers for language understanding. In: Proceedings of the 2019 Conference of the North American Chapter of the Association for Computational Linguistics: Human Language Technologies, Volume 1 (Long and Short Papers), pp. 4171–4186 (2016)
2. Vaswani, A., et al.: Attention is all you need. In: Advances in Neural Information Processing Systems, vol. 30, pp. 5998–6008 (2017)

3. Goldberg, Y., Levy, O.: word2vec explained: deriving Mikolov et al.'s negative-sampling word-embedding method. arXiv preprint arXiv:1402.3722 (2014)
4. Hendrycks, D., Gimpel, K.: Gaussian error linear units (GELUs). arXiv preprint arXiv:1606.08415 (2016)
5. Ba, J.L., Kiros, J.R., Hinton, G.E.: Layer normalization (2016)
6. Chen, D., Fisch, A., Weston, J., Bordes, A.: Reading Wikipedia to answer open-domain questions. In ACL (2017)
7. Choi, E., et al.: QuAC: question answering in context. In EMNLP (2018)
8. Kou, F., Junping, D., He, Y., Ye, L.: Social network search based on semantic analysis and learning. CAAI Trans. Intell. Technol. 1(4), 293–302 (2016)
9. Liang, Z., Junping, D., Li, C.: Abstractive social media text summarization using selective reinforced Seq2Seq attention model. Neurocomputing 410, 432–440 (2020)
10. Meng, D., Jia, Y., Junping, D., Fashan, Y.: Initial shift problem for robust iterative learning control systems with polytopic-type uncertainty. Int. J. Syst. Sci. 41(7), 825–838 (2010)
11. Li, W., Sun, J., Jia, Y., Junping, D., Xiaoyan, F.: Variance-constrained state estimation for nonlinear complex networks with uncertain coupling strength. Digit. Signal Process. 67, 107–115 (2017)
12. Meng, D., Jia, Y., Junping, D.: Robust iterative learning protocols for finite-time consensus of multi-agent systems with interval uncertain topologies. Int. J. Syst. Sci. 46(5), 857–871 (2015)

TGNN: A GNN-Based Method with Multi-entity Node for Personal Banking Time Prediction

Zhikang Mo[1], Qixiang Shao[1], Likang Wu[1], Runlong Yu[1], Qi Liu[1], Jiexin Xu[2], Hongmei Song[2], and Enhong Chen[1(✉)]

[1] Anhui Province Key Laboratory of Big Data Analysis and Application, State Key Laboratory of Cognitive Intelligence, School of Computer Science and Techonology, University of Science and Technology of China, Hefei, China
{mzk,qixiangshao,wulk,yrunl}@mail.ustc.edu.cn,
{qiliuql,cheneh}@ustc.edu.cn
[2] Department of Information Technology, China Merchant Bank, Shenzhen, China
{jiexinx,songhongmei}@cmbchina.com

Abstract. The offline business of banks is deeply involved in bank clients' financial lives and directly affects the satisfaction of clients. For offline banking scenarios, accurate prediction of clients' banking time is essential for the service system of the banks, which can be used for multiple downstream tasks, such as queuing time prediction, real-time queuing planning, etc. However, the problem of banking time prediction remains open due to many technical and domain challenges, such as Anonymous Client Problem (ACP) and Sparse Interaction Problem (SIP). The existing works mainly utilize the traditional machine learning method and are relatively plain in modeling this practical scenario thus leading to an unpromising performance. Different from existing works, we predict the personal banking time by modeling the clients and banking services in the banking process through mining a large number of banking records. In this paper, we propose a Tuple-node-based Graph Neural Network (TGNN) framework to learn representations of clients and services of banks and estimate the personal banking time based on the representations. Empirical studies on two real-world datasets collected from a fintech bank demonstrate the effectiveness of TGNN.

Keywords: Data mining · Graph neural networks · Banking time prediction

1 Introduction

Despite the trend of online banking in the Internet era, offline banking service is still an essential part of the financial activities of commercial bank clients. For commercial banks, it is an important task to improve clients' satisfaction in the banking service process which is vital for banks to retain clients and

L. Zhang et al. (Eds.): CINT 2022, CCIS 1714, pp. 68–79, 2022.
https://doi.org/10.1007/978-981-19-8915-5_7

increase revenue. With waiting in the queue being inevitable, clients may get upset for waiting too long. To reduce the clients' anxiety, an accurate estimation of waiting time or the improvement of the queuing system is urgently needed. In this context, an accurate estimation of banking time is valuable for commercial banks to improve the real-time queuing system and generate an estimated time of waiting for clients in the queue to reduce clients' anxiety.

Figure 1 shows the real-world scenario for offline banking in most commercial banks. When the clients arrive at the branch, they need to get the number on the queuing machine and enter the corresponding queue for queuing. Waiting is unavoidable and consistently makes clients anxious. Our task aims to predict the banking time for each client, so that the predicted duration time can be utilized as the input feature of downstream tasks, such as queuing time prediction, dynamic queuing planning, etc. However, we find that there are mainly two domain challenges hindering the predicting performance of the existing methods.

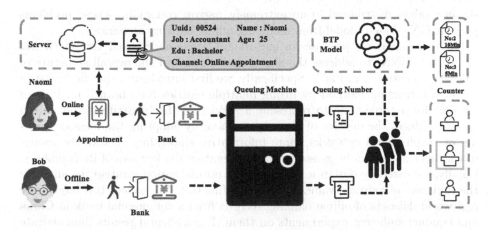

Fig. 1. Real-world scenario of offline banking.

Anonymous Client Problem. In real-world datasets collected from a fintech bank, we find that a large portion of data samples contains little information about the clients and we attribute it to the following characteristics of offline banking scenarios. As illustrated in Fig. 1, Naomi makes an appointment for offline bank service and we can make use of her profile to improve the banking time prediction accuracy. However, Bob arrives at the bank branch without an appointment thus causing the missing of Bob's profile. The existing methods cannot handle the problem of missing values in training and ignore the importance of clients' features for the BTP task.

Sparse Interaction Problem. The offline banking scenario intrinsically leads to the sparse interaction problem, i.e., having many missing record entries, as most clients tend to head for a small number of bank branches and handle specific banking business related to their wealth status. The lack of records for some clients prevents models from generating accurate predictions.

To overcome the mentioned challenges, inspired by [14,17], we present a novel graph-based learning paradigm for the BTP task. Considering the interactions between clients and bank services as a bipartite graph, Graph Neural Networks (GNN) [6,14] can aggregate the features of high-order collaborative clients to the target client node according to message passing. In this way, clients with similar interactions can be found and the negative impact of sparse interaction and missing values in clients' features is alleviated to a great extent.

However, achieving this goal via GNN is limited by some obstacles. First, there are usually only tens of types of banking services, so a simple construction of a bipartite graph that connects clients and types of services will make the bipartite graph extremely dense and the GNN-based model cannot train on such a graph. Second, the personal banking time varies greatly, from tens of seconds to hundreds of minutes. Using the ground truth directly will make the model unable to converge, yet a common solution of normalization will make the smaller values distributed in an extremely narrow codomain. These problems prevent GNN-based model from modeling offline banking scenarios.

In this paper, we propose an end-to-end Tuple-node-based Graph Neural Network (TGNN) to address the above challenges, and the overall structure of TGNN is illustrated in Fig. 2. Specifically, we first introduce a specific bipartite graph construction method by fusing multiple entities (i.e., branch id, type of service) for a tuple-node to represent a service in the bipartite graph, which greatly reduces the density of the edges. Then, by adopting the message passing of graph neural networks, more informative embedding vectors for anonymous client nodes can be generated by aggregating the features of its neighbors. Finally, we carefully design a ground truth normalization strategy to alleviate the influence of extreme values on the loss function. We collect two large-scale real-world datasets of offline banking records from a commercial bank in China and conduct sufficient experiments on them. Experimental results demonstrate the superiority of our proposed model and the novel predicting paradigm compared with all baselines. We summarize our major contributions as follows:

- We conduct a focused study on predicting the duration time of personal banking and point out two critical problems in a real-world scenario: Anonymous Client Problem and Sparse Interaction Problem. We formulate the problem as modeling the clients and services in each banking record via GNN, which is the first in this research area.
- We propose a novel method of constructing a bipartite graph specifically for the offline banking scenario. We define the bank service node in the bipartite graph by a tuple of multiple entities and stack GNN layers to explore the connectivity information between clients and services to learn better representations for the BTP task.
- We extract two large-scale datasets from a real-world database. Extensive experiments on these two datasets validate the effectiveness of TGNN.

2   Related Works

In this section, we will introduce the works related to the BTP task as well as Graph Neural Networks(GNN) which inspires the proposed GNN-based method that tackles the domain challenges in our practical scenario.

2.1   Personal Banking Time Prediction

Recent years have witnessed the vigorous development of artificial intelligence techniques in financial research and application [12,18]. However, the BTP task was rarely studied in the existing literature and most researchers paid attention to estimating the waiting time in personal banking scenarios. Mourõo et al. [1] aimed to study the overflow problem in bank queues, i.e., leaving the clients waiting in queue for a long time, and to detect the overflow cases. Four different models were compared in [1], including Queue Theory, Gradient Boosting Machine, Random Forest, Deep Learning, and the GBM method achieved the best performance. Some other works [7,9] tried to predict the waiting time based on some related features by utilizing machine learning and prove that machine learning can be a better way of predicting waiting time than Queue Theory.

However, the existing works mostly performed experiments on datasets that contain only a small set of input features. For instance, only date features were used to predict personal banking time in [5]. In our scenarios, we have access to various features which can be classified into client features, service features, and context features. In this research area, we still lack in-depth exploration of modeling the complex personal banking scenario via cutting-edge deep learning methods. To our knowledge, our approach is the first comprehensive attempt to exploit the BTP task in the clients and banking services modeling view.

2.2   Graph Neural Networks

Due to the completeness of the theoretical frame and the simplicity of the structure, Graph Neural Network (GNN) has been successfully applied to numerous research areas with structured graph data [6,8]. Moreover, GNN also shows promising performance in other tasks without explicit graph formation. Shi et al. [13] utilized the Heterogeneous Networks to learn better latent factors for users and items and to improve the performance of the recommendation system. Wu et al. [15,16] organized the connection between projects in the crowdfunding scenario as a graph and proposed a GNN-based approach to recognize the pattern of competitiveness and evolution in the market. Liu et al. [10] introduced GNN layers to automatically find the potential flow trends of technologies in patent mining. In this paper, we process the client banking records from a graph perspective which is the first attempt in this domain and propose a bipartite graph construction method specifically for the banking time prediction task to improve the performance of the GNN-based model.

3 Proposed Method

In this section, we introduce our Tuple-node based Graph Neural Network (TGNN) model by first formulating the BTP task and then presenting the details.

3.1 Problem Formulation

The task of Banking Time Prediction(BTP) is to estimate the time duration of a client being served on a banking service. Each instance can be described by three fields, i.e., the client information, the bank service information as well as the context information. We can represent each instance as follows:

$$\mathcal{X} = \{c_1, c_2, ..., c_j, s_1, s_2, ..., s_k, o_1, o_2, ..., o_m\},$$

where c_j, s_k, o_m represents the three fields of features respectively. Our proposed model is trained to make real-value predictions $\hat{y} \in \mathcal{R}$ as time duration estimation for each instance and the problem is defined as a regression task where our model serves as regression function $f(\mathcal{X}) \to \hat{y}$.

3.2 TGNN

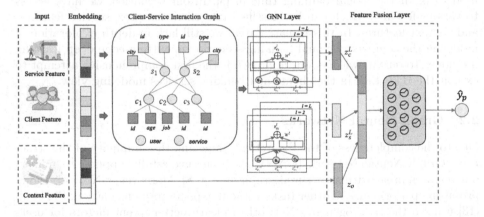

Fig. 2. The oveview of proposed model TGNN. Note that the client node c_1 denotes client with rich features while client node c_2 and c_3 denotes anonymous clients with only client id associated. All of the service nodes are associated with three features. After propagation of L GNN layers, we obtain graph embedding z_c^L, z_s^L for client and service nodes. Finally, we concatenate them with context feature embedding z_o and use MLP as feature fusion layer to generate predictions for the task.

Bipartite Graph. To exploit the collaborative signal of clients to learn the representation of the clients for more accurate predictions, we firstly build the bipartite graph by utilizing the event logs. We treat every bank service record as an interaction between a client and a tuple node with multi-entity and we define the resulting bipartite graph as follows:

Client-Service graph, denoted as $\mathcal{G} = (\mathcal{C}, \mathcal{S}, \mathcal{E}_{(c,s)})$, is a bipartite graph where $\mathcal{C}$ is a set of clients and $\mathcal{S}$ is a set of tuples of (branch id, type of service). And $\mathcal{E}_{(c,s)}$ is the set of undirected edges between clients and services. The client features and service features are attached to the nodes respectively as node features and the context features are attached to edges as edge features.

Node Embedding Initialization. In addition to the structure of the bipartite graph, we also assume that the associated features of nodes are also helpful to the BTP task.

For the i-th column of input features, we convert it into a dense vector and the embedding vector $e_i \in \mathbf{R}^{d'}$ via embedding matrix and d' denotes the dimension of feature embeddings. We concatenate these dense vectors of each feature and transform the output vector with a fully connected layer to generate the input embedding for nodes in the bipartite graph:

$$z_c^0 = \text{norm}\left(\sigma\left(W_c\left[e_1^c\|e_2^c\|...\|e_j^c\right] + b_c\right)\right), \tag{1}$$

$$z_s^0 = \text{norm}\left(\sigma\left(W_s\left[e_1^s\|e_2^s\|...\|e_k^s\right] + b_s\right)\right), \tag{2}$$

where $z_c^0, z_s^0 \in \mathcal{R}^d$ represent the initial embeddings of two types of nodes, $W_c \in \mathbf{R}^{d\times(jd')}, W_s \in \mathbf{R}^{d\times(kd')}$ are the trainable weight matrices, the $b_c, b_s \in \mathbf{R}^d$ are the bias vectors respectively, σ denotes the *ReLU* activation function.

As mentioned in the problem formulation, the nodes of offline clients are only associated with client id. To tackle the feature sparsity problem as such, we explicitly fuse the feature information into the initial embeddings of the nodes of online clients. Then, by adopting the message passing of graph neural networks, more informative embedding vectors for nodes of offline clients can be generated.

GNN Layer. For notational convenience and generality, we simply refer to the node set of the full graph with $\mathbf{V} = \mathcal{C} \cup \mathcal{S}$. The core function of the GNN layer is to learn how to aggregate the features of neighbors of the ego node so we first construct the aggregation of the neighborhood as follows:

$$z_{\mathcal{N}(i)}^{l+1} = \gamma\left(\left\{\frac{1}{c_{ij}}z_j^l, \forall j \in \mathcal{N}(i)\right\}\right), \tag{3}$$

where γ denotes mean pooling operation, z_j^l denotes the embedding of node j from the previous GNN layer, and $\mathcal{N}(i)$ stands for the Neighbor set of node i. Following graph convolutional network [8], we set the normalization term c_{ij} of message passing as $\sqrt{|\mathcal{N}_j||\mathcal{N}_i|}$ where $\mathcal{N}_i$ and $\mathcal{N}_j$ denotes the first-hop neighbors of node i and node j. From the viewpoint of representation learning, it can be interpreted as a discount factor that reflects how much the neighbors' information contributes to the representation learning of node i.

We then aggregate the messages propagated from node i's neighborhood and update the $l + 1$-th layer embedding for node i as follows:

$$z_i^{l+1} = \text{norm}\left(\sigma\left(W^{l+1} \cdot \left[z_i^l \| z_{\mathcal{N}(i)}^{l+1}\right] + b^{l+1}\right)\right),\qquad(4)$$

where W^{l+1} and b^{l+1} denotes the fully connected layer for the $(l+1)$-th GNN layer. By stacking L layers of information aggregation, we can fuse the feature of L-hop neighbors into the embedding of the ego node. We can stack more GNN layers to model connectivity between client and service node and enrich the embeddings of anonymous clients by fusing the collaborative signal. Inspired by [14], we utilize the high-order collaborative signal to enrich the initial embedding of node i by concatenating the initialization embedding and output embedding of the L-th layers GNN:

$$z_i = z_i^0 \| z_i^L.\qquad(5)$$

By combining the L-th layer embedding with initial embedding, we can utilize the high-order relations to improve the anonymous client nodes without features.

Feature Fusion Layer. After getting the node representation z_c and z_s for client and service nodes respectively, we concatenate z_c and z_s with the embedding of other context features z_o which are obtained as follows:

$$z_o = \text{norm}\left(\sigma\left(W_o\left[e_1^o \| e_2^o \| ... \| e_m^o\right] + b_o\right)\right),\qquad(6)$$

where $W_o \in \mathbf{R}^{d \times (md')}$ is the trainable weight matrixes, the $b_o \in \mathbf{R}^d$ is the bias vectors for context features, σ denotes the *ReLU* activation function. Then we apply multiple fully connected layers to predict the service time for each sample:

$$\hat{y}_i = W_2\left(\sigma_1\left(W_1\left([z_c \| z_s \| z_o]\right) + b_1\right)\right) + b_2,\qquad(7)$$

where W_x, b_x and σ_x denotes the trainable weight matrix, bias vector and *ReLU* activation function for the x-th layer of MLP respectively. And we remove the activation function of the last layer for generating real-value prediction.

3.3   Label Normalization and Optimization

As for model optimization, our method is trained by optimizing the L1 normalization loss function in a supervised fashion. However, since labels of the personal banking time vary in a large range from a few minutes to hundreds of minutes, the model is unable to converge. Inspired by [15], we apply a function $\log(\cdot)$ to normalize the labels and train the proposed model by calculating the L1 normalization loss of processed labels as follows:

$$L(\hat{y}, y) = \frac{1}{N} \sum_{i=0}^{N} |\hat{y} - \tilde{y}|,\qquad(8)$$

where $\hat{y}$ is the prediction value, $\tilde{y}$ is calculated by $\tilde{y} = \log(y)$ and N is the batch size. Finally, the parameters of TGNN are updated by gradient descent in an end-to-end fashion. When we evaluate or test the performance of TGNN, we compute the metrics with $\exp(\hat{y})$ and the original label y.

4   Experiment

In this section, we first describe the characteristics of the collected real-world datasets and then our experimental settings. And we present the experimental results to show the effectiveness of TGNN.

4.1   Dataset Description

Table 1. Statistics of datasets.

Dataset	#Client	#Service	#Records	Sparsity
BTP-300K	226,854	6,478	321,265	0.083%
BTP-1M	600,510	8,000	981,185	0.092%

To our best knowledge, there is no available public dataset for the BTP task. To evaluate the effectiveness of the proposed model, we construct two real-world datasets depending on the size, i.e., BTP-1M and BTP-300K, with all the client information desensitized to protect data privacy. The statistics of these two datasets are summarized in Table 1. Both the datasets share the same feature fields which contain 8 client feature fields, 3 service feature fields, and 3 context feature fields. The proportion of training/validation/testing is set as 20%/20%/60% by chronological order.

4.2   Experimental Settings

Evaluation Metrics. We evaluate the performance of baseline models and our proposed TGNN model with two metrics, including Mean Absolute Percentage Error (MAPE) and Mean Absolute Error (MAE) which are denoted as follows:

$$MAPE = \frac{1}{N}\sum_{i=0}^{N}\frac{|y_i - \exp(\hat{y})|}{y_i}, \quad MAE = \frac{1}{N}\sum_{i=0}^{N}|y_i - \exp(\hat{y}_i)|. \quad (9)$$

Baseline Models. To demonstrate the effectiveness of TGNN, Several regression models commonly used are chosen to compare with TGNN.

- **Support Vector Regression** [4] is a regression technique based on Support Vector Machine (SVM) which implicitly maps inputs into high-dimensional feature spaces to find decision boundaries to predict the output.
- **Random Forest** [1,11] is an ensemble learning method constructed by a large number of decision trees which are trained by sampling different training data and is popular for regression task for its interpretability.
- **XGBoost** [2] is a highly efficient implementation under the gradient boosting framework and achieves excellent performance in many regression tasks.
- **Wide&Deep** [3] uses nonlinear feature transforms for sparse features and is popular in many applications of nonlinear regression tasks due to its superiority in modeling the memorization and generalization in one structure.

Hyper-parameter Settings. We use Adam as model optimizer and tune the learning rate to 0.0005. The batch size is set to 1024. To deal with scalability issues of GNN, we adapt the mini-batch training and random neighbor sampling while training. The number of GNN layers is fixed to 3 and the number of neighbors for each ego node is set to [20,20,20] correspondingly. The embedding size for each feature is set to 20, and the dimension of the initial embedding is set to 64. The dimension of the transformed embedding for each GNN layer is set to [64,64,64]. We use a two-layer MLP for final prediction and the units for each fully connected layer are set to [200, 100].

Table 2. Overall Performance Comparison.

Method	BTP-300K		BTP-1M	
	MAE	MAPE	MAE	MAPE
SVR	17.57	1.853	17.501	1.829
RF	10.968	0.861	10.740	0.846
XGBoost	10.220	0.790	10.149	0.773
Wide&Deep	10.633	0.897	10.600	0.854
TGNN	**9.883**	**0.590**	**9.877**	**0.553**
TGNN w/o Feat	10.295	0.593	10.077	0.572
TGNN w/o LN	10.155	0.635	10.123	0.663
TGNN w/o TN	10.397	0.661	10.614	0.632

4.3 Experiment Results

Overall Performance. We report the average metrics on the test set in Table 2 and we have the following observations:

- XGBoost outperforms other traditional models as well as deep learning method Wide&Deep and we attribute it to its robustness and its ability to handle outliers. SVR suffers from the sparsity of input features and performs poorly and RF fails to achieve as good performance as XGBoost.
- The deep learning method Wide&Deep performs much worse than XGBoost and we observe the over-fitting problem in training which shows that it cannot handle the sparse interaction problem.
- The results demonstrate that TGNN achieves the best performance on both metrics. The TGNN method achieves 0.070/0.078 improvement on MAPE and 3.3%/2.7% on MAE for BTP-300K and BTP-1M respectively and we contribute the improvement to the effective modeling of client and service via high-order connectivities.

Ablation Study on TGNN. As our method focuses on designing the GNN-based model to improve prediction, we conduct experiments on different variants to investigate the impacts of components of TGNN and the performance of these variants are reported in Table 2. The conclusions can be drawn as follows:

- The TGNN w/o Feat is a variant of TGNN that learns the node embeddings without using the features for both client nodes and service nodes and it performs second-best on both metrics, indicating that the model can learn useful node representations by only leveraging the connectivity of the nodes.
- The performance of TGNN w/o Label Normalization (LN) drops on MAPE indicating that label normalization is effective for improving TGNN.
- The TGNN w/o Tuple-Node(TN) is trained on a bipartite graph without tuple-node and regards the *bank* as node entity. The performance of TGNN w/o TN drops significantly on both metrics compared with TGNN which indicates the effectiveness of our method of bipartite graph construction with multi-entity nodes.

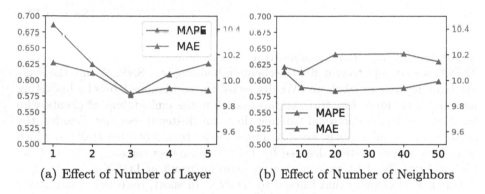

(a) Effect of Number of Layer   (b) Effect of Number of Neighbors

Fig. 3. Hyper-parameter Experiments on BTP-300K.

Hyper-parameter Experiments. As the GNN layer plays a significant role in learning the embedding representations for nodes, we investigate the impact of the number of layers and the number of sampled neighbors for each node. All the experiments are conducted on BTP-300K.

Effect of Number of Layers. To investigate the effect of the number of layers on TGNN, we adjust the layer numbers in the range of {1,2,3,4,5}. For convenience, we use TGNN-3 to indicate TGNN with 3 layers and the same notes for other variants. When varying the number of layers, TGNN is consistently superior to other methods on both metrics except for using only one layer. It again verifies the effectiveness of TGNN and empirically shows that explicit modeling of high-order connectivity can greatly facilitate the BTP task. And TGNN-2 and TGNN-3 achieve significant improvement over TGNN-1 and we attribute the improvement to the effective modeling of the clients through high-hop relations.

Effect of Number of Neighbors. We search the number of neighbors in the range of {5, 10, 20, 40, 50}, and the results are shown in Fig. 3(b). From the results we can conclude that increasing the number of neighbors can uplift the performance and it indicates that the more neighbors' information aggregated, the target node's embedding is learned better for the task.

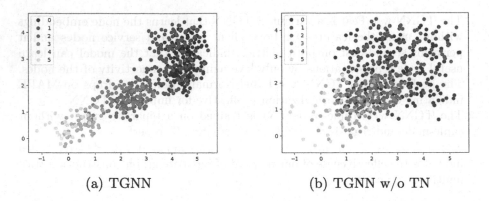

(a) TGNN   (b) TGNN w/o TN

Fig. 4. Visualization of client embeddings derived from TGNN and TGNN w/o TN.

Visualization of Client Embedding. For demonstrating the effectiveness of TGNN, we attempt to visualize the client embedding by t-SNE. We use the average banking time as labels and We discretize the continuous labels by bucketing for simplicity. From Fig. 4(a), we can find that the embeddings of clients who have similar average personal banking time are clustered together. Besides, the clusters with similar labels, are distributed closer than any other clusters, which means the representations learned by TGNN can reflect certain patterns of the clients. From Fig. 4(b), we can observe a similar result of TGNN w/o TN while it is not as obvious as that learned by TGNN. In short, both the visualization and evaluation metrics show that tuple-node bipartite graph construction helps to learn more expressive client representation for the BTP task.

5   Conclusions

In this paper, we investigated a new research problem of estimating the personal banking time and committed to addressing the major challenge of the anonymous client problem and sparse interaction problem which were not discussed in the existing works. Specifically, we first introduced a specific bipartite graph construction method for the Client-Service interaction which fused multiple entities for a tuple node. Then, we presented the TGNN model to learn node embeddings via stacking GNN layers on such a bipartite graph and predict the personal banking time in an end-to-end manner. Empirical studies on two real-world datasets collected from a fintech bank in China proved the effectiveness of our graph-based learning paradigm. In the future, we aim to further extend the framework to other applications in the banking scenario.

Acknowledgements. This research was partially supported by grants from the National Natural Science Foundation of China (Grants No. U20A20229, 61922073 and 62106244). Runlong Yu and Qi Liu thank the support of USTC-CMB Joint Laboratory of Artificial Intelligence. The collection and usage of user privacy data have been authorized by users to comply with Personal Information Protection Law of the P.R.C.

References

1. Carvalho, R.S., Carvalho, R.N., Ramos, G.N., Mouro, R.N.: Predicting waiting time overflow on bank teller queues. In: International Conference on Machine Learning and Applications (2017)
2. Chen, T., Guestrin, C.: Xgboost: A scalable tree boosting system. In: Knowledge Discovery and Data Mining (2016)
3. Cheng, H.T., et al.: Wide & deep learning for recommender systems. In: Conference on Recommender Systems (2016)
4. Drucker, H., Burges, C.J., Kaufman, L., Smola, A.J., Vapnik, V.: Support vector regression machines. In: Neural Information Processing Systems (1996)
5. Gomes, D., Nabil, R.H., Nur, K.: Banking queue waiting time prediction based on predicted service time using support vector regression. In: 2020 International Conference on Computation, Automation and Knowledge Management (ICCAKM), pp. 145–149. IEEE (2020)
6. Hamilton, W., Ying, Z., Leskovec, J.: Inductive representation learning on large graphs. In: Advances in Neural Information Processing Systems, vol. 30 (2017)
7. Hermanto, R.P.S., Suharjito, Diana, Nugroho, A.: Waiting-time estimation in bank customer queues using RPROP neural networks. Procedia Comput. Sci. **135**, 35–42 (2018)
8. Kipf, T.N., Welling, M.: Semi-supervised classification with graph convolutional networks. arXiv preprint arXiv:1609.02907 (2016)
9. Kyritsis, A.I., Deriaz, M.: A machine learning approach to waiting time prediction in queueing scenarios. In: International Conference on Artificial Intelligence (2019)
10. Liu, H., et al.: Technological knowledge flow forecasting through a hierarchical interactive graph neural network. In: 2021 IEEE International Conference on Data Mining (ICDM) (2021)
11. Sanit-in, Y., Saikaew, K.R.: Prediction of waiting time in one-stop service. Int. J. Mach. Learn. Comput. **9**(3), 322–327 (2019)
12. Shao, Q., et al.: Toward intelligent financial advisors for identifying potential clients: a multitask perspective. Big Data Min. Anal. **5**(1), 64–78 (2021)
13. Shi, C., et al.: Deep collaborative filtering with multi-aspect information in heterogeneous networks. IEEE Trans. Knowl. Data Eng. **33**(4), 1413–1425 (2019)
14. Wang, X., He, X., Wang, M., Feng, F., Chua, T.S.: Neural graph collaborative filtering. In: Proceedings of the 42nd International ACM SIGIR Conference on Research and Development in Information Retrieval, pp. 165–174 (2019)
15. Wu, L., Li, Z., Zhao, H., Pan, Z., Liu, Q., Chen, E.: Estimating early fundraising performance of innovations via graph-based market environment model. In: National Conference on Artificial Intelligence (2019)
16. Wu, L., Li, Z., Zhao, H., Qi, L., Chen, E.: Estimating fund-raising performance for start-up projects from a market graph perspective. Pattern Recogn. **121**, 108204 (2021)
17. Yu, R., Liu, Q., Ye, Y., Cheng, M., Chen, E., Ma, J.: Collaborative list-and-pairwise filtering from implicit feedback. IEEE Trans. Knowl. Data Eng. **34**(06), 2667–2680 (2022)
18. Zhao, H., et al.: A sequential approach to market state modeling and analysis in online p2p lending. IEEE Trans. Syst. Man Cybern. Syst. **48**(1), 21–33 (2017)

Spatial-Temporal Adaptive Graph Convolution with Attention Network for Traffic Forecasting

Weikang Chen[1]📷, Yawen Li[2](✉)📷, Zhe Xue[1]📷, Ang Li[1]📷, and Guobin Wu[3]

[1] Beijing Key Laboratory of Intelligent Telecommunication Software and Multimedia, School of Computer Science (National Pilot School of Software Engineering), Beijing University of Posts and Telecommunications,Beijing, People's Republic of China
{weikangchen,xuezhe,david.lee}@bupt.edu.cn
[2] School of Economics and Management, Beijing University of Posts and Telecommunications,China, People's Republic of China
warmly0716@126.com
[3] Didi Research Institute, Didi Chuxing,Beijing, People's Republic of China
wuguobin@didiglobal.com

Abstract. Traffic forecasting is one canonical example of spatial-temporal learning task in Intelligent Traffic System. Existing approaches capture spatial dependency with a pre-determined matrix in graph convolution neural operators. However, this explicit graph structure losses some hidden representations of relationships among nodes. Furthermore, traditional graph convolution neural operators cannot aggregate long-range nodes on the graph. To overcome these limitation, we propose a novel network, Spatial-Temporal Adaptive graph convolution with Attention Network (STAAN) for traffic forecasting. Firstly, we adopt an adaptive dependency matrix instead of using a pre-defined matrix during Graph Convolution Network (GCN) processing to infer the inter-dependencies among nodes. Secondly, we integrate PW-attention based on graph attention network, which is designed for global dependency, and GCN as spatial block. What's more, a stacked dilated 1D convolution, with efficiency in long-term prediction, is adopted in our temporal block for capturing the different time series. We evaluate our STAAN on two real-world datasets, and experiments validate that our model outperforms state-of-the-art baselines.

Keywords: Traffic forecasting · Graph attention network · Adaptive graph convolution · Spatial-temporal data

1 Introduction

Traffic forecasting is regarded as one of the key components of Intelligent Traffic System. Recent studies show that graph convolution neural network can deal with this complex data structure - graph structure data - better than traditional

L. Zhang et al. (Eds.): CINT 2022, CCIS 1714, pp. 80–91, 2022.
https://doi.org/10.1007/978-981-19-8915-5_8

convolution neural network. Spatial-temporal based on graph network models have been widely applied to solve these complex problems [1–5]. While in traffic speed forecasting, the dataset is collected by the speed sensors every time from the city's road network. Each sensor is viewed as a node in the traffic graph network. What's more, each node in practice is always affected by its surrounding neighbors. However, there are two problems when modeling the graph. On the one hand, most methods model the self-definition adjacent matrix based on Euclidean distance or Point of Interest as the relationship among the nodes. [5–7] process the adjacent matrix by road network distance with a thresholded Gaussian kernel. Firstly, the road status is changeable during the daytime. Secondly, using the distance to calculate the weight matrix, it ignores the third dimension information. Inspired by the [8], we propose graph convolution network with the adaptive matrix to represent the hidden relationship among nodes.

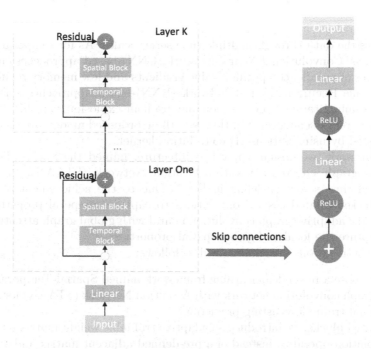

Fig. 1. The Architecture of our model STAAN. On the left, it consists of K spatial-temporal blocks which use different time steps. With the skip connections of those different time steps, there are two linear layers with activation layers on the right.

On the other hand, graph convolution operator aggregates neighbors' information by the adjacent matrix. For a long-term prediction, we need an operation to collect the global information among all nodes. Graph attention network [10,11] introduces an attention-based architecture to collect relevant information. [12] uses spatial attention to capture the spatiotemporal dynamic in road networks. [7,13] construct global and local extraction modules to consider the global information as well as local properties. To learn the similar conditions of any two roads of traffic network, we propose PW-attention mechanism based on graph to capture the global similarity information among nodes to enhance the ability of graph representation with the global graph.

Convolutional operation processes a local neighborhood, either in time or space. [7] adopts the gated mechanism to determine the ratio of information passed to the next layer. [14] proposes a non-local operation that computes the response at a position as a weighted sum of the features at all positions in the input feature maps. Traffic forecasting prediction is a long-term task. And non-local operations capture long-range dependencies directly by computing interactions between any two positions, regardless of their positional distance. With the assumption that similar roads have similar features, we combine the global graph attention as the similar function and graph convolution neural which is based on adaptive strategy, as the embedding function to enhance the ability to capture spatial features.

To accurately capture different time properties of traffic data, it is necessary to process the data through multiple time series scales. As for temporal prediction models, Convolutional Neural Network (CNN)-based approaches enjoy the advantages of parallel computing, stable gradients and low memory requirement [15,16] while Recurrent Neural Network (RNN)-based approaches suffer from time-consuming iterative propagation and gradient explosion/vanishing for capturing long-range sequences [17]. However, these proposed models are much more complicated by using various 1D convolution kernel.

In our work, we design a novel architecture, named the Spatial-Temporal Adaptive graph convolution with Attention Network (STAAN), for graph-structured time series modeling in Fig. 1. Due to the achievement of [5], we adopt stacked dilated casual convolutions to capture temporal properties. We combine the adaptive graph convolution neural with global graph attention neural to capture the local and global spatial properties.

Our contributions are summarized as follows:

- We propose a novel deep learning framework named Spatial-Temporal Adaptive graph convolution network with Attention Network (STAAN) for spatial-temporal traffic forecasting prediction.
- In spatial blocks, we introduce an adaptive trainable weight matrix into graph convolution operator, instead of a pre-defined adjacent matrix and attention mechanism named PW-attention function which aims for global information.
- We evaluate our STAAN on two real-world datasets, and experiments validate that our model outperforms state-of-the-art baselines.

2   Related Works

2.1   Graph Neural Network

Graph structured data is becoming more and more common in our daily life, like social connections, and traffic road networks. [18–20] design the graph convolution neural to deal with these graph-structured data. [21] introduces a Chebyshev polynomial parametrization for the spectral filter. Based on GCN, [6] combines graph convolution networks with recurrent neural networks in an encoder-decoder manner. [16] combines graph convolution with 1D convolution to tackle the time series prediction problem. To capture more information hidden in graph data, an adaptive matrix is a better ideal to extract properties during the processing of GCN.

Inspired by attention mechanism, graph attention network [22] proposes to learn the weighting function via self-attention mechanism which has been widely utilized in natural language processing etc. Graph attention network performs self-attention on the nodes with a shared attentional mechanism a:

$$e_{ij} = a(W[h_i, h_j]) \tag{1}$$

where $h_i \in R^C$ and $h_j \in R^C$ are both the input features, $W \in R^{C \times C'}$ is weight matrix, a is a shared attention function. Then normalize the coefficient $e_{ij} \in R$:

$$\alpha_{ij} = softmax_j(e_{ij}) = \frac{exp(e_{ij})}{\sum_{k \in N_i} exp(e_{ik})} \tag{2}$$

$$h_i' = \sigma(\sum_{j \in N_i} \alpha_{ij} W h_i) \tag{3}$$

where N_i is the set of neighbors of node i and $\sigma(\cdot)$ is an activation function. Recently, [22,23] propose a novel multi-level attention-based network. [24] propose Graph Multi-Attention Network (GMAN). [12] uses spatial attention to capture the spatiotemporal dynamic in road networks. [7] adopts the graph attention operation to extract the similar road conditions of traffic networks. Different from these works, our works adopt a dynamic trainable parameter matrix and attention mechanism as a similar measurement to automatically reflect and capture the hidden connection among all nodes.

2.2 Spatial-Temporal Prediction

In recent years, traffic forecasting problem has been viewed as a spatial-temporal forecasting task. However, there are two ways to capture the spatial-temporal. One is learning features with two components to capture temporal and spatial separately. [5] introduces self-adaptive graph and dilated convolution to capture spatial and temporal dependency. [12] is an end-to-end solution for traffic forecasting that captures spatial, short and long-term periodical dependencies. [25] uses spatial attention, temporal attention, and spatial sentinel vectors to capture the spatiotemporal dynamic in road networks. Others are to model spatial-temporal correlations simultaneously. Due to capturing heterogeneity of spatial and temporal properties simultaneously, those methods need to use more layers with different convolution operators. In all, to be computationally efficient heterogeneity between spatial feature and temporal feature, our model includes two components to capture spatial and temporal feature in traffic data separately.

3   Methodology

3.1   Traffic Prediction Problem

We target on the multi-step traffic forecasting problem. Consider multitudinous traffic series that contains history time series $X = \{X_{:,0}, X_{:,1}, ..., X_{:,t}\}$, and for each time step, $X_{:,t} = \{x_{1,t}, x_{2,t}, ..., x_{i,t}..., x_{N,t}\}^T \in R^{N \times C}$, where N is the number of all nodes and C denotes the features of each node. Our target is to predict the future features of all nodes by using the history data X.

$$[X_{:,0}, X_{:,1}, ..., X_{:,t}, G] \rightarrow F[X_{:,t+1}, ..., X_{:,t+T}] \tag{4}$$

where $G = (V, E, A)$, which denotes the road network. And V is a set of N nodes; E is a set of edges; $A \in R^{N \times N}$ corresponds to the adjacency matrix.

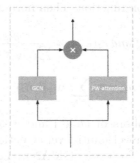

Fig. 2. Spatial Block. It contains of GCN and PW-attention components which captures the local and global spatial data.

3.2   Spatial Block with Graph Neural Network

Adaptive Matrix: Graph convolution is an essential operation to learn the nodes features. Most recent work in traffic forecasting deploys GCN to capture the spatial features. According to [20], the graph convolution operation can be well-approximated by 1st order Chebyshev polynomial expansion and generalized to high-dimensional GCN as:

$$Z = (I_N + D^{-\frac{1}{2}} A D^{-\frac{1}{2}}) X W \tag{5}$$

where $A \in R^{N \times N}$ is the normalized adjacency matrix, D is the degree matrix, and I_N is the identity matrix of n dimensions. And $X \in R^{N \times C}$ denote the input channels, $W \in R^{C \times F}$ is the layer-specific trainable weight matrix. GCN operator can divide into two operations: (1) aggregation the features from its neighbors. (2) transformation the features to a high dimensional space with the weight matrix. So in the first step, the effect of aggregation will be influenced by the adjacent matrix. Existing works mainly utilize the pre-defined adjacent matrix for GCN operation. [6] uses the distance to compute the pairwise road network and build the adjacency matrix using the thresholded Gaussian kernel. However, these calculated manually the matriax cannot truly reflect the hidden connections between the nodes. [5, 8] propose an adaptive matrix by multiplying the embedding of nodes $E_A \in R^{N \times d}$ and $E_A{}^T$ to replace the static adjacent matrix:

$$A_{adaptive} = g(E_A \bullet E_A{}^T) \tag{6}$$

where $g(\cdot)$ is a function to normalize the dynamic matrix. Instead of computing the degree matrix repeatedly, we can use the trainable E_A during the data training. Thus, the GCN can be formulated as:

$$Z = (I_N + A_{adaptive})XW \tag{7}$$

First, a dynamic trainable weight matrix, obtained by the dot product of the embedding nodes and its transposition, can truly reflect the hidden connections instead of using the pre-defined matrix. Rather than using the trainable parameter $A \in R^{N \times N}$, embedding function $E_A \in R^{N \times d}$ reduces the space complexity for faster training when $d \ll N$.

Graph Attention: A self-attention [9] module computes the response at a position in a sequence by attending to all positions and taking their weighted average in an embedding space. Graph attention network [17] is to compute the hidden representations of each node in the graph, following the self-attention strategy. With the assumption that similar roads have similar features. Like [7], we use the global graph attention networks to learn the similarity of the nodes instead of neighbors in graph attention networks. We define PW-attention:

$$a_{ij} = sigmoid(similarity(w_{ij}[x_i, x_j])) \tag{8}$$

$$output_i = \sum_{j \in N_i} a_{ij} w_{ij} x_j \tag{9}$$

where $similarity(\cdot)$ is a pairwise function compute a scalar which representing relationship between node i and j. And N_i is the all nodes. Different from GAT, we use the global graph to obtain relationship among nodes to enhance the ability to capture similar nodes' features.

Spatial Block: In our work, we use the GCN as the representation function and PW-attention as a similar function to learn the spatial features during the dataset. As shown in Fig. 2, the spatial block work as follows. First, we pass the input $H \in R^{N \times C}$ into GCN to capture the neighbors' feature, where N denotes the number of nodes, and C is the embedding dimension. On the other hand, we use the global graph PW-attention to learn similarity among different nodes. Then we combine above outputs with the element-wise Hadamard product. Experiments show that our spatial block performs well with the special module, which combines adaptive graph convolution network with PW-attention.

3.3 Temporal Block with Temporal Convolution Neural

We adopt the dilated causal convolution [27] as our temporal convolution neural layer to capture the temporal features trends. Figure 3 depicts dilated causal convolutions for dilations 1, 2, and 4. At the beginning of dilated causal convolution, it preserves the temporal causal order by padding zeros to the inputs. On the first layer, the dilated causal convolution operation slides over inputs by skipping values with the 1 step. And on the second layer, the step adds up to 2, which means the convolution just keeps some necessary information for the next layer. After stacked dilated convolutions, we will get a greatly large receptive field with a few layers. We adopt same gated mechanisms in dilated convolution in Fig. 4, which has been proved to control the features. For each layer:

$$z = g(W_{f,k}x) \otimes \sigma(W_{g,k}x) \tag{10}$$

where $\otimes$ denotes an element-wise product operator, function $g(\cdot)$ is an activation function of the output and $\sigma(\cdot)$ is the sigmoid function which decides whether the information should forget. K is the layer index, f and g denote filter and gate. And W is a learnable parameter. We set the $g(\cdot)$ as tangent hyperbolic function.

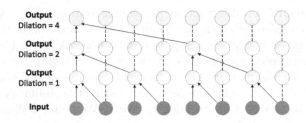

Fig. 3. A stack of dilated casual convolution layers.

3.4 Architecture of Network

As shown in Fig. 1, our framework of STAAN consists of stacked spatial-temporal blocks with skip connections to predict future traffic forecasting results. Each spatial-temporal block includes the temporal convolution neural (capture the time features) and the graph convolution networks (capture the space features). Our model can handle different temporal levels with different spatial-temporal blocks. For example, at the bottom block of our model, it can deal with the shortest-term time series, while from the bottom to the top, our model can receive more long-term time information. To keep the short-term information, we adopt a cascaded connection the higher-level uses the lower level's output as its input. So when the input of each block is a tensor H with the size of $[C, N, L]$ where C denotes embedding dimension, N is the number of all nodes, and L is the length sequence we want to predict. Spatial block is applied to each $h[:,:,i] \in R^{N \times C}$ to capture the spatial information. In the end, a skip connection is a great way to collect all the output from every block to predict the results.

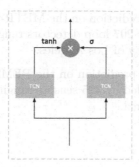

Fig. 4. Temporal Block.It contains dilated casual convolution layer with gated mechanisms.

3.5   Loss Function

We use the mean absolute error (MAE) to measure the performance of our model which is formulated as follows:

$$L(\hat{X}_{j:t+1}, ..., \hat{X}_{j:t+T}; \Theta) = \frac{1}{n} \sum_{i=1}^{T} \sum_{j=1}^{N} |\hat{X}_{j:i} - X_{j:i}| \tag{11}$$

where $X = \{X_{:,0}, X_{:,1}, ..., X_{:,t}\}$.

Table 1. Performance comparison of STAAN and other baseline models. STAAN achieves the best results on two datasets

Model	METR-LA(15/30/60 min)			PEMS-BAY(15/30/60 min)		
	MAE	MAPE(%)	RMSE	MAE	MAPE(%)	RMSE
ARIMA	3.99/ 5.15/ 6.90	9.60/ 12.70/ 17.40	8.21/ 10.45/ 13.23	1.62/ 2.33/ 3.38	1.62/ 2.33/ 3.38	1.62/ 2.33/ 3.38
FC-LSTM	3.44/ 3.77/ 4.37	9.60/ 10.90/ 13.20	6.30/ 7.23/ 8.69	2.05/ 2.20/ 2.37	4.80/ 5.20/ 5.70	4.19/ 4.55/ 4.69
DCRNN	2.77/ 3.15/ 3.60	7.30/ 8.80/ 10.50	5.38/ 6.45/ 7.59	1.38/ 1.74/ 2.07	2.90/ 3.90/ 4.90	2.95/ 3.97/ 4.74
GGRU	2.71/ 3.12/ 3.64	6.99/ 8.56/ 10.62	5.24/ 6.36/ 7.65	-	-	-
STGCN	2.87/ 3.48/ 4.45	7.40/ 9.40/ 11.80	5.54/ 6.84/ 8.41	1.46/ 2.00/ 2.67	3.01/ 4.31/ 5.73	2.90/ 4.10/ 5.40
APTN	2.76/ 3.15/ 3.70	7.30/ 8.80/ 10.69	5.38/ 6.43/ 7.69	1.38/ 1.97/ 2.33	2.91/3.69/4.65	2.96/ 3.95/ 4.60
ST-UNet	2.72/ 3.12/ 3.55	6.90/ 8.40/ 10.00	5.13/ 6.16/ 7.40	2.15/ 2.81/ 3.38	4.03/ 5.42/ 6.68	5.06/ 6.79/ 8.33
GWN	2.69/ 3.07/ 3.53	6.90/ 8.37/ 10.01	5.15/ 6.22/ 7.37	1.30/ 1.63/ 1.95	2.70/ 3.70/ 4.60	2.74/ 3.70/ 4.52
ST-GRAT	2.60/ 3.01/ 3.49	6.61/8.15/ 10.01	5.07/ 6.21/ 7.42	1.29/ 1.61/ 1.95	2.67/ 3.63/4.64	2.71/ 3.69/ 4.54
SLCNN	2.53/ 2.88/ 3.30	5.18/ 6.15/ 7.20	5.18/ 6.15/ 7.20	1.44/ 1.72/ 2.03	2.90/ 3.81/ 4.53	3.00/ 3.90/ 4.80
STAAN	2.49/ 2.85/ 3.29	5.15/ 6.13/ 7.23	5.10/ 6.10 / 7.15	1.27/ 1.57/ 1.92	2.67/ 3.63/ 4.51	2.58/ 3.57/ 4.40

4   Experiments

4.1   Dataset

In the experiment, we use the two real-world traffic datasets, namely METR-LA and PEMS-BAY released by [6]. More details for the datasets are in Table 2.

METR-LA. Traffic speed prediction on the METR-LA dataset, which contains 4 months of data recorded by 207 loop detectors ranging from March 1, 2012, to June 30, 2012, on the highway of Los Angeles.

PEMS-BAY. Traffic speed prediction on the PEMS-BAY dataset, which contains 6 months of data recorded by 325 sensors ranging from January 1, 2017, to June 30, 2017, in the Bay Area.

4.2 Baselines

We adopt Mean Absolute Errors (MAE), Mean Absolute Percentage Errors (MAPE), and Root Mean Squared Errors (RMSE) to compare the performance STAAN with the following state-of-the-art models:

- ARIMA. Auto-Regressive Integrated Moving Average model with Kalman filter [5].
- FC-LSTM. Recurrent neural network with fully connected LSTM hidden units [5].
- DCRNN. Diffusion convolution recurrent neural network [5], which combines graph convolution networks with recurrent neural networks in an encoder-decoder manner.
- GGRU. Graph gated recurrent unit network [17]. Recurrent-based approaches. GGRU uses attention mechanisms in graph convolution.
- STGCN. Spatial-temporal graph convolution network [16], which combines graph convolution with 1D convolution.
- GWN. A convolution network architecture [5], introduces a self-adaptive graph to capture the hidden spatial dependency, and uses dilated convolution to capture the temporal dependency.
- APTN. Attention-based Periodic-Temporal neural Network [12], which is an end-to-end solution for traffic forecasting that captures spatial, short-term, and long-term periodical dependencies.
- ST-UNet. Spatial-Temporal U-Net [13] adopts a U-shaped network to extract temporal and spatial properties simultaneously.
- ST-GRAT. Spatial-Temporal Graph attention [25], which uses spatial attention, temporal attention, and spatial sentinel vectors to capture the spatiotemporal dynamic in road networks.
- SLCNN. Spatial-temporal Graph Structure Learning [26] proposes pseudo three-dimensional convolution, which combines with the structure learning convolution to capture the temporal dependencies in traffic data.

4.3 Experimental Settings

All experiments are performed on a Linux server with one Intel(R) Xeon(R) Gold 5218 CPU @ 2.30 GHz and one NVIDIA GeForce RTX 2080 Ti CPU card. We use the eight blocks for capture the time sequence. And in temporal convolution neural, we use the sequence 1, 2, 1, 2, 1, 2, 1, 2 as the dilation sequence for each block. In spatial block, we use the softmax function as normalization in Eq. (1). During train model, we use the Adam optimizer as our optimizer, with initial value 0.001 and we adopt dropout with 0.3 for graph neural network. And we set the input dimension to 2, number of hidden layer to 40 and the output length sequence to 12. For dataset, we split it to 7:2:1 as the training data, valid data and the test data. All tests adopt 5 min as the time windows. And the target we want to get from our model is the future time in 15, 30, 60 min.

4.4 Experimental Results

Table 2. The details for the datasets

	METR-LA	PEMS-BAY
Nodes	207	325
Records	23974	52093
Time span	2012.03–2012.06	2017.01–2017.06
Time interval	5 min	
Daily range	0:00–24:00	

Table 1 shows the performance among these models for 15, 30, and 60 min ahead prediction on METR-LA and PEMS-BAY datasets. STANN gets the greatest performance in our experiment in particular. Several observations can be get by following analyses. Firstly, STAAN achieves a small improvement than SLCNN and GWN. We think our architecture is more capable of detecting spatial properties with PW-attention for global information instead of structure learning. Secondly, ST-GRAT uses spatial attention and temporal attention to capture the spatiotemporal properties. In contrast, STAAN employs stacked spatial-temporal blocks with different time steps for GCN blocks with different parameters. Thirdly, APTN, ST-GRAT have better results than STGCN, GGRU since APTN and ST-GRAT adopt attention mechanisms for both spatial and temporal properties. And ST-UNet adopts U-Net to capture spatial and temporal properties simultaneously, it performs the same as DCRNN at the short term prediction but shows better in the long term. FC-LSTM based on fully connected LSTM hidden units obtains a better than the traditional method.

5   Conclusion

In this paper, we present a Spatial-Temporal Adaptive graph convolution with the Attention mechanism Network, to address the traffic forecasting problem. STAAN composes spatial blocks based on GCN and temporal blocks based on TCN to capture heterogeneous graph structure data. Furthermore, STAAN utilizes an adaptive matrix and PW-attention mechanism which aims for learning global information. Validated on two real-world datasets, STAAN demonstrates the best performance than baselines for traffic forecasting.

Acknowledgements. This work was supported by the National Natural Science Foundation of China (No.62192784, No.62172056).

References

1. Chen, Z., Li, S., Yang, B., Li, Q., Liu, H.: Multi-scale spatial temporal graph convolutional network for skeleton-based action recognition. In Proceedings of the AAAI Conference on Artificial Intelligence **35**, 1113–1122 (2021)
2. Fang, Z., Long, Q., Song, G., Xie, K.: Spatial-temporal graph ode networks for traffic flow forecasting. In Proceedings of the 27th ACM SIGKDD Conference on Knowledge Discovery Data Mining, pp. 364–373 (2021)
3. Li, M., Zhu, Z.: Spatial-temporal fusion graph neural networks for traffic flow forecasting. In Proceedings of the AAAI conference on artificial intelligence **35**, 4189–4196 (2021)
4. Li, M., Jia, Y., Du, J.: LPV control with decoupling performance of 4WS vehicles under velocity-varying motion. IEEE Transactions on Control Systems Technology **22**(5), 1708–1724 (2014)
5. Wu, Z., Pan, S., Long, G., Jiang, J., Zhang, C. (2019). Graph wavenet for deep spatial-temporal graph modeling. arXiv preprint arXiv:1906.00121
6. Li, Y., Yu, R., Shahabi, C., Liu, Y.: Diffusion Convolutional Recurrent Neural Network: Data-Driven Traffic Forecasting. In International Conference on Learning Representations (2018)
7. Huang, R., Huang, C., Liu, Y., Dai, G., Kong, W.: LSGCN: Long Short-Term Traffic Prediction with Graph Convolutional Networks. In IJCAI, pp. 2355–2361 (2020)
8. Bai, L., Yao, L., Li, C., Wang, X., Wang, C.: Adaptive graph convolutional recurrent network for traffic forecasting. Advances in neural information processing systems **33**, 17804–17815 (2020)
9. Vaswani, A., Shazeer, N., Parmar, N., Uszkoreit, J., Jones, L., Gomez, A. N., ... Polosukhin, I.: Attention is all you need. Advances in neural information processing systems, 30 (2017)
10. Veličković, P., Cucurull, G., Casanova, A., Romero, A., Liò, P., Bengio, Y.: Graph Attention Networks. In International Conference on Learning Representations (2018)
11. Ashish Vaswani, Noam Shazeer, Niki Parmar, Jakob Uszkoreit, Llion Jones, Aidan N Gomez, Łukasz Kaiser, and Illia Polosukhin.: Attention is all you need. In NIPS, pp 5998–6008 (2017)
12. Park, C., Lee, C., Bahng, H., Tae, Y., Jin, S., Kim, K., ... Choo, J.: ST-GRAT: A Novel Spatio-temporal Graph Attention Networks for Accurately Forecasting Dynamically Changing Road Speed. In CIKM (2020)
13. Gao, H., Ji, S.: Graph representation learning via hard and channel-wise attention networks. In Proceedings of the 25th ACM SIGKDD International Conference on Knowledge Discovery & Data Mining, pp. 741–749 (2019)
14. Wang, X., Girshick, R., Gupta, A., He, K.: Non-local neural networks. In Proceedings of the IEEE conference on computer vision and pattern recognition, pp. 7794–7803 (2018)

15. Yan, Sijie, Yuanjun Xiong, and Dahua Lin.: Spatial Temporal Graph Convolutional Networks for Skeleton-Based Action Recognition. In Thirty-Second AAAI Conference on Artificial Intelligence, 2018
16. Bing Yu, Haoteng Yin, and Zhanxing Zhu.: Spatio-temporal graph convolutional networks: A deep learning framework for traffic forecasting. In IJCAI, pp 3634–3640, 2018
17. Defferrard, M., Bresson, X., Vandergheynst, P.: Convolutional neural networks on graphs with fast localized spectral filtering. Advances in neural information processing systems, 29 (2016)
18. Fang, Y., Deng, W., Du, J., Hu, J.: Identity-aware CycleGAN for face photo-sketch synthesis and recognition. Pattern Recognition **102**, 107249 (2020)
19. Lin, P., Jia, Y., Du, J., Yu, F.: Average consensus for networks of continuous-time agents with delayed information and jointly-connected topologies. In 2009 American Control Conference, pp. 3884–3889, (2009)
20. Shi, C., Han, X., Song, L., Wang, X., Wang, S., Du, J., Yu, P.S.: Deep Collaborative Filtering with Multi-Aspect Information in Heterogeneous Networks. IEEE Transactions on Knowledge and Data Engineering **33**(4), 1413–1425 (2021)
21. Welling, M., Kipf, T. N.: Semi-supervised classification with graph convolutional networks. In International Conference on Learning Representations (2016)
22. Liu, L., Zhang, R., Peng, J., Li, G., Du, B., Lin, L.: Attentive crowd flow machines. In Proceedings of the 26th ACM international conference on Multimedia, pp. 1553–1561 (2018)
23. Guo, S., Lin, Y., Feng, N., Song, C., Wan, H.: Attention based spatial-temporal graph convolutional networks for traffic flow forecasting. In Proceedings of the AAAI conference on artificial intelligence **33**, 922–929 (2019)
24. Zheng, C., Fan, X., Wang, C., Qi, J.: Gman: A graph multi-attention network for traffic prediction. In Proceedings of the AAAI conference on artificial intelligence **34**, 1234–1241 (2020)
25. Yu, B., Yin, H., Zhu, Z.: Spatio-Temporal Graph Convolutional Networks: A Deep Learning Framework for Traffic Forecasting. In IJCAI (2018)
26. Geng, X., Li, Y., Wang, L., Zhang, L., Yang, Q., Ye, J., Liu, Y.: Spatiotemporal multi-graph convolution network for ride-hailing demand forecasting. In Proceedings of the AAAI conference on artificial intelligence **33**, 3656–3663 (2019)
27. Shi, X., Qi, H., Shen, Y., Wu, G., Yin, B.: A spatial-temporal attention approach for traffic prediction. IEEE Transactions on Intelligent Transportation Systems **22**(8), 4909–4918 (2020)

Sentiment Analysis of Online Travel Reviews Based on Capsule Network and Sentiment Lexicon

Jia Wang(iD), Junping Du(✉)(iD), Yingxia Shao(iD), and Ang Li(iD)

Beijing Key Laboratory of Intelligent Telecommunication Software and Multimedia,
School of Computer Science (National Pilot School of Software Engineering),
Beijing University of Posts and Telecommunications, Beijing 100876, China
junpingdu@126.com, {Wangj2021110865,shaoyx,david.lee}@bupt.edu.cn

Abstract. With the development of online travel services, it has great application prospects to timely mine users' evaluation emotions for travel services and use them as indicators to guide the improvement of online travel service quality. In this paper, we study the text sentiment classification of online travel reviews based on social media online comments and propose the sentiment classification based on the Capsule Network and sentiment lexicon (SCCL). SCCL model aims at the lack of consideration of local features and emotional semantic features of the text in the language model. And make following improvements to the shortcomings. Capsule Network (CapNet) is introduced to extract local features while retaining good context features. On the other hand, the sentiment lexicon is introduced to extract the emotional sequence of the text to provide richer emotional semantic features for the model. To enhance the universality of the sentiment lexicon, the improved Semantic Orientation Pointwise Mutual Information (SO-PMI) algorithm based on Term Frequency-Inverse Document Frequency (TF-IDF) is used to expand the lexicon, so that the lexicon can also perform well in the field of online travel reviews.

Keywords: Capsule network · Sentiment lexicon · Travel reviews · BERT

1 Introduction

It is not difficult to see that the Internet has been deeply integrated into people's daily life. More and more people choose to release their emotions on social networks [1–4]. Therefore, how to use of Internet public opinion tendency to guide actual production and life has become a very important application prospect of text sentiment analysis. By introducing sentiment analysis technology, exploring online travel reviews can help online travel enterprises to analyze customers' needs promptly, to make timely feedback on their shortcomings, which has considerable application value.

Due to the use of BERT for pre-training to provide excellent upstream embedded training mode for downstream tasks, it has made a breakthrough in the field of Natural Language Processing (NLP). To improve the overall performance of an NLP model, we almost only need to consider how to obtain a downstream network structure with better performance. As the development of Recurrent Neural Network (RNN) seems to encounter some bottlenecks and Convolutional Neural Network (CNN) is more and more widely used in the NLP field, more and more people pay attention to the downstream task of text emotion classification using the hybrid network of CNN and RNN [5]. Despite the continuous progress of the RNN model structure, the application of the traditional CNN structure in the NLP field seems need to be improved.

In this paper, we proposed a text sentiment classification model based on CapNet and sentiment lexicon to analyze online travel reviews. We mainly improve the shortcomings of BERT-BiGRU from two aspects. At first, the Cap Net is introduced to enhance the learning of local features. What's more, the sentiment lexicon is used to provide more sufficient semantic features for the model. In order to solve these two problems, we took Weibo comments as an example and used capsule units instead of traditional convolution neurons. Meanwhile, manually selected sentiment seed words to expand the domain lexicon based on the SO-PMI algorithm to obtain a sentiment lexicon suitable for Weibo comments. Then we verified the effectiveness of our method on the labeled Weibo comment public data set and compared it with the BERT classification model. Finally, we crawled the travel related comments on the social platform through the crawler, screened and manually marked them, so that we completed the sentiment classification of online travel comments.

The contribution of this paper lies in 3 aspects:

- The capsule convolution cell is introduced to the BERT-BiGRU model instead of the traditional convolution neuron, so that the model can get the local features from the text sequence without destroying the well-extracted context features.
- The domain lexicon is extended based on the SO-PMI algorithm with the Weibo comment data set, and the extended domain lexicon is used to provide semantic features for the deep learning classification model.
- A hybrid model combining sentiment lexicon and deep neural network is used to process online travel reviews, which has achieved good performance in both public and self built data sets.

2   Related Work

Text sentiment classification is the basis of sentiment analysis and a branch of text classification. Sentiment classification is more based on the subjective emotional factors of the text sequence which represents the emotional tendency of the expression to distinguish different types, unlike the traditional text classification, which only focuses on the objective content of the text. Generally, the research related to text sentiment classification is classified from three technical levels: the method using sentiment lexicon, the method using machine learning, and the method based on hybrid models.

2.1   The Method Using Sentiment Lexicon

The sentiment classification method using the sentiment lexicon mainly matches the words used in the text with the lexicon, then analyzes the overall emotional tendency of the sequence pick up by processing a sentiment word sets which the words in this set hit the lexicon. Song et al. quantified the emotional intensity of the sequence at the word level by using the sentiment lexicon [6]. According to the number of words hitting the emotional dictionary and the weight of pre-related adverbs, they got the overall emotional score of the text. Yang et al. mined the emotional tendency of video comments through the SO-PMI algorithm and summarized and sorted out the sentiment lexicon in the field of video comments based on the standard sentiment lexicon [7]. Zhang et al. used a lexicon to analyze the emotion polarity of video barrage and expand the lexicon through the word2vec algorithm first [8]. Although it can efficiently recognize sentiment patterns with certain accuracy only by matching the lexicon quickly, this method does not consider the relationship between words. The emotional value of a single word can not change dynamically according to the article or sentence. At the same time, the effect of this method also depends heavily on the quality of the lexicon [9]. If you want to maintain a high level of the model, you need to maintain the dictionary quite often. Therefore, there are fewer and fewer methods to use lexicon alone.

2.2   The Method Using Machine Learning

The sentiment classification method using machine learning mainly focus on K-Nearest Neighbor [10], Naive Bayesian, and Support Vector Machines [11,12]. Compared with the way using sentiment lexicon, this method does not rely on manual construction, which reduces subjectivity. The classification model can be updated in time through the database. But this method usually cannot make full use of the contextual information which comes from contextual sequence and is pretty crucial in emotional analysis, so it eventually lead to a decline in accuracy. Therefore, the thinking of using deep learning has become the mainstream method.

Deep learning is a subset of machine learning and an application of multi-layer neural networks in learning [13–18]. For the problem of sentiment classification, there are two crucial network structures: CNN and RNN. CNN is usually used in image processing, but the research using CNN as text feature extraction has gradually increased recently. Shao combined Bert and TextCNN models and verified the effectiveness of the method through the takeaway review dataset [19]. Xu et al. constructed a hierarchical classification model pos-ACNN-CNN by introducing location coding and attention mechanism into the ordinary CNN model and achieved good results on the IMDB film review dataset [20].

Nowadays, bi-directional models such as BiLSTM and BiGRU have emerged, because these models are more in line with the characteristics of text information related to both front and back sequences. Yue et al. realized sentiment analysis through the BiLSTM network, before the word vector entered the neural network, they first increased the weight of the word vector of keywords through the pre-attention mechanism [21]. Compared with the traditional model, the accuracy can be improved by 1.7%. In order to handle the recursive net work, Lu et al. built an improved BiGRU that can easily adapt to this structure [22]. In addition, Textblob technology is used to correct spelling errors during preprocessing, so that the model can well avoid errors caused by spelling errors. These studies bring more semantic features to the methods based on deep learning.

2.3   The Method Based on Hybrid Models

At first, people thought that each CNN and RNN corresponds to different learning tasks, so a single network model was usually used to extract text feature [23–29]. Later, people gradually realized that the hybrid CNN and RNN model can extract text information more comprehensively [30–32].

However, due to the size of the convolution kernel and the application of the pooling layer, the traditional CNN model is insensitive to the spatial information of features, which is very unfriendly to text processing. Therefore, some researchers have used spatial information-sensitive Capsule Convolution Networks to deal with emotional text classification. Based on using CNN and BiGRU as feature extraction networks, Cheng et al. introduced capsule structure as a classifier to classify text emotion [33]. Xu achieved good performance in small sample data sets and cross-domain migration by integrating attention mechanism and capsule structure, using a multi-head self-attention-based feature extractor and capsule structure as a classifier [34]. Zhang used the capsule network to overcome the disadvantage of information loss in convolution neural network pooling operation and uses the capsule unit to replace the traditional convolution structure in a BiGRU-CNN model [35, 36].

Recently, some researchers have proposed sentiment text classification combining the sentiment lexicon method and deep learning method [37–39]. However, all these methods either lack the consideration of local features or lack the semantic feature information, so they cannot extract the text features comprehensively.

3   Model

This section will describe the overall situation of the SCCL model and introduce the key algorithms in the model in detail.

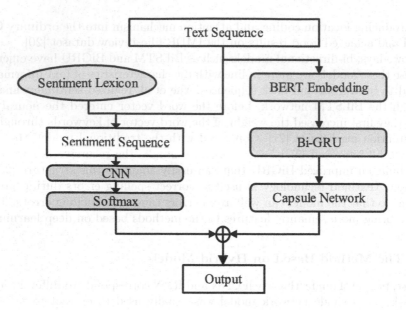

Fig. 1. Overall structure of SCCL

3.1 Overview

Figure 1 shows a simple block diagram of the overall situation of our SCCL structure. It can be seen that the SCCL model is generally divided into two routes to extract text features. On the one hand, the left half of Fig. 1 shows the sentiment semantic feature extraction route. First, the text sequence is segmented, and the stopped words are removed. Then the sentiment lexicon is used to match the text emotional feature words, the hit emotional feature words are combined into emotional sequences and embedded through the word2vec algorithm, and the emotional semantic features are extracted through the feature extraction network of CNN and Softmax. In the text context feature extraction part shown in the right half of Fig. 1, instead of word segmentation, Bert is directly used for character-level embedding, and then the combined network of BiGRU and CapNet is used to extract sequence's context features. Finally, the model will synthesize the results of the two parts of feature extraction and integrate the output.

3.2 BERT for Embedding

BERT is a pre-training language representation model based on the Transformers model. Figure 2 shows the simple structure of BERT and Tf modules represent Transformers block. BERT adopts a new training style called MLM for language mask training. This makes it possible to generate deep bi-directional linguistic representations. At the same time, BERT will embed each text sequence in three ways when inputting text sequences, namely token embeddings, segment

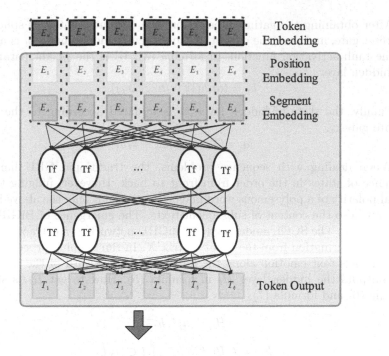

Fig. 2. Simple structure of BERT

embeddings, and position embeddings, which is also an indispensable feature for Bert to better extract context information. Since BERT was proposed, it achieved overwhelming advantages in many NLP tasks, and even aroused the pre-training frenzy in this field. Using BERT pre-training model has almost become the only choice for text processing.

3.3 BiGRU

GRU unit is a simplified and improved neural network model for LSTM. The LSTM module is composed of three gating units: input gate, forgetting gate, and output gate. In GRU neural network, the three gating units in LSTM are replaced by z_t and r_t, which represent the update gate and reset gate respectively. In this way, the parameters and tensors of the model are reduced, making GRU more concise and efficient than LSTM.

In an actual calculation process, GRU first obtains the gating information of z_t and r_t through x_t and h_{t-1} passed down from the previous node. In formula (1) and formula (2), σ represents the Sigmoid activation function, W_z and W_r are the weight parameters of the two gates respectively.

$$z_t = \sigma(W_z(h_{t-1}, x_t)) \tag{1}$$

$$r_t = \sigma(W_r(h_{t-1}, x_t)) \tag{2}$$

After obtaining the gating information, the current input x_t is spliced with the reset gate, and then the output of the currently hidden node $\tilde{h}_t$ is activated by the tanh activation function. In formula (3), W is the weight parameter of the hidden layer.

$$\tilde{h}_t = tanh(W(r_t h_{t-1}, x_t)) \tag{3}$$

Finally, the state of hidden layer h_t is updated according to the state of update gate z_t.

$$h_t = (1 - z_t)h_{t-1} + z_t \tilde{h}_t \tag{4}$$

When dealing with sequence problems, the traditional GRU handle the sequence of states in the order from front to back. However, judging the emotional polarity of a polysemous word maybe requires not only the above information, but also the content of subsequent texts. The emergence of BiGRU solves this problem. The SCCL model used the BiGRU network as a extractor of global semantic information from the input matrix X. In the training process, the network models text emotion along the forward and backward of the information and outputs the hidden layer H_t in formula (5). How to get H_t is shown in formula (6) and formula (7).

$$H_t = [h_t^{\rightarrow}, h_t^{\leftarrow}] \tag{5}$$

$$h_t^{\rightarrow} = GRU(X, h_{t-1}^{\rightarrow}), t \in [1, L] \tag{6}$$

$$h_t^{\leftarrow} = GRU(X, h_{t-1}^{\leftarrow}), t \in [L, 1] \tag{7}$$

3.4   Capsule Network

As an excellent feature detector, CNN can use a one-dimensional convolution kernel to extract local patterns from vector sequences, and then use the pooling operation to reduce parameters. However, these characteristics of CNN have also become an obstacle for the model to make an important breakthrough in the text field. First, the size of the convolution kernel determines the feature size that CNN can detect. For text processing, too large a convolution kernel will make it difficult for the model to learn the relationship between words, while too small a convolution kernel will make the model unable to deal with complex sentence structures such as inversion and preposition. On the other hand, the pooling operation will cause the CNN structure to lose a lot of spatial information. Text sequence is more sensitive to space, especially when the complex Chinese is the processing target, the pooling operation is easy to ignore the details hidden in the text. In contrast, the capsule network cannot be limited by the structure and size of the detection unit, and can automatically update the receptive domain, so that it can flexibly grasp the internal spatial relationship between the whole and local text, to learn the complex internal relationship of the text.

The core idea of the capsule network is to replace the traditional convolution neuron with the capsule layer. Therefore, the internal structure of the capsule layer is also different from that of ordinary neurons. In the capsule layer structure shown in Fig. 3, the primary capsule layer will divide the feature vector

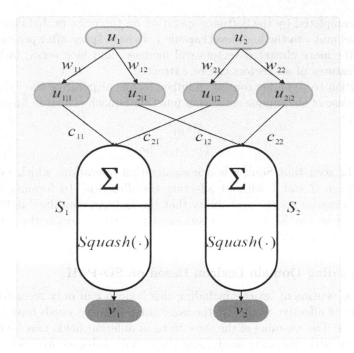

Fig. 3. Capsule layer structure

into multiple primary capsules through simple channel cutting. After the primary capsules enter the routing capsule layer, they first encode the position information through the affine transformation as formula (8). In this formula, u_i represents the ith primary capsule and $\bar{u}_{j|i}$ represents one of its high layer capsule, W_{ij} shows the affine metrics acting on it.

$$\bar{u}_{j|i} = W_{ij}u_i \tag{8}$$

Then, the capsule network will dynamically route the high-level capsules according to formula (9). In short, the dynamic routing is a weighted sum based on the weight c_{ij} in formula (10). c_{ij} determines how the vector after the affine matrix projection processing of this layer will enter the vector of the next layer. Unlike traditional neurons, the dynamic routing does not require bias.

$$S_j = \sum_i C_{ij}\bar{u}_{j|i} \tag{9}$$

$$C_{ij} = \frac{exp(b_{ij})}{\sum_k exp(b_{ik})} \tag{10}$$

It is not difficult to see that the key to dynamic routing is how to determine the weight coefficient c_{ij}. The capsule layer uses a method called Routing-by-agreement, which gives weight to the vector in a similar clustering way. This process is completed by the Softmax operation on the prior probability b_{ij} from the low-level unit i to the high-level capsule j. In each space after projection, the weight of the more clustered vectors will increase, and vice versa. In this way, the main features of all vectors can be extracted.

In addition to dynamic routing, another technical point of the capsule network is the use of the unique activation function Squash shown in formula (11).

$$v_j = \frac{||s_j||^2}{1 + ||s_j||^2} \frac{s_j}{||s_j||} \tag{11}$$

It can be seen that Squash is a normalization operation, which takes each vector between 0 and 1 without affecting the direction. In formula (11), the former term represents the probability that the features contained in the vector are perceived by the high-level network, and the latter term is the unit vector that maintains the direction.

3.5   Expanding Domain Lexicon Based on SO-PMI

The existing sentiment lexicon including this lexicon can only recognize a limited number of affective words. At the same time, Chinese words have polysemy and fuzziness. The meaning of the same word in different fields may be different, especially for text sentiment analysis in the social media environment [40]. On the one hand, because there are many new words in the text in the social media environment, the traditional sentiment lexicon is difficult to detect new words; On the other hand, the text content of social media has strong domain characteristics, and the general sentiment lexicon may bring serious misjudgment of information. Therefore, the emotional words in different fields should not be the same. We must build a unique domain sentiment lexicon for the field of Weibo comment text.

In order to identify the special emotion words in the field of online comments, this paper uses the combination of TF-IDF and SO-PMI to expand the sentiment lexicon. Compared with the traditional SO-PMI, this method can consider more semantic information of emotional words and reduce manpower [7]. TF-IDF algorithm can evaluate the importance of a word relative to a certain text in the whole corus. PMI is used to measure the relevance between two words. The calculation formula is shown in formula (12), which $P(w_1, w_2)$ shows the probability of word w_1 and w_2 in the same text. The SO-PMI algorithm judges whether a word is more likely to appear with positive words or negative words based on the PMI value of words. The calculation formula is shown in formula (13).

$$PMI(w_1, w_2) = log_2[\frac{P(w_1, w_2)}{P(w_1)P(w_2)}] \tag{12}$$

$$SO - PMI(word) = \sum_{seed \in Pos} PMI(word, seed)$$
$$- \sum_{seed \in Neg} PMI(word, seed) \tag{13}$$

We first rank the words in the corpus according to their TF-IDF values, and then manually select the 100 most important high-frequency emotional words. The 100 high-frequency emotion words include 50 positive emotion words and 50 negative emotion words represented by *Pos* and *Neg* in formula (13). Then the 100 emotion words are used as emotion seed words, and then the SO-PMI values of the words in the corpus are calculated to select 60 positives and 60 negatives with the most obvious emotional tendency, which are added to the sentiment to form a domain lexicon.

4   Experiment

This section mainly introduces the results of the experiment based on our SCCL model, including the used text datasets and sentiment lexicon, then briefly analyzes the experimental results.

4.1   Dataset

The text data set we used in this study for model training is from the public Weibo Review data set. This data set contains 40133 texts, which are divided into six categories. These data comes from 17133 items in the NLPCC Emotion Classification Challenge and 23000 labeled Weibo review data. During the training, 10% of the training data will be randomly selected as the test set. Then we use the crawler technology to crawl a number of travel comments on Weibo and other social platforms, filter and manually mark 2000 comments as the target set, we ensure that the category distribution is equivalent to the training set in this process. The classification of data sets is shown in Table 1.

Table 1. Classification of data sets

Dataset	Class	Label	Number
Training	Null	0	13993
	Like	1	6697
	Sad	2	5348
	Disgust	3	5978
	Anger	4	3167
	Happiness	5	4950
Target	Null	0	700
	Like	1	200
	Sad	2	300
	Disgust	3	300
	Anger	4	200
	Happiness	5	300

The collection of emotion words and their related emotion resources is called the sentiment lexicon. It is an important supporting resource for text sentiment analysis and mining [40]. HowNet's Chinese sentiment lexicon is used in our.

4.2   Effectiveness of Capsule Network

In order to prove that the Capsule network can perform well in text processing, we replace the capsule structure in the SCCL model with a multi-head CNN for comparison. At the same time, in order to verify whether other convolution structures sensitive to time and space can also surpass the performance of traditional CNN, we also try to use the Temporal Convolution Network TCN to replace the Capsule network. Causal Convolution, an important structure of TCN, is a convolution model proposed to deal with sequence problems. This convolution structure can combine the information of pre-sequence states when predicting a certain state, which gives the network time sensitivity. On the other hand, another important structure of TCN, Dilated Convolution can endow the model with spatial sensitivity.

Table 2. Text sequence feature extraction network

Model	acc	f1
CNN	48.68	46.59
Multi-head CNN	51.11	49.72
TCN	48.92	47.47
Capsule network	**52.45**	**51.0**

In Table 2, it can be seen that by using the Capsule structure can our SCCL model get an better performance using CNN or TCN, which also stems from the fact that the Capsule structure can better retain the space-time information of the feature vector and ensure that the features will not be lost in the deep network. On the contrary, although the traditional CNN has expanded the receptive fields as much as possible through the multi-head mechanism, the convolution results of connecting different receptive fields in parallel are not flexible enough, and the effect is not as good as the Capsule network. In addition, although TCN overcomes the disadvantage of space-time insensitivity, the prediction of this convolution model in a certain state cannot be related to the information at any future time, which also violates the trend of NLP using bi-directional structure. In particular, when it is used together with BERT and BiGRU, the bi-directional features obtained by the low-level network are lost to a certain extent, resulting in a decline in performance.

4.3   Effectiveness of Sentiment Lexicon

In order to choose which feature extraction network to use to extract the features of sentiment sequences, we also conducted a group of comparative experiments. Because the sentiment sequence is only composed of some intermittent emotional words, the context feature is weaker than the text sequence, or we don't want the model to learn wrong context information through it. Therefore, we don't use the feature extraction structure similar to the text but only use the simple convolution extraction structure. At the same time, we replace the simple convolution in SCCL with multi-head convolution, capsule convolution, and temporal convolution for comparison. In Table 3, it can be seen that the effects of several convolution structures are similar, but the simple CNN structure still has better performance.

Table 3. Sentiment sequence feature extraction network

Model	acc	f1
Multi-head CNN	52.09	49.6
TCN	52.01	49.9
Capsule network	52.27	51.13
CNN	**52.45**	**51.0**

4.4 Ablation Experiment

Finally, in order to verify all parts in SCCL is effective, we also conduct ablation experiments. The main method is to remove all parts of the SCCL model or replace them with other structures. In Table 4 it can be seen that the SCCL model is indeed better than the network of BERT direct classification or BERT words embedded in BiGRU to extract features. At the same time, the introduction of a Capsule network can bring greater improvement than the introduction of the sentiment lexicon, which is mainly limited by the quality of the sentiment lexicon. In particular, the sentiment lexicon we use only contains the emotional polarity of words, but the actual classification task has six categories. Positive emotion and negative emotion are divided into two categories and three categories respectively, which also limits the accuracy of classification. Nevertheless, the effect of using the lexicon with domain expansion is better than that of the common lexicon and the method without a lexicon. At the same time, the SCCL model can also achieve 48% accuracy on our target set, which proves that our model has certain generalization.

Table 4. Ablation experiment results

Model	acc	f1
BERT	50.04	47.94
BERT-BiGRU	51.05	49.14
BERT-CapsuleNet	50.75	48.86
BERT-BiGRU-CapsuleNet	51.63	49.98
BERT-BiGRU-Normal Lexicon	51.00	48.86
BERT-BiGRU-Expanded Lexicon	51.15	49.43
SCCL	**52.45**	**51.0**
SCCL-test	**48.58**	**47.43**

5   Conclusion

In this paper, we study a sentiment classification model SCCL based on capsule network and sentiment lexicon from two aspects: how to enhance the local feature extraction ability of the mixed language model and how to provide more emotional semantic features for the sentiment classification model. It is proved that the capsule network as a local feature extractor is better than the traditional CNN through experimental verification. It is also found that TCN and the bi-directional language model are not effective when used together. In addition, we also confirmed that the introduction of a sentiment lexicon into the deep learning model can add better semantic features to the model to improve performance, and this dictionary must be expanded in combination with the application field, otherwise, it is difficult to get excellent results.

As future work, we plan to start with building a better domain lexicon. In this experiment, the sentiment lexicon we used can only distinguish the positive and negative polarity of emotional words, but we are facing a problem of multiple classifications. Both positive and negative texts are divided into different categories, which makes it difficult for the lexicon to play a role in distinguishing these texts.

Acknowledgements. This work was supported by the National Natural Science Foundation of China (No. 62192784, No. 62172056).

References

1. Shi, W., Cue, G., He, S.: Literature review of network public opinion research from the perspective of sentiment. Doc. Inf. Knowl. **39**(1), 105–118 (2022)
2. Kou, F., Du, J., He, Y., Ye, L.: Social network search based on semantic analysis and learning. CAAI Trans. Intell. Technol. **1**(4), 293–302 (2016)
3. Li, A., et al.: Scientific and technological information oriented semantics-adversarial and media-adversarial cross-media retrieval. arXiv preprint arXiv:2203.08615 (2022)
4. Yang, Y., Du, J., Ping, Y.: Ontology-based intelligent information retrieval system. J. Softw. **26**(7), 1675–1687 (2015)
5. Chen, Z., Yue, Q.: Review of research on application of deep learning network model in text sentiment classification task. Libr. Inf. Stud. **15**(01), 103–112 (2022)
6. Song, G., Cheng, D., Zhang, S., Liu, W., Ding, X.: A model of textual emotion score calculation based on the emotion dictionary. China Comput. Commun. **33**(22), 56–58 (2021)
7. Yang, L., Zhai, T.: Research on affective tendency based on affective dictionary. Netw. Secur. Technol. Appl. **2022**(03), 53–56 (2022)
8. Zhang, T., Ni, Y., Mo, T.: Sentiment curve clustering and communication effect of barrage videos. J. Comput. Appl. 1–20 (2022)
9. Wang, Y., Zhu, J., Wang, Z., Bai, F., Gong, J.: Review of applications of natural language processing in text sentiment analysis. J. Comput. Appl. **42**(4), 1011–1020 (2022)

10. Sun, B., Du, J., Gao, T.: Study on the improvement of K-nearest-neighbor algorithm. In: 2009 International Conference on Artificial Intelligence and Computational Intelligence, no. 4, pp. 390–393 (2009)
11. Ajitha, P., Sivasangari, A., Rajkumar, R., Poonguzhali, S.: Design of text sentiment analysis tool using feature extraction based on fusing machine learning algorithms. J. Intell. Fuzzy Syst. **40**(1), 1–9 (2022)
12. Hu, M., Fan, C., Zhu, Y.: Emotional analysis of weibo comments based on machine learning. China Comput. Commun. **32**(12), 71–73 (2020)
13. Fang, Y., Deng, W., Du, J., Hu, J.: Identity-aware CycleGAN for face photo-sketch synthesis and recognition. Pattern Recogn. **102**, 107249 (2020)
14. Li, W., Jia, Y., Du, J.: Distributed consensus extended Kalman filter: a variance-constrained approach. IET Control Theory Appl. **11**(3), 382–389 (2017)
15. Xu, L., Du, J., Li, Q.: Image fusion based on nonsubsampled contourlet transform and saliency-motivated pulse coupled neural networks. Math. Probl. Eng. (2013)
16. Lin, P., Jia, Y., Du, J., Yu, F.: Average consensus for networks of continuous-time agents with delayed information and jointly-connected topologies. In: 2009 American Control Conference, pp. 3884–3889 (2009)
17. Meng, D., Jia, Y., Du, J.: Consensus seeking via iterative learning for multi-agent systems with switching topologies and communication time-delays. Int. J. Robust Nonlinear Control **26**(17), 3772–3790 (2016)
18. Li, M., Jia, Y., Du, J.: LPV control with decoupling performance of 4WS vehicles under velocity-varying motion. IEEE Trans. Control Syst. Technol. **22**(5), 1708–1724 (2014)
19. Shao, H.: Sentiment analysis of Chinese short text based on BERT-TextCNN. China Comput. Commun. **34**(01), 77–80 (2022)
20. Xu, Y., Lin, X., Lu, L.: Long text sentiment classification model based on hierarchical CNN. Comput. Eng. Des. **43**(04), 1121–1126 (2022)
21. Yue, W., Zhu, C., Gao, Y.: BiLSTM Chinese text sentiment analysis based on pre-attention. World Sci. Res. J. **7**(6), 33–42 (2021)
22. Lu, X., Zhang, H.: Sentiment analysis method of network text based on improved At-BiGRU model. Sci. Program. **2021**(12), 1–11 (2021)
23. Shi, C., et al.: Deep collaborative filtering with multi-aspect information in heterogeneous networks. IEEE Trans. Knowl. Data Eng. **33**(4), 1413–1425 (2019)
24. Li, Q., Du, J., Song, F., Wang, C., Liu, H., Lu, C.: Region-based multi-focus image fusion using the local spatial frequency. In: 2013 25th Chinese Control and Decision Conference (CCDC), pp. 3792–3796 (2013)
25. Li, W., Jia, Y., Du, J.: Distributed extended Kalman filter with nonlinear consensus estimate. J. Franklin Inst. **354**(17), 7983–7995 (2017)
26. Zhao, L., Jia, Y., Yu, J., Du, J.: H∞ sliding mode based scaled consensus control for linear multi-agent systems with disturbances. Appl. Math. Comput. **292**, 375–389 (2017)
27. Weiming, H., Gao, J., Bing Li, O.W., Junping, D., Maybank, S.: Anomaly detection using local kernel density estimation and context-based regression. IEEE Trans. Knowl. Data Eng. **32**(2), 218–233 (2018)
28. Li, W., Jia, Y., Du, J.: Variance-constrained state estimation for nonlinearly coupled complex networks. IEEE Trans. Cybern. **48**(2), 818–824 (2017)
29. Li, W., Jia, Y., Du, J., Yu, F.: Gaussian mixture PHD filter for multi-sensor multi-target tracking with registration errors. Sig. Process. **93**(1), 86–99 (2013)
30. Yan, C., He, L.: Research on text sentiment analysis of dual-channel neural model based on BERT. Intell. Comput. Appl. **12**(05), 16–22 (2022)

31. Deng, H., Ergu, D., Liu, F., Cai, Y., Ma, B.: Text sentiment analysis of fusion model based on attention mechanism. Procedia Comput. Sci. **199**, 741–748 (2022)
32. Li, Z., Yang, Y., Wu, L., Li, J.: Study of text sentiment analysis method based on GA-CNN-LSTM model. J. Jiangsu Ocean Univ. (Nat. Sci. Ed.) **30**(04), 79–86 (2021)
33. Cheng, Y., Sun, H., Chen, H., Li, M., Cai, Y., Cai, Z.: Text sentiment analysis capsule model combining convolutional neural network and bidirectional GRU. J. Chin. Inf. Process. **35**(05), 118–119 (2021)
34. Xu, L.: Short text sentiment analysis based on self-attention and capsule network. Comput. Modern. **2020**(07), 61–64+70 (2020)
35. Zhang, L.: Capsule text classification method combining GRU and attention mechanism. Technol. Innov. Appl. **12**(05), 15–17+21 (2022)
36. Hu, C., Xia, L., Zhang, L., Wang, C., Han, X.: Comparative study of news text classification based on capsule network and convolution network. Comput. Technol. Dev. **30**(10), 86–91 (2020)
37. Luo, H., Yang, Q.: Sentiment analysis based on sentiment lexicon and stacked residual BiLSTM network. J. Comput. Appl. **42**(04), 1099–1107 (2022)
38. Duan, R., Huang, Z., Zhang, Y., Liu, X., Dang, Y.: Sentiment classification algorithm based on the cascade of BERT model and adaptive sentiment dictionary. Wirel. Commun. Mob. Comput. (2021)
39. Yang, S., Zhang, N.: Text sentiment analysis based on sentiment lexicon and context language model. J. Comput. Appl. **41**(10), 2829–2834 (2021)
40. Wang, Z., Chen, Y., Zhou, H., Sun, T.: The construction of a domain sentiment lexicon based on chinese text. Inf. Res. **2020**(11), 48–56 (2020)

A Sentiment Analysis Model for Car Review Texts Based on Adversarial Training and Whole Word Mask BERT

Xingchen Liu[1] , Yawen Li[2]([⊠]) , Yingxia Shao[1] , Ang Li[1] , and Jian Liang[3]

[1] Beijing Key Laboratory of Intelligent Telecommunication Software and Multimedia,
School of Computer Science (National Pilot School of Software Engineering),
Beijing University of Posts and Telecommunications, Beijing 100876, China
{2021110866,shaoyx,david.lee}@bupt.edu.cn
[2] School of Economics and Management,
Beijing University of Posts and Telecommunications,
Beijing, People's Republic of China
warmly0710@120.com
[3] Didi Research Institute, Didi Chuxing, Beijing, People's Republic of China
liangjian@didiglobal.com

Abstract. In the automotive world, reviews will influence buyer decisions and word of mouth. As an important branch of natural language processing, sentiment analysis provides an effective research method for sentiment analysis of reviews. However, due to the large differences between the review texts in the automotive field and the pre-trained texts, and the large differences in the review texts, when the classification model is directly applied to the car reviews, some indicators of the model will be deteriorated. In order to overcome the above challenges, from the perspective of word vector, use whole-word masks of automotive domain-specific vocabulary and then train with an adversarial strategy. We propose a textual sentiment analysis model for car reviews based on adversarial training and whole-word mask BERT.

Keywords: Adversarial training · Whole word mask BERT · Sentiment analysis

1 Introduction

At present, there are many car information websites in China that provide platforms for publishing car reviews, such as Dongchedi, Autohome, etc. A large number of car-buying users post their car-buying experience and product usage experience on these websites. Therefore, in the face of a large number of text review data containing evaluation content such as automotive product performance, quality, and brand services, how to make full use of text mining and other related technologies to efficiently mine the user emotional information contained

L. Zhang et al. (Eds.): CINT 2022, CCIS 1714, pp. 107–121, 2022.
https://doi.org/10.1007/978-981-19-8915-5_10

in the review text, and find out the user's demand for products. Emotional tendencies, so as to assist consumers to make accurate purchasing decisions, help auto companies to improve products and services in a targeted manner, and enhance corporate competitiveness are important issues that need to be solved at present [1–4]. In this paper, we optimize the emotion recognition in the car review domain by increasing the whole word mask of the automotive domain vocabulary and adversarial training to the BERT model.

For emotion recognition in the automotive field, the current main methods are the method based on emotion dictionary, machine learning and deep learning, etc. [5–9]. In today's Internet environment, new words are generated every day, and a lot of manpower is required to construct the sentiment dictionary, and the sentiment dictionary-based method strongly relies on the sentiment dictionary, so it has great limitations [5,10]. Sentiment classification based on machine learning requires manual labeling of text features; secondly, machine learning needs to rely on multiple data, which is prone to ineffective work, and the model is not efficient, and it is difficult to adapt to today's rapidly-developing world. The sentiment analysis method based on deep learning has been developed rapidly in recent years [6,14,15], and the accuracy has been greatly improved, but it cannot accurately classify professional vocabulary in specific fields.

In this paper, we consider the special form of Chinese and its importance in natural language processing, introduce proper nouns in the automotive field, and construct a BERT with whole word mask. A lot of redundant punctuation marks in the training data, so based on this, we use adversarial training to train the BERT covered by the whole word to extract more robust vectors and bring them into the classification network, so that the model can better adapt to the car reviews generated by users. Has good practical value. The main contributions are as follows:

- A BERT algorithm based on whole word mask of automobile domain vocabulary is proposed, By introducing proper nouns in the automobile domain, supervised learning is performed, which is more suitable for classifying the sentiment tendency of automobile reviews.
- A method for adversarial training of the above model is proposed, which improves the anti-interference ability of the model by adding disturbance factors to the word Embedding and the final fully connected layer.
- Through experimental comparison, the BERT model with whole word mask based on adversarial training proposed in this paper is superior to the most cutting-edge sentiment analysis model in both the accuracy and F1 of car evaluation sentiment analysis.

2   Related Work

For emotion recognition in the automotive field, the current main methods are the method based on emotion dictionary, machine learning and deep learning, etc. [1,2,5,6,18].

The method of a sentiment dictionary is to construct a sentiment dictionary artificially first. The sentiment value of sentiment words in the document is obtained by using the sentiment dictionary, and the overall sentiment tendency of the document is determined by weighted calculation. This method can define the sentiment of words, which is easy to analyze and understand by readers. If the content of the dictionary is rich enough, a better effect of sentiment analysis can be obtained [8,32,33]. However, the method based on the sentiment dictionary relies too much on the sentiment dictionary and always has the limitation of the dictionary. In today's information age, new words appear every day, and the maintenance of the dictionary requires a great cost [21,36]; at the same time, this method also does not involove the relationship between words and the context.And the sentiment dictionary is not applied to processing multiple datasets. Gradually, researchers began to study sentiment analysis based on machine learning.

Compared with the method of using an emotional dictionary, machine learning does not rely on manual construction, which saves a lot of manpower. Through the database, the thesaurus can be updated in time. In machine learning, KNN [12,13], NB [16] and Support Vector Machine (SVM) [17] are commonly used learning algorithms. SVM and NB are better for the classification of text data [15]. Rodrigo Moraes proposed an SVM-based sentiment analysis method at the document level, which finally achieved 84.1% results on the Movies dataset [34]. V Narayanan demonstrating that the combination of word n-grams and mutual information feature selection can significantly improve accuracy [35]. The sentiment classification method needs to rely on a large amount of data, thus leading to ineffective results and slow execution speed. If the efficiency of the model is not high, it is difficult to adapt era of information explosion [19].

The introduction of deep learning has greatly promoted the development of sentiment classification. The deep learning method mainly uses embedding and multi-layer neural network [20–23] for forwarding propagation, and finally maps it into a set of vectors [24]. At present, the mainstream deep learning models for sentiment analysis include BiLSTM [25] proposed by S Hochreiter and Transformer [26] proposed by A Vaswani et al. Zhongdu has achieved the achievement of SOTA. Deep learning training models consume a lot of computing power, and the emergence of transfer learning and pre-training models has made deep learning popular [37]. A pre-trained model refers to a model that has been trained on a dataset. Researchers hope that the model that has spent a lot of time training can be retained and fine-tuned on their own dataset. The latest pre-training models for sentiment analysis include: Embeddings from Language Models (ELMo) [27], BERT, and other deep learning-based sentiment analysis methods have developed rapidly in recent years, and the accuracy has been greatly improved, but for specific fields The professional vocabulary cannot be accurately classified.

Adversarial training was originally proposed by Generative adversarial nets, which is a method of defending against malicious attacks in the image field to improve the robustness of the model [28–30]; then Miyato applied adversarial training to text classification tasks [31,38–40].

3 Method

We propose an adversarial training and whole-word mask BERT (ATWWM-BERT), which is mainly composed of two parts, which are the whole-word mask BERT model based on the car review domain (Sect. 3.1) and the adversarial learning-based text classification strategy (Sect. 3.2) composition. Next, each of them will be described in detail.

3.1   Whole-Word Mask BERT Model Based on Car Review Domain

In Chinese natural language processing, since the BERT model adopts the word segmentation method of word granularity in Chinese, a sentence is divided into an array composed of words. For example, the word 'Bi Ya Di" will be split into three words "Bi", "Ya" and "Di" when inputting. During pre-training, these words segmented by the tokenizer are randomly replaced by [MASK]. Obviously, such a pre-training method makes BERT unable to learn the semantic information in Chinese text very well. In this paper, the Bidirectional Encoder Representation from Transformers-whole word mask (BERT-wwm) pre-training model, When some words in a phrase related to the car review domain are covered by [MASK] during training, other words that belong to the same phrase will also be [MASK]. After the BERT pre-training based on the whole-word mask of the car review field, the BERT pre-training model can extract more representation information in the car review field, which can better solve the car review field. Semantic ambiguity and sparse key features. The specific whole-word mask pre-training process in the field of car reviews is as follows:

The MLM model is used to randomly block 15% of the entries in the car review corpus sentences, and then the model predicts what the removed entries are. For the randomly occluded words, the pre-training method of whole word mask in the field of car reviews is used: i). 80% of the word vectors are replaced by [MASK] when inputting, if the word is part of the relevant nouns in the field of car reviews, other characters that belong to the same word will also be covered accordingly; ii). The other 15% of the word vectors are replaced by other word vectors. Similarly, if the word is part of the relevant nouns in the field of car reviews, other characters that belong to the same word will also be replaced accordingly; iii), 5% of the word vector input remains normal. The generated samples of are shown in Table 1.

We have achieved the pre-training process for the whole word mask of the car review field through the above method. From Table 1, we can find that this pre-training method can extract more information in the car review field and better solve the problems that appear in the car review. Problems with sparse proper nouns and key features. The model structure is shown in Fig. 1:

Table 1. Generating examples of whole word mask in the domain of car reviews

Approach	Result
Original text	My Bi Ya Di drove 70,000 km and consumed 8 fuel per 100 km. The space and control are also good. Very satisfied with the purchase
Original BERT generation case	My Bi [MASK] Di drove 70,000 km and consumed 8 fuel per 100 km. The space and control are also good. Very [MASK] with the purchase
The whole word covers the field of car reviews	My [MASK][MASK][MASK] drove 70,000 km and consumed 8 fuel per 100 km. The space and control are also good. Very [MASK] with the purchase

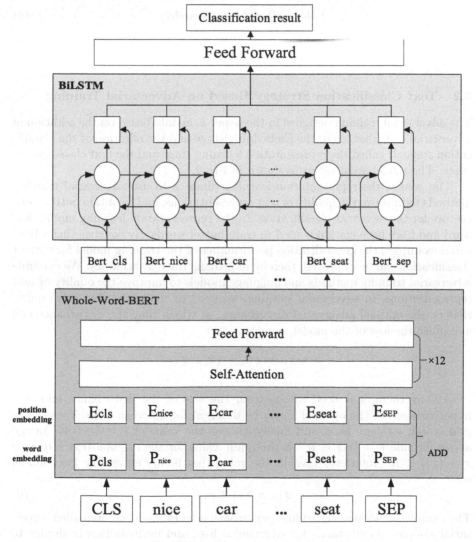

Fig. 1. Model structure diagram

When the reviews and car review entities are input into the BERT pretrained model based on the whole word mask of the car review domain, the model processing is calculated as follows:

$$Hmodel = BERT(Emb) \qquad (1)$$

$$Lmodel = LSTM(Hmodel) \qquad (2)$$

$$Mmodel = MLP(Lmodel) \qquad (3)$$

$$Label = SoftMax(Mmodel) \qquad (4)$$

MLP is used to compress the pre-trained features to the same feature dimension as the number of categories. The features are then classified by Softmax.

3.2   Text Classification Strategy Based on Adversarial Training

The adversarial training designed in the paper is mainly based on the addition of adversarial disturbances to the Embedding stage and the addition of the classification stage. It called the representation learning stage and the text classification stage. The model architecture is shown in Fig. 2.

The goal of the representation learning phase is to use adversarial training methods to improve the quality of text representations, and to obtain better word vectors for the next text classification. In the representation learning model, forward and back propagation is used to train better words. By constructing adversarial examples, the generalization performance of the training model for correct classification can be improved, thereby improving the text accuracy. We combine adversarial training methods and language models to improve the quality of text representations. In adversarial learning, we need to create the maximum noise, that is, the optimal adversarial disturbance, at which time the disturbance can maximize the loss of the model, namely:

$$\hat{r} = \arg\max_{r, \|r\| \leqslant \varepsilon} \left\{ L_{adv} \left(\hat{x}_{1:\ell}, \theta', r \right) \right\} \qquad (5)$$

Among them, ε is used to constrain the size of the disturbance and is a hyperparameter. The optimal ε may be different for different tasks. We use the grid search strategy here, and finally, choose the value of ε to be 0.17. in the above formula $r = \{r_i\} \subset \mathrm{R}^V$ is the input value for the original text sequence $x = \{x_i\} \subset \mathrm{R}^V$ interfere. That is, the value that finally enters the Bert model is:

$$\hat{x}_{1:\ell} = x_{1:\ell} + r_{1:\ell} \qquad (6)$$

The samples generated by adding perturbation to Embedding are called adversarial samples. $Ladv$ stands for adversarial loss, and its definition is similar to Llm. However, the value of this perturbation cannot be accurately calculated

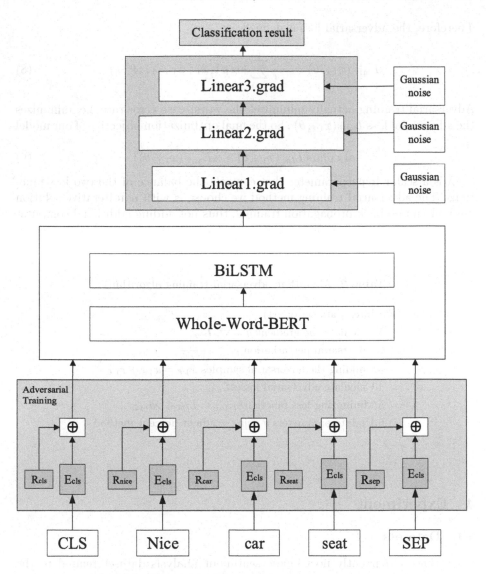

Fig. 2. Adversarial training framework diagram

in the BERT network. GoodFellow proposed an approximation algorithm, $Ladv$ linearize around $\hat{x}_{1:\ell}$. This method yields a non-iterative solution to $\hat{r}$

$$\hat{r}_i = \varepsilon \frac{g_i}{\|g_2\|_2}, g_i = \nabla_{x_i} L_{lm}(x_{1:\ell}, \theta') \tag{7}$$

Among them, $\|g_2\|_2$ presents L2 regularity. The worst direction of the perturbation is the positive direction of the gradient of the loss in the input value.

Therefore, the adversarial loss is defined as:

$$L_{\text{adv}}\left(\hat{x}_{1:\ell}, \theta\right) = -\frac{1}{\ell} \sum_{i=1}^{\ell} \log p\left(\left(\hat{x}_i \mid \hat{x}_{1:i-1}\right); \theta'; \hat{r}\right) \tag{8}$$

Adversarial training actually minimizes the worst-case error rate, i.e. minimizes the adversarial loss $L_{adv}(x_{1:\ell}, \theta)$. So the final optimization objective of our model is:

$$\arg\min\left\{L_{lm}\left(x_{1:\ell}, \theta\right) + \lambda L_{\text{adv}}\left(x_{1:\ell}, \theta\right)\right\} \tag{9}$$

λ is a scalar hyperparameter that controls the balance of the two loss functions. The adversarial training method we choose is with non-iterative solution method and no back-propagation training, thus not adding additional computational overhead. The specific steps of the adversarial training method are shown as follows Table 2.

Table 2. Algorithm: adversarial training algorithms

For bitch data set of x(t)
1.Calculate the gradient $g = \nabla_x L_{lm}$
2.Adversarial perturbation $\hat{r}_i = \varepsilon \frac{g_i}{\|g_2\|_2}$
3.Building the adversarial samples $\hat{x}_{1:\ell} = x_{1:\ell} + r_{1:\ell}$
4.Calculate adversarial losses L_{adv}
5.Minimizing loss function $L_{total} = L_{lm} + \lambda L_{adv}$
6.Update parameters θ using gradient descent method

4   Experiment

4.1   Datasets

Since there is currently no Chinese sentiment analysis dataset related to the field of bus reviews, a sentiment analysis dataset in the field of car reviews is designed and constructed. Crawled comments from car review websites such as Autohome[1] and Knowing Chedi[2]. 10543 car review news and comments were crawled through the Scrapy framework. After data cleaning and screening, 9947 items were selected as our dataset, and sentiment annotations were performed on them. We annotated a total of 3 categories of emotions: positive, neutral, and negative. The specific format is as follows: i) Positive emotion: It is recommended that 2.5T, CVT gearbox with dead weight, high body, China's road conditions are more complicated than Japan and the United States, the short-term power

---

[1] https://www.autohome.com.cn/.
[2] https://www.dongchedi.com/.

demand is still more, and the 2.5 fuel consumption is not high positive. ii) Neutral emotion: The new Forester will be officially unveiled at the North American Auto Show at the end of the month. At that time, I will be considering whether to buy the new model or the old model. I am now waiting and watching. Footpads, chassis armor, chassis guards neutral. iii) Negative emotions: The dodge I bought with my brother-in-law has high fuel consumption, almost power, and the interior space is not too large. For 7 seats, it costs 800 yuan for small maintenance. Negative. Among them, there are 3670 positive emotions, 3661 neutral emotions, and 2616 negative emotions. Strip. We evenly distributed 9947 pieces of data according to sentiment, including 5000 pieces of training set, 2000 pieces of validation set, and 2947 pieces of test set.

4.2   Evaluation Metrics

This task uses the accuracy rate and Macro-F1 as evaluation indicators for evaluation, and the calculation formula for the accuracy rate is:

$$Acc = \frac{\sum_{i=1}^{m} TP_i}{Total} \tag{10}$$

TP_i is the number of correct classifications for the i-th class. Total is the total number of data, and precision is the correct predictions by the model to the total number of predictions. It mainly measures the accuracy of the model.

$$Precision_i = \frac{TP_i}{TP_i + FP_i} \tag{11}$$

Recall measures the rate at which a class is correctly classified by the model. It measures the recall rate of the model, where TP_i is the number of correct predictions for a certain category, and FN_i is the number of misidentified texts of this type. Its formula is:

$$Recall_i = \frac{TP_i}{TP_i + FN_i} \tag{12}$$

So the formulas for average precision and average recall are as follows.

$$Precision_{mean} = \frac{\sum_{i=1}^{m} Precision_i}{m} \tag{13}$$

$$Recall_{mean} = \frac{\sum_{i=1}^{m} Recall_i}{m} \tag{14}$$

F1 is a comprehensive consideration of P and R. Its formula is.

$$F1_{Macro} = 2\frac{Recall_m * Precision_m}{Recall_m + Precision_m} \tag{15}$$

4.3   Settings

The experimental parameters are set as follows: the maximum sequence length is set to 512, title and comment segment length is set to 510, the learning rate is set to 21e5, and the hidden layer size of the BERT model is set to 768, the optimization of the model The algorithm adopts Adam, which is a gradient descent algorithm with adaptive learning rate adjustment, which has the advantage of automatically adjusting the learning rate and accelerating the convergence speed. And the total number of epochs for training is 3 epochs. The perturbation factor e for adversarial training is set to 0.17.

4.4   Compare Models

For a fine-tune mode and feature enhancement representation of our proposed BERT pre-training model, this section mainly compares three types of pre-training models, including basic BERT, BERT+LSTM and ERNIE:

- BERT: The Transformer-based pre-training model published by Google has achieved SOTA on multiple NLP tasks. On this basis, we add a multi-layer perceptron to the model for emotion recognition.
- BERT+CNN: The output vector of bert is used as embedding inputs as the input of convolution; three different convolution kernels are used for convolution and pooling, and finally the three results are concat, and finally they are fully connected for classification.
- BERT+LSTM: Based on the BERT output vector, a LSTM model is attached to the head to obtain a time-based deeper vector for classification.
- ERNIE: It is a knowledge enhancement model proposed by Baidu in 2019.

To further demonstrate our model follow-up, we perform ablation experiments below.

4.5   Experiment 1: Comparative Experimental Results

We compared several models proposed in Sect. 4.4, in which the BERT model was used as the benchmark model, and the comparison results are shown in the Table 3.

Table 3. Comparing the results

Model	ACC	Macro-F1
BERT	68.56	64.89
BERT+LSTM	69.75	65.76
BERT+CNN	68.98	65.12
ERNIE	70.23	67.45
ATWWM-BERT	**77.68**	**74.75**

Table 3 shows the comparison results proposed in this chapter and other models. The bolded place is the best result. The final model achieved 74.75 and 77.76 in the macro-F1 and ACC evaluation indicators respectively, and also has great advantages compared with the currently announced Chinese model (higher than ERNIE 7.3 points). It can be seen that our model can accurately analyze car reviews. In order to more intuitively show the comparative effect of the algorithm in this paper. Table 4 shows an example of the effect of whole word mask BERT based on adversarial learning on specific text classification. The bolded ones are the correctly classified results. The text of the classification is: Hong Qi is more official, although the fuel consumption is high, the driving is stable, and the interior is more atmospheric.

Table 4. Comparing the results of different models

Model	Classification result
BERT	Neutral
BERT+LSTM	Neutral
BERT+CNN	Neutral
ERNIE	Neutral
ATWWM-BERT	**Positive**

Experiments shows our model has better model expression, and has a better effect on the task of car review sentiment analysis. The Loss versus epoch curve is shown in Fig. 3.

It can be seen from the loss drop graph that the models tend to converge in the end. Among them, the BERT single model has the highest loss and the worst classification effect. The whole word mask BERT proposed by us based on adversarial learning has the best classification effect and the lowest loss. It is consistent with that shown in Table 4. It shows that our proposed model has good adaptability to the car review dataset.

4.6   Experiment 2: Ablation Experiment Result

In order to more clearly verify the collinearity of the two schemes proposed in the paper to the final model. In this paper, four ablation experimental schemes are mainly used to prove the experimental effect of the model, which are:

- The original BERT pre-training model was pre-trained, and the position of the multi-layer perceptron was added to the model for sentiment classification.
- BERT + adversarial training: The original BERT model is trained by adversarial training, and a fully connected layer is added.
- Our model + adversarial training in the field of car review: The original BERT pre-training model was pre-trained against the whole word mask of the car review field, and the position of the multi-layer perceptron was added to the model for sentiment classification.

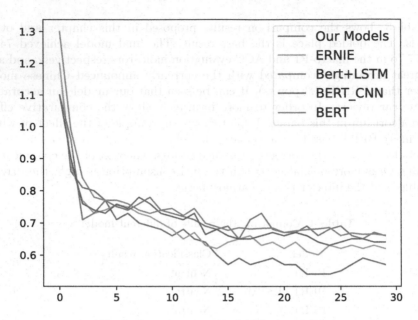

Fig. 3. Loss drop graph of different models

– Our model + adversarial training + LSTM: On the basis of the whole word mask and feature enhancement representation model in the field of car reviews, a bidirectional LSTM network is added to learn the sequence features between entries, and finally the whole word mask and feature enhancement representation model is added. Connection layer for classification.

Table 5. Ablation experiment results

Model	ACC	Macro-F1
BERT	68.56	64.89
BERT-wwm	71.23	69.32
BERT+ Adversarial	73.72	69.32
BERT-wwm + Adversarial	75.72	73.78
ATWWM-BERT	**77.68**	**74.75**

First, the experimental results of the BERT model show that it has the lowest value on both ACC and Macro-F1 results. The bolded place is the best result. At the same time, we tested the model after pre-training in the field of car reviews. Compared with the basic BERT language model, there was an improvement of 4.11 points in the results, confirming that the proposed pre-training of in the field of car reviews was effective. Effectiveness. On the basis of the BERT model, we used the adversarial training method to train the data set for the BERT model. The results show that compared with the method without adversarial training, its ACC has improved by 2.76%. Based on the BERT model pre-trained in the field of car reviews, adversarial learning is added to enhance the expressive ability of the language model. Compared with our BERT model, there is a 1.05% improvement in value, which proves that adversarial learning is effective for sentiment analysis tasks in the field of car reviews. Finally, a bidirectional LSTM network is added to learn the sequence features between terms to form the final model of this chapter, which continues to improve the ACC value by 1.96%. The validity of the sentiment analysis model proposed in this chapter based on whole-word mask and feature enhancement in the field of car reviews is verified (Table 5).

4.7 Error Analysis

At the same time, this paper conducts an error analysis of the model, such as typos, redundant punctuation, and different people's understanding of different things (for example, some reviews car weight as an advantage, some as a disadvantage). When the length of the comment is over 512 words, the BERT model cannot extract all the features of the comment at one time and it will generate inaccurate sentiment prediction. For this reason, although the model in this paper is superior to other models, it still needs further improvement and further optimization in the model in sentiment analysis of long texts.

5   Conclusion

Aiming at the task of text sentiment analysis in the field of car reviews, in order to improve the model in the professional field, we proposes a BERT preprocessing model based on whole word mask and adversarial training in the field of car reviews. Comparative experiments and ablation experiments were carried out on the model respectively. The experiments show that the model proposed has achieved higher classification accuracy in the task of sentiment analysis of car review texts. At the same time, the study also finds that when the length of the comment is over 512 words or the comment text has a lot of noise, the BERT model cannot extract all the features of the comment at one time, the accuracy of the model recognition will be reduced. We speculate that if the method in this paper is applied to other domains, similar improvements in classification performance can be obtained.

Acknowledgements. This work was supported by the National Natural Science Foundation of China (No. 62192784, No. 62172056).

References

1. Yang, H.: Research on sentiment classification and evaluation of car reviews based on evidence reasoning. Hefei University of Technology (2020). https://doi.org/10.27101/d.cnki.ghfgu.2020.001666

2. Ran, C.: Sentiment analysis of car review texts based on multi-label classification. Donghua University (2021). https://doi.org/10.27012/d.cnki.gdhuu.2021.000998
3. Kou, F., et al.: Hashtag recommendation based on multi-features of microblogs. J. Comput. Sci. Technol. **33**(4), 711–726 (2018)
4. Kou, F., Junping, D., He, Y., Ye, L.: Social network search based on semantic analysis and learning. CAAI Trans. Intell. Technol. **1**(4), 293–302 (2016)
5. Chundong, W., Hui, Z., Xiuliang, M., Wenjun, Y.: A review of sentiment analysis on Weibo. Comput. Eng. Sci. **44**(01), 165–175 (2022)
6. Yanxiang, H., Songtao, S., Feifei, N., Fei, L.: A deep learning model for sentiment enhancement of Weibo sentiment analysis. Chin. J. Comput. **40**(04), 773–790 (2017)
7. Devlin, J., Chang, M.W., Lee, K., et al.: BERT: pre-training of deep bidirectional transformers for language understanding. arXiv preprint arXiv:1810.04805 (2018)
8. Wang Zhitao, Yu., Zhiwen, G.B., Xinjiang, L.: Sentiment analysis of Chinese Weibo based on dictionary and rule set. Comput. Eng. Appl. **51**(08), 218–225 (2015)
9. Li, M., Jia, Y., Du, J.: LPV control with decoupling performance of 4WS vehicles under velocity-varying motion. IEEE Trans. Control Syst. Technol. **22**(5), 1708–1724 (2014)
10. Yang, Y., Junping, D., Ping, Y.: Ontology-based intelligent information retrieval system. J. Softw. **26**(7), 1675–1687 (2015)
11. Li, W., Jia, Y., Du, J.: Distributed extended Kalman filter with nonlinear consensus estimate. J. Franklin Inst. **354**(17), 7983–7995 (2017)
12. Peterson, L.E.: K-nearest neighbor. Scholarpedia **4**(2), 1883 (2009)
13. Sun, B., Du, J., Gao, T.: Study on the improvement of K-nearest-neighbor algorithm. In: 2009 International Conference on Artificial Intelligence and Computational Intelligence, vol. 4, no. 1, pp. 390–393 (2009)
14. Hu, W., Gao, J., Li, B., et al.: Anomaly detection using local kernel density estimation and context-based regression. IEEE Trans. Knowl. Data Eng. **32**(2), 218–233 (2018)
15. Meng, D., Jia, Y., Du, J.: Consensus seeking via iterative learning for multi-agent systems with switching topologies and communication time-delays. Int. J. Robust Nonlinear Control **26**(17), 3772–3790 (2016)
16. Webb, G.I., Keogh, E., Miikkulainen, R.: Naïve Bayes. Encyclopedia Mach. Learn. **15**(1), 713–714 (2010)
17. Shifei, D., Bingjuan, Q., Hongyan, T.: A review of support vector machine theory and algorithm research. J. Univ. Electron. Sci. Technol. China **40**(01), 2–10 (2011)
18. Ran, L., Zheng, L., Hailun, L., Weiping, W., Dan, M.: A review of text sentiment analysis. Comput. Res. Dev. **55**(01), 30–52 (2018)
19. Xu, L., Du, J., Li, Q.: Image fusion based on nonsubsampled contourlet transform and saliency-motivated pulse coupled neural networks. Math. Probl. Eng. (2013)
20. Shi, C., Han, X., Song, L., et al.: Deep collaborative filtering with multi-aspect information in heterogeneous networks. IEEE Trans. Knowl. Data Eng. **33**(4), 1413–1425 (2019)
21. Li, W., Jia, Y., Du, J.: Distributed consensus extended Kalman filter: a variance-constrained approach. IET Control Theory Appl. **11**(3), 382–389 (2017)
22. Lin, P., Jia, Y., Du, J., et al.: Average consensus for networks of continuous-time agents with delayed information and jointly-connected topologies. In: American Control Conference, pp. 3884–3889 (2009)
23. Li, Q., Du, J., Song, F., et al.: Region-based multi-focus image fusion using the local spatial frequency. In: 2013 25th Chinese Control and Decision Conference (CCDC), pp. 3792–3796 (2013)

24. LeCun, Y., Bengio, Y., Hinton, G.: Deep learning. Nature **521**(7553), 436–444 (2015)
25. Xu, G., Meng, Y., Qiu, X., et al.: Sentiment analysis of comment texts based on BiLSTM. IEEE Access **7**(1), 51522–51532 (2019)
26. Vaswani, A., Shazeer, N., Parmar, N., et al.: Attention is all you need. In: Advances in Neural Information Processing Systems, vol. 30 (2017)
27. Peters, M.E.: Deep contextualized word representations. arXiv e-prints (2018)
28. Goodfellow, I., Pouget-Abadie, J., Mirza, M., et al.: Generative adversarial nets. Advances in Neural Information Processing Systems, vol. 27 (2014)
29. Fang, Y., Deng, W., Du, J., Hu, J.: Identity-aware CycleGAN for face photo-sketch synthesis and recognition. Pattern Recogn. **102**(1), 107249 (2020)
30. Li, A., Du, J., Kou, F., et al.: Scientific and technological information oriented semantics-adversarial and media-adversarial cross-media retrieval. arXiv preprint arXiv:2203.08615 (2022)
31. Miyato, T., Dai, A.M., Goodfellow, I.: Adversarial training methods for semi-supervised text classification. arXiv preprint arXiv:1605.07725 (2016)
32. Rao, Y., Lei, J., Wenyin, L., et al.: Building emotional dictionary for sentiment analysis of online news. World Wide Web **17**(4), 723–742 (2014)
33. Zhang, S., Wei, Z., Wang, Y., et al.: Sentiment analysis of Chinese micro-blog text based on extended sentiment dictionary. Futur. Gener. Comput. Syst. **81**(1), 395–403 (2018)
34. Moraes, R., Valiati, J.F., Neto, W.P.G.O.: Document-level sentiment classification: an empirical comparison between SVM and ANN. Expert Syst. Appl. **40**(2), 621–633 (2013)
35. Narayanan, V., Arora, I., Bhatia, A.: Fast and accurate sentiment classification using an enhanced Naive Bayes model. In: Yin, H., et al. (eds.) IDEAL 2013. LNCS, vol. 8206, pp. 194–201. Springer, Heidelberg (2013). https://doi.org/10.1007/978-3-642-41278-3_24
36. Van Atteveldt, W., van der Velden, M.A.C.G., Boukes, M.: The validity of sentiment analysis: comparing manual annotation, crowd-coding, dictionary approaches, and machine learning algorithms. Commun. Methods Meas. **15**(2), 121–140 (2021)
37. Qiu, X.P., Sun, T.X., Xu, Y.G., Shao, Y.F., Dai, N., Huang, X.J.: Pre-trained models for natural language processing: a survey. Sci. China Technol. Sci. **63**(10), 1872–1897 (2020). https://doi.org/10.1007/s11431-020-1647-3
38. Liu, P., Qiu, X., Huang, X.: Adversarial multi-task learning for text classification. arXiv preprint arXiv:1704.05742 (2017)
39. Garg, S., Ramakrishnan, Bae, G.: BERT-based adversarial examples for text classification. arXiv preprint arXiv:2004.01970 (2020)
40. Song, L., Yu, X., Peng, H.T., et al.: Universal adversarial attacks with natural triggers for text classification. arXiv preprint arXiv:2005.00174 (2020)

Bi-convolution Matrix Factorization Algorithm Based on Improved ConvMF

Peiyu Liu(ID), Junping Du(✉)(ID), Zhe Xue(ID), and Ang Li(ID)

Beijing Key Laboratory of Intelligent Telecommunication Software and Multimedia, School of Computer Science (National Pilot School of Software Engineering), Beijing University of Posts and Telecommunications, 100876 Beijing, China
junpingdu@126.com, {xuezhe,david.lee}@bupt.edu.cn

Abstract. In order to solve the sparsity problem of the traditional matrix factorization algorithm and the problem of the low utilization for review document information, this paper proposes a BiconvMF algorithm based on improved ConvMF. This algorithm uses two parallel convolutional neural networks to extract deep features from the user review set and item review set respectively and fuses these features into the decomposition of the rating matrix, so as to construct the user latent model and the item latent model more accurately. The experimental results show that compared with traditional recommendation algorithms like PMF, ConvMF, and DeepCoNN, the method proposed in this paper has lower prediction error and can achieve a better recommendation effect. Specifically, compared with the previous three algorithms, the prediction errors of the algorithm proposed in this paper are reduced by 45.8%, 16.6%, and 34.9%, respectively.

Keywords: Recommendation algorithm · Matrix factorization · User review set · Item review set

1 Introduction

With the rapid development of information technology, related problems such as information overload also follow. Facing the exponential growth of data on the Internet, recommendation technology came into being [1, 2]. In order to meet the individual needs of users and efficiently provide relevant information to users in need, recommendation technology has been widely researched and promoted.

Recommendation algorithms are mainly divided into three types [3, 4]: collaborative filtering algorithm, content-based recommendation algorithm and hybrid recommendation algorithm. The collaborative filtering algorithm [3] is further divided into user-based and item-based. The former finds similar users by calculating the similarity between users, the latter finds similar users by calculating the similarity between items. The content-based recommendation algorithm [5] also calculates the similarity between items. However, the difference between a content-based recommendation and item-based collaborative filtering algorithm is that the former finds the similarity between items through metadata, such as the natural language description of the item by the merchant, the product label and other metadata; and the latter quantifies an item by all users' preferences for an item. The hybrid recommendation algorithm [6] is to combine multiple recommendation algorithms to complement each other and give play to their respective advantages.

Among them, the more mainstream is the collaborative filtering algorithm, of which matrix factorization is the most widely used collaborative filtering algorithm [9, 10]. Koren et al. [7] first applied matrix factorization (MF) to the recommendation field. The algorithm proposed the concept of latent vector based on the user's rating matrix for items, and used MF to decompose the rating matrix into user matrix and item matrix. On the basis of MF, Salakhutdinov et al. [8] proposed a probability matrix factorization (PMF) model, and further optimized MF by assuming that the implicit features of the user matrix and item matrix have a Gaussian probability distribution. Although the collaborative filtering algorithm based on matrix factorization has achieved good results in the field of recommendation, there are still problems such as the sparsity of the rat ing data, which has a greater impact on the system performance [11 15]. Therefore, as comment text data that can directly reflect user preferences, it has received more and more attention from scholars. McAuley et al. [16] proposed the Hidden Factors Topics (HTF) algorithm, which mines potential topics in user review texts based on topic models, and analyzes latent factors in user ratings based on matrix factorization algorithms. Hu Zhongkai et al. [17] calculated the similarity between items by mining the feature sentiment word pairs in the user reviews, and analyzed the user's personal preferences and interests based on the user review data. However, the above machine learning-based algorithms can only learn the shallow features of the review text and lose important text features such as word order, and with the wide application and development of deep learning, more and more scholars try to apply deep learning in the field of recommendation [18–22]. The convolution matrix factorization (ConvMF) proposed by Kim et al. [23] combines convolutional neural networks and probabilistic matrix factorization, they utilize convolutional neural networks [24, 25] to extract deep features of review content and fuse them into rating matrix factorization. But this method only utilizes the comment information of the item and ignores the user's comment information. Zheng et al. [26] proposed the deep cooperative neural network (DeepCoNN). This algorithm uses two parallel CNN to extract deep features in the item comment text and user comment text respectively, and finally map them to the same feature space by setting a shared layer.

To sum up, in order to solve the data sparsity of traditional matrix factorization algorithms and the incomplete utilization of review information in the ConvMF algorithm, this paper introduces the concepts of the item review set and the user review set and proposes a bi-convolution matrix factorization (BiConvMF) algorithm based on improved ConvMF.

2 Related Work

2.1 Item Review Set and User Review Set

As a way for users to directly evaluate and describe items, comments contain rich user preference information and product feature information. Using review documents as auxiliary information to add to the recommendation algorithm can effectively improve the efficiency of the recommendation system and alleviate the problem of data sparsity.

Among them, the item review set refers to the collection of all reviews on an item, which reflects the feature information of the item, is the most authentic experience of the user, and can more appropriately show the performance of the item on each feature. For example, for a specific restaurant, if 80% of people mention in the review that the restaurant's dining environment is poor, it means that the restaurant may have poor performance in terms of environmental hygiene.

A user review set is a collection of all reviews made by a user. Compared with monotonous rating data, user review sets can show user preferences in a more intuitive way. For example, the aspect mentioned most frequently in a user's review set may be the aspect that the user values most when purchasing this type of item, that is, the user may be more inclined to purchase items that perform better in this aspect.

2.2 Convolution Matrix Factorization

The traditional machine learning methods for text processing in the recommendation systems, such as LDA [27], are mostly based on the bag-of-words model, which ignores the word order of the text and cannot learn the deep features of the text. As the first algorithm to integrate deep learning into PMF, ConvMF solves the problem of the sparsity of the scoring matrix and the problem that machine learning cannot learn the deep features of the text, and has a good recommendation effect.

Figure 1 presents an overview of the ConvMF probabilistic model that integrates the CNN into the PMF. Among them, the part framed by dotted-blue on the left is PMF, and the part on the right which is framed by dashed-red is the part of CNN processing the item comment set. The goal of ConvMF is to find a user latent model and an item latent model ($U \in R^{k \times N}$ and $V \in R^{k \times M}$, where N is the number of users, M is the number of items, and K is the dimension of the latent model), whose product reconstructs the rating matrix R.

As a generative model for user latent models, ConvMF places a zero-mean spherical Gaussian prior on user latent models with variance σ_U^2, as shown in Eq. 1. Where $N(x|\mu, \sigma^2)$) is the probability density function of the Gaussian normal distribution with mean μ and variance σ^2.

$$p\left(U|\sigma_U^2\right) = \prod_i^N N\left(u_i|0, \sigma_U^2 I\right) \qquad (1)$$

In the generative model of item latent models, ConvMF integrates CNN and thinks that the item latent model is obtained by the following equations.

$$v_i = cnn(W, X_j) + \epsilon_j \qquad (2)$$

$$\epsilon_j \sim N\left(0, \sigma_V^2 I\right) \qquad (3)$$

Among them, W is the internal weights in CNN, X_j represents the document of item j, and ϵ_j is Gaussian noise. For the parameter W in the neural network, ConvMF places

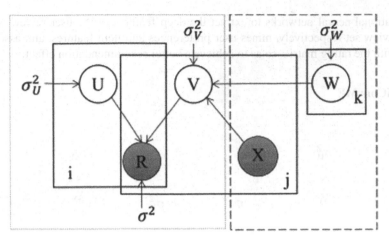

Fig. 1. Graphical model of ConvMF model

zero-mean spherical Gaussian prior. Accordingly, the conditional distribution over item latent model V is shown in the following formula.

$$p\left(V|W,X,\sigma_V^2\right) = \prod_{j}^{M} N\left(v_j|cnn(W,X_j),\sigma_V^2 I\right) \tag{4}$$

However, the ConvMF algorithm only uses the item review set, only pays attention to the characteristics of the item itself, does not integrate the user preference information, ignores the part of the information that can reflect the user preference in the review text, and cannot effectively combine the item characteristics with user preference combination. Therefore, this paper integrates the item review set and user review set, and proposes the BiConvMF algorithm based on the improved ConvMF,which more comprehensively integrates the rating matrix and the review document. The experimental results show that the algorithm proposed in this paper has a better recommendation effect than ConvMF.

3   Bi−convolution Matrix Factorization Algorithm Based on Improved ConvMF

In order to solve the data sparsity problem of the traditional matrix factorization algorithm and the problem that the ConvMF algorithm cannot fully utilize the review document information to make it better integrated with the rating matrix, this paper proposes a BiConvMF algorithm based on improved ConvMF. The algorithm uses two parallel convolutional neural networks to extract the deep features of the user review set and item review set respectively, mines user preferences and item features, and associates them with the rating matrix, so as to achieve a better recommendation effect.

3.1 BiConvMF

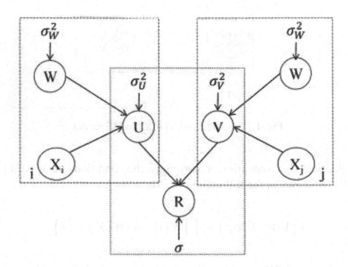

Fig. 2. Graphical model of BiConvMF model

Figure 2 shows the overall structure of the BiConvMF algorithm proposed in this paper. This figure shows how to fuse the deep features of the user review set and item review set extracted by the convolutional neural network into the PMF. Where X_j represents the review set of item j and Xi represents the review set of user i. In the algorithm proposed in this paper, as the assumptions of ConvMF and PMF, our task is to find the user latent model U and the item latent model V ($U \in \mathrm{R}^{k \times N}$ and $V \in \mathrm{R}^{k \times M}$, k is the latent model dimension, N and M are the number of users and the number of items respectively), whose product ($U^T V$) reconstructs the rating matrix $R(R \in \mathrm{R}^{N \times M})$.

From a probabilistic point of view, the conditional distribution over observed ratings is given by

$$p\left(R|U, V, \sigma^2\right) = \prod_{i}^{N} \prod_{j}^{M} N\left(r_{ij}|u_i^T v_j, \sigma^2\right)^{I_{ij}} \tag{5}$$

where I_{ij} is an indicator function such that it is 1 if user i rated item j and 0 otherwise. The definition of $N\left(x|\mu, \sigma^2\right)$ is the same as mentioned in Sect. 2.2.

However, unlike the probabilistic model for user latent models in ConvMF, the algorithm proposed in this paper believes that the user latent model U is also determined by the deep features of user comments extracted from the user comment set by the convolutional neural network, namely

$$u_i = cnn(W, X_i) + \epsilon_i \tag{6}$$

$$\epsilon_i \sim N\left(0, \sigma_U^2 I\right) \tag{7}$$

Therefore, the conditional distribution over user latent models is given by

$$p\left(U|W, X, \sigma_U^2\right) = \prod_i^N N\left(u_i|cnn(W, X_i), \sigma_U^2 I\right) \tag{8}$$

To sum up, in the BiConvMF algorithm, the conditional distribution of the user latent model U and the item latent model V and the determinants are shown by the following equations:

$$\begin{cases} v_i = cnn\left(W, X_j\right) + \epsilon_j, \epsilon_j \sim N\left(0, \sigma_V^2 I\right) \\ p\left(V|W, X, \sigma_V^2\right) = \prod_j^M N\left(v_j|cnn(W, X_j), \sigma_V^2 I\right) \\ u_i = cnn(W, X_i) + \epsilon_i, \epsilon_i \sim N\left(0, \sigma_U^2 I\right) \\ p\left(U|W, X, \sigma_U^2\right) = \prod_i^N N\left(u_i|cnn(W, X_i), \sigma_U^2 I\right) \end{cases} \tag{9}$$

3.2 Structure of Convolutional Neural Networks

In this algorithm, we use the convolutional neural network to extract the deep features in the review documents and use the extracted user review features and item review features to help construct the user latent model U and the item latent model V, so as to complete the reconstruction of the rating matrix and achieve the purpose of recommendation. In CNN, this paper generally sets up four layers: embedding layer, convolution layer, pooling layer, and output layer.

As shown in Fig. 3, first the data is preprocessed, and each comment text (all comments of a user or an item) is mapped into a long vector S. This long vector S will be transformed into a matrix $D \in R^{p \times l}$ through the embedding layer, where l refers to the length of S, and p refers to the embedding dimension of each word in S. Next, the matrix D goes through a certain number of convolutional layers with different sizes [28], extracts different features of the review text through different convolution kernels, and the extracted features are downsampled by pooling layer. Finally, in the output layer, all the extracted features are implied into a vector s of length k (that is, the dimension of the latent model) through full connection, and the vector is output to the user/item latent model as the latent feature of the comment text for scoring prediction.

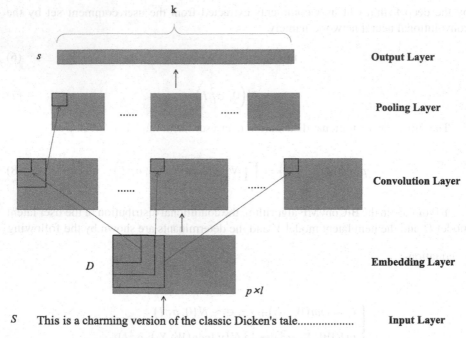

Fig. 3. Structure of convolutional neural networks

3.3 Optimization Methodology

In order to optimize the variables in Eq. (9), this paper adopts the maximum a posteriori (MAP) estimation [29] of the following equation.

$$\max U, V, W_U, W_V p\left(U, V, W_U, W_V | R, X, \sigma^2, \sigma_U^2, \sigma_V^2, \sigma_{W_U}^2, \sigma_{W_V}^2\right)$$
$$= \max\left[p\left(R|U, V, \sigma^2\right)p\left(V|W_V, X, \sigma_V^2\right)p\left(W|\sigma_{W_V}^2\right)p\left(V|W_U, X, \sigma_U^2\right)p\left(W|\sigma_{W_U}^2\right)\right]$$
(10)

By taking the negative logarithm of the above formula, Eq. (10) is converted into the form of the loss function shown in the following formula.

$$\mathcal{L}(U, V, W_U, W_V) = \sum_i^N \sum_j^M \frac{I_{ij}}{2}\left(r_{ij} - u_i^T v_j\right)_2 + \frac{\lambda_V}{2}\sum_j^M \left\|v_j - cnn\left(W_V, X_j\right)\right\|_2 +$$
$$\frac{\lambda_{W_V}}{2}\sum_k^{|\lambda_{W_V}|} \left\|w_k\right\|_2 + \frac{\lambda_U}{2}\sum_i^N \left\|u_i - cnn\left(W_U, X_i\right)\right\|_2 + \quad + \frac{\lambda_{W_U}}{2}\sum_k^{|\lambda_{W_U}|} \left\|w_k\right\|_2$$
(11)

where λU is σ^2/σ_U^2, λV is σ^2/σ_V^2, and λW is σ^2/σ_W^2.

In this paper, we optimize the variables U, V, and W in the above formula based on the coordinate descent method, that is, the variables are iteratively updated and optimized by fixing the remaining variables. Differentiating Eq. (11), we can get the following iterative update formula.

$$v_j \leftarrow \left(UI_jU^T + \lambda_V I_K\right)^{-1}\left(UR_j + \lambda_V cnn(W_V, X_j)\right) \tag{12}$$

$$u_i \leftarrow \left(VI_iV^T + \lambda_U I_K\right)^{-1}\left(VR_i + \lambda_U cnn(W_U, X_i)\right) \tag{13}$$

where I_i is a diagonal matrix with $I_{ij}, j = 1, \ldots, M$ as its diagonal elements and Ri is a vector with $(r_{ij})_{j=1}^M$ for user i. For item j, I_j and R_j are similarly defined as I_i and R_i, respectively.

For the parameter W in the convolutional neural network, we use the back-propagation algorithm [30] to iteratively update.

4 Experiment

In order to verify the effectiveness of the algorithm proposed in this paper, we conduct comparative experiments based on real datasets in this section. Using the public dataset provided by Amazon, this paper compares four models of BiConvMF, ConvMF, PMF, and DeepCoNN. The experimental results show that the proposed BiConvMF algorithm based on improved ConvMF has higher accuracy than the other three baseline models in the field of recommendation technology.

4.1 Experiment Introduction

Dataset
The dataset used in this paper comes from the public real dataset provided by Amazon [31, 32] named Movies and TV, which provides a large number of users' comment information and rating information for different movies or TV shows. In the experiment of this paper, we select the first 20,000 pieces of data, and there are 13,533 users and 311 movies or TV series in these 20,000 pieces of data. As shown in the Table 1 below.

Table 1. Data statistic

DataSet	#users	#items	#ratings	Density
Movies and TV	13,533	311	20000	0.46%

Competitors and Parameter Setting
We compared two versions of BiConvMF with the following baselines.

- PMF: Probabilistic Matrix Factorization is the most basic matrix factorization model in collaborative filtering algorithms. The model only uses the rating matrix to calculate the user latent model and the item latent model.

- ConvMF: Convolutional Matrix Factorization algorithm uses a convolutional neural network to integrate item reviews into matrix decomposition, and uses item review set and rating matrix to calculate user latent model and item latent model.
- DeepCoNN: The Deep Cooperative Neural Networks algorithm uses two parallel CNNs to extract deep features in item review text and user review text respectively, and finally map them to the same feature space by setting a shared layer, and introducing a decomposition machine as the corresponding score evaluator.
- BiConvMF +: Bi Convolutional Matrix Factorization with a pre-trained word embedding model is another version of BiConvMF. The model utilizes word vectors trained on word2vec [33, 34] for pre-trained word embedding model.

In this paper, we set the dimension K of user latent model U and item latent model V to 50 and initialized U and V randomly from 0 to 1. In the convolutional layers of the convolutional neural network, we use various window sizes (3, 4, and 5) to extract different features of the review text, and we used 100 shared weights per window size.

In this experiment, we use Python to write the experimental code of the algorithm proposed in this article and build a convolutional neural network based on PyTorch.

In calculating the accuracy of the model, we used root mean squared error (RMSE) [36], this evaluation measure calculates the prediction accuracy of each algorithm based on the actual score and the predicted score, as shown in the following formula.

$$RMSE = \sqrt{\frac{\sum_{i,j}^{N,M} \left(r_{ij} - \widehat{r_{ij}} \right)^2}{\# \, of \, ratings}} \tag{14}$$

4.2 Experiment Result

Table 2 shows the optimal values of λU and λV in each algorithm. These optimal values are the results of our continuous experiments. Based on these optimal values, we compare the overall rating prediction error of different algorithms.

Table 2. Optimal values of λU and λV

Algorithm	λ_U	λ_V
PMF	1	100
ConvMF	1	100
DeepCoNN	–	–
BiConvMF	100	100
BiConvMF +	100	100

In order to prevent the chance of the experiment, we conducted 5 experiments on the same training set and test set for each algorithm based on the above parameters, and compared the experimental results with averages. The overall rating prediction error of the model obtained by each training on the test set is shown in the following table.

Table 3. The overall rating prediction error on the test set

	PMF	ConvMF	DeepCoNN	BiConvMF	BiConvMF+
1	1.80828	1.17172	1.47178	0.98570	0.98651
2	1.80828	1.16598	1.51836	0.97707	0.99562
3	1.80828	1.17693	1.50119	0.98745	1.01396
4	1.80828	1.17512	1.52463	0.97122	0.98159
5	1.80828	1.18053	1.50492	0.97571	0.98470
Average	1.80828	1.17406	1.501177	0.97943	0.99248

In order to better compare the experimental results, we draw the average overall rating prediction error of each model above as a line graph, as shown below.

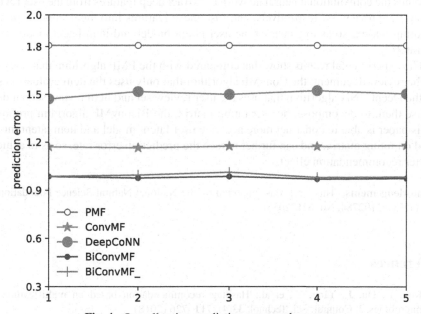

Fig. 4. Overall rating prediction error on the test set

From Fig. 4 we can clearly see that in every experiment, BiConvMF's prediction error was the lowest of all algorithms, while PMF has the highest error rate, DeepCoNN ranks second, and ConvMF ranks third.

Combining with Table 3, it can be seen that the average prediction error of the BiConvMF algorithm is reduced by 45.8% and 16.6% compared with PMF and ConvMF, respectively. It means the integration of the user review set and the user review set together into the matrix factorization can further improve the accuracy of rating prediction, and based on user review features and item review features, more deep correlations between review documents and rating matrices can be mined, so that the rating matrix can be decomposed into user latent models and item latent models more accurately.

Compared with DeepCoNN, the average prediction error of the BiConvMF algorithm is reduced by 34.9%, indicating that the method based on matrix decomposition in BiConvMF to find the user latent model and item latent model respectively is better than the method of fusion of user and item features in DeepCoNN, after all, user review features and item review features represent different things, and fusing them together may lose some of the individual features of users and items, thereby weakening the association between them and ratings.

In summary, the BiConvMF algorithm proposed in this paper can further reduce the score prediction error and achieve a better recommendation effect.

5 Conclusion

This paper proposes the BiconvMF algorithm based on the improved ConvMF, which combines the convolutional neural network to extract deep features from the user review set and item review set respectively, and fuse these features into the decomposition of the rating matrix, so as to construct the user latent model and item latent model more accurately.

The experimental results show that compared with the PMF algorithm that does not use the review document, the ConvMF algorithm that only uses the item evaluation set, and the DeepCoNN algorithm that uses the user review set and item review set but does not use them to decompose the user rating matrix, the BiconvMF algorithm proposed in this paper is able to construct more accurate user latent model and item latent model based on rating matrix, and can further reduce the prediction error rate, so as to achieve a better recommendation effect.

Acknowledgements. This work was supported by the National Natural Science Foundation of China (No. 62192784, No. 62172056).

References

1. Kou, F., Du, J., Yang, C., et al.: Hashtag recommendation based on multi-features of microblogs. J. Comput. Sci. Technol. **33**(4), 711–726 (2018)
2. Li, A., Du, J., Kou, F., et al.: Scientific and technological information oriented semantics-adversarial and media-adversarial cross-media retrieval. arXiv preprint arXiv:2203.08615 (2022)
3. Xu, H., Wu, X., Li, X., et al.: Comparison study of internet recommendation system. J. Softw. **20**(2), 350–362 (2009)
4. Zhao, L., Hu, N., Zhang, S.: Algorithm design for personalization recommendation systems. J. Comp

5. Xie, H., Li, Q., Cai, Y.: Community-aware resource profiling for personalized search infolksonomy. J. Comput. Sci. Technol. **27**(3), 599–610 (2012)
6. Noel, J., Sanner, S., Tran, K., et al.: New objective functions for social collaborative filtering. In: Proceedings of the 21st International Conference on World Wide Web, pp. 859–868. ACM Press (2012)
7. Koren, Y., Bell, R., Volinsky, C.: Matrix factorization techniques for recommender systems. Computer **42**(8), 30–37 (2009)
8. Mnih, A., Salakhutdinov, R.: Probabilistic matrix factorization. In: Proceedings of the Advances in Neural Information Processing Systems, Vancouver, Canada, pp. 1257–1264 (2008)
9. Shi, C., Han, X., Song, L., et al.: Deep collaborative filtering with multi-aspect information in heterogeneous networks. IEEE Trans. Knowl. Data Eng. **33**(4), 1413–1425 (2019)
10. Xue, Z., Junping, D., Dawei, D., Lyu, S.: Deep low-rank subspace ensemble for multi-view clustering. Inf. Sci. **482**, 210–227 (2019)
11. Sun, B., Du, J., Gao, T.: Study on the improvement of K-nearest-neighbor algorithm. In: 2009 International Conference on Artificial Intelligence and Computational Intelligence, vol. 4, pp. 390–393 (2009)
12. Li, Q., Du, J., Song, F., et al.: Region-based multi-focus image fusion using the local spatial frequency. In: 2013 25th Chinese control and decision conference (CCDC), pp. 3792–3796 (2013)
13. Li, W., Jia, Y., Du, J.: Distributed extended Kalman filter with nonlinear consensus estimate. J. Franklin Inst. **354**(17), 7983–7995 (2017)
14. Yang, Y., Du, J., Ping, Y.: Ontology-based intelligent information retrieval system. J. Softw. **26**(7), 1675–1687 (2015)
15. Hu, W., Gao, J., Li, B., et al.: Anomaly detection using local kernel density estimation and context-based regression. IEEE Trans. Knowl. Data Eng. **32**(2), 218–233 (2018)
16. McAuley, J., Leskovec, J.: Hidden factors and hidden topics: understanding rating dimensions with review text. In: Proceedings of the 7th ACM Conference on Recommender System (RecSys), Hong Kong, China, pp. 165–172 (2013)
17. Hu, Z., Zheng, X., Wu, Y., et al.: Product recommendation algorithm based on user comment mining. J. Zhejiang Univ. (Eng. Sci. Edn.) **47**(08), 1475–1485 (2013)
18. Fang, Y., Deng, W., Du, J., et al.: Identity-aware CycleGAN for face photo-sketch synthesis and recognition. Pattern Recogn. **102**, 107249 (2020)
19. Li, W., Jia, Y., Du, J.: Distributed consensus extended Kalman filter: a variance-constrained approach. IET Control Theory Appl. **11**(3), 382–389 (2017)
20. Xu, L., Du, J., Li, Q.: Image fusion based on nonsubsampled contourlet transform and saliency-motivated pulse coupled neural networks. Math. Probl. Eng. **2013**, 135182 (2013)
21. Lin, P., Jia, Y., Du, J., et al.: Average consensus for networks of continuous-time agents with delayed information and jointly-connected topologies. In: 2009 American Control Conference, pp. 3884–3889 (2009)
22. Meng, D., Jia, Y., Du, J.: Consensus seeking via iterative learning for multi-agent systems with switching topologies and communication time-delays. Int. J. Robust Nonlin. Control **26**(17), 3772–3790 (2016)
23. Kim, D., Park, C., Oh, J., et al.: Convolutional matrix factorization for document context-aware recommendation. In: Proceedings of the 10th ACM conference on recommender systems, pp. 233–240 (2016)
24. Li, W., Jia, Y., Du, J.: Recursive state estimation for complex networks with random coupling strength. Neurocomputing **219**, 1–8 (2017)
25. Zhao, L., Jia, Y., Yu, J., et al.: H∞ sliding mode based scaled consensus control for linear multi-agent systems with disturbances. Appl. Math. Comput. **292**, 375–389 (2017)

26. Zheng, L., Noroozi, V., Yu, P.: Joint deep modeling of users and items using reviews for recommendation. In: Proceedings of the Tenth ACM International Conference on Web Search and Data Mining, pp. 425–434. Cambridge (2017)
27. Wang, C., Blei, D.: Collaborative topic modeling for recommending scientific articles. In: Proceedings of the 17th ACM SIGKDD International Conference on Knowledge Discovery and Data Mining, KDD 2011, pp. 448–456. ACM Press, August 2011
28. Kim, Y.: Convolutional neural networks for sentence classification. In: Proceedings of the 2014 Empirical Methods in Natural Language Processing (EMNLP), pp. 1746– 1751 (2014)
29. Mordohai, P., Medioni, G., Fua, P., et al.: Maximum A-Posteriori Estimation (2009)
30. Nayak, G., Nayak, D.: Back Propagation Algorithm (2013)
31. He, R., McAuley, J.: Ups and downs: modelling the visual evolution of fashion trends with one-class collaborative filtering. In: Proceedings of the 25th International Conference on World Wide Web, pp. 507–517 (2016)
32. McAuley, J., Targett, C., Shi, Q., et al.: Image-based recommendations on styles and substitutes. In: Proceedings of the 38th International ACM SIGIR Conference on Research and Development in Information Retrieval, pp. 43–52 (2015)
33. Mikolov, T., Sutskever, I., Kai, C., et al.: Distributed representations of words and phrases and their compositionality. Adv. Neural. Inf. Process. Syst. **26**, 3111–3119 (2013)
34. Mikolov, T., Chen, K., Corrado, G., et al.: Efficient estimation of word representations in vector space. Comput. Sci. (2013)
35. Dupuy, D.: Root mean squared error (2016)

A Novel Defect Detection Method for Insulators of Power Transmission Line Based on YOLOv5

Jianrong Cao, Shuo Shang, Ming Wang$^{(\boxtimes)}$, and Yuan Zhuang

School of Information and Electrical Engineering, Shandong Jianzhu University,
Jinan 250101, China
xclwm@sdjzu.edu.cn

Abstract. Insulators are widely used in power transmission lines. They need to go through defect detection before being used on site. The traditional method is through manual detection, which is inefficient and costly. This paper proposes a novel defect detection method based on YOLOv5 for insulators of power transmission line. First, in order to solve the problem of dataset richness, the insulator defect dataset is enhanced and annotated. Then the data in the defect dataset is converted into a unified format and input into YOLOv5 network for training. The optimal defect detection YOLOv5 network model is obtained by adjusting the learning rate and optimizing the network structure. Finally, the YOLOv5 network model has been compared with SSD, YOLOv4, and faster RCNN network model. The experimental results show that the defect detection method based on YOLOv5 has faster detection speed, higher detection accuracy in defect detection for insulators of power transmission line than SSD, YOLOv4, and faster RCNN network model.

Keywords: Defect detection · YOLOv5 · Data enhancement

1 Introduction

Object defects mainly refer to the appearance or practicality of defects caused by physical or chemical factors that are lower than the engineering requirements [1]. The defects of objects caused by physical factors mainly include scratches, cracks, defects, etc. The defects of objects caused by chemical factors mainly include stains, corrosion, discoloration, etc. Insulator is one of the most important components of transmission line. It needs defect detection before engineering application. Common defects of insulators include wear, cracks, aging, discoloration, corrosion, stains, etc.

The traditional method of transmission circuit insulator detection is through manual detection. This detection method has low accuracy, long-time consuming

This work is supported by National Natural Science Foundation (NNSF) of China under Grant 62073196 and U1806204.

L. Zhang et al. (Eds.): CINT 2022, CCIS 1714, pp. 135–146, 2022.
https://doi.org/10.1007/978-981-19-8915-5_12

and low efficiency. With the development of power grid, an automatic and efficient insulator defect detection method is urgently needed. Deep learning is a new research direction in the field of machine learning [2]. It has the ability to learn the internal laws and representation levels of sample data, which is very helpful for image interpretation [3]. At present, deep learning method has been applied to defect detection [4]. In this paper, the deep learning method is applied to the insulator defect detection of transmission lines. The insulator defect detection method based on deep learning completes the defect detection task by training the defect detection model with a sufficiently accurate defect dataset. It is not only unaffected by the harsh environment and subjective factors, but also can detect the defects of products quickly and accurately.

With the development of computer vision technology, object surface defect detection methods emerge in continually. Fouda Yasser m et al. proposed a fabric defect detection method based on integral image [5]. Zhang et al. studied the defect detection methods of intelligent instruments, wood, PCB boards and distribution line conductors based on image processing technology, and summarized the advantages and disadvantages of various detection methods [6]. However, these methods are specific to the defects of specific artifacts. They are not suitable for transmission line insulators with various types of defects.

As a branch of machine learning, deep learning has become a research hotspot since 2012 [7]. It simulates the mechanism of the human brain to interpret data, and it forms more abstract high-level representation attribute categories or features by combining low-level features, so as to discover the distributed feature representation of data. In recent years, deep learning has been widely used in the fields of posture recognition, pedestrian detection, object classification, smart home, etc. The network model of deep learning has gradually changed from the first neural network LeNet based on convolution in 1998 to AlexNet in 2012, then to YOLO, SSD, R-CNN, etc. and also has been widely used in defect detect [8–10]. Zhang et al. proposed an improved MobileNet-SSD algorithm for automatic defect detection of vehicle body paint [11]. Chen et al. proposed surface defect detection method based on improved attention mechanism and feature fusion model [12]. Li et al. presented surface defect detection of vehicle light guide plates based on an improved RetinaNet [13]. Lin et al. proposed fabric defect detection based on the improved cascade R-CNN [14].

YOLO algorithm is one of the most popular deep learning algorithms at present. YOLOv1 was released in 2015, and five versions have been released with continuous improvement. Its advantages have been shown in defect detection [15]. Xian et al. realized copper elbow surface defect detection using improved YOLOv3 network [16]. Liao Xinting et al. realized the surface defect detection of printed circuit board using improved YOLOv4 network [17]. Li et al. realized the surface defect detection of hot rolled strip steel using YOLOv5 network [18]. YOLOv5 network model is adopted in this paper.

This paper presents a new method for insulator defect detection of transmission lines based on YOLOv5. Firstly, digital image processing technology is used for data enhancement to solve the problem of insufficient insulator dataset. Then the dataset is annotated with labelme tool for later training and verification. Then, the dataset is converted into a unified format and transmitted to the YOLO5 network model for training. Finally, the trained model is used to detect the defects of insulators. In order to verify the effectiveness of the proposed method, this paper compares the method based on YOLOv5 with neural network model SSD, YOLOv4 and faster RCNN.

2 A Defect Detection Method Based on YOLOv5

2.1 YOLOv5 Network Model

YOLOv5 is a single-stage target detection algorithm. Released shortly after the emergence of YOLOv4. YOLOv5 makes some improvements based on YOLOv4, which greatly improves its speed and accuracy. As shown in Fig. 1, the network architecture of YOLOv5 mainly includes input layer, backbone network, neck network and head output layer.

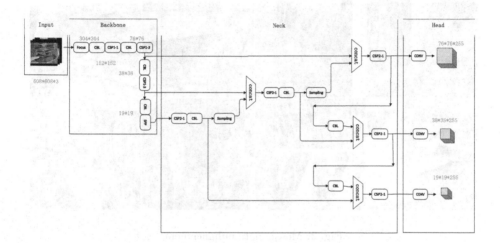

Fig. 1. YOLOv5 network model

Input Layer. The input performs mosaic data enhancement, adaptive anchor box calculation and adaptive image scaling on the image. Mosaic data enhancement is based on the CutMix data enhancement method. As shown in Fig. 2, four pictures are spliced in the way of random scaling, random clipping and random arrangement. Then training speed of the network is greatly improved while enriching the dataset, while the memory requirement of the model is reduced. Adaptive anchor box calculation mainly uses k-means clustering method to set the initial anchor box with specific length and width according to the annotation. The initial anchor box is used to output the prediction box during training. Adaptive image scaling is used to adjust the size of images. It scales the image to a specific size and reduce the black edge filling.

Fig. 2. Mosaic data enhancement

Backbone Network. Backbone network is a pretty deep network which overcomes the gradient descent very well. It is mainly composed of focus structure and CSP structure.

- Focus structure: As shown in Fig. 3, the focus structure cuts input pictures through slice operation, which is not available in YOLOv4. For YOLOv5s, the size of original image is $608 \times 608 \times 3$. After being input into focus structure, the image becomes a characteristic image which is $304 \times 304 \times 12$. Then through another convolution operation with 32 convolution kernels, the characteristic image finally becomes $304 \times 304 \times 32$.
- CSP structure: CSP structure has been proposed in YOLOv4. As a portable structure, CSP structure can be combined with a variety of network structures. Therefore, YOLOv5 applies CSP1_X structure in the backbone network based on YOLOv4, and applies CSP2_X structure in neck network. CSP

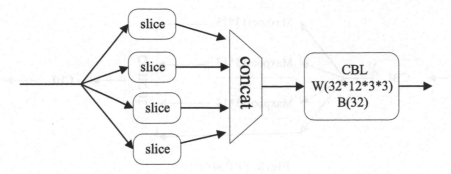

Fig. 3. Focus structure

network structure is shown in Fig. 4. CSP1_X structure divides the input into two branches. One branch first passes through CBL (Conv+BN+Leakyrelu), then passes through several Resunit structures (bottleneck * n), and then uses a convolution; The other branch convolutes directly. Then the two branches are concatenated, and then pass BN (batch norm), activate again, and pass CBL successively. The depth of CSP2_X structure is shallower than CSP1_X structure, and the resunit is replaced by 2 * x CBLS.

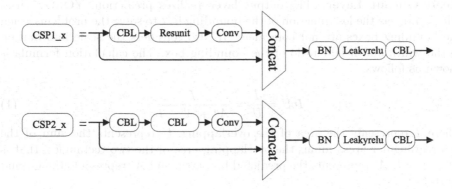

Fig. 4. CSP structure

– SPP structure: YOLOv5 uses max pools of 1×1, 5×5, 9×9 and 13×13 to perform multi-scale feature fusion. The SPP structure is shown in Fig. 5.

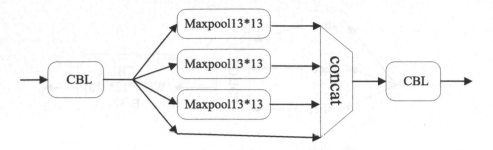

Fig. 5. SPP structure

Neck Network. In addition to the use of CSP2_X structure in the neck network to enhance the ability of feature fusion of network, YOLOv5 enhances the feature fusion of different layers and predicts on multiple scales through FPN+PAN structure. FPN (feature pyramid network) transfers high-level strong semantic features from top to bottom to enhance the semantic expression on multiple scales. PAN (path aggregation network) transfers strong positioning information from bottom to top to enhance the positioning ability on multiple scales.

Head Output Layer. The output layer realizes prediction. YOLOv5 uses GIoU_Loss as the loss function of the bounding box to solve the problems when the bounding boxes are not coincident. It also considers the scale information of the width and height ratio of the bounding box. The calculation formula is shown as follows.

$$IoU = \frac{I}{U} = \frac{I}{A^p + A^\theta - I} \tag{1}$$

where I represents the area of the overlapping, U represents the sum of the two rectangular areas minus the overlapping area of the two rectangles, that is $A^p + A^\theta - I$, A^p represents the predicted box area, and A^θ represents the ground truth box area.

GIoU considers the minimum closure of two rectangles. It is shown in (2):

$$GIoU = IoU - \frac{A^c - U}{A^c} \tag{2}$$

where A^c is the minimum outer area of two rectangles.

In the processing, NMS (non maximum suppression) algorithm will be applied to many boxes, because CIoU_Loss contains the influence factor v, which involves the information of the ground truth. When testing, there is no ground truth. YOLOv5 uses the weighted NMS method based on GIOU_Loss. It deletes the boxes whose overlapping area with the high score box is greater than a certain threshold value, and iterate continuously to suppress redundant boxes.

2.2 Configuration Files

There are four different weight files in YOLOv5: YOLOv5s, YOLOv5x, YOLOv5l, YOLOv5m. YOLOv5s is the most basic network structure. The others are based on YOLOv5s to expand the network depth and width to achieve higher detection performance. However their detection speeds are slower than that of YOLOv5s. The performance comparison of the four weight files is shown in Fig. 6. This paper focuses on defect detection of power transmission line insulators. The YOLOv5s network model is adopted here.

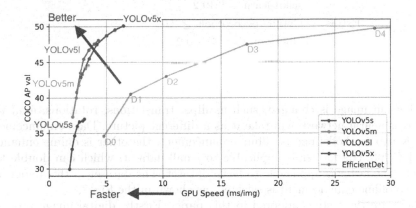

Fig. 6. Performance comparison of four kinds of weight files

3 Experiment

3.1 Parameter Settings

The experiment is based on Python, and uses pytorch as the architecture. The official requirements are python $\geq$ 3.7 and pytorch $\geq$ 1.5. The main experimental environment is shown in Table 1:

3.2 Dataset Preparation

The application performance of deep neural network depends on the quality of data inputed. It will look for the most obvious features that can distinguish the two classes. Because the training model has many parameters, it needs to provide enough sample data for the model. However, the training data set used for detection is often limited. When the data set is insufficient or the shooting scene is limited, it needs to expand the data set through data enhancement. By performing data enhancement, it can prevent the deep neural network from learning irrelevant features and fundamentally improve the overall performance.

Table 1. Experimental environment

Base	matplotlib $\geq$ 3.2.2 scipy $\geq$ 1.4.1
	numpy $\geq$ 1.18.5 torch $\geq$ 1.7.0
	opencv-python $\geq$ 4.1.2 torchvision $\geq$ 0.8.1
	Pillow PyYAML $\geq$ 5.3.1
Logging	tensorboard $\geq$ 2.4.1 wandb
Plotting	seaborn $\geq$ 0.11.0 pandas
Export	coremltools $\geq$ 4.1 onnx $\geq$ 1.9.0
	scikit-learn==0.19.2
Extras	Cython pycocotools $\geq$ 2.0
	albumentations $\geq$ 1.0.2
LabelImg	PyQt5 == 5.15.4 labelme == 4.5.9

When an image is changed, such as flips, translations, rotations, etc., the YOLOv5s neural network will take it as a different picture. Data enhancement involves two methods: one is offline enhancement, the other is online enhancement [19,20]. The former is applicable to small dataset, which can double the dataset. The latter is applicable to large dataset. The dataset in this paper are small, so offline enhancement is selected, as shown in the Fig. 7.

There are three steps adopted in this paper. Firstly, digital image processing technologies, such as image filtering, noise reduction, restoration, etc. are employed to pretreat images. Secondly, the insulator defect dateset is enhanced from 15 to 600 by performing data enhancement on the images, such as translation, rotation, affine, flipping, changing saturation, etc. Then labelme tool is used to annotate the images, and generate JSON files. Finally, the JSON file is transformed into a TXT file using Python coding.

3.3 Model Training

Due to the small scale of the data set, this paper adopts the form of full batch learning. It can better represent the sample population. Hence it has the ability to face the direction of extreme values more accurately. A defect tag is marked "flaw". The detection is relatively simple, so the number of records is 100. CUDA is used to accelerate the deep neural network. The tool wandb is used to help track experiments, record super parameters of operation, output indicators, visualize and share results.

During the training process, the results are divided into four categories, as shown in Table 2:

Accuracy, precision, recall, and error rate are regarded as the evaluation indicators of model training results. Since defect detection is a binary classification problem, so parameter precision and recall are employed as the evaluation indicators. The calculation formulas are shown in (3) and (4), see Table 2 for parameters:

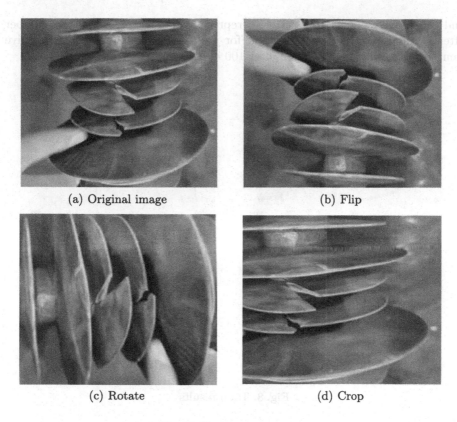

(a) Original image   (b) Flip

(c) Rotate   (d) Crop

Fig. 7. Data enhancement

Table 2. Forecast results

	Positive	Negative
Positive	TP($TruePositive$)	FP($FalsePositive$)
Negative	FN($FalseNegative$)	TN($TrueNegative$)

$$Precision = \frac{TP}{TP+FP} \tag{3}$$

$$Recall = \frac{TP}{TP+FN} \tag{4}$$

After training YOLOv5 model, the evaluation indicators are directly generated in results.png, as shown in Fig. 8. The performance is gradually improving. It reaches more than 0.9 after 100 epochs in Fig. 8. Box is the mean value of GIoU_Loss function. Objectness is the mean value of classification loss. Both of BOX and Objectness are gradually reduced to the minimum as they are iterated continuously. The value mAP is the area enclosed after drawing with precision and recall as two axes. The letter m represents the average, and the number after @ represents the threshold value for judging IoU as positive and negative samples, reaching the maximum after 100 epochs.

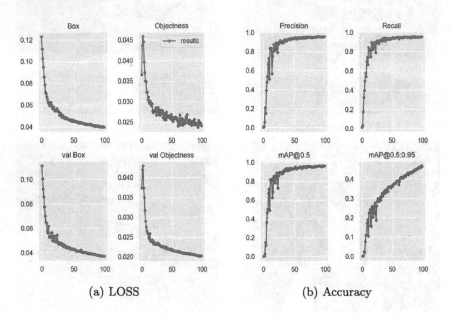

(a) LOSS   (b) Accuracy

Fig. 8. Train results

3.4   Comparative Experiment

When the YOLOv5s model is trained, the weights of the model are saved in last.pt and best.pt. The file detect.py is used for detection. Weight file uses best.pt. The detected results with YOLOv5s model are shown in Fig. 9. It can be seen that the defect detection is relatively accurate. The marked numbers represent the confidence level, which can be understood as the degree of similarity.

In order to verify the superiority of YOLOv5 network, SSD, fast RCNN and YOLOv4 networks are trained and tested under the same dataset and experimental conditions. The experimental results are shown in Table 3. Obviously, YOLOv5 has higher precision, lower loss and faster detection speed compared to the other methods.

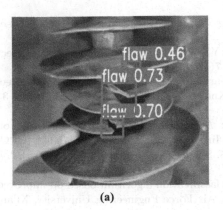
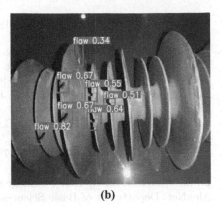

(a)   (b)

Fig. 9. Detection results

Table 3. Forecast results

	YOLOv5	SSD	YOLOv4	faster RCNN
Precision	0.95	0.92	0.85	0.87
LOSS	0.07	2.95	4.21	1.62
Detect speed (fps)	4.76	4.35	1.23	3.70

4 Conclusion

Because the defect types of transmission line insulators are diverse and irregular, it is difficult to extract and recognize by traditional digital image processing methods. This paper presents a method based on YOLOv5 for insulator defect detection of transmission lines. The proposed method first expands the defect dateset through data enhancement. Then the model setting and training are carried out. Finally, the insulator defect detection is carried out. In order to verify the effectiveness of this method, comparative experiments are also carried out. Compared with other neural networks, this proposed method has higher detection accuracy and faster detection speed.

References

1. Chen, Y., Ding, Y., Zhao, F., Zhang, E., Wu, Z., Shao, L.: Surface defect detection methods for industrial products: a review. Appl. Sci. **11**(16), 1–25 (2021)
2. Tulbure, A.-A., Tulbure, A.-A., Dulf, E.-H.: A review on modern defect detection models using DCNNs - deep convolutional neural networks. J. Adv. Res. **35**, 33–48 (2022)
3. Goni, I., Ahmadu, A.S., Malgwi, Y.M.: Image processing techniques and neuro-computing algorithms in computer vision. Adv. Netw. **9**(2), 33–38 (2021)
4. Gong, X., Bai, Y., Liu, Y., Mu H.: Application of deep learning in defect Detection. In: Journal of Physics: Conference Series, vol. 1684, no. 1 (2020)

5. Fouda, Y.M.: Integral images-based approach for fabric defect detection. Opt. Laser Technol. **147**, 1–15 (2022)
6. Zhang, H., Jing, H., Chen, T., Zhang, Y., Wei, P.: Partial application of defect detection in industry. Int. Core J. Eng. **7**(7), 144–147 (2021)
7. Sengupta, S., et al.: A review of deep learning with special emphasis on architectures, applications and recent trends. Knowl.-Based Syst. **194**(prepublish), 1–33 (2020)
8. Ni, H., Han, Y., Duan, X., Yang, G.: An improved LeNet-5 model based on encrypted data. In: Zeng, J., Qin, P., Jing, W., Song, X., Lu, Z. (eds.) ICPCSEE 2021. CCIS, vol. 1452, pp. 166–178. Springer, Singapore (2021). https://doi.org/10.1007/978-981-16-5943-0_14
9. Li, S., Wang, L., Li, J., Yao, Y.: Image classification algorithm based on improved AlexNet. Department of Basic Sciences, Air Force Engineering University, Xi'an, China, pp. 1–8 (2021)
10. Zhang, W., Fu, C., Xie, H., Zhu, M., Tie, M., Chen, J.: Global context aware RCNN for object detection. Neural Comput. Appl. **33**, 11627–11639 (2021)
11. Zhang, J., et al.: An improved MobileNet-SSD algorithm for automatic defect detection on vehicle body paint. Multimedia Tools Appl. **79**(prepublish), 23367–23385 (2020)
12. Chen, Y., Wang, G., Fu, Q., Chaudhary, G.: Surface defect detection method based on improved attention mechanism and feature fusion model. Comput. Intell. Neurosci. **2022**, 1–12 (2022)
13. Li, J., Wang, H.: Surface defect detection of vehicle light guide plates based on an improved RetinaNet. Meas. Sci. Technol. **33**(4), 1–11 (2022)
14. Xue, L., Li, Q., Lu, Y., Zhang, D., He, Q., Wang, H.: Fabric defect detection based on the improved cascade R-CNN. Acad. J. Comput. Inf. Sci. **4**(7), 81–87 (2021)
15. Jiang, P., Ergu, D., Liu, F., Cai, Y., Ma, B.: A review of YOLO algorithm developments. Procedia Comput. Sci. **199**, 1066–1073 (2022)
16. Xian, Y., Liu, G., Fan, J., Yu, Y., Wang, Z.: YOT-Net: YOLOv3 combined triplet loss network for copper elbow surface defect detection. Sensors **21**(21), 1–12 (2021)
17. Liao, X., Lv, S., Li, D., Luo, Y., Zhu, Z., Jiang, C.: YOLOv4-MN3 for PCB surface defect detection. Appl. Sci. **11**(24), 1–17 (2021)
18. Li, S., Wang, X.: YOLOv5-based defect detection model for hot rolled strip steel. In: Journal of Physics: Conference Series, vol. 2171, no. 1, pp. 1–6 (2022)
19. Fu, W., Qian, L., Zhu, X.: GAN-based intrusion detection data enhancement. In: Proceedings of the 33rd China Control and Decision Making Conference, no. 11, pp. 226–231 (2021)
20. Zhang, R., Liu, J., Zeng, Y., Pan, K., Huang, L.: Improved object detection using data enhancement method based on generative adversarial nets. In: Journal of Physics: Conference Series, vol. 1827, no. 1, pp. 1–6 (2021)

Multi-objective Optimization Based Viscosity Prediction for Inks in Direct Ink Writing Numerical Simulations

Yongqiang Tu[1,2(✉)], Alaa Hassan[3], Ali Siadat[2], Gongliu Yang[1], and Lihong Qiao[4]

[1] School of Instrumentation and Optoelectronic Engineering, Beihang University, Beijing 100191, People's Republic of China
tuyq_1992@163.com
[2] LCFC, Arts Et Métiers ParisTech, 57000 Metz, France
[3] ERPI, Université de Lorraine, 54000 Nancy, France
[4] School of Mechanical Engineering and Automation, Beihang University, Beijing 100191, China

Abstract. Direct ink writing (DIW) is one of the most popular additive manufacturing (AM) techniques. To fully understand the DIW, numerical simulations are used to model this process. The prediction accuracy of DIW numerical simulations is significantly influenced by the viscosity expression accuracy of inks. However, the previous works failed to realize an accurate viscosity prediction due to the lack of model selection and the low-accuracy parameters determination. Herein, this paper develops a novel multi-objective optimization based viscosity prediction method for inks in DIW numerical simulations. Firstly, rotational shear rate sweep tests are conducted to obtain shear rate-viscosity data. Then, four empirical shear-thinning viscosity models are selected as alternative models. The question of determining model parameters is then transformed into a multi-objective optimization problem (MOOP), and NSGA-II and TOPSIS are deployed to determine the model parameters and the final viscosity prediction result. Afterwards, the proposed method is validated by comparing the simulation and experimental results of profile of freeform extruded filaments (FEF). The proposed viscosity prediction method is validated as the predicted result using a cellulose-based ink has the minimum difference between simulation and experimental profile of FEF with 4.31% relative error. The work overcomes the limitations of the previous works in viscosity prediction of inks and demonstrates an effective and accurate approach for viscosity prediction of inks in DIW numerical simulations.

Keywords: Multi-objective optimization · Viscosity prediction · Direct ink writing · Numerical simulations

1 Introduction

Direct ink writing (DIW), also known as material extrusion based 3D printing, is one of the most popular additive manufacturing (AM) techniques due to its diversity in materials and flexibility in equipment [1]. In this process, the feedstock is prepared as

L. Zhang et al. (Eds.): CINT 2022, CCIS 1714, pp. 147–157, 2022.
https://doi.org/10.1007/978-981-19-8915-5_13

ink with shear-thinning rheological property and shape retention property [2]; then the ink is filled in a syringe and extruded by a piston from a nozzle into a substrate layer by layer forming a 3D part [3].

In recent years, to fully understand the DIW process and improve the geometrical quality of parts fabricated by DIW, numerical simulations have been widely established for DIW [4–7]. Comminal et al. established numerical models of deposited filaments [4] and corners [6] in extrusion based additive manufacturing, respectively. Göhl et al. [5] simulated deposited filaments in DIW based on a computational fluid dynamics (CFD) simulation tool. Tu et al. [7] modeled and evaluated freeform extruded filament for DIW based on numerical simulations. The prediction accuracy of numerical simulations results for DIW was significantly influenced by the viscosity expression of inks [8]. Thus, an accurate and reliable viscosity expression of the used ink is important for prediction accuracy of numerical simulations of DIW.

The previous works for viscosity prediction of inks regarded the viscosity model as a power law equation (PLE) and determined the parameters in the model using linear regression method (LRM) [9–11]. However, the previous work failed to realize an accurate viscosity prediction due to these two shortcomings as:

1) Lack of model selection: because ink in DIW is a typical shear-thinning fluid [12], PLE has been widely chosen as the viscosity model of ink due to its simplicity in parameter determination and high computational speed in numerical simulations [13]. However, there are many model structures for shear-thinning material and other viscosity model might be more accurate for the ink than PLE.
2) Restriction of determination of parameters: PLE was transferred to a linear equation and parameters were determined by LRM in the previous works. However, for other complex model structures which could not be transferred to linear equation, LRM is limited.

Thus, to overcome the shortcomings of the previous works for viscosity prediction of inks and improve simulation accuracy of DIW numerical simulations, it is crucial and desirable to propose an improved viscosity prediction method for inks in DIW numerical simulation. The main contribution of this work is choosing four commonly used viscosity models of shear-thinning materials as model alternatives of ink, and then proposing a novel multi-objective optimization method to determine parameters in each model alternative and select the best model for viscosity expression of ink to realize an accurate viscosity prediction for inks in DIW.

In this work, a novel multi-objective optimization based viscosity prediction of inks in DIW numerical simulations is proposed and the proposed method is validated by comparing experimental and simulation results of freeform extruded filaments (FEF) using a cellulose-based ink in a DIW 3D printer. The work overcomes the limitations of previous works in viscosity prediction of inks and demonstrates an effective and accurate approach for viscosity prediction of inks in DIW numerical simulations.

2 Data Acquisition and Viscosity Model Alternatives

2.1 Data Acquisition

Data for viscosity prediction are obtained by rotational shear rate sweep tests using a rheometer ARES (TA Instruments, USA) with a 25 mm plate-plate geometry at a gap distance of 1 mm. Shear rate-viscosity data are measured at 25 °C and controlled shear rate from 0.0125 to 100 (5 points per decade). Rotational shear rate sweep tests are performed in triplicate and mean values are used as shear rate-viscosity data for viscosity prediction.

2.2 Viscosity Model Alternatives

Four empirical viscosity models for shear-thinning inks including the power law equation (PLE), the Hershel-Bulkley equation (HBE), the Bird-Carreau equation (BCE) and the Cross Power Law equation (CPLE) are selected as viscosity model alternatives.

PLE is written as [14]:

$$\mu = k_P \dot{\gamma}^{n_P - 1} \tag{1}$$

where μ is the viscosity of the ink and $\dot{\gamma}$ is the shear rate; the parameters k_P and n_P are positive constants called the consistency index and power law index in PLE, respectively.

HBE is written as [15]:

$$\mu = min\left(\mu_{0,H}, \tau_{0,H}/\dot{\gamma} + k_H \dot{\gamma}^{n_H - 1}\right) \tag{2}$$

where the parameters $\mu_{0,H}$, $\tau_{0,H}$, k_H and n_H are positive constants called the limiting dynamic viscosity, yield stress, consistency index and flow index in HBE, respectively.

BCE is written as [16]:

$$\mu = \mu_{\infty,B} + \left(\mu_{0,B} - \mu_{\infty,B}\right) \times \left[1 + (k_B \dot{\gamma})^2\right]^{(n_B - 1)/2} \tag{3}$$

where the parameters $\mu_{0,B}$, $\mu_{\infty,B}$, k_B and n_B are positive constants called the zero-shear dynamic viscosity, infinite-shear dynamic viscosity, relaxation time and power law index in BCE, respectively.

CPLE is written as [17]:

$$\mu = \mu_{\infty,C} + \frac{\mu_{0,C} - \mu_{\infty,C}}{1 + (k_C \dot{\gamma})^{n_C}} \tag{4}$$

where the parameters $\mu_{0,C}$, $\mu_{\infty,C}$, k_C and n_C are positive constants called the zero-shear dynamic viscosity, infinite-shear dynamic viscosity, relaxation time and power law index in CPLE, respectively.

Table 1. Constraints of viscosity model alternatives.

Model	PLE	HBE	BCE	CPLE
Constraint	$\begin{cases} k_P > 0 \\ 0 < n_P < 1 \end{cases}$	$\begin{cases} \mu_{0,H} \geq 0 \\ \tau_{0,H} \geq 0 \\ k_H > 0 \\ 0 < n_H < 1 \end{cases}$	$\begin{cases} 0 \leq \mu_{\infty,B} < \mu_{0,B} \\ k_B > 0 \\ 0 < n_R < 1 \end{cases}$	$\begin{cases} 0 \leq \mu_{\infty,C} < \mu_{0,C} \\ k_C > 0 \\ 0 < n_C < 1 \end{cases}$

3 Parameters Determination and Viscosity Model Selection

3.1 Formalization of Multi-objective Optimization Problem

Parameters in each model are defined as design variables. Due to the shear-thinning property, constraints of each model are listed in Table 1.

The best model selection should have the highest trend correlation and lowest fitting error compared to experimental curve. In statistics, the coefficient of determination (R^2) represents the trend correlation between calculated and experimental curves and absolute average relative deviation ($AARD\%$) represents fitting error for data values. Thus, to compare the accuracy of both model selection and parameter determination, R^2 and $AARD\%$ are used as indicators as follows [18]:

$$R^2 = \frac{\sum_{i=1}^{N} \left(\mu_{i,e} - \overline{\mu}_e\right)^2 - \sum_{i=1}^{N} \left(\mu_{i,e} - \mu_{i,c}\right)^2}{\sum_{i=1}^{N} \left(\mu_{i,e} - \overline{\mu}_e\right)^2} \tag{5}$$

$$AARD\% = \frac{1}{N} \sum_{i=1}^{N} \left(\left|\frac{\mu_{i,e} - \mu_{i,c}}{\mu_{i,e}}\right|\right) \times 100 \tag{6}$$

where $\mu_{i,e}$ and $\mu_{i,c}$ denote the experimental and calculated values of ink viscosity, respectively; N is the number of datasets; $\overline{\mu}_e$ is the mean of experimental values for ink viscosity. In order to obtain an accurate and reliable model selection, the objectives are designated as $max(R^2)$ and $min(AARD\%)$ together. However, $max(R^2)$ and $min(AARD\%)$ may not be satisfied at the same time. Meanwhile, simply curve fitting method is hard to find the best model because the expressions of model alternatives are complex nonlinear equations. Thus, the model selection question is transferred to a multi-objective optimization problem (MOOP) to find the best compromise solution for the two objectives. The objective for determining the model parameters is written as: $min\left[-R^2, AARD\%\right]$.

3.2 Parameter Determination Using NSGA-II and TOPSIS

Unlike the single-objective optimization problem, solving MOOP will obtain a set of optimal points called a Pareto front instead of a unique optimal solution [19]. NSGA-II is used to obtain the Pareto front of the MOOP for each model alternative. Then, TOPSIS (technique for order preference by similarity to an ideal solution) is used to determine the best compromise solution from Pareto front as TOPSIS is a practical and classical approach for ranking and selecting alternatives [20].

The procedure of the NSGA-II is: first, the initial population $P(t)|t = 0$ is randomly generated by setting population size N_p; then, the genetic operators (selection, crossover and mutation) are performed on a parent population $P(t)$ to obtain the offspring population $Q(t)$; afterwards, the parent population $P(t)$ and the offspring population $Q(t)$ are merged as $R(t)$ to perform the fast non-dominant sorting; and the crowding distances are calculated for individuals in each non-dominating rank to select the new parent population $P(t + 1)$. The process is repeated until the stopping criteria are met.

In this study, NSGA-II are conducted using the software Matlab. The properties of NSGA-II are listed in Table 2.

Table 2. Properties of NSGA-II in this study.

Population type	Population size	Selection function	Crossover probability	Mutation probability	Stopping criteria
Double vector	200	Tournament	0.8	0.2	Max generation number: 20000

The procedure of the TOPSIS is illustrated as follows [21]:

1) Create a matrix $(x_{ij})_{m \times n}$ with m alternatives and n objectives. The element x_{ij} is the objective function value of i_{th} alternative with regard to the j_{th} objective function.
2) Normalize the matrix $(x_{ij})_{m \times n}$ to a normalized matrix $(t_{ij})_{m \times n}$ by using the equation below:

$$t_{ij} = \frac{x_{ij}}{\sqrt{\sum_{i=1}^{m} x_{ij}^2}}, i = 1, 2, ..., m, j = 1, 2, ..., n \quad (7)$$

3) Obtain the weighted normalized matrix $(a_{ij})_{m \times n}$ by:

$$a_{ij} = w_j \times t_{ij}, i = 1, 2, ..., m, j = 1, 2, ..., n \quad (8)$$

where w_j is the relative weight about the j_{th} objective and satisfied $\sum_{j=1}^{n} w_j = 1$. In this study, range weight is used to calculate w_j as:

$$w_j = \frac{(max(x_{ij}) - min(x_{ij}))/max(x_{ij})}{\sum_{j=1}^{n} ((max(x_{ij}) - min(x_{ij}))/max(x_{ij}))} \quad (9)$$

4) Determine the positive ideal alternative A^+ and the negative ideal alternative A^-:

$$A^+ = [min(a_{11,...}, a_{m1}), min(a_{12,...}, a_{m2}), .., min(a_{1n,...}, a_{mn})] \quad (10)$$

$$A^- = \left[max\left(a_{11,...,}a_{m1}\right), max\left(a_{12,...,}a_{m2}\right), .., max\left(a_{1n,...,}a_{mn}\right)\right] \tag{11}$$

5) Calculate the distance between the target alternative A and the positive ideal alternative A^+, and the distance between the target alternative A and the negative ideal alternative A^-:

$$d_i^+ = \sqrt{\sum_{j=1}^{n}\left(a_{ij} - A_j^+\right)^2}, i = 1, 2, ..., m, j = 1, 2, ..., n \tag{12}$$

$$d_i^- = \sqrt{\sum_{j=1}^{n}\left(a_{ij} - A_j^-\right)^2}, i = 1, 2, ..., m, j = 1, 2, ..., n \tag{13}$$

6) Calculate the relative closeness to the ideal solution of alternatives:

$$C_i = \frac{d_i^-}{d_i^+ + d_i^-}, i = 1, 2, ..., m \tag{14}$$

7) Rank the Pareto optimal points according to the values of C_i, and the final compromise solution A_{final} is selected when its C_i value is at the maximum of all Pareto optimal points:

$$A_{final} = A \in max(C_i) \tag{15}$$

In this study, $n = 2$ as two objectives were designated.

4 Validation

Viscosity predictions are imported to the numerical simulations of freeform extruded filaments (FEF) in DIW proposed in [7]. Then, a DIW 3D printer TM-081 (Tobeca Company, France) is used to extrude the ink into FEF and a camera (Canon LEGRIA HF R86 Noir, Canon Inc., Japan) is used to obtain experimental results as shown in Fig. 1. In this study, the main process parameters in numerical simulation and experiments are: for syringe, inner diameter is 21.6 mm; for nozzle, length is 18 mm; inner diameter is 0.84 mm and outer diameter is 1.22 mm; for extrusion velocity, piston velocity is 1.06×10^{-2} mm/s. Finally, simulation and experimental results of profiles of FEF are compared to validate the proposed viscosity prediction using the relative error as indicator. N_m measuring points are set along the filament length uniformly from nozzle bottom at fixed sampling intervals of 1 mm and diameter on each measuring point is measured as $d_i(i = 1, 2, ..., N_m)$. Relative error is defined as root mean square (RMS) of deviations for $d_i(i = 1, 2, ..., N_m)$ between simulation and experimental results.

5 Results and Discussion

A well printable cellulose-based ink is selected as ink reference to validate the method. The viscosity values of the cellulose ink with different shear rates are assessed by rotational shear rate sweep tests. Rotational shear rate sweep tests are performed in triplicate

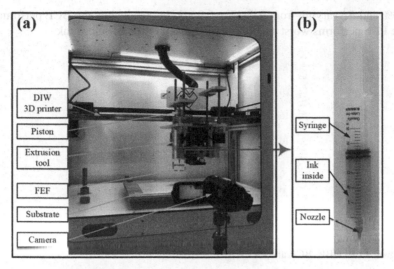

Fig. 1. Experimental setup for validation: (a) DIW 3D printer with a camera; (b) extrusion tool.

and mean values are used as data to reduce test errors. As shown in Fig. 2, the viscosity of the cellulose ink remains at a constant of about 903 $Pa \cdot s$ when shear rate is below $0.02\ s^{-1}$. When shear rate exceeds this value, the viscosity decreases as shear rate increases showing a shear-thinning property.

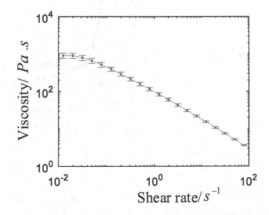

Fig. 2. Shear rate-viscosity data of the cellulose ink for viscosity prediction.

Pareto fronts obtained by the NSGA-II for the four model alternatives are plotted in Fig. 3. The Pareto front is on the highest right side of the performance curve of the PLE with *AARD*% varying from 19.00% to 22.41% and R^2 varying from 0.9100 to 0.9223. The Pareto fronts are nearly the same for the HBE and the CPLE as *AARD*% varies from 4.79% to 14.60% and R^2 varies from 0.9832 to 0.9971. The Pareto front is on the lowest left side of the performance curve of the BCE with *AARD*% varying from 3.51%

to 4.85% and R^2 varying from 0.9987 to 0.9993. In conclusion, the BCE performs best and the PLE performs worst as model alternatives for the cellulose ink.

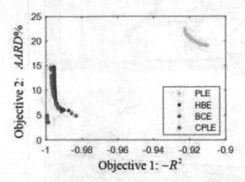

Fig. 3. Pareto fronts of the MOOP obtained by the NSGA-II for the four viscosity model alternatives: PLE, HBE, BCE and CPLE.

Parameters for each model are obtained by using the TOPSIS shown in Fig. 4 and the results are listed in Table 3. As BCE has the maximum R^2 and minimum $AARD\%$, the viscosity prediction result is the BCE with the determined parameters.

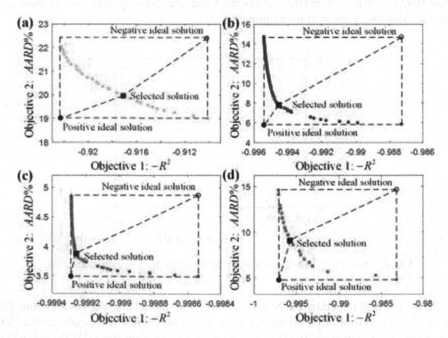

Fig. 4. Parameter determination from Pareto fronts by using the TOPSIS for: (a) PLE; (b) HBE; (c) BCE; (d) CPLE.

Table 3. Determined parameters in each model alternative.

Model alternative	Determined parameters	Performance	
		R^2	AARD%
PLE	$k_P = 79.39\ Pa \cdot s, n_P = 0.38$	0.9171	19.95%
HBE	$\mu_{0,H} = 865.57\ Pa \cdot s, \tau_{0,H} = 0.049\ Pa, k_H = 865.57\ Pa \cdot s, n_H = 0.32$	0.9945	7.80%
BCE	$\mu_{0,B} = 956.81\ Pa \cdot s, \mu_{\infty,B} = 0.0022\ Pa \cdot s, k_B = 26.63\ Pa \cdot s, n_B = 0.29$	0.9993	3.87%
CPLE	$\mu_{0,C} = 1105.81\ Pa \cdot s, \mu_{\infty,C} = 2.51\ Pa \cdot s, k_C = 13.94\ Pa \cdot s, n_C = 0.91$	0.9958	9.09%

Finally, the numerical simulation results using four models are compared with the experimental results. As shown in Fig. 5 and Table 4, BCE has the minimum difference between simulation and experimental results of profile of FEF with 4.31% relative error, which validates the effectiveness and accuracy of the proposed viscosity prediction method.

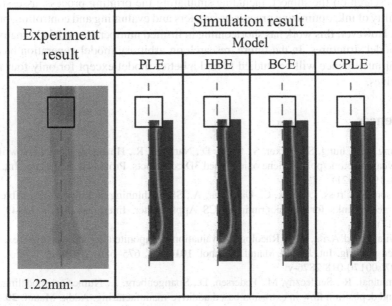

Fig. 5. Profiles of FEF in extrusion experiment and numerical simulations using the four model alternatives.

Table 4. Relative error between experimental and simulation results.

Model alternative	PLE	HBE	BCE	CPLE
Relative error (%)	30.29	12.54	4.31	19.78

6 Conclusion

This study proposed a novel multi-objective optimization viscosity prediction method for inks in DIW numerical simulations. Firstly, rotational shear rate sweep tests are conducted to obtain shear rate-viscosity data. Then, four empirical shear-thinning viscosity models – PLE, HBE, BCE and CPLE – are selected as alternative models. The question of determining model parameters is then transformed into a MOOP, and NSGA-II and TOPSIS are deployed to determine the model parameters and the final viscosity model selection result. Afterwards, the proposed method is validated by comparing the simulation and experimental results of profile of FEF.

The proposed viscosity prediction method can accurately and reliably express ink viscosity in DIW as the predicted result using a cellulose-based ink has the minimum difference between simulation and experimental profile of FEF with 4.31% relative error. Furthermore, the accurate and reliable viscosity prediction provides the basis for future research on the subject, including simulating the printing process, assessing the printability of ink, optimizing process parameters and evaluating and controlling product quality. However, this work has shortcoming in limited number of model alternative and fixed model structures. In the future, research on arbitrary model generation based on artificial intelligence will be studied to find a better model except for only four model alternatives.

References

1. Zhang, B., Chung, S., Barker, S., Craig, D., Narayan, R., Huang, J.: Direct ink writing of polycaprolactone/polyethylene oxide based 3D constructs. Prog. Nat. Sci. Mater. Int. **31**(2), 180–191 (2021)
2. Wilson, S., Cross, L., Peak, C., Gaharwar, A.: Shear-thinning and thermo-reversible nano-engineered inks for 3D bioprinting. ACS Appl. Mater. Interfaces. **9**(50), 43449–43458 (2017)
3. Dávila, J.L., d' Ávila, M.A.: Rheological evaluation of Laponite/alginate inks for 3D extrusion-based printing. Int. J. Adv. Manuf. Technol. **101**(1–4), 675–686 (2018). https://doi.org/10.1007/s00170-018-2876-y
4. Comminal, R., Serdeczny, M., Pedersen, D., Spangenberg, J.: Numerical modeling of the strand deposition flow in extrusion-based additive manufacturing. Addit. Manuf. **20**, 68–76 (2018)
5. Göhl, J., Markstedt, K., Mark, A., Håkansson, K., Gatenholm, P., Edelvik, F.: Simulations of 3D bioprinting: predicting bioprintability of nanofibrillar inks. Biofabrication **10**(3), 034105 (2018)
6. Comminal, R., Serdeczny, M., Pedersen, D., Spangenberg, J.: Motion planning and numerical simulation of material deposition at corners in extrusion additive manufacturing. Addit. Manuf. **29**, 100753 (2019)

7. Tu, Y., Hassan, A., Arrieta-Escobar, J., Zaman, U., Siadat, A., Yang, G.: Modeling and evaluation of freeform extruded filament based on numerical simulation method for direct ink writing. Int. J. Adv. Manuf. Technol. **120**(5), 3821–3829 (2022)

8. Liu, Q., et al.: Assessing the dynamic extrusion-based 3D printing process for power-law fluid using numerical simulation. J. Food Eng. **275**, 109861 (2020)

9. Ouyang, L., Yao, R., Zhao, Y., Sun, W.: Effect of bioink properties on printability and cell viability for 3D bioplotting of embryonic stem cells. Biofabrication **8**(3), 035020 (2016)

10. Kim, M., Lee, Y., Jung, W., Oh, J., Nam, S.: Enhanced rheological behaviors of alginate hydrogels with carrageenan for extrusion-based bioprinting. J. Mech. Behav. Biomed. Mater. **98**, 187–194 (2019)

11. Tu, Y., Arrieta-Escobar, J., Hassan, A., Zaman, U., Siadat, A., Yang, G.: Optimizing Process Parameters of Direct Ink Writing for Dimensional Accuracy of Printed Layers. 3D Printing and Additive Manufacturing, ahead of print (2021)

12. Armstrong, C., Yue, L., Deng, Y., Qi, H.: Enabling direct ink write edible 3D printing of food purees with cellulose nanocrystals. J. Food Eng. **330**, 111086 (2022)

13. Li, G., Liu, T., Xiao, X., Gu, M., Liao, W.: Numerical simulations of droplet forming, breaking and depositing behaviors in high-viscosity paste jetting. J. Manuf. Process. **78**, 172–182 (2022)

14. Rodriguez, M., Brown, J., Giordano, J., Lin, S., Omenetto, F., Kaplan, D.: Silk based bioinks for soft tissue reconstruction using 3-dimensional (3D) printing with in vitro and in vivo assessments. Biomaterials **117**, 105–115 (2017)

15. Rodríguez de Castro, A., Agnaou, M., Ahmadi-Sénichault, A., Omari, A.: Numerical investigation of Herschel–Bulkley fluid flows in 2D porous media: yielding behaviour and tortuosity. Comput. Chem. Eng. **140**, 106922 (2020)

16. Domurath, J., Saphiannikova, M., Férec, J., Ausias, G., Heinrich, G.: Stress and strain amplification in a dilute suspension of spherical particles based on a Bird-Carreau model. J. Nonnewton. Fluid Mech. **221**, 95–102 (2015)

17. Karimi, S., Dabagh, M., Vasava, P., Dadvar, M., Dabir, B., Jalali, P.: Effect of rheological models on the hemodynamics within human aorta: CFD study on CT image-based geometry. J. Nonnewton. Fluid Mech. **207**, 42–52 (2014)

18. Zheng, Y., Shadloo, M., Nasiri, H., Maleki, A., Karimipour, A., Tlili, I.: Prediction of viscosity of biodiesel blends using various artificial model and comparison with empirical correlations. Renewable Energy **153**, 1296–1306 (2020)

19. Tu, Y., Yang, G., Cai, Q., Wang, L., Zhou, X.: Optimal design of SINS's Stewart platform bumper for restoration accuracy based on genetic algorithm. Mech. Mach. Theory **124**, 42–54 (2018)

20. Mandal, P., Mondal, S.: Multi-objective optimization of Cu-MWCNT composite electrode in electro discharge machining using MOPSO-TOPSIS. Measurement **169**, 108347 (2021)

21. Ge, Y., Liu, Z., Sun, H., Liu, W.: Optimal design of a segmented thermoelectric generator based on three-dimensional numerical simulation and multi-objective genetic algorithm. Energy **147**, 1060–1069 (2018)

A Meta-learning-Based Object Detection Method for Custom Grasping in Human-Robot Collaboration

Song Yu[1]([✉]), Cheng Peng[1], and Lianyi Zhang[2,3]

[1] Beihang University, Beijing 100191, People's Republic of China
yusong0397@163.com, pengc@buaa.edu.cn
[2] Beijing Simulation Center, Beijing 100854, People's Republic of China
[3] Beijing Institute of Electronic System Engineering, Beijing 100854, People's Republic of China

Abstract. Industrial robots play an important role in a manufacturing system. While grasping is the first step for industrial robots in many tasks. Grasping the target object stably and accurately is of great significance for its subsequent operations. We propose a meta-learning-based grasping detection method, which takes RGB images as input and outputs the images with grasping points. We first obtained a feature extractor with strong generalization ability through large-scale datasets, and then introduced a meta-learning method, so that the grasp pose generator can be quickly adjusted according to different objects. The advantage of our method is that it can quickly adapt to new objects that have never been seen before. For new objects, we need to provide annotated grasping information. It can quickly obtain the grasping position we expected.

Keywords: Meta learning · Object detection · Custom grasping

1 Introduction

Industrial robots play an important role in a manufacturing system. While grasping is the first step for industrial robots in many tasks. Grasping the target object stably and accurately is of great significance for its subsequent operations.

Currently, the main grasping methods are traditional analytic and intelligent methods. The traditional method is the analytical method, which uses the geometry, material, position of the object, and the kinematic and dynamic characteristics of the robot itself to complete the generation of the grasping position. However, this method is only suitable for certain objects with certain positions and attitudes. In recent years, deep learning is now widely used in robot grasp detection. For example, by using a deep convolutional neural network to extract features from two-dimensional pictures, the grasping frame generated in the picture can be mapped to the grasping of three-dimensional space. In addition, there are many one-stage or two-stage deep learning algorithms in the field of object detection that have achieved good results, so many people transfer them to the grasp detection tasks. In addition, other works, such as [1] introduce a novel, end-to-end trainable CNN-based architecture to deliver high-quality results for grasp detection suitable for a parallel-plate gripper, and semantic segmentation and propose a novel refinement module that takes advantage of previously calculated grasp detection and semantic segmentation and further increases grasp detection accuracy. They implemented high-precision grasp detection on Cornell grasping datasets. Although deep learning methods have achieved good results in object detection, due to the complexity and uniqueness of customized tasks in IMS, deep learning cannot get excellent performance for different situations. [2, 3] learned a strategy using reinforcement learning and used this strategy to demonstrate the generalization of new objects. Other people use few-shot learning to quickly locate the target object.

One limitation of the prior studies is that they can't generate different grasping points based on the task to be performed, i.e., in a human-robot collaboration scene, simple operations can be performed independently by the robot, therefore the robot needs to obtain "operating" grasp locations, which means those easy-to-operate grasp locations. While complex operations are usually performed by robots assisted by humans, therefore "operating" grasp locations are usually reserved for humans and robots grasp other grasp locations. As mentioned above generating different grasping positions for the same object is necessary. Another limitation is that they cannot generate grasping points quickly and accurately for unseen objects.

To overcome the above limitations, this paper proposes a meta-learning-based grasping detection method, which takes RGB images as input and outputs the images with grasping points. The advantage of our method is that it can quickly adapt to new objects that have never been seen before. For new objects, we need to provide annotated grasping information. It can quickly obtain the grasping position we expected.

The main contribution of this paper is as follows:

(a) A meta-learning-based object detection method is proposed by adapting GrconvNet to industrial few-shot learning scenarios. We propose a new training process.
(b) We first obtained a feature extractor with strong generalization ability through large-scale datasets and then introduced MAML, which is a meta-learning method, so that the grasp pose generator can be quickly adjusted ac-cording to different objects.
(c) We also did some ancillary works. Such as dividing a publicly available Cornell datasets into several sub-datasets, which represents the similarity and difference between the data, so that the model takes attention to the connection between different classes. All of these works are important for few-shot learning task scenarios.

The rest of the paper is organized as follows: Sect. 2 briefly describes state-of-the-art methods to make robots fully autonomous. In Sect. 3, we introduce the proposed method and proposed model. Experiment results are shown in Sect. 4. Finally, Sect. 5 concludes the paper.

2 Background

This section briefly introduces few-shot learning.

2.1 Few-Shot Learning Method

Few-shot learning is widely studied in image classification tasks, we are inspired by the following methods. We divide it into two categories.

First, optimize the trained parameters. This method utilizes the parameters of the pretrained model of the related task as initialized parameters for the new task and fine-tunes the model parameters using the datasets of the new task. It is considered that some general structural information can be obtained from large-scale datasets. [6] used Convolutional Neural Networks to train on ImageNet for image classification tasks, then use large datasets for foreground segmentation, and finally uses a single sample to train objects to be segmented in target segmentation. If only a small sample datasets is used to fine-tune the model parameters by gradient descent, it will often cause overfitting. In order to solve this problem, the following attempts were made. [7] used a validation set to monitor the training progress. During training, stop the learning process when the performance on the validation set no longer improves. [8] considered that for a set of filters, only one strength parameter is learned that is multiplied by the filter, thus enabling the selection of which parameters of the filter to update. [9] had done the following experiments to group the filters in the CNN according to some auxiliary information, and then use the sample grouping back-propagation in the training set to achieve fine-tuning. [11] learned parameters from similar datasets for small sample datasets. [13] proposed a method of font style transfer by pretraining a network to recognize fonts in gray images. The old network is then fine-tuned while training a new additional network to generate color-style fonts. They jointly trained the new and old parameters.

Second, fine-tuning parameters are obtained through meta-learning. Model-agnostic Meta-learning [14] was the most representative method. There are many improvements to this method. [15] learned to choose from a subset of initialization parameters for a new task. After adding task-specific information, MAML is suitable for specific tasks. [16] argued that learning a model with a small number of samples inevitably leads to high uncertainty. [17] investigated the uncertainty.

3 The Proposed Method

In this section, we introduce the details of the proposed method.

3.1 Preliminaries

Rectangle in Grasping Detection. Grasping detection models take RGB images as input, and output the grasp representation of the target object. Different grasping representation methods will lead to a different grasping result. Currently, the representation methods can be divided into point-pair-based grasp representation and oriented rectangle-based grasp representation.

The point-pair-based representation method can be represented by (1).

$$G_{point} = \{x_1, y_1, x_2, y_2\} \tag{1}$$

where (x_1, y_1) is the location of the first point, (x_2, y_2) is the location of the second point. They represent the location of the gripper. Using these two points, we can infer the grasp configuration including position, direction, and gripper opening width.

The oriented rectangle-based grasp representation is most commonly used. It can be represented by (2).

$$G_{rect} = \{x, y, \theta, \omega, h\} \tag{2}$$

where (x, y) is the center point of the rectangle. θ represents the rotation angle of the rectangle from the image horizontal axis, ω and h represent the weight and height of the grasping rectangle.

The rectangle-based grasp uses the intersection over union (IoU) as a metric. IoU can be calculated by (3).

$$IoU = \frac{Area_{Intersection}}{Area_{Union}} \tag{3}$$

where Area Intersection represents the area of the intersection of two rectangles and Area Union represents the area of the union of two rectangles.

By definition, IoU is greater than or equal to 0 and less than or equal to 1. You can determine whether the grasping is successful by setting a threshold and compare with the threshold.

3.2 Structure

The structure of our model is shown in Fig. 1.

The GrConvNet model consists of three parts: 1. The feature extraction, which will be trained on the base datasets and shared with other processes. The feature extraction layer takes the processed image as input and outputs a feature map. 2. Grasp pose generator. For different objects, the parameters of this part are different. Inputting the previously extracted feature image into this part will outputs three images as grasp angle, grasp width, and grasp quality score. Finally infers grasp poses from three output images. The two parts are obtained by training the base datasets first, but then only the feature extractor obtained in this step is used, and the grasp pose locator is discarded. We will use meta-learning later to learn a code generator to get a class-specific grasp pose locator. 3. In order to remove the ambiguity of the representation of the rectangle-based representation, we convert rectangle-based representation to points-pair-based representation. We add a conversion module at the end to do this.

This structure is suitable for our proposed training process.

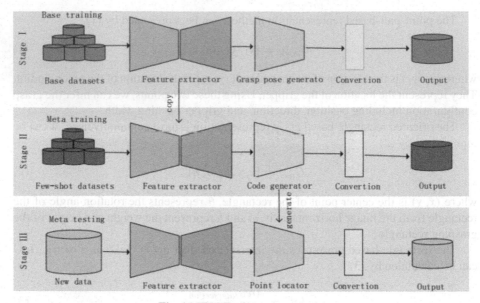

Fig. 1. The structure of our model

3.3 Training Process

In order to make full use of the rich original data while adapting to the few-shot learning, the whole process is divided into three parts.

Part 1: Basis Training Learning Feature Extractors. The aim of this part is to learn a class-agnostic feature extractor f. This can be achieved simply by standard supervised learning of base classes, simply to the original GrConvnet's training process. Specifically, we perform grasp pose generation and train the model (including feature extractor $f(\cdot)$ and grasp pose generator $h(\cdot)$) by Huber loss, which is represented by (4).

$$L_\delta(a) = \begin{cases} \frac{1}{2}a^2, & for |a| \leq \delta \\ \delta \cdot \left(|a| - \frac{1}{2}\delta\right), & \text{otherwise} \end{cases} \tag{4}$$

At this stage, we train a complete feature extractor and grasp pose generator, although the goal of this stage is only to learn a strong feature extractor $f(\cdot)$, The grasp pose generator in this stage is a regular grasp pose generator, which will be discarded in part2 but will be used at the test time for base classes.

The model training process is as follows.

First, the input data is preprocessed, and in order to make the image meet the input requirements of the network, it is cropped, resized, and normalized. The 224×224 n-channel processed RGB input images are fed into GrConvnet. Next, using the features extracted from the preprocessed images by GrConvNet, three images are generated as the grasp angle, grasp width, and grasp quality score as outputs. Finally, the grasping pose is inferred from the three output images.

Given the training datasets which contain ground-truth grasp pose $P_{ground-truth}$ and the predicted grasp pose P_{grasp}, we use Huber loss for model optimization on the parameters of feature extractor $f(\cdot)$ and grasp pose generator $h(\cdot)$, which can be represented by (5).

$$L\left(P_{grasp}, P_{ground-truth}\right) = \frac{1}{n} \sum z_k \tag{5}$$

where z_k is given by (6):

$$z_k = \begin{cases} 0.5(P_{grasp_k} - P_{ground-truthh_k})^2 \\ \left|P_{grasp_k} - P_{ground-truthh_k}\right| - 0.5 \end{cases} \tag{6}$$

Part 2: Meta Training Learning Code Generator. The basic idea of meta-learning is learning to learn, that is, to learn a code generator to generate the parameters of the grasp pose generator in our case. To learn a model agnostic grasp pose generator, we introduce the training mode in Model-Agnostic Meta-Learning (MAML).

First, we divided the base datasets into multiple sub-datasets according to data similarity. Each sub-datasets will be used to train code generator $g(\cdot)$ by episodic meta-learning strategy. Each sub-datasets can be seen as a few-shot task, thus simulating the time requirement of few-shot learning of new tasks. Specifically, each sub-dataset contains several images representing a class of objects, possibly from different angles or distances. We define each sub-datasets as a few-shot task T_i, which is uniformly distributed over the set of possible labelsets.

In meta-learning, we need to train in episodes. First, we randomly sample N sub-datasets as N tasks and each sub-dataset has K images, which are names N-ways K-shots mission. We should deal with this mission in episode E. Then, we sample a support set S for meta training and a query set Q for meta validation.

The support set S is used for the code generator. The code can be obtained by (7).

$$c_k = g(S_k) \tag{7}$$

where S_k are the images from the support set of class k. With these codes c_k, our method then performs object detection for query images I by using the feature extractor and grasp pose generator by (8) and (9):

$$m = f(I), I \in Q \tag{8}$$

$$Y = h(m, c_k) \tag{9}$$

Our model is then trained to minimize the mean prediction error on Q by updating solely the parameters of the code generator.

Part 3: Meta Testing Generate Point Locator. After base training and meta training, we obtain a feature extractor f and a code generator g. In meta testing, let's deal with unseen objects. We first obtain the parameters of grasp pose generator h by code generator g. Then input the test image to f and output the feature maps. Pass the feature map to h and we will get the grasp pose. The parameters of h can be updated a few times if we need them. Finally, we obtain all the parts of iFSgrNet.

4 Experiment

4.1 Experiment Settings

We choose a public datasets in the field of robotic grasping—Cornell datasets, which is widely used as a benchmark evaluation platform. It is collected in the real world with an RGBD camera. The datasets is composed of 885 images with a resolution of 640 × 480 pixels of 240 different objects with positive grasps (5110) and negative grasps (2909). RGB images and corresponding point cloud data of each object with various poses are provided.

As we mentioned above. The training process includes basic training, meta training, and meta testing.

For basis training, we do not need to process the datasets, just randomly sample data each epoch for training and validating. We use 80% of the datasets for training and 20% for validation, then we get the feature extractor and the grasp pose generator which are then discarded.

The other hyper parameters of our training process are shown in Table 1.

Table 1. Hyper parameters

Hyperparameter	Batch size	Training epochs	Batches per epoch	Optimizer
Setting	8	30	100	Adam

For meta training and meta testing, we divided Cornell datasets into 38 sub-datasets based on the similarities and differences between the grasped objects.

We use 30 sub-datasets for meta training and 8 sub-datasets for meta testing. We set a task as 5-ways 3-shots, which means we should choose 5 sub-datasets for 5 different categories and 3 images in each category.

4.2 Validation of the Structure

We choose remote control, mouse, scissors, and screwdriver as examples. The results are shown in Fig. 2. The original RGB images are shown in the first column. They are fed into our model after preprocessing such as cropping and scaling. The quality images are shown in the second column. They represent the location of a target object. Where the color difference is largest indicates the center coordinate. The shape of an object can be inferred from the difference in color. The angle images are shown in the third column. They also show location information. Besides, color information indicates the angle of the grasp rectangle. When the grasping rectangle is approximately horizontal, the color change is not obvious, and when the grasping rectangle is approximately vertical, the color difference is maximum. The fourth column represents the width images, similar to angle images, they contain position information and grasp rectangle width information. Quality images, angle images, and width images are generated by the grasp pose generator. Given these three images, we can deduce the grasp rectangle, which is shown in

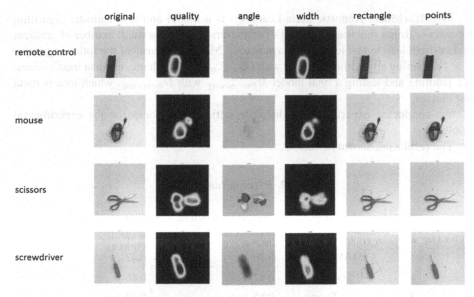

Fig. 2. The output of our model

the fifth column. The rectangle represents grasp position, grasp angle, and grasp width three kinds of information. The grasp point pairs are shown in the sixth column.

One can see that for different objects, it can generate grasp point pairs that meet our expectations. So we can tell that the model produces better results when given better guidance. Finally achieving better human-robot interaction.

4.3 Validation of the Optimization Strategy

The proposed incremental few-shot grasp points predictor is evaluated with the following baselines: 1. Fine-Tuning method. 2. MEML method.

The fine-tuning method means improving performance through minor alterations. It is a kind of transfer learning, in our case, the source datasets is 30 sub-datasets of the divided datasets and the target datasets is the remaining 8 sub-datasets. Fine-tuning consists of the following steps:

(1) Training a base model with a source datasets, where the base model is our improved GrConvnet. We merge the sub-datasets in the source datasets, and randomly select images for training. (2) Create a new neural network model. This copies all model designs and feature extractor's parameters on the base model and resets the grasp pose locator's parameters. We assume that these model parameters contain the knowledge learned from the source datasets and this knowledge will also be applicable to the target datasets. (3) Train the target model on the target datasets. We also merge the sub-datasets in the target datasets, and randomly select images for training. The grasp pose generator part will be trained from scratch, while the parameters of the feature extractor are fine-tuned based on the parameters of the base model.

MAML (Model Agnostic Meta-Learning) is a model and task agnostic algorithm for meta-learning that trains a model's parameters such that a small number of gradient updates will lead to fast learning on a new task. MAML consists of the following steps: (1) Training a base model M_{meta} with $D_{meta-train}$, , which means meta train classes. (2) Training and testing a final model $M_{fine-tuning}$ with $D_{meta-test}$, which means meta test classes.

We conducted experiments in different settings and compared the experimental results.

The results are shown in Table 2.

Table 2. Experimental results

Way	Shot	Method	Objects seen before	Objects unseen before
5	2	Fine-Tuning	0.86	0.31
		MAML	0.76	0.42
		iFSgrNet	0.87	0.46
5	3	Fine-Tuning	0.85	0.33
		MAML	0.76	0.44
		iFSgrNet	0.87	0.46
5	4	Fine-Tuning	0.86	0.34
		MAML	0.78	0.43
		iFSgrNet	0.90	0.49
5	5	Fine-Tuning	0.86	0.40
		MAML	0.77	0.45
		iFSgrNet	0.91	0.50

By analyzing the data, we find that iFSgrNet gives good results for both seen and unseen objects. Fine-Tuning gives good results for seen objects but gives a poor performance on unseen objects. Because Fine-Tuning makes full use of the information on the base datasets, it still requires several training epochs to adapt to new samples. MAML is effective for few-shot learning, so it performs well on unseen objects, but because it wants to find properties of globally optimal parameters, it does not generalize well to base datasets, which leads to its bad performance on objects seen before.

5   Conclusion and Future Works

This paper proposed an adaptive Incremental Few-shot grasp points prediction network and a new training paradigm. With our model iFSgrNet and training steps, grasp points for unseen objects can be generated quickly. For an unseen object, people only need to mark their grasp points on the RGB image, the purpose of human-robot cooperation is also achieved.

Our next step is to deploy our model into a simulated IMS or real IMS. And use the grasping success rate as an indicator to evaluate the performance of our proposed method. We hope that our proposed method can be truly applied to IMS and inspire other scholars.

References

1. Ainetter, S., Fraundorfer, F.: End-to-end Trainable Deep Neural Networkfor Robotic Grasp Detection and Semantic Segmentation from RGB (2021)
2. Zeng, A., et al.: Learning Synergies between Pushing and Grasping withSelf-Supervised Deep Reinforcement Learning. IEEE (2018)
3. Berscheid, L., Meiner, P., Krger, T.: Robot Learning of Shifting Objectsfor Grasping in Cluttered Environments (2019)
4. Bordel, B., Alcarria, R., Sánchez-de-Rivera, D., Robles, T.: Protecting industry 4.0 systems against the malicious effects of cyber-physical attacks. In: Ochoa, S.F., Singh, P., Bravo, J. (eds.) UCAmI 2017. LNCS, vol. 10586, pp. 161–171. Springer, Cham (2017). https://doi.org/10.1007/978-3-319-67585-5_17
5. Wang, L., et al.: Symbiotic human-robot collaborative assembly. CIRP Ann. Manuf. Technol. **68**(2), 701–726 (2019)
6. Caelles, S., et al.: One-shot video object segmentation. In: 2017 IEEE Conferenceon Computer Vision and Pattern Recognition (CVPR). IEEE (2017)
7. Arik, S.O., et al.: Neural Voice Cloning with a Few Samples (2018)
8. Keshari, R., et al.: Learning Structure and Strength of CNN Filters for SmallSample Size Training. IEEE (2018)
9. Yoo, D., et al.: Efficient K-Shot Learning with Regularized Deep Networks (2017)
10. Zhang, J., et al.: Recurrent neural network for motion trajectory prediction in human-robot collaborative assembly. CIRP Ann. **69**(1), 9–12 (2020)
11. Gidaris, S., Komodakis, N.: Dynamic few-shot visual learning without forgetting. In: 2018 IEEE/CVF Conference on Computer Vision and Pattern Recognition(CVPR). IEEE (2018)
12. Zhang, J., et al.: Artificial intelligence in advanced manufacturing: current status and future outlook. J. Manuf. Sci. Eng. **142**, 1–53 (2020)
13. Azadi, S., et al.: Multi-Content GAN for Few-Shot Font Style Transfer (2017)
14. Finn, C., Abbeel, P., Levine, S.: Model-Agnostic Meta-Learning for Fast Adaptation of Deep Networks (2017)
15. Lee, Y., Choi, S.: Gradient-Based Meta-Learning with Learned Layerwise Metric and Subspace (2018)
16. Finn, C., Xu, K., Levine, S.: Probabilistic Model-Agnostic Meta-Learning. arXiv (2018)
17. Kim, T., et al.: Bayesian Model-Agnostic Meta-Learning (2018)
18. Mahyar, A., Radji, K.M.: Grasp and stress analysis of an underactuated finger for proprioceptive tactile sensing. IEEE/ASME Trans. Mechatron. **23**(4), 1619–1629 (2018)

A Knowledge-Embedding-Based Approach for Process-Decision Knowledge Mining

Xinzheng Xu, Zhicheng Huang[✉], and Lihong Qiao

School of Mechanical Engineering and Automation, Beihang University, Beijing 100191, China
zc_huang@buaa.edu.cn

Abstract. Association rule mining algorithm is a main technique to discover and extract knowledge of rules represented with antecedents and consequents, which can be applied to mining process-decision knowledge. However, it is difficult to reflect the semantic association between process data items when only the support degree and confidence coefficient are used as indicators for judging whether the data items can be included in the content of knowledge. This usually results in amounts of invalid rules in output. To address this problem, a knowledge-embedding-based approach is presented in this study. To integrate semantic information into algorithm, a matrix of semantic correlation among data items is developed as the knowledge to be embed. The indicators of cohesion and relevancy are introduced based on the matrix of semantic correlation. Then two fusion models are developed to enhance the semantic correlation evaluation, one is built with the cohesion and support degree coupling while the other is proposed with the combination of relevancy and confidence coefficient. Based on these models, the proposed algorithm is able to identify the effectiveness of the composed knowledge expressed in rule form effectively. This method is carried out to mine process-decision knowledge with the machining data of gears and shafts. The results reveal that the number and proportion of correct rules are improved with knowledge imbedded, which validate the proposed method.

Keywords: Knowledge mining · Knowledge embedding · Process-decision knowledge · Semantic association

1 Introduction

Process-decision knowledge is a kind of process knowledge in common use, with which process designers can make process decisions. During the production and manufacturing activities, enterprises accumulate amounts of process specification documents as the guideline of machining and assembly activities. These files record the technological process data, such as part and product information, process sequence, equipment and tool employed. There are rich and useful process-decision knowledge hidden behind the data. It is an effective approach for enterprises to acquire and accumulate knowledge resources by mining process-decision knowledge from the technological process data. How to realize this kind of knowledge mining effectively has become the current research hotspot in the field of intelligent manufacturing.

© The Author(s), under exclusive license to Springer Nature Singapore Pte Ltd. 2022
L. Zhang et al. (Eds.): CINT 2022, CCIS 1714, pp. 168–180, 2022.
https://doi.org/10.1007/978-981-19-8915-5_15

Association rule mining algorithm is a main technique to discover and extract knowledge of rule representation with antecedents and consequents. It can be applied to mining process-decision knowledge [1]. Huang CM et al. [1] acquired lots of process-decision knowledge based on Apriori algorithm. J. Jiao et al. [2] introduced the hashing technique into Apriori algorithm, which improves the efficiency of process-decision knowledge mining. At present, the research on mining process-decision knowledge mainly focuses on how to improve the efficiency of algorithm. However, there are few studies on improving the proportion of valid process-decision knowledge in algorithm output to improve the quality of mining results.

Ana Cristina et al. [3] believed that it is hard to reflect the semantic association between process data items when only the support and confidence are used as indicators to assist in judging whether the data items can be included in the content of knowledge. In this way, some data items of high statistical level but irrelevance are retained, resulting in producing a large amount of invalid domain knowledge. In order to increase the number and proportion of correct knowledge in output, a knowledge-embedding-based method is proposed to mine process-decision knowledge. The method embeds the process knowledge used to describe the semantic association among process data items in the Apriori algorithm, and ascertains whether the analyzed data items can constitute process-decision knowledge based on two fusion models holding the semantic and statistical information of data items.

2 The Model of Process-Decision Knowledge Mining

The task of mining process-decision knowledge is to discover and acquire knowledge that can assist process designers with process planning from a large amount of historical process data. Given a process data set $T = \{t_1, t_2, t_3,... t_i... t_n\}$, t_i refers to a process record and it can be represented by two-tuple, as shown in Formula (1).

$$t_i = \{Operation, Step\} \tag{1}$$

where, *Operation* refers to the collection of process data items in the operation level of process, *Step* refers to the collection of process data items in the step level of process.

Process-decision knowledge consists of antecedents and consequents, which can be represented by generative rule, as shown in Formula (2).

$$Knowledge = \text{IF}\{ Antecedents\} \text{ Then}\{ Consequents\} \tag{2}$$

where, *Antecedents* refers to the set of process data items that antecedents include, *Consequents* refers to the set of process data items that consequents include. For example, it is one piece of knowledge that carbide-tipped tool of YT15 can be used for rough machining of 45-steel parts, which is described by natural language. According to Formula (2), this piece of knowledge can be represented as one generative rule, as shown in Formula (3).

$$\text{IF}\{Rough\,machining, 45\,steel\} \text{ Then}\{Carbide - tipped\,tool, YT15\} \tag{3}$$

According to Formula (1) and (2), it is necessary to find a series of related data items from the process data set T and then combine them orderly to produce process- decision knowledge. In general, this is a process with two steps. The first step is the search of the data items that can constitute process-decision knowledge from the process data set. The next is the generation of the *Antecedents* and the *Consequents* by traversing each generated set and organize them in the form of generative rule.

3   Process Knowledge Representation Based on Semantic-Correlation-Degree Matrix

Semantics is the specific meaning or interpretation that data is given in a specific domain [4]. Knowledge contains the semantic information of data, and the semantic association among data items reflects the inherent connection of knowledge content [3]. The information describing the semantic relationship between two data items can be used as a kind of knowledge. It can be embedded in the algorithm of knowledge mining to assist in searching for the elements of process-decision knowledge. To achieve this kind of process knowledge embedding effectively, the semantic correlation should be quantized among data items and the representation of the knowledge to embed should be established.

Process element, or entity, is a set of instances with the same properties and actions [5], such as *Machining feature, Machining operation, Machining equipment* and *Part material*, etc. Process element is the semantic embodiment of process data item and process data item is the instance of process element. There are many types of process elements in a large amount of historical process data, and each process element includes multiple instances. Common process elements and their instances in process planning are listed in Table 1.

Table 1. Common process elements and their instances

Process element	Instance
Feature	Hole, groove, plane and end face, etc
Machining operation	Rough turning, semi-finishing, fine turning, rough boring and fine boring, etc.
Machining equipment	C336-1, C368L, C385L and C512A, etc.
Gauge	Inner micrometer, cylindrical plug gauge and Vernier caliper, etc.
Fixture	Self-centering chucks, mandrels and top centers, etc.

Relational expression between process element and process data item is defined as shown in Formula (4).

$$f_1 : x \to y, x \in S_1, y \in S_2 \tag{4}$$

where, x refers to one process data item, and y refers to one process element, and S_1 refers to the set of process element instances, and S_2 refers to the set of process elements.

In the process planning, there is association among some process elements. For example, the value of *Machining operation* is related to *Machining feature*, and the selection of *Tool Grade* is related to *Part material*. Relational expression describing two elements that are related is defined as shown in Formula (5).

$$f_2 : y_1 \rightarrow y_2, y_1, y_2 \in S_2 \tag{5}$$

where, y_1 and y_2 refer to two different process elements, and S_2 refers to the set of process elements. When process element y_1 is one of the conditions to determine the process element y_2, y_1 and y_2 are related.

According to Formula (4) and (5), the formula that calculated the degree of semantic correlation between two data items is defined as follows.

$$\text{SR}_{ab} = R_{f_1(a)f_1(b)} = \begin{cases} 1, \exists f_2, f_2 : f_1(a) \rightarrow f_1(b) \\ 0, No\ f_2\ exists\ between\ f_1(a)\ and\ f_1(b) \end{cases} \tag{6}$$

where, SR_{ab} refers to the degree of semantic correlation between data item a and b, and $R_{f1(a)f1(b)}$ refers to the degree of correlation between element $f_1(a)$ and $f_1(b)$.

In process planning, when two process elements that data item a and b belong to are related, the value of their semantic-correlation degree is 1 and the correlation degree between their owning elements is 1. Otherwise, the value is 0. In a particular case, two identical process elements are not related and no semantic correlation exists between data item and itself.

If the relationships among some process elements are known before mining decision-making knowledge on a process data set, the knowledge describing the correlations among these process elements can be represented by semantic-correlation-degree matrix according to Formula (5), of which the matrix is shown in Formula (7).

$$M = \begin{pmatrix} R_{11} R_{12} \cdots R_{1,n-1} R_{1n} \\ \vdots \ddots \vdots \\ \vdots \ddots R_{ij} \vdots \\ \vdots \ddots \vdots \\ R_{n1} R_{n2} \cdots\cdots R_{nn} \end{pmatrix}_{n \times n} \tag{7}$$

where, M refers to the semantic-correlation-degree matrix of the process knowledge to embed, and n is the number of related elements that knowledge contains, and R_{ij} refers to the correlation degree between process element i and j.

Take the machining process data of a part as an example, the relationships among some process elements—*Part Material, Machining Feature, Machining Method and Tool Grade*—are known, the semantic-correlation-degree matrix to represent these pieces of knowledge can be established according to Formula (7), the construction of the matrix as shown in Fig. 1.

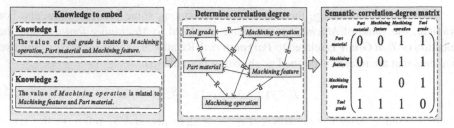

Fig. 1. The construction of semantic-correlation-degree matrix.

The semantic-correlation-degree matrix describes the correlation among the process elements in the knowledge to embed and quantifies the semantic correlation between two process data items, which can provide guidance for process-decision knowledge mining.

4   Construction of Knowledge Mining Algorithm Based on Process Knowledge Embedding

The knowledge describing the semantic correlations among process data items is embed into the Apriori algorithm for knowledge mining. This can make the algorithm retain the data items of high statistical level and interrelation in search of process-decision knowledge content, and the algorithm also excludes the data sets of condition-result type with high statistical level but low irrelevance.

4.1   The Adequacy of the Process Knowledge to Embed

In process-decision knowledge mining, the quality of algorithm output is also concerned with the amount of process knowledge to embed. To quantify the amount of knowledge to embed, the indicator of adequacy as shown in Formula (8).

$$KS = \frac{n\_elements}{N\_elements} n\_elements \leq N\_elements \tag{8}$$

where, KS refers to the adequacy of the knowledge to embed in the task of knowledge mining, and $n\_elements$ is the number of process elements that knowledge to embed contains, and $N\_elements$ is the number of process elements in the data set of this task.

The indicator KS reflects the completeness of process knowledge to embed relative to a specific task of knowledge mining.

4.2   The Calculation Models of Cohesion and Relevancy

Considering the characteristics of process-decision knowledge, the indicator of cohesion is introduced, which is used to quantify one process data item set and to reflect the possibility of this set constituting the content of process-decision knowledge; the indicator of relevancy is introduced, which is applied to quantify two sets and to reflect the correlation between antecedent set and consequent set.

The cohesion is a measure of the correlations among process data items and indicates how closely each data item is combined with each other in a set [4]. Given a process data set T, the cohesion of set T is defined as shown in Formula (9).

$$Cohesion(T) = \frac{C^2_{r\_itempairs}}{C^2_{n\_Set}} \times \ln\ r\_itempairs \tag{9}$$

where, n_set is the number of items in a set, and $r\_itempairs$ is the number of the correlated data items in a set.

The relevancy is a measure of the correlation between antecedent set and consequent set and indicates the possibility of their interacting as both antecedent and consequent in a rule. Given two process data set T_1 and T_2, the relevancy between two sets is defined as shown in Formula (10).

$$Relevence(ifT_1thenT_2) = \frac{q\_itempairs}{N\_TC} \times \ln q\_itempairs \tag{10}$$

where, N_TC refers to the number of items in a set, and $q\_itempairs$ refers to the number of paired combinations of data items that are correlated from antecedent set to consequent set.

4.3   Two Fusion Models Based on Knowledge Embedding

Combine the calculation model of cohesion with that of support in Apriori to build a fusion model as the criterion whether data items constituting the content of process-decision knowledge. Combine the calculation model of relevancy with that of confidence in Apriori to establish a fusion model and it determines whether a piece of process-decision knowledge can be generated from two subsets of condition-result type.

Given a set T defined in Formula (1) and a process data set $K = \{k_1, k_2, k_3,... k_i...$ $k_n\}$, $K \subset T$, the support of K upon the dataset T is defined as shown in Formula (11) [6].

$$Support(K) = \frac{|t(K)|}{n} \tag{11}$$

where, $|t(K)|$ is the number of occurrences of the transaction—process record—containing the set K, and n is the total number of the transactions that are the records of process plan.

The fusion model with cohesion and support coupling is defined as shown in Formula (12).

$$Fusion(Cohesion\&Support) = w_1 \times Cohesion(K) + w_2 \times Support(K) \tag{12}$$

where, w_1 and w_2 are weight coefficient, and $w_1 + w_2 = 1$.

Given two process data sets K_1 and K_2, the confidence of a rule to represent knowledge with K_1 antecedent and K_2 consequent is defined as shown in Formula (13) [6].

$$Confidence(if\ K_1\ then\ K_2) = \frac{|t(K_1 \cup K_2)|}{|t(K_1)|} \qquad (13)$$

where, $|t(K_1)|$ is the number of occurrences of the transactions containing the set K1, and $|t(K_1 \cup K_2)|$ is the number of the transactions containing K1 and K2.

The fusion model with relevancy and confidence coupling is defined as shown in Formula (13).

$$Fusion\ (Relevancy\ \&\ Confidence) = \begin{cases} Relevancy\ \times\ Confidence, & if\ Relevancy \neq 0 \\ Confidence, & if\ Relevancy = 0 \end{cases} \qquad (14)$$

4.4 The Improved Apriori Algorithm Based on Process Knowledge Embedding

Before the task of associate rule mining is performed based Apriori, the minimum support and minimum confidence—abbreviated as Min-Supp and Min-Confi—need to be set, and the set of data items whose support is beyond or equal to the Min-Supp is called frequent item set. Among the frequent item sets, the rule with confidence beyond or equal to Min-Confi is called strong association rule, the final and desirable rule. Data mining involves two steps: Traverse the dataset to retrieve all the data item sets that satisfy the Min-Supp, that is, to obtain the frequent item sets; traverse all the frequent itemsets and produce strong association rules that are to satisfy the Min-Confi.

Modify the indicators and thresholds in Apriori. According to Formula (12) and (14), replace the *support* with *Fusion(Cohesion&Support)*, set the minimum *Fusion(Cohesion&Support)*, abbreviated as Min-Co-Sup; Replace the *confidence* with *Fusion(Relevancy&Confidence)*, set the minimum *Fusion(Relevancy&Confidence)*, abbreviated as Min-Re-Conf. Through the search strategy of Apriori, find all the data sets that satisfy the Min-Co-Sup in the process dataset. On this basis, produce all the subsets that satisfy the Min-Re-Conf among those process data sets, and then organize them by generative rule to produce process-decision knowledge. The flow of the modified algorithm as shown in Fig. 2.

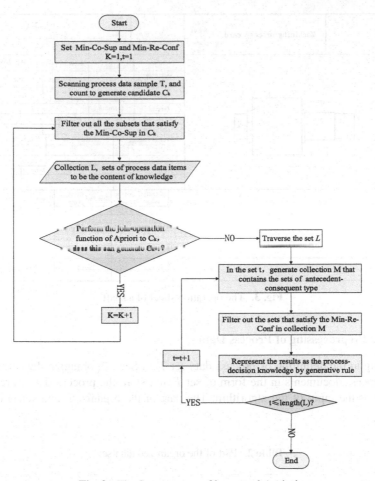

Fig. 2. The flow process of improved Apriori.

5 Case Study

In this section, the proposed approach is verified by knowledge mining in the process data set of gears and shafts. In this case, the process data is collected from the documents of machining process plan for gears and shafts. The operation sheet as one kind of documents as shown in Fig. 3.

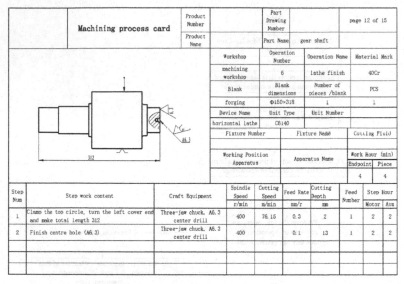

Fig. 3. The operation sheet of a shaft.

5.1 The Preprocessing of Process Data

According to the definition of process data set T in Sect. 2, organize the information of the process documents in the form of set T and store the process data in relational database as the input of the algorithm. The part of the organized data set is listed in Table 2.

Table 2. Part of the organized data set

Serial number	Part material	Machining feature	Dimension type	Nominal size/mm	Tool material	Tool grade	a_p/mm	...
1	End face	Rough turn	Length	66.4	Carbide	YT15	1.3	...
2	Outer circle	Rough turn	Diameter	91.5	Carbide	YT15	1.25	...
3	Step surface	Semi-finish turn	Length	118.5	Carbide	YT30	1.3	...
......	......	......	......	......	......	......	......	...

Data preprocessing is the key to provide data of high quality for algorithm, which is a critical step in knowledge mining [7]. In the raw data set, some process element— *Nominal size, Roughness, Feed rate* and *Spindle speed*, etc.— are continuous variables, whereas Apriori algorithm is oriented towards the disperse variables [6]. Therefore, the continuous variables should be processed into the disperse variables respectively, and correspondingly the value of continuous variable should be mapped into the value of disperse variable.

Through the approach of set partitioning [8], the values of continuous variables are divided into multiple sets. For example, the process element *Cutting speed* is continuous variable and it holds wide range of values in the dataset. It is by cluster analysis that the values are grouped into different subsets [9]. Correspondingly the process element *Cutting speed* becomes *Cutting speed group*, a disperse variable. Some preprocessed elements and their values are listed in Table 3.

Table 3. Some preprocessed elements and their values

Pre-preprocessed		Post-preprocessed	
Process element	Value	Process element	Value
Roughness	Ra6.3	Roughness group	Group 1
Nominal size/mm	64	Nominal size group	Group 3
Feed rate/(mm/r)	0.52	*Feed rate* group	Group 4
Spindle speed/(m/s)	1.79	*Spindle speed* group	Group 6

5.2 Experimental Results and Discussion

IN the experiment, the proposed approach and Apriori are applied respectively to the data set. They are both programmed by Python language. The parameters in proposed approach and Apriori are set as listed in Table 4.

Table 4. The parameters in proposed approach and Apriori

Parameter name	Symbol	Value
Minimum Fusion (Cohesion & Support)	Min-Co-Sup	0.15
Minimum Fusion (Relevancy & Confidence)	Min-Re-Conf	0.7
Knowledge adequacy	KS	1
Weight coefficient	W_1	0.1
Weight coefficient	W_2	0.9
Minimum support	Min-Supp	0.15
Minimum confidence	Min-Confi	0.9

The mining results is processed by knowledge reasoning to filter out the correct process knowledge [10]. The first task of knowledge mining is performing on the data set of shafts with 82 transactions, while the second task is performing on data set of gears with 93 transactions. Some mining results are listed in Table 5.

Table 5. Some mining results in proposed approach

Serial number	Antecedent items	Consequent items	Fusion (Cohesion & Support) value	Fusion (Relevance & Confidence) value	Check
1	{45 # steel, IT13, Ra12.5}	{Rough turn}	0.253	0.784	✓
2	{20CrMnTi, End face, Ra6.3, IT9}	{Semi-finish turn, YT15}	0.198	0.725	✓
3	{20CrMnTi, Outer circle, Spindle speed group2, Semi-finish turning}	{ Feed rate group 3}	0.154	0.704	✓

The comparison between two algorithms is shown in Table 6 and Fig. 4. Obviously, more valid knowledge can be captured and the proportion of correct rules is significantly increased with Apriori embedded knowledge. Meanwhile, the proposed approach produces less amount of results compared with general Apriori, which is partly convenient for the data post-processing.

Table 6. The comparison between the proposed approach and Apriori

Algorithm	Gear			Shaft		
	The total number of rules	Correct rules	Proportion of correct rules	The total number of rules	Correct rules	Proportion of correct rules
Apriori	98	12	12.24%	108	16	14.81%
Proposed approach	38	31	81.58%	51	42	82.35%

The impact of embedded process knowledge amount on the mining results are also studied. Various experiments have been conducted under different conditions of knowledge adequacy, of which the results are shown in Fig. 5. It can be concluded that the proportion of correct knowledge increases with more process knowledge embedding, which proves validates the proposed approach.

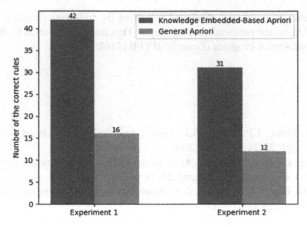

Fig. 4. The comparison between the proposed approach and Apriori.

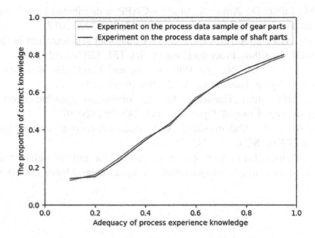

Fig. 5. The effect of algorithm under different conditions of knowledge adequacy.

6   Conclusion

In the proposed approach, the knowledge is represented as the semantic relationship among process data items through a semantic-correlation-degree matrix. Based on the semantic-correlation-degree, the calculation model of cohesion is built and combined with support degree, and the calculation model of relevancy is established and merged with confidence. These two fusion models determines whether the analyzed data items can constitute process-decision knowledge. The method embeds the process knowledge into knowledge mining algorithm, which improves the quantity and proportion of correct knowledge in mining results. It provides a new solution for enterprises to acquire and accumulate the process knowledge. Further research can be conducted on the update and accumulation of process-decision knowledge.

Acknowledgement. The author(s) disclosed receipt of the following financial support for the research, authorship, and/or publication of this paper: This study is supported by the National Key Research and Development Program (Grant 2021YFB1716200).

References

1. Huang, C.M., Hong, T.P., Horng, S.J.: Mining knowledge from object-oriented instances. Expert Syst. Appl. **33**(2), 441–450 (2007)
2. Jiao, J., Zhang, L., Zhang, Y., et al.: Association rule mining for product and process variety mapping. Int. J. Comput. Integr. Manuf. **21**(1), 111–124 (2013)
3. Garcia, A.C.B., Ferraz, I., Vivacqua, A.S.: From data to knowledge mining. Artif. Intell. Eng. Des. Anal. Manuf. **23**(4), 427–441 (2009)
4. Alnabhan, M., Hammad, M., Sarairah, S.A.: Combining structural and semantic cohesion measures to identify extract class refactoring. Int. J. Comput. Appl. Technol. **61**(3), 198–206 (2019)
5. Milosevic, M., Lukic, D., Antic, A., et al.: e-CAPP: a distributed collaborative system for internet-based process planning. J. Manuf. Syst. **42**, 210–223 (2017)
6. Silva, J., et al.: Association rules extraction for customer segmentation in the SMEs sector using the apriori algorithm. Procedia Comput. Sci. **151**, 1207–1212 (2019)
7. Glasgow, J., Jurisica, I.I., Ng, R.: Data mining and knowledge discovery in molecular databases. Pacific Symp. Biocomput. **5**(12), 365–366 (2015)
8. Foutlane, O., El Hallaoui, I., Hansen, P.: Integral simplex using double decomposition for set partitioning problems. Comput. Oper. Res. **111**, 243–257 (2019)
9. Abdulah, S., Atwa, W., Abdelmoniem, A.M.: Active clustering data streams with affinity propagation. ICT Exp. **8**(2), 276–282 (2022)
10. Wan, S., Li, D., Gao, J., Li, J.: A knowledge based machine tool maintenance planning system using case-based reasoning techniques. Rob. Comput. Integr. Manuf. **58**, 80–96(2021)

A Knowledge Content Matching Degree Calculation Method Supporting Process Knowledge Recommendation

Peilin Shao, Lihong Qiao, and Zhicheng Huang[✉]

School of Mechanical Engineering and Automation, Beihang University, Beijing 100191, China
zc_huang@buaa.edu.cn

Abstract. Product process design relies upon the process knowledge support acquired by process designers and enterprises. Process knowledge recommendation has been attached more importance by enterprises in that it can quickly provide process designers with accurate and appropriate process knowledge. In this paper, a "scene-label-classification" knowledge recommendation scheme for process knowledge graph is established, and a knowledge content matching degree calculation method supporting process knowledge recommendation is proposed. Design requirements are described by parameterized characteristics from various dimensions such as material, precision requirements. Based on knowledge coding, the attribute characteristics of process knowledge are uniformly identified and associated with requirement scene characteristics. A requirements-knowledge semantic vector space model is established, and a calculation method of matching degree between design requirements and knowledge content is proposed based on improved cosine distance. This scheme enables quickly positioning the corresponding process knowledge based on coding labels, and final process knowledge recommendation candidate set is obtained through matching degree calculation and filtering sort, which thus enables dynamic classification and appropriate recommendation of process knowledge.

Keywords: Knowledge recommendation · Knowledge coding · Matching degree calculation

1 Introduction

As a bridge connecting product design and product manufacturing, the current process design process relies upon the experience of process designers, as well as guide of existing process knowledge of the enterprise. During this process, inexperienced process designers frequently need to spend a lot of time searching for the required knowledge, resulting in the efficiency and quality difference of process design. In this case, due to the capacity to quickly provide appropriate process knowledge for process designers according to process design requirement, process knowledge recommendation technology has been widely used in machining [1], assembly [2], sheet metal and other different process.

With the continuous development and wide application, knowledge recommendation oriented to process knowledge graph has become a research focus, including process design requirement analysis, rapid positioning of requirements and knowledge, and knowledge matching algorithm design. According to the systematic analysis of process design requirements, Zhou et al. [3] obtained process requirements from five aspects such as users and design information, and converted them into corresponding process characteristics. Guo et al. [4] obtained hidden user requirements from user requirement data and established association mapping for product attributes. However, most of current process design requirements analysis is limited to the part information or user requirement, short of comprehensive analysis of design requirements. For the rapid positioning of requirements and knowledge, it is an effective method to construct the unified representation of knowledge attributes [5, 6]. For the matching between process knowledge and design requirements, currently semantic matching calculation methods such as vector space model-based matching calculation [7], ontology-based semantic matching calculation [8] and deep learn-based matching calculation are commonly used. Wang et al. [9] applied TF-IDF algorithm based on vector space model in the matching process of manufacturing knowledge and design requirements. Renu et al. [10] used the text matching algorithm to realize the knowledge retrieval and sharing of the text-based assembly process scheme.

To support the fast and high matching degree process knowledge recommendation, this paper proposes a method to map between process design requirements and process knowledge attributes by constructing the coding label of process knowledge graph. A requirements-knowledge semantic vector space model is established and the matching degree between requirements and knowledge is calculated based on improved cosine distance.

2 "Scene-Label-Classification" Process Knowledge Recommendation Framework

Oriented to knowledge graph, this paper proposed a process knowledge recommendation scheme-"scenario-label-classification", which is shown in Fig. 1. Different dimensions of process design requirements are described by parametric characteristics such as material, size characteristic, part type, precision, etc. At the same time, unified identification of process knowledge attributes are constructed using knowledge coding label, and parameterized requirement scenes are correlated with process knowledge attributes. Therefore, rapid positioning from process design requirements to process knowledge attributes is achieved and initial process knowledge recommendation candidate is generated. Process design requirement semantic vector is obtained by analyzing parameterized requirement scene. Meanwhile, process knowledge semantic vector of initial candidates is generated by TransE algorithm and dimensionality reduction to the same dimension as the process design requirement semantic vectors. Based on the improved cosine distance, the matching degree between them can calculated and filtrated according to matching degree threshold value. The final process knowledge recommendation candidate set is obtained so as to enable the dynamic classification of process knowledge under different requirement scenarios.

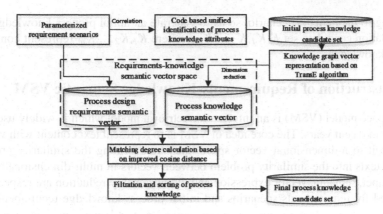

Fig. 1. "Scene-label-classification" process knowledge recommendation framework

3 Correlation Between Requirement Scenarios and Process Knowledge Attributes

The process design requirements of different dimensions are analyzed, and requirement scenarios of process knowledge recommendation are described through materials, dimension characteristics, part types and other parameterized characteristics. Meanwhile, the process knowledge attribute characteristics are identified uniformly by knowledge coding, and then requirement scene characteristics and process knowledge attribute characteristics are expressed in correlation.

According to the requirement scene of process knowledge recommendation, this paper divides process design requirement into three aspects: part information, product information and other information. Among them, part information contains the geometric information and non-geometric information including surface shape, size, precision information, part materials, technical requirements, etc. Compared with the part, product information contains the number of parts, the position relationship between parts, and the assembly relationship between parts, etc. Other information includes processing/assembly time limits, types of knowledge required, etc. Through parameterized characteristic description, the requirement scenarios set $R(R_1,R_2,...,R_q)$ is established, where $R_1,R_2,...,R_q$ represent the parameterized requirements characteristics, which facilitates the construction of association mapping between process design requirements and process knowledge attributes.

In this paper, process knowledge attributes are uniformly identified by constructing coding labels in the knowledge graph, enabling the quick positioning of knowledge attribute characteristics according to design requirements. However, when there are too many parameterized demand features, it may be impossible to find the process knowledge that meets all the demand characteristics. Therefore, the quantity threshold value S_n meeting the requirements of parameterized characteristics is set. And process knowledge that meets the conditions (including the number of requirement features $\geq S_n$) is selected according to the demand scenario, so as to generate an initial process knowledge recommendation candidate set $K(K_1, K_2, ..., K_m)$, where $K_1, K_2, ..., K_m$ represent contained process knowledge.

4 Construction of Requirements-Knowledge Semantic VSM

Vector space model (VSM) is an information retrieval model which is widely used and effective in recent years. The core idea of VSM is to represent text content with vectors and map it to n-dimensional vector space, thus transforming the similarity problem between texts into the similarity problem between vectors in multi-dimensional space. In this paper, semantic vector expression and dimensionality reduction are respectively conducted for requirements scenarios and initial process knowledge recommendation candidate set, thus obtaining requirement semantic vector and several process knowledge semantic vectors. Then the requirements-knowledge semantic VSM is established so as to calculate the matching degree between process design requirements and process knowledge.

4.1 Construction of Requirement Semantic VSM

The construction idea of semantic VSM is that text is regarded as a combination of several independent characteristic terms, and a high-dimensional space is constructed with these different characteristic terms. Each characteristic term is one dimension of this space, and text is regarded as a space vector. In this paper, parameterized characteristics such as material, dimension feature and part type are utilized to describe the process design requirements, so each parameterized characteristic is the characteristic term of requirement semantic VSM. Assuming that process design requirements consist of independent parameterized characteristics, it can be expressed as:

$$R = \{r_1, d_1; r_2, d_2; \ldots \ldots; r_n, d_n\} \tag{1}$$

Therein $r_i(1 \le i \le n)$ represents the parameterized characteristic name, and $d_i(1 \le i \le n)$ represents each parameter value/description content. For the parameterized characteristics such as technical requirements, the content is described in natural language, like "pay attention to temperature control and quenching transfer time of aluminum alloy materials in heat treatment process". In order to enable the matching between parameterized requirement characteristics described in natural language and the process knowledge content, it is necessary to generate text vector using NLP to calculate semantic matching degree.

Given different weights for each parameterized characteristic as the vector component, the text vector V_r used to represent the process design requirements can be expressed as:

$$V_r = \{Wr_1, d_1; Wr_2, d_2; \ldots \ldots; Wr_n, d_n\} \tag{2}$$

Therein $w_{ri}(1 \le i \le n)$ represents the weight of each parameterized characteristic, which is generally set by process designer according to the importance of each parameterized characteristic. Therefore, process design requirements can be represented by an N-dimensional characteristic vector.

4.2 Construction of Process Knowledge Semantic VSM

Aiming at each process knowledge graph in the process knowledge recommendation candidate set, the vector representation method of process knowledge graph based on TransE algorithm is adopted, so that each process knowledge could be represented by a p-dimension vector $V_{trans}(P \geq N)$. In order to calculate the matching degree between requirement vector and process knowledge vector, dimensionality reduction methods such as PCA is adopted to keep the dimension number and meanings of two vectors consistent. For the ith process knowledge of the initial process knowledge recommendation candidate set, its semantic vector $V_{k-i}(1 \leq i \leq m)$ can be expressed as:

$$V_{k-i} = \left\{ r_1, d_1'; r_2, d_2'; \ldots \ldots; r_n, d_n' \right\} \tag{3}$$

Therein $r_i(1 \leq i \leq n)$ represents n parameterized characteristics of process design requirements, and $d'_i(1 \leq i \leq n)$ represents the value/description content of this parameter (empty if no content). Different from requirement semantic vector, the weight of each parameterized characteristic of knowledge semantic vector is calculated based on statistics, among which the most commonly used method is TF-IDF method. Term Frequency (TF) weight indicates the number of times a characteristic item appears in this document. The more times it appears, the more important it is. However, for process knowledge, high appearance frequency of parameterized characteristic does not necessarily mean that it is more important. Therefore, in order to reduce the influence of TF weight, when the occurrence frequency of parameterized requirement characteristic is not 0, it can be expressed as:

$$\text{TF}_{(i-k)} = 1 + log(1 + logj) \tag{4}$$

Therein j represents the number of occurrences of parameterized characteristic r_k in process knowledge K_i. If this parameterized requirement characteristic is not included in K_i, then $TF_{(i-k)} = 0$.

IDF (Inverse Document Frequency) weight refers to the frequency of all process knowledge contained in initial knowledge candidate set for one parameterized characteristic. If this parameterized characteristic appears in multiple process knowledge, it proves that its distinguishing ability is low, and therefore, IDF weight is expressed as:

$$\text{IDF}_{(i-k)} = log(\frac{N}{n} + \alpha) \tag{5}$$

Therein α is a constant. In the similarity calculation between texts, if a keyword appears in all texts, its IDF value is extremely low. However, in the matching of requirements and process knowledge, if a parameterized characteristic appears in all process knowledge, it does not mean that this characteristic is unimportant. According to Formula (5), the larger α is, the weaker the distinguishing ability of this parameterized characteristic is. Therefore, α is set as 1 in this paper, N represents the number of process knowledge in the initial knowledge candidate set, and n represents the number of process knowledge with this parameterized characteristic. Finally, the weight of parameterized characteristic r_k in process knowledge K_i is:

$$w_{i-k} = \text{TF}_{(i-k)} * \text{IDF}_{(i-k)} \tag{6}$$

The semantic vector V_k used to represent a process knowledge can be expressed as:

$$V_k = \left\{ w_{k1}, d'_1; w_{k2}, d'_2; \ldots \ldots ; w_{kn}, d'_n \right\} \tag{7}$$

Therein $w_{ki}(1 \le i \le n)$ represents the weight of each parameterized characteristic obtained through Formula (6). For an initial process knowledge recommendation candidate set containing m process knowledge, a $m*n$ knowledge semantic VSM can be finally constructed:

$$V_{k-m} = \left\{ \begin{array}{c} w_{k11}, d'_{11}; \cdots ; w_{k1n}, d'_{1n} \\ \cdots \\ w_{km1}, d'_{m1}; \cdots ; w_{kmn}, d'_{mn} \end{array} \right\} \tag{8}$$

5 Knowledge Content Matching Degree Calculation

The calculation process of matching degree between requirements semantic vector and semantic vector of each process knowledge is shown in Fig. 2: Based on improved cosine distance, the matching degree of each process knowledge content in the initial candidate set and process design requirement is calculated. The matching degree threshold M_t and quantity threshold N_q is set in advance for comparison to filter out the process knowledge with low matching degree. The reserved process knowledge is sorted according to the matching degree value, and final process knowledge recommendation candidate set $K'(K_1, K_2, \ldots, K_q)$ is obtained and pushed to the process designer.

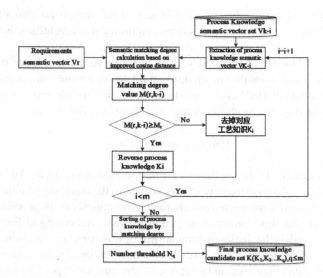

Fig. 2. The calculation process of matching degree

5.1   Matched-Degree Calculation Based on Improved Cosine Distance

After obtaining V_r and $V_{k\text{-}i}$, the semantic matching degree between requirements and process knowledge content can be expressed according to the matching degree between the vectors. In this paper, cosine distance between vectors is utilized:

$$M(i, k - i) = \cos \theta = \frac{V_r * V_{k-i}}{|V_r||V_{k-i}|} \tag{9}$$

For requirements semantic vector V_r and process knowledge semantic vector $V_{k\text{-}i}$, besides containing weights $w_{ri}(1 \leq i \leq n)$ and $w_{ki}(1 \leq i \leq n)$ of parameterized characteristics, descriptions $d_i(1 \leq i \leq n)$ and $d'_i(1 \leq i \leq n)$ of parameterized characteristics are also included. Compared with classical semantic calculation process based on cosine distance, this process also needs to calculate the matching degree between $d_i(1 \leq i < n)$ and $d'_i(1 \leq i \leq n)$. In this regard, this paper summarizes several situations that may occur when $d_i(1 \leq i \leq n)$ and $d'_i(1 \leq i \leq n)$ match:

a)   Numerical matching. In this case, $d_i(1 \leq i \leq n)$ and $d'_i(1 \leq i \leq n)$ can be directly compared, which is applicable to parameterized requirement characteristics described by numerical values such as surface roughness and machining accuracy. The result has two cases: a match of 1 and a mismatch of 0.

b)   Semantic matching. For parts material, parts type and other parameterized requirement characteristics described by simple text, $d_i(1 \leq i \leq n)$ and $d'_i(1 \leq i \leq n)$ can be directly compared, which is consistent with numerical matching. For parameterized requirement characteristics such as technical requirements that need to be processed by natural language, semantic matching degree between them should be calculated based on cosine distance. The matching result range is [0,1], where 0 indicates complete mismatch and 1 indicates complete match.

Therefore, based on classical cosine distance, this paper proposes a calculation method of matching degree between the requirements semantic vector V_r and the process knowledge semantic vector $V_{k\text{-}i}(1 \leq i \leq m)$ based on improved cosine distance. The calculation formula is:

$$M(r, k - i) = \frac{V_r * V_{k-i}}{|V_r||V_{k-i}|} = \frac{\sum\limits_{j=1}^{n} \left[w_{r_j} * w_{(k-i)_j} * M(d_{r_j}, d_{(k-i)_j}) \right]}{\left(\sqrt{\sum\limits_{j=1}^{n} (w_{r_j})^2} * \left(\sqrt{\sum\limits_{j=1}^{n} (w_{(k-i)_j})^2} \right. \right.} \tag{10}$$

Therein $M(d_{rj}, d_{(k-i)j}, 1 \leq j \leq n)$ represents the matching degree between parameterized characteristics description contents of two vectors. The range of $M(r,k\text{-}i)$ is [0,1], and the larger $M(r,k\text{-}i)$ is, the higher matching degree between requirements and process knowledge is.

5.2 Candidate Process Knowledge Filtering Ranking

The matching degree $M(r,k\text{-}i)$ between each knowledge and process design requirements is calculated and compared with threshold value M_t. If the matching degree value is greater than, the corresponding process knowledge is retained. Otherwise, corresponding process knowledge is eliminated. The reserved process knowledge is sorted from large to small according to matching degree value, and according to quantity threshold N_q, the final process knowledge recommendation candidate set is obtained and pushed to the designer.

6 Experimental Verification and Analysis

The validity of the proposed process knowledge recommendation scheme and knowledge content matching calculation method is verified by a shaft-hole part example of machining design. Firstly, according to the process specification of the part, the parameterized requirement characteristics information used to describe its process design requirements is summarized, as shown in Table 1.

Table 1. Parameterized requirement characteristics of a shaft-hole part

Requirement characteristics type	Requirement characteristics name	Description content
Part information	Part type	Shaft-hole
	Part material	45 steel
	Shape characteristic 1	Outer circle
	Dimensional information 1	$\varnothing 40$ mm $\times$ 180 mm
	Machining precision 1	IT7
	Surface roughness 1	1.6 μm
	Shape characteristic 2	Inner hole
	Dimensional information 2	$\varnothing 20$ mm $\times$ 180 mm
	Machining precision 2	IT8
	Surface roughness 2	3.2 μm
Non-part information	Technical requirement	Modulation hardness 220–250 HBW. Sharp edges blunt, remove edges and corners burrs

The corresponding process knowledge attributes are located in the knowledge base according to the knowledge coding, and the quantity threshold S_n value that meets the parameterized requirement characteristics is set as 8, and four characteristics including recommended knowledge category (machining route), part type (axle hole), and shape feature (1 is outer circle, 2 is inner hole) are must contained. An initial process knowledge recommendation candidate set containing 12 process knowledge is generated, and its description in "Machining Route" is shown in Table 2.

Table 2. Information of initial knowledge recommendation candidate set $K(K_1,K_2,...,K_{12})$

Serial number	Process knowledge information
1	Rough turning - Semi-finish turning - Drilling - Reaming - Semi-fine hinge - Finish turning
2	Rough turning - Semi-finish turning - Drilling - Reaming - Semi-fine hinge - Rough grinding – Semi-finish grinding
3	Rough turning - Semi-finish turning - Drilling - Semi-fine hinge - Finish hinge - Finish turning
4	Rough turning - Semi-finish turning - Drilling - Semi-fine hinge - Finish hinge - Rough grinding – Semi-finish grinding
5	Rough turning - Semi-finish turning - Drilling - Semi-fine hinge - Rough grinding hole - Rough grinding outer circle
6	Rough turning - Semi-finish turning - Drilling - Semi-fine hinge – Rough grinding hole - Finish turning
7	Rough milling - Semi-finish milling - Drilling - Reaming - Semi-fine hinge - Finish milling
8	Rough milling - Semi-finish milling - Drilling - Semi-fine hinge - Finish hinge - Finish milling
9	Rough milling - Semi-finish milling - Drilling - Semi-fine hinge - Rough grinding hole - Finish milling
10	Rough turning - Semi-finish turning - Rough pulling - Finish pulling – Finish turning
11	Rough turning - Semi-finish turning - Rough grinding - Rough pulling - Finish pulling – Semi-finish grinding
12	Rough milling - Semi-finish milling - Rough pulling - Finish pulling – Finish milling

According to Table 1 and the generated initial process knowledge recommendation candidate set, the requirements semantic vector $V_r = \{w_{r1},d_1;w_{r2},d_2;...;w_{r12},d_{12}\}$ and knowledge semantic vector $V_{k-i} = \{w_{r1},d'_1;w_{r2},d'_2;...;w_{r12},d'_{12}\}$ are respectively established. For requirements semantic vector V_r, its weight coefficient represents the key degree of this characteristic. Under the condition that the knowledge attributes of the parts type, material and shape characteristics must meet the requirement, it is assumed that the machining accuracy, surface roughness and technical requirements are the focus of the process designer to pay attention to whether the requirements and knowledge match. The weight coefficients of the machining accuracy, surface roughness and technical requirements are set as 0.2, and the weight coefficients of the other parameterized requirements are set as 0.1.

After the semantic vector weight coefficient of each process knowledge V_{k-i} in initial knowledge candidate set is calculated, the matching degree threshold $M_t = 0.7$ and quantity threshold $N_q = 6$ are set. By the matching degree calculation method based on improved cosine distance, the matching degree between requirements and each process knowledge is calculated. The results are shown as Fig. 3.

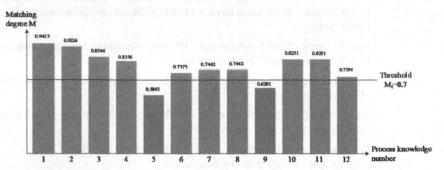

Fig. 3. Matching degree results between requirements and each process knowledge

Table 3. Information of final knowledge recommendation candidate set $K'(K_1, K_2, ..., K_6)$

Serial number	Process knowledge information	Matching degree value
1	Rough turning - Semi-finish turning - Drilling - Reaming - Semi-fine hinge - Finish turning	0.9413
2	Rough turning - Semi-finish turning - Drilling - Reaming - Semi-fine hinge - Rough grinding – Semi-finish grinding	0.9226
3	Rough turning - Semi-finish turning - Drilling - Semi-fine hinge - Finish hinge - Finish turning	0.8346
4	Rough turning - Semi-finish turning - Rough pulling - Finish pulling – Finish turning	0.8251
5	Rough turning - Semi-finish turning - Rough grinding - Rough pulling - Finish pulling – Semi-finish grinding	0.8251
6	Rough turning - Semi-finish turning - Drilling - Semi-fine hinge - Finish hinge - Rough grinding – Semi-finish grinding	0.8156

According to the matching degree threshold $M_t = 0.7$, 5th and 9th process knowledge are filtered out. Process knowledge numbered 6th, 7th, 8th and 12th process knowledge are filtered out according to the required process knowledge quantity threshold $N_q = 6$. The final process knowledge recommendation candidate set was obtained after reordering according to the matching degree from large to small, as shown in Table 3. After verification, the candidate set of process knowledge meets the machining requirements of the shaft-hole part.

7 Conclusion

In this paper, the "scene-label-classification" knowledge recommendation scheme for process knowledge graph is established to enable dynamic classification of process knowledge for different requirements scenarios. The multi-dimensional requirements for process knowledge recommendation are fully considered, and correlation mapping between requirements and process knowledge attributes was established by parameterized requirement characteristics and coding labels. The demand-knowledge semantic vector space model was constructed by taking parameterized requirement characteristics as dimensions of the space. The matching degree calculation method based on improved cosine distance is proposed, which considered both parameterized requirement characteristics and description content. A verification example with shaft-hole part showed that based on specific requirement scenarios, the proposed method achieved the process knowledge recommendation with strong pertinence and flexible number of knowledge candidates.

Acknowledgement. The author(s) disclosed receipt of the following financial support for the research, authorship, and/or publication of this paper: This work is supported by the National Key Research and Development Program (Grant 2021YFB1716200).

References

1. Geng, J., Zhang, S., Hui, W.: Knowledge Recommendation method for concept development of manufacturing technology using morphological similarity. Int. J. Softw. Eng. Knowl. Eng. **28**(08), 1121–1150 (2018)
2. Wu, Z., Li, L., Liu, H.: Process knowledge recommendation system for mechanical product design. IEEE Access PP(99), 1 (2020)
3. Hu, Y., Ding, Y., Xu, F., Liu, J., Xu, W., Feng, H.: Knowledge recommendation system for human-robot collaborative disassembly using knowledge graph. In: Proceedings of the ASME 2021 16th International Manufacturing Science and Engineering Conference, MSEC2021, vol. 2, pp. 1–6. ASME (2021)
4. Guo, Q., Xue, C., Yu, M., Shen, Z.: A New user implicit requirements process method oriented to product design. J. Comput. Inf. Sci. Eng. **19**(1), 011010.1–011010.11 (2019)
5. Kudryavtsev, D., Gavrilova, T.: From anarchy to system: a novel classification of visual knowledge codification techniques. Knowl. Process. Manag. **24**(01), 3–13 (2016)
6. Liu, D., Ray, G., Whinston, A.B.: The interaction between knowledge codification and knowledge-sharing networks. Inf. Syst. Res. **21**(04), 892–906 (2010)
7. Kadowaki, N., Kishida, K.: Empirical comparison of word similarity measures based on co-occurrence, context, and a vector space model. Korea Inst. Sci. Technol. Inf. **8**(02), 06–17 (2020)
8. Wen, Y., Gao, C., Pan, H.: Research on concept semantic similarity computation based on ontology. In: 2011 IEEE 2nd International Conference on Computing, Control and Industrial Engineering, vol. 2, pp. 284–287. IEEE, Wuhan (2011)
9. Wang, K., Liu, T., Tong, S., Zhang, X.: Research on matching of manufacturing knowledge and design requirements based on virus adsorption mechanism. Manuf. Automat. **36**(15), 116–120 (2014). (In Chinese)
10. Renu, R., Mocko, G.: Computing similarity of text-based assembly processes for knowledge retrieval and reuse. J. Manuf. Syst. **39**, 101–110 (2016)

Control of Intelligent Networked Things

Fault-Tolerant Control for Underwater Vehicle with Actuator Saturation and Faults

Hongfei Li$^{(\boxtimes)}$ ⓘ and Jing Xu

Chongqing Key Laboratory of Nonlinear Circuits and Intelligent Information Processing, College of Electronic and Information Engineering, Southwest University, Chongqing 400715, China
hongfli@126.com

Abstract. Underwater vehicle system, as a kind of special machine capable of underwater resource exploration, submarine pipeline maintenance, marine environment reconnaissance and submarine rescue, is a common tool in modern marine exploitation. Underwater vehicles play an important role in the survey and exploration of marine resource. The fault tolerant control for underwater vehicle system with external disturbance and actuator faults is studied in this paper. The fault observer can estimate the fault in the existence of disturbance environment. A sufficient condition for the existence of fault observer is proposed which guarantees the stability of the closed-loop system under actuator faults. Moreover, a fault-tolerant controller is developed to compensate for the failure effects on the system by updating the design feedback matrices online. For the fault-tolerant controller, Lyapunov function is used to obtain the stability for underwater vehicle system about actuator saturation. Finally, an example is included to show the effectiveness of the presented theory.

Keywords: Underwater vehicle model · Fault tolerant controller · Actuator saturation · Robust fault estimation

1 Introduction

Ocean is the second strategic space among the land, ocean, sky and outer space. It is the exploitation base of biology, energy, water, metal resources and the most practical and potential space. The development of ocean will have direct and enormous influence on the development of economics and society. With the continuous development of science and technology of mankind, the demand for the

---

Supported by the National Natural Science Foundation of China under Grant 62003008, and in part by the Zhejiang Lab's International Talent Fund for Young Professionals, and in part by Fundamental Research Funds for the Central Universities under Grant SWU-KQ22027.

L. Zhang et al. (Eds.): CINT 2022, CCIS 1714, pp. 195–208, 2022.
https://doi.org/10.1007/978-981-19-8915-5_17

development of the ocean is also becoming higher and higher. Marine resources gradually become an important target of exploitation and utilization of many countries. The abundance of marine resources goes far beyond the land and the ocean will become the main field for the future development of human, therefore, the marine exploration, research and protective development have become the main problem confronted by many coastal countries. As the intelligent tool which can replace humans for ocean exploration to a large extent, the underwater vehicle has been more and more applied into practice, including civil and military aspects where it is of irreplaceable importance. The underwater vehicle system is an intelligent system which requires high autonomy and security. Its motion control technology has always been a hot research topic [1–5]. When executing relevant tasks, the system needs to track specific curves efficiently and accurately, so the tracking ability of under-actuated AUV is the prerequisite to complete tasks. At the same time, the model of underwater vehicle is a complex system integrating nonlinearity, coupling and uncertainty, which will bring difficulties to the design of control. Underwater vehicles operate autonomously in marine environment without any umbilical cable. Safety and reliability are considered as underwater vehicles' important features. Thrusters are the main source to provide the forces required to control underwater vehicle, and thrusters are also one of the most likely sources of faults. After the occurrence of thruster fault, fault tolerant control is one of effective techniques to deal with thruster faults to maintain the safety of thrusters itself and the underwater vehicle. Therefore, research on thruster fault tolerant control will play an important role in improving underwater vehicles'safety [6–8]. Moreover, weak propeller fault features are faint and have relatively lower discrepancy compared with marine external random noises. Currently, there is no mature theory and agreed-upon solution. However, researches on weak propeller fault feature diagnosis theory and its application are of great significance and high practical values for improving the security of underwater vehicle and its development process.

Although the design and control of the underwater vehicle depends on the specific requirements of the underwater operation, its control principle is consistent while what is different is the design of the function module in upper layer. Currently, with the extensive application of underwater vehicle and the continuous innovation of its structure, there are still many problems to be solved or improved in the control of it. Under the improvement of effectiveness and reliability about underwater vehicle, they have been widely used in scientific, military etc. Because of the limitation of volume, energy and the navigation environment, a long time, stability performance is the important technical challenge of underwater vehicle. In recent years, underwater vehicles have been widely used in underwater exploration, underwater engineering maintenance, intelligent environmental protection and other fields. These rich application prospects have greatly promoted the innovation of motion control technology, so many good results have been investigated. Due to the complexity of underwater marine environment, actuator faults often occur. When actuator failure occurs, how to ensure the stable operation of the underwater vehicle system is an extremely important task. Aiming at the problem of actuator failure in underwater vehicles, fault-tolerant control technology is an important means to achieve robot stability.

In addition, state constraints caused by output nonlinearity should be considered. Due to the output transmission or sensor device will appear dead zone, saturation and hysteresis phenomena. Therefore, the system state is distorted through the output nonlinearity, resulting in the output state can not be used as an effective known signal, which brings great difficulties to the controller design and stability analysis, and seriously affects the performance of the system. For example, in the attitude control system of spacecraft, the actuator is one of the key components to achieve the precise attitude control goal. If the actuator fails, the realization of the attitude control goal of the spacecraft attitude control system will be affected, the accuracy will decrease, and the entire space mission will fail in serious cases. This requires a control strategy to improve the tolerance of the vehicle. The actuators and sensors in the system often have problems such as space limitation, and the communication signals often have problems such as packet loss and network delay in the process of transmission [9–14]. In order to accurately estimate and timely detect all kinds of fault information in the system, fault-tolerant controller is proposed to ensure the normal and stable operation of the underwater vehicle system [15–19]. Fault-tolerant technique is often used to solve some problems for component failure and communication failure. It has important advantages and research value compared with common controllers.

In more cases, due to the constraints of device physics and specific technical conventions in practical applications, the maximum control input is usually bounded, which may lead to actuator saturation. The actuator saturation phenomenon has a great impact on the performance of the control system, which will lead to the degradation of the system performance, and even lead to the instability of the system. But it is inevitable to appear in the robot control system, considering it can be more suitable for the practical application background. For example, Sakthivel et al. considered the finite time fault- tolerant strategy for neural control model about input saturation and time delay in [20]. Zuo et al. studied robust fault tolerant control for singular systems about time varying state-dependent nonlinear perturabation and actuator saturation in [21]. Hu et al. proposed an active fault-tolerant control system for spacecrafts with external disturbance and actuator fault in [22]. Moreover, Shen et al. designed an active fault-tolerant control system for spacecraft attitude control with actuator faults and input constraints in [23]. In this paper, the fault-tolerant control strategy is established for underwater vehicle system about actuator faults and input saturation. To cope with actuator faults, a fault detection observer is studied to detect the fault promptly. some LMI condition for the existence of fault observer is proposed which guarantees the stability of the closed-loop systema about actuator faults. Moreover, a fault-tolerant controller is developed to compensate for the failure effects on the system by updating the design feedback matrices online. For the fault-tolerant controller, Lyapunov function is used to obtain the stability for underwater vehicle system about actuator saturation.

Finally, an example is included to illustrate the effectiveness of the proposed method.

The structure of the article is as follows. Section 2 outlines the dynamic model. Section 3 shows the main results. The simulation results and discussion are presented in Sect. 4. Finally, Sect. 5 gives the conclusion.

2   Preliminaries

To facilitate the description of the AUV system, two coordinate systems (i.e., the geodetic coordinate system $O_g - xyz$, the carrier coordinate system $O_b - xyz$) are established. For a more intuitive description of the six degrees of freedom AUV system, define position vector $\eta_1 = \text{col}\{x, y, z\}$, orientation vector $\eta_2 = \text{col}\{\phi, \theta, \varphi\}$, velocity vector $v_1 = \text{col}\{u, v, w\}$ and angular velocity vector $v_2 = \text{col}\{p, q, r\}$.

Through the coordinate transformation of the underwater robot system, the following expression can be obtained:

$$\dot{\eta} = \mathcal{J}(\eta)v, \tag{1}$$

where $\eta = \text{col}\{\eta_1, \eta_2\}$, $v = \text{col}\{v_1, v_2\}$, the transformation matrix is $\mathcal{J}(\eta)$. By the previous works [1,24], the hydrodynamic model of AUV is constructed as

$$\mathbf{K}\dot{v} = -\mathbf{C}(v)v - \mathcal{M}(v)v - g(\eta) + \tau + \tau_w, \tag{2}$$

where $\mathbf{K}$ is the rigid body matrix, $\mathbf{C}(\cdot)$ is the matrix of Coriolis and Centripetal terms, $\mathcal{M}(\cdot)$ is viscous hydrodynamic coefficient matrix, $g(\cdot)$ is the restoring forces, τ is the control input, τ_w is the environment disturbance.

Let $y = 0, v = 0, p = 0, r = 0, \phi = 0, \varphi = 0$, $G = B$. The center of buoyancy Z_b and center of the gravity Z_g are located in the vertical plane. linearized damping forces/moments $(-X_u, -Z_w, -M_q)$ and quadratic damping terms $(-X_{u|u|}|u|, -Z_{w|w|}|w|, -M_{q|q|}|q|)$ on the diagonal.

Based on the above assumptions, the $\mathbf{K}$, $\mathbf{C}(v)$, $\mathcal{M}(v)$, $g(\eta)$, v, τ, τ_w are supposed to have the following structures:

$$\mathbf{K} = \begin{bmatrix} m_{11} & 0 & 0 \\ 0 & m_{22} & 0 \\ 0 & 0 & m_{33} \end{bmatrix}, \mathcal{M}(v) = \begin{bmatrix} d_{11} & 0 & 0 \\ 0 & d_{22} & 0 \\ 0 & 0 & d_{33} \end{bmatrix},$$

$$\mathbf{C}(v) = \begin{bmatrix} 0 & 0 & m_{22}w \\ 0 & 0 & -m_{11}u \\ -m_{22}w & m_{11}u & 0 \end{bmatrix}, v = \begin{bmatrix} u & w & q \end{bmatrix}^{\mathcal{T}},$$

$$g(\eta) = \begin{bmatrix} 0 \\ 0 \\ -(Z_bB - Z_gG)\sin\theta \end{bmatrix}, \tau = \begin{bmatrix} X & 0 & M \end{bmatrix}^{\mathcal{T}},$$

$$\mathcal{J}(\eta) = \begin{bmatrix} \cos\theta & \sin\theta & 0 \\ -\sin\theta & \cos\theta & 0 \\ 0 & 0 & 1 \end{bmatrix}, \tau_w = \begin{bmatrix} \tau_{uw} & \tau_{uw} & \tau_{uw} \end{bmatrix}^{\mathcal{T}},$$

where m_{11}, m_{22}, m_{33} is the mass in the $x-$, $z-$, and $q-$ direction, respectively. $d_{22} = -Z_w - Z_{w|w|}|w|$, $d_{33} = -M_q - M_{q|q|}|q|$, $-(Z_b B - Z_g G)\sin\theta = -\bar{B}\bar{G}_z B\sin\theta$, propulsion forces is X and pitch moments is M. $d_{11} = -X_u - X_{u|u|}|u|$,

By (1) and (2), we can get AUV model (3) as

$$\begin{cases} \dot{v} = -\mathbf{K}^{-1}[\mathbf{C}(v(s))v + \mathcal{M}(v)v + g(\eta) - \tau - \tau_w], \\ \dot{\eta} = \mathcal{J}(\eta)v. \end{cases} \tag{3}$$

Suppose the velocity and attitude measurements of the AUV are denoted as z_f.

As a strongly nonlinear system, the motion system of AUV can be simplified as

$$\dot{\vartheta}(s) = \mathcal{R}(\vartheta(s)) + \mathbf{W}u(s) + \mathbf{F}f(s) + w(s), \tag{4}$$

in which $\mathcal{R}(\cdot) = \text{col}\{-\mathbf{K}^{-1}[\mathbf{C}(v)v + \mathcal{M}(v)v + g(\eta)], \mathcal{J}(\eta(s))\}$, $\vartheta = \text{col}\{v, \eta\}$, $\mathbf{W} = \text{col}\{\mathbf{K}^{-1}, 0\}$, control input $u(s) = \tau$, $w(s) = \mathbf{K}^{-1}\tau_w$ is environment disturbance, $f(s)$ represents the actuator failure, $\mathbf{F}$ is a constant matrix with appropriate dimension.

The space $L_2[0, \infty)$ is composed of all continuous functions defined in the interval $[0, \infty)$ with 2-norm.

Assumption 1. The fault is bounded with known limit and its first-order time derivative belongs to $L_2[0, \infty)$.

Assumption 2. The environment disturbance $w(s)$ belongs to $L_2[0, \infty)$.

3   Main Results

3.1   The Design of Fault Observer

By introducing the fact that

$$\dot{f}(s) = \dot{f}(s) + \sigma f(s) - \sigma f(s), \tag{5}$$

where σ is a design constant, the dynamic system (4) can be reorganized as the following augmented system

$$\dot{\bar{\vartheta}}(s) = \mathcal{C}_f \bar{\vartheta}(s) + \mathcal{A}_f \mathcal{R}(\vartheta(s)) + \mathcal{W}_f u(s) + \mathcal{D}_f \varpi, \tag{6}$$

$$\bar{\vartheta}(s) = \text{col}\{\vartheta(s), f(s)\}, \quad \varpi = \text{col}\{w(s), \dot{f}(s), -\sigma f(s)\},$$

$$\mathcal{A}_f = \begin{bmatrix} \mathcal{I} \\ 0 \end{bmatrix}, \mathcal{C}_f = \begin{bmatrix} 0 & \mathbf{F} \\ 0 & \sigma\mathcal{I} \end{bmatrix}, \mathcal{W}_f = \begin{bmatrix} \mathbf{W} \\ 0 \end{bmatrix},$$

$$\mathcal{D}_f = \begin{bmatrix} \mathcal{I} & 0 & 0 \\ 0 & \mathcal{I} & -\mathcal{I} \end{bmatrix}.$$

The system fault and state observer is built to estimate the system fault and state.

$$\dot{\hat{\vartheta}}(s) = \mathcal{C}_f\hat{\vartheta}(s) + \mathcal{A}_f\mathcal{R}(\hat{\vartheta}(s)) + \mathcal{W}_f u(s) + \mathcal{K}(\vartheta(s) - \hat{\vartheta}(s)), \qquad (7)$$

$\hat{\vartheta}(s) = \text{col}\{\hat{\vartheta}(s), \hat{f}(s)\}$, $\hat{\vartheta}(s)$ and $\hat{f}(s)$ are the estimations of $\vartheta(s)$ and $f(s)$, respectively. $\mathcal{K}$ is the observer gain to be designed.

Let $\mathscr{E}(s) = \bar{\vartheta}(s) - \hat{\vartheta}(s)$, the error system is obtained as

$$\dot{\mathscr{E}}(s) = \mathcal{C}_f\mathscr{E}(s) + \mathcal{A}_f(\mathcal{R}(\vartheta(s)) - \mathcal{R}(\hat{\vartheta}(s))) + \mathcal{D}_f\varpi - \mathcal{K}\mathcal{L}\mathscr{E}(s), \qquad (8)$$

where $\mathcal{L} = \begin{bmatrix} \mathcal{I} & 0 \end{bmatrix}$.

Assumption 3. The nonlinear function $\mathcal{R}(\vartheta(s)) - \mathcal{R}(\hat{\vartheta}(s))$ satisfies Lipschitz condition i.e.,

$$\|\mathcal{R}(\vartheta(s)) - \mathcal{R}(\hat{\vartheta}(s))\| \le \beta\|\vartheta(s) - \hat{\vartheta}(s)\|. \qquad (9)$$

An effective theorem on the asymptotic stability of the system is proposed as follows:

Theorem 1. *For a given positive scalar α if there exist a symmetric positive definite matrix $\mathcal{G}$ and scalar ε such that the following LMI holds, i.e.,*

$$\Lambda_1 = \begin{bmatrix} \Lambda & \mathcal{G}\mathcal{D} \\ * & -\alpha^2\mathcal{I} \end{bmatrix} < 0, \qquad (10)$$

where $\Lambda = \mathcal{G}\mathcal{C}_f + \mathcal{C}_f^{\mathcal{T}}\mathcal{G} + \dfrac{\beta^2}{\varepsilon}\mathcal{I} + \mathcal{I} + \varepsilon\mathcal{G}\mathcal{A}_f\mathcal{A}_f^{\mathcal{T}}\mathcal{G} - \mathcal{G}\mathcal{K}\mathcal{L} - (\mathcal{K}\mathcal{L})^{\mathcal{T}}\mathcal{G}$. Then the error system (8) can be stable.

Proof: Choose a suitable Lyapunov function as

$$\mathscr{G}(s) = \mathscr{E}^{\mathcal{T}}(s)\mathcal{G}\mathscr{E}(s). \qquad (11)$$

By taking the time derivative of the Lyapunov function and applying (8), one gets

$$\dot{\mathscr{G}}(s) = \mathscr{E}^{\mathcal{T}}(s)\mathcal{G}\dot{\mathscr{E}}(s) + \dot{\mathscr{E}}^{\mathcal{T}}(s)\mathcal{G}\mathscr{E}(s)$$
$$= \mathscr{E}^{\mathcal{T}}(s)\mathcal{G}[\mathcal{C}_f\mathscr{E}(s) + \mathcal{A}_f(\mathcal{R}(\vartheta(s)) - \mathcal{R}(\hat{\vartheta}(s)))$$
$$+ \mathcal{D}\varpi - \mathcal{K}\mathcal{L}\mathscr{E}(s)] + [\mathcal{C}_f\mathscr{E}(s) + \mathcal{A}_f(\mathcal{R}(\vartheta(s))$$
$$- \mathcal{R}(\hat{\vartheta}(s))) + \mathcal{D}\varpi - \mathcal{K}\mathcal{L}\mathscr{E}(s)]^{\mathcal{T}}\mathcal{G}\mathscr{E}(s). \qquad (12)$$

By using Assumption 3 and (12), we have

$$\dot{\mathscr{G}}(s) \le \mathscr{E}^{\mathcal{T}}(s)\mathcal{G}\mathcal{C}_f\mathscr{E}(s) + \mathscr{E}^{\mathcal{T}}(s)\mathcal{C}_f^{\mathcal{T}}\mathcal{G}\mathscr{E}(s)$$
$$+ \mathscr{E}^{\mathcal{T}}(s)\mathcal{G}\mathcal{A}_f(\mathcal{R}(\vartheta(s)) - \mathcal{R}(\hat{\vartheta}(s)))$$
$$+ (\mathcal{R}(\vartheta(s)) - \mathcal{R}(\hat{\vartheta}(s)))^{\mathcal{T}}\mathcal{A}_f^{\mathcal{T}}\mathcal{G}\mathscr{E}(s)$$
$$+ \mathscr{E}^{\mathcal{T}}(s)\mathcal{G}\mathcal{D}\varpi + \varpi^{\mathcal{T}}\mathcal{D}^{\mathcal{T}}\mathcal{G}\mathscr{E}(s)$$
$$- \mathscr{E}^{\mathcal{T}}(s)\mathcal{G}\mathcal{K}\mathcal{L}\mathscr{E}(s) - \mathscr{E}^{\mathcal{T}}(s)(\mathcal{K}\mathcal{L})^{\mathcal{T}}\mathcal{G}\mathscr{E}(s). \qquad (13)$$

Apply Young's inequality to get

$$\mathscr{E}^{\mathscr{T}}(s)\mathcal{G}\mathcal{A}_f(\mathscr{R}(\vartheta(s)) - \mathscr{R}(\hat{\vartheta}(s)))$$

$$+ (\mathscr{R}(\vartheta(s)) - \mathscr{R}(\hat{\vartheta}(s)))^{\mathscr{T}}\mathcal{A}_f^{\mathscr{T}}\mathcal{G}\mathscr{E}(s)$$

$$\leq \varepsilon\mathscr{E}^{\mathscr{T}}(s)\mathcal{G}\mathcal{A}_f\mathcal{A}_f^{\mathscr{T}}\mathcal{G}\mathscr{E}(s) + \frac{1}{\varepsilon}(\mathscr{R}(\vartheta(s))$$

$$- \mathscr{R}(\hat{\vartheta}(s)))^{\mathscr{T}}(\mathscr{R}(\vartheta(s)) - \mathscr{R}(\hat{\vartheta}(s)))$$

$$= \varepsilon\mathscr{E}^{\mathscr{T}}(s)\mathcal{G}\mathcal{A}_f\mathcal{A}_f^{\mathscr{T}}\mathcal{G}\mathscr{E}(s) + \frac{1}{\varepsilon}\|\mathscr{R}(\vartheta(s)) - \mathscr{R}(\hat{\vartheta}(s))\|^2$$

$$\leq \varepsilon\mathscr{E}^{\mathscr{T}}(s)\mathcal{G}\mathcal{A}_f\mathcal{A}_f^{\mathscr{T}}\mathcal{G}\mathscr{E}(s) + \frac{\beta^2}{\varepsilon}\mathscr{E}^{\mathscr{T}}(s)\mathscr{E}(s). \tag{14}$$

Substituting from (14) into (13) results in:

$$\dot{\mathscr{G}}(s) \leq \mathscr{E}^{\mathscr{T}}(s)\mathcal{G}\mathcal{C}_f\mathscr{E}(s) + \mathscr{E}^{\mathscr{T}}(s)\mathcal{C}_f^{\mathscr{T}}\mathcal{G}\mathscr{E}(s)$$

$$+ \frac{\beta^2}{\varepsilon}\mathscr{E}^{\mathscr{T}}(s)\mathscr{E}(s) + \varepsilon\mathscr{E}^{\mathscr{T}}(s)\mathcal{G}\mathcal{A}_f\mathcal{A}_f^{\mathscr{T}}\mathcal{G}\mathscr{E}(s)$$

$$+ \mathscr{E}^{\mathscr{T}}(s)\mathcal{G}\mathcal{D}\varpi + \varpi^{\mathscr{T}}\mathcal{D}^{\mathscr{T}}\mathcal{G}\mathscr{E}(s)$$

$$- \mathscr{E}^{\mathscr{T}}(s)(\mathcal{G}\mathcal{K}\mathcal{L} + (\mathcal{K}\mathcal{L})^{\mathscr{T}}\mathcal{G})\mathscr{E}(s). \tag{15}$$

In order to measure this influence, assuming that $\mathscr{G}(0) = 0$ and the cost function $\mathscr{J}(s)$ can be established as

$$\mathscr{J}(s) = \int_0^t (\mathscr{E}^{\mathscr{T}}(c)\mathscr{E}(c) - \alpha^2\varpi^{\mathscr{T}}\varpi)ds$$

$$= \int_0^t (\mathscr{E}^{\mathscr{T}}(c)\mathscr{E}(c) - \alpha^2\varpi^{\mathscr{T}}\varpi + \dot{\mathscr{G}}(c))ds$$

$$- \int_0^t \dot{\mathscr{G}}(c))ds. \tag{16}$$

From (15), one gets

$$\dot{\mathscr{G}}(s) + \mathscr{E}^{\mathscr{T}}(s)\mathscr{E}(s) - \alpha^2\varpi^{\mathscr{T}}\varpi$$

$$\leq \zeta^{\mathscr{T}}(s)\Lambda_1\zeta(s) < 0, \tag{17}$$

where $\zeta(s) = \text{col}\{\mathscr{E}(s), \varpi\}$. On the basis of (16) and (17), one can get $\mathscr{J}(s) < 0$. For $t \in [0, \infty)$, the equation (16) can become as

$$\int_0^\infty (\mathscr{E}^{\mathscr{T}}(c)\mathscr{E}(c) - \alpha^2\varpi^{\mathscr{T}}\varpi)ds$$

$$= \lim_{t\to\infty} \int_0^t (\mathscr{E}^{\mathscr{T}}(c)\mathscr{E}(c) - \alpha^2\varpi^{\mathscr{T}}\varpi)ds < 0.$$

Therefore, the result $\|\mathscr{E}(s)\|_2^2 \leq \alpha^2\|\varpi\|_2^2$ is obtained, which means H_∞ performance α. The proof is done.   □

3.2 Fault-Tolerant Control for Underwater Vehicles with Sector Nonlinearity

In the following, the fault tolerant controller is presented as:

$$u(s) = \mathbf{sat}(\hbar(s)) - \mathbf{W}^+ \mathbf{F} \hat{f}(s), \tag{18}$$

where $\hbar(s) = \mathcal{E}\hat{\vartheta}(s)$, $\mathcal{E} = (e_{ij})_{n \times n}$ is the control gain. The matrix $\mathbf{W}^+$ satisfies $(\mathcal{I} - \mathbf{W}^+ \mathbf{W})\mathbf{F} = 0$. The saturation function $\mathbf{sat}(h(s)) = (\mathbf{sat}(\hbar_1(s)), \mathbf{sat}(\hbar_2(s)), \cdots, \mathbf{sat}(\hbar_n(s)))^{\mathcal{T}} : \mathbb{R}^n \to \mathbb{R}^n$ with $\mathbf{sat}(\hbar_i(s)) = \mathbf{sign}(\hbar_i(s)) \min \{\hbar_{oi}, |\hbar_i(s)|\}$ ($i \in \{1, 2, \cdots, n\}$), where $\hbar_{oi} \in \mathbb{R}_+$ is the ith element of the vector $\hbar_o \in \mathbb{R}_+^n$, and is the known saturation level.

Lemma 1 [20]. Let $v = (v_1, v_2, \ldots, v_n)^{\mathcal{T}} \in \mathbb{R}^n$ and $r = (r_1, r_2, \ldots, r_n)^{\mathcal{T}} \in \mathbb{R}^n$. If $-\hbar_{oi} \le r_i \le \hbar_{oi}$ for $i \in \{1, 2, ..., n\}$, then $\mathbf{sat}(v) \in \mathbf{co}\{\Upsilon_j v + \Upsilon_j^- r, j \in \Lambda\}$, where $\Lambda = \{1, 2, ..., 2^n\}$, $\hbar_{oi} \in \mathbb{R}_+$, and $\mathbf{co}\{v\}$ represents the convex hull defined by the vector v.

By applying Lemma 1 to $\mathbf{sat}(\hbar(s))$, for two matrices $\mathcal{E} \in \mathbb{R}^{n \times n}$, $\mathcal{S} \in \mathbb{R}^{n \times n}$, if $-\hbar_{oi} \le \mathcal{S}_i \hat{\vartheta}(s) \le \hbar_{oi}$ for $i \in M$, then $\mathbf{sat}(\mathcal{E}\hat{\vartheta}(s)) \in \mathbf{co}\{\Upsilon_j \mathcal{E}\hat{\vartheta}(s) + \Upsilon_j^- \mathcal{S}\hat{\vartheta}(s), j \in \Lambda\}$, where $\hbar_{oi} \in \mathbb{R}_+$, $\mathcal{S}_i$ represents the ith row of matrix $\mathcal{S}$.

Moreover, suppose that $\forall \hat{\vartheta}(s) \in \mathcal{S}(|\Gamma|, \hbar_o)$, $\hbar_o \in \mathbb{R}_+^n$, it follows that $\mathbf{sat}(\mathcal{E}\hat{\vartheta}(s)) \in \mathbf{co}\{\Upsilon_j \mathcal{E}\hat{\vartheta}(s) + \Upsilon_j^- \mathcal{S}\hat{\vartheta}(s), j \in \Lambda\}$, which implies that $\mathbf{sat}(\mathcal{K}\hat{\vartheta}(s)) = \sum_{j=1}^{2^n} \lambda_j(\hat{\vartheta}(s))(\Upsilon_j \mathcal{E} + \Upsilon_j^- \mathcal{S})\hat{\vartheta}(s)$, with $\sum_{j=1}^{2^n} \lambda_j(\hat{\vartheta}(s)) = 1$, $0 \le \lambda_j(\hat{\vartheta}(s)) \le 1$ and $j \in \Lambda$.

Under fault tolerant controller (18), systems (4) and (8) can be changed as

$$\dot{\mathcal{E}}_{\vartheta}(s) = \mathscr{C}_f \mathcal{E}_{\vartheta}(s) + \mathscr{A}_f g(\mathcal{E}_{\vartheta}(s)) + \mathscr{D}_f \varpi, \tag{19}$$

where $\mathcal{E}_{\vartheta}(s) = \mathbf{col}\{\mathcal{E}(s), \vartheta(s)\}$, $g(\mathcal{E}_{\vartheta}(s)) = \mathbf{col}\{\mathscr{R}(\vartheta(s)) - \mathscr{R}(\hat{\vartheta}(s)), \mathscr{R}(\vartheta(s))\}$, $\mathscr{S} = \sum_{j=1}^{2^n} \lambda_j(\hat{\vartheta}(s))(\Upsilon_j \mathcal{E} + \Upsilon_j^- \mathcal{S})$,

$$\mathscr{A}_f = \begin{bmatrix} \mathcal{A}_f \\ \mathcal{I} \end{bmatrix}, \mathscr{C}_f = \begin{bmatrix} -\mathcal{K}\mathcal{L} & \mathbf{F} & 0 \\ 0 & \sigma\mathcal{I} & 0 \\ \mathscr{S} & \mathbf{F} & \mathscr{S} \end{bmatrix},$$

$$\mathscr{D}_f = \begin{bmatrix} \mathcal{I} & 0 & 0 \\ 0 & \mathcal{I} & -\mathcal{I} \\ \mathcal{I} & 0 & 0 \end{bmatrix}.$$

Next, by constructing the Lyapunov function, we can get that the fault tolerant control error system (19) is stable.

Theorem 2. *For given positive scalars α and ξ if there exist a symmetric positive definite matrix $\mathcal{P}$ and some scalars ε such that the following LMIs hold, i.e.,*

$$\begin{bmatrix} \mathcal{P} & \mathcal{S}_i^{\mathcal{T}} \\ \star & \xi\hbar_{oi}^2 \end{bmatrix} \ge 0, \quad i \in M, \tag{20}$$

$$\Lambda_2 = \begin{bmatrix} \hat{\Lambda} & \mathcal{P}\mathscr{A}_f \\ * & (\frac{1}{\varepsilon_1} - \alpha_1)\mathcal{I} \end{bmatrix} < 0, \tag{21}$$

where $\hat{\Lambda} = \mathcal{P}\mathscr{C}_f + \mathscr{C}_f^{\mathcal{I}}\mathcal{P} + \mathcal{I} + \varepsilon_1 \mathcal{P}\mathscr{D}_f \mathscr{D}_f^{\mathcal{I}}\mathcal{P}$. *Then the fault tolerant control system* (19) *is stable.*

Proof: Choose a suitable Lyapunov function as

$$\mathscr{U}(s) = \mathscr{E}_x^{\mathcal{I}}(s)\mathcal{P}\mathscr{E}_\vartheta(s). \tag{22}$$

By taking the time derivative of the Lyapunov function and applying (8), one gets

$$\begin{aligned}
\dot{\mathscr{U}}(s) &= \mathscr{E}_x^{\mathcal{I}}(s)\mathcal{P}\dot{\mathscr{E}}_\vartheta(s) + \dot{\mathscr{E}}_x^{\mathcal{I}}(s)\mathcal{P}\mathscr{E}_\vartheta(s) \\
&= \mathscr{E}_x^{\mathcal{I}}(s)\mathcal{P}[\mathscr{C}_f\mathscr{E}_\vartheta(s) + \mathscr{A}_f g(\mathscr{E}_\vartheta(s)) + \mathscr{D}_f\varpi] \\
&\quad + [\mathscr{C}_f\mathscr{E}_\vartheta(s) + \mathscr{A}_f g(\mathscr{E}_\vartheta(s)) + \mathscr{D}_f\varpi]^{\mathcal{I}}\mathcal{P}\mathscr{E}_\vartheta(s). \tag{23}
\end{aligned}$$

Apply Young's inequality to get

$$\begin{aligned}
&\mathscr{E}_x^{\mathcal{I}}(s)\mathcal{P}\mathscr{D}_f\varpi + \varpi^{\mathcal{I}}\mathscr{D}_f^{\mathcal{I}}\mathcal{P}\mathscr{E}_\vartheta(s) \\
&\leq \varepsilon_1\mathscr{E}_x^{\mathcal{I}}(s)\mathcal{P}\mathscr{D}_f\mathscr{D}_f^{\mathcal{I}}\mathcal{P}\mathscr{E}_\vartheta(s) + \frac{1}{\varepsilon_1}\varpi^{\mathcal{I}}\varpi. \tag{24}
\end{aligned}$$

Substituting from (24) into (23) results in:

$$\begin{aligned}
\dot{\mathscr{U}}(s) &= \mathscr{E}_x^{\mathcal{I}}(s)\mathcal{P}\dot{\mathscr{E}}_\vartheta(s) + \dot{\mathscr{E}}_x^{\mathcal{I}}(s)\mathcal{P}\mathscr{E}_\vartheta(s) \\
&= \mathscr{E}_x^{\mathcal{I}}(s)\mathcal{P}[\mathscr{C}_f\mathscr{E}_\vartheta(s) + \mathscr{A}_f g(\mathscr{E}_\vartheta(s))] \\
&\quad + [\mathscr{C}_f\mathscr{E}_\vartheta(s) + \mathscr{A}_f g(\mathscr{E}_\vartheta(s))]^{\mathcal{I}}\mathcal{P}\mathscr{E}_\vartheta(s) \\
&\quad + \varepsilon_1\mathscr{E}_x^{\mathcal{I}}(s)\mathcal{P}\mathscr{D}_f\mathscr{D}_f^{\mathcal{I}}\mathcal{P}\mathscr{E}_\vartheta(s) + \frac{1}{\varepsilon_1}\varpi^{\mathcal{I}}\varpi. \tag{25}
\end{aligned}$$

In order to measure this influence, assuming that $\mathscr{U}(0) = 0$ and the cost function $\mathscr{J}_1(s)$ is established as :

$$\begin{aligned}
\mathscr{J}_1(s) &= \int_0^t (\mathscr{E}_x^{\mathcal{I}}(c)\mathscr{E}_x(c) - \alpha_1^2\varpi^{\mathcal{I}}\varpi)ds \\
&= \int_0^t (\mathscr{E}_x^{\mathcal{I}}(c)\mathscr{E}_x(c) - \alpha_1^2\varpi^{\mathcal{I}}\varpi + \dot{\mathscr{U}}(c))ds \\
&\quad - \int_0^t \dot{\mathscr{U}}(c))ds. \tag{26}
\end{aligned}$$

From (21), one gets

$$\begin{aligned}
&\dot{\mathscr{U}}(s) + \mathscr{E}_x^{\mathcal{I}}(s)\mathscr{E}_\vartheta(s) - \alpha_1^2\varpi^{\mathcal{I}}\varpi \\
&\leq \hat{\zeta}^{\mathcal{I}}(s)\Lambda_2\hat{\zeta}(s) < 0. \tag{27}
\end{aligned}$$

where $\hat{\zeta}(s) = \text{col}\{\mathscr{E}_\vartheta(s), g(\mathscr{E}_\vartheta(s)), \varpi\}$.

On the basis of (26) and (27), one can get $\mathscr{J}_1(s) < 0$. For $t \in [0, \infty)$, the equation (26) can become as

$$\int_0^\infty (\mathscr{E}_x^{\mathscr{T}}(c)\mathscr{E}_x(c) - \alpha_1^2 \varpi^{\mathscr{T}} \varpi)ds$$

$$= \lim_{t \to \infty} \int_0^t (\mathscr{E}^{\mathscr{T}}(c)\mathscr{E}(c) - \alpha_1^2 \varpi^{\mathscr{T}} \varpi)ds$$

$$< 0.$$

Therefore, the fault tolerant control system (19) is stable. The proof is thus completed. $\qquad\square$

4   Simulation Examples

The following simulation example is presented to verify the results obtained by the theorem.

Example 1. Based on [1], the parameters of underwater vehicle system is presented as follows: $m_{11} = 10.8\,kg, m_{22} = 13.3\,kg, m_{33} = 0.6\,kg * m^2$. $X_u = -1\,kg/m, X_{u|u|}|u| = -10\,kg/m, Z_w = -50\,kg/m, Z_{w|w|}|w| = -10\,kg/m, M_q = -50\,kg/m, M_{q|q|}|q| = -5\,kg/m, \bar{B}\bar{G}_z = 0.03\,m$. Choose

$$g(\cdot) = \begin{bmatrix} 0.2045q^2 - 0.0103uq \\ -0.0231q^2 - 0.0561uq \\ 0 \end{bmatrix},$$

Assume that external disturbance $\tau_w = 0$ and actuator fault $f(s)$ as

$$f(s) = \begin{cases} 0, & 0s \le t \le 5s, \\ sin2t, & 5s \le t \le 40s. \end{cases}$$

Solving LMIs (20) and (21), the parameter matrix $\mathcal{K}$ is obtained as follows

$$\begin{bmatrix} 2.236 & 1.458 & 3.962 & 0 & 1.267 & -1.254 \\ -.035 & 0 & 4.861 & 0 & 5.968 & 2.374 \\ 1.230 & -0.346 & 2.379 & 1.230 & 0.283 & 0.294 \\ 2.810 & 0 & 0.382 & -3.825 & 1.027 & 4.218 \\ 0 & 1.435 & 0 & 2.4365 & 0.427 & 5.241 \\ 0.927 & -1.457 & 2.461 & 4.538 & -0.067 & 0 \\ 1.557 & -0.567 & 1.453 & 2.126 & 0 & 0.734 \end{bmatrix}.$$

Figures 1 and 2 show the state motion trajectory of the system and the system state estimation in the case of failure. Figure 3 depicts the diagnostic value $\hat{f}(s)$ and the true value $f(s)$ in the case of actuator failure.

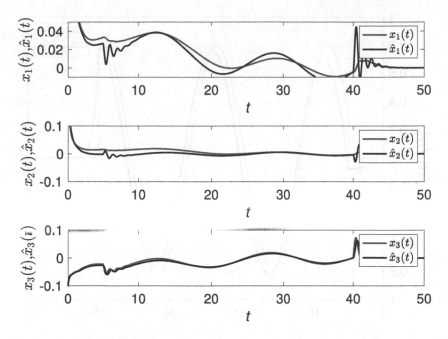

Fig. 1. Trajectories of actual state $x_1(s), x_2(s)$ and $x_3(s)$ and the corresponding estimated state $\hat{\vartheta}_1(s), \hat{\vartheta}_2(s)$ and $\hat{\vartheta}_3(s)$.

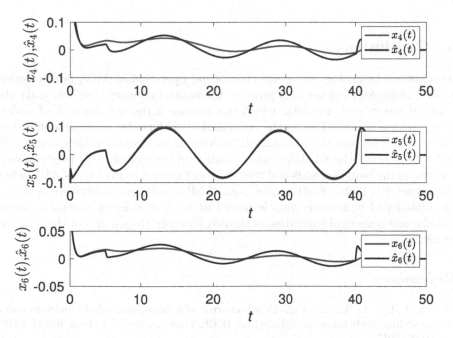

Fig. 2. Trajectories of actual state $x_4(s), x_5(s)$ and $x_6(s)$ and the corresponding estimated state $\hat{\vartheta}_4(s), \hat{\vartheta}_5(s)$ and $\hat{\vartheta}_6(s)$.

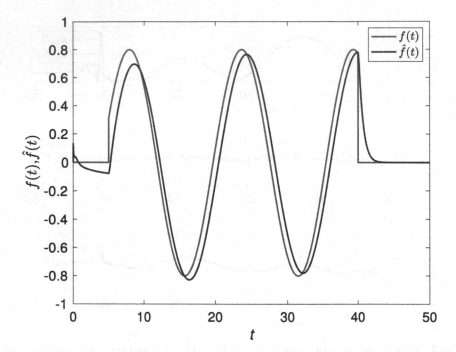

Fig. 3. Trajectories of fault true value $f(s)$ and the corresponding diagnostic value $\hat{f}(s)$.

5   Conclusions

As a control technology to ensure the normal operation of AUV, fault-tolerant control technology can not only improve the control accuracy, but also make the faulty thruster work normally, which has become a research hotspot of underwater vehicle control. Due to the complicated underwater environment, safety and stability become the technical difficulties of underwater vehicle control. In order to improve the reliability and stability of the system, this paper mainly focuses on the fault diagnosis and fault-tolerant control technology of AUV when the actuator is faulty. Furthermore, some LMI conditions is obtained to ensure the stability of underwater vehicle model under fault-tolerant control strategy. Finally, one numerical simulation is showed to verify the validity of the theorem result.

References

1. Yu, J., Liu, J., Wu, Z., et al.: Depth control of a bioinspired robotic dolphin based on sliding-mode fuzzy control method. IEEE Trans. Industr. Electron. **65**(3), 2429–2438 (2017)
2. Peymani, E., Fossen, T.I.: Path following of underwater robots using Lagrange multipliers. Robot. Auton. Syst. **67**, 44–52 (2015)

3. Scaradozzi, D., Palmieri, G., Costa, D., et al.: BCF swimming locomotion for autonomous underwater robots: a review and a novel solution to improve control and efficiency. Ocean Eng. **130**, 437–453 (2017)
4. Wang, R., Wang, S., Wang, Y., et al.: Development and motion control of biomimetic underwater robots: A survey. IEEE Trans. Syst. Man Cybern. Syst. **52**(2), 833–844 (2022)
5. Sun, X., Shi, J., Liu, L., et al.: Transferring deep knowledge for object recognition in low-quality underwater videos. Neurocomputing **275**, 897–908 (2018)
6. Yang, Y., Wang, J., Wu, Z., et al.: Fault-tolerant control of a CPG-governed robotic fish. Engineering **4**(6), 861–868 (2018)
7. Van, M., Do, X.P., Mavrovouniotis, M.: Self-tuning fuzzy PID-nonsingular fast terminal sliding mode control for robust fault tolerant control of robot manipulators. ISA Trans. **96**, 60–68 (2020)
8. Kadiyam, J., Parashar, A., Mohan, S., et al.: Actuator fault-tolerant control study of an underwater robot with four rotatable thrusters. Ocean Eng. **197**, 106929 (2020)
9. Bahreini, M., Zarei, J.: Robust finite-time fault-tolerant control for networked control systems with random delays: A Markovian jump system approach. Nonlinear Anal. Hybrid Syst. **36**, 100873 (2020)
10. Li, L., Yao, L., Jin, H., et al.: Fault diagnosis and fault-tolerant control based on Laplace transform for nonlinear networked control systems with random delay. Int. J. Robust Nonlinear Control **30**(3), 1223–1239 (2020)
11. Hu, J.W., Zhan, X.S., Wu, J., et al.: Analysis of optimal performance of MIMO networked control systems with encoding and packet dropout constraints. IET Control Theory Appli. **14**(13), 1762–1768 (2020)
12. Amani, A.M., Afshar, A., Menhaj, M.B.: Fault tolerant networked control systems subject to actuator failure using virtual actuator technique. IFAC Proc. Vol. **44**(1), 5465–5470 (2011)
13. Zhang, C.H., Yang, G.H.: Event-triggered adaptive output feedback control for a class of uncertain nonlinear systems with actuator failures. IEEE Trans. Cybern. **50**(1), 201–210 (2018)
14. He, X., Wang, Z., Ji, Y.D., et al.: Active fault tolerant control for a class of networked systems with partial actuator failures. IFAC Proc. Vol. **45**(20), 1299–1304 (2012)
15. Sakthivel, R., Saravanakumar, T., Kaviarasan, B., et al.: Finite-time dissipative based fault-tolerant control of Takagi-Sugeno fuzzy systems in a network environment. J. Franklin Inst. **354**(8), 3430–3454 (2017)
16. Zhang, G., Liu, J., Liu, Z., et al.: Adaptive fuzzy discrete-time fault-tolerant control for permanent magnet synchronous motors based on dynamic surface technology. Neurocomputing **404**, 145–153 (2020)
17. Ju, Y., Wei, G., Ding, D., et al.: Finite-time fault tolerant control for stochastic parameter systems with intermittent fault under stochastic communication protocol. Int. J. Robust Nonlinear Control **30**(15), 6112–6129 (2020)
18. Duan, K., Zhang, W.: Event-triggered fault-tolerant control for networked systems with dynamic quantiser. IET Control Theory Appli. **10**(9), 1088–1096 (2016)
19. Wang, Y., Wang, Z.: Model free adaptive fault-tolerant tracking control for a class of discrete-time systems. Neurocomputing **412**, 143–151 (2020)
20. Sakthivel, R., Joby, M., Wang, C., et al.: Finite-time fault-tolerant control of neutral systems against actuator saturation and nonlinear actuator faults. Appl. Math. Comput. **332**, 425–436 (2018)

21. Zuo, Z., Ho, D.W.C., Wang, Y.: Fault tolerant control for singular systems with actuator saturation and nonlinear perturbation. Automatica **46**(3), 569–576 (2010)
22. Hu, H., Wang, B., Cheng, Z., et al.: A novel active fault-tolerant control for spacecrafts with full state constraints and input saturation. Aerosp. Sci. Technol. **108**, 106368 (2021)
23. Shen, Q., Yue, C., Goh, C.H., et al.: Active fault-tolerant control system design for spacecraft attitude maneuvers with actuator saturation and faults. IEEE Trans. Industr. Electron. **66**(5), 3763–3772 (2018)
24. Antonelli, G.: Underwater Robots. Springer, Cham (2014). https://doi.org/10.1007/978-1-4613-1419-6

Event-Triggered Kernel Recursive Least Squares Algorithm

Yawen Li[1] and Wenling Li[2(✉)] [iD]

[1] School of Economics and Management, Beijing University of Posts and Telecommunications, Beijing 100876, People's Republic of China
[2] School of Automation Science and Electrical Engineering, Beihang University (BUAA), Beijing 100191, People's Republic of China
lwlmath@buaa.edu.cn

Abstract. This paper proposed a kernel recursive least squares algorithm for a kind of nonlinear models with coupled inputs. In such models, the output is generated with multiple inputs in a coupled fashion. A distinct feature of the proposed algorithm is that any two inputs should be computed in the kernel functions. As the existing sparsification techniques are not applicable to such models, the event-triggered strategy is devised to prune the linear growing structure. It is shown that the event-triggered threshold provides a compromise between computational cost and estimation performance. Numerical results show the superior performance of the algorithm.

Keywords: Kernel adaptive filter · Coupled inputs · Event-trigger

1 Introduction

Kernel adaptive filters have gained considerable attention due to their excellent nonlinear approximation capabilities. The aim of kernel adaptive filters is to solve nonlinear filtering problems using linear filtering structures in a reproducing kernel Hilbert space (RKHS). The linear filtering methods are applied in the RKHS and nonlinear filtering results are obtained in the original input space [1]. Many kernel adaptive filters have been developed such as kernel least mean square [2], multikernel LMS [3], kernel recursive least squares [4], kernel affine projection [5], extended kernel recursive least squares [6], and so on.

The drawback of kernel adaptive filters is their linear growing structure, which results in the high computation cost and memory requirement in practical implementations. To overcome this problem, sparsification techniques have been devised include approximate linear dependence (ALD) criterion [4], surprise [7], coherence [8], quantization approach [9–11] and nearest-instance-centroid-estimation [12,13]. In comparison with sparsification methods, another way to address computational and memory issues is to select a fixed-dimensional network structure such as Nystrom approach [14] and random Fourier features

---

Supported by NSFC under Grant 61976013.

[15]. Although many kernel adaptive filters have been developed, they are not designed for nonlinear models with coupled inputs. Moreover, all the existing sparsification techniques focus on designing appropriate selection criteria on input data, which can not be applied for nonlinear models with multiple inputs.

In this paper, a KRLS algorithm is designed for nonlinear models with coupled inputs. Instead of the existing sparsification selection criteria on input data, an event-triggered strategy is designed by using output errors to reduce the computational and storage requirements. It is shown that the event-triggered threshold provides a compromise between computational cost and estimation performance.

The reminder of the paper is organized as follows. The problem formulation is given in Sect. 2 . In Sect. 3, a KRLS algorithm is proposed by using event-triggered strategy. In Sect. 4, numerical results are provided to show the performance of the algorithm, followed by conclusion in Sect. 5.

2   Problem Formulation

We consider the nonlinear model with coupled inputs

$$d_k = \sum_{i=1}^{N} a_i f(u_{i,k}) + v_k \tag{1}$$

where $u_{i,k} \in \mathcal{U}$ is the input data from the i-th node and $d_k \in R$ is the output data. N denotes the number of nodes. $\mathcal{U}$ is a compact subspace of R^p. a_i is the coupling weight satisfying $a_i > 0$ and $\sum_{i=1}^{N} a_i = 1$. f is a nonlinear function. v_k is the additive noise process.

The aim of this paper is to estimate a nonlinear function f by using input-output data pairs $\{(u_{i,k}, d_k), i = 1, 2, \cdots, N\}_{k=1}^{M}$. Similar problems have been extensively studied for a nonlinear input-output model. Following the existing formulation of finding the true function, we try to minimize the mean square errors

$$J_k = \sum_{l=1}^{k} \left(d_l - \sum_{i=1}^{N} a_i f(u_{i,l}) \right)^2 + \lambda ||f||^2 \tag{2}$$

where the positive scalar λ is a regularization factor.

In the framework of kernel adaptive filtering theory, the input data $u_{i,k}$ is transformed into a feature space $\mathcal{F}$ as $\psi(u_{i,k})$ where ψ is a function from $\mathcal{U}$ to $\mathcal{F}$. Meanwhile, the nonlinear function f defined in $\mathcal{U}$ can be represented as a linear operator Ω defined in $\mathcal{F}$ such that [1]

$$f(u) = \Omega^T \psi(u) \tag{3}$$

By replacing f with the linear operator Ω in the nonlinear input-ouput model (1) and the optimization cost (2), we can obtain

$$d_k = \Omega^T \sum_{i=1}^{N} a_i \psi(u_{i,k}) + v_k \tag{4}$$

$$J_k = \sum_{l=1}^{k} \left(d_l - \Omega^T \sum_{i=1}^{N} a_i \psi(u_{i,l}) \right)^2 + \lambda ||\Omega||^2 \tag{5}$$

Then, the problem of estimating the nonlinear function f can be transformed to find the linear operator Ω in the feature space by using data $\{(\psi(u_{i,k}), d_k), i = 1, \cdots, N\}_{k=1}^{M}$. This can be computed recursively using the classic RLS algorithm. However, the feature space $\mathcal{F}$ may be infinite dimensional and the mapping φ is often difficult to be derived explicitly. Hence, it is almost impossible to do all calculations in the feature space. Fortunately, the Mercer's Theorem provides a connection between $\mathcal{U}$ and $\mathcal{F}$ [1]

$$\kappa(u, u') = \psi^T(u)\psi(u') \tag{6}$$

where $\kappa(\cdot, \cdot)$ denotes a continuous, positive-definite, symmetric kernel function. The Eq (6) is known as kernel trick. A well-known kernel function is the Gaussian kernel $\exp\{-(u - u')^T(u - u')/2\rho^2\}$ with width parameter ρ.

The advantage of using kernel trick is that the explicit calculations on $\psi(u)$ are not required for finding Ω and they can be derived directly with respect to calculations on u.

3   The Proposed Algorithm

In this section, the KRLS algorithm is designed for the nonlinear model with coupled inputs. Then the event-triggered strategy is designed by using output errors to reduce the computation and storage requirements.

3.1   KRLS Algorithm

To derive the optimal solution for the cost function (5), we define the following augmented vectors

$$D_k = [d_1, \cdots, d_k]^T \tag{7}$$

$$\Psi(u_k) = \left[\sum_{i=1}^{N} a_i \psi(u_{i,1}), \cdots, \sum_{i=1}^{N} a_i \psi(u_{i,k}) \right] \tag{8}$$

Then the optimal solution can be obtained by taking derivative of J_k with respect to Ω

$$\Omega_k = [\lambda I + \Psi(u_k)\Psi^T(u_k)]^{-1}\Psi(u_k)D_k \tag{9}$$

where I is the identity matrix.

Applying matrix inverse lemma to (9) yields

$$\Omega_k = \Psi(u_k)[\lambda I + \Psi^T(u_k)\Psi(u_k)]^{-1}D_k$$
$$= \Psi(u_k)w_k \tag{10}$$

where $w_k = [\lambda I + \Psi^T(u_k)\Psi(u_k)]^{-1}D_k$.

Define $Q_k = [\lambda I + \Psi^T(u_k)\Psi(u_k)]^{-1}$, we have

$$Q_k^{-1} = \lambda I + \Psi^T(u_k)\Psi(u_k)$$
$$= \begin{bmatrix} \lambda I & 0 \\ 0 & \lambda \end{bmatrix} + \begin{bmatrix} \Psi^T(u_{k-1})\Psi(u_{k-1}) & h_k \\ h_k^T & \delta_k \end{bmatrix}$$
$$= \begin{bmatrix} Q_{k-1}^{-1} & h_k \\ h_k^T & \lambda + \delta_k \end{bmatrix} \tag{11}$$

where

$$\delta_k = \sum_{i=1}^{N} a_i \psi^T(u_{i,k}) \sum_{j=1}^{N} a_j \psi(u_{i,k})$$
$$= \sum_{i=1}^{N} \sum_{j=1}^{N} a_i a_j \kappa(u_{j,k}, u_{i,k}) \tag{12}$$

$$h_k = \Psi^T(u_{k-1})\left(\sum_{i=1}^{N} a_i \psi(u_{i,k}) \right)$$
$$= \begin{bmatrix} \sum_{i=1}^{N} \sum_{j=1}^{N} a_i a_j \psi^T(u_{j,1})\psi(u_{i,k}) \\ \sum_{i=1}^{N} \sum_{j=1}^{N} a_i a_j \psi^T(u_{j,2})\psi(u_{i,k}) \\ \vdots \\ \sum_{i=1}^{N} \sum_{j=1}^{N} a_i a_j \psi^T(u_{j,k-1})\psi(u_{i,k}) \end{bmatrix}$$
$$= \begin{bmatrix} \sum_{i=1}^{N} \sum_{j=1}^{N} a_i a_j \kappa(u_{j,1}, u_{i,k}) \\ \sum_{i=1}^{N} \sum_{j=1}^{N} a_i a_j \kappa(u_{j,2}, u_{i,k}) \\ \vdots \\ \sum_{i=1}^{N} \sum_{j=1}^{N} a_i a_j \kappa(u_{j,k-1}, u_{i,k}) \end{bmatrix} \tag{13}$$

By using the block matrix inverse identity [1], Q_k can be further rewritten as

$$Q_k = r_k^{-1} \begin{bmatrix} Q_{k-1}r_k + z_k z_k^T & -z_k \\ -z_k^T & 1 \end{bmatrix} \tag{14}$$

where

$$z_k = Q_{k-1}h_k \tag{15}$$
$$r_k = \lambda + \delta_k - z_k^T h_k \tag{16}$$

Now, w_k is obtained by

$$
\begin{aligned}
w_k &= Q_k D_k \\
&= \begin{bmatrix} Q_{k-1} + z_k z_k^T r_k^{-1} & -z_k r_k^{-1} \\ -z_k^T r_k^{-1} & r_k^{-1} \end{bmatrix} \begin{bmatrix} D_{k-1} \\ d_k \end{bmatrix} \\
&= \begin{bmatrix} w_{k-1} - z_k r_k^{-1}(d_k - h_k^T w_{k-1}) \\ r_k^{-1}(d_k - h_k^T w_{k-1}) \end{bmatrix}
\end{aligned}
\tag{17}
$$

Finally, the function can be estimated by using (3)

$$
\begin{aligned}
f_k(u) &= \Omega_k^T \psi(u) \\
&= (\Psi(u_k) w_k)^T \psi(u) \\
&= w_k^T \Psi^T(u_k) \psi(u) \\
&= w_k^T \left[\sum_{i=1}^N a_i \kappa(u_{i,1}, u), \cdots, \sum_{i=1}^N a_i \kappa(u_{i,k}, u) \right]^T \\
&= \sum_{l=1}^k \sum_{i=1}^N w_k^l a_i \kappa(u_{i,l}, u)
\end{aligned}
\tag{18}
$$

where w_k^l is the l-th element of w_k.

The estimated output at time instant k should be

$$
\begin{aligned}
\hat{d}_k &= \sum_{i=1}^N a_i f_k(u_{i,k}) \\
&= \sum_{l=1}^k \sum_{i=1}^N \sum_{j=1}^N w_k^l a_i a_j \kappa(u_{j,l}, u_{i,k})
\end{aligned}
\tag{19}
$$

It can be observed that the event-triggered KRLS is different from the one for a single node [4] since any two inputs $u_{j,l}$ and $u_{i,k}$ should be computed in the kernel function (19).

The main challenge of the KRLS algorithm is that the model order grows every time when a new input-output data pair arrives, which leads to increasing computational cost and storage requirements. Thus, sparsification techniques should be designed to reduce the linear growing structure in (19). With the development of the kernel adaptive filters, many sparsification techniques have been proposed [4,7–13]. A remarkable feature is that almost all the sparsification techniques are proposed with respect to the input data. Generally, a part of the existing inputs is formulated as a dictionary and the new input is compared with the dictionary via distance. The model order of the filter is not increased if the distance is less than a threshold so that the linear growing structure can be controlled.

The existing sparsification techniques can not be directly applied to the nonlinear model with coupled inputs (1) since the inputs are taken from different nodes and the new inputs can not be compared with a common dictionary. An alternative way for sparsification is by designing a dictionary for each node. However, the input indexes in the dictionaries might be different. For example, we consider two nodes with ten inputs for each node. Two dictionaries are designed where the inputs from the first node $\{u_{1,1}, u_{1,5}, u_{1,9}\}$ are stored in the first dictionary and the inputs from the second node $\{u_{2,2}, u_{2,6}, u_{2,10}\}$ are stored in the second dictionary. According to (19), any two inputs should be computed in the kernel functions and therefore the weight w_k should be computed for each input. In other words, the model order of the filter is not reduced and the filter remains a linear growing structure. To overcome this problem, we propose an event-triggered strategy using the output data.

3.2   Event-Triggered Strategy for Sparsification

To reduce the linear growing structure of the KRLS algorithm, we consider an event-triggered strategy so that the model order is increased only at certain trigger time instants $\alpha_1, \alpha_2, \cdots, \alpha_{m(k)}$, where $m(k)$ is the total number of triggering time at time instant k. Note that the set of trigger time instants $\{\alpha_l\}_{l=1}^{m(k)}$ is a subset of $\{j\}_{j=1}^{k}$ and $m(k)$ is usually less than k by using event-triggered strategy. Based on the trigger time instants, a dictionary is designed to store the input-output data pairs as $\mathcal{D}_k = \{\mathcal{U}_{\alpha_l}\}_{l=1}^{m(k)}$, where $\mathcal{U}_{\alpha_l} = \{(u_{i,\alpha_l}, d_{\alpha_l}), i = 1, 2, \cdots, N\}$ represents the input-output data pair at time instant α_l. Specifically, the new data pair is stored in this dictionary and the KRLS is implemented normally if the event is triggered. Otherwise, the data pair is considered to be redundant and it is discarded to save computational cost and memory requirement. Then the estimated function (18) and the estimated output can be represented as

$$f_k(u) = \sum_{l=1}^{m(k)} \sum_{i=1}^{N} w_k^l a_i \kappa(u_{i,\alpha_l}, u) \tag{20}$$

$$\hat{d}_k = \sum_{l=1}^{m(k)} \sum_{i=1}^{N} \sum_{j=1}^{N} w_k^l a_i a_j \kappa(u_{j,\alpha_l}, u_{i,k}) \tag{21}$$

In this paper, the output errors is used to devise the event-triggered strategy, i.e., the event is triggered whenever

$$|d_k - \hat{d}_k| > \gamma \tag{22}$$

where $\gamma > 0$ is the threshold and $\hat{d}_k$ is computed as (20).

The event-triggered condition (22) shows that the KRLS algorithm update its parameters only when there is sufficient innovation, which is measured by the output error. Thus, by choosing an appropriate threshold, the KLRS algorithm reaches a compromise between computational cost and estimation accuracy. For clarity, the pseudo-code that summarizes the event-triggered KRLS is shown in Algorithm 1.

Algorithm 1. Event-triggered KRLS

1. Initialization:

Initialize w_1, Q_1

Kernel width parameter ρ

Regularization parameter λ

Event-triggered threshold γ

Denote the input-output $\mathcal{U}_1 = \{u_{1,1}, \cdots, u_{N,1}, d_1\}$

Dictionary $\mathcal{D}_1 = \{\mathcal{U}_{\alpha_1}\}$ and $\alpha_1 = 1$

Size of dictionary $m(1) = 1$

2. Filtering:

if $\mathcal{U}_k$ is available

Compute

$$
h_k = \begin{bmatrix}
\sum_{i=1}^{N} \sum_{j=1}^{N} a_i a_j \kappa(u_{j,\alpha_1}, u_{i,k}) \\
\sum_{i=1}^{N} \sum_{j=1}^{N} a_i a_j \kappa(u_{j,\alpha_2}, u_{i,k}) \\
\vdots \\
\sum_{i=1}^{N} \sum_{j=1}^{N} a_i a_j \kappa(u_{j,\alpha_{m(k-1)}}, u_{i,k})
\end{bmatrix}
$$

Compute $e_k = d_k - h_k^T w_{k-1}$

if $|e_k| > \gamma$ ▷ Event-triggered condition

Size of dictionary $m(k) = m(k-1) + 1$

Set $\alpha_{m(k)} = k$

Insert $\mathcal{U}_k$ into the dictionary $\mathcal{D}_k = \{\mathcal{D}_{k-1}, \mathcal{U}_{\alpha_{m(k)}}\}$

Compute $\delta_k = \sum_{i=1}^{N} \sum_{j=1}^{N} a_i a_j \kappa(u_{j,k}, u_{i,k})$

Compute $z_k = Q_{k-1} h_k$

Compute $r_k = \lambda + \delta_k - z_k^T h_k$

Compute

$$
Q_k = r_k^{-1} \begin{bmatrix} Q_{k-1} r_k + z_k z_k^T & -z_k \\ -z_k^T & 1 \end{bmatrix}
$$

Compute

$$
w_k = \begin{bmatrix} w_{k-1} - z_k r_k^{-1} e_k \\ r_k^{-1} e_k \end{bmatrix}
$$

Compute

$$
f_k(u) = \sum_{l=1}^{m(k)} \sum_{i=1}^{N} w_k^l a_i \kappa(u_{i,\alpha_l}, u)
$$

else

Size of dictionary $m(k) = m(k-1)$

Dictionary $\mathcal{D}_k = \mathcal{D}_{k-1}$

Weight $w_k = w_{k-1}$

end if

end while

Table 1. Performance comparison between KRLS and ET-KRLS

Algorithm	MSE	Model order	Run Time (Sec)
KRLS	0.0293	500	40.42
ET-KRLS-0.1	0.0298	70	8.11
ET-KRLS-0.2	0.0320	42	5.44
ET-KRLS-0.3	0.0342	28	3.58
ET-KRLS-0.4	0.0388	20	2.61
ET-KRLS-0.5	0.0445	15	1.74

4   Numerical Results

In this section, the performance of the event-triggered KRLS (ET-KRLS) is verified for nonlinear models with coupled inputs.

Consider the following nonlinear input-output model with five coupled nodes

$$d_k = \sum_{i=1}^{5} a_i [u_{i,k}(w_1 - w_2 \exp(-u_{i,k}^2))$$
$$- (w_3 + w_4 \exp(-u_{i,k}^2)) + w_5 \sin(u_{i,k}\pi)] + v_k \qquad (23)$$

where the input data $u_{i,k}$ is drawn from uniform distribution of interval $[-1, 1]$, and v_k is Gaussian noise with zero-mean and standard deviation $\sigma_i = 0.001$. Similar models with a single node have been investigated in [8,11]. As in [11], the coefficients are taken to be $w_1 = 0.128$, $w_2 = 0.448$, $w_3 = 0.512$, $w_4 = 0.512$, $w_5 = 0.128$. In the simulations, Gaussian kernel is applied with kernel width

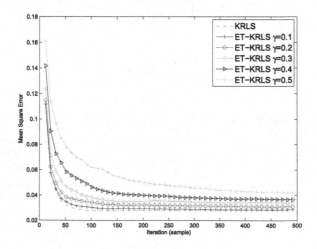

Fig. 1. MSE with different event-triggered thresholds.

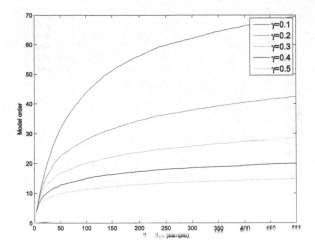

Fig. 2. Model order with different event-triggered thresholds.

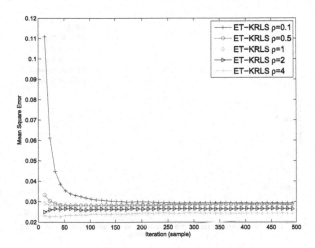

Fig. 3. MSE of ET-KRLS ($\gamma = 0.1$) with different kernel widths.

$\rho_i = 0.1$. The regularization factor is set $\lambda = 0.01$. The mean square error (MSE) is obtained using 100 Monte Carlo runs for performance comparison.

First of all, we show how the even-triggered threshold affects the performance. the number of training data is 500, and the number of testing data is 100. The behavior of the ET-KRLS algorithm with different thresholds $\gamma = 0.1, 0.2, 0.3, 0.4, 0.5$ are presented in Fig.1. They are compared with the KRLS algorithm without event-triggered strategy. Note that the performance of the ET-KRLS algorithm with $\gamma = 0.1$ is very close to the KRLS algorithm. Moreover, the performance will become worse when the threshold increases. This is due to the fact that less data are used to update the filter parameters as the threshold increases. The model order growth curves versus different thresh-

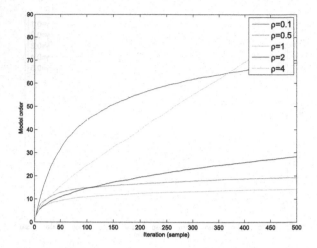

Fig. 4. Model order of ET-KRLS ($\gamma = 0.1$) with different kernel widths.

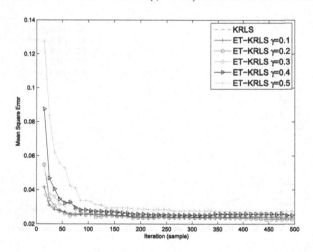

Fig. 5. MSE with different event-triggered thresholds (polynomial kernel).

olds are demonstrated in Fig.2. The model order is decreased as the threshold increases. Testing MSE and model order at final iteration are shown in Table 1, as well as the execution time for one simulation run. It is clear that the event-triggered strategy provides a desirable compromise between computational cost and estimation performance.

Secondly, the performance of ET-KRLS algorithm is verified with respect to Gaussian kernel widths. For $\gamma = 0.1$, the Gaussian kernel widths are taken to be $\rho = 0.1, 0.5, 1, 2, 4$ and the MSEs are presented in Fig. 3. The results suggest that the proposed ET-KRLS algorithm works well with different kernel widths.

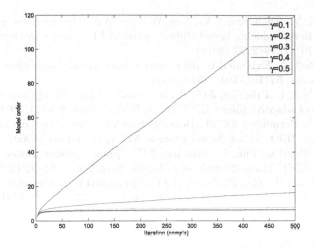

Fig. 6. Model order with different event-triggered thresholds (polynomial kernel).

The model order growth curves are given in Fig. 4. It is clear that the model order will be increased if the kernel width is chosen large or small.

Thirdly, we show the performance of the proposed ET-KRLS algorithm with other types of kernel functions. A polynomial kernel $\kappa(u_1, u_2) = (1 + u_1^T u_2)^3$ is applied. The MSEs with different event-triggered thresholds are given in Fig. 5 and the model orders are shown in Fig. 6 It can be observed that the proposed ET-KRLS algorithm can still achieve accurate performance with other forms of kernel functions.

5   Conclusion

We designed a KRLS algorithm for a kind of nonlinear models with coupled inputs. An event-triggered strategy is designed to cut the linear growing structure. Simulation results show that the event-triggered threshold provides a compromise between the computational cost and estimation accuracy.

References

1. Liu, W., Principe, J.C., Haykin A.: Kernel Adaptive Filtering: A Comprehensive Introduction. John Wiley & Sons (2010)
2. Liu, W., Pokharel, P., Principe, J.C.: The kernel least mean square algorithm. IEEE Trans. Signal Process. **56**(2), 543–554 (2008)
3. Tobar, F.A., Kung, S., Mandic, D.P.: Multikernel least mean square algorithm. IEEE Trans. Neural Netw. Learn. Syst. **25**(2), 265–277 (2014)
4. Engel, Y., Mannor, S., Meir, R.: The kernel recursive least squares algorithm. IEEE Trans. Signal Process. **52**(8), 2275–2285 (2004)

5. Wu, Q., Li, Y., Zakharov, Y.V., Xue, W., Shi, W.: A kernel affine projection-like algorithm in reproducing kernel Hilbert space. IEEE Trans. Circ. Syst. II: Express Briefs **67**(10), 2249–2253 (2019)
6. Liu, W., Park, I.: Extended kernel recursive least squares algorithm. IEEE Trans. Signal Process. **57**(10), 3801–3814 (2009)
7. Liu, W., Park, I., Principe, J.C.: An information theoretic approach of designing sparse kernel adaptive filters. IEEE Trans. Neural Netw. **20**(12), 1950–1961 (2009)
8. Richard, C., Bermudez, J.C.M., Honeine, P.: Online prediction of time series data with kernels. IEEE Trans. Signal Process. **57**(3), 1058–1067 (2009)
9. Chen, B., Zhao, S., Zhu, P., Principe, J.C.: Quantized kernel least mean square algorithm. IEEE Trans. Neural Netw. Learn. Syst. **23**(1), 22–32 (2012)
10. Chen, B., Zhao, S., Zhu, P., Principe, J.C.: Quantized kernel recursive least squares algorithm. IEEE Trans. Neural Netw. Learn. Syst. **24**(9), 1484–1491 (2013)
11. Wang, S., Wang, W., Duan, S.: A class of weighted quantized kernel recursive least squares algorithms, IEEE Trans. Circ. Syst. II: Express Briefs **64**(6), 730–734 (2017)
12. Li, K., Principe, J.C.: Transfer learning in adaptive filters: the nearest-instance-centroid-estimation kernel least-mean-square algorithm. IEEE Trans. Signal Processing **65**(24), 6520–6535 (2017)
13. Zhang, H., Wang, L., Zhang, T., Wang, S.: The nearest-instance-centroid-estimation kernel recursive least squares algorithms. IEEE Trans. Circ. Syst. II: Express Briefs **67**(7), 1344–1348 (2020)
14. Zhang, T., He, F., Zheng, Z., Wang, S.: Recursive minimum kernel mixture mean p-power error algorithm based on the Nystrom method. IEEE Trans. Circ. Syst. II: Express Briefs **67**(11), 2772–2776 (2020)
15. Xiong, K., Zhang, Y., Wang, S.: Complex-valued adaptive filtering based on the random Fourier features method. IEEE Trans. Circ. Syst. II: Express Briefs **67**(10), 2284–2288 (2020)

Distributed Fault-Tolerant Formation Control of Nonholonomic Mobile Robots with SSA Parameter Optimization

Jing Wang[1(✉)], Hao Wang[1], Meng Zhou[1], and Shuang Ju[2]

[1] School of Electrical and Control Engineering, North China University of Technology, Beijing 100144, People's Republic of China
jwang@ncut.edu.cn
[2] College of Information Science and Technology, Beijing University of Chemical Technology, Beijing 100029, People's Republic of China

Abstract. A distributed fault-tolerant cooperative scheme for nonholonomic mobile robots under a directed network is proposed in a leader-follower framework. The cooperative scheme consists of a fault-tolerant control protocol and an adaptive estimation of actuator fault factor. In order to obtain optimal parameters, a sparrow search algorithm is combined with a distributed consensus protocol. Moreover, the designed distributed consensus fault-tolerant control protocol is verified by seven robots, which are guaranteed to move along the reference trajectory with a predefined formation pattern. Finally, the simulation results show that the control performance is improved with the optimized parameters.

Keywords: Fault-tolerant control · Sparrow search algorithm · Leader-follower consensus · Nonholonomic mobile robots

1 Introduction

Multi-agent systems have been drawn much attention, of which formation control is a pretty popular trend. In [1–5], agents were viewed as mass points to study. He et al. modeled multiple nonholonomic vehicles and proposed a leaderless formation controller [6]. Mohamed et al. solved a formation control problem for a network of mobile vehicles with time-varying delays [7]. Liu et al. adopted a backstepping approach and a sliding mode technique for robots to achieve a consensus tracking objective [8]. Emmanuel et al. solved a leaderless consensus control for robots under communication delays [9]. Zhang et al. investigated a consensus tracking problem for robots under a directed graph [10]. Ju et al. studied mobile robots with input constraints by a model predictive control method

This work is funded by the National Natural Science Foundation of China (61973023), Beijing Natural Science Foundation (4202052), Beijing Municipal Education Commission Science and Technology Program (KM202110009013) and Research Foundation for Talents of NCUT (107051360022XN694, 107051360021XN090/010).

[11]. Zhao et al. proposed a formation control approach for multiple UAV systems derived from iterative learning [12]. The above achievements have promoted the control of multi-agent systems, but they do not consider the faults that may happen to the systems.

The actuator faults in a multi-agent system is worth researching because it may lead to degraded system performances or even lead to system instability. Wang et al. investigated an adaptive fault-tolerant control problem for multi-agent systems under actuator faults [13]. Dan et al. designed distributed event-triggered consensus protocol considering the case of actuator saturation [14]. Ranjith et al. integrated an artificial potential field method and a nonsingular terminal sliding mode control, and they did some real-time experimentations [15]. Wang et al. investigated a fault tolerant control for an unmanned aerial vehicle by a nonsingular fast terminal sliding mode technique [16]. Wang et al. investigated an adaptive distributed fault-tolerant formation control for a group of wheeled robots under actuator faults [17]. Chang et al. considered kinematics and dynamics of differential wheeled mobile robots [18]. Besides, the optimization of controller parameters is also worth studying.

Note that the consensus error will be reduced apparently if parameters of an controller are selected appropriately. Li et al. used a grey wolf optimize scheme to tune variables of controllers [19]. Mehran et al. applied a multi-objective bat algorithm for optimization to tune the parameters [20]. Sparrow search algorithm(SSA), a novel swarm optimization approach, with the unique algorithmic solution, is less likely to fall into a local optimum than similar algorithms [21]. As far as we know, few optimization algorithms have been used to optimize parameters of controllers in multi-agent systems.

This paper investigates a distributed fault-tolerant formation problem for nonholonomic robots subject to actuator faults under directed communication, which is inspired by [10,13]. Compared with [10], this paper considers actuator faults. In comparison with [13], the modeled object is mobile robots which have a predefined pattern in this paper. Besides, SSA, which is combined with a distributed consensus protocol, is designed to tune the controller parameters.

The paper is organized as follows. In Sect. 2, the nonholonomic mobile robots are modeled and a transformation is presented. An adaptive fault-tolerant protocol is proposed in Sect. 3. Section 4 shows that a combination of SSA and the distributed consensus controller. Section 5 describes the simulation results. Section 6 concludes this paper.

2   Problem Formulation

2.1   Notations

$1_n = [1,\ldots,1]^T \in R^n$. For vector $y = [y_1,\ldots,y_n]^T \in R^n$, $|y| = [|y_1|,\ldots,|y_n|]^T$. Denote $\text{sign}(y) = [y_1/|y_1|,\ldots,y_n/|y_n|]^T$, where $y_i \neq 0$ for i $\in \{1,\ldots,n\}$, and sign(0) = 0. Set $\text{diag}(y) = \text{diag}\{y_1,\ldots,y_n\}$, and $\text{sig}(y) = [|y_1|\text{sign}(y_1),\ldots,|y_n|\text{sign}(y_n)]^T$.

2.2 Graph Theory

Consider a multiple nonholonomic mobile robot system consisting of one leader and n followers. The interaction among robots can be modeled by a directed network $\mathcal{G}_n = (\mathcal{V}, \mathcal{E})$. $\mathcal{V}$ is a set representing n followers, and $\mathcal{E}$ is a set of edges. $\mathcal{A}$ is regarded as a weighted adjacency matrix with element a_{ij}. One has $a_{ij} > 0$ if $(v_j, v_i) \in \mathcal{E}$ and $a_{ij} = 0$ otherwise.

The Laplacian matrix is $\mathcal{L} = [l_{ij}]_{n \times n}$ with $\mathcal{L} = \mathcal{D} - \mathcal{A}$, where $\mathcal{D} = \mathrm{diag}\{d_1, \ldots, d_n\}$ with $d_i = \sum_{j=1, j \neq i}^{n} a_{ij}, i \in \{1, \ldots, n\}$. When robot i is connected to leader, b_i is a positive constant, $b_i = 0$ otherwise. b_i is the element of $\mathcal{B}$ where $\mathcal{B} = \mathrm{diag}\{b_1, \ldots, b_n\}$. $\mathcal{M}$ is defined as $\mathcal{M} = \mathcal{B} + \mathcal{L}$. If a directed graph contains a spanning tree, there exits a node that is called the root without the parent node. Then, the root owns a directed path to each other node of the graph [22].

2.3 System Description

Consider the multiple nonholonomic mobile robot system contains one leader and n followers, whose kinematic model is described by

$$\dot{x}_i(t) = v_i(t) \cos \theta_i(t)$$
$$\dot{y}_i(t) = v_i(t) \sin \theta_i(t) \tag{1}$$
$$\dot{\theta}_i(t) = \omega_i(t)$$

where x_i and y_i denote the position of the ith robot in x and y direction, respectively, θ_i is the orientation, v_i is the linear velocity, and ω_i is the angular velocity of robot i. Robot i refers to the leader for $i = 0$, and followers for $i = 1, 2, \ldots, n$.

Assumption 1: Angular velocity ω_i of robot $i(i \in \{0, \ldots, n\})$ is bounded, i.e. $|\omega_i| \leq K_w$, where K_w is a positive constant.

Introduce a transformation [23] as follows

$$q_{i1} = \theta_i$$
$$q_{i2} = (x_i - z_{ix}) \sin \theta_i - (y_i - z_{iy}) \cos \theta_i$$
$$q_{i3} = (x_i - z_{ix}) \cos \theta_i + (y_i - z_{iy}) \sin \theta_i \tag{2}$$
$$\bar{u}_{i1} = \omega_i$$
$$\bar{u}_{i2} = v_i - \bar{u}_{i1} q_{i2}$$

where q_{ik}, $i \in \{0, 1, \ldots, n\}$ and $k \in \{1, 2, 3\}$, is the kth state of the ith robot, and $\bar{u}_{ip}$ is the pth control input of ith robot for $p \in \{1, 2\}$. $z_{ix} = |x_i - x_0|$ and $z_{iy} = |y_i - y_0|$ are referenced distances between follower i and the leader, z_{0x} and z_{0y} are set to be 0. The dynamic system (2) is converted to

$$\dot{q}_{i1} = \bar{u}_{i1}$$
$$\dot{q}_{i2} = \bar{u}_{i1} q_{i3} \tag{3}$$
$$\dot{q}_{i3} = \bar{u}_{i2}$$

In practice, the actuators of robots are inevitable to have faults. The loss of effectiveness fault is considered as

$$\bar{u}_{ip}^f = (1 - \rho_{ip})\bar{u}_{ip} \tag{4}$$

where ρ_{ip} is the actuator fault factor for $i \in \{1,2,\ldots,n\}$, satisfying $1 > \bar{\rho} \geq \rho_{ip} \geq \underline{\rho} > 0$, where $\bar{\rho}$ and $\underline{\rho}$ denote the upper and lower bounds of ρ_{ip}, respectively. The dynamic system (3) can be written as

$$\dot{q}_{i1} = \bar{u}_{i1}^f = (1 - \rho_{i1})\bar{u}_{i1}$$
$$\dot{q}_{i2} = \bar{u}_{i2}^f q_{i3} = (1 - \rho_{i1})\bar{u}_{i1}q_{i3} \tag{5}$$
$$\dot{q}_{i3} = \bar{u}_{i2}^f = (1 - \rho_{i2})\bar{u}_{i2}$$

3   Distributed Fault-Tolerant Consensus Protocol

The robot i possesses the relative state information between itself and its neighbors. The consensus error of robot i is defined as

$$e_{ik} = \sum_{j \in N_i} a_{ij}(q_{ik} - q_{jk}) + b_i \tilde{q}_{ik} \tag{6}$$

with

$$\tilde{q}_{ik} = q_{ik} - q_{0k} \tag{7}$$

where $k \in \{1, 2, 3\}$.

The compact form of (6) is shown as

$$e_1 = \mathcal{M}\tilde{q}_1 \tag{8}$$
$$e_2 = \mathcal{M}\tilde{q}_2 \tag{9}$$
$$e_3 = \mathcal{M}\tilde{q}_3 \tag{10}$$

where $e_1 = [e_{11},\ldots,e_{n1}]^T$, $e_2 = [e_{12},\ldots,e_{n2}]^T$, $e_3 = [e_{13},\ldots,e_{n3}]^T$, $\tilde{q}_1 = [\tilde{q}_{11},\ldots,\tilde{q}_{n1}]^T$, $\tilde{q}_2 = [\tilde{q}_{12},\ldots,\tilde{q}_{n2}]^T$, and $\tilde{q}_3 = [\tilde{q}_{13},\ldots,\tilde{q}_{n3}]^T$.

In order to achieve a consensus formation, a distributed fault-tolerant consensus protocol is proposed as follows

$$\bar{u}_{ip} = \frac{u_{ip}}{1 - \hat{\rho}_{ip}} \tag{11}$$

where $\hat{\rho}_{ip}$ is the estimation of the actuator-fault factor, and u_{ip} ($p \in \{1,2\}$) is the control input. It is proposed as

$$u_{i1} = \frac{1}{l_1 \sum_{j \in N_i} a_{ij} + b_i} [(-k_1) \operatorname{sig}(e_{i1}) \operatorname{sign}(l_1) + b_i u_{01}$$

$$+ l_1 \sum_{j \in N_i} a_{ij} u_{j1} - k_4 u_{i1}^* \operatorname{sign}(e_{i1} u_{i1}^*)] \tag{12}$$

$$u_{i2} = \frac{1}{l_2 \sum\limits_{j \in N_i} a_{ij} + b_i}[(-k_3)\operatorname{sig}(e_{i3})\operatorname{sign}(l_2) + b_i u_{02} + l_2 \sum\limits_{j \in N_i} a_{ij}u_{j2}$$

$$- k_2 \operatorname{sign}(e_{i3})|\bar{e}_{i2}|\operatorname{sign}(l_2)] \tag{13}$$

with

$$u_{i1}^* = \frac{1}{\sum\limits_{j \in N_i} a_{ij} + b_i}\{(\frac{1-\rho}{1-\bar{\rho}})u_{i2}[\sum\limits_{j \in N_i} a_{ij}(\bar{e}_{i2} - \bar{e}_{j2}) + b_i \bar{e}_{i2}] + \sum\limits_{j \in N_i} a_{ij}u_{j1}^*\} \tag{14}$$

where k_1, k_2, k_3 are positive constants, and $k_2 > K_w$. l_1, l_2, k_4 are adjustable parameters. $\bar{e}_{i2}$ is the relative consensus error whose vector form is defined as

$$\bar{e}_2 = e_2 - \mathcal{M}\operatorname{diag}(q_3)\tilde{q}_1 \tag{15}$$

where $q_3 = [q_{13}, \ldots, q_{n3}]^T$ and $\bar{e}_2 = [\bar{e}_{12}, \ldots, \bar{e}_{n2}]^T$.

Note that (14) can be written in a compact form as

$$u_1^* = (\mathcal{M}^T)^{-1}\operatorname{diag}(\frac{1-\rho}{1-\bar{\rho}})\operatorname{diag}(u_2)\mathcal{M}^T\bar{e}_2 \tag{16}$$

According to (16), the compact form of (12)–(13) is calculated by

$$u_1 = \frac{1}{l_1}\mathcal{M}^{-1}[(-k_1)\operatorname{sig}(e_1)\operatorname{sign}(l_1) + \mathcal{B}\mathbf{1}_n u_{01}$$

$$- k_4(\mathcal{M}^T)^{-1}\operatorname{diag}(\frac{1-\rho}{1-\bar{\rho}})\operatorname{diag}(u_2)\mathcal{M}^T\bar{e}_2 \tag{17}$$

$$\operatorname{sign}(e_1^T(\mathcal{M}^T)^{-1}\operatorname{diag}(\frac{1-\rho}{1-\bar{\rho}})\operatorname{diag}(u_2)\mathcal{M}^T\bar{e}_2)]$$

$$u_2 = \frac{1}{l_2}\mathcal{M}^{-1}[(-k_3)\operatorname{sig}(e_3)\operatorname{sign}(l_2) + \mathcal{B}\mathbf{1}_n u_{02}$$

$$- k_2 \operatorname{diag}(\operatorname{sign}(e_3))|\bar{e}_2|\operatorname{sign}(l_2)] \tag{18}$$

where $u_1 = [u_{11}, \ldots, u_{n1}]^T$ and $u_2 = [u_{12}, \ldots, u_{n2}]^T$.

To obtain the estimation of fault factors, $\hat{\rho}_{fip}$ is regarded as the low-pass filter of $\hat{\rho}_{ip}$, which can effectively reduce the possible high-frequency disturbance. An adaptive fault-factor estimation algorithm is proposed as follows

$$\dot{\hat{\rho}}_{ip} = \operatorname{Proj}\{H_{ip}\} = \begin{cases} 0 & \text{if } \hat{\rho}_{ip} = \underline{\rho}_{ip} \text{ and } H_{ip} \leq 0 \\ & \text{or } \hat{\rho}_{ip} = \bar{\rho}_{ip} \text{ and } H_{ip} \geq 0 \\ H_{ip} & \text{otherwise} \end{cases} \tag{19}$$

$$\dot{\hat{\rho}}_{fip} = \operatorname{Proj}\{H_{fip}\} = \begin{cases} 0 & \text{if } \hat{\rho}_{fip} = \underline{\rho}_{ip} \text{ and } H_{fip} \leq 0 \\ & \text{or } \hat{\rho}_{fip} = \bar{\rho}_{ip} \text{ and } H_{fip} \geq 0 \\ H_{fip} & \text{otherwise} \end{cases} \tag{20}$$

with

$$H_{ip} = -\eta_{ip}[\xi_i (\hat{\rho}_{ip} - \hat{\rho}_{fip})]$$
$$H_{fip} = \eta_{fip} (\hat{\rho}_{ip} - \hat{\rho}_{fip}).$$

(21)

where Proj{.} is the projection operator, restricting both $\hat{\rho}_{ip}$ and $\hat{\rho}_{fip}$ to the set $[\underline{\rho}, \bar{\rho}]$. $\eta_{ip} > 0$ and $\eta_{fip} > 0$ are adaptive gains and $\xi_i > 0$ is the modified gain.

Based on the estimation of fault factors, the compact form of (11) is

$$\bar{u}_1 = \text{diag}(\lambda_1')^{-1} u_1$$

(22)

$$\bar{u}_2 = \text{diag}(\lambda_2')^{-1} u_2$$

(23)

where $\bar{u}_1 = [\bar{u}_{11}, \ldots, \bar{u}_{n1}]^T$, $\bar{u}_2 = [\bar{u}_{12}, \ldots, \bar{u}_{n2}]^T$, $\lambda_1' = [1 - \hat{\rho}_{11}, \ldots, 1 - \hat{\rho}_{n1}]^T$ and $\lambda_2' = [1 - \hat{\rho}_{12}, \ldots, 1 - \hat{\rho}_{n2}]^T$.

Combining (3), (5) and (7), one obtains that

$$\dot{\tilde{q}}_{i1} = \lambda_{i1} \bar{u}_{i1} - u_{01}$$

(24)

$$\dot{\tilde{q}}_{i2} = \lambda_{i1} \bar{u}_{i1} q_{i3} - u_{01} q_{03}$$

(25)

$$\dot{\tilde{q}}_{i3} = \lambda_{i2} \bar{u}_{i2} - u_{02}$$

(26)

where $\lambda_{i1} = 1 - \rho_{i1}$ and $\lambda_{i2} = 1 - \rho_{i2}$.

According to (6)–(7) and (24), we can get

$$\dot{e}_{i1} = \sum_{j \in N_i} a_{ij} (\dot{\tilde{q}}_{ik} - \dot{\tilde{q}}_{jk}) + b_i \dot{\tilde{q}}_{ik}$$

$$= \sum_{j \in N_i} a_{ij} \left(\frac{\lambda_{i1}}{\lambda_{i1}'} u_{i1} - \frac{\lambda_{j1}}{\lambda_{j1}'} u_{j1} \right) + b_i \left(\frac{\lambda_{i1}}{\lambda_{i1}'} u_{i1} - u_{01} \right)$$

$$= \left(\sum_{j \in N_i} a_{ij} + b_i \right) \frac{\lambda_{i1}}{\lambda_{i1}'} u_{i1} - \sum_{j \in N_i} a_{ij} \frac{\lambda_{j1}}{\lambda_{j1}'} u_{j1} - b_i u_{01}$$

$$= \left(\sum_{j \in N_i} a_{ij} + b_i \right) \frac{\lambda_{i1}}{\lambda_{i1}'} \frac{1}{l_1 \sum\limits_{j \in N_i} a_{ij} + b_i} \left[b_i u_{01} - k_1 \, \text{sig} \, (e_{i1}) \, \text{sign}(l_1) + l_1 \sum_{j \in N_i} a_{ij} u_{j1} \right.$$

$$\left. - k_4 u_{i1}^* \, \text{sign}(e_{i1} u_{i1}^*) \right] - \sum_{j \in N_i} a_{ij} \frac{\lambda_{j1}}{\lambda_{j1}'} u_{j1} + b_i u_{01}$$

$$= \frac{1}{l_1} \frac{\lambda_{i1}}{\lambda_{i1}'} [(-k_1) \, \text{sig} \, (e_{i1}) \, \text{sign}(l_1) - b_i u_{01}$$

$$+ l_1 \sum_{j \in N_i} a_{ij} u_{j1} - k_4 u_{i1}^* \, \text{sign}(e_{i1} u_{i1}^*)] - \sum_{j \in N_i} a_{ij} \frac{\lambda_{j1}}{\lambda_{j1}'} u_{j1} + b_i u_{01}$$

$$= \frac{1}{l_1} \frac{\lambda_{i1}}{\lambda_{i1}'} [(-k_1) \, \text{sig} \, (e_{i1}) \, \text{sign}(l_1) - k_4 u_{i1}^* \, \text{sign}(e_{i1} u_{i1}^*) + b_i u_{01}] - b_i u_{01}$$

(27)

Similarly, one can get

$$\dot{e}_{i3} = \frac{1}{l_2} \frac{\lambda_{i2}}{\lambda_{i2}'} [(-k_3) \, \text{sig} \, (e_{i3}) \, \text{sign}(l_2)$$

$$- k_2 \, \text{sign} \, (e_{i3}) \, |\bar{e}_{i2}| \, \text{sign}(l_2) + b_i u_{02}] - b_i u_{02}$$

(28)

A compact form of (24)–(26) can be written as

$$\dot{\tilde{q}}_1 = \mathrm{diag}(\lambda_1)\bar{u}_1 - \mathbf{1}_n u_{01} \tag{29}$$

$$\dot{\tilde{q}}_2 = u_{01}\tilde{q}_3 + \mathrm{diag}(q_3)[\mathrm{diag}(\lambda_1)\bar{u}_1 - \mathbf{1}_n u_{01}] \tag{30}$$

$$\dot{\tilde{q}}_3 = \mathrm{diag}(\lambda_2)\bar{u}_2 - \mathbf{1}_n u_{02} \tag{31}$$

where $\lambda_1 = [\lambda_{11},\ldots,\lambda_{n1}]^T$ and $\lambda_2 = [\lambda_{12},\ldots,\lambda_{n2}]^T$.

According to (9), (16)–(18) and (27)–(31), one obtains that

$$\dot{e}_1 = \frac{1}{l_1}\,\mathrm{diag}(\frac{\lambda_{i1}}{\lambda'_{i1}})[(-k_1)\,\mathrm{sig}(e_1)\,\mathrm{sign}(l_1) - k_4(\mathcal{M}^T)^{-1}\,\mathrm{diag}(\frac{1-\rho}{1-\bar{\rho}})\,\mathrm{diag}(u_2)\mathcal{M}^T\bar{e}_2$$

$$\mathrm{sign}(e_1^T(\mathcal{M}^T)^{-1}\,\mathrm{diag}(\frac{1-\rho}{1-\bar{\rho}})\,\mathrm{diag}(u_2)\mathcal{M}^T\bar{e}_2) + \mathcal{B}\mathbf{1}_n u_{01}] - \mathcal{B}\mathbf{1}_n u_{01} \tag{32}$$

$$\dot{e}_2 = \mathcal{M}\dot{\tilde{q}}_2$$
$$= u_{01}e_3 + \mathcal{M}\,\mathrm{diag}(q_3)[\mathrm{diag}(\lambda_1)\bar{u}_1 - \mathbf{1}_n u_{01}] \tag{33}$$

$$\dot{e}_3 = \frac{1}{l_2}\,\mathrm{diag}(\frac{\lambda_{i2}}{\lambda'_{i2}})[(-k_3)\,\mathrm{sig}(e_3)\,\mathrm{sign}(l_2)$$
$$- k_2\,\mathrm{sign}(e_3)|\bar{e}_2|\,\mathrm{sign}(l_2) + \mathcal{B}\mathbf{1}_n u_{02}] - \mathcal{B}\mathbf{1}_n u_{02} \tag{34}$$

$$\dot{\bar{e}}_2 = \dot{e}_2 - \mathcal{M}\,\mathrm{diag}(q_3)\dot{\tilde{q}}_1 - \mathcal{M}\,\mathrm{diag}(\dot{q}_3)\tilde{q}_1$$
$$= u_{01}e_3 - \mathcal{M}\,\mathrm{diag}(\lambda_2)\,\mathrm{diag}(\bar{u}_2)\tilde{q}_1 \tag{35}$$

Theorem 1. *The fault-tolerant protocol (11)–(14) with the fault parameter adaptive law (19)–(21) guarantee the leader-follower consensus tracking of multiple robots (1), i.e., $\lim\limits_{t\to\infty} q_{ik} = q_{0k}$, where $i = 1,2,\ldots,n$ and $k = 1,2,3$, if the following condition is satisfied*

$$\begin{cases} l_1 < 0 \ or \ l_1 > \frac{1-\rho}{1-\bar{\rho}} & if \ u_{01} \geq 0 \\ 0 < l_1 < \frac{1-\bar{\rho}}{1-\rho} & if \ u_{01} \leq 0 \\ -\frac{1-\bar{\rho}}{1-\rho} \leq l_2 < 0 \ or \ l_2 = \frac{1-\bar{\rho}}{1-\rho} & if \ u_{02} \geq 0 \\ 0 < l_2 \leq \frac{1-\bar{\rho}}{1-\rho} & if \ u_{02} \leq 0 \\ k_4 \geq \frac{l_1(1-\rho)}{1-\bar{\rho}} & if \ l_1 > 0 \\ k_4 \leq \frac{l_1(1-\rho)}{1-\bar{\rho}} & if \ l_1 < 0 \end{cases}$$

meanwhile, $k_2 > K_w$, and $\mathcal{G}_n$ owns a directed spanning tree.

Proof. The Lyapunov function is chosen as follows

$$V = \frac{1}{2}\left(e_1^T e_1 + \bar{e}_2^T \bar{e}_2 + e_3^T e_3\right) \tag{36}$$

Then the time derivative of the Lyapunov function is calculated as

$$\dot{V} = \left(e_1^T \dot{e}_1 + \bar{e}_2^T \dot{\bar{e}}_2 + e_3^T \dot{e}_3\right)$$

$$= e_1^T \left[\frac{1}{l_1} \operatorname{diag}\left(\frac{\lambda_{i1}}{\lambda'_{i1}}\right)\left[(-k_1)\operatorname{sig}(e_1)\operatorname{sign}(l_1) - k_4(\mathcal{M}^T)^{-1}\operatorname{diag}\left(\frac{1-\rho}{1-\bar{\rho}}\right)\operatorname{diag}(u_2)\right].$$

$$\mathcal{M}^T \bar{e}_2 \operatorname{sign}(e_1^T(\mathcal{M}^T)^{-1}\operatorname{diag}\left(\frac{1-\rho}{1-\bar{\rho}}\right)\operatorname{diag}(u_2)\mathcal{M}^T \bar{e}_2) + \mathcal{B}1_n u_{01}] - \mathcal{B}1_n u_{01}]$$

$$+ e_3^T \left[\frac{1}{l_2}\operatorname{diag}\left(\frac{\lambda_{i2}}{\lambda'_{i2}}\right)\left[(-k_3)\operatorname{sig}(e_3)\operatorname{sign}(l_2) - k_2\operatorname{sign}(e_3)|\bar{e}_2|\operatorname{sign}(l_2)\right.$$

$$+ \mathcal{B}1_n u_{02}] - \mathcal{B}1_n u_{02}] + \bar{e}_2^T\left[u_{01}e_3 - \mathcal{M}\operatorname{diag}\left(\frac{\lambda_{i2}}{\lambda'_{i2}}\right)\operatorname{diag}(u_2)\tilde{q}_1\right] \tag{37}$$

It yields to

$$\dot{V} = e_1^T\left[\frac{1}{l_1}\operatorname{diag}\left(\frac{\lambda_{i1}}{\lambda'_{i1}}\right)\mathcal{B}1_n u_{01} - \mathcal{B}1_n u_{01}\right]$$

$$+ \left[-e_1^T \frac{k_4}{l_1}(\mathcal{M}^T)^{-1}\operatorname{diag}\left(\frac{1-\rho}{1-\bar{\rho}}\right)\operatorname{diag}(u_2)\mathcal{M}^T \bar{e}_2 \cdot \operatorname{sign}(e_1^T(\mathcal{M}^T)^{-1}\right.$$

$$\cdot \operatorname{diag}\left(\frac{1-\rho}{1-\bar{\rho}}\right)\operatorname{diag}(u_2)\mathcal{M}^T \bar{e}_2) - \bar{e}_2^T \mathcal{M}\operatorname{diag}\left(\frac{\lambda_{i2}}{\lambda'_{i2}}\right)\operatorname{diag}(u_2)\tilde{q}_1]$$

$$+ \left[\bar{e}_2^T u_{01}e_3 - e_3^T \frac{k_2}{|l_2|}\operatorname{sign}(e_3)|\bar{e}_2|\right]$$

$$- e_1^T \frac{k_1}{|l_1|}\operatorname{diag}\left(\frac{\lambda_{i1}}{\lambda'_{i1}}\right)\operatorname{sig}(e_1) - e_3^T \frac{k_3}{|l_2|}\operatorname{diag}\left(\frac{\lambda_{i2}}{\lambda'_{i2}}\right)\operatorname{sig}(e_3)$$

$$+ e_3^T\left[\frac{1}{l_2}\operatorname{diag}\left(\frac{\lambda_{i2}}{\lambda'_{i2}}\right)\mathcal{B}1_n u_{02} - \mathcal{B}1_n u_{02}\right] \tag{38}$$

According to the conditions in Theorem 1, one can obtain that the first term and the last term of (38) are both non-positive, where u_{01} and u_{02} are known inputs of leader.

For the second term of (38), one has

$$- e_1^T\operatorname{diag}\left(\frac{\lambda_{i1}}{\lambda'_{i1}}\right)\frac{k_4}{l_1}\left(\mathcal{M}^T\right)^{-1}\operatorname{diag}\left(\frac{1-\rho}{1-\bar{\rho}}\right)\operatorname{diag}(u_2)\mathcal{M}^T \bar{e}_2$$

$$\operatorname{sign}(e_1^T\left(\mathcal{M}^T\right)^{-1}\operatorname{diag}\left(\frac{1-\rho}{1-\bar{\rho}}\right)\operatorname{diag}(u_2)\mathcal{M}^T \bar{e}_2)$$

$$\leq - \frac{k_4}{l_1}\frac{1-\bar{\rho}}{1-\rho}e_1^T\left(\mathcal{M}^T\right)^{-1}\operatorname{diag}\left(\frac{1-\rho}{1-\bar{\rho}}\right)\operatorname{diag}(u_2)\mathcal{M}^T \bar{e}_2$$

$$\operatorname{sign}(e_1^T\left(\mathcal{M}^T\right)^{-1}\operatorname{diag}\left(\frac{1-\rho}{1-\bar{\rho}}\right)\operatorname{diag}(u_2)\mathcal{M}^T \bar{e}_2)$$

$$\leq - e_1^T\left(\mathcal{M}^T\right)^{-1}\operatorname{diag}\left(\frac{1-\rho}{1-\bar{\rho}}\right)\operatorname{diag}(u_2)\mathcal{M}^T \bar{e}_2$$

$$\operatorname{sign}(e_1^T\left(\mathcal{M}^T\right)^{-1}\operatorname{diag}\left(\frac{1-\rho}{1-\bar{\rho}}\right)\operatorname{diag}(u_2)\mathcal{M}^T \bar{e}_2) \tag{39}$$

what we can learn is

$$-e_1^T \left(\mathcal{M}^T\right)^{-1} \mathrm{diag}(\frac{1-\rho}{1-\bar{\rho}}) \, \mathrm{diag}\,(u_2) \, \mathcal{M}^T \bar{e}_2$$

$$\mathrm{sign}(e_1^T \left(\mathcal{M}^T\right)^{-1} \mathrm{diag}(\frac{1-\rho}{1-\bar{\rho}}) \, \mathrm{diag}\,(u_2) \, \mathcal{M}^T \bar{e}_2)$$

$$-\bar{e}_2^T \mathcal{M} \, \mathrm{diag}(\frac{\lambda_{i2}}{\lambda'_{i2}}) \, \mathrm{diag}(u_2) \tilde{q}_1 \leq 0 \tag{40}$$

Therefore, the second term of (38) is non-positive. For the third term of (38), one has

$$-\frac{k_2}{|l_2|} |e_3|^T \mathrm{diag}(\frac{\lambda_{i2}}{\lambda'_{i2}})| \, |\bar{e}_2| \leq -\frac{k_2}{|l_2|} \frac{1-\bar{\rho}}{1-\rho} |e_3|^T |\bar{e}_2| \tag{41}$$

$$< -k_2 |e_3|^T |\bar{e}_2|$$

since $k_2 > K_w \geq |u_{01}|$, the third term of (38) is non-positive. Therefore, one obtains

$$\dot{V} \leq -e_1^T \frac{k_1}{|l_1|} \mathrm{diag}(\frac{\lambda_{i1}}{\lambda'_{i1}}) \, \mathrm{sig}(e_1) - e_3^T \frac{k_3}{|l_2|} \mathrm{diag}(\frac{\lambda_{i2}}{\lambda'_{i2}}) \, \mathrm{sig}(e_3)$$

$$= -\frac{k_1}{|l_1|} \sum_{i=1}^{n} (\frac{\lambda_{i1}}{\lambda'_{i1}}) e_{i1} \, \mathrm{sig}\,(e_{i1}) - \frac{k_3}{|l_2|} \sum_{i=1}^{n} (\frac{\lambda_{i2}}{\lambda'_{i2}}) e_{i3} \, \mathrm{sig}\,(e_{i3})$$

$$= -\frac{k_1}{|l_1|} \sum_{i=1}^{n} (\frac{\lambda_{i1}}{\lambda'_{i1}}) |e_{i1}|^2 - \frac{k_3}{|l_2|} \sum_{i=1}^{n} (\frac{\lambda_{i2}}{\lambda'_{i2}}) |e_{i3}|^2$$

$$< 0 \tag{42}$$

4   Controller Parameter Optimization by SSA

To obtain the optimal parameters of controllers quickly, the SSA is used for parameter tuning. The adjustable parameters l_1, l_2, k_4 don't participate in that process. Sparrows in SSA are divided into producers and scroungers, and there are alerters scattered around [21].

The number of sparrows is m, and the dimension of optimization variables is 3. The process is shown in Fig. 1, and the optimal parameters corresponding to the minimum value of the fitness function are obtained. Here the fitness function is as follows

$$F = \kappa_1 \sum_{1}^{n} \sqrt{\frac{\sum_{t=0}^{T_e} (v_i(t) - \bar{v}_i)^2}{T_e - 1}}$$

$$+ \kappa_2 \sum_{1}^{n} \sqrt{\frac{\sum_{t=0}^{T_e} (\omega_i(t) - \bar{\omega}_i)^2}{T_e - 1}}$$

$$+ \kappa_3 \sum_{1}^{n} \sqrt{\frac{\sum_{t=0}^{T_e} (\theta_i(t) - \bar{\theta}_i)^2}{T_e - 1}} \tag{43}$$

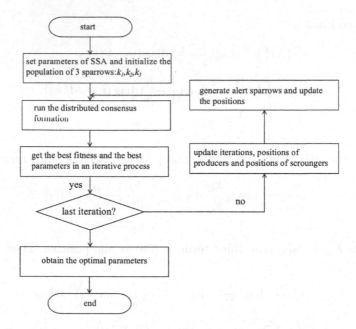

Fig. 1. The flowchart of SSA parameter optimization.

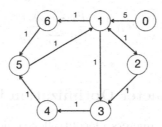

Fig. 2. The communication topology of robots.

Table 1. Initial conditions of robots

	x	y	θ
Leader	8.4	−17.5	0.52
Follower 1	11.3	−16.1	0.5
Follower 2	7.9	−16.3	0.37
Follower 3	6.9	−15.6	0.47
Follower 4	5.9	−16.2	0.58
Follower 5	6.2	−18.2	0.6
Follower 6	9.7	−17.3	0.51

where κ_1, κ_2 and κ_3 are the weighted factors, and $T_e > 1$ is the time of end for $i = 1, 2, \ldots, n$. $\bar{v}_i$, $\bar{\omega}_i$ and $\bar{\theta}_i$ are the arithmetic mean of linear velocity, angular velocity, and orientation for follower i, respectively.

5   Simulation

In this section, a simulation example is presented to demonstrate the effectiveness of the distributed fault-tolerant algorithm. The system containing 1 leader and 6 followers with a directed topology is considered in Fig. 2. The number of populations in SSA is 50, each sparrow corresponds to a set of parameters (k_1, k_2, k_3), iterations is 100, $\kappa_1 = 0.3$, $\kappa_2 = 0.3$, $\kappa_3 = 0.4$ and $T_e = 10$. The linear and angular velocities of the leader are $v_0 = 5$, $w_0 = -1$, respectively. The desired distances between each follower and the leader are chosen as $z_{1x} = 2$, $z_{2x} = 1$, $z_{3x} = -1$, $z_{4x} = -2$, $z_{5x} = -1$, $z_{6x} = 1$, $z_{1y} = 0$, $z_{2y} = \sqrt{3}$, $z_{3y} = \sqrt{3}$, $z_{4y} = 0$, $z_{5y} = -\sqrt{3}$, $z_{6y} = -\sqrt{3}$. Initial conditions are set in Table 1.

Let the second follower suffer from an actuator fault at 4s where $\rho_{21} = \rho_{22} = 0.75$, $\bar{\rho} = 0.8$ and $\rho = 0.1$. The adaptive gains in the fault estimation are chosen as $\eta_{\rho 1} = \eta_{\rho 2} = 0.33$, $\eta_{f 21} = \eta_{f 22} = 1.51$ and the modified gain $\xi_2 = 16.75$.

The parameters optimized by SSA are: $k_1 = 45.1$, $k_2 = 0.17$, $k_3 = 43.6$, while a set of parameters are chosen arbitrarily: $k_1 = 15.5$, $k_2 = 0.2$, $k_3 = 19$. Set $l_1 = 0.1$, $l_2 = -0.1$, and $k_4 = 0.5$. The errors of the orientation are shown in Figs. 3 and 4, respectively. It is observed that the error is smaller and the convergence is faster with the optimal parameters.

From Figs. 5 and 6, adaptive fault-tolerant algorithms can compensate for the effects of actuator faults quickly. The fault-tolerant trajectories of six robots

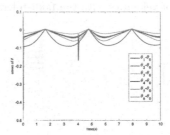

Fig. 3. Orientation errors between followers and leader: $k_1 = 15.5$, $k_2 = 0.2$, $k_3 = 19$, $k_4 = 0.5$.

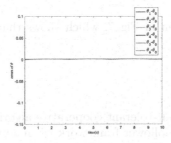

Fig. 4. Orientation errors between followers and leader: $k_1 = 45.1$, $k_2 = 0.17$, $k_3 = 43.6$, $k_4 = 0.5$.

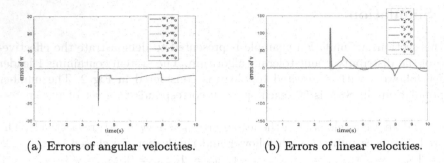

(a) Errors of angular velocities.   (b) Errors of linear velocities.

Fig. 5. Errors of velocities without fault-tolerant controller.

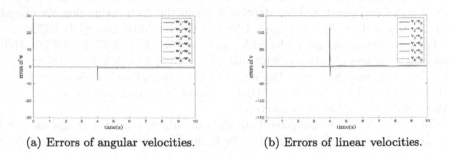

(a) Errors of angular velocities.   (b) Errors of linear velocities.

Fig. 6. Errors of velocities with the fault-tolerant controller.

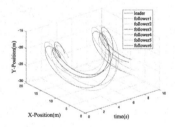

Fig. 7. The trajectories of robots.

and the leader can be seen in Fig. 7, which shows that the followers can track the trajectory of leader.

6   Conclusion

A distributed adaptive fault-tolerant cooperative algorithm for mobile robots is proposed based on leader-follower framework when actuator faults occur in one of the followers. SSA is used to obtain the optimal parameters. The effectiveness of the designed adaptive distributed fault-tolerant protocol is illustrated by a simulation experiment.

References

1. Chu, H., Cai, Y., Zhang, W.: Consensus tracking for multi-agent systems with directed graph via distributed adaptive protocol. Neurocomputing **50**, 8–13 (2015)
2. Meng, T., Lin, Z.: Leader-following almost output consensus for linear multi-agent systems with disturbance-affected unstable zero dynamics. Syst. Control Lett. **145**, 104787 (2020)
3. Alouache, A., Wu, Q.: Consensus based least squares estimation for single-integrator multi-agent systems with a time-varying reference state. J. Electron. Sci. Technol. **18**(2), 190–200 (2020)
4. Li, X., Tang, Y., Reza Karimi, H.: Consensus of multi-agent systems via fully distributed event-triggered control. Automatica **116**, 108898 (2020)
5. Ju, S., Wang, J., Dou, L.: Enclosing control for multiagent systems with a moving target of unknown bounded velocity. IEEE Trans. Cybern. **52**, 11561–11570 (2022). https://doi.org/10.1109/TCYB.2021.3072031
6. He, X., Geng, Z.: Consensus-based formation control for nonholonomic vehicles with parallel desired formations. Int. J. Control **94**(2), 507–520 (2021)
7. Maghenem, M., Loría, A., Nuño, E., Panteley, E.: Consensus-based formation control of networked nonholonomic vehicles with delayed communications. IEEE Trans. Autom. Control **66**(5), 2242–2249 (2021)
8. Liu, L., Yu, J., Ji, J., Miao, Z., Zhou, J.: Cooperative adaptive consensus tracking for multiple nonholonomic mobile robots. Int. J. Syst. Sci. **50**(8), 1556–1567 (2019)
9. Nuño, E., Loría, A., Hernández, T., Maghenem, M., Panteley, E.: Distributed consensus-formation of force-controlled nonholonomic robots with time-varying delays. Automatica **120**, 109114 (2020)
10. Zhang, X., Peng, Z., Yang, S., Wen, G., Rahmani, A.: Distributed fixed-time consensus-based formation tracking for multiple nonholonomic wheeled mobile robots under directed topology. Int. J. Control **94**(1), 248–257 (2019)
11. Ju, S., Wang, J., Dou, L.: MPC-based cooperative enclosing for nonholonomic mobile agents under input constraint and unknown disturbance. IEEE Trans. Cybern. (2022). https://doi.org/10.1109/TCYB.2022.3164713
12. Zhao, Z., Wang, J., Chen, Y., Ju, S.: Iterative learning-based formation control for multiple quadrotor unmanned aerial vehicles. Int. J. Adv. Robot. Syst. **17**(2), 1–12 (2020)
13. Wang, Z., Wu, Y., Liu, L., Zhang, H.: Adaptive fault-tolerant consensus protocols for multiagent systems with directed graphs. IEEE Trans. Cybern. **50**(1), 25–35 (2018)
14. Ye, D., Chen, M., Yang, H.: Distributed adaptive event-triggered fault-tolerant consensus of multiagent systems with general linear dynamics. IEEE Trans. Cybern. **49**(3), 757–767 (2017)
15. Nair, R., Karki, H., Shukla, A., Behera, L., Jamshidi, M.: Fault-tolerant formation control of nonholonomic robots using fast adaptive gain nonsingular terminal sliding mode control. IEEE Syst. J. **13**(1), 1006–1017 (2019)
16. Wang, J., Zhao, Z., Zheng, Y.: NFTSM-based fault tolerant control for quadrotor unmanned aerial Vehicle with finite-time convergence. In: 10th IFAC Symposium on Fault Detection, Supervision and Safety for Technical Processes SAFEPROCESS, pp. 441–446. Publisher, IFAC, Warsaw, Poland (2018)
17. Wang, Y., Jiang, B., Wu, Z., Xie, S., Peng, Y.: Adaptive sliding mode fault-tolerant fuzzy tracking control with application to unmanned marine vehicles. IEEE Trans. Syst. Man Cybern. Syst. **51**(11), 6691–6700 (2021)

18. Chang, Y., Wu, C., Lin, H.: Adaptive distributed fault-tolerant formation control for multi-robot systems under partial loss of actuator effectiveness. Int. J. Control Autom. Syst. **16**, 2114–2124 (2018)
19. Li, Q., et al.: An enhanced grey wolf optimization based feature selection wrapped kernel extreme learning machine for medical diagnosis. Comput. Math. Methods Med. **2017**, 9512741 (2017)
20. Rahmani, M., Komijani, H., Ghanbari, A., Ettefagh, M.: Optimal novel super-twisting PID sliding mode control of a MEMS gyroscope based on multi-objective bat algorithm. Microsyst. Technol. **24**(6), 2835–2846 (2018)
21. Xue, J., Shen, B.: A novel swarm intelligence optimization approach: sparrow search algorithm. Syst. Sci. Control Eng. Open Access J. **8**(1), 22–34 (2020)
22. Ren, W., Beard, R.: Consensus seeking in multiagent systems under dynamically changing interaction topologies. IEEE Trans. Autom. Control **50**(5), 655–661 (2005)
23. Murray, R., Sastry, S.: Nonholonomic motion planning: steering using sinusoids. IEEE Trans. Autom. Control **38**(5), 700–716 (1993)

Set-Membership Estimation for Nonlinear Parameter-Varying Systems

Hui Zhang and Fei Liu$^{(\boxtimes)}$

Key Laboratory of Advanced Control for Light Industry Processes, Ministry of
Education, Jiangnan University, Wuxi 214122, Jiangsu, China
`fliu@jiangnan.edu.cn`

Abstract. For discrete nonlinear parameter varying systems (NLPV),
the set-membership estimation problem is investigated. First, the characteristics of NLPV systems are managed by using polytopic decomposition of parameter varying matrices and reconstructing the Lipschitz
nonlinear condition. Then, a sufficient condition for the set-membership
estimation under unknown-but-bounded (UBB) noise is derived. Moreover, a semi-definite programming (SDP) problem and the related linear
matrix inequality (LMI) condition are formulated. The minimal feasible
ellipsoidal state set is obtained by solving this problem. Finally, a simulation of a road vehicle suspension is used to confirm the viability of the
proposed method.

Keywords: Set-membership estimation · Nonlinear parameter varying
systems · Lipschitz nonlinearity

1 Introduction

The safety of industrial process has received more and more attention. When
evaluating the industrial process's safety and dependability, the system's state
is crucial. While the data collected by the sensor does not reveal the state of the
system clearly. As a result, the state estimation issue [1] requires us to determine the estimated value closely approaching the actual value of the state in
accordance with the system model, sensor measurement, and noise assumptions.
Depending on different noise assumptions, the problem of state estimation is also
different. When the noise is based on probability assumption, it is a bayesian
estimation problem. It is a issue of set-membership estimation when the noise
is on the premise that it is unknown-but-bounded (UBB) [2]. Within the probabilistic framework, even if the probability of large noise is very low, it can not be
guaranteed that it will not occur. The set-membership estimation stipulates that
the noise belongs to a certain set, and the estimated feasible state set includes
all possible state variables, which meets the safety needs of industrial processes.
The most popular set descriptions for set-membership estimation are intervals
[3], ellipsoids [4], and zonotopes [5]. Multi-agent systems [6], information physics
systems [7], biochemical processes [8], and other systems are examples of current
applications for set-membership estimation. Although the real models are often

L. Zhang et al. (Eds.): CINT 2022, CCIS 1714, pp. 235–244, 2022.
https://doi.org/10.1007/978-981-19-8915-5_20

nonlinear, the majority of set-membership estimation methods are intended for linear systems. Consequently, designing set-membership estimation methods for nonlinear systems has always been challenging [9].

Because the analysis of the nonlinear system is very complex, researchers hope to use mature linear system theories to deal with nonlinear systems. So the linear parameter varying (LPV) system is developed. The LPV system is a special kind of nonlinear system [10], which has the form of the linear system, and the nonlinear term changes with measurable parameters. Because a great number of nonlinear components may be integrated in varying parameters in order to turn a nonlinear system into a comparable quasi-LPV version, it has been shown in recent decades that the framework of LPV systems is ideal for addressing nonlinear control problems. As a result, the LPV framework enables the application of linear technology to the system identification, controller design, and state estimation of nonlinear systems. In many instances, it may be preferable to keep the nonlinear structure rather than the linear structure [11], which minimizes conservatism and is more faithful to the original model. Recent research has addressed design and analysis tools for Lipschitz or quadratic nonlinearity [12] constrained parameter-varying systems. Alternatively, in the controller, the nonlinear function may be preserved in parameter varying terms via a linear fractional transform or nonlinear interpolation. Currently, state estimation [13], model predictive control [14], singular systems [15], quadratic nonlinear constrained systems [16], and sliding mode control [17] are the key topics of study on nonlinear parameter varying (NLPV) systems.

Motivated by the above considerations, in the present work, a set-membership estimation method for a class of NLPV system with UBB noise is proposed. The characteristics of NLPV systems are managed by using polytopic decomposition of parameter varying matrix and reconstructing the Lipschitz nonlinear condition. A semi-definite programming (SDP) problem with a constraint of linear matrix inequality (LMI) is calculated recursively to obtain the minimal ellipsoidal feasible state set.

The remaining sections of the paper are structured as follows. In Sect. 2, the set-membership estimation design issue for NLPV systems is defined. Section 3 develops a brand-new set-membership estimation method. To demonstrate the viability of the proposed approach, Sect. 4 includes a simulation of the suspension system of a road vehicle. In Sect. 5, conclusions are made.

2   Problem Formulation

Consider the following discrete NLPV system

$$x_{k+1} = Ax_k + F(\rho_k)\Phi(x_k) + Bw_k \tag{1}$$

$$y_k = Cx_k + Dv_k \tag{2}$$

where $x_k \in R^{n_x}$, $u_k \in R^{n_u}$, $y_k \in R^{n_y}$ are the state variable, control input and measurement output of the system at time k. $\Phi(x_k)$ is a nonlinear term regarding to state variable x_k. w_k and v_k are process noise and measurement noise. The real matrices A, B, C, and D are with known dimensions. The parameter varying matrix $F(\rho_k)$ meets the polytopic structure, which is obtained by weighting the vertex matrix F_i ,

$$F(\rho_k) = \sum_{i=1}^{2^L} \xi(\rho_k)F_i, \tag{3}$$

$$\sum_{i=1}^{2^L} \xi(\rho_k) = 1, \xi(\rho_k) \geq 0, \tag{4}$$

where weighting parameter ξ is related to scheduling variable $\rho_k \in R^L$, which is usually known or measurable.

The nonlinear term $\Phi(x_k)$ satisfies the Lipschitz condition

$$\|\Phi(x_k) - \Phi(\hat{x}_k)\| \leq \|\Gamma(x_k - \hat{x}_k)\|, \tag{5}$$

where Γ is a known constant matrix.

The process noise w_k and measurement noise v_k are compatible with the UBB condition

$$\mathcal{E}(\cdot, Q_k) : w_k^T Q_k^{-1} w_k \leq 1, \tag{6}$$

$$\mathcal{E}(\cdot, R_k) : v_k^T R_k^{-1} v_k \leq 1, \tag{7}$$

where both ellipsoid centers are the coordinate origin, and the shape matrix are Q_k and R_k.

An ellipsoidal feasible state set contains the initial state x_0

$$\mathcal{E}(\hat{x}_0, P_0) : (x_0 - \hat{x}_0)^T P_0^{-1}(x_0 - \hat{x}_0) \leq 1, \tag{8}$$

where $\hat{x}_0$ is an estimate of x_0, which is presumed to be given, and $P_0 = P_0^T > 0$ is a matrix that is already known.

Here a set-membership estimator is applied as

$$\hat{x}_{k+1} = A\hat{x}_k + F(\rho_k)\Phi(\hat{x}_k) + L(\rho_k)(y_k - C\hat{x}_k), \tag{9}$$

where estimator parameter $L(\rho_k)$ is to be designed.

Consequently, the primary challenge of this paper is to develop an appropriate set-membership estimator for NLPV systems, recursively calculate the minimal ellipsoidal feasible state set

$$\mathcal{E}(\hat{x}_{k+1}, P_{k+1}) : (x_{k+1} - \hat{x}_{k+1})^T P_{k+1}^{-1}(x_{k+1} - \hat{x}_{k+1}) \leq 1, \tag{10}$$

for the state x_{k+1}, in light of the current measurement information y_k, the process noise set $w_k \in \mathcal{E}(\cdot, Q_k)$, and the measurement noise set $v_k \in \mathcal{E}(\cdot, R_k)$.

3 Set-Membership Estimation for NLPV Systems

This section introduces the design method of set-membership estimation for NLPV systems.

Lemma 1. *If $x_k \in \mathcal{E}(\hat{x}_k, P_k)$, then x_k can be treated as a affine function of a hyperball z with a displacement $\hat{x}_k$.*

$$x_k = \hat{x}_k + E_k z, \tag{11}$$

where $E_k E_k^T = P_k$, and $\|z\| \le 1$.

Theorem 1. *For the system (1-2), if there exist matrices $L(\rho_k)$ and non-negative scalars τ_1, τ_2, τ_3 and τ_4 such that*

$$\sum_{i=1}^{2^L} \begin{bmatrix} P_{k+1} & \Pi_i \\ \Pi_i^T & -\Theta(\tau_1, \tau_2, \tau_3, \tau_4) \end{bmatrix} \le 0 \tag{12}$$

where Π_i is given in (18), $\theta(\tau_1, \tau_2, \tau_3, \tau_4)$ is given in (25), then the ellipsoidal feasible state set $\mathcal{E}(\hat{x}_{k+1}, P_{k+1})$ contains the state variable x_{k+1}.

Proof. By mathematical induction, if the provided ellipsoidal feasible state set $x_0 \in \mathcal{E}(\hat{x}_0, P_0)$ contains the true state variable x_0 initially. Assuming that the state variable x_k at time k still belongs to the ellipsoidal state feasible set $x_k \in \mathcal{E}(\hat{x}_k, P_k)$, the ellipsoidal state feasible set $\mathcal{E}(\hat{x}_{k+1}, P_{k+1})$ that contains the real state x_{k+1} should be identified at time k+1.

The estimation error can be obtained by making a difference between the system model (1–2) and the estimator (9) at time k+1, then

$$\begin{aligned} x_{k+1} - \hat{x}_{k+1} =& A x_k + F(\rho_k)\Phi(x_k) + B w_k - A\hat{x}_k - F(\rho_k)\Phi(\hat{x}_k) \\ & - L(\rho_k)(y_k - C\hat{x}_k) \\ =& (A - L(\rho_k)C)(x_k - \hat{x}_k) + F(\rho_k)(\Phi(x_k) - \Phi(\hat{x}_k)) \\ & + B w_k - L(\rho_k) D v_k. \end{aligned} \tag{13}$$

Using LEMMA 1, it is capable of writing (13) as

$$\begin{aligned} x_{k+1} - \hat{x}_{k+1} =& (A - L(\rho_k)C)E_k z + F(\rho_k)(\Phi(x_k) - \Phi(\hat{x}_k)) \\ & + B w_k - L(\rho_k) D v_k. \end{aligned} \tag{14}$$

Because $\Phi(x_k)$ meets the Lipschitz condition, then

$$\begin{aligned} (\Phi(x_k) - \Phi(\hat{x}_k))^T(\Phi(x_k) - \Phi(\hat{x}_k)) &\le (\Gamma(x_k - \hat{x}_k))^T(\Gamma(x_k - \hat{x}_k)) \\ &\le z^T(E_k^T \Gamma^T \Gamma E_k)z. \end{aligned} \tag{15}$$

Utilizing polytopic decomposition, (14) could be expressed as

$$x_{k+1} - \hat{x}_{k+1} = \sum_{i=1}^{2^L} \xi_i \Pi_i \eta, \tag{16}$$

where

$$\eta = \begin{bmatrix} 1 \\ z \\ \Phi(x_k) - \Phi(\hat{x}_k) \\ w_k \\ v_k \end{bmatrix}, \tag{17}$$

and

$$\Pi_i = \begin{bmatrix} 0 & (A - L_iC)E_k & F_i & B & -L_iD \end{bmatrix}. \tag{18}$$

Therefore, feasible state set $\mathcal{E}(\hat{x}_{k+1}, P_{k+1})$ may be expressed as

$$\eta^T[(\sum_{i=1}^{2^L} \xi_i \Pi_i)^T P_{k+1}^{-1} \sum_{i=1}^{2^L} \xi_i \Pi_i - diag\,\{1,0,0,0,0\}]\eta \le 0. \tag{19}$$

Use η to turn constraints $\|x\| \le 1$, $w_k^T Q_k^{-1} w_k \le 1$, $v_k^T R_k^{-1} v_k \le 1$, and restructured Lipschitz condition (15) into quadratic inequality constraints

$$\eta^T diag\,\{-1, I, 0, 0, 0\}\,\eta \le 0, \tag{20}$$

$$\eta^T diag\,\{0, -E_k^T \Gamma^T \Gamma E_k, I, 0, 0\}\,\eta \le 0, \tag{21}$$

$$\eta^T diag\,\{-1, 0, 0, Q_k^{-1}, 0\}\,\eta \le 0, \tag{22}$$

$$\eta^T diag\,\{-1, 0, 0, 0, R_k^{-1}\}\,\eta \le 0. \tag{23}$$

Using S-procedure to integrate inequality constraints, equation (19–23) can be written in a single inequation in the following form

$$\begin{aligned}
&\sum_{i=1}^{2^L} \xi_i \Pi_i^T P_{k+1}^{-1} \sum_{i=1}^{2^L} \xi_i \Pi_i - diag\{1,0,0,0,0\} - \tau_1 diag\{-1, I, 0, 0, 0\} \\
&- \tau_2 diag\{0, -E_k^T \Gamma^T \Gamma E_k, l, 0, 0\} - \tau_3 diag\{-1, 0, 0, Q_k^{-1}, 0\} \\
&- \tau_4 diag\{-1, 0, 0, 0, R_k^{-1}\} \le 0
\end{aligned} \tag{24}$$

Then the LMI (12) can be obtained by using Schur complement, where

$$\begin{aligned}
\theta(\tau_1, \tau_2, \tau_3, \tau_4) = &diag\{1 - \tau_1 - \tau_3 - \tau_4, \tau_1 I - \tau_2 E_k^T \Gamma^T \Gamma E_k, \tau_2 I, \\
&\tau_3 Q_k^{-1}, \tau_4 R_k^{-1}\}
\end{aligned} \tag{25}$$

After obtaining the sufficient condition for the ellipsoidal feasible state set $\mathcal{E}(\hat{x}_{k+1}, P_{k+1})$ containing real state variable x_{k+1}, the size of which also needs to be optimized. Usually, the volume of the set or the trace of the shape matrix is considered. Because volume optimization always leads to a narrow ellipsoidal set, it is more appropriate to minimized trace of P_{k+1}.

The optimization problem is described as

$$\begin{aligned}
&\min \quad tr(P_{k+1}). \\
&subject \quad to \quad (12)
\end{aligned} \tag{26}$$

Since the optimization objective is convex and the constraint condition is LMI, it is a typical SDP problem [18]. Hence, using the interior point approach, it may be resolved successfully.

Algorithm 1. Set-membership Estimation for NLPV Systems
step 1: Initialize the values of $\hat{x}_0$, P_0, Q_k, R_k, ρ_k; and set k = 0.
step 2: Calculate vertice matrix F_i, and weighting parameter ξ_i
step 3: Calculate the estimator parameter $L(\rho_k)$ and P_{k+1} by solving (26); and update $\hat{x}_{k+1}$ by (9).
step 4: Set $k = k + 1$. If $k = k_n$ (k_n is the last sampling step), then stop; else go to **step 2**.

4   Simulation

This section uses a road vehicle suspension system [19] as an illustration of the validity and efficacy of the suggested method. The schematic diagram of a 1/4 road vehicle suspension system is demonstrated in Fig. 1.

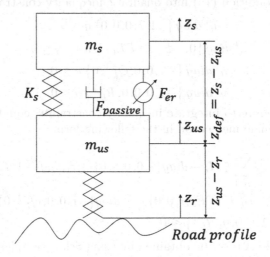

Fig. 1. 1/4 road vehicle suspension system.

The process dynamics takes the form as follows:

$$\dot{x} = \begin{bmatrix} 0 & 1 & 0 & -1 & 0 \\ -\frac{k_s+k_0}{m_s} & -\frac{c_0}{m_s} & 0 & \frac{c_0}{m_s} & -\frac{1}{m_s} \\ 0 & 0 & 0 & 1 & 0 \\ \frac{k_s+k_0}{m_s} & \frac{c_0}{m_s} & -\frac{k_t}{m_s} & -\frac{c_0}{m_{us}} & \frac{1}{m_s} \\ 0 & 0 & 0 & 0 & -\frac{1}{\tau} \end{bmatrix} x + \begin{bmatrix} 0 \\ 0 \\ 0 \\ 0 \\ -\frac{f_c}{\tau}\rho \end{bmatrix} tanh(\Gamma x) + \begin{bmatrix} 0 & 0 \\ 0 & 0 \\ -1 & 0 \\ 0 & 0 \\ 0 & 0 \end{bmatrix} w, \quad (27)$$

$$y = \begin{bmatrix} -\frac{k_s+k_0}{m_s} & -\frac{c_0}{m_s} & 0 & \frac{c_0}{m_s} & -\frac{1}{m_s} \\ \frac{k_s+k_0}{m_s} & \frac{c_0}{m_s} & -\frac{k_t}{m_s} & -\frac{c_0}{m_{us}} & \frac{1}{m_s} \end{bmatrix} x + \begin{bmatrix} 0.01 \\ 0.01 \end{bmatrix} v, \quad (28)$$

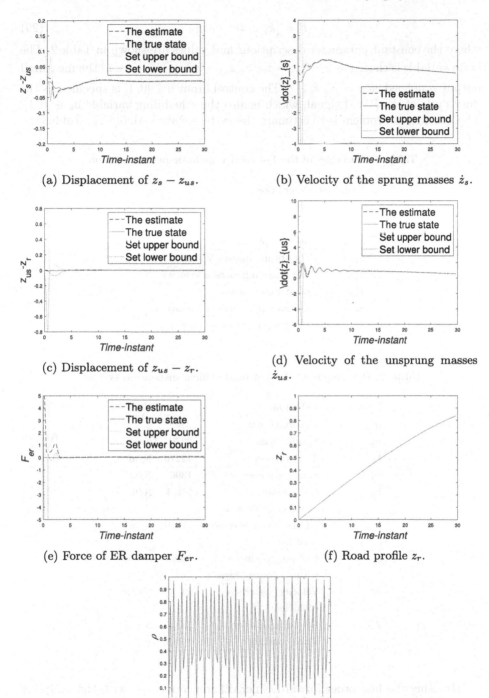

(a) Displacement of $z_s - z_{us}$.

(b) Velocity of the sprung masses $\dot{z}_s$.

(c) Displacement of $z_{us} - z_r$.

(d) Velocity of the unsprung masses $\dot{z}_{us}$.

(e) Force of ER damper F_{er}.

(f) Road profile z_r.

(g) Scheduling variable ρ_k.

Fig. 2. Simulation results

$$\Gamma = \begin{bmatrix} k_1 & c_1 & 0 & -c_1 & 0 \end{bmatrix} \tag{29}$$

where the constant parameter descriptions and values are shown in Table 2. The state variable is chosen as $x = \begin{bmatrix} z_s - z_{us} & \dot{z}_s & z_{us} - z_r & \dot{z}_{us} & F_{er} \end{bmatrix}^T$, and the measured output is defined as $y = \begin{bmatrix} \ddot{z}_s & \ddot{z}_{us} \end{bmatrix}^T$. The control input $u \in [0, 1]$ is specified as the duty cycle of the PWM signal, which is also the scheduling variable $\rho_k \in [0, 1]$. The considered problem is to estimate the system state variable x_k (Table 1).

Table 1. Variables of the 1/4 road vehicle suspension system

Variables	Description
z_s	The sprung masses displacement
z_{us}	The unsprung masses displacement
z_r	Road displacement input
$\dot{z}_s$	The sprung masses Velocity
$\dot{z}_{us}$	The unsprung masses Velocity
F_{er}	ER damper force
$\ddot{z}_s$	The sprung masses acceleration
$\ddot{z}_{us}$	The unsprung masses acceleration

Table 2. Parameters of the 1/4 road vehicle suspension system

Parameters	Definition	Value	Unit
m_{us}	Unsprung mass	250	g
m_s	Sprung mass	2270	g
k_t	Tire stiffness	12270	N/m
k_s	Spring stiffness	1396	N/m
k_0	Gas pressure Stiffness coefficient	170.4	N/m
k_1	Displacement hysteresis coefficient	218.16	N/m
c_0	Damping coefficient without control input	68.83	N·s/m
c_1	Velocity hysteresis coefficient	21	N·s/m
f_c	ER fluid yield force	28.07	N
τ	Time constant	0.043	s

By using the first-order forward Euler difference method with the sampling interval $T = 0.3$ s, and terminal time $T_n = 30$ s, the discrete dynamic of the road vehicle suspension system is written as

$$x_{k+1} = (I + TA)x_k + TF(\rho_k)\Phi(x_k) + TBw_k, \tag{30}$$

$$y_k = TCx_k + TDv_k. \tag{31}$$

The initial state $x_0 = \begin{bmatrix} 0\ 0\ 0\ 0\ 0 \end{bmatrix}^T$ belongs to the initial feasible state set $\mathcal{E}(\hat{x}_0, P_0)$, where $\hat{x}_0 = \begin{bmatrix} 0.015\ -0.15\ 0.0015\ -0.15\ 3 \end{bmatrix}^T$, and $P_0 = diag \begin{bmatrix} 0.02^2\ 0.2^2\ 0.002^2\ 0.2^2\ 9 \end{bmatrix}$. The shape matrix describing process and measurement noise are $Q_k = R_k = 1$. Because the scheduling variable $\rho \in [0,1]$, the vertex matrix $F_1 = \begin{bmatrix} 0\ 0\ 0\ 0\ 0 \end{bmatrix}^T$ with weighting parameter $\xi(\rho = 0) = 1 - \rho$, $F_2 = \begin{bmatrix} 0\ 0\ 0\ 0\ fc/\tau \end{bmatrix}^T$ with weighting parameter $\xi(\rho = 1) = \rho$.

According to Figs. 2a–e, the red solid line of true state variable x_k belongs to the feasiable state set $\mathcal{E}(\hat{x}_k, P_k)$, which provides a green dotted line of upper bound, a blue dotted line of lower bound, and a black dashed line of estimated state variable $\hat{x}_k$. Although the initial fluctuation is large, the algorithm converges rapidly after $3s$. It is assumed that the choice of model parameters or the selection of initial feasible state set $\mathcal{E}(\hat{x}_0, P_0)$ accounts for this fluctuation. Figure 2f shows the road profile z_r of this simulation is uphill. Figure 2g shows the change of scheduling variable ρ_k.

5   Conclusion

This work proposes a set-membership estimation method for NLPV systems. First, the polytopic structure is used to decompose the parameter varying matrix. Then Lipschitz nonlinear condition is used to construct quadratic constraints, and then all state and noise constraints are written as LMI. Finally, the ellipsoidal feasible state set is minimized by solving a SDP problem. The simulation analysis of the suspension system of a road vehicle testifies to the efficacy of the proposed method. The design of the set-membership estimation approach for highly nonlinear systems requires more research.

Acknowledgements. This work is supported by National Natural Science Foundation (NNSF) of China under Grant 61833007.

References

1. Simon, D.: Optimal State Estimation: Kalman, H Infinity, and Nonlinear Approaches. John wiley & sons, Hoboken (2006)
2. Schweppe, F.: Recursive state estimation: unknown but bounded errors and system inputs. IEEE Trans. Automat. Contr. **13**(1), 22–28 (1968)
3. Efimov, D., Perruquetti, W., Raïssi, T., Zolghadri, A.: Interval observers for time-varying discrete-time systems. IEEE Trans. Automat. Contr. **58**(12), 3218–3224 (2013)
4. Maksarov, D.G., Norton, J.P.: Computationally efficient algorithms for state estimation with ellipsoidal approximations. Int. J. Adapt. Control Signal Process. **16**(6), 411–434 (2002)
5. Alamo, T., Bravo, J.M., Camacho, E.F.: Guaranteed state estimation by zonotopes. Automatica **41**(6), 1035–1043 (2005)

6. Ge, X., Han, Q., Yang, F.: Event-based set-membership leader-following consensus of networked multi-agent systems subject to limited communication resources and unknown-but-bounded noise. IEEE Trans. Ind. Electron. **64**(6), 5045–5054 (2016)
7. Ding, D., Han, Q., Wang, Z., Ge, X.: A survey on model-based distributed control and filtering for industrial cyber-physical systems. IEEE Trans. Industr. Inform. **15**(5), 2483–2499 (2019)
8. Shen, X., Budman, H.: Set membership estimation with dynamic flux balance models. Processes **9**(10), 1762 (2021)
9. Wang, Z., Shen, X., Liu, H., Meng, F., Zhu, Y.: Dual set membership filter with minimizing nonlinear transformation of ellipsoid. IEEE Trans. Automat. Contr. **67**(5), 2405–2418 (2021)
10. Tóth, R.: Modeling and Identification of Linear Parameter-Varying Systems. Springer, Berlin (2010). https://doi.org/10.1007/978-3-642-13812-6
11. Sename, O., Rotondo, D.: Emerging approaches for nonlinear parameter varying systems. Int. J. Robust Nonlinear Control **31**(17), 8121–8123 (2021)
12. Németh, B., Gáspár, P.: Ensuring performance requirements for semiactive suspension with nonconventional control systems via robust linear parameter varying framework. Int. J. Robust Nonlinear Control. **31**(17), 8165–8182 (2021)
13. Pham, T.P., Sename, O., Dugard, L.: Real-time damper force estimation of vehicle electrorheological suspension: a nonlinear parameter varying approach. IFAC-PapersOnLine **52**(28), 94–99 (2019)
14. Menezes Morato, M., Elias Normey Rico, J., Sename, O.: An input-to-state stable model predictive control framework for Lipschitz nonlinear parameter varying systems. Int. J. Robust Nonlinear Control. **31**(17), 8239–8272 (2021)
15. Righi, I., Aouaouda, S., Chadli, M., Khelil, K.: Robust controllers design for constrained nonlinear parameter varying descriptor systems. Int. J. Robust Nonlinear Control **31**(17), 8295–8328 (2021)
16. Rotondo, D., Buciakowski, M., Witczak, M.: Simultaneous state and process fault estimation in linear parameter varying systems using robust quadratic parameter varying observers. Int. J. Robust Nonlinear Control **31**(17), 8390–8407 (2021)
17. Gómez-Peñate, S., R. López-Estrada, F., Valencia-Palomo, G., Rotondo, D., Guerrero-Sánchez, M.E.: Actuator and sensor fault estimation based on a proportional multiple-integral sliding mode observer for linear parameter varying systems with inexact scheduling parameters. Int. J. Robust Nonlinear Control. **31**(17), 8420–8441 (2021)
18. Boyd, S., Boyd, S.P., Vandenberghe, L.: Convex Optimization. Cambridge University Press, Los Angeles (2004)
19. Pham, T.P., Sename, O., Dugard, L.: A nonlinear parameter varying observer for real-time damper force estimation of an automotive electro-rheological suspension system. Int. J. Robust Nonlinear Control **31**(17), 8183–8205 (2021)

Adaptive Synchronization
of Fractional-Order Multiplex Networks
via Quantized Control

Yunzhan Bai, Cheng Hu, Juan Yu[✉], and Haijun Jiang

Xinjiang University, Urumqi 830017, People's Republic of China
xjuyjmathmatic@xju.edu.cn

Abstract. This paper investigates adaptive synchronization of fractional order multiplex networks. Firstly, an efficient fractional-order adaptive strategy with logarithmic quantizer is designed to achieve asymptotic synchronization. Subsequently, the synchronization of the networks is rigorously analyzed by using Lyapunov function method and the fractional differential inequality. Note that the developed control strategy is also feasible for the first-order multiplex networks. The feasibility of theoretical results is verified finally by providing a numerical model.

Keywords: Fractional-order · Multiplex network · Adaptive quantized control · Synchronization

1 Introduction

Various complex systems in practice can be abstracted as complex networks(CNs), such as social networks, neural networks, biological networks, etc. Although considerable efforts have been devoted to CNs based on simple graphs in recent decades [1,2], numerous real networks cannot be fully characterized by single CNs. For example, social networks are CNs composed of many interacting groups such as families, friends, colleagues. Therefore, a multiplex network composed of many layers, in which the layers represent different relations, seems to be more illustrative [3].

Fractional-order(FO) calculus has been extensively utilized to depict various models of engineering applications, including fluid mechanics [4], processes of electrochemistry [5], and viscoelastic systems [6]. As a result, the FO calculus is spontaneously introduced in CNs to more accurately reveal the feature of long-term memory and hereditary in some materials, processes and systems [7]. In view of this, it is worth noticing that the fractional-order multiplex networks

This work was supported jointly by National Natural Science Foundation of China (61866036), by the Special Project for Local Science and Technology Development Guided by the Central Government (ZYYD2022A05), and by Xinjiang Key Laboratory of Applied Mathematics (XJDX1401).

(FMNs) play important roles in abstracting the real world, and the study of their dynamical behaviors has become a hot topic, such as stability [8] and synchronization [9].

Synchronization is a fundamental dynamic feature of CNs and is widely applied in signal processing [10], secure communications [11] and other fields. Recently, the synchronization control of FOCNs has boomed rapidly, and many various control means have been explored, such as pinning control [12], sliding control [13] and event-triggered control [14]. Note that the control gain is often designed as a constant, which may larger than the actual demand gain. Fortunately, adaptive control can perfectly address this trouble, where the control gain varies about the time and can be automatically tuned according to different situations. Nowadays, many excellent results about adaptive synchronization have been obtained for integer-order complex or multilayer networks [15,16].

Conversely, few reports have been published to study adaptive synchronization of FMNs. By introducing effective adaptive control, Liu et al. addressed the synchronization in [17] for FO multiple neural networks. Based on a new FO Halanay-type inequality, Luo et al. analyzed adaptive synchronization of FMNs with time delays by utilizing graph-theoretic method and Lyapunov method in [18]. Different from these adaptive schemes, a type of edge-based FO adaptive law was proposed for FO spatiotemporal networks with boundary coupling by Yang et al. in [19]. In addition, Yang et al. also developed a rigorous analytic approach for adaptive control of FO models, which provides an important guidance for this paper.

On the other hand, signal transmission is usually limited by channel width or channel capacity, which inevitably leads to incomplete signal transmission. Consequently, signal quantization was proposed by Kalman [20], in which only discrete values need to be transmitted, and the signal transmission burden is greatly reduced. Since then, the synchronization of CNs via quantitative control has attracted extensive attention. In [21], Li et al. designed pinning quantized control to achieve finite-time synchronization of CNs. Combining adaptive technique with quantized output control, Bao et al. discussed adaptive synchronization in [22] for FO coupled networks with output coupling. Nevertheless, there are few researches on adaptive quantized control of FMNs.

Based on the aforementioned discussion, the main aim of this article is to the asymptotic synchronization of FMNs via adaptive quantization control. The main contributions are summarized as follows.

1. To reduce signal transmission frequency and improve the effective utilization rate of network resources, an FO adaptive quantization controller is designed. This control scheme is also applicable to integer-order multiple networks, which can be regarded as an extension of the previous works [15,16].
2. Based on the above control scheme, a rigorous theoretical analysis is developed to realize the synchronization of FMNs by using vector transformation and fractional differential inequality, which provides a referable analytic method for adaptive control of FO system.

The remainder is organized as follows. In Sect. 2, some important preliminaries are presented. An adaptive quantized controller is developed and some synchronization conditions are derived for FMNs in Sect. 3. Section 4 gives an example to test the synchronization controller and criteria. A summary is provided in Sect. 5.

Notation: In this paper, $\mathbb{R} = (-\infty, +\infty)$, $\mathbb{R}^n$ denotes the n-dimensional Euclidean space. T represents the transposition of a vector. $\mathfrak{N} = \{1, 2, \ldots, N\}$ and $\mathfrak{M} = \{1, 2, \ldots, M\}$. $\|\cdot\|$ is the Euclidean norm. For a matrix $\mathfrak{A} \in \mathbb{R}^{n \times n}$, $\mathfrak{A} > 0$ represents that $\mathfrak{A}$ is positive definite, $\lambda_{\max}(\mathfrak{A})$ is the largest eigenvalue of the matrix $\mathfrak{A}$. $\mathrm{diag}(\cdot)$ represents a diagonal matrix. $\otimes$ denotes the Kronecker product.

2   Problem Statement

Definition 1 *[23]. For an integrable function $\phi(t) : [t_0, +\infty) \to \mathbb{R}$ and $0 < \mathfrak{a} < 1$, the FO integral is defined as*

$$_{t_0}I_t^{\mathfrak{a}}\phi(t) = \frac{1}{\Gamma(\mathfrak{a})} \int_{t_0}^t \frac{\phi(s)}{(t-s)^{1-\mathfrak{a}}} ds,$$

where $\Gamma(\mathfrak{a}) = \int_0^{+\infty} t^{\mathfrak{a}-1}e^{-t}dt$.

Definition 2 *[23]. For a differentiable function $\phi(t) : [t_0, +\infty) \to \mathbb{R}$ and $0 < \mathfrak{a} < 1$, the Caputo FO derivative is defined by*

$$_{t_0}^{C}D_t^{\mathfrak{a}}\phi(t) = \frac{1}{\Gamma(1-\mathfrak{a})} \int_{t_0}^t \frac{\phi'(s)}{(t-s)^{\mathfrak{a}}} ds.$$

Lemma 1 *[24]. Suppose that $\psi(t) : [t_0, +\infty) \to \mathbb{R}$ be a differentiable function, then*

$$\frac{1}{2}{}_{t_0}^{C}D_t^{\mathfrak{a}}\psi^T(t)\psi(t) \leq \psi^T(t){}_{t_0}^{C}D_t^{\mathfrak{a}}\psi(t), \quad 0 < \mathfrak{a} < 1.$$

Lemma 2 *[23]. If a continuous differentiable function $\psi(t) : [t_0, +\infty) \to \mathbb{R}$,*

$$_{t_0}I_t^{\mathfrak{a}}{}_{t_0}^{C}D_t^{\mathfrak{a}}\psi(t) = \psi(t) - \psi(t_0), \quad 0 < \mathfrak{a} < 1.$$

In this paper, a class of FMNs composed of N layers is considered and each layer has M dynamical nodes. The dynamic evaluation of FMNs is described by

$$_{t_0}^{C}D_t^{\alpha}v_i^{(\varrho)}(t) = g(v_i^{(\varrho)}(t)) + \sigma \sum_{j=1, j \neq i}^{M} a_{ij}^{(\varrho)} E(v_j^{(\varrho)}(t) - v_i^{(\varrho)}(t))$$

$$+ \delta \sum_{k=1, k \neq \varrho}^{N} b_{\varrho k} F(v_i^{(k)}(t) - v_i^{(\varrho)}(t)) + \omega_i^{(\varrho)}(t), \qquad (1)$$

where $i \in \mathfrak{M}$, $\varrho \in \mathfrak{N}$, $0 < \alpha < 1$, $v_i^{(\varrho)}(t) = (v_{i1}^{(\varrho)}(t), v_{i2}^{(\varrho)}(t), \ldots, v_{in}^{(\varrho)}(t))^T \in \mathbb{R}^n$ denotes the state of the ith node in the ϱth layer, $g(\cdot) : \mathbb{R}^n \to \mathbb{R}^n$ is a smooth nonlinear vector function, σ and δ are the intra-layer and inter-layer coupling strengths, respectively. $E = \mathrm{diag}\,(E_1, E_2, \ldots, E_n) > 0$ represents an internal coupling matrix in each layer, $F = \mathrm{diag}\,(F_1, F_2, \ldots, F_n) > 0$ is an internal coupling matrix among nodes cross layer, $\omega_i^{(\varrho)}(t)$ is a control input of the ith node at the ϱth layer, $A^{(\varrho)} = (a_{ij}^{(\varrho)}) \in \mathbb{R}^{M \times M}$, in which $a_{ij}^{(\varrho)} > 0$ ($i \neq j$) if there exists a link between the node i and the node j at the ϱth layer, or else, $a_{ij}^{(\varrho)} = 0$, $i, j \in \mathfrak{M}$, $B = (b_{\varrho k}) \in \mathbb{R}^{N \times N}$, in which $b_{\varrho k} > 0$ ($\varrho \neq k$) if and only if there exists an edge between the ith node of the ϱth layer and the ith node of the kth layer, otherwise $b_{\varrho k} = 0$, $\varrho, k \in \mathfrak{N}$. The corresponding Laplacian matrix $\hat{A}^{(\varrho)} = (\hat{a}_{ij}^{(\varrho)})_{M \times M}$ in layer ϱ is defined as $\hat{a}_{ij}^{(\varrho)} = -a_{ij}^{(\varrho)}$ ($i \neq j$), and $\hat{a}_{ii}^{(\varrho)} = \sum_{j=1, j \neq i}^{M} a_{ij}^{(\varrho)}$, the inter-layer Laplacian matrix $\hat{B} = (\hat{b}_{\varrho k})_{N \times N}$ is defined as $\hat{b}_{\varrho k} = -b_{\varrho k}$ ($\varrho \neq k$), and $\hat{b}_{\varrho \varrho} = \sum_{k=1, k \neq \varrho}^{N} b_{\varrho k}$.

The dynamics of the isolated node of the FMN (1) is given by

$$\,^{C}_{t_0}D_t^\alpha s(t) = g(s(t)), \tag{2}$$

where $s(t) = (s_1(t), s_2(t), \cdots, s_n(t))^T \in \mathbb{R}^n$.

Assumption 1. For each $v_i, v_j \in \mathbb{R}^n$, there has a positive constant ℓ satisfying

$$\|g(v_i) - g(v_j)\| \le \ell \|v_i - v_j\|, \quad i, j \in \mathfrak{M}.$$

3   Main Results

The synchronization error is defined as $\jmath_i^{(\varrho)}(t) = v_i^{(\varrho)}(t) - s(t)$, then the error dynamics as following

$$\,^{C}_{t_0}D_t^\alpha \jmath_i^{(\varrho)}(t) = \tilde{g}(\jmath_i^{(\varrho)}(t)) + \sigma \sum_{j=1, j \neq i}^{M} a_{ij}^{(\varrho)} E(\jmath_j^{(\varrho)}(t) - \jmath_i^{(\varrho)}(t))$$

$$+ \delta \sum_{k=1, k \neq \varrho}^{N} b_{\varrho k} F(\jmath_i^{(k)}(t) - \jmath_i^{(\varrho)}(t)) + \omega_i^{(\varrho)}(t), \quad i \in \mathfrak{M}, \varrho \in \mathfrak{N},$$

$$\tag{3}$$

where $\tilde{g}(\jmath_i^{(\varrho)}(t)) = g(v_i^{(\varrho)}(t)) - g(s(t))$.

Definition 3. the FMN (1) is called to be asymptotically synchronized provided that

$$\lim_{t \to +\infty} \| \jmath_i^{(\varrho)}(t)\| = 0, i \in \mathfrak{M}, \varrho \in \mathfrak{N}.$$

The adaptive quantized controller $\omega_i^{(\varrho)}(t)$ is designed by

$$\begin{cases} \omega_i^{(\varrho)}(t) = -\vartheta_i^{(\varrho)}(t)p(\mathfrak{z}_i^{(\varrho)}(t)), \\ {}_{t_0}^{C}D_t^{\alpha}\vartheta_i^{(\varrho)}(t) = \beta_i^{(\varrho)}\|\,\mathfrak{z}_i^{(\varrho)}(t)\|^2, \end{cases} \tag{4}$$

where $i \in \mathfrak{M}, \varrho \in \mathfrak{N}, \beta_i^{(\varrho)} > 0, \vartheta_i^{(\varrho)}(t_0) \geq 0, p(\mathfrak{z}_i^{(\varrho)}(t)) = \big(\bar{p}(\mathfrak{z}_{i1}^{(\varrho)}(t)), \bar{p}(\mathfrak{z}_{i2}^{(\varrho)}(t)), \ldots, \bar{p}(\mathfrak{z}_{in}^{(\varrho)}(t))\big)^T$.

The quantizer $\bar{p}(\cdot) : \mathbb{R} \to \mathcal{V}$ is defined as follows

$$\bar{p}(\mu) = \begin{cases} \Psi_\varsigma, & \frac{1}{1+\chi}\Psi_\varsigma < \mu \leq \frac{1}{1-\chi}\Psi_\varsigma, \\ 0, & \mu = 0, \\ -\bar{p}(-\mu), & \mu < 0, \end{cases}$$

where $\mathcal{V} = \{\pm\Psi_\varsigma : \Psi_\varsigma = \lambda^\varsigma\Psi_0, \varsigma = 0, \pm1, \pm2, \ldots\} \cup \{0\}$ with $\Psi_0 > 0$, and $\chi = \frac{1-\lambda}{1+\lambda}$, $0 < \lambda < 1$. In the sense of Filippov, there exists $\Delta \in [-\chi, \chi]$ such that $\bar{p}(\mu) = (1+\Delta)\mu$, $\mu \in \mathbb{R}$.

Theorem 1. *The FMN (1) achieves asymptotical synchronization under Assumption 1 and the adaptive quantized control scheme (4).*

Proof. Select a Lyapunov function as

$$V(t) = \frac{1}{2}\sum_{r=1}^{N}\sum_{i=1}^{M}(\mathfrak{z}_i^{(\varrho)}(t))^T\,\mathfrak{z}_i^{(\varrho)}(t) + \frac{1}{2}\sum_{\varrho=1}^{N}\sum_{i=1}^{M}\frac{1-\chi}{\beta_i^{(\varrho)}}\left(\vartheta_i^{(\varrho)}(t) - \tilde{\vartheta}\right)^2,$$

where $\tilde{\vartheta}$ is a constant.

In view of Lemma 1, one has

$$\begin{aligned} {}_{t_0}^{C}D_t^{\alpha}V(t) \leq{} & \sum_{\varrho=1}^{N}\sum_{i=1}^{M}(\mathfrak{z}_i^{(\varrho)}(t))^T {}_{t_0}^{C}D_t^{\alpha}\,\mathfrak{z}_i^{(\varrho)}(t) + \sum_{\varrho=1}^{N}\sum_{i=1}^{M}\frac{1-\chi}{\beta_i^{(\varrho)}}(\vartheta_i^{(\varrho)}(t) - \tilde{\vartheta}){}_{t_0}^{C}D_t^{\alpha}\vartheta_i^{(\varrho)}(t) \\ ={} & \sum_{\varrho=1}^{N}\sum_{i=1}^{M}(\mathfrak{z}_i^{(\varrho)}(t))^T\tilde{g}(\mathfrak{z}_i^{(\varrho)}(t)) - \sum_{\varrho=1}^{N}\sum_{i=1}^{M}d_i^{(\varrho)}(t)(\mathfrak{z}_i^{(\varrho)}(t))^Tp(\mathfrak{z}_i^{(\varrho)}(t)) \\ & + \sigma\sum_{\varrho=1}^{N}\sum_{i=1}^{M}\sum_{j=1,j\neq i}^{M}(\mathfrak{z}_i^{(\varrho)}(t))^Ta_{ij}^{(\varrho)}E(\mathfrak{z}_j^{(\varrho)}(t) - \mathfrak{z}_i^{(\varrho)}(t)) \\ & + \delta\sum_{\varrho=1}^{N}\sum_{i=1}^{M}\sum_{k=1,k\neq\varrho}^{N}(\mathfrak{z}_i^{(\varrho)}(t))^Tb_{\varrho k}F(\mathfrak{z}_i^{(k)}(t) - \mathfrak{z}_i^{(\varrho)}(t)) \\ & + (1-\chi)\sum_{\varrho=1}^{N}\sum_{i=1}^{M}(\vartheta_i^{(\varrho)}(t) - \tilde{\vartheta})\|\,\mathfrak{z}_i^{(\varrho)}(t)\|^2. \end{aligned} \tag{5}$$

According to Assumption 1, one obtains that

$$\sum_{\varrho=1}^{N}\sum_{i=1}^{M}(\mathfrak{z}_i^{(\varrho)}(t))^T\tilde{g}(\mathfrak{z}_i^{(\varrho)}(t)) \leq \sum_{\varrho=1}^{N}\sum_{i=1}^{M}\ell(\mathfrak{z}_i^{(\varrho)}(t))^T\,\mathfrak{z}_i^{(\varrho)}(t) = \ell\|\,\mathfrak{z}(t)\|^2. \tag{6}$$

For the convenience of subsequent analysis, denote

$$\jmath^{(\varrho)}(t) = \left((\jmath_1^{(\varrho)}(t))^T, (\jmath_2^{(\varrho)}(t))^T \ldots, (\jmath_M^{(\varrho)}(t))^T\right)^T,$$

$$\jmath(t) = \left((\jmath^{(1)}(t))^T, (\jmath^{(2)}(t))^T, \ldots, (\jmath^{(N)}(t))^T\right)^T,$$

$$\jmath_i(t) = \left((\jmath_i^{(1)}(t))^T, (\jmath_i^{(2)}(t))^T \ldots, (\jmath_i^{(N)}(t))^T\right)^T,$$

$$\bar{\jmath}(t) = \left((\jmath_1(t))^T, (\jmath_2(t))^T, \ldots, (\jmath_M(t))^T\right)^T,$$

it follows that

$$\sigma \sum_{\varrho=1}^{N} \sum_{i=1}^{M} \sum_{j=1,j\neq i}^{M} (\jmath_i^{(\varrho)}(t))^T a_{ij}^{(\varrho)} E(\jmath_j^{(\varrho)}(t) - \jmath_i^{(\varrho)}(t))$$

$$= \sigma \sum_{\varrho=1}^{N} \sum_{i=1}^{M} (\jmath_i^{(\varrho)}(t))^T \left(\sum_{j=1,j\neq i}^{M} a_{ij}^{(\varrho)} E \jmath_j^{(\varrho)}(t) - \sum_{j=1,j\neq i}^{M} a_{ij}^{(\varrho)} E \jmath_i^{(\varrho)}(t) \right)$$

$$= \sigma \sum_{\varrho=1}^{N} \sum_{i=1}^{M} (\jmath_i^{(\varrho)}(t))^T \left(- \sum_{j=1,j\neq i}^{M} \hat{a}_{ij}^{(\varrho)} E \jmath_j^{(\varrho)}(t) - \hat{a}_{ii}^{(\varrho)} E \jmath_i^{(\varrho)}(t) \right)$$

$$= -\sigma \sum_{\varrho=1}^{N} \sum_{i=1}^{M} \sum_{j=1}^{M} (\jmath_i^{(\varrho)}(t))^T \hat{a}_{ij}^{(\varrho)} E \jmath_j^{(\varrho)}(t)$$

$$= \sigma(\jmath(t))^T (-\hat{A} \otimes E) \jmath(t) \leq \sigma \lambda_1 \|\jmath(t)\|^2, \tag{7}$$

and

$$\delta \sum_{\varrho=1}^{N} \sum_{i=1}^{M} \sum_{k=1,k\neq\varrho}^{N} (\jmath_i^{(\varrho)}(t))^T b_{\varrho k} F(\jmath_i^{(k)}(t) - \jmath_i^{(\varrho)}(t))$$

$$= \delta \sum_{\varrho=1}^{N} \sum_{i=1}^{M} (\jmath_i^{(\varrho)}(t))^T \left(\sum_{k=1,k\neq\varrho}^{N} b_{\varrho k} F \jmath_i^{(k)}(t) - \sum_{k=1,k\neq\varrho}^{N} b_{\varrho k} F \jmath_i^{(\varrho)}(t) \right)$$

$$= \delta \sum_{\varrho=1}^{N} \sum_{i=1}^{M} (\jmath_i^{(\varrho)}(t))^T \left(- \sum_{k=1,k\neq\varrho}^{N} \hat{b}_{\varrho k} F \jmath_i^{(k)}(t) - \hat{b}_{\varrho\varrho} F \jmath_i^{(\varrho)}(t) \right)$$

$$= -\delta \sum_{\varrho=1}^{N} \sum_{i=1}^{M} \sum_{k=1}^{N} (\jmath_i^{(\varrho)}(t))^T \hat{b}_{\varrho k} F \jmath_i^{(k)}(t)$$

$$= \delta \bar{\jmath}^T(t)(-I_M \otimes \hat{B} \otimes F)\bar{\jmath}(t) \leq \delta \lambda_2 \|\bar{\jmath}(t)\|^2 = \delta \lambda_2 \|\jmath(t)\|^2, \tag{8}$$

where

$$\hat{A} = \mathrm{diag}(\hat{A}^{(1)}, \hat{A}^{(2)}, \ldots, \hat{A}^{(N)}),$$

$$\lambda_1 = \lambda_{\max}(-\hat{A} \otimes E), \lambda_2 = \lambda_{\max}(-I_M \otimes \hat{B} \otimes F).$$

By the property of quantization, it has

$$-\sum_{\varrho=1}^{N}\sum_{i=1}^{M} d_i^{(\varrho)}(t)(\jmath_i^{(\varrho)}(t))^T p(\jmath_i^{(\varrho)}(t)) = -\sum_{\varrho=1}^{N}\sum_{i=1}^{M}\sum_{\iota=1}^{n} d_i^{(\varrho)}(t)\,\jmath_{i\iota}^{(\varrho)}(t)\bar{p}(\jmath_{i\iota}^{(\varrho)}(t)).$$

If $\jmath_{i\iota}^{(\varrho)}(t) \geq 0$,

$$\sum_{\varrho=1}^{N}\sum_{i=1}^{M}\sum_{\iota=1}^{n} d_i^{(\varrho)}(t)\,\jmath_{i\iota}^{(\varrho)}(t)\bar{p}(\jmath_{i\iota}^{(\varrho)}(t)) \geq (1-\chi)\sum_{\varrho=1}^{N}\sum_{i=1}^{M}\sum_{\iota=1}^{n} d_i^{(\varrho)}(t)\,\jmath_{i\iota}^{(\varrho)}(t)\,\jmath_{i\iota}^{(\varrho)}(t),$$

when $\jmath_{i\iota}^{(\varrho)}(t) < 0$,

$$\sum_{\varrho=1}^{N}\sum_{i=1}^{M}\sum_{\iota=1}^{n} d_i^{(\varrho)}(t)\,\jmath_{i\iota}^{(\varrho)}(t)\bar{p}(\jmath_{i\iota}^{(\varrho)}(t)) = -\sum_{\varrho=1}^{N}\sum_{i=1}^{M}\sum_{\iota=1}^{n} d_i^{(\varrho)}(t)\,\jmath_{i\iota}^{(\varrho)}(t)\bar{p}(-\jmath_{i\iota}^{(\varrho)}(t))$$

$$> (1-\chi)\sum_{\varrho=1}^{N}\sum_{i=1}^{M}\sum_{\iota=1}^{n} d_i^{(\varrho)}(t)\,\jmath_{i\iota}^{(\varrho)}(t)\,\jmath_{i\iota}^{(\varrho)}(t).$$

Based on the above analysis, it follows that

$$-\sum_{\varrho=1}^{N}\sum_{i=1}^{M}\vartheta_i^{(\varrho)}(t)(\jmath_i^{(\varrho)}(t))^T p(\jmath_i^{(\varrho)}(t)) \leq -(1-\chi)\sum_{\varrho=1}^{N}\sum_{i=1}^{M}\vartheta_i^{(\varrho)}(t)(\jmath_i^{(\varrho)}(t))^T \jmath_i^{(\varrho)}(t). \quad (9)$$

Substituting (6)–(9) into (5), and choosing $\tilde{\vartheta} = \frac{1}{1-\chi}(\ell + \sigma\lambda_1 + \delta\lambda_2 + 1)$,

$$\begin{aligned}
{}_{t_0}^{C}D_t^{\alpha}V(t) &\leq (\ell + \sigma\lambda_1 + \delta\lambda_2)\,\|\jmath(t)\|^2 - (1-\chi)\sum_{r=1}^{N}\sum_{i=1}^{M}\tilde{\vartheta})\|\jmath_i^{(\varrho)}(t)\|^2 \\
&= (\ell + \sigma\lambda_1 + \delta\lambda_2 - (1-\chi)\tilde{\vartheta})\,\|\jmath(t)\|^2 \\
&= -\|\jmath(t)\|^2 = -2V(t), \quad\quad (10)
\end{aligned}$$

where $V(t) = \dfrac{1}{2}\sum_{r=1}^{N}\sum_{i=1}^{M}(\jmath_i^{(\varrho)}(t))^T \jmath_i^{(\varrho)}(t)$. By means of Lemma 2, one gets

$$V(t) - V(t_0) \leq -2{}_{t_0}^{C}I_t^{\alpha}V(t) \leqslant 0,$$

which implies that $V(t)$ and ${}_{t_0}^{C}I_t^{\alpha}V(t)$ are bounded for $t \geqslant 0$. Furthermore,

$$\lim_{t \to +\infty} V(t) = 0,$$

which is derived by the proof of Theorem 2 in [17]. Thus, the synchronization of FMN (1) is guaranteed via the adaptive quantized controller (4).   □

Remark 1. When $\delta = 0$, the system (1) is reduced to

$$\begin{aligned}
{}_{t_0}^{C}D_t^{\alpha}v_i^{(\varrho)}(t) =&\ \sigma\sum_{j=1,j\neq i}^{M} a_{ij}^{(\varrho)} E(v_j^{(\varrho)}(t) - v_i^{(\varrho)}(t)) \\
&+ g(v_i^{(\varrho)}(t)) + \omega_i^{(\varrho)}(t), \quad i \in \mathfrak{M}, r \in \mathfrak{N}. \quad (11)
\end{aligned}$$

From the analysis of Theorem 1, it is easy to conclude that the FMN without inter-layer coupling (11) is also asymptotically synchronized under Assumption 1 and the controller (4).

Remark 2. Similarly to Remark 1, $\sigma = 0$, the system (1) is reduced as

$$
{}^{C}_{t_0}D^{\alpha}_t v_i^{(\varrho)}(t) = \delta \sum_{k=1,k\neq\varrho}^{N} b_{\varrho k} \Gamma(v_i^{(k)}(t) \quad v_i^{(\varrho)}(t))
$$
$$
+ g(v_i^{(\varrho)}(t)) + \omega_i^{(\varrho)}(t), \quad i \in \mathfrak{M}, \varrho \in \mathfrak{N}. \tag{12}
$$

Under Assumption 1 and the controller (4), the FMN without intra-layer coupling (12) can achieve asymptotic synchronization.

Remark 3. Compared with the control scheme in [17,18], the factor that signal transmission is limited by channel capacity and width is fully considered, and adaptive quantized control is designed in this paper, which greatly reduce the transmission burden of the signal and the control cost.

If $\alpha = 1$, the FMN (1) becomes the following integer-order multiplex network

$$
\dot{v}_i^{(\varrho)}(t) = g(v_i^{(\varrho)}(t)) + \sigma \sum_{j=1,j\neq i}^{M} a_{ij}^{(\varrho)} E(v_j^{(\varrho)}(t) - v_i^{(\varrho)}(t))
$$
$$
+ \delta \sum_{k=1,k\neq\varrho}^{N} b_{\varrho k} F(v_i^{(k)}(t) - v_i^{(\varrho)}(t)) + \omega_i^{(\varrho)}(t), \quad i \in \mathfrak{M}, \varrho \in \mathfrak{N}. \tag{13}
$$

In light of this, the adaptive quantized controller (4) becomes the following form

$$
\begin{cases}
\omega_i^{(\varrho)}(t) = -\vartheta_i^{(\varrho)}(t) p(\varepsilon_i^{(\varrho)}(t)), \\
\dot{\hat{\vartheta}}_i^{(\varrho)}(t) = \beta_i^{(\varrho)} \|\varepsilon_i^{(\varrho)}(t)\|^2,
\end{cases} \tag{14}
$$

where $i \in \mathfrak{M}, \varrho \in \mathfrak{N}, \beta_i^{(\varrho)} > 0, \vartheta_i^{(\varrho)}(t_0) \geq 0$.

Corollary 1. *Under Assumption 1, the network (13) realizes asymptotic synchronization via the adaptive quantized control (14).*

Proof. Construct the same Lyapunov function as Theorem 1, one has

$$
\dot{V}(t) = \sum_{\varrho=1}^{N}\sum_{i=1}^{M}(\jmath_i^{(\varrho)}(t))^T \dot{\jmath}_i^{(\varrho)}(t) + \sum_{\varrho=1}^{N}\sum_{i=1}^{M}\frac{1-\chi}{\beta_i^{(\varrho)}}(\vartheta_i^{(\varrho)}(t) - \tilde{\vartheta})\dot{\vartheta}_i^{(\varrho)}(t)
$$
$$
= \sum_{\varrho=1}^{N}\sum_{i=1}^{M}(\varepsilon_i^{(\varrho)}(t))^T \left[\tilde{g}(\varepsilon_i^{(\varrho)}(t)) + \sigma \sum_{j=1,j\neq i}^{M} a_{ij}^{(\varrho)} E(\jmath_j^{(\varrho)}(t) - \jmath_i^{(\varrho)}(t)) \right.
$$
$$
\left. + \delta \sum_{k=1,k\neq\varrho}^{N} b_{\varrho k} F(\jmath_i^{(k)}(t) - \jmath_i^{(\varrho)}(t)) + \omega_i^{(\varrho)}(t) \right]
$$

$$+ (1 - \chi) \sum_{\varrho=1}^{N} \sum_{i=1}^{M} (\vartheta_i^{(\varrho)}(t) - \tilde{\vartheta}) \| \jmath_i^{(\varrho)}(t) \|^2$$

$$\leq (\ell + \sigma\lambda_1 + \delta\lambda_2 - (1 - \chi)\tilde{\vartheta}) \| \jmath(t) \|^2 .$$

Choosing $\tilde{\vartheta} \geq \frac{1}{1-\chi}(\ell + \sigma\lambda_1 + \delta\lambda_2)$, which leads to $\dot{V}(t) \leq 0$. Thus, the controlled system (13) is asymptotically synchronized.   □

Remark 4. In [15,16], the dynamics of integer-order models were considered. From Corollary 1, the results of this paper are also applicable for the integer-order multiplex networks, so it can be considered as the valuable extension from integer-order multiplex networks to FO ones.

4   Numerical Verification

Consider a three-layer FMN with three nodes in model (1), where $\alpha = 0.98$, $\sigma = 0.03$, $\delta = 0.02$, $\Psi_0 = 1$, $\lambda = 0.8$, $E = \text{diag}(2, 2, 2)$, $F = \text{diag}(3, 3, 3)$,

$$A^{(1)} = A^{(2)} = A^{(3)} = \begin{pmatrix} 0 & 1 & 1 \\ 1 & 0 & 1 \\ 1 & 1 & 0 \end{pmatrix}, B = \begin{pmatrix} 0 & 1 & 0 \\ 1 & 0 & 1 \\ 0 & 1 & 0 \end{pmatrix}.$$

Select the chaotic Lü's system as the synchronization system (2), which is described as

$$_{t_0}^{C}D_t^{\alpha} s(t) = g(s(t)) = \begin{pmatrix} 10s_2(t) - 10s_1(t) \\ 35s_1(t) - 2.5s_1(t)s_3(t) \\ -3s_3(t) + 4s_1^2(t) \end{pmatrix}. \tag{15}$$

The topology of the FMN (1) is depicted in Fig. 1, in which the dotted line indicates the connection between layers, and the solid line indicates the connection within the same layer. And the dynamic trajectory of model (15) is shown

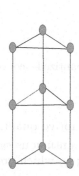

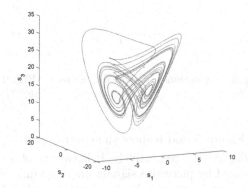

Fig. 1. Topology of the multiplex network (1).

Fig. 2. The chaotic behavior of system (15).

in Fig. 2 with the initial state $s(0) = (1, 2.5, 6)^T$, which reveals that system (15) possesses chaotic behavior.

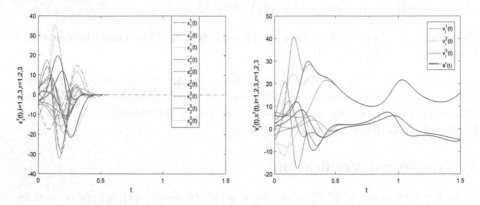

Fig. 3. Synchronization error $\varepsilon_i^{(\varrho)}(t)$.   **Fig. 4.** Trajectories of $v_i^{(\varrho)}(t)$ and $s^{(\varrho)}(t)$.

Choose the control parameters $\beta_i^1 = \beta_i^3 = 1, \beta_i^2 = 1.5$ and $\vartheta_i^\varrho(t_0) \in [0, 1]$. By Theorem 1, the synchronization is ensured and the numerical results are displayed in Figs. 3 and 4.

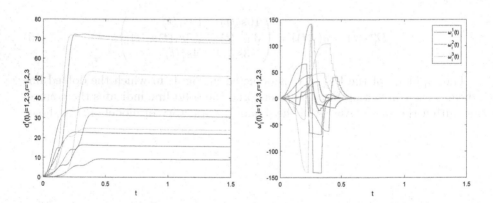

Fig. 5. Evolutions of control gains $\vartheta_i^{(\varrho)}(t)$.   **Fig. 6.** Adapt quantized controller $\omega_i^{(\varrho)}(t)$.

Figures 5 and 6 show the control gains $d_i^{(r)}(t)$ and adaptive quantized controller $\omega_i^{(r)}(t)$, respectively. It is easy to observe that the continuous signals are replaced by piecewise signals under quantized controller (4), which greatly cut the control cost and the communication burden.

5   Conclusion

The problem of asymptotic synchronization of FMNs has been investigated in this article. By developing an adaptive quantization controller and using Lyapunov method, the asymptotic synchronization of FMNs has been analyzed and proved strictly. At last, the theoretical results has been confirmed via numerical simulations. Note that delays are inevitable in large-scale networks [8,9,17], and the next step will be devoted to the synchronization problem of FMNs with delays.

References

1. Wu, Y., Shen, B., Ahn, C., Li, W.: Intermittent dynamic event-triggered control for synchronization of stochastic complex networks. IEEE Trans. Circuits Syst. I Regul. Pap. **68**(6), 2639–2650 (2021)
2. Kazemy, A., Lam, J., Zhang, X.: Event-triggered output feedback synchronization of master-slave neural networks under deception attacks. IEEE Trans. Neural Netw. Learn. Syst. **33**(3), 952–961 (2022)
3. Wu, T., Liu, X., Qin, J., Herrera, F.: Trust-consensus multiplex networks by combining trust social network analysis and consensus evolution methods in group decision-making. IEEE Trans. Fuzzy Syst. (2022). https://doi.org/10.1109/3158432
4. Ezzat, M.: State space approach to thermoelectric fluid with fractional order heat transfer. Heat Mass Transf. **48**(1), 71–82 (2012)
5. Allagui, A., Freeborn, T., Elwakil, A.: Review of fractional-order electrical characterization of supercapacitors. J. Power Sour. **400**, 457–467 (2018)
6. Niedziela, M., Wlazło, J.: Notes on computational aspects of the fractional-order viscoelastic model. J. Eng. Math. **108**(1), 91–105 (2017). https://doi.org/10.1007/s10665-017-9911-0
7. Arena, P., Caponetto, R., Fortuna, L., Porto, D.: Bifurcation and chaos in noninteger order cellular neural networks. Int. J. Bifurc. Chaos **8**(7), 1527–1539 (1998)
8. He, B.-B., Zhou, H.-C., Kou, C.-H., Chen, Y.Q.: New integral inequalities and asymptotic stability of fractional-order systems with unbounded time delay. Nonlinear Dyn. **94**(2), 1523–1534 (2018). https://doi.org/10.1007/s11071-018-4439-z
9. Liu, P., Kong, M., Zeng, Z.: Projective synchronization analysis of fractional-order neural networks with mixed time delays. IEEE Trans. Cybern. (2020). https://doi.org/10.1109/3027755
10. Wei, G., Jia, Y.: Synchronization-based image edge detection. Europhys. Lett. **59**, 814–819 (2015)
11. Xie, Q., Chen, G., Bollt, E.: Hybrid chaos synchronization and its application in information processing. Math. Comput. Model. **35**, 145–163 (2002)
12. Shi, T., Hu, C., Yu, J., Jiang, H.: Exponential synchronization for spatio-temporal directed networks via intermittent pinning control. Neurocomputing **451**, 337–349 (2021)
13. Ma, Z., Liu, Z., Huang, P., Kuang, Z.: Adaptive fractional order sliding mode control for admittance-based telerobotic system with optimized order and force estimation. IEEE Trans. Industr. Electron. **69**(5), 5165–5174 (2022)

14. Yang, Y., Hu, C., Yu, J.: Event-triggered quasi-synchronization of fractional-order reaction-diffusion networks with disturbance. J. Xinjiang Univ. **39**(2), 134–143 (2021)
15. Hu, C., Jiang, H.: Pinning synchronization for directed networks with node balance via adaptive intermittent control. Nonlinear Dyn. **80**(1), 295–307 (2015)
16. Wu, Y., Liu, L., Hu, J., Feng, G.: Adaptive antisynchronization of multilayer reaction-diffusion neural networks. IEEE Trans. Neural Netw. Learn. Syst. **29**(4), 807–818 (2018)
17. Liu, P., Xu, M., Sun, J., Zeng, Z.: On pinning linear and adaptive synchronization of multiple fractional-order neural networks with unbounded time-varying delays. IEEE Trans. Cybern. (2021). https://doi.org/10.1109/3119922
18. Luo, T., Wang, Q., Jia, Q., Xu, Y.: Asymptotic and finite-time synchronization of fractional-order multiplex networks with time delays by adaptive and impulsive control. Neurocomputing **493**, 445–461 (2022)
19. Yang, Y., Hu, C., Yu, J., Jiang, H.: Synchronization of fractional-order spatiotemporal complex networks with boundary communication. Neurocomputing **450**, 197–207 (2021)
20. Kalman, R.: Nonlinear aspects of sampled-data control systems. In: Proceedings of the 1956 Symposium on Nonlinear Circuit Analysis, vol. 6, pp. 273–313 (1956)
21. Li, Y., Yang, Z., Xia, D., Mei, J.: Finite-time synchronization for complex networks via guaranteed cost intermittent pinning quantized control. In: 33rd Chinese Control and Decision Conference Proceedings, pp. 5321–5326. IEEE, Kunming, China (2021)
22. Bao, H., Park, J., Cao, J.: Adaptive synchronization of fractional-order output-coupling neural networks via quantized output control. IEEE Trans. Neural Netw. Learn. Syst. **32**(7), 3230–3239 (2021)
23. Kilbas, A., Srivastava, H., Trujillo, J.: Theory and Applications of Fractional Differential Equations. Elsevier Science Press, Holland (2006)
24. Aguila, N., Duarte, M., Gallegos, G.: Lyapunov functions for fractional order systems. Commun. Nonlinear Sci. Numer. Simul. **19**(9), 2951–2957 (2014)

Synchronization in Fixed/Preassigned Time of Inertial Neural Networks with Time-Varying Delays

Conghui Yang, Cheng Hu [ID], Juan Yu[(✉)], and Haijun Jiang

Xinjiang University, Urumqi 830017, People's Republic of China
xjuyjmathmatic@xju.edu.cn

Abstract. This article mainly investigates the fixed-/preassigned-time synchronization of inertial neural networks (INNs) with time-varying delays. Above all, the underlying INNs is transformed into two subsystems by applying reduced-order transformation, and an effective control scheme is developed to explore fixed-time (FXT) synchronization. Furthermore, the corresponding synchronization criteria are derived under the p-norm. In addition, the preassigned-time (PAT) synchronization is also investigated via designing some control strategies with finite gains, in which the settling time (ST) can be preset in advance. The theoretical results are further verified at last via a numerical example.

Keywords: Fixed/preassigned-time synchronization · Inertial neural network · Time-varying delay

1 Introduction

Various neural network systems have been extensively applied for many years among diverse fields, including pattern recognition, optimizations and secure communication [1–3]. Note that delays are ubiquitous in NNs due to the finite information transmission and switching speed among different neurons. Currently, various kinds of NN models with delays have been explored and numerous achievements have been presented [4]. However, many practical matters in applications are not easy to be accurately described and effectively solved by the classical first-order NNs, such as hair cells of mammalian [5] and squid's axon [6]. Fortunately, Babcock and Westervelt proposed an INN model, which is described as the second-order differential system. Up to now, many outstanding works have been reported for different kinds of delayed INNs [7].

As one of the significant dynamical behaviors, synchronization indicates that drive-response systems tend to an identical behavior. At present, various types

Supported by National Natural Science Foundation of China (61866036), by the Special Project for Local Science and Technology Development Guided by the Central Government (ZYYD2022A05) and by Xinjiang Key Laboratory of Applied Mathematics (XJDX1401).

of synchronization for INNs with delays were developed and many interesting results were obtained by means of different control techniques, including complete synchronization [8], lag synchronization [9], quasi synchronization [10]. In [9], the exponential lag synchronization of delayed INNs was studied in view of inequality techniques. In [10], the quasi synchronization problem for the discrete-time INNs was studied by utilizing the generalized matrix measure.

However, the synchronization type mentioned above is asymptotic synchronization, which belongs to infinite-time synchronization. To accelerate synchronization convergence time, the definition of finite-time (FNT) synchronization was proposed, which implies that synchronization can be guaranteed in a finite time. Presently, the FNT synchronization of delayed INNs has attracted much attention [11–13]. In [11], the FNT synchronization for delayed INNs was considered via integral inequality skills and standard reduced-order transformation. In [12], the FNT synchronization of memristive INNs with time-delay was concerned via applying standard reduced-order method.

It is worth noting that the ST mentioned above heavily relies on initial state of system, but the initial state cannot be accurately obtained in advance due to the influence of external factors, which causes some troubles to the estimation of synchronization time. In order to overcome this tough problem, the FXT stability was proposed in [14], in which the ST only depends on the parameters of the considered system and independents of the initial state. Nowadays, the FXT synchronization of delayed INNs was discussed in the framework of the theory of FXT stability [15–17]. In [15], the FXT synchronization of delayed Cohen-Grossberg INNs with external disturbances was studied via event-triggered strategy. In [16], the FXT synchronization of fuzzy BAM memristive INNs with neutral-type and proportional delays was investigated via differential inclusion and analysis methods. Note that the linear term in the controller designed in the aforementioned FNT and FXT synchronization is essential. Hence, an interesting issue is how to develop a compact controller without linear term to explore FXT synchronization of delayed INNs.

Although the ST of FXT synchronization is related to system parameters, it is expected that the synchronization time can be preset in advance based on the actual needs [18,19]. In [18], the PAT synchronization of competitive NNs was researched based on two different PAT stability theorems. To our knowledge, it seems that there are few results about PAT synchronization of delayed INNs, which will be studied in this article.

Based on the aforementioned discussion, this paper will concern about FXT/PAT synchronization of delayed INNs.

(1) Distinguish from the existing FXT synchronization results [15–17], a novel controller without linear term is developed for delayed INNs to explore FXT synchronization based on p-norm and the ST obtained is more accurate via FXT stability given by [19].
(2) The PAT synchronization for the addressed INNs is investigated via developing some controllers with bounded control gains and several more simple synchronization criteria are derived.

The remainder of this article is arranged below. The INN system and some preliminaries are given in Sect. 2. FXT/PT synchronization is concerned in Sect. 3 based on p-norm. The derived results are confirmed via an illustrative example in Sect. 4. A simple summary is made in Sect. 5.

Notations: $\mathbb{R} = (-\infty, +\infty)$, $\mathbb{R}^n$ is a space consisting of $n-$dimensional real vectors. For any $\breve{\eta} = (\breve{\eta}_1, \breve{\eta}_2, \ldots, \breve{\eta}_n)^T \in \mathbb{R}^n$, $\|\breve{\eta}\|_p = (|\breve{\eta}_1|^P + |\breve{\eta}_2|^P + \cdots + |\breve{\eta}_n|^P)^{\frac{1}{p}}$ ($p \geq 1$). $\mathbf{C}([-\tau, 0], \mathbb{R}^n)$ is a space consisting of continuous differentiable functions from $[-\tau, 0]$ to $\mathbb{R}^n$ with the norm defined $\|\breve{\varphi}(\varsigma)\|_p = \sup\limits_{-\tau \leq \varsigma \leq 0} (\sum\limits_{l=1}^{n} |\breve{\varphi}_l(\varsigma)|_p^P)^{\frac{1}{p}}$ for $\breve{\varphi}(\varsigma) \in \mathbf{C}([-\tau, 0], \mathbb{R}^n)$. For each $\breve{\gamma} \in \mathbb{R}$, $\text{sign}(\breve{\gamma})$ is the standard sign function of $\breve{\gamma}$, $\csc(\breve{\gamma})$ is the cosecant function of $\breve{\gamma}$. $\bar{n} = \{1, 2, \ldots, n\}$.

2 Preliminaries

Consider a type of delayed INNs characterized by

$$\frac{d^2 x_i(\mathrm{t})}{dt^2} = -\kappa_i \frac{dx_i(\mathrm{t})}{dt} - \varrho_i x_i(t) + \sum_{j=1}^{n} c_{ij} g_j(x_j(t))$$

$$+ \sum_{j=1}^{n} d_{ij} g_j(x_j(t - \tau(t))) + I_i(t), \quad i \in \bar{n}, \tag{1}$$

in which $x_i(t)$ stands for the state variable of the ith neuron at time t, $\kappa_i > 0$, $\varrho_i > 0$, c_{ij}, d_{ij} are connection weights related to neurons without or with delays. $g_j(x_j(t))$ represents the activation function of the jth neuron at time t, $\tau(t) \in [0, \tau]$ is the time-varying delay, $I_i(t)$ denotes a bias or external input on the ith neuron at time t.

The initial state of network (1) is provided by

$$x_i(\mathrm{t}) = \widehat{\varphi}_i(\varsigma), \quad \frac{dx_i(\mathrm{t})}{dt} = \widehat{\phi}_i(\varsigma), \quad \varsigma \in [-\tau, 0],$$

here $i \in \bar{n}$, $\widehat{\varphi}_i(\varsigma), \widehat{\phi}_i(\varsigma) \in \mathbf{C}([-\tau, 0], \mathbb{R}^n)$.

Next, let $y_i(t) = \frac{dx_i(\mathrm{t})}{dt} + \omega_i x_i(\mathrm{t})$, then the model (1) is equivalent to the following equation

$$\begin{cases} \dfrac{dx_i(\mathrm{t})}{dt} = -\omega_i x_i(\mathrm{t}) + y_i(\mathrm{t}), \\ \dfrac{dy_i(\mathrm{t})}{dt} = -\alpha_i x_i(\mathrm{t}) - \beta_i y_i(\mathrm{t}) + \sum\limits_{j=1}^{n} c_{ij} g_j(x_j(t)) \\ \quad + \sum\limits_{j=1}^{n} d_{ij} g_j(x_j(t - \tau(t))) + I_i(t), i \in \bar{n}, \end{cases} \tag{2}$$

where $\omega_i \in \mathbb{R}$, $\alpha_i = \varrho_i + \omega_i(\omega_i - \kappa_i)$, $\beta_i = \kappa_i - \omega_i$.

Considering model (2) as the master model, the slave model is given as

$$
\begin{cases}
\dfrac{dz_i(t)}{dt} = -\omega_i z_i(t) + v_i(t) + u_{1i}(t), \\[2mm]
\dfrac{dv_i(t)}{dt} = -\alpha_i z_i(t) - \beta_i v_i(t) + \displaystyle\sum_{j=1}^{n} c_{ij} g_j(z_j(t)) \\[4mm]
\qquad\qquad + \displaystyle\sum_{j=1}^{n} d_{ij} g_j(z_j(t - \tau(t))) + I_i(t) + u_{2i}(t), \quad i \in \bar{n},
\end{cases}
\tag{3}
$$

in which $u_{1i}(t), u_{2i}(t)$ represent the control inputs to reach FXT or PT synchronization.

Let $e(t) = \big(e_{11}(t), e_{12}(t), \ldots, e_{1n}(t), e_{21}(t), e_{22}(t), \ldots, e_{2n}(t)\big)^T$ be the synchronization error, where $e_{1i}(t) = z_i(t) - x_i(t)$, $e_{2i}(t) = v_i(t) - y_i(t)(i \in \bar{n})$, then

$$
\begin{cases}
\dot{e}_{1i}(t) = -\omega_i e_{1i}(t) + e_{2i}(t) + u_{1i}(t), \\[2mm]
\dot{e}_{2i}(t) = -\alpha_i e_{1i}(t) - \beta_i e_{2i}(t) + \displaystyle\sum_{j=1}^{n} c_{ij} G_j(e_{1j}(t)) \\[4mm]
\qquad\qquad + \displaystyle\sum_{j=1}^{n} d_{ij} G_j(e_{1j}(t - \tau(t))) + u_{2i}(t), i \in \bar{n},
\end{cases}
\tag{4}
$$

here $G_j(e_{1j}(\cdot)) = g_j(z_j(\cdot)) - g_j(x_j(\cdot))$.

Definition 1. *The neural models (2) and (3) are called to be FXT synchronized provided that there have a positive number $\mathfrak{T} > 0$ which does not rely on the initial state but may be related to network or control parameters, and a time instant $\mathfrak{T}(e(\varsigma)) \geq 0$ called the settling time satisfying $\mathfrak{T}(e(\varsigma)) \leq \mathfrak{T}$ for any $e(\varsigma) \in \mathbb{R}^{2n}$ and $\varsigma \in [-\tau, 0]$, such that*

$$
\lim_{t \to \mathfrak{T}(e(\varsigma))} \|e(t)\| = 0, \quad \|e(t)\| = 0 \quad \text{for any} \ \ t \geq \mathfrak{T}(e(\varsigma)).
$$

Definition 2. *For a preset time $\mathfrak{T}_p > 0$ which is totally independent of initial state and system parameters, the neural models (2) and (3) are called to achieve PT synchronization within $\mathfrak{T}_p$ if*

$$
\lim_{t \to \mathfrak{T}_p} \|e(t)\| = 0, \quad \|e(t)\| = 0 \quad \text{for any} \ \ t \geq \mathfrak{T}_p.
$$

Lemma 1 *[20]. Let $\widetilde{\alpha}_k \geq 0$, $k \in \bar{m}$, $0 \leq \acute{p} \leq 1$, $\acute{q} > 1$ then*

$$
\sum_{k=1}^{m} \widetilde{\alpha}_k^{\acute{p}} \geq \Big(\sum_{k=1}^{m} \widetilde{\alpha}_k\Big)^{\acute{p}}, \quad \sum_{k=1}^{m} \widetilde{\alpha}_k^{\acute{q}} \geq m^{1-\acute{q}}\Big(\sum_{k=1}^{m} \widetilde{\alpha}_k\Big)^{\acute{q}}.
$$

Lemma 2 *[20]. If u, v are nonnegative real numbers, positive real numbers $\acute{p}, \acute{q}$ satisfy $\frac{1}{\acute{p}} + \frac{1}{\acute{q}} = 1$, then*

$$
uv \leq \frac{u^{\acute{p}}}{\acute{p}} + \frac{v^{\acute{q}}}{\acute{q}}.
$$

Lemma 3 *[19]. Function $V(f(t)) : \mathbb{R}^n \to \mathbb{R}$ is C-regular, if*

$$\dot{V}(f(t)) \leq kV(f(t)) - \bar{\xi}_1 V^\delta(f(t)) - \bar{\xi}_2 V^\theta(f(t)), \quad f(t) \in \mathbb{R}^n \setminus \{0\},$$

in which $k \in \mathbb{R}$, $\bar{\xi}_1$, $\bar{\xi}_2 > 0$, $\delta > 1$ and $0 \leq \theta < 1$, the following results are true.

1) If $k \leq 0$, $f(t) = 0$ for $t \geq \mathfrak{T}_1$, here

$$\mathfrak{T}_1 = \frac{\pi}{(\delta - \theta)\bar{\xi}_2} \left(\frac{\bar{\xi}_2}{\bar{\xi}_1}\right)^\epsilon csc(\epsilon\pi).$$

in which $\epsilon = (1 - \theta)/(\delta - \theta)$.

2) If $0 < k < 2\sqrt{\bar{\xi}_1\bar{\xi}_2}$ and $\delta + \theta = 2$, $f(t) = 0$ for $t \geq \mathfrak{T}_2$, here

$$\mathfrak{T}_2 = \frac{1}{\delta - 1} \frac{2}{\sqrt{4\bar{\xi}_1\bar{\xi}_2 - k^2}} \left(\frac{\pi}{2} + \arctan\left(\frac{k}{\sqrt{4\bar{\xi}_1\bar{\xi}_2 - k^2}}\right)\right).$$

Lemma 4 *[19]. Function $V(f(t)) : \mathbb{R}^n \to \mathbb{R}$ is C-regular, if there have several numbers $\delta > 1$, $0 \leq \theta < 1$, $k \in \mathbb{R}$, $\bar{\xi}_1$, $\bar{\xi}_2 > 0$, and a time instant $\mathfrak{T}_p$ such that*

$$\dot{V}(f(t)) \leq -\frac{\hat{\mathfrak{T}}}{\mathfrak{T}_p}\left(-kV(f(t)) + \bar{\xi}_1 V^\delta(f(t)) + \bar{\xi}_2 V^\theta(f(t))\right), \quad f(t) \in \mathbb{R}^n \setminus \{0\},$$

then $f(t) = 0$ for $t \geq \mathfrak{T}_p$, here

$$\hat{\mathfrak{T}} = \begin{cases} \mathfrak{T}_1, & k \leq 0, \\ \mathfrak{T}_2, & 0 < k < \sqrt{\bar{\xi}_1\bar{\xi}_2}, \ \delta + \theta = 2. \end{cases}$$

Assumption 1. *There have numbers $l_j, M_j > 0$, such that for any $\tilde{x}, \tilde{y} \in \mathbb{R}$,*

$$|g_j(\tilde{x}) - g_j(\tilde{y})| \leq l_j|\tilde{x} - \tilde{y}|, \qquad |g_j(\tilde{x})| \leq M_j, \qquad j \in \bar{n}.$$

3   Main Results

Denote

$$\tilde{k}_i = -p\omega_i + (p - 1) + \alpha_i + \sum_{j=1}^{n} |c_{ji}| l_i, \quad \varphi_1 = p\rho_2, \quad \varphi_2 = (2n)^{\frac{1-\gamma}{p}} p\rho_3,$$

$$k_i^* = 1 + \alpha_i(p - 1) - p\beta_i + \sum_{j=1}^{n}(p - 1)|c_{ij}| l_j, \mathcal{K} = \max_{i \in \bar{n}}\{\tilde{k}_i, k_i^*\}.$$

Theorem 1. *Based on Assumption 1, the control laws in model (3) are designed as*

$$\begin{cases} u_{1i}(t) = -\text{sign}(e_{1i}(t))\left(\rho_2|e_{1i}(t)|^\eta + \rho_3|e_{1i}(t)|^\gamma\right), \\ u_{2i}(t) = -\text{sign}(e_{2i}(t))\left(\rho_1 + \rho_2|e_{2i}(t)|^\eta + \rho_3|e_{2i}(t)|^\gamma\right), \end{cases} \quad i \in \bar{n}, \qquad (5)$$

where ρ_1, ρ_2, $\rho_3 > 0$, $0 \leq \eta < 1$ and $\gamma > 1$ and satisfy

(H_1) $\alpha_i > 0$, $\displaystyle\sum_{j=1}^{n} 2|d_{ij}|M_j < \rho_1$, $i \in \bar{n}$,

then the following statements are derived.

1) *If $\Re \leq 0$, the models (2) and (3) reach FXT synchronization and the ST $\mathfrak{T}$ satisfies*

$$\mathfrak{T} \leq \mathfrak{T}_1 = \frac{p\pi}{(\gamma - \eta)\varphi_1}\left(\frac{\varphi_1}{\varphi_2}\right)^\epsilon \csc(\epsilon\pi).$$

   in which $\epsilon = (1 - \eta)/(\gamma - \eta)$.

2) *If $0 < \Re < 2\sqrt{\varphi_1\varphi_2}$ and $\eta + \gamma = 2$, the models (2) and (3) realize FXT synchronization and the ST $\mathfrak{T}$ satisfies*

$$\mathfrak{T} \leq \mathfrak{T}_2 = \frac{p}{\gamma - 1}\frac{2}{\sqrt{4\varphi_1\varphi_2 - \Re^2}} \times \left(\frac{\pi}{2} + \arctan(\frac{\Re}{\sqrt{4\varphi_1\varphi_2 - \Re^2}})\right).$$

Proof. Obviously, the control strategy $u_{2i}(t)$ is discontinuous, so according to the measurable selection theory [21], there has a function $\theta_{2i}(t) \in \text{sign}(e_{2i}(t))$ such that

$$\dot{e}_{2i}(t) = -\alpha_i e_{1i}(t) - \beta_i e_{2i}(t) + \sum_{j=1}^{n} c_{ij}G_j(e_{1j}(t)) + \sum_{j=1}^{n} d_{ij}G_j(e_{1j}(t - \tau(t)))$$
$$- \theta_{2i}(t)\rho_1 - \text{sign}(e_{2i}(t))(\rho_2|e_{2i}(t)|^\eta + \rho_3|e_{2i}(t)|^\gamma), \qquad i \in \bar{n}.$$

Establish the following Lyapunov function

$$V(t) = \sum_{i=1}^{n}(|e_{1i}(t)|^p + |e_{2i}(t)|^p), \quad p \geq 1. \tag{6}$$

For $e(t) \in \mathbb{R}^{2n} \setminus \{0\}$, one has

$$\dot{V}(t) \leq -p\sum_{i=1}^{n} \omega_i|e_{1i}(t)|^p + p\sum_{i=1}^{n} |e_{1i}(t)|^{p-1}|e_{2i}(t)| - p\sum_{i=1}^{n} \rho_1|e_{2i}(t)|^{p-1}$$
$$- p\sum_{i=1}^{n} \beta_i|e_{2i}(t)|^p + \sum_{i=1}^{n}\sum_{j=1}^{n} |c_{ij}||e_{2i}(t)|^{p-1}|G_j(e_{1j}(t))|$$
$$+ \sum_{i=1}^{n}\sum_{j=1}^{n} |d_{ij}||e_{2i}(t)|^{p-1}|G_j(e_{1j}(t - \tau(t)))| + p\sum_{i=1}^{n} \alpha_i|e_{2i}(t)|^{p-1}|e_{1i}(t)|$$
$$- p\sum_{i=1}^{n} \rho_2\left[|e_{1i}(t)|^{p+\eta-1} + |e_{2i}(t)|^{p+\eta-1}\right]$$
$$- p\sum_{i=1}^{n} \rho_3\left[|e_{1i}(t)|^{p+\gamma-1} + |e_{2i}(t)|^{p+\gamma-1}\right]. \tag{7}$$

Based on Lemma 2 and Assumption 1,

$$p\sum_{i=1}^{n}|e_{1i}(t)|^{p-1}|e_{2i}(t)| \leq \sum_{i=1}^{n}(p-1)|e_{1i}(t)|^{p} + \sum_{i=1}^{n}|e_{2i}(t)|^{p}, \qquad (8)$$

$$p\sum_{i=1}^{n}\alpha_{i}|e_{2i}(t)|^{p-1}|e_{1i}(t)| \leq \sum_{i=1}^{n}\alpha_{i}\big((p-1)|e_{2i}(t)|^{p} + |e_{1i}(t)|^{p}\big), \qquad (9)$$

$$p\sum_{i=1}^{n}\sum_{j=1}^{n}|c_{ij}||e_{2i}(t)|^{p-1}|G_{j}(e_{1j}(t))|$$
$$\leq \sum_{i=1}^{n}\sum_{j=1}^{n}(p-1)|c_{ij}|l_{j}|e_{2i}(t)|^{p} + \sum_{i=1}^{n}\sum_{j=1}^{n}|c_{ji}|l_{i}|e_{1i}(t)|^{p}, \qquad (10)$$

$$p\sum_{i=1}^{n}\sum_{j=1}^{n}|d_{ij}||e_{2i}(t)|^{p-1}|G_{j}(e_{1j}(t-\tau(t)))| \leq 2p\sum_{i=1}^{n}\sum_{j=1}^{n}|d_{ij}||e_{2i}(t)|^{p-1}M_{j}. \quad (11)$$

According to Lemma 1,

$$-p\sum_{i=1}^{n}\rho_{2}\Big[|e_{1i}(t)|^{p+\eta-1} + |e_{2i}(t)|^{p+\eta-1}\Big]$$
$$-p\sum_{i=1}^{n}\rho_{3}\Big[|e_{1i}(t)|^{p+\gamma-1} + |e_{2i}(t)|^{p+\gamma-1}\Big]$$
$$\leq -p\rho_{3}(2n)^{\frac{1-\gamma}{p}}V^{\frac{p+\gamma-1}{p}}(t) - p\rho_{2}V^{\frac{p+\eta-1}{p}}(t). \qquad (12)$$

Submitting (8)–(12) into (7) yields

$$\dot{V}(t) \leq \sum_{i=1}^{n}\tilde{k}_{i}|e_{1i}(t)|^{p} + \sum_{i=1}^{n}k_{i}^{*}|e_{2i}(t)|^{p} - p\rho_{3}(2n)^{\frac{1-\gamma}{p}}V^{\frac{p+\gamma-1}{p}}(t) - p\rho_{2}V^{\frac{p+\eta-1}{p}}(t)$$
$$\leq \Re V(t) - \varphi_{1}V^{\frac{p+\eta-1}{p}}(t) - \varphi_{2}V^{\frac{p+\gamma-1}{p}}(t).$$

Based on Lemma 3, the neural models (2) and (3) realize FXT synchronization within the ST $\mathfrak{T}$, here

$$\mathfrak{T} = \begin{cases} \mathfrak{T}_{1}, & \Re \leq 0, \\ \mathfrak{T}_{2}, & 0 < \Re < \sqrt{\varphi_{1}\varphi_{2}}, \quad \gamma + \eta = 2. \end{cases}$$

The proof is finished.

Remark 1. In the previous FXT synchronization works [14–17], the linear term in the control law is necessary. Note that there is no linear term in the control strategy (5), so our designed control strategy is more effective and the corresponding criteria are less conservative.

The PAT synchronization of the models (2) and (3) will be investigated as follows.

Theorem 2. *Under Assumption 1 and* H_1*, the control laws are designed as*

$$\begin{cases} u_{1i}(t) = -\frac{\mathfrak{T}_2}{\mathfrak{T}_p} sign(e_{1i}(t))\big(\rho_2|e_{1i}(t)|^\eta + \rho_3|e_{1i}(t)|^\gamma\big), \\ u_{2i}(t) - -sign(e_{2i}(t))\rho_1 - \frac{\mathfrak{T}_2}{\mathfrak{T}_p}\big(\rho_2|e_{2i}(t)|^\eta + \rho_3|e_{2i}(t)|^\gamma\big), \qquad i \in \bar{n}, \end{cases} \quad (13)$$

where $\rho_1, \rho_2, \rho_3 > 0$, $0 \leq \eta < 1$, $\gamma > 1$, $0 < \mathfrak{K} < 2\sqrt{\varphi_1\varphi_2}$, $0 < \mathfrak{T}_p \leq \mathfrak{T}_2$, $\mathfrak{T}_2$ *is defined in Theorem 1, then the neural models (2) and (3) are PAT synchronized within* $\mathfrak{T}_p$.

Proof. Similarly, for $e(t) \in \mathbb{R}^{2n} \setminus \{0\}$,

$$\dot{V}(t) \leq -\frac{\mathfrak{T}_2}{\mathfrak{T}_p}\Big(-\mathfrak{K}V(t) + \varphi_1 V^{\frac{p+\eta-1}{p}}(t) + \varphi_2 V^{\frac{p+\gamma-1}{p}}(t)\Big).$$

By Lemma 4, the neural models (3) and (4) achieve PAT synchronization within the time $\mathfrak{T}_p$.

Remark 2. Note that the ST of PAT synchronization is unrelated to system parameters and initial states, and the synchronization time can be preset in advance based on actual needs. As a result, PAT synchronization has a wider range of applications than FXT synchronization.

Remark 3. In the result [18], several control laws with infinite control gains was designed to ensure the PAT synchronization. Dissimilarly, the PAT synchronization of INNs is researched in this article via applying several control schemes with bounded control gains and the obtained synchronization criteria are more compact and more easily checked.

4   Numerical Simulations

Consider the following INNs composed of two neurons

$$\frac{d^2x_i(t)}{dt^2} = -\kappa_i \frac{dx_i(t)}{dt} - \varrho_i x_i(t) + \sum_{j=1}^{2} c_{ij}g_j(x_j(t))$$

$$+ \sum_{j=1}^{2} d_{ij}g_j(x_j(t - \tau(t))) + I_i(t), \quad i = 1, 2, \quad (14)$$

here $I_1(t) = I_2(t) = 0$, $\tau(t) = \frac{e^t}{1+e^t}$, $g_1(x) = g_2(x) = \sin(10x)$, $\kappa_1 = 4.0, \kappa_2 = 2.8$, $\varrho_1 = 1.5, \varrho_2 = 0.1$ and

$$C = (c_{ij})_{2\times2} = \begin{pmatrix} 0.8 & -0.4 \\ -3.3 & -2.1 \end{pmatrix}, D = (d_{ij})_{2\times2} = \begin{pmatrix} -1.5 & -0.2 \\ -0.7 & 1.3 \end{pmatrix}.$$

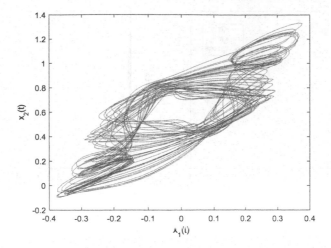

Fig. 1. The phase trajectory of system (16).

Through reduced-order transformation, the drive system (14) is translated into

$$
\begin{cases}
\dfrac{dx_i(t)}{dt} = -\omega_i x_i(t) + y_i(t), \\[2mm]
\dfrac{dy_i(t)}{dt} = -\alpha_i x_i(t) - \beta_i y_i(t) + \displaystyle\sum_{j=1}^{2} c_{ij} g_j(x_j(t)) \\[4mm]
\qquad\quad + \displaystyle\sum_{j=1}^{2} d_{ij} g_j(x_j(t - \tau(t))), \qquad i = 1, 2,
\end{cases}
\tag{15}
$$

in which $w_1 = w_2 = 0$, $\alpha_1 = 1.5$, $\alpha_2 = 1$, $\beta_1 = 4$, $\beta_2 = 2.8$.

The trajectory of inertial network (15) is displayed in Fig. 1, where the initial state is chosen as $x_1(\varsigma) = -0.2, y_1(\varsigma) = 0.4, x_2(\varsigma) = -0.5, y_2(\varsigma) = 0.4$.

The controlled response network is described by

$$
\begin{cases}
\dfrac{dz_i(t)}{dt} = -\omega_i z_i(t) + v_i(t) + u_{1i}(t), \\[2mm]
\dfrac{dv_i(t)}{dt} = -\alpha_i z_i(t) - \beta_i v_i(t) + \displaystyle\sum_{j=1}^{2} c_{ij} g_j(z_j(t)) \\[4mm]
\qquad\quad + \displaystyle\sum_{j=1}^{2} d_{ij} g_j(z_j(t - \tau(t))) + u_{2i}(t), \quad i = 1, 2.
\end{cases}
\tag{16}
$$

Select $p = 3$, $\gamma = 1.97$, $\eta = 0.03$. $\rho_1 = 4, \rho_2 = 10, \rho_3 = 16, \varphi_1 = 30$ and $\varphi_2 = 30.6602$. It is easy to calculate that $l_1 = l_2 = 10$, $M_1 = M_2 = 1$ and $\mathcal{K} = 60$. By Theorem 1, the neural models (15) and (16) reach FXT synchronization within $\mathfrak{T}_3 = 2.0809$, which is shown in Fig. 2.

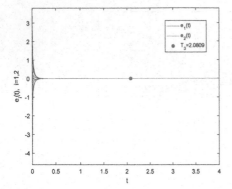

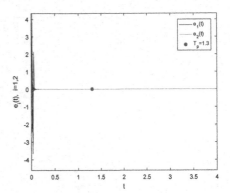

Fig. 2. FXT synchronization under controller (5).

Fig. 3. PAT synchronization under controller (13).

In what follows, the PAT synchronization of the models (15) and (16) is verified under the controller (13). Choose $p = 3$, $\gamma = 1.97$, $\eta = 0.03$. From Theorem 2, the neural models (15) and (16) reach PAT synchronization within $\mathfrak{T}_p = 1.3$, which is revealed in Fig. 3.

Remark 4. In the numerical example, it is calculated from Lemma 3 that the settling time is 2.0809. However, under the same parameters, the ST is calculated as 2.8284 and 2.2214 based on the results [22] and [23]. Clearly, our estimate for ST is more precise in comparison with the previous works.

5 Conclusion

The FXT and PT synchronization of delayed INNs has been studied. At first, the considered INN was transformed into two the first-order subsystems by using standard reduced-order transformation and the corresponding control strategy without linear term was developed to analyze FXT synchronization. Furthermore, under the p-norm, some simple and effective synchronization criteria were derived by utilizing inequality technique. In addition, the PAT synchronization has been also investigated by developing some a control law with bounded control gains, in which the ST can be assigned in advance on account of the actual needs. The designed control law and theoretical results have been confirmed finally via a numerical example.

Note that the asymptotic synchronization of INNs has been widely investigated by using non-reduced transformation, but there are few studies on FXT and PT synchronization of INNs by applying direct analysis approach, which is a topic of our future research.

References

1. Haken, H.: Pattern recognition and synchronization in pulse-coupled neural networks. Nonlinear Dyn. **44**(1), 269–276 (2006)

2. Bouzerdoum, A., Pattison, T.: Neural network for quadratic optimization with bound constraints. IEEE Trans. Neural Netw. **4**(2), 293–304 (1993)
3. Lakshmanan, S., Prakash, M., Lim, C., Rakkiyappan, R., Balasubramaniam, P., Nahavandi, S.: Synchronization of an inertial neural network with time-varying delays and its application to secure communication. IEEE Trans. Neural Networks Learn. Syst. **29**(1), 195–207 (2016)
4. Chen, L., Chen, Y., Zhang, N.: Synchronization control for chaotic neural networks with mixed delays under input saturations. Neural Process. Lett. **53**(5), 3735–3755 (2021)
5. Angelaki, D., Correia, M.: Models of membrane resonance in pigeon semicircular canal type II hair cells. Biol. Cybern. **65**(1), 1–10 (1991)
6. Mauro, A., Conti, F., Dodge, F., Schor, R.: Subthreshold behavior and phenomenological impedance of the squid giant axon. J. Gen. Physiol. **55**(4), 497–523 (1970)
7. Wei, X., Zhang, Z., Lin, C., Chen, J.: Synchronization and anti-synchronization for complex-valued inertial neural networks with time-varying delays. Appl. Math. Comput. **403**, 126194 (2021)
8. Korneev, I., Semenov, V., Slepnev, A., Vadivasova, T.: Complete synchronization of chaos in systems with nonlinear inertial coupling. Chaos, Solitons Fractals **142**, 110459 (2021)
9. Shi, J., Zeng, Z.: Global exponential stabilization and lag synchronization control of inertial neural networks with time delays. Neural Netw. **126**, 11–20 (2020)
10. Xiao, Q., Huang, T.: Quasisynchronization of discrete-time inertial neural networks with parameter mismatches and delays. IEEE Trans. Cybern. **51**(4), 2290–2295 (2019)
11. Zhang, Z., Chen, M., Li, A.: Further study on finite-time synchronization for delayed inertial neural networks via inequality skills. Neurocomputing **373**, 15–23 (2020)
12. Guo, Z., Gong, S., Huang, T.: Finite-time synchronization of inertial memristive neural networks with time delay via delay-dependent control. Neurocomputing **293**, 100–107 (2018)
13. Hui, J., Yu, J.: Exponential synchronization of complex-valued inertial neural networks based on a periodically intermittent control. J. Xinjiang Univ. (Nat. Sci. Edn. Chin. English) **39**(2), 151–160 (2022)
14. Polyakov, A.: Nonlinear feedback design for fixed-time stabilization of linear control systems. IEEE Trans. Autom. Control **57**(8), 2106–2110 (2012)
15. Jia, H., Luo, D., Wang, J., Shen, H.: Fixed-time synchronization for inertial Cohen-Grossberg delayed neural networks: an event-triggered approach. Knowl.-Based Syst. 109104 (2022)
16. Duan, L., Li, J.: Fixed-time synchronization of fuzzy neutral-type BAM memristive inertial neural networks with proportional delays. Inf. Sci. **576**, 522–541 (2021)
17. Feng, L., Hu, C., Yu, J.: Fixed-time synchronization of coupled memristive complex-valued neural networks. J. Xinjiang Univ. (Nat. Sci. Edn. Chin. English) **38**(02), 129–143 (2021)
18. Chen, C., Mi, L., Liu, Z., Qiu, B., Zhao, H., Xu, L.: Predefined-time synchronization of competitive neural networks. Neural Netw. **142**, 492–499 (2021)
19. Hu, C., He, H., Jiang, H.: Fixed/Preassigned-time synchronization of complex networks via improving fixed-time stability. IEEE Trans. Cybern. **51**(6), 2882–2892 (2021)
20. Hardy, G., Littlewood, J., Pólya, G.: Inequalities. Cambridge, U.K.: Cambridge University Press (1952)

21. Filippov, A.: Differential Equations with Discontinuous Right-Hand Sides. Kluwer, Dordrecht, The Netherlands (1988)
22. Hu, C., Yu, J., Chen, Z., Jiang, H., Huang, T.: Fixed-time stability of dynamical systems and fixed-time synchronization of coupled discontinuous neural networks. Neural Netw. **89**, 74–83 (2017)
23. Zeng, K., Wang, L., Cheng, J.: Fixed-time and preassigned-time synchronization of delayed inertial neural networks. In: 36th Youth Academic Annual Conference of Chinese Association of Automation, vol. 2021, pp. 558–563 (2021)

A Deep Reinforcement Learning Based Leader-Follower Control Policy for Swarm Systems

Di Cui, Huiping Li$^{(\boxtimes)}$ [ID], and Rizhong Wang

School of Marine Science and Technology, Northwestern Polytechnical University, Xi'an, China
{dicui,rizhingwang}@mail.nwpu.edu.cn, lihuiping@nwpu.edu.cn

Abstract. This paper is concerned with the learning-based control problem for large-scale robotic swarm systems, which makes the single leader able to herd the follower swarm systems to form a target distribution. We use the mean-field model to describe the spatio-temporal evolution of the probability density of the follower swarm, under which the physical space is divided into several bins and the leader control policy only depends on the density distribution over these bins. Therefore, the designed control policy is free from the computation issue raised by the large number of follower agents N. A deep reinforcement learning (DRL) algorithm is designed here to learn the leader control policy and accommodate the variation of the follower density. It is verified that the proposed control policy is much more efficient than existing results in terms of control performance and training time.

Keywords: Swarm systems · Leader-follower control · Mean-field model · Deep reinforcement learning (DRL)

1 Introduction

Swarm systems take a dominant role in various practical applications, such as area exploration and environmental monitoring, because of the flexibility and adaptability properties [1,2]. As one of the most promising control protocols, leader-follower control method is able to control a swarm of low-cost follower agents using the sophisticated leader with powerful performance.

In the framework of the leader-follower control, there has been a great majority of the related works concerning with three fundamental issues: consensus control [3], containment control [4] and formation control [5]. Leader-follower consensus control aims at designing a control policy steering the follower agents

This work was partially supported by the National Natural Science Foundation of China (NSFC) under Grant 61922068, 61733014; Shaanxi Provincial Funds for Distinguished Young Scientists under Grant 2019JC-14; Aoxiang Youth Scholar Program.

to track the leader. However, for the situations that a team of leaders is required to provide guidance for the follower agents, the study of leader-follower containment control is necessary, in which the control law is designed to drive the follower agents into a convex hull spanned by the multiple leaders. In the leader-follower formation control case, the control objective is to form a prescribed formation by maintaining a relative distance between the leader and the follower. Note that the follower agents in the above control protocols work in a cooperative way and the leaders have an attractive effect on the follower agents, which put high requirements on the communication networks among agents.

In this paper, we study the leader-follower control policies that the leaders herd the swarm of follower robotics into a predefined target distribution, in which a repulsive effect is forced on the follower by the leader and the follower agents work in a noncooperative fashion. Such ideas could find a wild range of applications in the field of crowd control, wildlife management and coverage control, etc. The work in [6] proposed control strategies for the multiple leaders to herd the follower agents in 2D and 3D, respectively, and the convergence results were derived by mapping the system dynamics to nonholonomic robot model. For the single leader case, Paranjape et al. [7] studied the herding strategy that enables a single unmanned aerial vehicle to divert a swarm of birds away from a specified region. However, the designing process of these controllers is not optimization-based, which results in poor swarm performance.

Recently, reinforcement learning (RL) methods have attracted particular interests to design the control policy for the multi-agent systems [8,9], in which the policy is optimized by minimizing an expected performance cost. For the leader-follower framework, Go et al. [10] studied the optimal control policy for the leader using SARSA, an RL algorithm. Then, the follower agents were herded to the target position. Note that both the optimization and the non-optimization based algorithms mentioned above adopt the individual-agent-based Lagrangian framework, which shows poor scalability with the swarm population size because of the expensive computation cost. To resolve this issue, in this paper, we use the so-called *mean-filed model* (MFM) to describe the spatio-temporal evolution of the probability density of the follower swarm [11,12], such that the density distribution, the collective property of the swarm, is controlled over time in the Euclerian framework using a probabilistic control method.

Lots of previous works have applied MFM to different swarm application scenarios, such as coverage [13], task allocation [14], etc. Additionally, some RL-based methods are also developed using MFM. For example, to solve the rendezvous and pursuit evasion problems of the swarm, Hüttenrauch et al. [15] proposed to calculate the state dependent control policies for each agent in the framework of RL. However, since the control policies of each agent will be redesigned once the task changes, these prior works show poor performance in view of versatility. In contrast, due to the utilization of the leader-follower control paradiam, only the leader control policy is redesigned in our approach.

In this paper, we study the learning based leader-follower controller for swarm systems with MFM. The control objective is to learn the leader control policy such that the follower robotic swarm is quickly herded to form a target distribution over several bins derived by dividing the physical space. Although the traditional learning based leader-follower controller uses the tabular Temporal-Difference (TD) method, the continuous state space (follower population fraction) of the system is analysed by discretization [16], which results in an inaccurate expression of the real swarm density distribution and leads to a longer time to form the target distribution.

Therefore, we design a deep reinforcement learning (DRL) based leader-follower controller for swarm systems to resolve the aforementioned issue, which learns the leader control policy through a deep neural network (DNN). The main contributions of this study are summarized as follows:

1) A leader-follower control protocol is designed to herd the swarm with a single leader using MFM, thus ensuring the versatility of the proposed algorithm.
2) A novel DRL based leader-follower control algorithm is developed to resolve the inaccuracy of the traditional tabular TD based RL method. In addition, due to the fast calculation speed of DNN, the proposed DRL algorithm shows strong real-time calculation capability.

The rest of this paper is organized as follows. Section 2 introduces mean-field model of the leader-follower swarm and states the problem formulation. In Sect. 3, a novel DRL based leader-follower control algorithm is designed. Then, simulation and comparison studies are given in Sect. 4. Finally, Sect. 5 makes the conclusion.

Notations: $\mathbb{N}_{\geq 0}$ and $\mathbb{R}$ denote the non-negtive integers and real number, respectively. $\boldsymbol{v} \in \mathbb{R}^n$ represents an n-dimensional column vector, and $\boldsymbol{v}_i$ is the ith element of the vector. $\forall \boldsymbol{x} \in \mathbb{P}^n$ indicates a $n \times 1$ column-stochastic vector, which satisfies $\boldsymbol{x}^T \cdot \mathbf{1} = 1$ and $\boldsymbol{x}_i \geq 0, \forall i = 1, \cdots, n$. For two nonempty sets A and B, $A/B = \{x | x \in A, x \notin B\}$. $\chi_x(y) : \mathbb{N}_{\geq 0} \rightarrow \{0,1\}$ is the indicator function of y, and $\chi_x(y) = 1$ only if $x = y$. $\mathbb{R}_{(a,b)}$ and $\mathbb{I}_{[a,b]}$ denote the set $\{x \in \mathbb{R} | a < x < b\}$ and the integer set $\{x \in \mathbb{N}_{\geq 0} | a \leq x \leq b\}$, respectively.

2 Preliminaries and Problem Formulation

2.1 Preliminaries

This subsection provides the basic concept and presents some necessary definitions to construct our leader-follower based MFM.

Consider a swarm consisting of a single leader and N homogeneous follower agents. Assume that N agents are distributed over a physical space B, which is divided into n disjoint bins B_i and satisfies $B = \cup_{i=1}^{n} B_i$, as shown in Fig. 1 ($n = 25$). Note that the number and partition fashion of the bins are problem specifically. For example, a bin means the local physical space in coverage control problem and a detailed task in task allocation. Therefore, our approach provides an intelligent paradiam for the large-scale swarm control with the leader-follower architecture, which could be employed to settle other issues for robotic swarm with a slight modification.

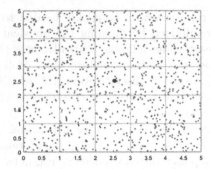

Fig. 1. 1000 follower agents distributed over 25 bins.

To facilitate the presentation of the MFM, we denote the bins and the relationship among them using some notations in graph theory. For a directed graph $G = (\mathcal{V}, \mathcal{E})$, the vertex in the set $\mathcal{V} = \{1, 2, \cdots, n\}$ represents the collection of bins, and the edge belongs to the set $\mathcal{E} = \{(i, j)|i, j \in \mathcal{V}\}$ means that any agent in bin B_i is able to transition to bin B_j. Then, we make the following standard assumptions:

Assumption 1 *(Connectivity)*. *The graph G is strongly connected and the set $\bar{\mathcal{E}} = \{(i, i)|i \in \mathcal{V}\}$ belongs to $\mathcal{E}$.*

Assumption 2 *(Leader's capability)*. *The leader is able to determine the vertex at which it stays and count the number of the follower agents at each vertex. In addition, only the follower agents located at the same vertex with the leader could be repelled.*

Definition 1 *(Current swarm distribution)*. *The current population fraction of the follower swarm at vertex i (bin B_i) at time step k is denoted as:*

$$\Theta_i(k) = \frac{1}{N}\sum\nolimits_{j=1}^{N}\chi_i(X_j(k)), \tag{1}$$

where $i \in \mathcal{V}$, $j \in \mathbb{I}_{[1,N]}$. $X_j(k) \in \mathcal{V}$ is the vertex at which the follower agent j is located. Then, the column-stochastic current swarm distribution $\Theta(k) = [\Theta_1(k), \cdots, \Theta_n(k)]^T$.

Using Definition 1, the desired column-stochastic target swarm distribution $\bar{\Theta}$ is well defined.

2.2 Problem Formulation

In this subsection, we first construct the leader-follower based MFM and then present the problem formulation.

Note that the follower agents move in a random fashion, the leader has no prior knowledge of the detailed follower behavior model. For the known leader location $l(k) \in \mathcal{V}$ at time instant $k \in \mathbb{N}_{\geq 0}$, the state of the follower agent i is represented by a stochastic process $X_i(k)$, which evolves according to the following conditional probabilities:

$$\text{Prob}(X_i(k+1) = C(e)|X_i(k) = P(e)) = u_e(k) \tag{2}$$

for each $e = (P(e), C(e)) \in \mathcal{E}$. We call $P(e)$ and $C(e)$ the parent and child vertices of e, respectively. $u_e : \mathbb{N}_{\geq 0} \to \mathbb{R}_{(0,1)}$ is the transition rate from bins $B_{P(e)}$ to $B_{C(e)}$. Here, we assume that only the follower agents at vertex $l(k)$ could be repelled, that is

$$u_e(k) = \begin{cases} \tau_e & P(e) = l(k), \\ 0 & P(e) \neq l(k), \end{cases} \tag{3}$$

$\forall e \in \mathcal{E}/\bar{\mathcal{E}}$. where $\tau_e \in \mathbb{R}_{[0,1]}$ is a predetermined parameter and satisfies

$$\sum_{e \in \mathcal{E}/\bar{\mathcal{E}}, P(e)=i} \tau_e < 1.$$

Then, for the pair $(i,i) \in \bar{\mathcal{E}}$, we have:

$$u_{(i,i)} = 1 - \sum_{e \in \mathcal{E}/\bar{\mathcal{E}}, P(e)=i} u_e(k)$$

Denote the probability density $\mathcal{P}(\mathcal{V}) = \{x \in \mathbb{R}^n | \mathbf{1}^T x = 1, x_j \in \mathbb{R}_{[0,1]}\}$ on $\mathcal{V}$. By utilizing the stochastic process defined in (2), the spatio-temporal evolution of the probability density $\text{Prob}(X_i(k) = v) = x_v^i(k) \in \mathbb{R}_{[0,1]}$ for the follower agent i is:

$$x^i(k+1) = \sum_{e \in \mathcal{E}} u_e(k) M_e x^i(k), \tag{4}$$

$$x^i(0) \in \mathcal{P}(\mathcal{V}),$$

where the entries in matrix $M_e \in \mathbb{R}^{n \times n}$ are defined as follows:

$$M_e^{ij}(k) = \begin{cases} 1 & i = C(e), j = P(e), \\ 0 & otherwise. \end{cases} \tag{5}$$

Since the random variables $X_i(k), \forall i \in \mathbb{I}_{[1,N]}$ are independent and identically distributed (IID), the evolution of the probability density for the follower swarm can be redefined by the MFM, a single discrete-time *Kolmogorov Forward Equation* in (4):

$$x(k+1) = \sum_{e \in \mathcal{E}} u_e(k) M_e x(k), \tag{6}$$

$$x(0) \in \mathcal{P}(\mathcal{V}).$$

According to the law of large numbers, the swarm distribution defined in (1) converges to the probability density $x(k)$. Therefore, the control issues raised in the large-scale swarm could be settled by resorting to the deterministic quantity $x(k)$, which is free from the influence of the swarm size and only decided by the number of bins n.

Then, in order to design a learning-based control policy for the leader to herd the swarm of the follower to the target distribution $\bar{\Theta}$ as quickly as possible, DRL is studied here to formulate such an optimization problem, and the reward function is designed using the deterministic quantity $x(k)$ as follows:

$$R(k) = -\mathbb{E}_\pi \|x(k) - \bar{x}\|^2 \tag{7}$$

where $\bar{x}$ is the target probability density of the swarm.

Now, we summerize the problem to be studied as follows: For the given target probability density $\bar{x}$, learn a control policy $\pi : \mathcal{P}(\mathcal{V}) \times \mathcal{V} \to A$ for the leader using the discounted return:

$$\begin{aligned} G(k) &= R(k) + \gamma R(k+1) + \cdots + \gamma^{\infty-k} R(\infty) \\ &= \sum_{i=k}^{\infty} \gamma^{i-k} R(i), \end{aligned} \tag{8}$$

such that $x(k) \to \bar{x}$, where $\gamma \in \mathbb{R}_{(0,1)}$ is the discount rate. A is the action space for the leader defined by the collection of the possible transition A_i at each vertex i, where

$$A_i = \cup_{e \in \mathcal{E}, P(e)=i} \{e\}, i \in \mathcal{V} \tag{9}$$

Finally, we can easily conclude that $\Theta(k) \to \bar{\Theta}$, when $x(k) \to \bar{x}$ holds. We show the key steps in the learning-based leader-follower swarm controller in Fig. 2.

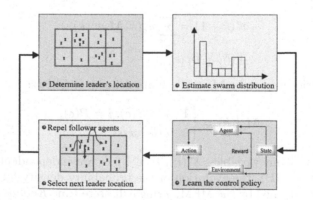

Fig. 2. Flowchart of the learning-based leader-follower swarm controller.

3 DRL Based Leader-follower Controller

3.1 Deep Neural Network

In this subsection, we give the brief description of DNN.

We use $S = \{[x(k), l(k)] | x(k) \in \mathcal{P}(\mathcal{V}), l(k) \in \mathcal{V}\}$ to denote the state of the environment, and the action set A of the leader has been defined in (9). The goal of RL in this paper is to interact with the environment and learn the control policy which maximises the expected return $Q(s, a) = \mathbb{E}_\pi[G(k) | s(k) = s, a(k) = a]$ (the state action value function) starting from $\forall s \in S$ and $\forall a \in A$. Generally, $Q(s, a)$ is estimated from experience and bootstrapping technology.

In traditional tabular-based RL, such as SARSA and Q-learning [16], $Q(s, a)$ is trained and saved as a multi-dimensional tabular form. Then, the leader control policy is calculated by importing the current state s. However, these methods define S as a vector that only contains limited discrete quantities of the continuous population fractions of the swarm and the leader's location $l(k)$. Therefore, the control performance is strongly influenced by the discretization precision, and the issues such as the memory needed for the large tables become particular urgent with the increase of the accuracy requirements. To cope with this issue, this article uses DNN to approximate $Q(s, a)$ with the experiences in a limited subset of the state space.

A typical structure of DNN, as shown in Fig. 3, is comprised of three parts: input layer, hidden layer and output layer, which is able to fit arbitrary finite discontinuous nonlinear function using a series of composited nonlinear mapping functions [17]

$$f_\theta(y) = h_l(h_{l-1}(\cdots h_1(y))) \tag{10}$$

where the network has l layers, and $h_i(y) = \delta(\omega_\theta^i y + b_\theta^i)$. δ is the nonlinear activation function, commonly designed as: sigmoid function, tanh function or ReLU function.

Using the limited experiences of $Q(s, a)$, the optimal weight parameters $\theta = \{\omega_\theta, b_\theta\}$ of the neural network is obtained by minimizing a predefined loss function, which extends the learning capacity from discrete-time state space to continuous-time.

3.2 DRL Based Leader-Follower Controller Design

In this subsection, the detailed procedures for DRL based leader-follower controller are presented as follows.

First, construct the training data set. Different from the supervised learning, DRL improves its control policy with the knowledge obtained by interaction with the environment. Therefore, by starting an episode from the given initial swarm distribution $x(0)$, we will obtain a sequence of actions, rewards and observations of the state $s_1, a_1, r_1 \cdots, s_T, a_T$ as the training data.

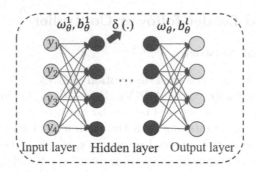

Fig. 3. A typical structure of DNN.

Then, approximate function $Q(s, a)$ using DNN introduced in Sect. 3.1. Defining the loss function at iteration step i in an episode as

$$L_i(\boldsymbol{\theta}_i) = \mathbb{E}_{s_i, a_i \sim \rho(\cdot)}(\|U_i - Q(s_i, a_i; \boldsymbol{\theta}_i)\|^2) \tag{11}$$

where $Q(s_i, a_i; \boldsymbol{\theta}_i)$ is the approximated state action value function, and $U_i = r_i + \gamma \max a_{i+1} Q(s_{i+1}, a_{i+1}; \boldsymbol{\theta}_i)$ is the target. The behavior distribution $\rho(s, a)$ denotes the probability distribution over s and a. Under the guidance of the stochastic gradient-descent (SDG) and the semi-gradient method, differentiating the loss function in (11) with respect to $\boldsymbol{\theta}_i$, we arrive at

$$\nabla_{\boldsymbol{\theta}_i} L_i(\boldsymbol{\theta}_i) = (U_i - Q(s_i, a_i; \boldsymbol{\theta}_i)) \nabla_{\boldsymbol{\theta}_i} Q(s_i, a_i; \boldsymbol{\theta}_i) \tag{12}$$

Next, update the weight vector $\boldsymbol{\theta}_i = \boldsymbol{\theta}_{i-1} - \alpha \nabla_{\boldsymbol{\theta}_i} L_i(\boldsymbol{\theta}_i)$ with the learning rate α, and choose the leader control policy using the approximated $Q(s_i, a_i; \boldsymbol{\theta}_i)$ with the ε-greedy policy. By executing the policy, the environment will output new training datas s_i, a_i, r_i.

Then, iteratively execute the above procedures.

In order to further improve the training performance, the following two steps are considered:

1) Set an experience reply unit. To break the data dependence in the training process, an experience reply bool is built to store the observed data and provide sample training data for DNN. The training process is activated only if the bool is full.

2) Employ a separate target DNN. It should be noticed that the target in (11) shares a common DNN with $Q(s_i, a_i; \boldsymbol{\theta}_i)$, which may raise the data dependence and lead to the instability of the training process. Therefore, we calculate the target using different weight parameters $\boldsymbol{\theta}'$, and $U_i = r_i + \gamma \max a_{i+1} Q(s_{i+1}, a_{i+1}; \boldsymbol{\theta}')$. Then, let $\boldsymbol{\theta}' = \boldsymbol{\theta}$ for every fixed step.

Finally, the leader control policy is quickly calculated using the trained DNN. The detailed training process for DRL based leader control policy is shown in Fig. 4.

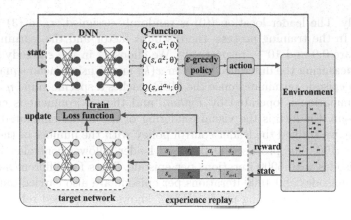

Fig. 4. Training process for DRL based leader control policy

4 Numerical Example

Consider a swarm system distributed in four bins, the corresponding graph is shown in Fig. 5. Here, we choose the action set of the leader as follows:

$$A_i = \mathbb{I}_{[0,4]}, i \in \mathcal{V} \tag{13}$$

which denotes the leader move to the left, right, up, down and stay in the current bins, respectively.

The initial distribution $x(0)$ and the target distribution $\bar{x}$ of the swarm of the follower agents are set as

$$x(0) = [0.4, 0.1, 0.1, 0.4]^T$$

and

$$\bar{x} = [0.1, 0.4, 0.4, 0.1]^T,$$

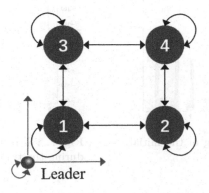

Fig. 5. The directed graph of the bins

respectively. The leader location $l(0)$ is randomly assigned. τ_e in (3) is 0.1 for all $e \in \mathcal{E}$. In the training process, the discount factor and the learning rate to update $\boldsymbol{\theta}$ are 0.9 and 10^{-3}, respectively. We choose ε in the ε-greedy policy as 0.01. By measuring the difference between $\boldsymbol{x}(k)$ and $\bar{\boldsymbol{x}}$ using mean squared error (MSE), an episode terminates once the MSE reaches a specific value $\eta = 0.0005$.

The simulation is operated by *Python*, and the environment is created in *OpenAI Gym*. Figure 6 is the visual rendering of the initial simulated environment. Here, we trained the leader control policy with the number of the follower agents $N = 100$. The proposed DRL based leader-follower controller is trained on 100 episodes with 5000 iterations per episode. Tests for different swarm size with 1000 episodes and 1000 iterations per episode are also carried out.

First, during the training process, Fig. 7 shows the detailed returns in each episode, which shows that the returns converge in five episodes. That is, $Q(s, a)$ is quickly learned.

Then, during the test process, the distribution of the follower swarm at the end of an arbitrary episode is shown in Fig. 8. The policies were also tested on scenarios with 1000 followers. The results are shown in Fig. 9, which verify the robustness of the proposed policy with the variation of the agents populations.

Tabular based Q-learning methods [16] are also carried out for comparison. Using the same environment in Fig. 5, we test the average number of iterations of the leader control policy for different value of N. Here, we choose the terminate threshold value $\eta = 0.005$. Figure 10 is the comparison results, which shows that the proposed DRL based controller has the following two advantages: 1) It provides an improved performance from the perspective of fewer average iterations until convergence. 2) It has stonger robustness in terms of the swarm size because of the lower variation of the average iterations. Figure 11 shows the simulation results using $\eta = 0.0025$. Compared with Fig. 10, the average iterations decrease with the increase of η for both the two algorithms, which is reasonable beacause that a relaxed terminate condition will close an episode in advance.

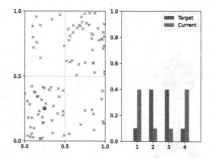

Fig. 6. Visual rendering of the initial simulated environment.

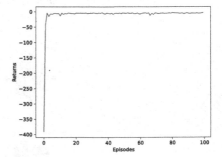

Fig. 7. The returns for the 100 episodes during the training

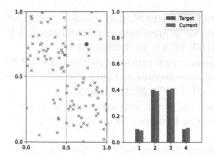

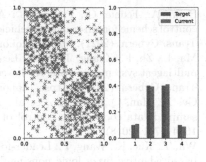

Fig. 8. Visual rendering of the final distribution for $N = 100$

Fig. 9. Visual rendering of the final distribution for $N = 1000$

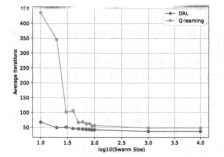

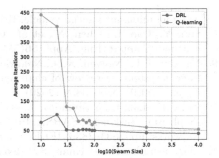

Fig. 10. The comparision results for the variation of the average iterations with $\eta = 0.005$

Fig. 11. The comparision results for the variation of the average iterations with $\eta = 0.0025$

5 Conclusions

In this paper, we have proposed a DRL based leader-follower swarm control algorithm that enables a single leader to herd the follower agents to form a target distribution. Different from the individual-agent-based Lagrangian framework, we have established a mean-filed model for the leader follower case at the macroscopic level, which scaled well with the swarm population size. The simulation and comparison studies have also been carried out to verify the effectiveness and advantages of the proposed algorithm.

References

1. Elamvazhuthi, K., Kakish, Z., Shirsat, A., et al.: Controllability and stabilization for herding a robotic swarm using a leader: a mean-field approach. IEEE Trans. Rob. **37**(2), 418–432 (2021)

2. Bono, A., Fedele, G., Franze, G.: A swarm-based distributed model predictive control scheme for autonomous vehicle formations in uncertain environments. IEEE Trans. Cybern. (2021). https://doi.org/10.1109/TCYB.2021.3070461

3. Ma, L., Zh, F., Zhang, J., et al.: Leader-follower asymptotic consensus control of multiagent systems: an observer-based disturbance reconstruction approach. IEEE Trans. Cybern. (2021). https://doi.org/10.1109/TCYB.2021.3125332

4. Ge, X., Han, Q., Ding, D., et al.: A survey on recent advances in distributed sampled-data cooperative control of multi-agent systems. Neurocomputing **275**, 1684–1701 (2018)

5. Wu, T., Xue, K., Wang, P.: Leader-follower formation control of USVS using APF-based adaptive fuzzy logic nonsingular terminal sliding mode control method. J. Mech. Sci. Technol. **36**(4), 2007–2018 (2022)

6. Pierson, A., Schwager, M.: Controlling noncooperative herds with robotic herders. IEEE Trans. Rob. **34**(2), 517–525 (2018)

7. Paranjape, A.A., Chung, S.J., Kim, K., et al.: Robotic herding of a flock of birds using an unmanned aerial vehicle. IEEE Trans. Rob. **34**(4), 901–915 (2018)

8. Sun, Y., Cao, L., Chen, X., et al.: Overview of multi-agent deep reinforcement learning. Comput. Eng. Appl. **56**(5), 13–24 (2020)

9. Nguyen, T.T., Nguyen, N.D., Nahavandi, S.: Deep reinforcement learning for multiagent systems: a review of challenges, solutions, and applications. IEEE Trans. Cybern. **50**(9), 3826–3839 (2020)

10. Go, C.K., Lao, B., Yoshimoto, J., et al.: A reinforcement learning approach to the shepherding task using SARSA. In: 2016 International Joint Conference on Neural Networks, pp. 3833–3836. IEEE, Vancouver (2016)

11. Elamvazhuthi, K., Berman, S.: Mean-field models in swarm robotics: a survey. Bioinspiration Biomimet. **15**(1), 015001 (2019)

12. Zheng, T., Han, Q., Lin, H.: Transporting robotic swarms via mean-field feedback control. IEEE Trans. Autom. Control (2021). https://doi.org/10.1109/TAC.2021.3108672

13. Bandyopadhyay, S., Chung, S., Hadaegh, F.Y.: Probabilistic and distributed control of a large-scale swarm of autonomous agents. IEEE Trans. Rob. **33**(5), 1103–1123 (2017)

14. Berman, S., Halasz, A., Hsieh, M.A., et al.: Optimized stochastic policies for task allocation in swarms of robots. IEEE Trans. Rob. **25**(4), 927–937 (2009)

15. Hüttenrauch, M., Adrian, S., Neumann, G.: Deep reinforcement learning for swarm systems. J. Mach. Learn. Res. **20**(54), 1–31 (2019)

16. Kakish, Z.M., Elamvazhuthi, K., Berman, S.: Using reinforcement learning to herd a robotic swarm to a target distribution. Comput. Sci. arXiv:2006.15807

17. Hornik, K., Stinchcombe, M., White, H.: Multilayer feedforward networks are universal approximators. Neural Netw. **2**, 359–366 (1989)

Research on the Key Technology of Digital Twin-Driven Fracture Reduction Robot Force Control

Peng Wang$^{(\boxtimes)}$, Lingling Yang, and Yanran Wang

Beijing Institute of Petrochemical Technology, Beijing 102617, China
2020310807@bipt.edu.cn

Abstract. In order to make a breakthrough in the bottleneck of the current technology of medical robots, this article focuses on the problem of difficult human position precision control of the fracture reduction machine, introducing the digital twin into the construction of the robot reduction surgical systems. And we propose a solution from the high-level control architecture to the terminal controller optimization. Firstly, there is no effective connection between the current clinical surgical pathological data acquisition and robot control system. In this paper, the key factor of robot control--force position control accuracy is taken as the specific object, and a closed-loop technical framework for force position error is constructed. In addition, the existing construction methods of force bit control cannot meet the dynamics of human-computer interaction. Therefore, this paper tries to deeply integrate the robot dynamics mechanism model, real data and finite element three-dimensional model, and proposes a dynamic model method with additional robot dynamic mechanism. Besides, according to the environmental complexity problem in the process of force bit control. A multimodal fusion control scheme is proposed to design a high-precision force bit controller by using intraoperative multi-source information.

Keywords: Robot dynamics mechanism model · Error dynamic modeling · Multi-modal fusion control

1 Introduction

Medical systems have developed into a huge and complex system, in which a large number of emerging technologies, including artificial intelligence and big data, have poured into it, making the medical system move from unitization to integration, and from people-oriented to man-machine collaboration. Intelligent medical treatment is a complex interdisciplinary subject based on the integration of life science and information technology. The connotation of intelligent medical treatment is based on the integration of advanced technologies such as information technology, artificial intelligence and mechanical technology, so as to complete the construction of intelligent medical modes, means and formats of medical systems in the closed loop, man-machine cooperation and all things interconnection, so as to meet the particularity of individual cases and the needs

L. Zhang et al. (Eds.): CINT 2022, CCIS 1714, pp. 281–287, 2022.
https://doi.org/10.1007/978-981-19-8915-5_24

of the whole process of treatment. However, in this point of view, there is still a lack of a complete set of theoretical and technical systems. Therefore, it has become urgent to determine to research the scope of smart medicine and its boundary and relationship with other related disciplines. Then it gives the technical system and key technologies of smart transformation and upgrading. The construction of medical human-computer interaction system is the mainstream idea and scheme for the implementation of smart medicine, that is, to let robots participate in the whole treatment process, and the application field of medical robots representing its development level is facing great opportunities and challenges. As a new industry, it drives the new growth of the world economy, and thus has attracted the attention and attention of all countries. The research of medical robots mainly includes many medical fields such as diagnosis, treatment, rehabilitation, nursing and functional assistance. The combination of medical robot technology and information technology is the research direction in the field of modern and contemporary medical robots.

The participation of auxiliary robots in surgery is the main idea of intelligent medical landing and implementation. In the early 1990s, an example of robot-assisted surgery with doctors began to appear, and it was proved to have good clinical practicability. Multiple research institutions have developed the prototype system of orthopedic surgery auxiliary robots, and some have been successfully commercialized, which have been promoted and used worldwide. Overseas began to develop orthopedic surgery auxiliary robot time is relatively early, relatively speaking technology is more mature, more achievements. The University of California has introduced a robot system based on an innovative system for total bone marrow replacement surgery. The robot system is developed on the basis of traditional industrial robot systems, which can be used for total bone replacement, knee replacement, bone marrow replacement and repair. At present, ZEUS surgical robot system and Da Vinci robot system are mature in clinical application, which are characterized by high precision and high stability. Due to the manual fixation of fracture reduction, motion can usually be decomposed into movement or rotation along a certain axis, so it is suitable to be replaced by robot motion, which creates favorable preconditions for robot reduction.

The development of orthopedic surgery auxiliary robots in China is still in its infancy. Doctors successfully completed the remote operation from Beijing to Yan' an and from Beijing to Shijiazhuang. The remote operation function was realized based on the network platform. Based on this, Beijing Tianzhihang Medical Co., Ltd. has successfully developed the first orthopedic surgical robot with completely independent intellectual property rights in China. The system has the functions of autonomous positioning and man-machine cooperative control. In addition, Nankai University has developed a set of auxiliary minimally invasive spine robot positioning system, which is mainly based on medical image data to assist the positioning of percutaneous vertebroplasty. The image display and processing technology of the system can correct the artifacts of metal objects and perform effective image segmentation. Minimally invasive surgical robots were developed by a Chinese university and Institute of Automation, Chinese Academy of Sciences. Shenzhen Institute of Advanced Technology, Chinese Academy of Sciences independently developed a spinal surgical robot system, which is mainly composed of a five-degree-of-freedom manipulator, an preoperative autonomous planning system, an infrared tracking and positioning system and an intraoperative computer navigation system.

In view of the fact that there is no effective connection between the acquisition of clinical surgical pathological data and the robot control system, the existing force and position control construction methods cannot meet the dynamic nature of human-computer interaction and the complex environment in the process of force and position control. This paper introduces the human-robot cooperative force and position control system for fracture reduction driven by digital twins. The overall framework is shown in Fig. 1, emphasizing the platform design idea of 'top-down' and 'inside-out'. That is, first of all, the digital twin architecture of the human-computer system for fracture reduction should be clarified, and the interactive mapping relationship between the physical entity and the simulation model should be established. Then, the mechanism of the operation should be started. It is emphasized that all intelligent transformation must be carried out under the guidance of mechanism rather than medical statistical laws (statistical laws can only be used as auxiliary and reference). The key problems to be solved in this paper can be summarized as the following three aspects: the construction method of human-machine digital twin system for fracture reduction, the dynamic accurate modeling technology of force-position error and the multi-modal human cooperative control technology.

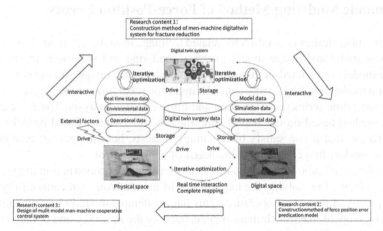

Fig. 1. Overall architecture of collaborative control for reset robot driven by digital twinning

2   Construction Method of Man - Machine Digital Twin System for Fracture Reduction

Firstly, the collection of pathological data and the construction of human-machine virtual model have made great progress. However, there is no effective connection between them. In response to this demand, this paper introduces the concept of digital twinning into the construction of robot reduction surgery system, and puts forward a new human-computer collaborative architecture. The focus is to establish the connection between human-computer entities and virtual models of reduction surgery, which offers a novel point of view for the optimization of surgical scheme. Therefore, this paper studies the man-machine digital twin system architecture for fracture reduction surgery, and clarifies the connotation, requirements, characterization, composition and level of the system. This paper researches how to establish the interactive mapping relationship between physical system and virtual system, real data and simulation data, mechanism module and simulation model, and provides a standardized solution for the real implementation of intelligent medical treatment in the operation process.

The essential of building digital twin systems is how to establish the relation between the physical space and the virtual space, real data and virtual model, and the unified modeling language Modelica is proposed to complete the construction of kernel system. The whole system should include data resource module, capability module and interaction module.

The data resource module is used for integrating clinical information and simulation data to form a data-driven library. Capability modules should use a unified modeling approach to dynamically simulate data. The interactive module gives the analysis results according to the simulation results and the actual effect. The whole process design data analysis, modeling and simulation, mechanical analysis, etc.

3   Dynamic Modeling Method of Force-Position Errors

Robot controller design is not directly related to image models. There are two common methods of traditional image models: surface rendering and volume rendering. However, the model constructed in this way is essentially static image and cannot be called simulation model. For the existing control simulation prediction model, there are mainly two methods: time series reconstruction and finite element analysis. The finite element analysis method based on mechanics simplifies the three-dimensional model to a certain degree, so that it can satisfy biodynamics analysis, but the analysis results of the simplified model often cannot meet the needs of actual control.

Therefore, the traditional sample-based predictive model construction method or the controller obtained by solving the mechanism differential equation cannot fully reflect the complexity of the actual operation. This paper attempts to study the dynamic modeling technology of machine human error, especially the accuracy and dynamics of the model. Accuracy focuses on how the model can truly reflect the operation process. In the face of external interference, the changes in biomechanical properties and physical characterization, involving muscle and bone density, soft tissue viscoelasticity and deformation nonlinearity are the key factors that directly affect the operation process. The key to dynamics is the adaptive ability of the model, that is, how the model can dynamically respond and optimize according to the changes in the actual surgical process. Therefore, a dynamic modeling method of force-position error with robot dynamics mechanism is proposed, which is a dynamic modeling method of six-axis machine force-position error based on multi-source deep network.

As shown in Fig. 2, during the operation of the multi-axis robot system, there are many factors affecting the force-position error. Among them, the mechanical characteristic parameters (natural frequency and damping ratio, etc.) of the feed system are represented by Rp; the motion control parameters (proportional integral coefficient, etc.) are represented by Cp; the environmental interference (friction force, inertia force, etc.) is represented by Ed; other nonlinear influencing factors (physiological environment change, etc.) are represented by Nl; and the interactive information (voice gesture) is represented by Ci. The influence factors are coupling and influencing each other, such as: mechanical characteristic parameters directly affect all kinds of controller parameters, especially model-based controller parameters; nonlinear interference will change the dynamic response of the system; interaction information is an important constraint of robot motion, and the environmental changes caused by motion will affect the dynamic response and controller parameters of the system. In addition, the torque (force) and position (position) errors and their influencing factors are always changing during the operation of the multi-axis feed system. The relationship between them is time-varying and dynamic, and this relationship is difficult to be characterized by a single mechanism model or data. In order to accurately predict the change of force-position error, describe the complex relationship between force-position error and its influencing factors, and ensure the efficiency of model calculation, we use the idea of multi-source information fusion to obtain the dynamic mapping model between force-position error and its various influencing factors. The measured data, soft sensor data, calculation data, instruction data, mechanism formula, etc. are fused. The artificial intelligence algorithms such as deep neural network (such as convolutional neural network) are used to train and correct the dynamic mapping model, and finally the force level prediction model is obtained.

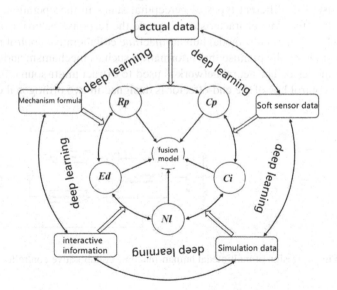

Fig. 2. Multi-source dynamic modeling based on deep network

4   Multimodal Human-Machine Collaborative Control System

When the virtual space and physical space are effectively connected, and the robot reset process is fully characterized by the dynamic model, the controller design can be carried out on this basis. Similarly, the complexity of the actual clinical environment also needs to be considered in designing the controller. Multimodal robots are widely used in the industrial field. However, for complex surgical processes, the main problems of multimodal robot control technology are embodied in the following two facets. Firstly, the characteristic representation of industrial multimodal robots cannot be shared in multiple modes, which leads to the unreliable application of the existing multimodal robot control methods. Secondly, the environmental factors of industrial production are quite different from the state environment of medical surgery. Both classical force control and modern force control are the model structures of known systems, but the actual situation is not ideal. The control system is very complex, and the system model is often unclear. The structure and parameters of the model have great fuzziness and unknowns. Industrial robots operate in various postures and interact with the environment. The dynamics itself also has great uncertainty, which brings many difficulties to the modeling. In robot trajectory planning, the robot and the environment usually have physical contact, especially when the rigidity of the robot and the working environment is large, it will produce very large contact force. The traditional robot control system based on position control has its own defects.

Therefore, this paper attempts a new idea, using the method of feature fusion to extract the characteristics of different types of perceptual states in the operation, and finally connect and fuse the state characteristics to guide the response behavior of the robot. As shown in Fig. 3, the multi-modal human-machine collaborative control proposed in this paper is based on the premise that information such as mechanism and data can be interactively modeled. The neural network is used to extract multi-source features, and the nonlinear control law of the end-effector is designed in two orthogonal directions.

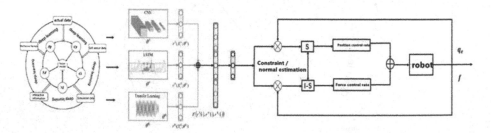

Fig. 3. Design of multimodal human-machine collaborative controller

5   Conclusion

Aiming at the problem of difficult control of human position accuracy of fracture reduction machine, this paper introduces digital twin into the construction of robot reduction surgery systems, and proposes a solution from high-level control architecture to terminal controller optimization. Firstly, the 'modeling-prediction-control' closed-loop control system based on digital twinning is designed to establish the mapping interaction between the physical space of the surgical site and the virtual simulation space. Even if the virtual simulation model evolves with the real surgical process, the corresponding control rate is given based on the state prediction of the virtual space, thereby affecting the robot control based on the physical space and forming the information closed-loop. In order to meet the dynamic of human-computer interaction, a dynamic modeling method of six-axis machine human position error based on multi-source deep network is proposed. Since the state environment of medical surgery is very complex, the feature fusion method is attempted to guide the response behavior of the robot. The final purpose is to design a high-precision force-position controller using intraoperative multi-source information.

References

1. Fangfang, G., Xizhuo, S., Jun, L., et al.: Construction of smart medical construction in China. Modern Hosp. Manag. **11**(2), 12 (2013)
2. Paul, G.J.: Privacy implications of wearable health devices. In: International Conference on Security of Information and Networks, pp. 117–121. ACM (2014)
3. Xiaoguang, H., Yaiun, L., Mingxing, F., et al.: Development and clinical application of orthopaedic surgical robotics. Sci. Technol. Guide **35**(10), 19–25 (2017)
4. Bargar, W.L., Bauer, A., Borner, M.: Robodoc: combined United States and German experience in over 1000 cases. J. Arthroplasty **14**(2), 251 (1999)
5. Nishihara, S., Sugano, N., Nishii, T., et al.: comparison between hand rasping and robotic milling for stem implantation in cementless total hip arthroplasty. J. Arthroplasty **21**(7), 957–966 (2006)
6. Nogler, M., Polikeit, A., Wimmer, C., et al.: Primary stability of a robodoc® implanted anatomical stem versus manual implantation. Clin. Biomech. **19**(2), 123–129 (2004)
7. Lee, S., Lim, J., Kim, K.: Control performance of a motion controller for robot-assisted surgery. In: Proceedings of the IEEE Workshop on Advanced Robotics and its Social Impacts (ARSO2010), Seoul, Korea, pp. 52–52 (2010)
8. Kazanzides, P., Zuhars, J., Mittelstadt, B., et al.: Force sensing and control for a surgical robot. Ion: Proceedings of the IEEE International Conference on Robotics and Automation, pp. 612–617 (1992)
9. Wang Junqiang, S., Yonggang, S., Lei, H., et al.: Design and application of medical robot and computer-aided navigation surgical system in tibial intramedullary nail surgery. Chin. J. Trauma Orthoped. **7**(12), 1108–1113 (2005)
10. Hao, J., Jianxun, Z., Gang, A., et al.: Design and implementation of a robot-assisted spinal minimally invasive surgery system. J. Nankai Univ. (Nat. Sci. Edn.) **41**(4), 32–35 (2008)
11. Ju, H., Zhang, J., An, G., et al.: A Robot-assisted system for minimally invasive spine surgery of percutaneous vertebroplasty based on CT Images. In: Proceedings of the IEEE International Conference on Robotics, Automation and Mechatronics, pp. 290–295 (2008)
12. He, Z.: Minimally invasive spinal surgery and its human system (remote control) and key technology research. The Third Military Medical University (2012)
13. Luo, H., Jia, F., Zheng, Z., et al.: An IGSTK-based surgical navigation system connected with medical robot. In: Proceedings of the IEEE Youth Conference on Information Computing and Telecommunications, pp. 49–52 (2011)

A Data-driven Feedforward Control Design Method for Nonlinear Systems

Luan Li[2], Bin Zhu[3], Yinpei Wang[4], and Xiaoqiang Ji[1,2(✉)]

[1] The Shenzhen Institute of Artificial Intelligence and Robotics for Society, The Chinese University of Hong Kong, Shenzhen, Guangdong, China
jixiaoqiang@cuhk.edu.cn
[2] The School of Science and Engineering, The Chinese University of Hong Kong, Shenzhen, Guangdong, China
[3] Department of Automation, Tsinghua University, Beijing, China
[4] University of California, Irvine, USA

Abstract. Feedforward controllers are widely used in industries with high demand for tracking accuracy. Model-based control design methods face modeling difficulty and uncertainty when dealing with increasingly complicated systems. In this paper, we present a new data-driven feedforward control design method. With the assistance of Koopman operator theory, nonlinear systems are lifted to high-dimensional space. Then the inverse of the lifted system is found and a feedforward controller is designed, which can directly work on the original system. Two simulation examples are presented, testifying the efficiency of the proposed method, and the comparison to the generally used local linearization approach is presented.

Keywords: Feedforward control · Data-driven control · Koopman operator · Nonlinear systems

1 Introduction

In tracking problems, the controlled system is required to track a desired trajectory. Feedforward control methods can tremendously improve the tracking accuracy in scenarios with high demand for control accuracy compared to feedback-only methods [1,2].

With a known system model, a feedforward controller is typically designed from the inverse model of the control system [2,3]. Such traditional model-based design methods typically require system identification to ensure that the system model is highly accurate. Another strategy is to directly identify the inverse

This work was partially supported by Shenzhen Science and Technology Program (Grant No. RCBS20210706092219050), Guangdong Basic and Applied Basic Research Foundation (Grant No. 2022A1515110411), and Shenzhen Institute of Artificial Intelligence and Robotics for Society (AC01202201001). Li Luan and Zhu Bin contribute equally to this work.
X. Ji—*IEEE Member*.

model of the system [4,5]. While in many complicated scenarios, system modeling can be very hard.

Data-driven control methods have drawn much attention in recent years and achieved significant success. Some advanced intelligent control methods are developed [6,7]. Neural networks are used in inverse model identification and feedforward control design [8,9]. However, such techniques treat control systems as a black box. The structure of those neural network-based methods often brings heavy computation and tuning effort.

Koopman operator theory [10] was first proposed in the 1930s. Various data-driven methods have been presented to find an approximation in finite dimension. Traditional control methods for linear systems can be implemented using the approximate Koopman operator.

In this paper, we present a new feedforward control method for nonlinear systems based on Koopman operator theory. System states are lifted to a high dimension space by a set of observable functions. Then the system inverse can be found from the linear lifted space. The proposed method does not require information on the system model and thus is a data-driven control method and possesses strong flexibility.

This paper is organized as follows: In Sect. 2 we describe the system inverse problem formulation. In Sect. 3 we describe the proposed data-driven feedforward control method. In Sect. 4 we describe simulation results and comparison. Section 5 presents the conclusion.

2   Problem Formulation

2.1   Feedforward Control by Inverting Nonlinear Systems

A feedforward controller takes in the desired output and generates the corresponding control signals. For example, consider such a nonlinear system

$$y(k) = g[y(k), y(k-1), \cdots, y(k-n), u(k), u(k-1)]. \tag{1}$$

Let $\hat{g}^{-1}(k)$ be the estimated nonlinear inverse dynamics of the controlled system $g(k)$. When g is a nonlinear function, the exact inverse of the dynamics is hard to find. Neural networks(NN) are strong tools to fit nonlinearity, and thus are widely used in model inverse identification.

Having the inverse dynamics $\hat{g}^{-1}(k)$ and actual dynamics $g(k)$ canceling each other out, the output $y(k)$ will equal to the reference input signal $y^\star(k)$

$$y(k) = \frac{g(k)}{\hat{g}^{-1}(k)} y^\star(k). \tag{2}$$

2.2   Feedforward Control by Inverting Lifted Linear System

In contrast to the linear system inverse method, those analytical methods for nonlinear systems usually bring more complexity and computational load. The complexity in network structure also could cause much tuning effort.

In this paper, we aim to find a data-driven method for system inverse. Rather than local linearization techniques, we seek a global linear representation for a nonlinear system, which is constructed from collected data only. For a nonlinear system

$$x_{k+1} = f(x_k, u_k), \tag{3}$$

we look for a transformation from original state x_k to another variable z_k, i.e. $x_k \rightarrow z_k$ where z_k is in linear state space. Such transformation enables us to apply the inverse method for linear systems.

3　Feedforward Control by Inverting Lifted Linear System

In this section, we first recall the feedforward control method for linear systems. Then a feedforward control design method is proposed based on the Koopman operator. The proposed control design method is totally based on collected data.

3.1　Direct Inverse for Linear Systems

Consider a typical discrete-time LTI system:

$$x_{k+1} = Ax_k + Bu_k, \quad y_k = Cx_k, \tag{4}$$

where A, B and C are general state space model matrixes. Besides a desired trajectory $y^\star \in \mathbb{R}^m$ is defined and initial state is x_0. We can write input-output equations recursively and stack all above variables and write in matrix form

$$
\begin{bmatrix} y_1 \\ y_2 \\ \vdots \\ y_m \end{bmatrix} = \begin{bmatrix} CA \\ CA^2 \\ \vdots \\ CA^m \end{bmatrix} x_0 + \begin{bmatrix} CB & & \\ CAB & CB \cdots & \\ \vdots & \vdots & \ddots \\ CA^{m-1}B & CA^{m-2}B & \cdots \end{bmatrix} \begin{bmatrix} u_0 \\ u_1 \\ \vdots \\ u_{m-1} \end{bmatrix}. \tag{5}
$$

With known initial state x_0 and desired trajectory $y^\star$, the target control input can be computed by

$$u^\star = P^{-1}(y^\star - Qx_0), \tag{6}$$

where

$$
P = \begin{bmatrix} CB & & \\ CAB & CB \cdots & \\ \vdots & \vdots & \ddots \\ CA^{m-1}B & CA^{m-2}B & \cdots \end{bmatrix}, Q = \begin{bmatrix} CA \\ CA^2 \\ \vdots \\ CA^m \end{bmatrix}. \tag{7}
$$

3.2　Koopman Operator

Here we describe the Koopman operator extended to controller systems. For a discretized nonlinear controlled system

$$x_{k+1} = f(x_k, u_k), \tag{8}$$

there are several ways to extend the Koopman operator to such controlled systems [11,12]. One basic idea is including the control input u and state x into an extended state space (x, u) [13].

Let the original dynamics be rewritten as $\mathcal{X}_{k+1} = F(\mathcal{X}_k) = [f(x_k, \mathbf{u}(0)), \mathcal{S}\mathbf{u}]^T$, where $\mathcal{X} = [x, \mathbf{u}]^T$ is the extended state and $\mathcal{S}$ is the shifting operator. The extended Koopman operator $\mathcal{K}_d : \mathcal{H} \to \mathcal{H}$ can be defined as

$$(\mathcal{K}_d \phi)(\mathcal{X}_k) = \phi(F(\mathcal{X}_k)). \tag{9}$$

In order to find an approximation [14,15] $\tilde{\mathcal{K}}_d$, one chooses a set of observable functions $\phi(\mathcal{X}) = [\phi_1(\mathcal{X}), \phi_2(\mathcal{X}), \cdots, \phi_w(\mathcal{X})]^T \in \mathbb{R}^w$. Assume a collection of data sets $(\mathcal{X}_j, \mathcal{X}_j^+)$ is available, where $\mathcal{X}_j^+ = F(\mathcal{X}_j)$. The finite-dimensional approximation of $\mathcal{K}_d$ can be directly calculated by

$$\tilde{\mathcal{K}}_d = \phi(\mathcal{X}_j^+)\phi(\mathcal{X}_j)^\dagger. \tag{10}$$

By splitting the matrix

$$\tilde{\mathcal{K}}_d = \begin{bmatrix} \mathcal{A}_{w \times w} & \mathcal{B}_{w \times p} \\ \mathcal{C}_{p \times w} & \mathcal{D} \end{bmatrix}, \tag{11}$$

we can get the approximate linear equation in the lifted state space

$$z_{k+1} = \mathcal{A}z_k + \mathcal{B}u_k, \quad \hat{x}_k = \mathcal{C}z_k, \tag{12}$$

where $z_k = \phi(x_k, u_k)$ is lifted state and $\hat{x}_k$ is the state estimation from lifted space.

3.3   System Inverse from Lifted Space

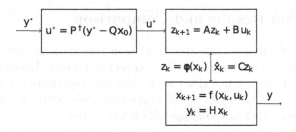

Fig. 1. Feedforward control based on Koopman operator.

As shown in Fig. 1, for a class of nonlinear system functions

$$x_{k+1} = f(x_k, u_k), \quad y_k = Hx_k, \tag{13}$$

where the output y_k is linear combination of states x_k. Define a set of observable functions $\phi(x_k) \in \mathbb{R}^w$ and let $z_k = \phi(x_k)$. As illustrated in last section, the lifted state space can be approximated according to Eq. (12)

$$z_{k+1} = \mathcal{A}z_k + \mathcal{B}u_k, \quad x_k = \mathcal{C}z_k. \tag{14}$$

Then $y_k = Hx_k = HCz_k$. With known initial state x_0, the initial lifted state is set to $z_0 = \phi(x_0)$. Similar to (5), replacing C with HC, the feedforward control input can be computed by

$$u^\star = \mathcal{P}^\dagger(y^\star - \mathcal{Q}x_0),\qquad(15)$$

where

$$\mathcal{P} = \begin{bmatrix} HCB & & \\ HCAB & HCB & \cdots \\ \vdots & \vdots & \ddots \\ HCA^{m-1}B & HCA^{m-2}B & \cdots \end{bmatrix}, \mathcal{Q} = \begin{bmatrix} HCA \\ HCA^2 \\ \vdots \\ HCA^m \end{bmatrix}.\qquad(16)$$

The workflow of the proposed method is illustrated in Algorithm. 1.

Algorithm 1. Data-driven feedforward control design for nonlinear systems

---

Require: The set of collected data $(\mathcal{X}_j, \mathcal{X}_j^+), j = 1, \cdots, M$, where $\mathcal{X}_j = [x_j, u_j]^T$. For each j, $\mathcal{X}_j^+$ is the one time step ahead measurement of $\mathcal{X}_j$; Desired trajectory $y^\star$; Initial system state x_0;

Ensure: Feedforward control $u^\star$;

  1: Choose a set of observable functions ϕ ;
  2: Compute approximate $\tilde{\mathcal{K}}_d = \phi(\mathcal{X}_j^+)\phi(\mathcal{X}_j)^\dagger$ and split to matrices $\mathcal{A}$, $\mathcal{B}$ and $\mathcal{C}$;
  3: Compute matrix $\mathcal{P}$ and $\mathcal{Q}$ in Eq. (16);
  4: $u^\star = \mathcal{P}^\dagger(y^\star - \mathcal{Q}x_0)$;
  5: **return** $u^\star$;

---

4   Simulation Results and Comparison

In this section, we demonstrate the simulation results using proposed methods and a comparison to the local linearization method. Both dynamics are used to generate measurement data, added with Gaussian distributed noise with standard deviation σ scaled to 10% of the maximum measurement. Then a comparison with the local linearization approach is presented.

4.1   Van der Pol Oscillator

We first consider a frequently used forced Van der Pol oscillator system

$$\dot{x}_1 = 2x_2, \quad \dot{x}_2 = -0.8x_1 + 2x_2 - 10x_1^2x_2 + u.\qquad(17)$$

We use Runge-Kutta 4 method with a sample period of 0.01s to get the discrete model. Measurement data is collected from 20 trajectories over 100 time steps, with random initial states on $[-1, 1]^2$ and random control input on $[-1, 1]$. Lift functions are combined with the state and 50 thin plate spline radial basis functions centering randomly on $[-5, 5]$.

We show the control performance tracking over two desired trajectories: 1 $y^\star = \alpha_1(1 - cos(\frac{4\pi}{N}k))^2$ and 2 $y^\star = \alpha_2 sin(\frac{4\pi}{N}k)$ The initial state is set to $[0, 0]$ and output $y = x_1$. The simulation results are shown in Fig. 2.

4.2   Bilinear Motor

In this section the proposed method is applied to control a DC motor with bilinear dynamics

$$\dot{x}_1 = -(R/L)x_1 - (k/L)x_2 u + u_a/L,$$
$$\dot{x}_2 = -(B/J)x_2 + (k/J)x_1 u - \tau_l/Jy. \tag{18}$$

Simulation parameters chosen for the motor model dynamics are referred to [16].

The same discretization and data collection procedure is conducted, with control signal random distributed on $[-1, 1]$ and initial conditions on $[-1, 1]^3$. We choose lifting functions as state itself and 20 polyharmonic radial basis functions centering randomly on $[-1, 1]$. Simulation results are presented in Fig. 3.

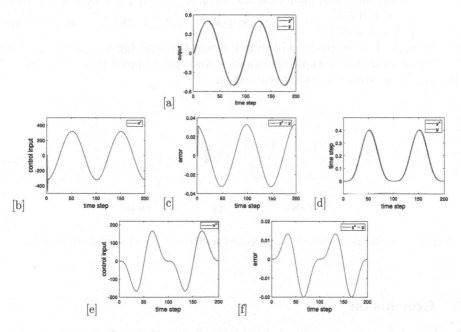

Fig. 2. Van der Pol oscillator simulation results. (a)-(c) output, control input and error for trajectory 1, (d)-(f) output, control input and error for trajectory 2

4.3   Comparison with Local Linearization

We compare the proposed method to the local linearization approach. Again, we use the model of the DC motor, and linearize the dynamics around the initial

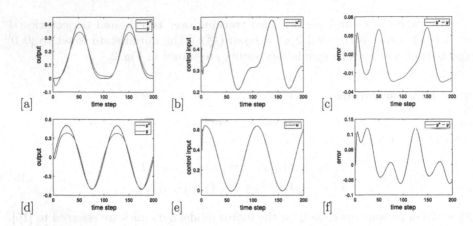

Fig. 3. Bilinear motor simulation results. (a)-(c) output, control input and error for trajectory 1, (d)-(f) output, control input and error for trajectory 2

state $[0, 0]$, the linearized model has the form $x_{k+1} = A_{lin}x_k + B_{lin}u_k + c$ where $A_{lin} = \begin{bmatrix} 0.654 & 0.228 \\ -0.162 & 0.957 \end{bmatrix}$, $B_{lin} = [0.028, 0.005]^T$ and $c = [0.175, -0.012]^T$. Then we can apply Eq. (6) to design the feedforward control input $u^\star$ for trajectory 2. Figure 4 shows the tracking performance and control input from the proposed data-driven method and local linearization.

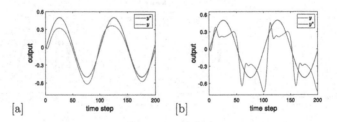

Fig. 4. Tracking performance (a) proposed method (b) local linearization method.

5   Conclusion

In the previous two examples, the proposed data-driven feedforward control method has achieved satisfying tracking accuracy. It appears that the tracking accuracy is determined by the accuracy of the predictor, which is evaluated by the gap between the state prediction and the true state. Unlike those based on NNs, where Neural networks are used to learn the inverse system function, the proposed method seeks a linear representation, or transformation, of the original system to allow for inverse techniques for linear systems. The numerical examples demonstrate the effectiveness of the proposed method.

References

1. Broussard, J., O'Brien, M.: Feedforward control to track the output of a forced model. IEEE Trans. Autom. Control **25**(4), 851–853 (1980)
2. Tomizuka, M.: Zero phase error tracking algorithm for digital control. J. Dyn. Syst. Meas. Contr. **109**(1), 65–68 (1987)
3. Tomizuka, M.: Feedforward digital tracking controllers for motion control applications. Adv. Robot. **7**(6), 575–586 (1992)
4. Butterworth, J., Pao, L., Abramovitch, D.: Analysis and comparison of three discrete-time feedforward model-inverse control techniques for nonminimum-phase systems. Mechatronics **22**(5), 577–587 (2012)
5. Boeren, F., Oomen, T., Steinbuch, M.: Iterative motion feedforward tuning: a data-driven approach based on instrumental variable identification. Control. Eng. Pract. **37**, 11–19 (2015)
6. Chen, S.-S.: Intelligent control of semiconductor manufacturing processes. In: IEEE International Conference on Fuzzy Systems, pp. 101–108. IEEE, (1992)
7. Kim, H., Lee, K., Jeon, B., Song, C.: Quick wafer alignment using feedforward neural networks. IEEE Trans. Autom. Sci. Eng. **7**(2), 377–382 (2009)
8. Li, Q., Qian, J., Zhu, Z., Bao, X., Helwa, M., Schoellig, P.: Deep neural networks for improved, impromptu trajectory tracking of quadrotors. In: 2017 IEEE International Conference on Robotics and Automation, pp. 5183–5189. IEEE, Singapore (2017)
9. Frye, M., Provence, R.: Direct inverse control using an artificial neural network for the autonomous hover of a helicopter. In: 2014 IEEE International Conference on Systems. Man, and Cybernetics, pp. 4121–4122. IEEE, San Diego (2014)
10. Koopman, B.: Hamiltonian systems and transformation in Hilbert space. Proc. Natl. Acad. Sci. **17**(5), 315–318 (1931)
11. Proctor, J., Brunton, S., Kutz, J.: Generalizing Koopman theory to allow for inputs and control. SIAM J. Appl. Dyn. Syst. **17**(1), 909–930 (2018)
12. Williams, M., Hemati, M., Dawson, J.: Extending data-driven Koopman analysis to actuated systems. IFAC-PapersOnLine **49**(18), 704–709 (2016)
13. Korda, M., Mezic, I.: Linear predictors for nonlinear dynamical systems: Koopman operator meets model predictive control. Automatica **93**, 149–160 (2018)
14. Mauroy, A., Goncalves, J.: Linear identification of nonlinear systems: a lifting technique based on the Koopman operator. In: IEEE 55th Conference on Decision and Control, pp. 6500–6505. IEEE, Las Vegas (2016)
15. Williams, M., Kevrekidis, I., Rowley, C.: A data-driven approximation of the Koopman operator: extending dynamic mode decomposition. J. Nonlinear Sci. **25**(6), 1307–1346 (2015)
16. Daniel-Berhe, S., Unbehauen, H.: Experimental physical parameter estimation of a thyristor driven DC-motor using the HMF-method. Control. Eng. Pract. **6**(5), 615–626 (1998)

Tracking Error Boundary of Novel Stable Inversion Based Feedforward Control for a Class of Non-minimum Phase Systems

Shaoqin Zhu[2], Yinpei Wang[3], Bin Zhu[4], and Xiaoqiang Ji[1,2(✉)]

[1] The Shenzhen Institute of Artificial Intelligence and Robotics for Society, The Chinese University of Hong Kong, Shenzhen, Guangdong, China
jixiaoqiang@cuhk.edu.cn
[2] School of Science and Engineering, The Chinese University of Hong Kong, Shenzhen, Guangdong, China
[3] University of California, Irvine, USA
[4] Department of Automation, Tsinghua University, Beijing, China

Abstract. Feedforward control methods enable discrete-time control systems to perform tasks with high tracking performance. Discrete-time systems very often have unstable inverses, with the instability being introduced when producing the discrete analogy of a continuous-time system. The problem statements for two novel stable inverses are given. The aim of this paper is to derive the tracking error bounds realized by the novel stable inversion-based feedforward control, under uncertainties from both measurement noise and model parameters. Simulation results are conducted to justify the validity.

Keywords: Stable inversion · Non-minimum phase systems · Tracking error bounds

1 Introduction

Among many control methods, feedforward control can bring extremely high precision and throughput to perform various complex motion tasks [1], so it is used in more and more scenarios [18–20]. The inverse model calculation is an important part of accurate tracking control. At the beginning this calculation was limited to finding the causal inversion of the minimum-phase system [21,22], while non-minimum phase (NMP) system has unstable inversion.

Theoretically, this method can achieve zero error control. However, unstable solution to the NMP system cannot be used in practice. There is much literature

This work was partially supported by Shenzhen Science and Technology Program (Grant No. RCBS20210706092219050), Guangdong Basic and Applied Basic Research Foundation (Grant No. 2022A1515110411), and Shenzhen Institute of Artificial Intelligence and Robotics for Society (AC01202201001). Li Luan and Zhu Bin contribute equally to this work.
X. Ji—*IEEE Member.*

studying on methods to solve instability problem of NMP systems to obtain a stable solution [2,3,8–14,17,23–25]. Zou et al., Bayo and Hunt [17,23,24] used a limited preview window of the desired output trajectory to achieve accurate desired output of NMP systems. However, if the preview window becomes larger, a bounded zero-tracking error solution may not be obtained by using this preview stable inversion method.

Di Benedetto and Lucibello [25] obtained the particular solution to the problem for time-varying NMP systems by selecting the initial conditions of the system. Wang [3] designed a general algorithm for solving inverse problems, which is suitable for both minimum-phase systems with time constant uncertainties and NMP systems. Jeong [10,11] proposed that the method of calculating the stable inversion of the maximum phase system can be extended to calculate stable inversion of the NMP system. Ji and colleagues [8,12–14] developed the minimum control energy method and noncausal finite impulse response (FIR) method. These two methods can relax the constraint on the system's initial-termination state and achieve accurate output tracking in finite time.

However, these methods are all based on the assumption that the original model is perfect and the measurement of desired output is correct. In this paper, two methods above are used to analyze the error boundary with model imperfection and measurement errors. In terms of error's magnitude, the total error is divided into three parts: error from the stable inversion method, the error caused by measurement error, and error from model imperfection. The boundaries of the three parts are estimated, and the boundaries' validity is verified.

The main contributions of this paper are listed as follows: (1) For both novel stable inversion methods, closed-form relationships between the tracking error boundary and the scalar of error are derived under the measurement noise and model parameters uncertainty; (2) By simulation, we show that the boundaries are valid and find that for both the minimum control energy method and the noncausal-FIR method, the main source of tracking error is from the imperfection of the model.

This paper is structured as follows. In Sect. 2, unstable inversion problem of the n-order NMP system and two existing stable inversion methods are introduced. In Sect. 3, measurement uncertainty and model parameter uncertainty are considered, and we explicitly derive the error boundary for two stable inversion methods. In Sect. 4, various simulation results are conducted, showing the validity of the derived error boundary. Results and contributions are discussed in Sect. 5.

2   Problem Statement for Finite Time Stable Inversion

2.1   Inverse Instability of Non-minimum Phase System

For a differential equation, given its output at sample time, it can be represented by a discrete-time system. If the transfer function of the system has zeros outside the identity element, the exact inverse will be unstable. Consider the following linear n-order NMP system

$$y[k+n] + a_1 y[k+(n-1)] + \cdots + a_n y[k]$$
$$= b_1 u[k+(n-1)] + b_2 u[k+(n-1)] + \cdots + b_n u[k]. \tag{1}$$

where there is one zero outside the unit circle. According to literature [8], this system has unstable inversion.

2.2   Two Stable Inversion Methods

To solve the inverse instability problem, methods have been developed. Among them, two methods give the stable inversion method with only the first few errors perfectly by assuming the model. We use the discrete form of 3rd order linear time-invariant NMP system to illustrate these two methods.

$$y(k+3)+a_1y(k+2)+a_2y[k+1]+a_3y(k) = b_1u(k+2)+b_2u(k+1)+b_3u(k). \quad (2)$$

Factoring. According to the characteristic equation $b_1Z^2 + b_2Z + b_3 = b_1(Z - z_1)(Z - z_2)$, where Z means forward shift operator, (2) can be expressed in matrix form with lower multi-diagonal coefficient matrix P and Z_1, Z_2. Use $y^* = b_1^{-1}Py$ to simplify the problem, then the inverse problem is $u^* = Z_2^{-1}Z_1^{-1}y^*$. The problem becomes computing two inverses. If $\exists\, i, |z_i| > 1$, the inverse is unstable. Under the assumption that the model is perfect, the following two methods give stable inversions of the problem.

Minimum Control Energy Method. A modified non-causal F is used to approximate the inverse in a stable way $F_i =$
$$\begin{bmatrix} 1 & -z_i^{-1} & \cdots & -z_i^{-(n-1)} \\ & 1 & \cdots & -z_i^{-(n-2)} \\ & & \ddots & \vdots \\ & & & 1 \end{bmatrix}.$$

The formula of F can be derived from a problem to minimize the Euclidean norm (control energy) of input with correct tracking of the desired output [8]. Reference [12] proved that, by replacing Z_i^{-1} with F_i, a stable solution to the inverse problem could be obtained. When n_s zeros are outside the unit circle, the final error is only in the first n_s terms.

Noncausal-FIR Method. This method replaces Z_i^{-1} with the pseudo-inverse of Z_i with the first row removed: $Z_{id} =$
$$\begin{bmatrix} -z_i & 1 & & \\ & -z_i & \ddots & \\ & & \ddots & 1 \\ & & & -z_i & 1 \end{bmatrix}_{(p-1)\times p}.$$

The first line removed represents the pulse signal after receiving input, and this operation causes the system to be unstable. With SVD factorization, $Z_{id} = USV^T$, pseudo-inverse $Z_{id}^\dagger$ is given by $Z_{id}^\dagger = VS^{-1}U^T$. In literature [12], it is shown that for a system with n_s zeros outside, this method gives a stable inversion, and also only has errors in the first n_s terms, and in particular, for the current system (2) of order 3, if there are two zeros outside, then only the first two terms have errors.

3   Tracking Error Boundary Under Uncertainties

Uncertainty Introduced by Measurement Noise. In a practical application scenario, the output of the system usually contains measurement disturbances. According to [15], this disturbance can be written as

$$y_m(k) = y(k) + w(k). \tag{3}$$

where $y_m(k)$ is the true measurement output and $w(k)$ is the disturbance. To illustration, we simply assume the distribution of $w(k)$ satisfies $w(k) \equiv w, w \sim N(0,1)$.

Uncertainty Introduced by Parameters Noise. The model's parameters may change during the control process for various external reasons, such as temperature and durability. Reference [16] considered that the model itself has errors, by using ϵ as the vector of uncertain parameters. We assume that the uncertainty of parameters makes the original nth order model (1) become

$$y[k+n] + a_1 y[k+(n-1)] + \cdots + a_n y[k]$$
$$= (b_1 + \epsilon_1)u[k+(n-1)] + \cdots + (b_n + \epsilon_n)u[k]. \tag{4}$$

and assume their distribution: $\epsilon_i \overset{i.i.d.}{\sim} N(0,1)$. It is also assumed that they are independent of w. If ϵ_1 is not 0, the zeros change proportionally with ϵ_1, so the parameters of the model have a huge mutation near the original model. To avoid this situation, we set $\epsilon_1 \equiv 0$, and assume that ϵ_1 perturbs the parameter in the form of addition.

3.1   Error Boundary of Minimum Control Energy Method

Using the minimum control energy method

$$\hat{y}^* = (Z_1 Z_2 + \epsilon)F_2 F_1 (y^* + w), \quad \epsilon = \epsilon_1 I + \epsilon_2 J + \epsilon_3 J^2. \tag{5}$$

J is the backward shift matrix and the error in terms of y^* is

$$e_f = \hat{y}^* - y^* = (Z_1 Z_2 F_2 F_1 - I)y^* + Z_1 Z_2 F_2 F_1 w + \epsilon F_2 F_1 (y^* + w). \tag{6}$$

The first part of (6) measures the estimated error caused purely by the inverse method used to estimate the inverse of the system. The second part means that the measurement error contributes to the final error with a transformation related to the inverse method. The third part shows the error caused by model's imperfection combined with the measurement error and method error.

   To find the boundary of the model error is to find the boundary of $||e_f||_2$. For the first part, according to literature [12], it can be bounded by

$$||(Z_1 Z_2 F_2 F_1 - I)y^*||_2 \leq |\delta_2' F_1 y^* + \delta_1' y^*| + |z_1 \delta_2' F_1 y^*|$$
$$\leq [(1+z_1)||\delta_2'||_2 ||F_1|| + ||\delta_1'||_2]||y^*||_2 \tag{7}$$
$$||F_i|| = ||\Sigma_{j=1}^{\infty} - z_i^{-j}(J')^j|| \leq \frac{1}{z_i - 1}.$$

where $\delta_i' = [0 \ -z_i^{-1} \ \cdots \ -z_i^{-(n-1)}]$. Notice that $||\delta_i'||_2 < \frac{1}{1-z_i^{-2}}$ and F_i can be divided into a series. The norm of J' can be bounded by 1 because $J'J = \text{diag}\{0, 1, \cdots, 1\}, \sigma_i = 0$ or $1, \forall i$, so $||J'|| \leq 1$. Then the first part can be bounded by $B_{f1} = \left[\frac{1+z_1}{(z_1-1)(1-z_2^{-2})} + \frac{1}{1-z_1^{-2}}\right]||y^*||_2$. For the second part, norm of Z_i can also be bounded. Then the second part is bounded by the norm of w.

$$||Z_i|| = ||I - z_iJ|| \leq |1 - z_i| = z_i - 1, \quad ||Z_1Z_2F_2F_1w||_2 \leq ||w||_2 \triangleq B_{f2}, \quad (8)$$

$||\epsilon||$ is bounded by $|\epsilon_1| + |\epsilon_2| + |\epsilon_3|$. So the third part is bounded by $B_{f3} = \frac{|\epsilon_1|+|\epsilon_2|+|\epsilon_3|}{(z_1-1)(z_2-1)}(||y^*||_2 + \sqrt{n}|w|)$. Combine the three boundaries, it gives the bound of total error: $B_f = B_{f1} + B_{f2} + B_{f3}$.

3.2   Error Boundary of Noncausal-FIR Method

For the noncausal-FIR method, controller removes the first row of the measured desired output and use $(y + w)_d$ to calculate the corresponding input, and the actual output is

$$\hat{y}^* = (Z_1Z_2 + \epsilon)Z_{2d}^\dagger[Z_{1d}^\dagger(y + w)_d]_d. \quad (9)$$

and the error between actual output here and the desired output is

$$e_p = \hat{y}^* - y^* = (Z_1Z_2Z_{2d}^\dagger[Z_{1d}^\dagger y_d]_d - y) + Z_1Z_2Z_{2d}^\dagger[Z_{1d}^\dagger w_d]_d + \epsilon Z_{2d}^\dagger[Z_{1d}^\dagger(y^* + w)_d]_d \quad (10)$$

The three parts are also explain how the imperfection of model and the measurement error works in this method. The first part:

$$Z_1Z_2Z_{2d}^\dagger[Z_{1d}^\dagger y_d]_d - Z_1Z_{1d}^\dagger y_d^* + Z_1Z_{1d}^\dagger y_d^* - y^* = \begin{bmatrix} Z_{21}Z_{2d}^\dagger x_d - x[1] + Z_{11}Z_{1d}^\dagger y_d^* - y^*[1] \\ -z_1(Z_{21}Z_{2d}^\dagger x_d - x[1]) \\ 0_{(n-2)\times 1} \end{bmatrix}. \quad (11)$$

where $x = Z_{1d}^\dagger y_d^*$. Its norm is bounded by $(1+z_1)|Z_{21}Z_{2d}^\dagger x_d - x[1]| + |Z_{11}Z_{1d}^\dagger y_d^* - y^*[1]|$. Observed that $Z_{11}Z_{1d}^\dagger y_d^* - y^*[1] = [-1 \ \ Z_{11}Z_{1d}^\dagger]y^*, |Z_{11}Z_{1d}^\dagger y_d^* - y^*[1]| \leq (1 + ||Z_{1d}^\dagger||)||y^*||_2$, and $|Z_{21}Z_{2d}^\dagger x_d - x[1]| \leq (1 + ||Z_{2d}^\dagger||)||x||_2$. The boundary of $||Z_{id}^\dagger||$ can be derived from the singular values of Z_{id} according to [8], which is $1/(z_i - 1)$. Then $||x||_2 \leq ||Z_{1d}^\dagger||\,||y_d^*||_2 \leq \frac{1}{z_i-1}||y^*||_2$, and the boundary of the first part is $B_{p1} = \frac{z_2-z_1+2z_1z_2}{(z_2-1)(z_1-1)}||y^*||_2$. For the second part, it is similar to minimum control energy method by just ignoring the $[\cdot]_d$ sign: $||Z_1Z_2Z_{2d}^\dagger[Z_{1d}^\dagger w_d]_d||_2 \leq ||w||_2 \triangleq B_{p2}$. The third part can be also calculated

$$||\epsilon Z_{2d}^\dagger[Z_{1d}^\dagger(y^* + w)_d]_d||_2 \leq ||\epsilon||||Z_{2d}^\dagger||||Z_{1d}^\dagger||||y^* + w||_2$$
$$\leq \frac{|\epsilon_1| + |\epsilon_2| + |\epsilon_3|}{(z_1 - 1)(z_2 - 1)}(||y^*||_2 + \sqrt{n}|w|) \triangleq B_{p3}, \quad (12)$$

which is also the same as the model imperfection error of minimum control energy method. So the only difference in the boundary of these two methods is in the model itself. The measurement error and the imperfection error are similar between them. Combine the three boundaries, the total boundary is: $B_p = B_{p1} + B_{p2} + B_{p3}$.

4   Simulation Results

To test the boundaries' validity given in the last section, this section simulates a feedforward control for a third-order system (n=100). It is assumed that $z_1 = 2, z_2 = 3$ for convenience. The equivalent desired output y^* is generated as a periodic trajectory, that is, $y^*(k) = \sin(k)$. In addition, the corresponding errors and boundaries are calculated by the formulas of $B_f, B_{f1}, B_{f2}, B_{f3}$ and $B_p, B_{p1}, B_{p2}, B_{p3}$. Finally, the relative errors and relative boundaries (boundaries are divided by $||y^*||_2$) are used for comparison.

Simulation Results for Minimum Control Energy Method. Simulation results using the minimum control energy method are shown as follows. It can be found that the estimated boundary is valid, the relative boundary (the blue line at the left of Fig. 1) is greater than the relative actual error (the red line at the left of Fig. 1) in every simulation, and the main source of error boundary is caused by model parameter uncertainty (the green line at the right graph of Fig. 1).

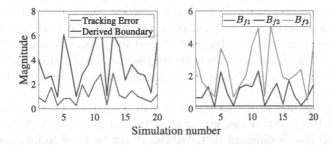

Fig. 1. Left: The total error and boundary for minimum control energy method when $y^*(k) = \sin(k)$. Right: The three error factors for minimum control energy method when $y^*(k) = \sin(k)$. Derived boundary is $B = B_{f1} + B_{f2} + B_{f3}$, B_{f1} means the boundary of inversion method error. B_{f2} is the boundary of measurement error. B_{f3} is the boundary of parameters uncertainty error.

Simulation Results for Noncausal-FIR Method. By using the noncausal-FIR method, simulation results are shown in Fig. 2. For comparing different inversion methods, we use the same y^* and same error realization to conduct an experiment. The estimated boundary is still valid, and the results are similar to the case where using the minimum control energy method, which means that, with the same desired output and same error realization, these two methods have similar estimated error boundaries and even similar actual output error, though the procedures of them are different.

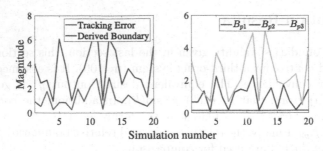

Fig. 2. Left: The total error and boundary for noncausal-FIR method when $y^*(k) = \sin(k)$. Right: The three error factors for noncausal-FIR method when $y^*(k) = \sin(k)$. Derived boundary is $B = B_{p1} + B_{p2} + B_{p3}$. B_{p1} means the boundary of inversion method error. B_{p2} is the boundary of measurement error. B_{p3} is the boundary of parameters uncertainty error.

5 Conclusion

This paper gives an explicit closed-form boundary of output error for two kinds of feedforward control methods when the model is inaccurate and measurement error exists. Furthermore, the total error is divided into the error from using the stable inversion method, the error caused by inaccurate measurement, and the error resulting from imperfect model parameters. In simulation part, the boundaries' validity is verified and the main source of the error boundary is found.

Since the boundary in this paper is still an expression of random terms, future researchers can consider giving statistical property of the boundary when random terms have a different distribution. It can be tried to find a more strict boundary than this paper.

References

1. van Hulst, J., Poot, M., Kostic, D., Yan, K.W., Portegies, J., Oomen, T.: Feedforward control in the presence of input nonlinearities: a learning-based approach. IFAC. **55**, 235–240 (2022)
2. Devasia, S., Chen, D., Paden, B.: Nonlinear inversion-based output tracking. IEEE Trans. Autom. Control **41**(7), 930–942 (1996)
3. Wang, X., Chen, D.: An inversion-based iterative learning control algorithm for a class of nonminimum-phase systems. IEE Proc. Control Theory App. **152**(1), 72–78 (2005)
4. LeVoci, P., Longman, R.: Intersample error in discrete time learning and repetitive control. In: AIAA/AAS Astrodynamics Specialist Conference and Exhibit (2004)
5. Li, Y., Longman, R.W.: Characterizing and addressing the instability of the control action in iterative learning control. Adv. Astronaut. Sci. **136**(01), 1967–1985 (2010)
6. Li, T.: Eliminating the internal instability in iterative learning control for nonminimum phase systems. Columbia University (2017)

7. Li, T., Longman, R. W.: Designing iterative learning control of non-minimum phase systems to converge to zero tracking error. In: AIAA/AAS Astrodynamics Specialist Conference (2016)
8. Longman, R.W., Li, T.: On a new approach to producing a stable inversion of discrete-time systems. In: Narendra (ed.) Proceedings of the 18th Yale Workshop on Adaptive and Learning Systems, Yale University, New Haven, CN (2017)
9. Kinosita, K., Sogo, T., Adachi, N.: Iterative learning control using adjoint systems and stable inversion. Asian J. Control 4(1), 60–67 (2002)
10. Jeong, G.M., Choi, C.II.: Iterative learning control with advanced output data for nonlinear non-minimum phase systems. Int. J. Syst. Sci. 37(14), 1051–1058 (2006)
11. Jeong, G.M., Choi, C.H.: Iterative learning control for linear discrete time non-minimum phase systems. Automatica 38(2), 287–291 (2002)
12. Ji, X., Li, T., Longman, R.W.: Proof of two stable inverses of discrete time systems. Adv. Astronaut. Sci. 162, 123–136 (2018)
13. Ji, X., Longman, R.W.: The insensitivity of the iterative learning control inverse problem to initial run when stabilized by a new stable inverse. In: Bock, H.G., Jäger, W., Kostina, E., Phu, H.X. (eds.) Modeling, Simulation and Optimization of Complex Processes HPSC 2018, pp. 257–275. Springer, Cham (2021). https://doi.org/10.1007/978-3-030-55240-4_13
14. Ji, X., Longman, R.W.: Two new stable inverses of discrete-time systems. Adv. Astronaut. Sci. 171, 4137–4143 (2022)
15. Bu, X., Hou, Z., Yu, F., Wang, F.: Robust model free adaptive control with measurement disturbance. IET Control Theory App. 6(9), 1288–1296 (2012)
16. Pakshin, P., Emelianova, J., Gałkowski, K., Rogers, E.: Iterative learning control under parameter uncertainty and failures. In: 2012 IEEE International Symposium on Intelligent Control, pp. 1249–1254. IEEE (2012)
17. Zou, Q.: Optimal preview-based stable-inversion for output tracking of nonminimum-phase linear systems. Automatica 45(1), 230–237 (2009)
18. Blanken, L., Koekebakker, S., Oomen, T.: Data-driven feedforward tuning using non-causal rational basis functions: with application to an industrial flatbed printer. Mechatronics 71, 102424 (2020)
19. Bruijnen, D., van Dijk, N.: Combined input shaping and feedforward control for flexible motion systems. In: 2012 American Control Conference (ACC), pp. 2473–2478. IEEE (2012)
20. Lambrechts, P., Boerlage, M., Steinbuch, M.: Trajectory planning and feedforward design for electromechanical motion systems. Control. Eng. Pract. 13(2), 145–157 (2015)
21. Silverman, L.M.J.P.: Inversion of multivariable linear systems. IEEE Trans. Autom. Control 14(3), 270–276 (1969)
22. Hirschorn, R.: Invertibility of multivariable nonlinear control system. IEEE Trans. Autom. Control 24(6), 855–865 (1979)
23. Bayo, E.: A finite-element approach to control the end-point motion of a single-link flexible robot. J. Robot. Syst. 4(1), 63–75 (1987)
24. Hunt, L.R., Meyer, G., Su, R.: Noncausal inverses for linear systems. IEEE Trans. Autom. Control 41(4), 608–611 (1996)
25. Di Benedetto, M.D., Lucibello, P.: Inversion of nonlinear time-varying systems. IEEE Trans. Autom. Control 38(8), 1259–1264 (1993)

Modeling, Simulation and Optimization of Intelligent Networked Things

Resource Scheduling Algorithm for Heterogeneous High-Performance Clusters

Lu Han[1,2(✉)]

[1] School of Automation Science and Electrical Engineering, Beihang University, Beijing 100191, China
luhan@buaa.edu.cn
[2] Engineering Research Center of Complex Product Advanced Manufacturing System, Ministry of Education, Beijing 100191, China

Abstract. Distributed computing resources are aggregated in a high-performance computing environment. The resources are appropriately allocated according to the user assignments. However, current resources scheduling strategies overly focus on system performance rather than the user fairness. Moreover, most strategies lack the environment adaptability. In order to solve these problems, this paper selects five different priority variables and proposes a multi-dimensional intelligent heterogeneous resource scheduling method for a high-performance cluster. It introduces the job environment queue, refines the state of the job system layer, optimizes the job priority scheduling strategy, and uses the genetic algorithm to optimize the priority parameters to increase the configurability of the job scheduling strategy. Using the algorithm, the overall performance of the platform is enhanced by 12.3% based on the PBS (Portable Batch System) scheduling system.

Keywords: High-performance cluster · Heterogeneous resource · Scheduling strategy · Optimization algorithm · User fairness

1 Introduction

Cluster is a kind of parallel or distributed processing system, and its efficient execution needs to rely on a reasonable scheduling strategy. The choice of job scheduling policy may affect the time when user jobs start to execute, and further affect whether users can apply computing resources fairly and reasonably [1]. In massively parallel processing systems, job scheduling algorithms have been a key factor affecting system CPU utilization [2, 3].

Currently, the common scheduling strategies are FCFS (First Come First Served) [4], SPT (Shortest Processing Time) [5], First Fit, Best Fit, Greedy, etc. [6]. There is also a large base of work on job scheduling within traditional clusters. Some of the more mature job management systems are platform LSF (Load Sharing Facility), PBS Pro, Torque and Slurm. Later on, improved algorithms based on backfilling and so on appeared [7]. Although backfilling algorithm can improve CPU utilization to some extent, there would be no jobs to fill the free CPU space when the job parameters in the queue cannot satisfy the conditions of Backfilling algorithm.

One of the objectives of performance evaluation methods is to provide a unified measure for the design and analysis of parallel algorithms. The goal of job scheduling in a cluster environment is assigning user submitted jobs to the most appropriate cluster nodes to run, achieving optimal scheduling, fully utilizing the resources in the cluster, and improving the overall throughput. The specific performance metrics of a clustered system include Optimal, QoS (Quality of Service), Load Balancing, Economic Principles, etc. [8]. From the perspective of target computing resource selection, the current just-in-time job scheduling model used in HPC (High Performance Computing) environments only considers to a certain extent the objective of minimizing the estimated queuing time of the environment.

In response to the problems encountered so far and the new demands arising from the development of HPC environment, this paper proposes an optimized job scheduling mechanism for the environment using five different priority factor variables. The jobs submitted by users will be submitted to the PBS system. The system will select the right tasks to be scheduled to the right HPC resources at the right time according to the overall usage of the environment.

2   Research Review

A cluster is a parallel or distributed processing system in which the computational nodes can be either single-processor systems or multi-processor systems. A cluster consisting of multiple single-processor systems is called a thin-node cluster, while a cluster consisting of multi-processor systems is called a fat-node cluster [9].

From the technical point of view of implementing the performance evaluation of parallel systems, the main approaches are: Measurement, Benchmark, Simulation, Performance Model, etc. Javadi, etc. [10] constructed an analytical model for the interconnection network of heterogeneous computing systems. Smith, etc. [11] developed a performance analysis model for high-performance reconfigurable computing systems. The model considers the division of tasks between workstations and reconfigurable components, the different computational demands of different workstation applications and the heterogeneity of workstations, etc. The model can guide users to optimize the management of resources.

The cluster job management system is responsible for the management of job queues in HPC systems. The job scheduling policy is the core of the cluster job management system. The choice of job scheduling policy determines the response time of user jobs and the fair and reasonable utilization of resources [12, 13]. The literature [14] uses the area of the two-dimensional space composed of CPU number and time as the job size criterion, and the jobs with larger area are scheduled first to solve the shortage of traditional backfilling favoring small jobs, and to facilitate finding backfilling jobs. The literature [15] proposes an improved algorithm based on the Backfilling algorithm. This algorithm is based on the CPU utilization rate of running jobs, and the CPU space available for backfill is expanded by dynamically adjusting the number of CPUs of running jobs, which makes up for the shortcomings of Backfilling algorithm. The literature [16] proposes an overhead and time based heuristic algorithm to minimize the execution cost, communication cost and overall completion time of scheduling workflow tasks in a cloud environment. The literature [17] proposes an index-based heuristic scheduling to execute parallel tasks on available cloud resources using an opportunity scheduling policy. Some scholars use intelligent optimization algorithms for scheduling, for example, the literature [18] proposes a Particle Swarm Optimization (PSO) based scheduling algorithm to minimize the execution cost of work-flow applications in cloud computing. The literature [19] proposes an improved priority-based task scheduling algorithm based on multi-criteria and multi-indicator decision models, which ultimately shortens the maximum completion time of tasks. The literature [20] uses a heuristic scheduling algorithm based on the Min-Min algorithm and balanced the processing of all resources, which eventually shortened the maximum completion time of task execution while improving the utilization of resources. The literature [21] uses a balanced spiral method on a meta-scheduler to optimize the traditional backfilling algorithm, which improved the efficiency of the backfilling operation and eventually shortened the maximum completion time of the task. In the literature [21], a "P-Backfill" algorithm is proposed to divide the incoming tasks into four categories for Backfilling scheduling according to their priority and frequency, which reduces the task execution time and average waiting delay. In the literature [22], based on the Backfilling algorithm, the value weight function of tasks is calculated in real time to assign tasks to idle VMs or request new VMs, which reduces the resource overhead of the server.

In terms of scheduling methods, static task assignment algorithms for clustered systems can be classified into algorithms based on optimization ideas, algorithms based on unguided search techniques, algorithms based on heuristic search, and algorithms based on graph theory [23]. The literature [24] proposes the use of Branch-and-Bound to solve the optimal solution. In the literature [25], the optimal solution is found from all possible solutions according to the corresponding objective function. In terms of algorithms based on unguided search techniques, the literature [26] proposes the simulated annealing algorithm. The literature proposes [27] genetic algorithm. The algorithm in the literature [28] applies the uniprcessor's earliest deadline first, EDF, algorithm to the dynamic scheduling of real-time tasks in multiprocessors; the algorithm in the literature [29] extends the uniprocessor's Least Laxity First (LLF) algorithm and thus uses it to solve the dynamic scheduling problem of real-time tasks in clustered systems. A modified Least Laxity First algorithm is proposed in the literature [30]. In time-slice based scheduling algorithm, the literature [31] proposes a dynamic scheduling algorithm for shared multi-processor systems, which utilizes the concept of time slices, where each processor uses a certain length of time slice to run the tasks on it. The length of the time slice allocated to the task is proportional to the task utilization.

3 Multi-objective Heterogeneous High-Performance Resource Scheduling Model Evaluation

Improving the resource utilization of the whole system is the core of HPC cluster management [32]. Also, since the task requests to be processed in the cluster often originate from different users, user fairness should be one of the metrics to be considered in the system. Therefore, combining the above two aspects, this paper proposes a model evaluation index based on resource utilization and user fairness.

Two forms of resource utilization are considered, i.e., real-time resource utilization and total resource utilization, and these two resource utilizations are introduced separately below.

3.1   Real-Time Resource Utilization

The real-time resource utilization refers to the system resource utilization at the current moment, and its expression can be given by Eq. 3-1.

$$\eta_r = \frac{\sum_{i=1}^{n} C_i^u}{\sum_{j=1}^{N} C_j^t} \tag{3-1}$$

where η_r is the real-time resource utilization, n is the total number of currently executing tasks, C_i^u is the number of cores required by each executing task, N is the total number of active nodes (including all free and busy nodes), and C_j^t is the number of available cores for each active node.

3.2   Total Resource Utilization

Total resource utilization refers to the utilization of system resources during the statistical time period, and its expression is represented by the following equation.

$$\eta_s = \frac{\sum_{i=1}^{n} C_i^u * t_i}{\sum_{j=1}^{N} C_j^t * t_j} \tag{3-2}$$

where η_s is the total resource utilization, t_i is the execution time of each task running in the statistical time period, and t_j is the running time of each node that was active in the statistical time period. The rest of the symbols have the same meaning as real-time resource utilization. The total resource utilization is one of the main indicators of the system scheduling capability.

3.3   User Fairness

The scheduling algorithm takes into account user fairness and its formula is defined as follows.

$$F = 1 - \frac{1}{2 * (D - 1)} \sum_{i=1}^{D} \frac{\sqrt{(W_i^u - W^s)^2}}{W^s} \tag{3-3}$$

F is the fairness value of the scheduling system, D is the number of users who have used the system in the statistical time period (if $D = 1$, the system has only 1 user, F is set to 1), W_i^u is the average waiting time of each user in the statistical time period, and W^s is the average waiting time of the system. The formula for calculating the average waiting time of users is as follows.

$$W^u = \frac{\sum\limits_{i=1}^{n} \frac{t_i^w}{C_i^u}}{n} \tag{3-4}$$

where n is the number of completed jobs for the user in the statistical time period, t_i^w is the waiting time for each task, and C_i^u is the number of kernels required for each task. It can be seen that the "average" of the average waiting time has an average meaning not only at the level of the number of tasks, but also at the level of the number of demand kernels. The system average waiting time formula is as follows.

$$W^s = \frac{\sum\limits_{j=1}^{D} W_j^u}{D} = \frac{\sum\limits_{j=1}^{D} \frac{\sum\limits_{i=1}^{n} \frac{t_{ij}^w}{C_{ij}^u}}{n_j}}{D} \tag{3-5}$$

where D is the number of users who submitted tasks to the system during the statistical time period, and each subscript j in the equation denotes the user j.

The fairness value is monotonically decreasing, i.e., the overall fairness is higher when the average waiting time of each user in the system is closer to the average waiting time of the system, at which point the calculated value is closer to 1, and vice versa, closer to 0.

4 Heterogeneous High-Performance Simulation Resource Scheduling Model

The function of the scheduling model is to assign jobs of different types of resources requested to nodes, so it is necessary to study how to reasonably assign jobs to scheduling so that the optimal evaluation metrics can be achieved.

4.1 Scheduling Strategy Design

The commonly used scheduling policies are often based on priority and backfill policies, which can result in infinite backfill. To overcome this drawback, this paper de-signs a scheduling policy that combines multiple policies based on a multi-queue dynamic scheduling model, considering a variety of factors.

When a task resource requirement can be satisfied by more than one queue, the queue closest to its requirements is selected first to place the task, and if the resources of the queue closest to the requirements are full, the task is placed to the next closest queue, and so on. If a task requires 12 cores for computation, both C12 and C144 queues can satisfy the task demand and are placed in the C12 queue first. When faced with multiple heterogeneous resources, the proximity of the resources to the demand is determined according to the following formula.

$$D = \sqrt{\frac{1}{n} \sum_{i=1}^{n} \left(S_i^d - S_i^s \right)^2} \tag{4-1}$$

where D is the degree of proximity, with smaller values implying closer proximity. n is the type of heterogeneous resource, S_i^d is the demand for each resource examined, and S_i^s is the supply available for each resource examined.

4.2 Scheduling Policy

There are three characteristics.

(1) The scheduling rules in this paper support cross-queue picking.
(2) The scheduling rules in this paper support custom scheduling policies, which mainly contain 2 types: priority examination of resource compliance and priority examination of priority value order.
(3) The scheduling rules proposed in this paper also support manual intervention in the scheduling order.

Based on the above scheduling policy premise, a scheduling policy based on Eq. 4-2 is proposed.

$$P_i = A_1 * C_i + A_2 * T_i - A_3 * S_i - A_4 * N_i + A_5 * I_i \tag{4-2}$$

where P_i is the priority value of each task. $A_1 \sim A_5$ represents the relative importance of each factor, which plays an important role in task prioritization and therefore needs to be optimized by the algorithm, C_i is the number of cores required for the task, T_i is the waiting time for the task, S_i is the amount of system resources used by the submitter of the task, N_i is the total number of tasks currently being executed or waiting to be executed by the user submitting the task, I_i is the "importance" of the task parameter. The formula involved is as follows.

$$S_i = \sum_{i=1}^{n} C_i^u * t_i \tag{4-3}$$

where n is the total number of tasks submitted by the user, C_i^u is the number of cores required for each task, and t_i is the duration of the task.

5 Intelligent Optimization Method for Heterogeneous Resource Scheduling Model

The rational use of scheduling algorithms enables the high-performance cluster job scheduling server to achieve a reasonable allocation of resources among the nodes.

Parameter optimization plays a key role in this. Evolutionary computation is a mature global optimization method with high robustness and wide applicability, which has the characteristics of self-organization, self-adaptation and self-learning, and can effectively deal with complex problems that are difficult to be solved by traditional optimization algorithms regardless of the nature of the problem. Among them, genetic algorithm is one of the most mature and widely used evolutionary computational methods. It is a computational model of biological evolutionary process that simulates the natural selection and genetics mechanism of Darwinian biological evolution, and is a method to search for optimal solutions by simulating the natural evolutionary process.

5.1 Genetic Algorithms Optimization

In conjunction with this heterogeneous high-performance simulation cluster scheduling, the objective is to maximize the value of the linear combination of the identified multiple objectives of job scheduling, like resource utilization and cluster fairness. The process is conducted by finding the appropriate parameters A1, A2, A3, A4, and A5 in the priority calculation formula, combined with the priority scheduling strategy proposed in Eq. 4-2, and the overall algorithmic steps are described as follows.

Step 1 Population initialization:

The appropriate initialization operation is designed according to the characteristics of the problem to be solved in this study. In this study, each gene value represents the value of the parameter to be optimized, i.e., the fractional coefficient A1 related to the number of nuclei required by the task, which takes the range [−1000, 1000], the fractional coefficient A2 related to the length of time the task has been waiting, which takes the range [0,1000], and the fractional coefficient A3 related to the amount of system resources already used by the submitter of this task, which takes the range [0, 1000]. The fractional coefficient A4 related to the total number of tasks currently being executed or waiting to be executed by the user who submitted the task, taking values in the range [0, 1000], and A5 is the influence factor of the importance parameter, all taking values in the range [1, 1000]. A population satisfying the constraints is obtained by the initialization operation.

Step 2 Determine the scheduling sequence:

This step is implemented using the Hook mechanism of PBS: according to the defined priority calculation formula and the parameter values determined by initialization, the priority value of each task itself is calculated and the queuing order of tasks is obtained according to the formulated multitask scheduling policy, i.e., the priority scheduling policy obtained using Eq. 4-2, and the task arrangement process is implemented.

Step 3 Evaluation of queuing strategies:

The objective function value to be optimized is calculated based on the queuing order obtained from Step 2, i.e., the fitness value of the individuals in the population is calculated. In this study, the fitness value of individuals is a linear combination of resource utilization and cluster fairness, and the default ratio is resource utilization: 0.9 and fairness: 0.1. Different queuing strategies are evaluated, and the queuing strategy with the largest fitness value of individuals is selected to obtain the corresponding priority strategy under this queuing strategy by backpropagation, and further backpropagation is performed to obtain the values of the coefficients in the priority calculation formula.

Step 4 Individual selection:

A suitable selection operator is designed to select individuals in the population. The selected individuals will enter the mating pool to form the parent population for crossover transformation to generate new individuals. The selection strategy is to be performed based on the individual fitness values. The aim of this study is to make the value of linear combination of cluster resource utilization and cluster fairness as large as possible, so individuals with larger fitness values should be selected with a correspondingly larger probability. The commonly used selection strategies are roulette selection, tournament selection, etc.

Step 5 Crossover operation:

The crossover probability pc (pre-set, usually 0.9) is used to determine whether the parent individuals need to perform the crossover operation. The crossover operator is designed according to the characteristics of the problem being optimized, and can be classified as single-point crossover, two-point crossover and multi-point crossover, etc. By crossover transformation, individuals that are not present in the parent population can be formed. The random multi-point crossover method is used in this system, i.e., a number from 2 to 5 is randomly selected for the crossover operator application before each crossover.

Step 6 Variational arithmetic:

Based on the mutation probability pm (pre-set, usually 0.1) to determine whether the parent individuals need to perform mutation operation. The main role of the mutation operator is to maintain the diversity of the population and prevent the population from falling into local optimum, so it is generally designed as a random transformation. New individuals can also be generated through the mutation operation.

After the three main operations of the genetic algorithm, i.e., selection, crossover and mutation, the parent population generates a new population of children, at which time the number of population iterations is increased by one, and the population jumps to Step 2 for the next round of priority calculation, and the corresponding values of the updated children are obtained and input to the specified scheduling strategy for determining the queuing order, so that the corresponding fitness values are calculated and evaluated to obtain The new priority parameters are evaluated, and the next round of iteration is performed until the maximum number of iterations is reached, and the optimal optimization result is output.

6 Case Study

6.1 Test Environment

In this paper, the test environment is arranged on a server with Centos7 operating system, and 17 virtual machines with Centos7 operating system are opened by VMware software: 1 PBS Server is used as a management node, and the remaining 16 PBS Clients are used as compute nodes. 4 of the 16 compute nodes are organized into a queue, corresponding to 12 cores, 32 cores, 144 cores and GPU queues.

In the simulation environment, the labeling method is used to match the task requirements with the compute queues. First, the platform label is customized in the PBS system, and the queue names are labeled for each compute node: "C12", "C32", "C144" and "GPU". Secondly, in the first hook the requirements of the task will be read and this information will be recorded in a list of tasks independent of the system. Finally, the system will set the demand as 1 core after the information is recorded (each VM is assigned 1 core, which will be recognized by the PBS system) and arrange the tasks in the corresponding queue according to the demand matching rules to achieve the simulation of the real scheduling environment.

6.2 Parameter Optimization Verification of PBS-Based Task Scheduling System

It is now possible to capture the performance index of PBS system in the set time period by the parameter optimization prototype system, calculate the fitness, and gradually evolve the improved parameters through the steps of screening, crossover, and variation.

(1) 3 users are randomly selected every 7 to 9 s and each user randomly submits 3 to 5 assignments. The job duration is randomly 1 to 10 s, where 12 core nodes are required for 1 to 4 s, 32 core nodes for 5 to 8 s, and 144 core nodes for 9 to 10 s.

(2) The prototype system triggers the tasks every 2 s, accesses the task record and user record data after 90 times (about 3 min), calculates the corresponding system resource utilization and user fairness, fuses them into fitness according to the set ratio, and clears them after backing up the historical data to start a new round of triggering and recording.

(3) Each round of testing a group of A1 to A5 parameters of fitness, if the racial ceiling number set to 20, a total of 30 iterations, so that it takes 30 h to complete a round of testing, you can observe whether there is a better trend of parameter optimization.

6.3 Test Results and Analysis

Fig. 1. Initial results of the test

The first is the randomly generated results of the first 2 generations, and it can be seen that the changes are very large. Even the initial top ranked genes are ranked bottom in the second round of testing, such as the gene group starting with 167.4694, which dropped from the third place to the bottom third. This indicates that in an environment where the job attributes and the time of being placed are random, even the same set of gene parameters may be tested with different fitness values. Thus, the goal of parameter optimization in this environment is not simply to find a set of genes with the largest fitness, but to find a set of genes with higher fitness in several consecutive tests. The final result is to allow the scheduling system to have a better scheduling effect in all situations (Figs. 1 and 2).

Fig. 2. Final results of the test

Observing the results near the end, a stabilization trend of genes can be observed.

(1) Observe the longitudinal genes: 257 and 768 appear in high frequency in the first column of genes, and 333, 640 and 894 in the second column of genes.
(2) Observe the horizontal genes. The first ranked gene groups, in which the gene segments are more stable, such as 637 and 791 at the end of the first gene group, still ranked at the end of the first gene group in the second test.

6.4   Test Results for Parameter Immobilization

Due to the specificity of the task, the complete evolution requires a long training time, and the more random test task is more difficult to get significant convergence results in a short-simplified process, so the random parameter part is fixed to get better convergence results. The parameters were set as follows.

3 users including pbs0, pbs1 and pbs2, submit 5 jobs in sequence every 10 s. The job durations are 1, 3, 5, 7, and 9, where 12core nodes are required from 1 to 4 s, 32core nodes are required from 5 to 8 s, and 144core nodes are required from 9 to 10 s.

The test results are as follows (Fig. 3).

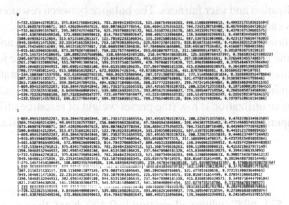

Fig. 3. Initial results of the test

It can be seen that the genomic morphology in the preliminary test results varied, and the fitness values are largely scattered in the [0.2, 0.5] (Fig. 4).

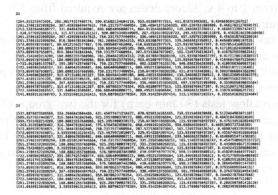

Fig. 4. Final results of the test

It can be seen that the optimization of scheduling parameters has a significant convergence effect for a more stable workflow.

(1) Observe the longitudinal genes: the first column of genes is roughly concentrated around 260 and 570; the second column of high-quality genes is roughly concentrated around 330 (180 also appears more often, but is mostly ordered in the middle and latter part); the third column of genes is roughly concentrated around 800; the fourth column of genes is roughly concentrated around 900 and 330 (900 is ordered more forward); the fifth column of genes is roughly concentrated around 140.

(2) Observe the lateral genes. 260 and 570 are alternately in the front of the genomic pattern.

Therefore, in this workflow, the gene parameters can be set as "570, 330, 800, 900, 140" or "260, 330, 800, 900, 140", which can achieve a better balance of resource utilization and user fairness. The balance between resource utilization and user fairness can be achieved.

(3) In this workflow mode, tasks are scheduled at an interval of 10 s and the maximum execution time is 9 s, so that the tasks are executed faster and the idle waiting time is longer. This situation is also reflected in the results: the adaptation values after parameter optimization are roughly concentrated in [0.4, 0.5], indicating that the system resource utilization is low (the preset weight of resource utilization is 80%), and the computing nodes can be closed appropriately to save resources.

6.5   Performance Improvement of Test Results

In the initial group under the parameter fixation environment, the highest adaptation is "−722, 375, 781, 521, 698", whose adaptation is 0.499. Next, the same environment as 6.4.2.2 is used to test the performance of the initial highest adaptation group and the optimization result group, as follows.

(1) Set the environment as follows: 3 users pbs0, pbs1, pbs2, and 5 jobs are submitted in sequence every 10 s. The job durations are 1, 3, 5, 7, and 9, where 12core nodes are required from 1 to 4 s, 32core nodes are required from 5 to 8 s, and 144core nodes are required from 9 to 10 s.

(2) Turn off the random generation function and evolution function of the genome, and keep only the highest initial fitness group "−722, 375, 781, 521, 698" and the optimized result group "570, 330, 800, 900, 140" (The test was performed on one of the result groups).

(3) Conduct 30 workflow tests (30 min each) for the two groups of parameters, and test the delayed version of step 2 in 6.4.1, and calculate the fitness value after each workflow test, and take the average of 30 values as the fitness result. The performance improvement can be obtained by comparing the adaptation results of the two groups of parameters, as shown in the following Table 1.

Table 1. Performance test results

	Parameters	Average fitness value for 30 tests
Initial maximum group	722, 375, 781, 521, 698	0.4233
Optimization results group	570, 330, 800, 900, 140	0.4752

As a result, the new parameters have been optimized to improve the overall performance of the platform by 12.3%.

6.6 Tests Conclusion

The above tests results show that the optimization system can optimize the parameters of the scheduling algorithm of the PBS-based high-performance scheduling environment, so that the range of values of high-quality genes can be obtained more quickly for a more stable workflow, and a higher resource utilization can be achieved on the basis of balancing resource utilization and user fairness. In addition, after a period of parameter optimization, the computing nodes can be turned on or off appropriately according to the high or low resource utilization, so as to better match the resources with the demand.

7 Conclusions

In this paper, a multi-parameter scheduling evaluation method is proposed for the highly concurrent job scheduling problem, and a multi-parameter optimization system based on genetic algorithm is developed and tested in a simulation environment.

Firstly, this paper proposes two metrics to measure the scheduling effectiveness of the system and their calculation formulas: system resource utilization and user fairness, and normalizes them and fuses them into fitness values that can be provided to the genetic algorithm optimization system. Secondly, this paper proposes a formula for calculating the scheduling priority value involving five parameters, develops a prototype system for parameter optimization based on natural genetic algorithm, and quickly achieves better convergence with a given fitness objective function. Then, the simulation environment of the PBS-based high-performance scheduling environment is built through a virtual machine system, which performs more stably in the subsequent testing sessions and provides a better scheduling simulation environment. Finally, this paper integrates the parameter optimization operation system with the simulation environment and designs a set of simulation test methods to verify the effect of the parameter optimization prototype system in a more realistic scheduling environment. The result is that the prototype system can better train a quality genome with certain robustness and provide a better parameter set for the scheduling algorithm.

References

1. Cao, Z.Y., Zhao, Y., Niu, T., et al.: User evaluation-based priority scheduling for cluster jobs. J. Huazhong Univ. Sci. Technol. Nat. Sci. Edn. **39**(S1), 134–138 (2011)
2. Mu'alem, A.W., Feitelson, D.G.: Utilization, predictability, workloads, and user runtime estimates in scheduling the IBM SP2 with backfilling. IEEE Trans. Parallel Distrib. Syst. **12**(6), 529–543 (2001)
3. Schwiegeishohn, U., Yahyapour, R.: Improving first-come-first-serve job scheduling by gang scheduling. In: Feitelson, D.G., Rudolph, L. (eds.) Job Scheduling Strategies for Parallel Processing. JSSPP 1998. LNCS, vol. 1459. Springer, Berlin, Heidelberg (1998). https://doi.org/10.1007/BFb0053987
4. Sun, J.H., Deng, Q.X., Meng, Y.K.: Modeling and approximation algorithm for two-stage load scheduling problem on GPU. J. Softw. **25**(2), 298–313 (2014)
5. Bobelin, L., Martineau, P., Zhao, D., et al.: Shortest processing time first algorithm for Hadoop. In: 2016 IEEE 3rd International Conference on Cyber Security and Cloud Computing (CSCloud), pp. 119–123. IEEE (2016)

6. Zhou, K.: Research on Job Scheduling Technology and Cluster Management System in High Performance Computing. Jiangsu University of Science and Technology, Zhenjiang (2015)
7. Bai, S.R., Fu, Y.H.: A backfill-based parallel job scheduling algorithm. J. Hunan Univ. Nat. Sci. Edn. **34**(1), 81–84 (2007)
8. Zhu, X.M.: Research on several scheduling problems of real-time tasks in heterogeneous clustered systems. Fudan University (2009)
9. Zhang, G.T., Zhao, J.Y., Bai, Z.Y.: A cluster job scheduling system based on LT-backfilling algorithm. Comput. Eng. **33**(21), 69–71 (2007)
10. Javadi, B., Akbari, M.K., Abawajy, J.H.: A performance model for analysis of heterogeneous multi-cluster systems. Parallel Comput. **32**(11–12), 831–851 (2006)
11. Smith, M.C., Peterson, G.D.: Parallel application performance on shared high performance reconfigurable computing resources. Perform. Eval. **60**(1–4), 107–125 (2005)
12. Liang, Y., Meng, D., Fan, J.P.: RB-FIFT a swarm job scheduling algorithm combining firstfit and reservation backfill strategies. Comput. Res. Dev. **41**(11), 1902–1910 (2004)
13. Arndt, O., Freisleben, B., Kielmann, T., et al.: A comparative study of online scheduling algorithms for networks of workstations. Clust. Comput. **3**(2), 95–112 (2000)
14. Liu, S.Q., Meng, L.F., Shuo, J., et al.: A reservation backfill algorithm for area maximum priority scheduling. Microcomput. Appl. **29**(12), 5–9 (2008)
15. Fu, Y.H., Bai, S.R., Fang, J.: Backfilling scheduling algorithm based on the "expanded footprint" improvement algorithm. Comput. Eng. Sci. **28**(9), 94–96 (2006)
16. Bessai, K., Youcef, S., Oulamara, A., et al.: Bi-criteria workflow tasks allocation and scheduling in cloud computing environments. In: 2012 IEEE Fifth International Conference on Cloud Computing, pp. 638–645. IEEE (2012)
17. He, T., Chen, S., Kim, H., et al.: Scheduling parallel tasks onto opportunistically available cloud resources. In: 2012 IEEE Fifth International Conference on Cloud Computing, pp. 180–187. IEEE (2012)
18. Wu, Z., Ni, Z., Gu, L., et al.: A revised discrete particle swarm optimization for cloud workflow scheduling. In: 2010 International Conference on Computational Intelligence and Security, pp. 184–188. IEEE (2010)
19. Patel, S.J., Bhoi, U.R.: Improved priority based job scheduling algorithm in cloud computing using iterative method. In: 2014 Fourth International Conference on Advances in Computing and Communications, pp. 199–202. IEEE (2014)
20. Bey, K.B., Benhammadi, F., Benaissa, R.: Balancing heuristic for independent task scheduling in cloud computing. In: 2015 12th International Symposium on Programming and Systems (ISPS), pp. 1–6. IEEE (2015)
21. Suresh, A., Vijayakarthick, P.: Improving scheduling of backfill algorithms using balanced spiral method for cloud metascheduler. In: 2011 International Conference on Recent Trends in Information Technology (ICRTIT), pp. 624–627. IEEE (2011)
22. Liu, S., Ren, K., Deng, K., et al.: A task backfill based scientific workflow scheduling strategy on cloud platform. In: 2016 Sixth International Conference on Information Science and Technology (ICIST), pp. 105–110. IEEE (2016)
23. Qiao, Y.: Research on integrated dynamic scheduling algorithm for real-time heterogeneous systems. Thesis, Institute of Software, Chinese Academy of Sciences (2001)
24. Xu, J., Parnas, D.L.: Scheduling processes with release times, deadlines, precedence and exclusion relations. IEEE Trans. Softw. Eng. **16**(3), 360–369 (1990)
25. Blazewicz, J., Ecker, K.: Multiprocessor task scheduling with resource requirements. Real-Time Syst. **6**(1), 37–53 (1994)
26. Di, N.M., Stankovic, J.A.: Scheduling distributed real-time tasks with minimum jitter. IEEE Trans. Comput. **49**(4), 303–316 (2000)
27. Golberg, D.E.: Genetic algorithms in search, optimization, and machine learning. Addion Wesley **1989**(102), 36 (1989)

28. Stankovic, J.A., Spuri, M., Di, N.M., et al.: Implications of classical scheduling results for real-time systems. Computer **28**(6), 16–25 (1995)
29. Dertouzos, M.L., Mok, A.K.: Multiprocessor online scheduling of hard-real-time tasks. IEEE Trans. Softw. Eng. **15**(12), 1497–1506 (1989)
30. Dominic, M., Jain, B.N.: Conditions for on-line scheduling of hard real-time tasks on multiprocessors. J. Parallel Distrib. Comput. **55**(1), 121–137 (1998)
31. Baruah, S.K., Cohen, N.K., Plaxton, C.G., et al.: Proportionate progress: a notion of fairness in resource allocation. Algorithmica **15**(6), 600–625 (1996)
32. Ma, X., Liu, G.M., Zhang, X.R.: A high performance computing based job scheduling management optimization research and application. Commun. World Second Half Month **3**, 1–2 (2015)

ieSTGCN:A Mining Model of Skeleton Spatio-temporal Graph

Guojun Mao[1,2(✉)] and Yijin Wang[1]

[1] Fujian University of Technology, Fuzhou 350118, People's Republic of China
2201901008@smail.fjut.edu.cn
[2] Key Laboratory of Big Data Mining and Application in Fujian Province,
Fuzhou 350118, People's Republic of China
19662092@fjut.edu.cn

Abstract. Traditional methods of human action recognition focus on internal links between human joints, that is, local neighbor connections. However, some external links that cannot exist in the skeleton graph are also important for identifying human behaviors, such as hands and feet in harmonious movement. To capture richer spatial features in a skeleton graph, it is necessary to add external links and distinguish internal links from external links in a skeleton graph. Therefore, this paper designs two different adjacency matrices to characterize the internal links and external links of the human body respectively, and set different edge weights and feature weights to them for autonomous learning during the convolution process. Furthermore, a spatio-temporal graph convolution network called ieSTGCN is proposed. It consists of two modules: graph convolution network supporting internal and external links (ieGCN) and temporal convolution network in human joints (joTCN). Experiments on the Kinetics and the NTU-RGB+D datasets demonstrate that our model can obtain better recognition accuracy than some benchmark models.

Keywords: Skeleton graph · Internal link · External link · Spatio-temporal graph convolution

1 Introduction

Human action recognition are playing an important role in video surveillance, human-computer interaction, virtual reality and other fields [5,8,14]. Of course, actions can be identified in a variety of ways, such as RGB image sequences [6], depth image sequences [18], and human dynamic skeleton [12]. Compared with other existing methods, dynamic skeleton data contains rich spatial and temporal information and is more robust for video analysis under complex backgrounds and scene changes.

This work was supported by the National Natural Science Foundation of China (61773415) and National Key Research and Development Project (2019YFD090 0800/05).

Skeleton sequence methods mainly encode the human joint coordinates into vectors and then applied time series analysis methods to perform pattern learning [7,16]. However, these methods lack the exploitation of the spatial relationships between human joints and mainly focus on the time change analysis of a single joint. In fact, Human skeleton naturally constitutes a graph structure, So the graph-based methods are naturally applied to action recognition.

Graph convolution network (GCN) has made progress in graph classification, semi supervised learning and so on [3,17], which can help solve the analysis of skeleton graphs. However, using gcn alone for dynamic skeleton sequences cannot extract valid temporal information [19]. Therefore, this paper makes use of spatio-temporal convolution block to integrate spatial location and temporal evolution relationship, so as to more effectively process dynamic skeleton graph data.

In addition, this paper also introduces the concept of external link, and creates an internal-external linking spatio-temporal graph convolution network (ieSTGCN) to mine skeleton graphs effectively.

2   Related Work

From the perspective of feature extraction, the methods of skeleton based action recognition are generally classified into two categories: hand-crafted methods and deep learning methods. Hand-crafted methods design node features by physical intuition, including covariance matrix analysis of joint trajectories [9], joint feature extraction based on relative position calculation [16], feature analysis based on evaluation of translation and rotation [15], etc. Undoubtedly, these methods are subjective and skillful, so their recognition results are difficult to be satisfactory.

Deep learning methods can automatically extract the features of skeleton data, so the analysis effects will be better. Currently, recurrent neural networks (RNN) and convolutional neural networks (CNN) have taken an important place in skeleton data analysis. The RNN-based approaches generally can well achieve the extraction of temporal features of skeleton data [4,11,12]. The CNN-based approaches are more conducive to spatial feature extraction of skeleton data [10,13]. In 2018, Yan et al. designed a new model ST-GCN(spatio-temporal graph convolutional neural network model ST-GCN) [19], which provides a novel solution for mining spatio-temporal skeleton graphs. However, ST-GCN only considers internal connections between local joints, which cannot support the interaction between farther joints. In many cases, these potential or perceived relations between long-distance joints are very valuable. For example, for the "clap hands" motion, the interaction between the two hands is very important, but in most skeleton data or graphs, the two hands are not considered to be naturally connected. Therefore, this paper introduces the external link relations to supplement the deficiency of natural connections in popular skeleton graphs.

In short, it is feasible to analyze human skeleton data by using spatio-temporal graphs, and the effectiveness of graph learning can be further enhanced by setting external links between skeleton joints.

3   Model Design

We denote skeleton graph as $G = \{V, E_a, E_b\}$. Specifically, V represents a set of all joints in the skeleton, E_a represents internal links, and E_b represents external links. Such, $\{V, E_a\}$ and $\{V, E_b\}$ are two sub graphs of G, represented by adjacency matrices $A \in \mathbb{R}^{|V| \times |V|}$ and $B \in \mathbb{R}^{|V| \times |V|}$ respectively. If $A_{ij} = 1$, there is an internal link between the i-th joint and the j-th joint. If $B_{ij} = 1$, it means we set an external link between the i-th joint and j-th joint.

Based on the above representation, this section will design our ieSTGCN model. It consists of a group of spatio-temporal convolution blocks. Each block consists of a spatial convolution module and a temporal convolution module. Next, the design of these units will be introduced step by step from bottom to top.

3.1   Spatial Convolution Module

The spatial convolution module (denoted as ieGCN) needs to consider internal and external links, so it is a fusion of internal graph convolution network (iGCN) and external graph convolution network (eGCN).

Internal Graph Convolution. Given a skeleton graph $G = \{V, E_a, E_b\}$, $\forall v_i \in V$, let its internal links correspond to a neighborhood $\mathcal{B}(v_i) = \{v_j | \langle v_j, v_i \rangle \in E_a\}$. Suppose there exists a mapping function $l_i : \mathcal{B}(v_i) \rightarrow \{0, 1, .., K-1\}$, so that each node maps only one numerical label. The multi-label graph convolution is formulated as follows:

$$f_{out}(v_i) = \sum_{v_j \in \mathcal{B}(v_i)} \frac{f_{in}(v_j) \cdot w(l_i(v_j))}{\mathcal{Z}_i(v_j)} \tag{1}$$

Where: f_{in} is the input features; f_{out} is the output features; w is the weight function; $\mathcal{Z}_i(v_j) = \left|\{v_m | l_i(v_m) = l_i(v_j)\}\right|$ is a the base of the corresponding subset.

For the human action recognition, we divide the neighborhood into three subsets based on the distance from a joint to the human center of gravity: root node, centripetal node set, and centrifugal node set, and the corresponding numerical labels are set to 0, 1, and 2 respectively. For an investigated node, root node is the itself; its set of centripetal nodes includes all nodes closer to the body's center of gravity than the root node; and the set of centrifugal nodes have ones which away from the body's center of gravity than the root node. That is:

$$l_i(v_j) = \begin{cases} 0 \text{ if } v_j \in V, \langle v_j, v_i \rangle \in E_a, d_{v_j,c} = d_{v_i,c} \\ 1 \text{ if } v_j \in V, \langle v_j, v_i \rangle \in E_a, d_{v_j,c} < d_{v_i,c} \\ 2 \text{ if } v_j \in V, \langle v_j, v_i \rangle \in E_a, d_{v_j,c} > d_{v_i,c} \end{cases} \tag{2}$$

Where: $l_i(v_j)$ is the numerical label of the neighboring node v_j;c is the position of the body's center of gravity;d is the distance function of two joint positions.

Using the multi-label technique, the original adjacency matrix A of internal links of a skeleton graph can be decomposed into 3 sub-adjacency matrices. That is

$$A + I = A^r + A^p + A^f = \sum_{q \in Q} A^q \tag{3}$$

Where A^r, A^p and A^f are called root adjacency matrix, centripetal adjacency matrix and centrifugal adjacency matrix respectively. Assuming $Q = \{r, p, f\}$, corresponding internal graph convolution is formulated as follows:

$$F_a = \sum_{q \in Q} M_a^q \odot \left((D^q)^{-\frac{1}{2}} A^q (D^q)^{-\frac{1}{2}} \right) F_{in} W_a^q \tag{4}$$

where: $F_{in} \in \mathbb{R}^{n \times d_{in}}$ is the input features in the skeleton graph and d_{in} represents the input feature dimension; $A^q, D^q \in \mathbb{R}^{n \times n}$ are the corresponding adjacency matrix and degree matrix of the q sub-graph respectively; $\odot$ is the Hadamard inner product multiplied by elementary bits; $M_a^q \in \mathbb{R}^{n \times n}$) and $W_a^q \in \mathbb{R}^{d_{in} \times d_{out}}$ are the edge weights and feature weights of the q sub-graph respectively; $F_a \in \mathbb{R}^{n \times d_{out}}$ and d_{out} is the output features and the dimension; $(D^q)^{-\frac{1}{2}} A^q (D^q)^{-\frac{1}{2}}$ is the normalized adjacency matrix of the corresponding q sub-graph, which is often used in GCN models [17].

External Graph Convolution. We use adjacency matrix B to indicate external links, the external graph convolution operation is formulated as follows:

$$F_b = M_b \odot \left((D_b)^{-\frac{1}{2}} B (D_b)^{-\frac{1}{2}} \right) F_{in} W_b \tag{5}$$

Where: D_b is the degree adjacency matrix of the B; M_b and W_b are the edge weight matrix and feature weight matrix of the external dependence graph convolution, respectively; F_{in} and F_b represent the input and output features of the graph convolution under the external dependence respectively.

Internal-External Graph Convolution. The internal links represent the natural associations of human body structures, while the external links express the non-physical implicit relationship . In order to capture the spatial dependence more comprehensively, we further fuse internal graph convolution and external graph convolution to form the internal-external graph convolution (denoted as ieGCN).

Given a skeleton graph with internal links adjacency matrices A and external links adjacency matrices B, the internal-external graph convolution is computed as follows:

$$F_{out} = F_a + F_b = \sum_{q \in Q} M_a^q \odot \left((D^q)^{-\frac{1}{2}} A^q (D^q)^{-\frac{1}{2}} \right) F_{in} W_a^q +$$
$$M_b \odot \left((D_b)^{-\frac{1}{2}} B (D_b)^{-\frac{1}{2}} \right) F_{in} W_b \tag{6}$$

Where F_{out} is the output feature, and the other symbols are the same as Eq. (4) and Eq. (5).

3.2 Temporal Convolution Module

The variation of node features in the time direction can be characterized by time series and extracting the temporal features form time series is very critical. In this work, we design a suitable temporal convolution module for joints in the human body (denoted by joTCN) to mine the temporal features.

Assume that the corresponding time series of a joint is $x_{in} \in \mathbb{R}^M$. We represent the kernel size of the one-dimensional convolution as Γ and write the neighborhood of the moment t as $\mathcal{B}(t) = \{p \mid |p - t| \leq \lfloor \Gamma/2 \rfloor\}$. Then, the output value of the temporal convolution at the moment of t is:

$$x_{out} = \sum_{p \in B(t)} x_{in}(p) \, \mathrm{w}(p) \tag{7}$$

where w represents the weight function; x_{out} is the output features of the temporal convolution.

3.3 Spatio-temporal Convolutional Block

Spatio-temporal convolutional Block is the basic computational unit in our learning model. It consists of the graph convolutional module ieGCN, the temporal convolutional module joTCN, and the necessary connection operations.

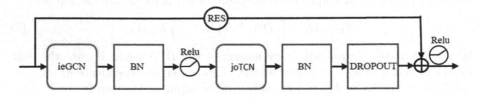

Fig. 1. Spatio-temporal convolutional block.

As shown in Fig. 1, the basic computational flow of this block is the following.

(1) Using ieGCN module to extract spatial features that integrated internal links and external links.
(2) The output of ieGCN is batch normalized(BN).
(3) The normalized spatio-temporal data are fed to the temporal module joTCN through the Relu() activation function to implement temporal convolution of features.
(4) The output of joTCN is batch normalized again and dropout operation is implemented to prevent overfitting of the model.
(5) A residual mechanism is introduced to make the model training more stable, and at the end of the bock, Relu() function is used again to perform nonlinear activation.

3.4 Network Structure in IeSTGCN

Figure 2 gives the schematic structure of ieSTGCN designed by this paper. It consists of three main parts: data preprocessing layer, backbone network, and prediction output layer.

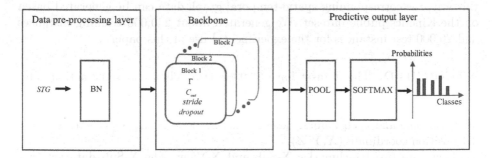

Fig. 2. Network structure of ieSTGCN.

In the data preprocessing layer, the input data is the spatio-temporal graph (STG), a time series of skeleton graphs. A batch normalization(BN) is set to standardize the scale of the input data.

The backbone network consists of multiple blocks stacked together. The main parameters of the each block include the convolution kernel size Γ in the time direction, the step of the temporal convolution *stride*, the number of output channels C_{out}, and the output clipping ratio *dropout*.

The predictive output layer consists of a global average pooling layer(POOL) and a softmax layer. POOL layer pools the feature graphs of different samples to the same size, and then the class prediction is done by the classifier.

4 Experiments

We conduct experiments on two different datasets: Kinetics [2] in the unconstrained environment and NTU-RGB+D [12] in the indoor environment. Some typical benchmark models are selected for comparison experiments to evaluate our model.

4.1 Datasets

Kinetics. There are more than 300,000 video clips with more than 400 human action types labeled, covering a wide range of human activity scenarios such as daily activities and sports competitions. Each video lasts about 10 s.

Using the OpenPose [1], we generated the spatio-temporal data for training from the original Kinetics videos. The node features include the two-dimensional coordinates (X, Y) and the confidence level C. Considering the case of at most two people, if there are more than two people in the scene, only the two people with the highest average confidence level of the joints are selected for the training sample. If there are less than 2 people in the picture, the corresponding entity is filled with 0. The size of each video clip is 300 frames. When some clips don't have enough frames, we replenish through the video replay method. In this way, the corresponding spatio-temporal graph data can be generated based on the Kinetics public dataset. We generated about 240,000 training instances and 20,000 test instances for the experimental use in this paper.

NTU-RGB+D. The dataset have 56,000 action clips and sixty action categories. All clips were taken by forty volunteers in an indoor experimental environment with three different viewpoints of the camera. Each clip has a maximum of two people and each human skeleton has 25 nodes. The node feature is the 3D position coordinate (X, Y, Z).

There are two benchmarks: X-Sub and X-View. The X-Sub data sets are divided by different cameras. It have 40,320 training instances and 16,560 test instances. X-View datasets are divided by different volunteers. It have 37,920 training instances and 18,920 test instances.

4.2 Evaluation Metrics

We select Top-1 and Top-5 as the evaluation indexes of the experiment. For each test sample, the output is the classification probability of all actions that ranked in the order of the highest to lowest. For Top-1, a sample is correctly classified if the real category is the fist class in the rank. For Top-5, the classification is correct if the real category of the sample is among the top five classes in the rank. Top-1 and Top-5 is formulated as follows:

$$
\begin{aligned}
top-1 &= \frac{\sum_{i}^{\kappa} \epsilon \left(class_i^{real} = rank_1 \left(class_i^{pred} \right) \right)}{\kappa} \\
top-5 &= \frac{\sum_{i}^{\kappa} \epsilon \left(class_i^{real} \in rank_5 \left(class_i^{pred} \right) \right)}{\kappa}
\end{aligned}
\tag{8}
$$

where: κ is the total number of instances; ϵ is a judgment function, if the condition is true, $\epsilon = 1$, otherwise, $\epsilon = 0$; $class_i^{real}$ represents the ground-truth label of the i-th instance; $rank_1 \left(class_i^{pred} \right)$ and $rank_5 \left(class_i^{pred} \right)$ represent the first and the top five labels of the i-th instance in the predicted probability rank respectively.

4.3 Experimental Setup

After repeated experimental tests, we set the appropriate network parameters. Specifically, the number of bloks is nine; Let $\Gamma = 9$ and $dropout = 0.5$; C_{out} of all blocks is set to 64,64,64,128,128,128,256,256,256. In this way, as the number of output channels increases exponentially, the acquired action features becomes richer; The step of the temporal convolution *stride* is set to two in the forth block and the seventh block, and one in the rest of the blocks. In this way, the total number of frames in the temporal dimension is reduced by half after the forth and seventh block, thus reducing the redundant information between frames and improving the computational efficiency.

For the Kinetics, the total epochs is fifty and the batch size is sixteen. The optimization strategy is SGD. Initially, the learning rate was kept at 0.1. Later, it was decays by 0.1 times at the twenty, thirty, and forty epoch.

For the NTU-RGB+D, the total epochs is fifty and the batch size is sixteen. The Original learning rate is 0.1 and decays by 0.1 times at the thirty and forty epochs.

4.4 Comparative Experiments

On the Kinetics dataset, four models, Feature Enc [7], Deep LSTM [12], Temporal Conv [13] and ST-GCN [19], are selected for accuracy comparison experiments. The results of the comparison experiments on Top-1 and Top-5 metrics are given in Fig. 3.

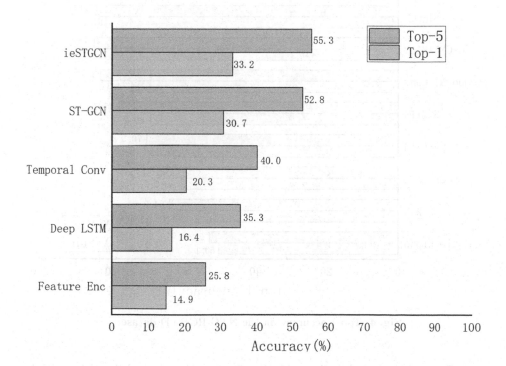

Fig. 3. Top-1 and Top-5 accuracy on the Kinetics dataset.

Figure 3 shows that the ieSTGCN outperforms the accuracy of the comparison methods on the Kinetics which is a typical dataset in an unconstrained environment, so such results reflect the advantages of the ieSTGCN model for human action recognition in an unconstrained environment.

The different types of models in Fig. 3 have different levels of accuracies. Firstly, Feature Enc based on manual feature extraction has the worst effect, which is mainly due to the subjectivity and arbitrariness of manual feature extraction. Secondly, although RNN or CNN based methods (Deep LSTM, Temporal Conv) can automatically extract motion features using deep learning techniques, they are based on single joint feature analysis without using the graph structure of skeleton data, so the accuracy is also difficult to improve. In contrast, the ST-GCN and ieSTGCN based on graph convolutional networks can improve the recognition performance by using both the graph structure of the skeleton graph and the node feature data. In particular, this paper introduces the external links of the skeleton graph, which effectively compensates for the local physical connection of the ST-GCN model and achieves the best experimental results.

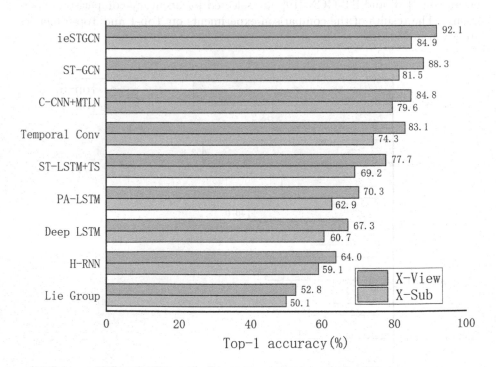

Fig. 4. Top-1 accuracy on the NTU-RGB+D dataset.

It is worth noting that since the Kinetics is a live video data with multiple motion modes coexisting in an outdoor complex scene, the action recognition accuracies in such environments are generally not high. In order to further testing the validity of ieSTGCN, next comparison experiments were conducted on the 3D skeleton dataset NTU-RGB+D in the indoor scene.

On two representative subsets of NTU-RGB+D dataset, X-Sub and X-View, the experiments were completed by selecting different recognition algorithms including Lie Group [15], H-RNN [4], Deep LSTM [12], PA-LSTM [12], ST-LSTM+TS [11], Temporal Conv [13], C-CNN+MTLN [10], and ST-GCN [19] to compare with our model. The experimental results for Top-1 accuracy are given in Fig. 4.

It is easy to see from Fig. 4:

(1) The latter three models ST-GCN, DPRL+GCNN, and ieSTGCN are graph learning models. Compared with the single-node feature learning methods, the experimental data reveals that the graph learning-based methods has significant technical advantages.
(2) ieSTGCN achieves 84.9% and 92.1% Top-1 index on X-Sub and X-View respectively, which surpasses the existing models. It indicates that the model in this paper has the ability to handle 3D data of skeleton without constraint environment and improve the accuracy.

5   Conclusion

This paper has presented a human skeleton action recognition model ieSTGCN. Firstly, internal and external links are fused in the spatial graph convolution module, which enhancing the model's spatial expression. Secondly, in order to distinguish different movement trends, the internal links are further divided into root nodes, centripetal node sets, and centrifugal node sets. Then, we construct the spatio-temporal convolution block as basic calculation unit to capture spatio-temporal features. Finally, model comparison experiments are completed in two typical public datasets, Kinetics and NTU-RGB+D. The results indicate that the accuracies of ieSTGCN in different environments are better than the existing comparative models.

References

1. Cao, Z., Simon, T., Wei, S.E., Sheikh, Y.: Realtime multi-person 2d pose estimation using part affinity fields. In: Proceedings of the IEEE Conference on Computer Vision and Pattern Recognition, pp. 7291–7299 (2017)
2. Carreira, J., Zisserman, A.: Quo vadis, action recognition? A new model and the kinetics dataset. In: proceedings of the IEEE Conference on Computer Vision and Pattern Recognition, pp. 6299–6308 (2017)
3. Defferrard, M., Bresson, X., Vandergheynst, P.: Convolutional neural networks on graphs with fast localized spectral filtering. In: Advances in Neural Information Processing Systems, vol. 29 (2016)
4. Du, Y., Wang, W., Wang, L.: Hierarchical recurrent neural network for skeleton based action recognition. In: Proceedings of the IEEE Conference on Computer Vision and Pattern Recognition, pp. 1110–1118 (2015)

5. Duric, Z., et al.: Integrating perceptual and cognitive modeling for adaptive and intelligent human-computer interaction. Proc. IEEE **90**(7), 1272–1289 (2002)
6. Feichtenhofer, C., Fan, H., Malik, J., He, K.: Slowfast networks for video recognition. In: Proceedings of the IEEE/CVF International Conference on Computer Vision, pp. 6202–6211 (2019)
7. Fernando, B., Gavves, E., Oramas, J.M., Ghodrati, A., Tuytelaars, T.: Modeling video evolution for action recognition. In: Proceedings of the IEEE Conference on Computer Vision and Pattern Recognition, pp. 5378–5387 (2015)
8. Gaur, U., Zhu, Y., Song, B., Roy-Chowdhury, A.: A "string of feature graphs" model for recognition of complex activities in natural videos. In: 2011 International Conference on Computer Vision, pp. 2595–2602. IEEE (2011)
9. Hussein, M.E., Torki, M., Gowayyed, M.A., El-Saban, M.: Human action recognition using a temporal hierarchy of covariance descriptors on 3d joint locations. In: Twenty-Third International Joint Conference on Artificial Intelligence (2013)
10. Ke, Q., Bennamoun, M., An, S., Sohel, F., Boussaid, F.: A new representation of skeleton sequences for 3d action recognition. In: Proceedings of the IEEE Conference on Computer Vision and Pattern Recognition, pp. 3288–3297 (2017)
11. Liu, J., Shahroudy, A., Xu, D., Wang, G.: Spatio-temporal LSTM with trust gates for 3D human action recognition. In: Leibe, B., Matas, J., Sebe, N., Welling, M. (eds.) ECCV 2016. LNCS, vol. 9907, pp. 816–833. Springer, Cham (2016). https://doi.org/10.1007/978-3-319-46487-9_50
12. Shahroudy, A., Liu, J., Ng, T.T., Wang, G.: NTU RGB+ D: a large scale dataset for 3d human activity analysis. In: Proceedings of the IEEE Conference on Computer Vision and Pattern Recognition, pp. 1010–1019 (2016)
13. Soo Kim, T., Reiter, A.: Interpretable 3d human action analysis with temporal convolutional networks. In: Proceedings of the IEEE Conference on Computer Vision and Pattern Recognition Workshops, pp. 20–28 (2017)
14. Sudha, M., Sriraghav, K., Jacob, S.G., Manisha, S., et al.: Approaches and applications of virtual reality and gesture recognition: a review. Int. J. Amb. Comput. Intell. (IJACI) **8**(4), 1–18 (2017)
15. Vemulapalli, R., Arrate, F., Chellappa, R.: Human action recognition by representing 3d skeletons as points in a lie group. In: Proceedings of the IEEE Conference on Computer Vision and Pattern Recognition, pp. 588–595 (2014)
16. Wang, J., Liu, Z., Wu, Y., Yuan, J.: Mining actionlet ensemble for action recognition with depth cameras. In: 2012 IEEE Conference on Computer Vision and Pattern Recognition, pp. 1290–1297. IEEE (2012)
17. Welling, M., Kipf, T.N.: Semi-supervised classification with graph convolutional networks. In: International Conference on Learning Representations (ICLR 2017) (2016)
18. Xu, C., Govindarajan, L.N., Zhang, Y., Cheng, L.: Lie-x: Depth image based articulated object pose estimation, tracking, and action recognition on lie groups. Int. J. Comput. Vision **123**(3), 454–478 (2017)
19. Yan, S., Xiong, Y., Lin, D.: Spatial temporal graph convolutional networks for skeleton-based action recognition. In: Thirty-Second AAAI Conference on Artificial Intelligence (2018)

Deep Recurrent Q-Network for Cloud Manufacturing Scheduling Problems

Xiaohan Wang[1], Lin Zhang[1]([✉]), Yongkui Liu[2], and Yuan Yang[1]

[1] School of Automation Science and Electrical Engineering, Beihang University,
Beijing 100191, China
zhanglin@buaa.edu.cn
[2] School of Mechano-Electronic Engineering, Xidian University, Xi'an 710071, China

Abstract. As a new manufacturing mode, cloud manufacturing integrates distributed manufacturing resources and capabilities into services, providing services to consumers with manufacturing requirements. Assigning consumers' tasks to services requires many-to-many scheduling. An effective scheduling algorithm can reduce production expenditure and increase processing efficiency. However, the cloud manufacturing environment takes the characteristics of dynamics, complexity, and diversity, making the task scheduling intractable. Deep reinforcement learning has been gradually applied to various scheduling problems and shows the potential of little hand-craft and non-trivial generalizability. This paper proposes a deep recurrent q-network-based scheduling algorithm to address task scheduling problems in cloud manufacturing. The environment is modeled as a partially observable Markov decision process. The long-short-term-based policy trained by reinforcement learning is utilized to choose service providers for each task in step. A case study of the automobile structure part processing indicates that our proposal outperforms deep q-network by 5.7% and proximal policy optimization by 7.7% on scheduling accuracy.

Keywords: Cloud manufacturing · Deep reinforcement learning ·
Task scheduling · Recurrent neural network

1 Introduction

As a new manufacturing mode, cloud manufacturing (CMfg) integrates information technologies such as cloud computing, Internet of things (IoT), and artificial intelligence (AI) with traditional manufacturing [1,2]. It packages different types of manufacturing resources and capabilities into services provided by service providers. In CMfg, scheduling services or tasks in the complex and dynamic cloud environment has become crucial in reducing manufacturing costs

This work is supported by the National Key R&D Program Funded Projects of China (2020AAA0109202) and the national natural science foundation of China (NSFC) under Grant Nos. 61873014 and 61973243.

and improving production efficiency. Compared to traditional manufacturing systems, the dynamic and uncertainty of CMfg are more prominent. For example, orders submitted by consumers are online and real-time, and their number is tough to be predicted. Additionally, the manufacturing resources and services may dynamically change, and their distributions are easily affected by external interference factors. Efficient scheduling algorithms can reduce manufacturing cost and improve efficiency and increase consumers' trust in CMfg platforms.

Methods for solving cloud manufacturing scheduling problems (CMfg-SP) are classified into two categories, namely priority dispatching rules (PDR) and heuristic algorithms. PDR represents the manually defined rule-based program, which is simple but effective. PDRs are able to schedule tasks in a short period as they consume little computing time, so some works focus on solving the dynamic scheduling in CMfg using PDRs [3]. However, effective PDRs need to be customized by experienced managers, thus increasing the dependence on expert knowledge and human-labor expenditure. Besides, PDRs' scheduling performance is another concern because they do not take optimal searches when generating scheduling solutions. As a result, more researchers choose to leverage heuristic algorithms to solve CMfg-SP. Heuristic algorithms decompose the scheduling problem into sub-problems and find the optimal local solution through optimization search processes. Heuristic algorithms automatically optimize the scheduling and are widely adopted in various manufacturing systems. However, the optimization depends on the searching procedure, in which calculating consumption is high [4]. Besides, they need re-calculation when data distributions of the scheduling environment change, resulting in low generalizability and can hardly be applied to dynamic environments. Although some researchers have alleviated these issues by parallel computing and transfer learning, the optimization search of heuristic algorithms still limits their applications. Therefore, a new scheduling framework for CMfg-SP is urgently needed, which should meet scheduling requirements of accuracy, dynamic, and fast time-respond simultaneously and reduce the dependence on expert knowledge.

Deep reinforcement learning (DRL) has been gradually adopted to solve scheduling problems [5]. DRL learns the decision-making policy automatically through the online interaction between agents and the environment and shows competitive performance in many scheduling problems, such as job shop scheduling problems (JSSPs). DRL learns to schedule tasks by trial-and-error and based on the knowledge of the CMfg environment and has been applied to solve CMfg-SPs. Previous works mainly focus on modeling CMfg environments as the Markov decision process (MDP), where the agent makes decisions based on the global state of the environment in each timestep, and commonly adopted DRL algorithms are deep-q-network (DQN) and its variants such as double deep q-network (DDQN) and dueling deep q-network (Dueling DQN). This paper proposed a deep recurrent q-network (DRQN) based scheduling method, in which the CMfg scheduling environment is modeled as a partially observed Markov decision process (POMDP). The contributions are summarized as follows: 1) The CMfg environment is modeled as a POMDP, where the agent only partially observes the environment's state. This modeling is more reasonable than MDP as the agent can hardly observe the global state in CMfg-SP. 2) We use long short-term memory (LSTM) as our agent's policy network, and LSTM is a variant of recurrent neural network (RNN) that can effectively extract temporal information in observations. 3) DRQN has rarely been applied to CMfg scheduling problems and other scheduling problems, and our simulation experiments verify its scheduling performance on an automobile structure part processing case. Experiment results indicate that our proposal outperforms DQN and proximal policy optimization (PPO) on scheduling performance and generalizability.

The remainder of this paper is organized as follows. Section 2 presents the literature review. Section 3 describes the statement of CMfg-SP. The POMDP modeling and the detailed design of our proposal are introduced in Sect. 4. In Sect. 5, experiments are implemented based on an automobile processing case. Section 6 presents the conclusion of this paper.

2   Related Works

In the early cloud manufacturing task scheduling stage, most researchers utilized heuristic algorithms to solve the CMfg-SP. Literature [6] combined advantages of genetic algorithm (GA), ant colony optimization (ACO), and other algorithms, and proposed an improved scheduling algorithm, which improved the efficiency of CMfg scheduling. Literature [7] improved the convergence speed of the algorithm by expanding the search space and proposed a collaborative particle swarm algorithm (PSA), which optimized the processing time and production cost and further improved the efficiency of the CMfg-SP. Literature [8] proposed a fast genetic algorithm for the optimal allocation of computing resources in CMfg, and their proposal further reduced the completion time and greatly improved scheduling efficiency in CMfg. A new cloud-based dismantling system proposed in literature [9] and the hybrid artificial bee colony algorithm proposed in literature [10] were optimized in terms of minimum completion time, production cost, and reliability, which improved the scheduling efficiency to a higher level. The fatal problem of heuristic algorithms is that they are only suitable for one scenario, meaning that the generalizability is poor. Once the scene changes, the algorithm needs to be modified, so it cannot meet the dynamic requirement of CMfg-SP.

With the development of AI, Deep Reinforcement Learning (DRL) has been proposed to solve CMfg-SP. Literature [11] proposed a CMfg scheduling algorithm based on DQN using the makespan as the optimization target. The algorithm constructs the state space with variables such as the start and end time of the task process and the task status of each provider. Literature [11] compared their DQN-based scheduling algorithm with four traditional heuristic algorithms such as HEFT, CPOP, LOOPAHEAD, and PEFT in different scenarios. The results showed that their proposal could complete the task well. Literature [12] proposed a Deep Q-Network with priority replay based on Dueling architecture to solve CMfg-SP. The algorithm established a reward function based on the logistic regression model and took the quality of service as the optimization target. Their experiments showed that DQN had improved effectiveness, robustness, adaptability, and scalability compared with traditional Q-learning.

3   Problem Statement

Scheduling in CMfg contains many procedures, such as converting orders into manufacturing tasks and assessing the quality of services, while this paper only concentrates on the task scheduling procedure. The CMfg-SP is similar to that described in [12]. Given n^{mt} manufacturing tasks to be scheduled among n^{mp} manufacturing providers. A task is processed alternatively in one or many providers, and the transferring of tasks among providers relies on logistics. The terminal of the scheduling is that all n^{mt} tasks have been completed. Three significant variables are described as follows, including the manufacturing task $mt^i \in \{mt^1, mt^2, ..., mt^{n^{mt}}\}$, the manufacturing provider $mp^i \in \{mp^1, mp^2, ..., mp^{n^{mp}}\}$, and the logistics $lg^{i,j}, i, j \in \{1, 2, 3, ..., n^{mp}\}$.

$$mt^i = < MST^i, Seq^i > \tag{1}$$

$$mst^{i,j} = < fc^{i,j}, pre^{i,j} > \tag{2}$$

A manufacturing task mt^i contains a subtask set MST^i and its sequence Seq^i, and subtasks need to be processed according to the sequence Seq^i. As for each subtask $mst^{i,j} \in MST^i$, it includes the functional type of services $fc^{i,j}$ for processing $mst_{i,j}$ and the successor subtask $pre^{i,j}$. A task is finished when all its subtasks are completed.

$$mp^i = < MS^i, loc^i > \tag{3}$$

$$ms^{i,j} = < fc^{i,j}, tm^{i,j}, ct^{i,j}, cp^{i,j} > \tag{4}$$

A manufacturing provider mp^i contains a service set MS^i and the location loc^i. As for each service $ms^{i,j} \in MS^i$, it includes the functional type $fc^{i,j}$, time comsumption $tm^{i,j}$, cost $ct^{i,j}$, and maximum capacity $cp^{i,j}$.

$$lg^{i,j} = < lt^{i,j}, lc^{i,j} > \tag{5}$$

The logistics $lg^{i,j}$ contains two elements, including logistic time and cost between mp_i and mp_j. Generally, the logistic time and cost are proportional to the distance between two providers.

Based on these variables, the target of CMfg-SP is to minimize the makespan and cost. Two objectives $Obj_{makespan}$ and Obj_{cost} are represented as:

$$\min Obj_{makespan} = \max_i (\sum_t (lt_{mp_{t-1,i}, mp_{t,i}} + tm_{mp_{t,i}, ms_{t,i}})) \tag{6}$$

$$\min Obj_{cost} = \sum_i \sum_t (lc_{mp_{t-1,i},mp_{t,i}} + ct_{me_{t,i},ms_{t,i}}) \tag{7}$$

where $mp_{t,i}, ms_{t,i}$ are the selected provider and the needed service for the task mt^i at the t timestep.

4 Design and Methodology

In this section, we introduce our proposal in two steps. Firstly, the POMDP of CMfg-SP is presented. Then, the DRQN-based scheduling framework is described.

4.1 Formulate as a POMDP

The POMDP of CMfg-SP can be described as a tuple $< O, A, r, \pi, \gamma >$. $o \in O$ represents the observation of the CMfg environment. A denotes the discrete action space. $r(s, a) : S \times A \to R$ is the reward function. π is the policy model, and the relationship between o, a, π in the t step is $a_{t+1} = \pi(o_t)$. The environment state transition is triggered by the action a_t and means that a task has just finished a subtask. $\gamma \in [0, 1]$ is the discount factor. The most significant difference between POMDP and MDP is whether the global state is feasible to the agent. The reason that most DRL algorithms are based on the MDP rather than POMDP is that most benchmarks for evaluating DRL performance are video games, and screen images contain all information in the environment [13]. However, the state in CMfg-SP refers to the combination of some core environmental variables, and these variables cannot represent the whole state of the scheduling environment. As a result, the CMfg-SP is more like a POMDP rather than an MDP.

Action Definition. The action $a_t \in A_t$ represents the selected provider in the t timestep. $A = \{a^0, a^1, a^2, ..., a^{n^{mp}}, a^{n^{mp}+1}\}$ is the action space, where a^0 represents the initial location mp_0, and $a^1, a^2, ..., a^n$ represent providers $mp_1, mp_2, ..., mp_n$. $a^{n^{mp}+1}$ represents that there is no available provider. During the scheduling, all tasks leave from the initial location mp^0 and are assigned to providers according to the selected actions.

Observation Definition. The observation $o \in O$ is the direct input to the policy model π_θ, and in the t timestep it is represented by:

$$o_t = < o_t^{order}, o_t^{dist}, o_t^{time}, o_t^{cost} > \tag{8}$$

where $o_t^{order} \in [0, 1]$ denotes the current processing progress. o_t^{dist} means distances between the current location and all providers. o_t^{time}, o_t^{cost} represent time and cost of the next required service in n^{mp} providers. o_t changes with the environment changes, and we scale each element in o_t to $(0, 1)$ to accelerate training.

Algorithm 1: Reward function

---

if *This episode is done* **then**
  | Return $-1 \cdot objective$;
else
  | **if** $a_t == a^{n^{mp}+1}$ **then**
  | | Return -10.0;
  | **else**
  | | **if** $a_t == a^0$ **then**
  | | | Return -1.0;
  | | **else**
  | | | Calculate the time and cost in the t timestep as c_t^{time}, c_t^{cost};
  | | | Return $-1 \cdot (w1 \cdot ||c_t^{time}|| + w2 \cdot ||c_t^{cost}||)$;
  | | **end**
  | **end**
end

Reward Definition. DRL solves the optimization problem by maxmizing the expectation of rewards [14]. We first convert two optimization targets of makespan and cost to one objective by weighted sum method (WSM) [4]:

$$\min Objective = w1 \cdot ||Obj_{makespan}|| + w2 \cdot ||Obj_{cost}|| \qquad (9)$$

where $w1, w2$ are weight factors denoting importance of makespan and cost, and $|| \cdot ||$ means the scaling operation. The definition of the reward function is reported in Algorithm 1. As an episodic problem, we use $-1 \cdot objective$ as the final reward. Additionally, we set some leading signals in each timestep to promote convergence.

4.2 DRQN-based Scheduling Algorithm

DRQN-Based Policy. Based on the constructed POMDP model, the agent policy model π_θ predicts the action a_t with respect to the observation o_t. As the agent cannot observe the global state of the environment, recording temporal information of observations is necessary. We choose LSTM to extract the temporal features of CMfg-SP. As shown in Fig. 1, the observation o_t is first projected into an embedding e_t by a multi-layer perceptron (MLP):

$$e_t = W^1 \cdot o_t + b^1 \qquad (10)$$

where W^1, b^1 are parameters of MLP. Then, the embedding is inputted to the LSTM layer with hidden states h_t, c_t from the last iteration. For the first iteration, h_t, c_t are initialized as zero vectors. The calculation of the LSTM layer is represented as:

$$l_t, h_{t+1}, c_{t+1} = LSTM(e_t, h_t, c_t) \qquad (11)$$

We leverage another MLP to project l_t to Q-values of each action:

$$q_t = W^2 \cdot l_t + b^2 \qquad (12)$$

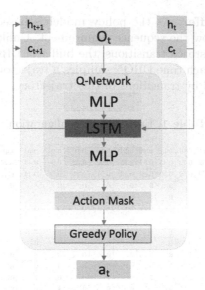

Fig. 1. DRQN-based policy model

where the dimension of q_t is equal to the action space size. We add an action mask layer after obtaining q_t to avoid the policy model to choose unexpected actions, and the masked q-value is represented as:

$$\hat{q}_t = q_t \cdot m_t \tag{13}$$

where m_t is the mask. For example, $m_t =< 1, -\infty, 1, ... >$ denotes that a^0 is feasible (the first value equals 1) and a^1 is infeasible (the second value in m_t is $-\infty$). Then, we choose the action a_t based on the $\epsilon - greedy$ strategy.

Training. The training of DRQN is similar to that of DQN [15]. In addition to the Q-network that chooses actions according to observations, DRQN also has a target-Q-network with the same structure of the Q-network as shown in Fig. 1. In each training step, o, a, o', r are sampled from the replay buffer, and the loss is calculated by temporal difference error (TD-error) as:

$$Loss = (r + \gamma \cdot max_{a'} Q(o', a'|\theta^-) - Q(o, a|\theta))^2 \tag{14}$$

where $Q(\cdot|\theta)$ is the Q-network, and $Q(\cdot|\theta^-)$ is the target Q-network. Compared to the training in DQN, we take two variants, including soft update and episode repaly buffer.

Soft Update. With the loss function, parameters θ in Q-network are updated by backpropagation. After some training cycles, parameters θ^- in the target Q-network is updated by:

$$\theta^- \leftarrow \alpha \cdot \theta + (1 - \alpha) \cdot \theta^- \tag{15}$$

where $\alpha \in (0, 1)$ is the soft updating rate.

Episode Replay Buffer. As the policy model is based on LSTM, sampled transitions should follow the sequence requirement. Unlike the replay buffer of DQN that shuffles the stored transitions, the buffer of DRQN stores trajectories of different episodes. Each time DRQN samples a trajectory from the buffer, the policy model is trained by transitions of this trajectory.

Table 1. Environment configuration

	mp1	mp2	mp3	mp4	mp5	mp6	mp7	mp8	mp9	mp10	mp11	mp12	mp13	mp14	mp15	mp16	mp17	mp18	mp19	mp20
Lx	0.65	0.83	0.35	0.64	0.14	0.62	0.72	0.43	0.87	0.75	0.92	0.32	0.6	0.44	0.24	0.7	0.58	0.79	0.95	0.44
Ly	0.97	1	0.49	0.91	0.33	0.29	0.52	0.79	0.99	0.54	0.91	0.75	0.36	0.44	0.41	0.88	0.11	0.41	0.12	0.9
ms1	6	0	6	0	0	6	0	0	0	0	6	0	0	8	0	0	0	0	0	0
ms2	0	6	0	9	0	0	6	0	5	0	0	7	0	7	9	0	0	0	0	0
ms3	0	0	5	8	5	9	9	0	9	0	8	0	8	0	7	5	0	0	5	5
ms4	9	0	5	6	0	7	0	6	7	0	0	0	0	7	8	0	0	5	0	0
ms5	0	0	0	0	8	0	6	9	0	0	6	5	0	7	0	0	6	0	9	0
ms6	6	8	7	0	0	5	0	0	8	6	5	0	7	0	0	0	0	0	7	5
ms7	0	9	0	0	0	9	5	8	0	0	0	0	0	8	0	0	0	0	0	5
ms8	9	6	5	7	5	6	0	7	0	0	0	6	0	0	6	5	8	0	0	5
ms9	9	0	0	0	0	6	9	7	7	0	7	9	0	7	0	7	0	0	5	0
ms10	0	6	0	0	8	5	6	9	0	6	9	9	8	0	6	5	0	0	0	0
ms11	9	7	0	6	6	6	0	0	0	8	6	0	8	6	5	0	5	5	0	7
ms12	5	6	0	0	0	7	6	8	6	0	8	7	0	6	0	0	8	9	5	6
ms13	9	7	6	8	6	6	5	0	7	0	0	7	6	8	8	0	6	0	9	5
ms14	0	0	0	8	9	0	9	0	9	5	8	0	7	8	8	0	0	0	0	0
ms15	0	0	9	9	0	8	5	0	7	9	6	0	7	0	5	7	7	6	7	5
ms16	0	0	8	7	0	5	6	0	6	0	8	7	0	0	0	6	0	5	8	9
ms17	9	5	0	6	8	6	8	0	9	9	7	0	9	0	0	0	9	5	0	5
ms18	0	0	0	5	9	6	6	0	7	8	0	9	8	0	5	9	0	5	5	7
ms19	5	7	5	0	0	0	0	5	0	8	0	9	0	0	0	7	9	6	5	6
ms20	5	0	9	9	0	0	0	0	9	0	7	0	0	9	0	7	9	0	7	8

5   Experimental Results

This section presents simulation experiments to evaluate the effectiveness of the proposed DRQN-based scheduling algorithm. First, configurations of the experimental scene and algorithms are introduced. Then, the comparison between DRQN and other scheduling algorithms, including DQN and proximal policy optimization (PPO), is conducted to verify the accuracy and generalizability of DRQN.

Table 2. Algorithm configuration

	DQN	DRQN	PPO
Training episodes	40000	40000	40000
Learning rate	0.01	0.001	0.005
Batch size	512	256	/
Dicounted factor	0.99	0.99	0.95
Linear hidden units	64	64	64
gradient clipping	5	5	7

5.1   Configurations

The scheduling scene is based on the case of automobile structure part processing, where a batch of structure parts needs to be processed from blanks to products. There are twenty service providers in this case, and their location is scaled to two-dimensional coordinates within the scope of $(0, 1)$. Totally there are twenty types of manufacturing services distributed in different providers, and the time and cost of each type of servce may be diverse as different providers provide them. As for the weighted factors of time and cost, we set $w1 = 0.3, w2 = 0.7$, denoting that cost is about twice important as makespan. To get an intuition for the environment data distribution, we report the service distribution in Table 1. The second and third rows in Table 1 are locations of providers, and the remaining rows represent the capacity for each type of service.

To compare the scheduling performance with other algorithms, we also implement the random rule, DQN, and PPO. DQN and PPO are DRL-based algorithms usually applied to CMfg-SP, and they share the same POMDP modeling with DRQN. The random rule means selecting feasible actions randomly in each step, and we set it to serve as a baseline. The hype-parameters of these algorithms are reported in Table 2.

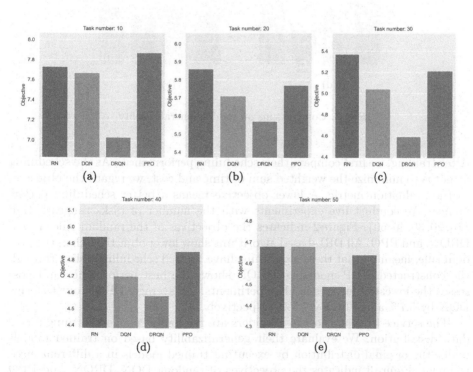

Fig. 2. Comparisons on scheduling performance

5.2 Comparisons

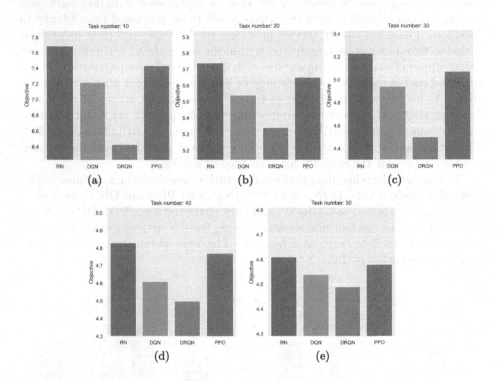

Fig. 3. Comparisons on model generalizability

After training, we first compare their scheduling performances. As the scheduling target is to minimize the weighted sum of time and cost, we regard the objective as the evaluation metric. A lower objective means a better scheduling performance. We conduct five experiments with the number of tasks ranges within $\{10, 20, 30, 40, 50\}$. Figure 2 indicates the objectives of the random rule, DQN, DRQN, and PPO. All DRL-based algorithms show lower objectives than the random rule, meaning that these algorithms have learned scheduling policy through the constructed MDP modeling. DRQN shows the best performance and possesses the lowest objectives in all experiments. On average, DRQN outperforms DQN by 5.7% and PPO by 7.7%, respectively.

The service time and cost in providers are randomly changed, forming a new data distribution. We evaluate their generalizability based on trained models under the original distribution by executing trained models in a different environment. Figure 3 indicates the objectives of random, DQN, DRQN, and PPO in the changing environment, where DRQN surpasses DQN and PPO by 5.9% and 8.4% on average, respectively.

6 Conclusion

This paper proposes a DRQN-based scheduling algorithm to tackle the CMfg-SP. The CMfg environment is modeled as a POMDP, where the agent can observe only partial environment state. Compared to the previous modeling of CMfg-SP that regards the environment as an MDP, POMDP is more suitable for the CMfg environment. Additionally, we construct an LSTM-based agent policy to select actions according to observations and train it with the loss function of TD-error. To facilitate the training of LSTM, we adopt the soft updating and episode replay buffer. Finally, simulation experiments prove that DRQN showed a competitive performance than DQN and PPO.

References

1. Li, B., et al.: Cloud manufacturing: a new service-oriented networked manufacturing model. Comput. Integr. Manuf. Syst. **16**(1), 1–7 (2010)
2. Zhang, L., et al.: Cloud manufacturing: a new manufacturing paradigm. Enterp. Inf. Syst. **8**(2), 167–187 (2014)
3. Zhou, L., Zhang, L., Ren, L., Wang, J.: Real-time scheduling of cloud manufacturing services based on dynamic data-driven simulation. IEEE Trans. Ind. Inf. **15**(9), 5042–5051 (2019)
4. Liu, Y., Wang, L., Wang, X.V., Xu, X., Zhang, L.: Scheduling in cloud manufacturing: state-of-the-art and research challenges. Int. J. Prod. Res. **57**(15–16), 4854–4879 (2019)
5. Mao, H., Schwarzkopf, M., Venkatakrishnan, S.B., Meng, Z., Alizadeh, M.: Learning scheduling algorithms for data processing clusters. In Proceedings of the ACM Special Interest Group on Data Communication, pp. 270–288 (2019)
6. Laili, Y., Tao, F., Zhang, L., Sarker, B.R.: A study of optimal allocation of computing resources in cloud manufacturing systems. Int. J. Adv. Manuf. Technol. **63**(5), 671–690 (2012)
7. Jian, C., Wang, Y.: Batch task scheduling-oriented optimization modelling and simulation in cloud manufacturing. Int. J. Simul. Model. **13**(1), 93–101 (2014)
8. Lin, Y.K., Chong, C.S.: Fast GA-based project scheduling for computing resources allocation in a cloud manufacturing system. J. Intell. Manuf. **28**(5), 1189–1201 (2017)
9. Jiang, H., Yi, J., Chen, S., Zhu, X.: A multi-objective algorithm for task scheduling and resource allocation in cloud-based disassembly. J. Manuf. Syst. **41**, 239–255 (2016)
10. Zhou, J., Yao, X.: A hybrid artificial bee colony algorithm for optimal selection of QOS-based cloud manufacturing service composition. Int. J. Adv. Manuf. Technol. **88**(9), 3371–3387 (2017)
11. Dong, T., Xue, F., Xiao, C., Li, J.: Task scheduling based on deep reinforcement learning in a cloud manufacturing environment. Concurrency Comput. Pract. Experience **32**(11), 5654 (2020)
12. Liang, H., Wen, X., Liu, Y., Zhang, H., Zhang, L., Wang, L.: Logistics-involved QOS-aware service composition in cloud manufacturing with deep reinforcement learning. Robot. Comput.-Integr. Manuf. **67**, 101991 (2021)

13. Henderson, P., Islam, R., Bachman, P., Pineau, J., Precup, D., Meger, D.: Deep reinforcement learning that matters. In: Proceedings of the AAAI Conference on Artificial Intelligence, vol. 32, no. 1 (2018)
14. Wang, X., Zhang, L., Lin, T., Zhao, C., Wang, K., Chen, Z.: Solving job scheduling problems in a resource preemption environment with multi-agent reinforcement learning. Robot. Comput.-Integr. Manuf. **77**, 102324 (2022)
15. Mnih, V., Kavukcuoglu, K., Silver, D., Rusu, A.A., Veness, J., Bellemare, M.G., Graves, A., Riedmiller, M., Fidjeland, A.K., Ostrovski, G., et al.: Human-level control through deep reinforcement learning. Nature **518**(7540), 529–533 (2015)

Fixed-Time Bipartite Consensus for Multi-Agent Systems Subjected to External Disturbances

Kaili Xiang, Zhiyong Yu$^{(\boxtimes)}$, and Haijun Jiang

College of Mathematics and System Sciences, Xinjiang University,
Urumqi 830017, China
yzygsts@xju.edu.cn

Abstract. This paper considers the leader-follower fixed-time bipartite consensus problem for multi-agent systems (MASs) with external disturbances. Firstly, in the leader framework, a new fixed-time integral sliding mode control strategy under a directed signed graph is designed, which can effectively handle the external disturbances. Secondly, according to inequality techniques and Lyapunov stability theory, some sufficient conditions for achieving fixed-time leader-follower bipartite consensus are obtained. Moreover, Zeno phenomenon can be avoided through the designed triggering mechanism. Finally, an example is presented to prove the correctness of obtained results.

Keywords: Fixed-time convergence · Leader-follower bipartite consensus · External disturbances · Event-triggered control

1 Introduction

Consensus was proposed by DeGroot in 1974 [1]. As a fundamental and important issue in cooperative control of MASs, it has been extensively studied owing to its extensive applications in sensor networks [2], unmanned vehicles [3] and formation of robots [4]. In existing works, the consensus results were mainly based on cooperative relationship or non-competitive relationship among agents [5,6]. However, in some social networks [7], when the interests and goals of agents are different, they are not only cooperative but also competitive. In this situation, the information transmission among agents can be represented by a signed graph, in which the cooperative and antagonistic relationships are described by the positive and negative edges, respectively. Along this line, the bipartite consensus was presented for the first time [8]. Afterwards, considering agents' second-order dynamics and more general high-order dynamics, the bipartite consensus problems of MASs were discussed in [9,10].

It is worth emphasizing that the results mentioned above [8–10] only can achieve asymptotical consensus. A faster convergence rate is worth studying, then

This work was supported by the National Natural Science Foundation of China (Grant Nos. 62003289, 62163035).

the finite-time consensus problems was considered [11,12]. For MASs with heterogeneous dynamics, the output bipartite consensus was investigated by designing finite-time convergence protocol [11]. Considering more general detail-balanced signed graph, the bipartite consensus was also studied based on finite-time stability theory [12]. Yet, under the finite-time control, the estimation of convergence time is related to the initial states. To improve this disadvantage, Polyakov [13] firstly proposed the fixed-time theory. Afterwards, the fixed-time protocols for different MASs with antagonistic relationship [14–16] were widely studied.

It is further to be observed that these works [14–16] were studied based on continuous communication. In practical applications, especially for limited communication resources, the continuous communication is not practical. Therefore, it is very meaningful to design some protocols to reduce the control cost and controller update. The event-triggered control can save resources and cut the cost, in which the controller will be triggered and updated when the triggering conditions are satisfied. Hence, the event-triggered control was extended the bipartite consensus [17–19]. For example, by using event-triggered control strategy, the bipartite consensus for high-order MASs under input saturation was investigated [19]. However, all these bipartite consensus results [14–19] were considered for some certain systems.

In practical cases, the disturbances and uncertain factors always exist, which will change or affect the stability of system. So, the consensus study of MASs with exogenous disturbances is essential. The sliding mode control strategy was introduced due to its robustness to model uncertainty and disturbance [20]. In the presence of disturbances, the consensus protocol was attained in finite-time by using integral sliding mode technology [21]. However, the competitive interactions were not considered in mentioned research. Based on above analysis, the more general antagonistic relationship should be discussed in consensus of MASs, which provides the purpose of this study. In comparison with existing works, the main innovation points are as follows:

1) Although the fixed-time bipartite consensus was studied [22,23], the disturbances were not considered in the system, and the communication graph [22] is undirected. However, we consider the case of MASs with external disturbances, and employ the integral sliding mode control strategy to effectively suppress the disturbances.
2) In existing results [24,25], the finite-time convergence protocols were designed, in which the convergence time relies on the initial states and only the cooperative relationship was considered. However, in this paper, we consider both cooperative relationship and competitive relationship and design a fixed-time control protocol, in which the estimation of settling time is independent of the initial states.
3) In contrast with [20], the event-triggered control method is used to avoid continuous communication among agents in this paper.

The rest of this article includes the components as follows. The preliminaries are given in Sect. 2. In Sect. 3, the main achievements are given, including the structure of integral sliding surface and the controller. Section 4 gives some simulations to verify the rationality of main results. In Sect. 5, a simple conclusion is drawn.

Notations. In this paper, $\text{sig}^v(\cdot) = \text{sign}(\cdot)|\cdot|^v$, $\text{sign}(\cdot)$ is the sign function. The notations $\text{diag}(\cdot)$ and $\text{rank}(\cdot)$ denote the diagonal matrix and rank of matrix, respectively. For a vector, $\text{abs}(\cdot)$ represents the absolute values of its elements.

2 Preliminaries

2.1 Graph Theory

A digraph is described by a triple $\mathscr{G} = (\mathscr{V}, \mathscr{E}, \mathscr{A})$, in which $\mathscr{V} = \{v_1, \ldots, v_N\}$ denotes the node set, $\mathscr{E} \subseteq \mathscr{V} \times \mathscr{V}$ is the edge set and $\mathscr{A} = [a_{ij}]_{N \times N}$ means the signed adjacency matrix. If $(v_i, v_j) \in \mathscr{E}$, $a_{ij} \neq 0$; $a_{ij} = 0$, otherwise. In addition, $a_{ij} > 0 (< 0)$ indicates a cooperative (competitive) relationship between agent i and j. v_0 represents the leader. Define $H - \text{diag}(u_{10}, u_{i0}, \ldots, u_{N0})$ where $u_{i0} > 0$ expresses that the follower i can directly get the information of the leader, and $a_{i0} = 0$, otherwise. Let $\bar{\mathscr{G}} = v_0 \cup \mathscr{G}$ describes a topology with leader. The Laplacian matrix $L = [L_{ij}]_{N \times N}$, in which $L_{ii} = \sum_{j=1,j\neq i}^{N} |a_{ij}|$ and $L_{ij} = -a_{ij}$ for $i \neq j$. Let $L_H = L + H$.

Definition 1 ([26]). A signed graph is structurally balanced if there is a bipartition of the node set $\mathscr{V}$ satisfying $\mathscr{V} = \mathscr{V}_1 \bigcup \mathscr{V}_2$ and $\mathscr{V}_1 \bigcap \mathscr{V}_2 = \emptyset$, such that $a_{ij} \geq 0, \forall \mathscr{V}_i, \mathscr{V}_j \in \mathscr{V}_q \ (q = 1, 2)$; $a_{ij} \leq 0, \forall \mathscr{V}_i \in \mathscr{V}_q, \mathscr{V}_j \in \mathscr{V}_r, q \neq r(q, r \in (1, 2))$. It is said structurally unbalanced otherwise.

Lemma 1 ([26]). A connected signed digraph $\mathscr{G}$ is structurally balanced when and only when, $\exists D \in \mathscr{D}$ such that all elements of $D\mathscr{A}D$ are nonnegative. Moreover, D can be divided into two parts, i.e., $\mathscr{V}_1 = \{i|d_i > 0\}$ and $\mathscr{V}_2 = \{i|d_i < 0\}$, where $\mathscr{D} = \text{diag}(\sigma_1, \ldots, \sigma_N)$ with $\sigma_i \in (1, -1)$.

2.2 Problem Statement

Consider a MAS with one leader and N followers, in which the dynamics of each follower is given by:

$$\dot{x}_i(t) = Ax_i(t) + B(u_i(t) + w_i(t)), \quad i = 1, 2, \ldots, N, \qquad (1)$$

where $x_i(t) \in R^n$, $w_i(t) \in R^m$ and $u_i(t) \in R^m$ are the ith agent's state, the unknown bounded disturbance and control input. $A \in R^{n \times n}$ and $B \in R^{n \times m}$ are the matrices with proper dimension.

The leader's dynamics is as follows:

$$\dot{x}_0(t) = Ax_0(t), \qquad (2)$$

where $x_0(t) \in R^n$ is the leader's state.

Definition 2. The MASs (1)–(2) can realize fixed-time bipartite consensus, if there exists a $T > 0$ such that

$$\lim_{t \to T} \|x_i(t) - \sigma_i x_0(t)\| = 0, \quad \text{and} \quad \|x_i(t) - \sigma_i x_0(t)\| \equiv 0, \quad \forall t \geq T, \qquad (3)$$

where $T > 0$ is called the convergence time.

Assumption 1. (A, B) is stabilizable.

Assumption 2. There exist constants $W_i > 0$, such that $\|w_i(t)\| \leq W_i$, $i = 1, 2, \ldots, N$.

Assumption 3. The communication topology $\mathscr{G}$ is structurally balanced and contains a directed spanning tree with the leader as the root.

Lemma 2 ([27]). If Assumption 3 holds, then there is a matrix $P = \text{diag}(p_1, p_2, \ldots, p_N) > 0$ such that $L_H P + L_H^T P > 0$ where P can be found out from $p = [p_1, p_2, \ldots p_N]^T = \text{abs}((L_H^T)^{-1})1_N$.

Lemma 3 ([28]). For a positive definite matrix $X \in R^{n \times n}$ and a matrix $B \in R^{n \times m}$ with full column rank, the matrix $B^T X B$ is positive definite.

Consider the following nonlinear system

$$\dot{z}(t) = \mathcal{G}(z(t)), \quad z(0) = z_0, \tag{4}$$

where $z(t) \in R^n$, $\mathcal{G}(\cdot) : R^n \to R^n$ is a nonlinear function with $\mathcal{G}(0) = 0$.

Lemma 4 ([29]). For any solution of (4), if there is a nonnegative and continuous function $\mathbb{V}(z) : R^n \to R^+$ satisfying

$$\dot{\mathbb{V}}(z(t)) \leq -(\alpha_1 \mathbb{V}^p(z(t)) + \alpha_1 \mathbb{V}^q(z(t)))^k, \quad z(t) \in R^n \backslash \{0\}, \tag{5}$$

in which $\alpha_1, \alpha_2, p, k > 0$, $q \geq 0$ and $pk > 1, qk < 1$, then the zero solution of (4) is fixed-time stable, and the estimation of convergence time $\mathcal{T}(z_0)$ satisfies

$$\mathcal{T}(z_0) \leq \frac{1}{\alpha_2^k} \left(\frac{\alpha_1}{\alpha_2} \right)^{\frac{1-qk}{p-q}} \left(\frac{1}{(1-qk)} + \frac{1}{(pk-1)} \right). \tag{6}$$

3   Main Results

In practical application, the interference exists in system (1). The integral sliding surface is designed as below

$$s_i(t) = B^T X B K e_i(t) - \int_0^t B^T X \big(B K (BB^T) \eta_i^\beta(v) + B K (BB^T) \text{sign}(\eta_i(v)) \big) dv, \tag{7}$$

where $\eta_i(t) = -\sum_{j \in N_i}^N |a_{ij}|(e_i(t) - \text{sign}(a_{ij})e_j(t)) + a_{i0}(e_i(t))$, $X \in R^{n \times n}$ is a positive definite matrix and $K = B^T X$. β is the ratio of two positive odd numbers and satisfies $\beta > 1$. $e_i(t) = x_i(t) - \sigma_i x_0(t)$.

Remark 1. The construction of integral sliding mode variable (7) is mainly referred to [28], in which the time-varying formation under leaderless MASs subjected to disturbances was investigated where the finite-time sliding surface was proposed. However, we extend it to leader-follower bipartite consensus and a fixed-time sliding surface is designed, which greatly improves its convergence rate and anti-interference.

To reduce the cost and energy consumption, the event-triggering control is introduced. Triggering time sequence of agent i can be represented by $t_0^i, t_1^i, t_2^i, \ldots$, and t_k^i represents the kth triggering time. The triggering instants $t_0^i, t_1^i, t_2^i, \ldots$ are given by triggering function $f_i(t)$. If $f_i(t) > 0$, the controller will be triggered, and the status information of agent i will be updated, then the agent i will transmit its updated information to neighbor node. The event-triggering instants are defined as follows

$$t_{k+1}^i = \inf\{t > t_k^i : f_i(t) > 0\}, \quad k \in \mathbb{N}, \quad t_0^i = 0,$$

where $f_i(t)$ will be given below.

Combined with the integral sliding mode (7), the controller is designed as below

$$u_i(t) = B^T \eta_i^\beta(t_k^i) + B^T \text{sign}(\eta_i(t_k^i)) - \gamma \|KA\| \|e_i(t_k^i)\| \text{sign}(s_i(t_k^i))$$
$$- \rho_1 \text{sign}(s_i(t_k^i)) - \rho_2 \text{sig}^\phi(s_i(t_k^i)), \quad t \in [t_k^i, t_{k+1}^i), \tag{8}$$

where $\phi > 1$, γ, ρ_1 and $\rho_2 > 0$ are parameters.

The control error is given as

$$\epsilon_i(t) = B^T \eta_i^\beta(t_k^i) + B^T \text{sign}(\eta_i(t_k^i)) - \gamma \|KA\| \|e_i(t_k^i)\| \text{sign}(s_i(t_k^i))$$
$$- \rho_1 \text{sign}(s_i(t_k^i)) - \rho_2 \text{sig}^\phi(s_i(t_k^i)) - \left(B^T \eta_i^\beta(t) + B^T \text{sign}(\eta_i(t))\right.$$
$$\left. - \gamma \|KA\| \|e_i(t)\| \text{sign}(s_i(t)) - \rho_1 \text{sign}(s_i(t)) - \rho_2 \text{sig}^\phi(s_i(t))\right). \tag{9}$$

The trigger function is as follows

$$f_i(t) = \|\epsilon_i(t)\| - \frac{(\lambda_{\min}(B^T X B)\rho_1 - W_i \|B^T X B\| - \mu)}{\|B^T X B\|}, \tag{10}$$

where $\lambda_{\min}(B^T X B)\rho_1 > (W_i \|B^T X B\| + \mu), 0 < \mu \leq 1$.

Theorem 1. *For MASs (1)–(2), suppose that Assumptions 1–3 hold, then the leader-follower bipartite consensus will be obtained in a fixed-time interval under the control protocol (8) with integral sliding mode (7), if the following conditions hold*

(i) $1 - \gamma \lambda_{\min}(B^T X B) < 0$,

(ii) $\|\epsilon_i(t)\| - \frac{(\lambda_{\min}(B^T X B)\rho_1 - W_i \|B^T X B\| - \mu)}{\|B^T X B\|} \leq 0$.

Proof. First, we prove that the sliding mode surface is achieved in a fixed-time. The time derivative of (7) is

$$\dot{s}_i(t) = B^T X B K \dot{e}_i(t) - B^T X B K B B^T \eta_i^\beta(t) - B^T X B K B B^T \text{sign}(\eta_i(t)).$$

Based on Lemma 3, the matrix $B^T X B > 0$. Select the Lyapunov function as

$$V_i(t) = \frac{1}{2} s_i(t)^T (B^T X B)^{-1} s_i(t). \tag{11}$$

For $t \in [t_k^i, t_{k+1}^i)$, the derivative of $V_i(t)$ is

$$
\begin{aligned}
\dot{V}_i(t) &= s_i(t)^T (B^T X B)^{-1} \big(B^T X B K \dot{e}_i(t) - B^T X B K B K \eta_i^\beta(t) \\
&\quad - B^T X B K B K \mathrm{sign}(\eta_i(t)) \big) \\
&= s_i(t)^T \big(K A e_i(t) + K B w_i(t) + K B \epsilon_i(t) - \gamma K B \| K A \| \| e_i(t) \| \mathrm{sign}(s_i(t)) \\
&\quad - \rho_1 K B \mathrm{sign}(s_i(t)) - \rho_2 K B \mathrm{sig}^\phi(s_i(t)) \big) \\
&\leq (1 - \gamma \lambda_{\min}(KB)) \| KA \| \| e_i(t) \| \| s_i(t) \| + W_i \| KB \| \| s_i(t) \| \\
&\quad + \| KB \| \| \epsilon_i(t) \| \| s_i(t) \| - \rho_1 \lambda_{\min}(B^T X B) \| s_i(t) \| \\
&\quad - \rho_2 \lambda_{\min}(B^T X B) \| s_i(t) \|^{\phi+1} \\
&= -\big(\lambda_{\min}(B^T X B) \rho_1 - W_i \| B^T X B \| - \| B^T X B \| \| \epsilon_i(t) \| \big) \| s_i(t) \| \\
&\quad + \big(1 - \gamma \lambda_{\min}(B^T X B) \big) \| B^T X A \| \| e_i(t) \| \| s_i(t) \| \| \\
&\quad - \rho_2 \lambda_{\min}(B^T X B) \| s_i(t) \|^{\phi+1}. \tag{12}
\end{aligned}
$$

Based on triggering condition (11) and $1 - \gamma \lambda_{\min}(B^T X B) < 0$, one has

$$
\begin{aligned}
\dot{V}_i(t) &\leq -\mu \| s_i(t) \| - \rho_2 \lambda_{\min}(B^T X B) \| s_i(t) \|^{\phi+1} \\
&\leq -c_1 V_i(t)^{\frac{1}{2}} - c_2 V_i(t)^{\frac{\phi+1}{2}}, \tag{13}
\end{aligned}
$$

where $c_1 = \mu \big(2 \lambda_{\min} \{ B^T X B \} \big)^{\frac{1}{2}}$, $c_2 = \frac{\rho_2}{2} \big(2 \lambda_{\min} \{ B^T X B \} \big)^{\frac{\phi+3}{2}}$.

Using Lemma 4, we can deduce that $V_i(t)$ converge to zero in a fixed-time under the control protocol (8). The convergence time T_i is

$$T_i \leq \frac{1}{c_1} \left(\frac{c_2}{c_1} \right)^{\frac{1}{\phi-1}} \left(2 + \frac{2}{\phi-1} \right). \tag{14}$$

Define $T_1 = \max_{1 \leq i \leq N} \{ T_i \}$. Then $s_i(t) = 0$ can be achieved for $t > T_1$. Therefore, it has

$$B^T X B K \dot{e}_i(t) - B^T X B K B B^T \eta_i^\beta(t) - B^T X B K B B^T \mathrm{sign}(\eta_i(t)) = 0. \tag{15}$$

Since $B^T X B$ is invertible, we can obtain

$$K \dot{e}_i(t) - K B B^T \eta_i^\beta(t) - K B B^T \mathrm{sign}(\eta_i(t)) = 0. \tag{16}$$

Furthermore, one has

$$K^T K \dot{e}_i(t) - K^T K B B^T \eta_i^\beta(t) - K^T K B B^T \mathrm{sign}(\eta_i(t)) = 0. \tag{17}$$

When $K^T K$ and BB^T are reversible, we can easily get $\dot{e}_i(t)$. However, when they are irreversible, in order to get $\dot{e}_i(t)$, we need to do transformations of $K^T K$ and BB^T. According to perturbation method in linear algebra, there exist some sufficiently small $\delta' > 0$ and $\delta > 0$ so that $K^T K = (K^T K + \delta' I_n)$ and $B^T B = (BB^T + \delta I_n)$, as δ' and δ tend to 0. Noting $G = (BB^T + \delta I_n) = B^T B$, through simplification, we further obtain the following expression

$$\dot{e}_i(t) = G\eta_i^\beta(t) + G\text{sign}(\eta_i(t)). \tag{18}$$

It yields

$$\eta(t) = -(L_H \otimes I_n)e(t), \quad \dot{e}(t) = (I_N \otimes G)(\eta^\beta(t) + \text{sign}(\eta(t))),$$

By employing Lemma 2, one has $Q = PL_H + L_H^T P > 0$.

We consider the Lyapunov candidate function as

$$V(t) = \eta^T(t)(P \otimes I_n)\eta(t). \tag{19}$$

Then, the derivative of $V(t)$ is

$$
\begin{aligned}
\dot{V}(t) &= 2\eta^T(t)(P \otimes I_n)\dot{\eta}(t) \\
&= -2\eta^T(t)(P \otimes I_n)((L_H \otimes I_n))((I_N \otimes G)(\eta^\beta(t) + \text{sign}(\eta(t)))) \\
&\leq -\eta^T(t)(Q \otimes G)\eta^\beta(t) - \eta^T(t)(Q \otimes G)\text{sign}(\eta(t)) \\
&\leq -\frac{\lambda_{\min}(Q \otimes G)}{\lambda_{\max}(P)}V^{\frac{\beta+1}{2}}(t) - \frac{\lambda_{\min}(Q \otimes G)}{\lambda_{\max}(P)}V^{\frac{1}{2}}(t). \tag{20}
\end{aligned}
$$

Using Lemma 4, we can conclude that the systems (1)–(2) achieve bipartite consensus in a fixed-time under control protocol (8). The convergence time T is

$$T \leq T_1 + \frac{\lambda_{\max}(P)}{\lambda_{\min}(Q \otimes G)}\left(2 + \frac{1}{(\beta-1)}\right). \tag{21}$$

Remark 2. For MASs with disturbances, the finite-time consensus was considered in [30]. In [31] and [32], the leaderless asymptotical consensus and prescribed-time consensus were considered, in which the consensus results were obtained under the undirected graph. Yet, in this research, the fixed-time integral sliding mode control is proposed for MASs with directed networks.

Remark 3. In [33,34], the disturbances were handled by the sign function, which makes the controller with high-frequency chattering. To avoid this phenomenon and enhance the stability of the system, we use the integral sliding mode to handle the disturbances.

Theorem 2. *For MASs (1)–(2), the Zeno behavior can be avoided by the controller (8) with the triggering function (10), if all conditions of Theorem 1 are satisfied.*

Proof. This proof is split into two steps. The one is before achieving the sliding surface, and the other step is after reaching the sliding surface.

Firstly, we will show that there is no Zeno phenomenon before reaching the sliding surface. For the convenience of simplification, let $k = \max_{0 \le t \le T}\{\|\eta_i^{\beta-1}(t)\|\}$, $k_1 = \max_{0 \le t \le T}\{\|\eta_i^{\beta}(t)\|\}$, $k_2 = \max_{0 \le t \le T}\{\|\mathrm{sig}^{\phi-1}(s_i(t))\|\}$, $\sqrt{n} = \max\{\mathrm{sign}(\eta_i(t))\}$.

The derivative of $\|\epsilon_i(t)\|$ is

$$\frac{d\|\epsilon_i(t)\|}{dt} \le \|\dot{\epsilon}_i(t)\|$$

$$\le \|B^T\|\left\|\frac{d}{dt}\eta_i^{\beta}(t)\right\| + \left\|\frac{d}{dt}\rho_2\mathrm{sig}^{\phi}(s_i(t))\right\|$$

$$\le \left[\beta\kappa\sqrt{Nn}L_{Hii}\|B\| + \rho_2\phi k_2\|B^T XBK\|\right]\left[k_3\|A\| + (k_4 + W_i)\|B\|\right]$$

$$+ \rho_2\phi k_2(k_1 + \sqrt{n})\|B^T XBK\|\|BB^T\|, \tag{22}$$

where $k_3 = \max_{0 \le t \le T}\{\|e_i(t)\|\}$, $k_4 = \max_{0 \le t \le T}\{\|u_i(t)\|\}$, and L_{Hii} represents the element in i-th column and row of L_{H_i}.

According to $\|\epsilon_i(t_k^i)\| = 0$, it yields

$$\|\epsilon_i(t)\| \le (t - t_k^i)\nu, \tag{23}$$

where
$\nu = \left[\beta\kappa\sqrt{Nn}L_{Hii}\|B\| + \rho_2\phi k_2\|B^T XBK\|\right]\left[k_3\|A\| + (k_4 + W_i)\|B\|\right] + \rho_2\phi k_2(k_1 + \sqrt{n})\|B^T XBK\|\|BB^T\|$.

The event is triggered if $f_i(t) > 0$, then one has

$$\|\epsilon_i(t)\| > \frac{(\lambda_{\min}(B^T XB)\rho_1 - W_i\|B^T XB\| - \mu)}{\|B^T XB\|} > 0. \tag{24}$$

Let $t_{k+1}^i - t_k^i = \Delta T_k^i$, thus it follows that

$$0 < \frac{(\lambda_{\min}(B^T XB)\rho_1 - W_i\|B^T XB\| - \mu)}{\|B^T XB\|} < \|\epsilon_i(t)\| \le \Delta T_k^i \nu. \tag{25}$$

Consequently

$$\Delta T_k^i \ge \frac{(\lambda_{\min}(B^T XB)\rho_1 - W_i\|B^T XB\| - \mu)}{\nu\|B^T XB\|} > 0. \tag{26}$$

Then, based on above analysis, the inter-event times are strictly positive. Finally, we can also exclude Zeno's behavior after reaching the sliding surface. When reaching the sliding surface, then, $s_i(t) = 0$. Similarly, we can state

$$\frac{d\|\epsilon_i(t)\|}{dt} \le \left[\beta\kappa\sqrt{Nn}L_{Hii}\|B\|\right]\left[\|A\|\|e_i(t)\| + \|B\|(\|u_i(t)\| + W_i)\right]$$

$$\le (\beta\kappa\sqrt{Nn}L_{Hii}\|B\|)(k_3\|A\| + (k_4 + W_i)\|B\|). \tag{27}$$

Combination with $\|\epsilon_i(t_k^i)\| = 0$, one has

$$\|\epsilon_i(t)\| \le (t - t_k^i)\nu', \tag{28}$$

where $\nu' = [\beta\kappa\sqrt{Nn}L_{Hii}\|B\|][k_3\|A\| + (k_4 + W_i)\|B\|]$.
Similar to the proof of the first step, we can also get

$$\Delta T_k^i \ge \frac{(\lambda_{\min}(B^T X B)\rho_1 - W_i\|B^T X B\| - \mu)}{\nu'\|B^T X B\|} > 0. \tag{29}$$

Therefore, there is no Zeno behavior.

4 Simulation Example

In this part, a numerical simulation is performed to prove the feasibility of our results.

Example 1. For MAS (1)–(2) contains 4 followers and one leader, in which $A = \begin{bmatrix} 0 & 1 \\ -1 & 0 \end{bmatrix}$, $B = [1, 1]^T$. The disturbances are considered as $w_i(t) = 0.01\sin(it)$, $i = 1,2,3,4$. The topology among agents is described by Fig. 1, in which the 0 represents the leader and $i = 1, 2, 3, 4$ are followers. Based on Definition 2, $\mathcal{V}_1 = \{3, 4\}$, $\mathcal{V}_2 = \{1, 2\}$, and $D = \mathrm{diag}(-1, -1, 1, 1)$.

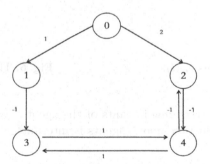

Fig. 1. The graph $\mathcal{G}$.

We choose $\phi = 1.5$, $\beta = 1.6$, $\mu = 1$, $\gamma = 1.3$, $W_i = 0.01$ and $\rho_1 = 1.1$, $\rho_2 = 1$. The initial states are $x_0(0) = [3, 1]^T$, $x_1(0) = [-2, 1]^T$, $x_2(0) = [-4, -1]^T$, $x_3(0) = [2, -1]^T$, and $x_4(0) = [4, 1]^T$. The matrix $X = \begin{bmatrix} 0.15 & 0.05 \\ 0.05 & 0.15 \end{bmatrix}$.

By solving the inequality in Lemma 2, we can obtain $P = \mathrm{diag}(0.1427, 2.3650, 1.4536, 0.6821)$. Under protocol (8), all agents can reach bipartite consensus in fixed-time and $T = 24.542s$. Figure 2 and Fig. 3 present the states $x_{i1}(t)$ and $x_{i2}(t)$ for $i = 0, 1, 2, 3, 4$. From Fig. 2 and Fig. 3, the states x_1 and x_2 converge to the opposite value of the x_0, while the states x_3 and x_4 track the leader's value.

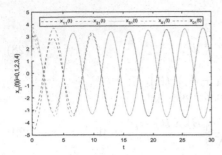

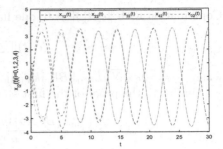

Fig. 2. The states $x_{01}(t)$ and $x_{i1}(t)$.   **Fig. 3.** The states $x_{02}(t)$ and $x_{i2}(t)$.

Figure 4 and Fig. 5 display the bipartite consensus errors, in which the errors approach to zero at T.

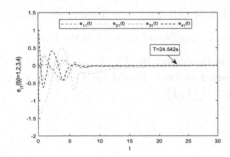

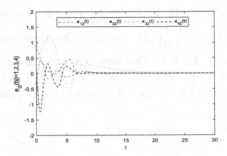

Fig. 4. The errors $e_{i1}(t)$.   **Fig. 5.** The errors $e_{i2}(t)$.

Figure 6 shows the triggering instants of the agent i, $i = 1, 2, 3, 4$, which also indicates the communication among agents is intermittent.

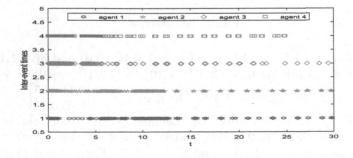

Fig. 6. Triggering instants of agent i

5 Conclusion

In this paper, we studied the leader-follower bipartite consensus for MASs subjected external disturbances. The disturbances suppressed by integral sliding mode function. Using event-triggered mechanism and applying fixed-time stability theory, we proved that the leader-follower bipartite consensus can be obtained in fixed-time. Besides, the Zeno phenomenon can be excluded. Our future work will focus on the bipartite consensus of MASs with switching topologies.

References

1. DeGroot, M.: Reaching a consensus. J. Am. Stat. Assoc. **69**(345), 118 121 (1974)
2. Halakarnimath, B., Sutagundar, A.: Multi-agent-based acoustic sensor node deployment in underwater acoustic wireless sensor networks. J. Inf. Technol. Res. **13**(4), 136–155 (2020)
3. Hu, Y., Lam, J., Liang, J.: Consensus of multi-agent systems with Luenberger observers. J. Franklin Inst. **350**(9), 2769–2790 (2013)
4. Liu, T., Wang, Z.: Coordinated formation control of wheeled mobile robots with switching communication topologies. IET Control Theory Appl. **13**(18), 3164–3173 (2019)
5. You, X., Hua, C., Li, K.: Fixed-time leader-following consensus for high-order time-varying nonlinear multi-agent systems. IEEE Trans. Autom. Control **65**(12), 5510–5516 (2020)
6. Gong, P., Lan, W.: Adaptive robust tracking control for multiple unknown fractional-order nonlinear systems. IEEE Trans. Cybern. **49**(4), 1365–1376 (2019)
7. Lee, S.: Predator's attack-induced phase-like transition in prey flock. Phys. Lett. A **357**(4), 270–274 (2006)
8. Altafini, C.: Consensus problems on networks with antagonistic interactions. IEEE Trans. Autom. Control **58**(4), 935–946 (2013)
9. Ding, T., Ge, M., Xiong, C.: Second-order bipartite consensus for networked robotic systems with quantized-data interactions and time-varying transmission delays. ISA Trans. **108**, 178–187 (2021)
10. Wu, Y., Hu, J.: Bipartite consensus control of high-order multi-agent systems. IFAC-PapersOnLine **52**(24), 201–206 (2019)
11. Duan, J., Zhang, H., Liang, Y.: Bipartite finite-time output consensus of heterogeneous multi-agent systems by finite-time event-triggered observer. Neurocomputing **365**, 86–93 (2019)
12. Lu, J., Wang, Y., Cao, J.: Finite-time bipartite consensus for multiagent systems under detail-balanced antagonistic interactions. IEEE Trans. Syst. Man Cybern. **51**(6), 3867–3875 (2019)
13. Polyakov, A.: Nonlinear feedback design for fixed-time stabilization of linear control systems. IEEE Trans. Autom. Control **57**(8), 2106–2110 (2011)
14. Zhao, M., Peng, C., Tian, E.: Finite-time and fixed-time bipartite consensus tracking of multi-agent systems with weighted antagonistic interactions. IEEE Trans. Circuits Syst. I: Regul. Pap. **68**(1), 426–433 (2021)
15. Xiao, Q., Liu, H., Wang, X.: A note on the fixed-time bipartite flocking for nonlinear multi-agent systems. Appl. Math. Lett. **99**, 105973 (2020)

16. Zhan, X., Hao, L., Han, T.: Adaptive bipartite output consensus for heterogeneous multi-agent systems with quantized information: a fixed-time approach. J. Franklin Inst. **358**(14), 7221–7326 (2021)
17. Yu, H., Chen, X., Chen, T.: Event-triggered bipartite consensus for multi-agent systems: a zeno-free analysis. IEEE Trans. Autom. Control **65**(11), 4866–4873 (2019)
18. Ren, J., Song, Q., Lu, G.: Event-triggered bipartite leader-following consensus of second-order nonlinear multi-agent systems under signed digraph. J. Franklin Inst. **356**(12), 6591–6609 (2019)
19. Xu, Y., Wang, J., Zhang, Y.: Event-triggered bipartite consensus for high-order multi-agent systems with input saturation. Neurocomputing **379**, 284–295 (2020)
20. Yu, S., Long, X.: Finite-time consensus for second-order multi-agent systems with disturbances by integral sliding mode. Automatica **54**, 158–165 (2015)
21. Ravindranathan, R., Behera, L., Kumar, S.: Event-triggered finite-time integral sliding mode controller for consensus-based formation of multirobot systems with disturbances. IEEE Trans. Control Syst. Technol. **27**(1), 39–47 (2017)
22. Shi, X., Lu, J., Liu, Y.: A new class of fixed-time bipartite consensus protocols for multi-agent systems with antagonistic interactions. J. Franklin Inst. **355**(12), 5256–5271 (2018)
23. Liu, X., Cao, J., Xie, C.: Finite-time and fixed-time bipartite consensus of multi-agent systems under a unified discontinuous control protocol. J. Franklin Inst. **356**(2), 734–751 (2017)
24. Fan, X., Wang, Z.: Event-triggered integral sliding mode control for linear systems with disturbance. Syst. Control Lett. **138**(3), 104–669 (2020)
25. Wang, X., Wang, G.: Distributed finite-time optimisation algorithm for second-order multi-agent systems subject to mismatched disturbances. IET Control Theory Appl. **14**(18), 2977–2988 (2020)
26. Wen, G., Wang, H., Yu, X.: Bipartite tracking consensus of linear multi-agent systems with a dynamic leader. IEEE Trans. Circuits Syst. II: Express Briefs **65**(9), 1204–1208 (2017). https://doi.org/10.1109/TCSII.2017.2777458
27. Bhowmick, S., Panja, S.: Leader-follower bipartite consensus of linear multi-agent systems over a signed directed graph. IEEE Trans. Circuits Syst. II: Express Briefs **66**(8), 1436–1440 (2018). https://doi.org/10.1109/TCSII.2018.2884006
28. Wang, J., Xu, Y., Yang, D.: Time-varying formation for high-order multi-agent systems with external disturbances by event-triggered integral sliding mode control. Appl. Math. Comput. **359**(2), 333–343 (2019)
29. Yu, Z., Yu, S., Jiang, H.: Distributed fixed-time optimization for multi-agent systems over a directed network. Nonlinear Dyn. **103**, 775–789 (2021)
30. Fan, X., Wang, Z.: Event-triggered integral sliding mode control for linear systems with disturbance. Syst. Control Lett. **138**(3), 104669 (2020)
31. Li, J., Chen, X., Hao, F.: Event-triggered bipartite consensus for multi-agent systems with antagonistic interactions. Int. J. Control Autom. Syst. **17**(8), 2046–2058 (2019)
32. Chen, X., Yu, H., Hao, F.: Prescribed-time event-triggered bipartite consensus of multi-agent systems. IEEE Trans. Circuits **52**(4), 2589–2598 (2022)
33. Deng, Q., Wu, J., Han, T.: Fixed-time bipartite consensus of multi-agent systems with disturbances. Phys. A **516**, 37–49 (2019)
34. Xu, Z., Liu, X., Cao, J.: Fixed-time bipartite consensus of nonlinear multi-agent systems under directed signed graphs with disturbances. J. Franklin Inst. **359**(6), 2693–2709 (2022). https://doi.org/10.1016/j.jfranklin.2022.02.023

Study on Method of Extraction and Clustering of Model Construction Style

Nana Shen, Chun Zhao$^{(\boxtimes)}$, and Hao Yang

Computer School, Beijing Information Science and Technology University,
Beijing 100101, China
zhaochun@bistu.edu.cn

Abstract. With the development of modeling and simulation technology in various fields, more and more modeling and simulation software are springing up. The diversity and complexity of software make the integration of heterogeneous models a significant challenge. The purpose of this paper is to address the issue of characteristics extraction for heterogeneous models in multi-fields. In this paper, the characteristics of heterogeneous models are abstracted into Model Construction Style (MCS), and a method of extraction and clustering of model construction style is presented. In this process, the general features of the model are extracted to form the model template, namely MCS, and model templates are clustered to establish the model construction style. The results show that this method can abstract the characteristics of multi-domain heterogeneous models and support the construction of a heterogeneous model style library.

Keywords: Heterogeneous models · Model integration · Model style library · Machine learning

1 Introduction

With the rapidly development of computer and simulation technology, modeling and simulation, as an important means of theoretical research and engineering practice, are widely used in various scientific research and national defense fields [1]. In the context of multi-domain complex system modeling and simulation, the development of complex products involves multiple disciplines and is developed by professionals in different fields using different languages, architectures, and tools [2]. In the process of model development, due to the lack of unified standard specification, the repeatedly development and isomerization of the model are serious [3]. Therefore, integration and reuse of models is a challenging issue.

Reusing existing models or model components can reduce development time and cost, thus speeding up the entire modeling and design process [4,5]. Therefore, using existing simulation resources to realize model reuse, reduce the complexity of modeling, and improve the flexibility and credibility of simulation modeling is the inevitable choice for complex system simulation [6].

Supported by the National Key R&D Program of China (No. 2018YFB1701600).

Nowadays, there are many researches on software design patterns [7], but few researches on design patterns of multi-domain models. Aiming at integrating and reusing heterogeneous models in complex products, constructing a style library of multi-domain complex product model construction based on model design patterns is proposed. This method is described by a new generation of intelligent integrated modeling and simulation language (X language) [8] for complex systems. The model construction style library supports the integrated modeling description of multi-level and multidisciplinary heterogeneous models of complex products and can realize fast model construction, integration, and reuse.

Based on the Modelica model, this paper extracted the features of multi-domain heterogeneous models and generated templates and established a model construction style.

First of all, in order to ensure the unity of the whole system model and the consistency among all levels of systems, these models are described in X language. Secondly, the general features of the X model are extracted to form model templates. Thirdly, the dataset is generated by analyzing and extracting the features of the template, and the Missing Values in the dataset are filled. By analyzing the influence of each dimension's data on the clustering result, a weight is added to each dimension's data. Finally, the datasets are clustered to verify the accuracy of classification.

The main contributions of this paper are as follows:

- General features of heterogeneous models are extracted to form templates.
- Using k-means algorithm, model templates are clustered, and model construction style is established.

The rest of the paper is structured as follows:

Modeling language and clustering algorithms are introduced in Sect. 2. The feature extraction and clustering of the model are implemented in Sect. 3. In Sect. 4, the clustering results are analyzed and evaluated. Section 5 concluded the paper and looked into future work.

2   Related Work

2.1   Modeling Language

Modelica is an object-oriented modeling language for multi-domain physical systems [9]. The language supports continuous and discrete system modeling and simulation, spanning different domains [10]. Modelica can be used to build large, complex, and heterogeneous physical systems in recent years [11]. The Modelica model covers many characteristics such as electrical, mechanical, thermal, control, etc., providing convenience for a unified description of physical systems [12]. In the existing studies, Modelica [13] modeling language carries the following four characteristics:

- Noncausal modeling based on equations: a declarative modeling method in which the causality of variables is determined by solving an equation system.

- Multi-domain modeling: objects in different disciplines such as electricity, machinery, and thermodynamics can be built into model components through Modelica.
- Object-oriented modeling: Modelica has a generic class concept that unifies classes, generics, and subtypes into a single language structure. The language improves component reuse and model development.
- Modelica provides a flexible software component model for creating and wiring component constructs.

At present, system modeling and simulation languages mostly focus on a single stage or a specific field and lack support for the whole life cycle of the complex system [14]. Although some systems modeling languages (such as SysML) and multi-physical modeling languages (such as Modelica) work together to achieve both modeling and simulation [15]. However, this approach does not guarantee model consistency due to the cross-platform implementation.

X language is an intelligent modeling and simulation language which supports the modeling of whole-system models, complex agent models, and the simulation of continuous, discrete, and mixed events [8].

2.2   Clustering Algorithm

Clustering is dividing a group of unknown samples into several categories by some algorithm without knowing the category of each sample in advance [16]. The method of cluster structure maximizes the similarity within the same cluster and maximizes the dissimilarity between different clusters [17]. Clustering is very useful in machine learning [18], data mining [19], image segmentation, and model recognition.

The K-means algorithm is an unsupervised algorithm used to group different objects into clusters. This algorithm is an efficient clustering method to classify massive high-dimensional numerical data [20]. The k-means algorithm is described as follows:

Algorithm 1. K-means algorithm

Input: dataset $D = \{x1, x2...xn\}$, cluster k of clusters
Output: K disjoint clusters
    Step1, choose k data at random from D as the initial centroid.
    Step2, each data is assigned to the centroid with the shortest distance.
    Step3, according to the cluster to which each sample belongs, the centroid points in the cluster are updated.
    Step4, the clustering result is output if the centroid does not change; otherwise, the iteration starts from step 2.

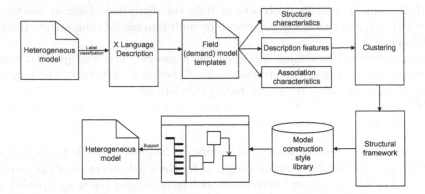

Fig. 1. Model construction style library

3 Materials and Methods

In this section, the method of feature extraction and clustering of heterogeneous models are introduced. First, the heterogeneous model is described by X language, and then the template is formed by extracting the general features of the model. Next, the dataset is generated by analyzing and extracting the structural features, description features, and association features of the template. Finally, the model construction style is constructed by clustering the datasets. The process is shown in Fig. 1.

3.1 Conversion of Model Template

There are many heterogeneous models (e.g., Modelica, SysML, AADS, etc.). X language is a modeling and simulation language that supports the unified description of heterogeneous models to ensure the consistency of models at all levels of the whole system. In order to build a model quickly and accurately for a certain domain or a certain problem, a template is generated by extracting the features of the model.

This paper takes 150 Modelica models as examples and transforms them into templates. The Modelica model starts with the keyword model followed by the name of the model. There are usually several keywords in the Modelica model, such as parameter, variable, initial equation, and equation. The parameter keyword is used to specify the variability of a variable, which can be thought of as a variable that must provide an assignment. The initial value of a variable that is not qualified by the keyword parameter is uncertain at the beginning of the simulation and can be assigned by the equations in the model. The initial equation section is used to initialize a variable. The equation section describes the characteristics of the model.

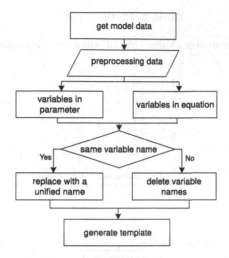

Fig. 2. Template generation flowchart

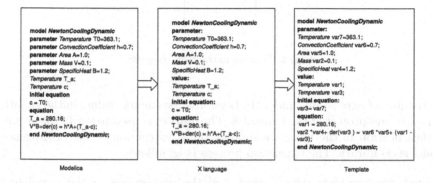

Fig. 3. Model to template process

The template extraction process is shown in Fig. 2.

- First, extract the variable name for the parameter part and the part not qualified by the parameter, and store that variable name in string 1.
- Next, extract the variable names for the initial equation part and equation part into string 2.
- Finally, if the variable names in string 1 occur in string 2, use the uniform variable names (e.g., var1, var2...varN). Otherwise, delete the variable name. Finally, form a template.

The effect diagram of the template is shown in Fig. 3.

3.2 Extraction of Model Features

After analyzing the structural characteristics, correlation characteristics, and description characteristics of 150 templates, the dataset is generated by counting

Table 1. Partial dataset

	Parameter	Value	Initial equation	Equation	Protect
Data 1	1	2	0	1	0
Data 2	3	1	0	4	1
Data 3	0	3	0	2	1
Data 4	4	2	1	3	0
Data 5	1	3	0	4	1

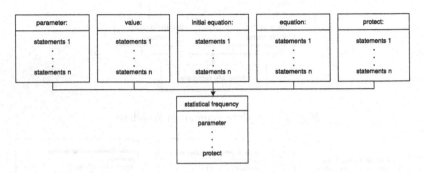

Fig. 4. Feature extraction diagram

the number of expressions under the keywords parameter, value, initial equation, equation, and protect in the templates. The dataset is used to verify the accuracy of classification in the future to support the construction of the heterogeneous model style library. The extraction process is as follows:

- First, the template data is read, and the expressions in the template are segmented by keywords and stored separately.
- Next, the frequency of expressions under each keyword is counted in a line-by-line traversal.
- Finally, the dataset is generated.

The process of feature extraction is shown in Fig. 4. Partial datasets are shown in Table 1.

3.3   Filling of Missing Value

Some data in a dataset miss partial values, and the partial values are called Missing Values. In the process of extracting model features, the lack of some features in the model leads to the generation of Missing Values in the dataset. Missing Values have a certain influence on the clustering effect. Therefore, in order to improve the performance of clustering, Missing Values need to be processed.

Missing Values can be processed in two ways. Filling the dataset with partially null values and removing data with partially null values in a dataset.

Table 2. Dataset with filled Missing Values

	Parameter	Value	Initial equation	Equation	Protect
Data 1	1	2	1	1	1
Data 2	3	1	1	4	1
Data 3	2	3	1	2	1
Data 4	4	2	1	3	1
Data 5	1	3	1	4	1

Missing Values filling methods include mean filling, mode filling, median filling, etc. If the data with Missing Values is less than the original dataset, the Missing Values can be deleted. If the proportion of Missing Values is relatively large, deleting Missing Values may lose a lot of information, thus affecting the clustering result. Therefore, a common method is to fill in Missing Values during data preprocessing.

In this paper, the Missing Values in the dataset are filled through the median filling. The filled partial dataset is shown in Table 2.

3.4 Entropy Value Method

The entropy method calculates the weight of each index by the degree of change of each index. Weight tends to be contribution or importance, which refers to the importance of an indicator relative to something. After processing the Missing Values of the dataset, 150 5-dimensional data are obtained. Since each dimension of data has a different influence on the clustering result, a weight should be added to each dimension in the evaluation and analysis of the dataset. If a feature has a great influence on the clustering result, the weight of the feature may be larger. If a feature has little influence on the clustering result, the weight of the feature may approach 0.

The steps to calculate the weight are as follows:

- In standardized data processing, the function is as follows:

$$z_{ij} = \frac{x_{ij} - \min\{x_{1j}, ...x_{nj}\}}{\max\{x_{1j}, ...x_{nj}\} - \min\{x_{1j}, ...x_{nj}\}} \tag{1}$$

x_{ij} indicates each indicator in the data, and z_{ij} represents the standardized value of each indicator data.
- Calculating the proportion of the i sample value of item j in this index:

$$p_{ij} = \frac{z_{ij}}{\sum\limits_{i=1}^{n} z_{ij}} \tag{2}$$

Table 3. Data weight

	Accuracy
Parameter	0.08
Value	0.06
Initial equation	0.32
Equation	0.06
Protect	0.47

Table 4. Weighted dataset

	Parameter	Value	Initial equation	Equation	Protect
Data 1	0.08	0.12	0.32	0.06	0.47
Data 2	0.24	0.06	0.32	0.24	0.47
Data 3	0.16	0.18	0.32	0.12	0.47
Data 4	0.32	0.12	0.32	0.18	0.47
Data 5	0.08	0.18	0.32	0.24	0.47

– Calculating the entropy value of each indicator:

$$e_j = -k \sum_{i=1}^{n} p_{ij} \ln(p_{ij}) \tag{3}$$

Among them, $k = \frac{1}{\ln(n)} > 0$, with $e_j \geq 0$.
– Calculating of index utility value:

$$d_j = 1 - e_j \tag{4}$$

– Calculating the weight of each indicator:

$$w_j = \frac{d_j}{\sum_{i=1}^{m} d_i}, (j = 1, ..., m) \tag{5}$$

Table 3 shows the weight value of each one-dimensional data calculated, and Table 4 shows a partial weighted dataset.

3.5   Clustering of Models

In this paper, models are divided into five categories: differential equation, connector, electrical, vector and array, and component. In this paper, the k-means algorithm is used to cluster five kinds of processed datasets to verify the accuracy of classification, thus supporting the construction of the heterogeneous model style library. The k-means algorithm is iterated based on the mean value between data and the distance from the centroid. The clustering process is shown in Fig. 5.

Algorithm 2. K-means implements feature clustering of templates

Step1, in the 150 datasets, 5 data are selected as the initial centroid.

Step2, assign each data to the nearest centroid to form 5 classes.

Step3, the mean value of data in each cluster is recalculated and used as the new centroid.

Step4, repeat steps 2, and 3 until the centroid no longer changes and the clustering ends.

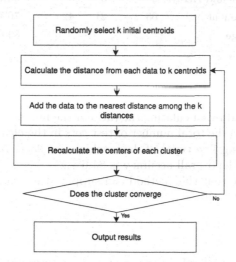

Fig. 5. K-means clustering flow chart

4   Experiments and Analysis

In this paper, 150 Modelica models are divided into five categories: differential equation, connector, electrical, vector, and array models and component models. In order to ensure the consistency of models at all levels of the whole system, these models are uniformly described in X language. In order to build a model quickly and accurately for a certain domain or a certain problem, a template is generated by extracting the general features of the model. The dataset is generated by analyzing and extracting the structural features, description features, and association features of the template. The dataset consists of five characteristics, which are parameter, value, initial equation, equation, and protect. The Missing Values in the dataset are filled by the median. Since each dimension of data has a different influence on the clustering result, the entropy weight method is adopted to add weight to the data of each dimension.

To verify the accuracy of the classification and support the construction of a heterogeneous model style library. This paper divides the dataset into a training set and a test set. The training set is 70% for training data, and five clustering centers are obtained. The test set is 30%, and the test set is assigned to the five cluster centers according to the distance between the test set and these

Table 5. Experiment results

Classification	Amount	Test	Training	Accuracy
Equation	31	10	21	95%
Connector	14	5	9	75%
Electric items	34	11	22	82%
Vectors and Arrays	8	3	5	95%
Component	63	21	42	76%
Average				84.6%

five cluster centers. Finally, the accuracy of clustering is calculated to test the similarity between clustering results and classification results. The accuracy of clustering is obtained by calculating the ratio of the number of test sets assigned to a cluster center to the total number of test sets in the class. Table 5 shows the accuracy of clustering five types of data, which are 95%, 75%, 82%, 95%, and 76%, respectively. The overall accuracy is 84.6%.

The results show that this method can support the construction of the heterogeneous model style library.

5   Conclusion

A method for extraction and clustering of model construction style is proposed. In this method, the heterogeneous model is described in X language, and the general features of the model are extracted to form the template. The dataset is generated by analyzing and extracting the features of templates. Finally, the accuracy of classification is verified by clustering datasets, and the model construction style is constructed. Next, the model design pattern is extracted and the heterogeneous model style library is constructed for the rapid construction, integration, and reuse of the model.

Acknowledgement. This work is supported by the National Key R&D Program of China (No. 2018YFB1701600).

References

1. Zhang, L., et al.: Modeling and simulation in intelligent manufacturing. Comput. Ind. **112**, 103123 (2019)
2. Ji, H., Zhai, X., Song, X., Liu, X., Liang, Y., Jia, Z.: HLA-based federation development framework supporting model reuse. In: Li, L., Hasegawa, K., Tanaka, S. (eds.) AsiaSim 2018. CCIS, vol. 946, pp. 72–81. Springer, Singapore (2018). https://doi.org/10.1007/978-981-13-2853-4_6
3. Liu, Y., Zhang, L., Zhang, W., Hu, X.: An overview of simulation-oriented model reuse. In: Zhang, L., Song, X., Wu, Y. (eds.) AsiaSim/SCS AutumnSim -2016. CCIS, vol. 646, pp. 48–56. Springer, Singapore (2016). https://doi.org/10.1007/978-981-10-2672-0_6

4. Overstreet, C.M., et al.: Issues in enhancing model reuse. In: International Conference on Grand Challenges for Modeling and Simulation (2002)
5. Liu, W., et al.: Simulation-oriented model reuse in cyber-physical systems: a method based on constrained directed graph. Int. J. Model. Simul. Sci. Comput. **13**(02), 2241005 (2022)
6. Xu, G.B., et al.: Development tendency of digital simulation. Comput. Simul. (2013)
7. Onarcan, M.O., et al.: A case study on design patterns and software defects in open source software. J. Softw. Eng. Appl. **11**(05), 249 (2018)
8. Zhang, L., et al.: X language: an integrated intelligent modeling and simulation language for complex products. In: 2021 Annual Modeling and Simulation Conference (ANNSIM). IEEE (2021)
9. Sanz, V., et al.: Cyber-physical system modeling with Modelica using message passing communication. Simul. Model. Pract. Theory **117**, 102501 (2022)
10. Hinkelman, K., et al.: Modelica-based modeling and simulation of district cooling systems: a case study. Appl. Energy **311**, 118654 (2022)
11. Masoom, A., et al.: Modelica-based simulation of electromagnetic transients using Dynawo: current status and perspectives. Electr. Power Syst. Res. **197**, 107340 (2021)
12. Qin, D., et al.: Modeling and simulating a battery for an electric vehicle based on Modelica. Automot. Innov. **2**(3), 169–177 (2019)
13. Fritzson, P.: Modelica: equation-based, object-oriented modelling of physical systems. In: Carreira, P., Amaral, V., Vangheluwe, H. (eds.) Foundations of Multi-Paradigm Modelling for Cyber-Physical Systems, pp. 45–96. Springer, Cham (2020). https://doi.org/10.1007/978-3-030-43946-0_3
14. Zhang, L., et al.: Model engineering for complex system simulation. In: The 58th CAST Forum on New Viewpoints and New Doctrines. Li (2011)
15. Zhang, L., et al.: Modeling & simulation based system of systems engineering. J. Syst. Simul. **34**(2), 179 (2022)
16. Garcia-Dias, R., et al.: Clustering analysis. In: Machine Learning, pp. 227–247. Academic Press (2020)
17. Sinaga, K.P., et al.: Unsupervised K-means clustering algorithm. IEEE Access **8**, 80716–80727 (2020)
18. Sarker, I.H.: Machine learning: algorithms, real-world applications and research directions. SN Comput. Sci. **2**, 1–21 (2021)
19. Dogan, A., et al.: Machine learning and data mining in manufacturing. Expert Syst. Appl. **166**, 114060 (2021)
20. Yu, S.-S., et al.: Two improved k-means algorithms. Appl. Soft Comput. **68**, 747–755 (2018)

Evaluation of Motion Planning Algorithms for Underground Mobile Robots

Desheng Zhu[1] , Yuanyuan Zhang[1] , Jiawen Wang[1] , Kaiqi Ren[2] ,
and Kehu Yang[1(✉)]

[1] School of Mechanical Electronic and Information Engineering, China University
of Mining and Technology, Beijing, China
ykh@cumtb.edu.cn
[2] Industrial and Commercial Bank of China, Beijing, China

Abstract. The underground coal mine is an extremely hard environment for workers due to geological hazard, poisonous gas, and harmful dusts. In such environment, coal mining robots are very helpful for coal mines to reduce the number of onsite workers, enhance safety, and improve efficiency. However, the autonomous movement of coal mine robots in the underground tunnel is still a big challenge. This paper gives a detailed evaluation of the commonly used motion planning algorithms for underground mobile robots. Firstly, the motion planning framework for mine mobile robots is proposed. It considers the global path planning, local path planning ,and the recovery behavior. Then, a motion testing framework in a simulated coal mine environment is constructed based on the ROS platform to test the commonly used motion planning algorithms, such as the the Dijistra, A*, rrt* and Hybrid A* algorithms. The test results shows that RRT* of DWA algorithm runs faster than other algorithm but Hybrid A* of DWA algorithm gets the shortest and smoothest path.

Keywords: Motion planning · Coal mine robot · Evaluation · ROS

1 Introduction

Coal is the most important energy in China, which accounts for 56% of the total primary energy consumption in 2021. Coal consumption is expected to grow at a compound annual growth rate of 2.3 % between 2021 and 2025 to reach 5.6 billion in 2025 [1]. However, the labor shortages due to aging population become the biggest challenge in the mining industry. To solve the problem, intelligent robots can be used in a variety of mining scenarios, such as tunnelling, excavating and inspection [2]. Consequently, the use of robotic devices powered by artificial

This work is supported by National Natural Science Foundation (NSFC) of China under Grant 61973307 and 61936008.

intelligence will transformed the coal industry, where safety and efficiency are the main issues.

The basic function for a coal mining robot is autonomously and agilely in the underground tunnel [3]. The autonomous movement of robots is a comprehensive engineering problem including perception, localization, planning, and control, shown as Fig. 1. The coal mine robot gets the environmental information of the mining space through cameras or lidars, and position and orientation of robot are calculated by positioning fusion algorithms such as Kalman filtering. By calculating a passable path used the motion planning algorithm, the robot is able to avoids obstacles such as hydraulic struts on the coal mine face, and sends motion commands to the motion controller for execution [4].

Coal mine is make up of curvy, irregular tunnel, meanwhile obstacles are various and complicate. Due to the special underground tunnel environment, mining robots need to travel in complex and rugged areas, making motion planning become a difficult problem. Many mature algorithms commonly used by ground robots may be not suitable for coal mine environment, and never be experimental tested before. This paper mainly focuses on the research on motion planning of the coal mine robot.

The paper is organized as follows. Related work was given in Sect. 2. The motion planning framework illustrated in Sect. 3. Then, in Sect. 4, it was shown how to test the real robot in simulated coal mine environment and evaluated the operation effect of various motion planning algorithms. Finally, the experiment results was analyzed in Sect. 5.

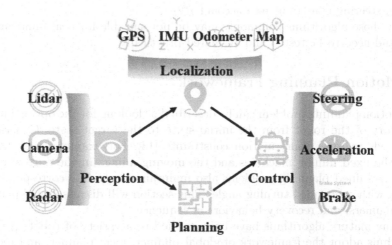

Fig. 1. The framework of autonomous movement

2   Related Work

Over the past few decades, many path planning technologies have been proposed, such as search-based method,sampling-based methods, potential field method and intelligent algorithm method.

Search-based method is a classic global path planning algorithm in the two-dimensional grid map. Representative algorithm include Dijkstra algorithm [5], A* algorithm [6], Hybrid A* [7] algorithm, D* algorithm [8], etc. Among them, A* is an improved version of Dijkstra, aimed at solving Dijkstra's inefficiency. Hybrid A* algorithm is combination of A* algorithm and vehicle kinematics to deal with kinematic constraint. D* is Dynamic A Star to apply at dynamic environment. a two level A-path planning calculation method to overcome computation complexity has been proposed [9].

Sampling-based methods is path planning algorithm based on graph structure. Representative algorithm include Probabilistic Roadmap Method(PRM), Rapidly-Exploring Random Trees(RRT), and their improved algorithm RRT* [10]. These algorithms find not relatively optimized paths but feasible paths.

The artificial potential field method is an collision avoidance approach, which the obstacle gives the robot a repulsive force and the target points give it attractive force. However, the artificial potential field method suffers from the local minimum and goal non-reachable with obstacles nearby problem. A improved artificial potential field method has been proposed to make mining robot go out of local minimum point autonomously [11]. Y. Lei proposed a fuzzy logic-based adaptive DWA, which considering obstacle avoidance is designing by taking Ackermann steering constraint into account [12].

But those algorithms commonly may be not suitable for coal mine environment,and need to be tested and evaluated practically.

3   Motion Planning Framework

The motion planning problem can be described as looking for the optimal motion trajectory of the robot from the initial state to the target state. Generally, it also needs to meet some motion constraints [13]. For example, they need to avoid the fixed mining machines and the moving miners in the narrow tunnel. The constrained planning problems also maintain constraints corresponding to motion with a bounded turning angle. This section will discuss global planners, local planners, and recovery behaviors in sequence.

Many mature algorithms have been applied to a variety of robots [14]. Our algorithms adopt the framework of global planner, local planner, and recovery behaviors, shown as Fig. 2:

- **Global planner:** Through global planner, the robot has gained a map to plan out a feasible path roughly, known as the global route.
- **Local planner:** Within the scope of the local sensor detection, local planner detects dynamic obstacles and actual traffic area around the robot's motion, as well as follows control rules and global path to calculate a local path.

- **Recovery behaviors:** Vehicle controller algorithm transforms the planning path into the control instruction. If the robot encounters an impassable path or gets lost, the recovery system is activated to reset the robot situation.

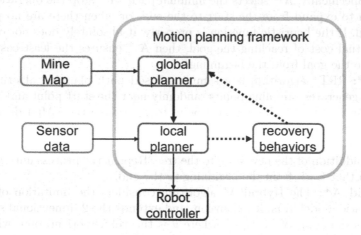

Fig. 2. The framework of motion planning

3.1 Global Planner

The global planner gives information about obstacles and environments contained in the map, the robot's position, and targets in the world.It creates a global path to reach the target position. The generated paths do not consider the dynamics and kinematics of the vehicle, resulting in a impassable path for the robot. Commonly used algorithms are Dijkstra, A*, rrt*, Hybrid A*.

- **Dijkstra:** Dijkstra is a shortest path algorithm for searching one vertex to other vertexes, which solves the shortest path problem in directed graph. The main characteristic of Dijkstra algorithm is that it starts from the starting point to traverse to the adjacent nodes of the nearest and unvisited vertex at the beginning point each time until it extends to the end point. The Dijkstra algorithm is breadth-first search, which is a kind of divergent search, so the space complexity and time complexity of Dijkstra algorithm are relatively high.
- **A*:** A* algorithm is classical heuristic search algorithm, which is the improvement algorithm from classical search algorithm Dijkstra. The most significant characteristic of the algorithm is that the heuristic function is given in the process of search to reduce the search nodes, thus improving the efficiency of path search. Beginning from the start point, A* algorithm targets at the terminal point with iterating over the adjacent points around the start point

and the traversed starting point, and calculates the total movement cost from the starting point to each node.

In each iteration of the main loop, A * needs to decide which paths to extend. It based on an estimate of the cost of the path and extending the path to the goal. Specifically, A * selects the minimal path. A * stop the operation when a path to expand from the start to the end, or when there are no paths to expand. If the heuristic function is properly, it absolutely does not overstate the actual cost of reaching the goal, then A * ensures the least costly path back to the goal from the beginning.

- **RRT***: RRT* algorithm is a sampling-based path planning algorithm. An RRT* generates sampling points randomly near the start point and connects the start point with the sampling point to generate a tree. After drawing the random tree, check that the path of the branch is passable. If the connection is feasible (completely through free space and with constraints), this results in the addition of the new state to the tree. Repeat the process until you have a path that leads from the beginning to the end.

- **Hybrid A***: The Hybrid A* algorithm considers the limitation of vehicle kinematic model in node expansion, and extends the 2-dimensional search to 3-dimensional space [x, y, θ], where θ is the vehicle orientation, which can plan the continuous pose change of unmanned parking spaces in discrete grid. Based on Hybrid A* algorithm, node expansion mode, collision detection, design of cost function and other aspects are improved to make the improved algorithm can faster search for the initial path.

3.2 Local Planner

The global path planner generates the general path of the vehicle motion without fast obstacle avoidance. The effect is not ideal when the vehicle directly executes the global path. On the one hand, the robustness of the global path planner is poor, reflected in the weak ability to avoid dynamic obstacles, and leads to planning on inaccurate maps. On the other hand, the search time of the global planner increases greatly with the search space. When searching in a high-dimensional search space, considering the increase in the amount of computation, the increase in computation time brought by re-planning is unbearable [15].

Local planners are responsible for getting trajectory to move the robot target position safely. The local planner tries to follow the global planner's plan while taking into account the kinematics and dynamics of the robot. To generate safe speed instructions, the local planner uses the Dynamic Window Approach (DWA) or Trajectory Rollout to simulate and select possible path according to the cost function.

- **Trajectory Rollout:** Trajectory Rollout discretely sample in the robot's control space, and generate a series of tracks. The set of trajectories is generated by changing the turning angle while maintaining a certain speed. The positions of trajectories are determined by calculating the turning angle every time step. After that, the Trajectory Rollout will identify which path collision-free. In this case, the optimization algorithm elects the shortest path between the ideal future position and the final position of the trajectory.

- **DWA:** The principle of the DWA algorithm is to search in the state space, constrain the search space to a suitable range, generate multiple prediction paths, select the optimal path according to the path evaluation function, and send the state control command of the optimal path directly to the chassis implement.

Just like Trajectory Rollout, DWA searchs for commands controlling the robot in the space of velocities. Firstly, the search space is reduced in circular trajectories, admissible velocities and dynamic window. Secondly, the trajectory is chosen which maximize objective function from the remaining trajectory. The objective function as:

$$G(v, \omega) = \alpha \cdot heading(v, \omega) + \beta \cdot dist(v, \omega) + \gamma \cdot vel(v, \omega) \qquad (1)$$

heading represents the deviation towards target, and is the largest when the robot moves towards the target. *dist* is the distance to the nearest obstacle on the trajectory. The shorter the distance to the obstacle, the greater the desire of the robot to move around the obstacle. *vel* is the forward speed of the robot and supports high speed movement. The larger the value, the faster the movement speed. α, β, γ denotes adjustable coefficient for heading, dist and vel, setting as defaults. v and ω are the vehicle speed and orientation.

3.3   Recovery Behavior

The motion planning system can works well in most cases. However, when there are some dramatically changes in the mine, the robot need to reset. To make the system robust, the recovery system was built into the mine motion planning framework.

- **Rotation:** When the robot gets trapped,the robot rotates to scan for free space. If this fail,a more aggressive recovery behavior will be attempted.
- **Back to the start point**: The robot returns along the path that it has traveled, meanwhile, it robot reroutes based on real-time environment. When if find another path, it will execute it. If this fail,a more aggressive recovery behavior will be attempted.
- **Rebuild the map**: The robot will abandon the previous map and re-plan the path with the real-time surrounding environment map.

4   Performance of Simulated Environment Experiment

In this section, we present the setup, evaluation environment and detailed experiment results.

4.1 Platform

Our experimental platform is built upon an Autolabor differential vehicle with an embedded computer(NVIDIA Jetson AGX Xavier), 2d Lidia(Slamtec RPLI-DAR A2), high precision MEMS Inertial Sensor(ADIS16495), and 360 pulse per revolution wheel odometer attached in wheels.

The platform is driven by some subsystems: hardware drivers, controllers, perception, planning, higher-level control. We use ros to communicate between subsystems, which is a common communication framework for robots. Experiments in this paper were performed with an Autolabor Pro 1 mobile platform, The maximum speed of the Pro1 base is 0.8 m/s (Figs. 3 and 4).

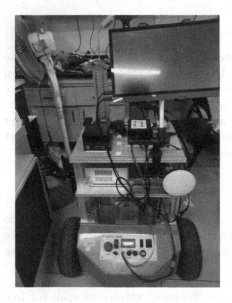 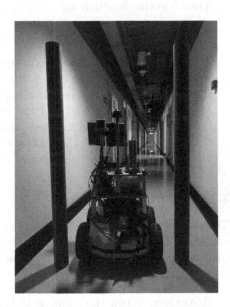

Fig. 3. The overview of autonomous robot   **Fig. 4.** The static obstacle avoidance test

4.2 Test Method of Coal Mine Simulation Conditions

Limited by the requirements of coal mine safety regulations, it is inconvenient to test on the actual site. However, to meet the actual production needs of coal mines, the production conditions of coal mines are imitated and 3 test experiments are set up to simulate the actual scene of coal mine roadways.

– **Roadway following test:** The operation of coal mine robot needs to reach the position accurately, so we carry out the inspection test of the task point. The task is to set the different target point in the corridor. The whole journey is 50 m in total. Every time the car reaches a target point, it will automatically go to the path planned for the next target point. When it reaches a target point, it will be recorded as a successful navigation plan. The path released by the car and relevant data of operation are recorded.

- **Static obstacle avoidance test:** In the coal mine production environment, the single hydraulic prop is widely used in underground mining support equipment. The diameter of the commonly used single hydraulic prop cylinder is 10cm. As simulating a single hydraulic prop cylinder, paper cylinders of the same size are set in the middle to simulate the mining environment obstacles. The operation ability of various algorithms is tested in the narrow passages between the obstacles of the props.
- **Dynamic obstacle avoidance test:** In the coal mine environment, workers often move around when they at work, and the moving person is a dynamic obstacle that the robot must avoid. This paper takes the moving person as the moving obstacle and tests the obstacle avoidance capability.

4.3   Evaluation Metrics

For performance evaluation, we use the following metrics, shown as Table 1.

Table 1. Evaluation metrics

Evaluation metrics	Description
Success rate	The proportion of no intervention or collision in trial
Path length	Average length of the walking route when the task is successfully completed
Runtime	The whole time from sending the target point command to running to the final point
Global path planning time	The time between the acceptance of the target point and the release of the first planned route by the global planner
Number of Obstacle collision	Number of collisions during running tests including dynamic and static obstacles
Minimum/maximum allowable width	The minimum passing distance without collision/ no collision will occur through space that exceed this width
Temporal coefficient	The ratio of the actual time to the minimum travel time representing the time of planner execution
Spatial coefficient	Spatial coefficient is the ratio of the actual distance traveled to the planned distance representing the efficiency of local planner execution
Smooth coefficient	The ratio of the actual Angle turned to the accumulated Angle of the planned path representing the curvature of the path executed by the local planner

- **Success rate:** Success rate refers to the proportion of no intervention or collision in trial.
- **Path length:** The length of the path is the key to evaluating the quality of the route. is recorded as the average length of the walking route when the task is successfully completed, and if it cannot be completed, the longest distance traveled is recorded.
- **Runtime:** The running time is the whole time from sending the target point command to running to the final point.
- **Global path planning time:** The time between the acceptance of the target point and the release of the first planned route by the global planner.

- **Number of obstacle collision:** Number of collisions during running tests, including dynamic and static obstacles.
- **Minimum/maximum allowable width:** The minimum allowable width refers to the minimum passing distance without collision. The maximum allowable width means that no collision will occur through roadways that exceed this width.
- **Temporal cocfficient:** Spatial coefficient is the ratio of the actual time to the minimum travel time, representing the time of planner execution.
- **Spatial coefficient:** Spatial coefficient is the ratio of the actual distance traveled to the planned distance, representing the efficiency of local planner execution.
- **Smooth coefficient:** Smooth coefficient is the ratio of the actual Angle turned to the accumulated Angle of the planned path, representing the curvature of the path executed by the local planner.

4.4 Experiment Results

To evaluate the moiton planning framework on our test vehicle described in Sect. 3, the combination algorithms are run based on the simulation mining robot tasks in Sect. 4.2. We test our framework used the mentioned metrics in Table 1, the running state of the test is shown as Figs. 5, 6, 7 and 8.

As shown in the Table 2, all of the global planner can gain connected path. RRT* has the highest planning efficiency, with planning time of 230.1 ms, while Hybrid A* is tens of times longer than RRT*, that of 5957.2 ms. In the same planning task, the performance of the four algorithms is relatively close, so the global path searched by all used algorithms is relatively close to the optimal path in the coal mine roadway. A* and RRT* can more suitable for global path planning.

Table 3 shows that in the static obstacle avoidance test, DWA has more collisions than Trajectory Rollout. As the DWA algorithm is more aggressive in plan, it can get through narrower tunnels. The minimum passable distance of DWA is 80 cm, but DWA needs a wider safety pass width to ensure stable and safe passage. To meet the safety requirement of mine, mining robots are forbidden to collide and fall down the safety supports to the ground. However, there are lots of hydraulic props in mines. So the operation of the mining robot must ensure that it can not hit the safety support. The robust Trajectory Rollout algorithm is more suitable for the complex down-hole environment.

Table 2. Comparison of global planning

Gobal planner	Success rate	Path length	Spatial coefficient
A*	100%	289.9 ms	1.02
Dijkstra	100%	306.3 ms	1.03
RRT*	100%	230.1 ms	1.02
Hybrid A*	100%	5957.2 ms	1.04

Fig. 5. Dijstra of DWA

Fig. 6. A* of DWA

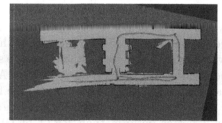

Fig. 7. RRT* of Trajectory Rollout

Fig. 8. Hybrid A* of Trajectory Rollout

Table 3. Comparison of local planning

Gobal planner	Success rate	Recovery behavior	Static obstacle collision	Dynamic obstacle Collision	Minimum allow width	Maximum allow width
Trajectory rollout	98.3%	4	1	0	86 cm	86 cm
DWA	85.8%	2	6	0	80 cm	95 cm

Table 4. Comparison of assembly planner

Gobal planner	Local planner	Runtime	Temporal coefficient	Travel distance	Spatial coefficient	Smooth coefficient
Dijkstra	Trajectory rollout	9.3 min	5.44	76.39 m	1.49	1.67
A*		9.1 min	5.41	**69.46 m**	**1.38**	**1.41**
RRT*		10.7 min	6.26	74.73 m	1.46	5.32
Hybrid A*		**8 min**	**4.70**	72.34 m	1.42	1.80
Dijkstra	DWA	8.6 min	4.99	94.66 m	2.25	2.05
A*		7.5min	4.37	72.07 m	1.40	1.65
RRT*		**6.1 min**	**3.55**	67.77 m	1.31	1.74
Hybrid A*		12.2 min	6.98	**62.03 m**	**1.18**	**1.63**

Table 4 is a comparison of assembly planner, runtime, travel distance, and path smoothness. The global path generated by RRT* and Hybrid A* is the most suitable for the local planner of DWA. The running time of RRT* of DWA is the shortest, which is 6.1 min, indicating RRT* of DWA has the highest planning efficiency. The running distance and smoothness indexes of Hybrid A* of DWA are the best, indicating that DWA can best follow the global path of Hybrid A*. The travel distance of Hybrid A* of DWA is the shortest, which is 62.03 m. However, Hybrid A* of DWA has the longest running time to reach each task point due to excessive constraints and long operation time. In terms of running distance results, little difference is founded between the two assembly planners but RRT* of DWA is considerably faster than Hybrid A* of DWA. So RRT* of DWA is the best among the four DWA combination algorithms tested.

The most suitable global path for Trajectory Rollout is generated by A* and Hybrid A*. A* of Trajectory Rollout has the shortest running distance (69.46 m), and its running time is second only to that of Hybrid A* of Trajectory Rollout. Hybrid A* of Trajectory Rollout has the shortest running time, which is 8 minus, and the shortest running distance after A* of Trajectory Rollout. This indicates that Trajectory Rollout is very suitable for A* and its improved algorithm.

As the shortest runtimes of the two groups, Hybrid A* of Trajectory Rollout has a better perform than RRT* of DWA. Meanwhile, Hybrid A* of DWA's path is shorter than the A*-Trajectory Rollout's path. Among the measured algorithms, RRT* of DWA's running time has obvious advantages compared with other algorithms, which is suitable for the requirements of fast passage tasks such as underground rescue. Additionally, Hybrid A* of DWA has the shortest distance and better smoothness, but the execution time is the longest, indicating that it is suitable for the application of narrow tunneled traffic and other scenarios that need to strictly follow the route.

5   Conclusion

This paper set a mining robot motion testing framework for simulated conditions of the coal mine, including roadway following test, static obstacle avoidance test, and dynamic obstacle avoidance test. This paper using a differential wheeled robot platform to test the effect of the assembly planner. Several indicators, planning speed, travel distance, and trajectory smoothness have been evaluated. This paper provides some guidelines for the application of coal mine robots.

In the study findings, it is clear that RRT* is the fastest planning global path. Additionally, RRT* of DWA can reach the target point faster than other algorithm combinations in the simulated mining environment. It is suitable for fast arrival scenarios, such as rescue and transport missions. Due to considering kinematic constraints, the planning time of Hybrid A* is much longer than that of other algorithms, but the path by Hybrid A* is the easiest to execute. Among various algorithm combinations, Hybrid A* of DWA algorithm has the shortest travel distance and the smoothest path, indicating that it is suitable for slow but strict path implementation scenes, such as narrow roadways with many obstacles.

References

1. Wang, G., Liu, F., Pang, Y.: Coal mine intellectualization: the core technology of high quality development. J. China Coal Soc. **44**(2), 349–357 (2019)
2. Ge, S., Hu, E., Pei, W.: Classification system and key technology of coal mine robot. J. China Coal Soc. **45**(1), 455–463 (2020)
3. Marder, E., Berger, E., Foote, T., Gerkey, B., Konolige, K.: The office marathon: robust navigation in an indoor office environment. In: IEEE International Conference on Robotics & Automation, pp. 300–307 (2010)
4. Li, X., Sun, Z., Cao, D., et al.: Real-time trajectory planning for autonomous urban driving: framework, algorithms, and verifications. IEEE/ASME Trans. Mechatron. **21**, 740–753 (2015)
5. Luecken, M., Büttner, M., Chaichoompu, K.: Benchmarking atlas-level data integration in single-cell genomics. Nat. Methods **19**, 41–50 (2022)
6. Shivam, J., Soumya, S.: Low-cost path planning in 2D environment using A* algorithm by considering slope of the obstacle. IFAC-Papers OnLine **55**(1), 783–788 (2022)
7. Richards, N., Sharma, M., Ward, D.: A hybrid A*/automaton approach to on-line path planning with obstacle avoidance. In: AIAA 1st Intelligent Systems Technical Conference, vol. 19, pp. 9–10 (2004)
8. González, R., Jayakumar, P., Iagnemma, K.: Stochastic mobility prediction of ground vehicles over large spatial regions: a geostatistical approach. Auton. Robots **41**(2), 311–331 (2017)
9. Qin, Y.: Research on detection system for coal mine detection robot based on the technology of information fusion. In: International Technology and Innovation Conference, pp. 151–152 (2009)
10. Palmieri, L., Kai, O.A.: A novel RRT extend function for efficient and smooth mobile robot motion planning. In: IEEE/RSJ International Conference on Intelligent Robots and Systems, pp. 205–211 (2014)
11. Tian, Z., Gao, X.: Path planning of disaster relief robot based on improved artificial potential field method. Ind. Mining Autom. **42**(09), 37–42 (2016)
12. Lei, Y., Wang, Y., Wu, S., Gu, X., Qin X.: A fuzzy logic-based adaptive dynamic window approach for path planning of automated driving Mining Truck. In: 2021 IEEE International Conference on Mechatronics, pp. 1–6 (2021)
13. Roesmann, C., Feiten, W., Woesch, T.: Trajectory modification considering dynamic constraints of autonomous robots. In: Robotics Proceedings of ROBOTIK 2012 7th German Conference on VDE, pp. 1–6 (2012)
14. Steve, M.: The marathon 2: a navigation system. In: 2020 IEEE/RSJ International Conference on Intelligent Robots and Systems, pp. 2718–2725 (2020)
15. Lu, D., David, V., Dave, H., William, D.: Layered costmaps for context-sensitive navigation. In: IEEE/RSJ International Conference on Intelligent Robots and Systems, pp. 709–715 (2014)

Optimization of Ethanol Fermentation Based on Design of Dynamic Experiments

Yangyang Liu and Fei Liu[✉]

Key Laboratory of Advanced Control for Light Industry Processes, Ministry of
Education, Jiangnan University, Wuxi 214122, Jiangsu, China
fliu@jiangnan.edu.cn

Abstract. For the fed-batch ethanol production process, the feed rate is
the key to determining the total yield. This paper optimizes the feed rate
based on the Kriging model by using the design of dynamic experiments
(DoDE). Firstly, a global approximation model is established by sequentially adding points to the initial experimental data set. And virtual samples are generated through the mega-trend-diffusion (MTD) technique
to enrich the experimental data set and balance the distribution of data
points. Then, a 1/2-fraction factorial design is performed in the optimal
solution region to augment the experimental data set, and the locally
enhanced global model is built and optimized. Finally, the modeling and
optimization process is iterated until the optimal solution meets the convergence criterion. The iterative update and optimization algorithm is
applied to ethanol production, which is the free terminal fed-batch fermentation process. The optimal solution of feed rate is convergent, and
is of guiding significance for practical production.

Keywords: Design of dynamic experiments · Kriging model ·
Fed-batch fermentation · Mega-trend-diffusion technique · Ethanol
production

1 Introduction

Fed-batch fermentation has been a commonly used fermentation technique for
ethanol production. This process mode can reduce the inhibition of substrate
and end-product, shorten fermentation time, and increase ethanol yield by regu-
lating the feed rate [1]. The early industrial feeding approach is relatively simple
to operate and is an empirical method. The most commonly used approach is
to weigh a certain amount of nutrients into the fermentation broth when the
culture is carried out for a certain period [2]. This approach is less effective
for controlling and optimizing fermentation. With the deepening of theoretical
research and practice, new feed strategies for ethanol production have been put
forward. Aiba, Shoda and Nagatani studied the inhibition of ethanol concentration on the specific growth rate of biomass and ethanol yield by controlling the
feed concentration in culture, and proposed a kinetic model of ethanol production [3]. According to this kinetic model, Hong obtained the optimal feed rate for
ethanol production using the Pontryagin maximum principle combined with the

L. Zhang et al. (Eds.): CINT 2022, CCIS 1714, pp. 380–391, 2022.
https://doi.org/10.1007/978-981-19-8915-5_33

transformation method [4]. A two-stage mixing method based on control vector parameterization was proposed by Banga et al. to dynamically optimize the feed rate of ethanol fermentation [5].

The above two typical methods are mechanistic model-based optimization (MMBO). What both have in common is the need for accurate mechanistic models. However, for complex biological processes, the identification, construction, and optimization of mechanistic models are not trivial problems [6]. Moreover, the parameter estimation of mechanistic models is inseparable from experimental data support, and it is well known that experiments are expensive. On the contrary, the data-driven model hardly relies on prior knowledge such as process mechanism but approximates the appropriate functional model with experimental data. Building and optimizing function models are relatively simple, effectively improving optimization efficiency. Therefore, data-driven optimization is a good alternative.

Design of Experiments (DoE) is a data-driven modeling and optimization method [7] for optimizing problems with time-invariant manipulated variables. However, the batch process has no steady-state operating point, and each state changes nonlinearly with time, so non-constant feed operation needs to be considered. Fiordalis and Georgakis innovatively proposed the design of dynamic experiments (DoDE) to optimize batch crystallization [8]. DoDE can reveal the influence of time-varying manipulated variables on process performance. This method has also been further applied and studied [9–12].

The optimization based on DoE faces two problems [13]: the number of experiments increases exponentially with the number of manipulated variables, which significantly increases the experimental cost; finding the global optimal solution to nonlinear problems is difficult using low-order polynomial models. Therefore, this paper uses the Kriging model instead of the polynomial model to improve model prediction accuracy. Through sequential experiments and the MTD technique [14,15], a more robust Kriging model is constructed with fewer experiments, and the region where the optimal solution is located as soon as possible.

2   DoDE Based on Kriging Method

2.1   Design of Dynamic Experiments

The experimental optimization is carried out for a batch process with n_I manipulated variables u_i $(i = 1, \ldots, n_I)$ and a single response y; the response is the key performance indicator. With data collected from a set of experiments, the relationship between the response and manipulated variables is estimated as

$$y = f(u_1, \ldots, u_{n_I}), \tag{1}$$

where the form of the function f is unknown.

To eliminate dimensions and simplify calculations, define the manipulated variable u_i with a dimensionless factor w_i:

$$u_i = u_{i0} + \Delta u_i w_i, \tag{2}$$

where $u_{i0} = (u_{i,max} + u_{i,min})/2$, $\Delta u_i = (u_{i,max} - u_{i,min})/2$. $u_{i,max}$ and $u_{i,min}$ are the maximum and minimum values of the manipulated variable u_i, respectively. The relationship between the response and manipulated variables is transformed into the relationship between the response and factors:

$$y = f(w_1, \ldots, w_{n_I}). \tag{3}$$

The above factor setting is a traditional DoE method. Its primary limitation is that it cannot effectively reveal the effect of time-varying manipulated variables on the process response. However, most batch processes have manipulated variables that vary over time. To resolve this situation, Georgakis and Fiordalis proposed and refined the DoDE approach [8,9]. The idea of the DoDE is to replace the dimensionless factor w_i with a dynamic factor $w_i(\tau)$. A time-varying manipulated variable $u_i(\tau)$ is defined as

$$u_i(\tau) = u_{i0}(\tau) + \Delta u_i(\tau) w_i(\tau), \tag{4}$$

where $u_{i0}(\tau) = (u_{i,max}(\tau) + u_{i,min}(\tau))/2$ and $\Delta u_i(\tau) = (u_{i,max}(\tau) - u_{i,min}(\tau))$ $/2$. $u_{i,max}(\tau)$ and $u_{i,min}(\tau)$ are the upper and lower bounds of the manipulated variable at time τ, respectively; $\tau = t/t_f$ is the dimensionless time, and t_f is the duration of a batch. $w_i(\tau)$ is a function of time, which changes with time and is therefore called a dynamic factor. Equation (1) is rewritten as

$$y = f(u_1(\tau), \ldots, u_{n_I}(\tau)). \tag{5}$$

$w_i(\tau)$ is expressed by a set of Shifted Legendre Polynomials (SLP) expansion:

$$w_i(\tau) = \sum_{j=1}^{n_J} x_{ij} \varphi_{j-1}(\tau), \tag{6}$$

where the coefficient x_{ij} is called the jth dynamic sub-factor of the ith manipulated variable. The coefficient vector x_i is defined by $x_i = [x_{i1}, \ldots, x_{in_J}]^T$. $\varphi_{j-1}(\tau)$ is the jth item of SLP, and the first three parameters of SLP are used to parameterize dynamic factors:

$$\varphi_0(\tau) = 1, \varphi_1(\tau) = -1 + 2\tau, \varphi_2(\tau) = 1 - 6\tau + 6\tau^2. \tag{7}$$

Eq. (5) can be rewritten as

$$y = f(x_i, \ldots, x_{n_I}). \tag{8}$$

When $\tau \in [-1, 1]$, the value of SLP is between -1 and 1. Let the variation range of $u_i(\tau)$ be $u_{i0}(\tau) - \Delta u_i(\tau)$ to $u_{i0}(\tau) + \Delta u_i(\tau)$, namely $-1 \leq w_i(\tau) \leq 1$, so dynamic sub-factors should meet the following inequality constraints:

$$-1 \leq x_{i1} \pm x_{i2} \pm x_{i3} \leq 1. \tag{9}$$

A low-order polynomial model is often used to construct function relationship between the response and factors. However, the global approximation of complex nonlinear processes by low-order polynomial models is limited, and finding a good optimal solution is difficult. Therefore, it is necessary to adopt a method with higher prediction accuracy for modeling.

2.2 Kriging Method

Kriging is a semi-parametric model that estimates unknown points through known points, with flexible application and high prediction accuracy. The Kriging model is used instead of the polynomial model. Suppose there is a known set of experiment points $X = [\mathbf{x}^1, \ldots, \mathbf{x}^{n_L}]^T$, where $\mathbf{x}^l$ is the lth designed experiment point, defined by $\mathbf{x}^l = [(x_1^l)^T, \ldots, (x_{n_I}^l)^T]^T$, $\mathbf{x}^l \in \mathbb{R}^{3n_I}$; and $x_i^l = [x_{i1}^l, x_{i2}^l, x_{i3}^l]^T$, where $l = 1, \ldots, n_L$, and n_L is the number of designed experiments. The corresponding response is $Y = [y^1, \ldots, y^{n_L}]^T$, $y^l \in \mathbb{R}$. The relationship between the response and experiment points is

$$y = \sum_{p=1}^{n_P} \beta_p g_p(\mathbf{x}) + z(\mathbf{x}). \tag{10}$$

The above equation consists of two parts. The first part is a linear model describing the overall trend of the response. β_p is the regression coefficient, where $p = 1, \ldots, n_P$, and n_P is the number of terms of a linear model; $\mathbf{x}$ represents the experiment point, and $g_p(\mathbf{x})$ is the polynomial basis function about $\mathbf{x}$, which can be zero-order, first-order or second-order [16]. The specific form is determined by the principle of minimizing the root mean square error.

The latter part is a random process $z(\mathbf{x})$ representing the local characteristics of the response, which satisfies the following properties: the mean is zero, the variance is σ^2, and the covariance is

$$cov\left[z\left(\mathbf{x}^l\right), z\left(\mathbf{x}^{l'}\right)\right] = \sigma^2 R\left(\Re\left(\mathbf{x}^l, \mathbf{x}^{l'}\right)\right), \tag{11}$$

where R is the correlation matrix, and $\Re(\mathbf{x}^l, \mathbf{x}^{l'})$ is the correlation function of any two experiment points $\mathbf{x}^l$ and $\mathbf{x}^{l'}$. In this paper, the Gaussian correlation function is used, that is,

$$\Re\left(\mathbf{x}^l, \mathbf{x}^{l'}\right) = \prod_{i=1}^{n_I} \prod_{j=1}^{3} exp\left(-\theta_{ij}\left\|x_{ij}^l - x_{ij}^{l'}\right\|^2\right), \tag{12}$$

where θ_{ij} $(\theta_{ij} > 0)$ is the unknown correlation parameter; x_{ij}^l and $x_{ij}^{l'}$ are the jth dynamic sub-factor of the ith manipulated variable at experiment points $\mathbf{x}^l$ and $\mathbf{x}^{l'}$, respectively.

After the correlation function is determined, the correlation matrix between the known experiment points is

$$R = \begin{bmatrix} \Re\left(\mathbf{x}^1, \mathbf{x}^1\right) & \cdots & \Re\left(\mathbf{x}^1, \mathbf{x}^{n_L}\right) \\ \vdots & \ddots & \vdots \\ \Re\left(\mathbf{x}^{n_L}, \mathbf{x}^1\right) & \cdots & \Re\left(\mathbf{x}^{n_L}, \mathbf{x}^{n_L}\right) \end{bmatrix}. \tag{13}$$

The correlation between any unknown point $\mathbf{x}$ and known points is $r(\mathbf{x}) = [\Re(\mathbf{x}, \mathbf{x}^1), \ldots, \Re(\mathbf{x}, \mathbf{x}^{n_L})]^T$. The predicted response of the Kriging model at the unknown point $\mathbf{x}$ is

$$\hat{y}(\mathbf{x}) = g(\mathbf{x})^T \hat{\beta} + r(\mathbf{x})^T \hat{\gamma}, \tag{14}$$

where $g(\mathbf{x}) = [g_1(\mathbf{x}), \ldots, g_{n_P}(\mathbf{x})]^T$ is the polynomial basis function vector. The coefficient $\hat{\beta} = (G^T R^{-1} G) G^T R^{-1} Y$ is estimated by generalized least squares, and the coefficient $\hat{\gamma} = R^{-1}(Y - G\hat{\beta})$ and the regression matrix is

$$G = \begin{bmatrix} g_1\left(\mathbf{x}^1\right) & \cdots & g_{n_P}\left(\mathbf{x}^1\right) \\ \vdots & \ddots & \vdots \\ g_1\left(\mathbf{x}^{n_L}\right) & \cdots & g_{n_P}\left(\mathbf{x}^{n_L}\right) \end{bmatrix}. \tag{15}$$

According to maximum likelihood estimation [16], the correlation parameter θ_{ij} is determined by maximizing Eq. (16).

$$max\left(-1/2\left[n_L \ln\left(\sigma^2\right) + \ln|R|\right]\right), \tag{16}$$

where σ is estimated as

$$\hat{\sigma}^2 = \frac{1}{n_L}\left(Y - G\hat{\beta}\right)^T R^{-1}\left(Y - G\hat{\beta}\right). \tag{17}$$

3 Iterative Update and Optimization Algorithm of the Kriging Model

It should be noted that DoDE is usually applied to the small sample set modeling optimization. For few representative data, MTD technique generates virtual samples can increase the amount of sample information and make the model more suitable for the actual process. y^l is the experiment value, and $\hat{y}^l$ is the model predicted value. The mean absolute percentage error (MAPE) is used to quantify how close the predicted Kriging model is to the actual process:

$$\mathrm{MAPE} = \frac{100}{n_L} \times \sum_{l=1}^{n_L}\left|\frac{y^l - \hat{y}^l}{y^l}\right|. \tag{18}$$

If MAPE $\leq 10\%$, it is considered that the predictive model can be used to estimate the response of virtual samples [17]. This paper uses a stricter condition of no more than 5% for more precise optimization. Since these designed experiments are *in silico*, add measurement error to the simulated response y^{sim}, i.e., $y^l \sim N\left(y^{sim}, 0.005 y^{sim}\right)$ [10].

In order to reduce the optimization cost and improve the optimization efficiency, an iterative update and optimization algorithm of the Kriging model is proposed. The initial experiments in this paper used the D-optimal designs [18], and the subsequent experiments used the Latin hypercube sampling (LHS) design [19]. Figure 1 shows the flowchart of the iterative optimization method. As shown, the iterative algorithm of the Kriging model can be summarized as follows.

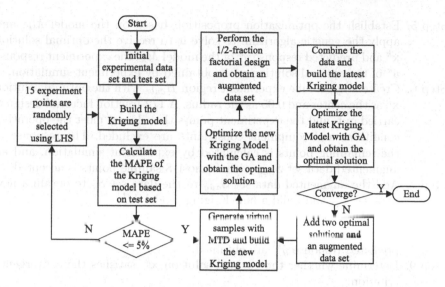

Fig. 1. Flowchart of the iterative update and optimization algorithm of the Kriging model

Specific calculation steps:

Step 1. Obtain the initial experimental data set S_0 and test set S_{test}. First, the experiment region is determined with the feed setting and equipment constraints. Second, an initial experiment arrangement with the quadratic polynomial structure and 20 sample points is constructed using the D-optimal designs. The corresponding response is received through the experimental simulation; and the initial experimental data set S_0 is obtained. Next, LHS is used to randomly select 15 sample points, and conduct experiments to obtain the test set S_{test}.

Step 2. Build the Kriging model M_0 based on the initial data set S_0.

Step 3. Calculate the MAPE of model M_0 with the test set S_{test}.
   a. If MAPE $\leq 5\%$ is satisfied, step 4 is performed.
   b. Otherwise, LHS is used to randomly select another 15 samples and add them to S_0 to obtain a new data set S_0', and Step 2 is performed. The prediction model built in this step is expressed as M_0'.

Step 4. Generate the virtual sample set S_{vir} according to the data set S_0' and the prediction model M_0'. MTD technique is applied to generate 100 virtual experiment points. The corresponding predicted response is calculated with M_0' to obtain the virtual experiment sample set S_{vir}. S_0' and S_{vir} are combined to obtain the synthetic experiment data set S_k, which is used as the training set. The Kriging model M_k is built based on the data set S_k; and set $k = 1$. The number of virtual samples is determined to be 100 after many trials.

Step 5. Establish the optimization proposition based on the model M_k, and apply the genetic algorithm to solve it to receive the optimal solution $\mathbf{x}^k$ and predicted response $\hat{y}^k$ of the model M_k; the experiment response y^k of the optimal solution $\mathbf{x}^k$ is obtained by experiment simulation.

Step 6. Create a hypercube experiment region H_{cube} with the optimal solution $\mathbf{x}^k$ as the center and 0.05 as the radius. A 1/2-fraction factorial design is carried out, and the experiment points that do not meet the operating conditions and equipment constraints are excluded. The response of the remaining points is calculated by experiment simulation, and an augmented data set S_{aug} with at most 8 sample points is accepted.

Step 7. Add the augmented data set S_{aug} to the data set S_k to obtain a new data set S'_k, and build a new Kriging model M'_k.

Step 8. The genetic algorithm (GA) is used to solve the optimization proposition based on the model M'_k, and the optimal solution $\mathbf{x}^{k'}$ and the predicted response $\hat{y}^{k'}$ are obtained.

Step 9. Determine whether the optimal solution $\mathbf{x}^{k'}$ satisfies the convergence criterion.

    a. If the optimal solution $\mathbf{x}^{k'}$ is located in the experiment region H_{cube}, it is considered that a local optimal result of the optimization problem is obtained, and the calculation process is finished;

    b. Otherwise, perform a experiment at the optimal solution $\mathbf{x}^{k'}$ to obtain the response $y^{k'}$, and step 10 is performed.

Step 10. Add the two optimization points $(\mathbf{x}^k, y^k)$ and $(\mathbf{x}^{k'}, y^{k'})$ and the augmented data set S_{aug} to the data set S'_0. Set $k = k + 1$, and then step 4 is performed.

In Step 1 to Step 5, by adding points sequentially and the MTD technique, the optimal solution region can be located as soon as possible with fewer data points. From Step 6 to Step 9, the augmented experiment are performed in the optimal solution region, and a locally augmented global model is established to ensure the optimality of the results.

4   Optimization of Fed-Batch Ethanol Fermentation Process

The fed-batch ethanol fermentation process with a batch time of 55 to 85 h is taken as the simulation experiment object to optimize the fed-batch process to maximize ethanol yield at the terminal time [5].

4.1   Feeding Process Settings

Let $u(\tau)$ be the feed rate, L/h. The reference feed rate is set according to the process of the fed-batch ethanol production with substrate and product inhibition kinetics [4]:

$$u_0(\tau) = \begin{cases} 0, & t \le t_s \\ \frac{t-t_s}{t_f-t_s} \frac{2\Delta V}{t_{fr}-t_{sr}}, & t_s < t \le t_f \end{cases}, \tag{19}$$

where
$$\tau = (t - t_s)/(t_f - t_s), \tag{20}$$
$$t_s = t_{sr} + \Delta t_{sr}w_1, \tag{21}$$
$$t_f = t_{fr} + \Delta t_{fr}w_2, \tag{22}$$

where t_{fr}, t_f, t_{sr}, t_s, Δt_{fr} and Δt_{sr} are reference fermentation time, specific fermentation time, reference feed switching time, specific feed switching time, and fermentation time offset and switching time offset, respectively. ΔV is the total amount of feed, where $t_{fr} = 70\,\text{h}$, $\Delta t_f = 15\,\text{h}$, $t_{sr} = 12\,\text{h}$, $\Delta t_s = 2\,\text{h}$, $\Delta V = 190\,\text{L}$.

The feed rate $u(\tau)$ is as in Eq. (4), and $\Delta u(\tau) = u_0(\tau)$. This paper only considers the feed rate $u(\tau)$, a time-varying manipulated variable. Then its corresponding dynamic factor $w(\tau)$ is expressed by the first three terms of SLP as

$$\begin{aligned} w(\tau) &= x_1^T [\varphi_0(\tau), \varphi_1(\tau), \varphi_2(\tau)]^T \\ &= x_{11}\varphi_0(\tau) + x_{12}\varphi_1(\tau) + x_{13}\varphi_2(\tau) \end{aligned} \tag{23}$$

Because $w(\tau) \in [-1, 1]$, the feed rate $u(\tau)$ varies from 0 to $2u_0(\tau)$. The fermenter volume is 200 L, and the fermentation broth volume has the following equation constraint at the end.

$$V_0 + \int_0^{t_f} u(\tau)dt = 200, \tag{24}$$

where V_0 is the initial fermentation broth volume, which is 10 L. According to Eqs. (19–23), Eq. (24) is simplified to $x_{12} = 3\,(t_{fr} - t_{sr})/(t_f - t_s) - 3x_{11} - 3$.

It can be seen that x_{12} can be represented by other factors, so it is not used as an independent factor to arrange experiments. To sum up, the factors involved in the experimental design are: feed switching time w_1 and fermentation time w_2, and dynamic sub-factors x_{11} and x_{13}.

An approximate model of ethanol production is built based on DoDE using the Kriging method. According to this model, the optimization proposition such as Eq. (25) is constructed.

$$\begin{aligned} &\underset{w_1,w_2,x_{11},x_{13}}{max} \quad y \\ &s.t. \quad 0 \le u(\tau) \le 12, \\ &\quad\quad -1 \le w_1, w_2 \le 1, \\ &\quad\quad -1 \le x_{11}, x_{12}, x_{13} \le 1, \\ &\quad\quad -1 \le x_{11} \pm x_{12} \pm x_{13} \le 1, \\ &\quad 174/(58 - 2w_1 + 15w_2) - 3x_{11} - x_{12} - 3 = 0. \end{aligned} \tag{25}$$

4.2   Results and Discussion

The optimization proposition of Eq. (25) is solved based on the iterative update and optimization algorithm of the Kriging model. The MAPE of the established model M_0 based on the initial experimental data set S_0 is 7.35%. After two experiment points are added and modeled, the Kriging model M_0' MAPE is 2.20%, which satisfies the preset accuracy. Solving the optimization proposition based on the model M_0', the obtained feed rate is shown by the blue dotted line in Fig. 2. The predicted yield of the model M_0' is 20470 g. The experiment is run at this feed rate, resulting in the expeiment yield of 19532 g. It can be seen that the Kriging model M_0' has a large deviation in the prediction of the ethanol production process. No measurement error is added to this result, but measurement error is added when used as modeling data. The same is true for the discussion that follows in this article.

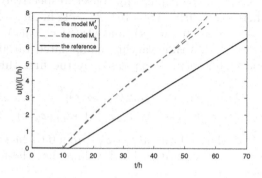

Fig. 2. Comparison of feed rate for model M_0' and model M_k. (Color figure online)

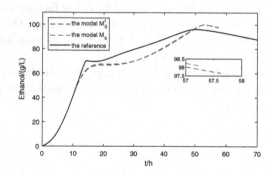

Fig. 3. Comparison of ethanol concentration for model M_0' and model M_k

Then, virtual samples are generated, and the model M_k is built and optimized again; the obtained feed rate is shown in the red dotted line in Fig. 2. The predicted ethanol yield is 20515 g, and the experiment yield is 19622 g. In Fig. 2, the solid black line is the reference feed rate. Figure 3 is the ethanol concentration corresponding to the feed rate in Fig. 2. The augmented experimental design and modeling optimization are carried out, and the experimental yield is 19664 g. So far, the first cycle execution of the algorithm as shown in Fig. 1 is completed. There is still a large deviation between the established prediction model and the ethanol production process, and the algorithm iteration needs to be continued. After three iterations again, the optimal solution $\mathbf{x} = [0.2625, 0.0625, -1.0000, -0.9000]$ that satisfies the convergence condition is obtained. The experiment is run under this solution $\mathbf{x}$ to obtain a maximum ethanol yield of 20210 g.

Under the condition of not generating virtual samples, the Kriging model iterative update and optimization algorithm is performed. After three iterations, the optimal solution satisfies the convergence condition; the optimal ethanol yield obtained by optimization is 19750 g. Comparing the results with and without adding virtual samples, it shows the effectiveness of introducing MTD technique for modeling optimization.

MDT technique generates an appropriate amount of virtual data based on experiment data, which reduces the proportion of augmented experiment data in the total modeling data. In this way, the influence of augmented data on the overall trend of the model is weakened. While improving the local accuracy of the model, it avoids the decline of global accuracy. At the same time, each generation of virtual samples is regenerated based on the experiment data in the entire experiment region, preventing the optimal solution from falling into a small region continuously.

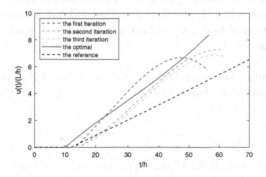

Fig. 4. Feed rate for algorithm iterations

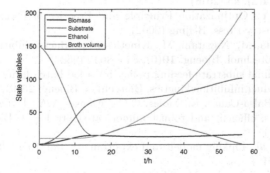

Fig. 5. State variable trajectory

Figure 4 shows the feed rate trajectory of each iteration of the Kriging iterative update and optimization method; the red solid line is the optimal feed rate corresponding to the optimal solution, and the black dotted line is the reference feed rate. Figure 5 shows the state change of biomass concentration, substrate concentration, ethanol concentration and fermentation broth volume under the optimal feed rate.

5 Conclusions

This article has presented the design of dynamic experiments method based on the Kriging model to optimize fed-batch ethanol production process. Firstly, a low-precision global model is built by sequentially adding points to the initial data set. Virtual samples are generated using MTD technique to construct a more stable new Kriging model for determining the optimal solution region. Then, a 1/2-fractional factorial design is performed in the optimal solution region to obtain the augmented experiment data set. A locally enhanced global model is built and optimized. Finally, the modeling and optimization process is iterated until the optimal solution meets the convergence criterion. The validity of MTD technique in this paper is verified by a comparative study of whether to add virtual samples. The iterative update and optimization algorithm is applied to ethanol production, which is the free terminal fed-batch fermentation process. The optimal solution of feed rate is convergent, and is of guiding significance for practical production.

Acknowledgements. This work is supported by National Natural Science Foundation (NNSF) of China under Grant 61833007.

References

1. Chang, Y.H., Chang, K.S., Chen, C.Y., Hsu, C.L., Chang, T.C., Jang, H.D.: Enhancement of the efficiency of bioethanol production by Saccharomyces cerevisiae via gradually batch-wise and fed-batch increasing the glucose concentration. Fermentation **4**(2), 45 (2018)
2. Chen, J., Li, Y.: Optimization Principle and Practice of Fermentation Process. Chemical Industry Press, Beijing (2002)
3. Aiba, S., Shoda, M., Nagatani, M.: Kinetics of product inhibition in alcohol fermentation. Biotechnol. Bioeng. **10**(6), 845–864 (1968)
4. Hong, J.: Optimal substrate feeding policy for a fed batch fermentation with substrate and product inhibition kinetics. Biotechnol. Bioeng. **28**(9), 1421–1431 (1986)
5. Banga, J.R., Balsa-Canto, E., Moles, C.G., Alonso, A.A.: Dynamic optimization of bioprocesses: efficient and robust numerical strategies. J. Biotechnol. **117**(4), 407–419 (2005)
6. Bonvin, D., et al.: Linking models and experiments. Ind. Eng. Chem. Res. **55**(25), 6891–6903 (2016)
7. Jacyna, J., Kordalewska, M., Markuszewski, M.J.: Design of Experiments in metabolomics-related studies: an overview. J. Pharm. Biomed. **164**, 598–606 (2019)

8. Fiordalis, A., Georgakis, C.: Data-driven, using design of dynamic experiments, versus model-driven optimization of batch crystallization processes. J Process Control. **23**(2), 179–188 (2013)
9. Georgakis, C.: Design of dynamic experiments: a data-driven methodology for the optimization of time-varying processes. Ind. Eng. Chem. Res. **52**(35), 12369–12382 (2013)
10. Wang, Z., Georgakis, C.: An in silico evaluation of data-driven optimization of biopharmaceutical processes. AIChE J. **63**(7), 2796–2805 (2017)
11. Jia, R., Mao, Z., He, D., Chu, F.: Hierarchical batch-to-batch optimization of cobalt oxalate synthesis process based on data-driven model. Chem. Eng. Res. Des. **144**, 185–197 (2019)
12. Georgakis, C., et al.: Data-driven optimization of an industrial batch polymerization process using the design of dynamic experiments methodology. Ind. Eng. Chem. Res. **50**(33), 11868–14000 (2020)
13. Myers, R.H.: Response surface methodology-current status and future directions. J. Qual. Technol. **31**(1), 30–44 (1999)
14. Li, D.C., Wu, C.S., Tsai, T.I., Lina, Y.S.: Using mega-trend-diffusion and artificial samples in small data set learning for early flexible manufacturing system scheduling knowledge. Comput. Oper. Res. **34**(4), 966–982 (2007)
15. Li, D.C., Chen, C.C., Chang, C.J., Lin, W.K.: A tree-based-trend-diffusion prediction procedure for small sample sets in the early stages of manufacturing systems. Expert Syst. Appl. **39**(1), 1575–1581 (2012)
16. Sacks, J., Welch, W.J., Mitchell, T.J., Wynn, H.P.: Design and analysis of computer experiments. Stat. Sci. **4**(4), 409–423 (1989)
17. Li, D.C., Wen, I.H.: A genetic algorithm-based virtual sample generation technique to improve small data set learning. Neurocomputing **143**, 222–230 (2014)
18. Montgomery, D.C.: Design and Analysis of Experiments. John wiley & sons, Hoboken (2017)
19. McKay, M.D., Beckman, R.J., Conover, W.J.: A comparison of three methods for selecting values of input variables in the analysis of output from a computer code. Technometrics **42**(1), 55–61 (2000)

Uncertain Economic Order Quantity Model for Perishable Items with Shelf Life

Yulin Yang and Yuhong Sheng[✉]

College of Mathematics and System Science, Xinjiang University, Urumqi, China
shengyuhong1@sina.com

Abstract. The early economic order quantity (EOQ) model is based on ideal conditions. It is called the traditional EOQ model. Its appearance marks the beginning of the quantitative scientific management stage in the field of operation and management. Based on it, a large number of quantitative analysis models and methods have emerged. In this paper, we study the EOQ model in which the demand for perishable items with shelf life varies with the sales price and inventory under an uncertain environment. This paper regards order cost, purchase cost, holding cost, deterioration cost, and deterioration recovery income as uncertain variables. According to the method of uncertainty theory, the expected value model of the EOQ model in an uncertain environment is established. By using the properties of uncertainty theory, it is proved that the expected value model can be transformed into the corresponding deterministic equivalent form. Based on these equivalence relations, a simulated annealing algorithm can be used to solve the optimal profit solution of an uncertain programming model. Finally, a numerical example is provided to highlight how the model is applied.

Keywords: Uncertainty theory · Uncertain programming · Expected value model · EOQ model · Inventory management

1 Introduction

With the development of e-commerce, the logistics industry ushered in rapid development. Inventory management is one of the significant branches of logistics science. The origins of inventory models can be traced back to the problem of bank cash flow in the late 19th century when Harris [1] investigated the reserve problem of bank money and developed a deterministic cash reserve model, which resulted in a simple formula for calculating the number of cash reserves, the originator of the later inventory control models. Wilson [2] derived the now well-known economic order quantity model (EOQ model) based on Harris' simple formula, also known as the Wilson model, and since then many scholars have conducted extensive research on the EOQ model.

In recent years, scholars all over the world have done the following research on the EOQ model. Datta et al. [3] established a relationship between stock quantities and inventory impact thresholds, giving an EOQ model in the case of impermissible stock-outs. Based on the findings of Datta et al., Urban [4] developed a model for the fluctuation of demand rate with stock quantity. Padmanabhan and Vrat [5] studied the impact of the level of shortage on lagged supply as customers' confidence in waiting for replenishment is more likely to be lost in the case of greater shortage phenomenon. Chang and Dye [6] considered that customers' confidence in waiting is more lost in the case of longer waiting time. However, Luo et al. [7] emphasized that it is crucial to take into account the impact of waiting time, selling price, as well as the customer's trust in waiting during a shortage period. However, Luo et al. [7] argued that it is crucial to consider both the customer's confidence in waiting in shortage times and the effect of waiting time and selling price on the lagged supply of shortage quantities, as well as the realistic inventory that affects the sales threshold. Tripathi [8] researched the novel use of an EOQ model for deteriorating items with time-sensitive demand, cash discounts, shortages, and allowable payment delays. In an EOQ model with upstream partial order-quantity-dependent trade credit and downstream full trade credit, Molamohamadi et al. [9] investigated ordering policies for a depreciating item. Sundararajan [10] investigated the EOQ model for non-transient perishable items. Arindum and Adrijit [11] proposed a time-variable linear demand EOQ model for defective items. Cenk [12] investigates the EOQ model for deteriorating items with optimal solutions for planned back orders. Noura [13] researched EOQ models of imperfect quality items and replenishment from different suppliers.

Due to the reality being very complex, many variables in the model can not be estimated. To complete the relevant replenishment task, we need to invite experts familiar with the field to estimate the relevant data. The estimated value given by experts is called "Belief Degree". By using the belief degree, we can give the budget and estimate of the problem, and then get a relatively reliable result. If probability theory is used to deal with the belief degree given by experts and models to solve practical problems, sometimes it may produce large errors. To avoid such mistakes, Liu [14] put forward the uncertainty theory in 2007 and improved it in 2009. Liu [15] introduced uncertainty theory into mathematical programming in 2009 and established uncertain programming. In recent years, uncertain programming has made new development. Some instances of these discoveries include uncertain single and bicriteria solid transportation problem [16,17], uncertain grain supply chain design [18], uncertain single-period supply chain problems [19], uncertain empty container allocation model [20], uncertain machine scheduling problem [21], uncertain inventory problem [22] and single-period inventory problem [23].

This paper proposes an EOQ model in which the demand for perishable items with shelf life varies with the sales price and inventory under an uncertain environment. The remainder of this paper is organized as follows. The expectation value model is used in Sect. 2 to create an EOQ model for uncertain environments. The model is resolved using the simulated annealing algorithm. After that, Sect. 3 conducts a numerical experiment. In Sect. 4, several conclusions are drawn.

2   Problem Description

In this section, this paper gives an uncertain EOQ model. In some actual inventory systems, the nature of the goods themselves will change over time. The most common is food products. With time, the products may deteriorate, rot, and so on. Therefore, in addition to the market demand, the factors causing the change in inventory are also caused by the goods themselves. This kind of product can be divided into two situations. First, products with a shelf life, which are valid before the shelf life, will become worthless goods after the shelf life. The second one is the continuous rotten products. The products are rotten continuously over time. The rotten goods are removed from the storage system, and the remaining goods are effective. This is the second case, and after deterioration can be recycled to the original manufacturer at a very low price.

2.1   Establishment of Uncertain EOQ Model

To begin with, this paper gives the corresponding assumptions and the notations are shown in Table 1.

(1) The demand for goods depends on the stock quantity and the selling price.
(2) The product has a shelf life and cannot be sold beyond the shelf life.
(3) The holding cost is nonlinear and changes with the change of stock.
(4) The replenishment capacity is unlimited, that is, no matter how much goods are replenished, it can be realized immediately.
(5) There is no replenishment lead time, that is, the goods are replenished immediately after the replenishment request is issued.
(6) Shortage is not allowed, that is, when the inventory is reduced to zero, the goods should be replenished.
(7) Assume that ξ_i are independent and the uncertainty distributions are Φ_i, $i = 1, 2, \cdots, 6$.
(8) In general, the recovery price of deteriorated goods is less than or equal to the purchase price, and the purchase price is less than or equal to the sales price.

In the inventory cycle of $[0, t]$, goods deterioration at a constant rate of η. According to the following function, the demand is determined by the retail price and stock quantity of goods,

$$P(x, S(t)) = \rho(x) + \gamma S(t). \tag{1}$$

Table 1. The corresponding notations.

Notations	Descriptions
ξ_1	The salvage price of unit deteriorated product
ξ_2	Deterioration cost per unit product
ξ_3	The purchase cost per unit product
ξ_4	The fixed holding cost per unit per unit time
ξ_5	The coefficient of holding cost function
ξ_6	Ordering cost(OC)
Γ	Order quantity
W	Maximum carrying capacity of warehouse
η	Product deterioration rate, $0 \leq \eta \leq 1$
γ	Sensitivity parameter of current stock quantities, $0 \leq \gamma \leq 1$
$S(t)$	Stock quantity at time t
$\rho(x)$	The function of demand changing with purchase price
$H(t)$	The function of holding cost changing with stock
$f(x,y)$	Total profit function
x	Selling price, which is a decision variable
y	Replenishment cycle, which is a decision variable
Φ_i	The uncertain distribution of ξ_i, $i = 1,2,3,4,5,6$

According to the demand Eq. (1) and the deterioration rate, the differential equation of stock quantity can be obtained as follows,

$$\frac{dS(t)}{dt} = -\rho(x) - \gamma S(t) - \eta S(t). \tag{2}$$

When the time is y, the stock quantity is 0, i.e.,

$$S(y) = 0. \tag{3}$$

According to the differential Eq. (2) and the initial condition (3), we can get the function of stock quantity changing with time as follows,

$$S(t) = \frac{\rho(x)}{\gamma + \eta} \left[\exp((\gamma + \eta)(y - t)) - 1 \right].$$

When $t = 0$, the stock quantity is equal to the order quantity of Γ, and the order quantity must be less than the maximum carrying quantity of the warehouse of W, i.e.,

$$\Gamma = S(0) = \frac{\rho(x)}{\gamma + \eta} \left[\exp((\gamma + \eta)y) - 1 \right] \leq W.$$

The change function of holding cost with stock quantity is as follows,

$$H(t) = \xi_4 + \xi_5 \cdot S(t) + (S(t))^2$$

$$= \frac{1}{(\gamma+\eta)^2} \cdot \{\xi_4(\gamma+\eta) + \xi_5\rho(x)(\gamma+\eta)\left[\exp((\gamma+\eta)(y-t)) - 1\right]$$

$$+ \{\rho(x)\left[\exp((\gamma+\eta)(y \quad t)) \quad 1\right]\}^2\}.$$

Sales income (SI) is

$$SI = x \int_0^y P(x, S(t))dt$$

$$= \frac{1}{(\gamma+\eta)^2} \cdot \{xy\eta\rho(x)(\gamma+\eta) + x\gamma\rho(x)\left(\exp((\gamma+\eta)y) - 1\right)\}.$$

Recovery Income (RI) of Deteriorated Products is

$$RI = \xi_1\left(\Gamma - \int_0^y (\rho(x) + \gamma S(t))\, dt\right)$$

$$= \frac{\xi_1}{(\gamma+\eta)^2}\{\rho(x)\left[\exp((\gamma+\eta)y) - 1\right]$$

$$- \left[y\eta(\gamma+\eta)\rho(x) + \gamma\rho(x)\left(\exp((\gamma+\eta)y) - 1\right)\right]\}.$$

Holding Cost (HC) is

$$HC = \int_0^y H(t)S(t)dt$$

$$= y\xi_4 + \left(y + \frac{\exp((\gamma+\eta)y)\cdot(\exp((\gamma+\eta)y) - 4) + 3}{2(\gamma+\eta)}\right)\left(\frac{\rho(x)}{\gamma+\eta}\right)^2$$

$$- \frac{1}{(\gamma+\eta)^2}\left(\xi_5 y\rho(x)(\gamma+\eta) + \xi_5\rho(x)\left[\exp(y(\gamma+\eta)) - 1\right]\right).$$

Purchase Cost (PC) is

$$PC = \xi_3\Gamma = \frac{\rho(x)\xi_3}{\gamma+\eta}\left[\exp((\gamma+\eta)y) - 1\right].$$

Deterioration Cost (DC) is

$$DC = \xi_2\left(\Gamma - \int_0^y (\rho(x) + \gamma S(t))\, dt\right)$$

$$= \xi_2\left\{\Gamma - \left[\rho(x)\cdot y \cdot \frac{\eta}{\gamma+\eta} + \frac{\gamma\rho(x)}{(\gamma+\eta)^2}\left(\exp((\gamma+\eta)y) - 1\right)\right]\right\}.$$

Therefore, the total profit of each cycle = Sales Income + Recovery Income of Deteriorated Products - Order cost - Holding Cost - Purchase Cost - Deteriorating Cost, i.e.,

$$f(x, y) = SI + RI - OC - HC - PC - DC$$

$$= \frac{1}{(\gamma + \eta)^2} \cdot \{xy\eta\rho(x)(\gamma + \eta) + x\gamma\rho(x) (\exp((\gamma + \eta)y) - 1)\} + \frac{\xi_1}{(\gamma + \eta)^2}$$

$$\cdot \{\rho(x) [\exp((\gamma + \eta)y) - 1] - [y\eta(\gamma + \eta)\rho(x) + \gamma\rho(x) (\exp((\gamma + \eta)y) - 1)]\}$$

$$- \xi_6 - y\xi_4 + \left(y + \frac{\exp((\gamma + \eta)y) \cdot (\exp((\gamma + \eta)y) - 4) + 3}{2(\gamma + \eta)}\right) \left(\frac{\rho(x)}{\gamma + \eta}\right)^2$$

$$+ \frac{1}{(\gamma + \eta)^2} (\xi_5 y\rho(x)(\gamma + \eta) + \xi_5\rho(x) [\exp(y(\gamma + \eta)) - 1])$$

$$- \frac{\rho(x)\xi_3}{\gamma + \eta} [\exp((\gamma + \eta)y) - 1] - \frac{\xi_2}{(\gamma + \eta)^2} \{\rho(x)(\gamma + \eta) [\exp((\gamma + \eta)y) - 1]$$

$$- [y\eta(\gamma + \eta)\rho(x) + \gamma\rho(x) (\exp((\gamma + \eta)y) - 1)]\} .$$

Since the total profit function itself is an uncertain variable, it is meaningless to minimize the total profit function. Assumed the expected value of variable ξ_i exists, then the expected value of $f(x, y)$ also exists. Therefore, in order to maximize the anticipated value of the total profit, x and y must be solved in the best possible way. The expectation model we have is shown below.

$$\begin{cases} \max E\left[f\left(x, y\right)\right] \\ \text{subject to:} \\ \quad \mathcal{M}\{\xi_3 \leq x\} \geq \alpha \\ \quad 0 \leq \eta \leq 1 \\ \quad y \geq 0 \end{cases}$$

where x is the selling price of goods, which is a decision variable. Due to ξ_3 being an uncertain variable and cannot be directly compared with a constant, we compare the expected value of purchase cost and sales price. We must find the best value of x and y and assume x^* and y^* to maximize the value of $E\left[f\left(x, y\right)\right]$. Where $E\left[f\left(x, y\right)\right]$ is as follows.

$$E\left[f\left(x,y\right)\right] = \int_0^1 \Psi^{-1}(\alpha)\mathrm{d}\alpha$$

$$= \int_0^1 \frac{1}{(\gamma+\eta)^2} \cdot \{xy\eta\rho(x)(\gamma+\eta) + x\gamma\rho(x)\left(\exp((\gamma+\eta)y) - 1\right)\} + \frac{\Phi_1^{-1}(\alpha)}{(\gamma+\eta)^2}$$

$$\cdot \{\rho(x)\left[\exp((\gamma+\eta)y) - 1\right] - \left[y\eta(\gamma+\eta)\rho(x) + \gamma\rho(x)\left(\exp((\gamma+\eta)y) - 1\right)\right]\}$$

$$- \Phi_6^{-1}(\alpha) - y\Phi_4^{-1}(\alpha) + \left(y + \frac{\exp((\gamma+\eta)y) \cdot (\exp((\gamma+\eta)y) - 4) + 3}{2(\gamma+\eta)}\right)$$

$$\cdot \left(\frac{\rho(x)}{\gamma+\eta}\right)^2 + \frac{1}{(\gamma+\eta)^2}\left(\Phi_5^{-1}(\alpha)y\rho(x)(\gamma+\eta) + \Phi_5^{-1}(\alpha)\rho(x)\left[\exp(y(\gamma+\eta)) - 1\right]\right)$$

$$- \frac{\rho(x)\Phi_3^{-1}(\alpha)}{\gamma+\eta}\left[\exp((\gamma+\eta)y) - 1\right] - \frac{\Phi_2^{-1}(\alpha)}{(\gamma+\eta)^2}\{\rho(x)(\gamma+\eta)\left[\exp((\gamma+\eta)y) - 1\right]$$

$$- \left[y\eta(\gamma+\eta)\rho(x) + \gamma\rho(x)\left(\exp((\gamma+\eta)y) - 1\right)\right]\}\,\mathrm{d}\alpha$$

$$= \frac{1}{(\gamma+\eta)^2} \cdot \{xy\eta\rho(x)(\gamma+\eta) + x\gamma\rho(x)\left(\exp((\gamma+\eta)y) - 1\right)\} + \frac{\int_0^1 \Phi_1^{-1}(\alpha)\mathrm{d}\alpha}{(\gamma+\eta)^2}$$

$$\cdot \{\rho(x)\left[\exp((\gamma+\eta)y) - 1\right] - \left[y\eta(\gamma+\eta)\rho(x) + \gamma\rho(x)\left(\exp((\gamma+\eta)y) - 1\right)\right]\}$$

$$- y\int_0^1 \Phi_4^{-1}(\alpha)\mathrm{d}\alpha + \left(y + \frac{\exp((\gamma+\eta)y) \cdot (\exp((\gamma+\eta)y) - 4) + 3}{2(\gamma+\eta)}\right)\left(\frac{\rho(x)}{\gamma+\eta}\right)^2$$

$$+ \frac{1}{(\gamma+\eta)^2}\left(\int_0^1 \Phi_5^{-1}(\alpha)\mathrm{d}\alpha y\rho(x)(\gamma+\eta) + \int_0^1 \Phi_5^{-1}(\alpha)\mathrm{d}\alpha\rho(x)\left[\exp(y(\gamma+\eta)) - 1\right]\right)$$

$$- \frac{\rho(x)\int_0^1 \Phi_3^{-1}(\alpha)\mathrm{d}\alpha}{\gamma+\eta}\left[\exp((\gamma+\eta)y) - 1\right] - \frac{\int_0^1 \Phi_2^{-1}(\alpha)\mathrm{d}\alpha}{(\gamma+\eta)^2}\{\rho(x)(\gamma+\eta)$$

$$\cdot \left[\exp((\gamma+\eta)y) - 1\right] - \left[y\eta(\gamma+\eta)\rho(x) + \gamma\rho(x)\left(\exp((\gamma+\eta)y) - 1\right)\right]\} - \int_0^1 \Phi_6^{-1}(\alpha)\mathrm{d}\alpha.$$

Such an uncertain optimization model is transformed into a crisp optimization model. This paper uses the expected value model to solve this uncertain model, and the uncertain objective constraint is also replaced by its expected value. The model is resolved using the simulated annealing algorithm.

2.2 Model Implementation

In this subsection, to determine the best profit margin for perishable goods in an uncertain environment, a simulated annealing algorithm will be applied. The simulated annealing (SA) was first proposed by Metropolis [24] in 1953, which is a probabilistic technique for estimating the global optimum of a function. And then the concept of annealing was effectively incorporated into combinatorial optimization by Kirkpatrick [25] in 1983.

The SA algorithm is based on the solid annealing principle, in which the solid is heated to a high enough temperature and then progressively cooled (that is, annealing) to make it reach the lowest energy point. On the contrary, if the temperature drops rapidly (i.e. quenching), it will not reach the lowest point. When the temperature is high, the internal energy of the internal particles is large, and the particles may move anywhere inside the solid. When the temperature slowly cools down, the internal energy of the particles decreases, and the particles become ordered. Finally the solid cools down or reaches equilibrium and stability, the position of the particle is fixed, where the internal energy is minimized and the optimal solution can be obtained.

The algorithm steps is as follows.

Step 1. Given initial temperature T_0, and initial point $x_0 = (x_{01}, x_{02})$, determine the point's function value $f(x_0)$.

Step 2. Randomly generate disturbance Δx, and get new point $x_0^* = x_0 + \Delta x$, calculate the new point function value $f(x_0^*)$, and the difference of function values $\Delta f = f(x_0^*) - f(x_0)$.

Step 3. If $\Delta f \leq 0$, as the starting point for the following simulation, the new position is accepted.

Step 4. If $\Delta f > 0$, we calculate the new point acceptance probability: $P(\Delta f) = \exp(-\Delta f K \cdot T)$ and generate pseudo-random numbers r with uniform distribution on $[0, 1]$. If $P(\Delta f) \geq r$, the new point will be accepted as the initial point of the next simulation. Otherwise, the original point will continue to be used as the starting point of the following simulation and the new point will be abandoned.

Step 5. The temperature is attenuated, and the second to fourth steps are repeated under the new temperature until the end temperature is reached.

Step 6. Output results x_0^* and $f(x_0^*)$.

3   Numerical Examples

In this section, a numerical example is provided to highlight how the model is applied.

Example. A supermarket orders milk products. The purchase cost ξ_3, deterioration cost ξ_2, and salvage price of unit deteriorated product ξ_1 of each box of the milk products are linear uncertain variables. And $\xi_1 \sim \mathcal{L}(5, 15)$, $\xi_2 \sim \mathcal{L}(3, 7)$, $\xi_3 \sim \mathcal{L}(20, 40)$. The constant holding cost ξ_4 per box of milk per unit time, the holding cost function coefficient ξ_5, and the order cost ξ_6 are all normal uncertain variables. And $\xi_4 \sim \mathcal{N}(5, 8)$, $\xi_5 \sim \mathcal{N}(2, 4)$, $\xi_6 \sim \mathcal{N}(300, 9)$. Suppose that the maximum carrying capacity of the warehouse W is 10000 cases, the deterioration rate η of the product is 0.01, the sensitivity parameter γ of current stock quantities is 0.4, and the demand function of the change of the sales price is $\rho(x) = 100 - 0.5x - 0.01x^2$. Find the best selling price x^* and the best cycle y^*, and then calculate the maximum total profit $f(x^*, y^*)$ of each cycle.

The total profit function $f(x, y)$ per cycle is also an uncertain variable. The inverse distribution and expectation values of the uncertain variable ξ_i, where $i = 1, 2, \cdots, 6$, are obtained.

Next, a simulated annealing algorithm is used to solve this example. Given initial temperature $T_0 = 100$, the annealing rate is 0.96. Use step 1 to step 6 above to get the results x^*, y^* and $f(x^*, y^*)$.

This paper uses MATLAB to implement this algorithm. The results are shown in Fig. 1. We know that when $x = 68.4$ and $y = 1.35$, the maximum profit margin is $f(x^*, y^*) = 492.4992$.

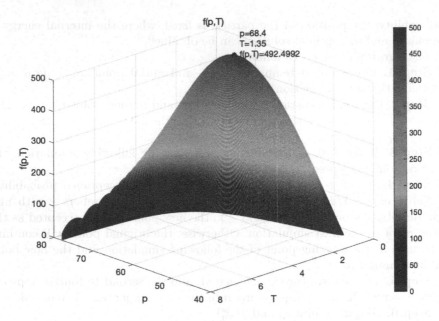

Fig. 1. The model result

Therefore, the milk purchased by the supermarket is sold at 68.4, the order cycle is 1.35 days, and the best profit is 492.4992.

4   Conclusion

Uncertainty theory provides a new method to solve the EOQ model. This paper takes perishable goods with a shelf life as the research object, takes order cost, purchasing cost, holding cost, deterioration cost, and deterioration recovery income as uncertain variables, takes holding cost as a function of stock, and the demand is driven by stock amount and sales price. The EOQ model's expected value model is established utilizing the uncertainty theory. Based on the uncertainty theory, the model is transformed into the form of certainty, and the simulated annealing algorithm is used to solve the maximum total profit. Finally, taking the sales and storage of dairy products in a supermarket as an example, the simulated annealing algorithm is utilized to solve the optimal solution, that is, the largest overall profit of the uncertain model, and the calculation process is given. The innovation of this paper: an uncertain programming model of economic replenishment lot size model is proposed, which considers the fact that demand and holding cost are nonlinear.

Acknowledgements. This research is funded by the National Natural Science Foundation of China (Grant No. 12061072), the Natural Science Foundation of Xinjiang (Grant No. 2020D01C017) and the Xinjiang Key Laboratory of Applied Mathematics (Grant No. XJDX1401).

References

1. Harris, F.: How many parts to make at once. Factory Maga. Manag. **10**(2), 135–136 (1913)
2. Wilson R. H.: A scientific routine for stock control. Harvard University (1934)
3. Datta, T.K., Pal, A.K.: A note on an inventory model with inventory-level-dependent demand rate. J. Oper. Res. Soc. **41**(10), 971–975 (1990)
4. Urban, T.L.: An inventory model with an inventory-level-dependent demand rate and relaxed terminal conditions. J. Oper. Res. Soc. **43**(7), 721–724 (1992)
5. Padmanabhan, G., Vrat, P.: Inventory model with a mixture of back orders and lost sales. Int. J. Syst. Sci. **21**(8), 1721–1726 (1990)
6. Chang, H., Dye, C.: An EOQ model for deteriorating items with time varying demand and partial backlogging. J. Oper. Res. Soc. **50**(11), 1176–1182 (1999)
7. Luo, B., Wang, J., Pan, X.: An EOQ Model of price increasing and two-level stock-dependent selling rate. Ind. Eng. 1 **15**(6), 32 36 (2012)
8. Tripathi, R.P.: Innovative approach of EOQ structure for decaying items with time sensitive demand, cash- discount, shortages and permissible delay in payments. Int. J. Appl. Comput. Math. **7**(3), 1–16 (2021). https://doi.org/10.1007/s40819-021-01003-8
9. Molamohamadi Z., Mirzazadeh A., Konstantaras I.: Ordering policies of a deteriorating item in an EOQ model under upstream partial order-quantity-dependent trade credit and downstream full trade credit. Adv. Oper. Res. **2021** (2021)
10. Sundararajan, R., Palanivel, M., Uthayakumar, R.: An EOQ model of non-instantaneous deteriorating items with price, time-dependent demand and backlogging. J. Control Decis. **8**(2), 135–154 (2021)
11. Arindum, M., Goswami, A.: Application of uncertain programming to an inventory model for imperfect quantity under time varying demand. Adv. Model. Optim. **15**(3), 565–582 (2013)
12. Cenk, C.: A simple derivation of the optimal solution for the EOQ model for deteriorating items with planned backorders. Appl. Math. Model. **89**(2), 1373–1381 (2021)
13. Noura Y.: The EOQ model with items of imperfect quality and replenishment from different suppliers. Int. J. Oper. Res. **40**(1) (2020)
14. Liu, B.: Uncertainty Theory, 2nd edn. Springer, Berlin (2007). https://doi.org/10.1007/978-3-540-73165-8
15. Liu, B.: Theory and Practice of Uncertain Programming, 2nd edn. Springer, Berlin (2009). https://doi.org/10.1007/978-3-540-89484-1
16. Chen, L., Peng, J., Zhang, B.: Uncertain goal programming models for bicriteria solid transportation problem. Appl. Soft Comput. **51**, 49–59 (2017)
17. Cui Q., Sheng Y.: Uncertain programming model for solid transportation problem. Inf. Int. Interdisc. J. **16**(2A), 1207–1214 (2013)
18. Ding S.: A new uncertain programming model for grain supply chain design. Inf. Int. Interdisc. J. **16**(2), 1069–1076 (2013)
19. Ding, S.: Belief degree of optimal models for uncertain single-period supply chain problem. Soft Comput. **22**(17), 5879–5887 (2018)
20. Jiang G.: An uncertain programming model of chance constrains for empty container allocation. Inf. Int. Interdisc. J. **16**(2A), 1119–1124, (2013)
21. Li, R., Liu, G.: An uncertain goal programming model for machine scheduling problem. J. Intell. Manuf. **28**(3), 689–694 (2017)

22. Rong, L.: Two new uncertainty programming models of inventory with uncertain costs. J. Inf. Comput. Sci. **8**(2), 280–288 (2011)
23. Qin, Z., Samarjit, K.: Single-period Inventory Problem under Uncertain Environment. Appl. Math. Comput. **219**(18), 9630–9638 (2013)
24. Metropolis, N., Rosenbluth, A., Rosenbluth, M., Teller, A., Teller, E.: Equation of state calculations by fast computing machines. J. Chem. Phys. **21**(6), 1087–1092 (1953)
25. Kirkpatrick, S., Gelatt, J., Vecchi, M.: Optimization by simulated annealing. Science **220**(4598), 671–680 (1983)

Distributed Processing of Continuous Range Queries over Moving Objects

Hui Zhu[1] and Ziqiang Yu[1,2(✉)]

[1] Yantai University, Yantai, China
zqyu@ytu.edu.cn, wumie698@163.com
[2] Key Laboratory of Urban Land Resources Monitoring and Simulation, MNR,
Shenzhen, China

Abstract. Monitoring range queries over moving objects is essential to extensive location-based services. The challenge faced with these location-based services is having to process numerous concurrent range queries over a large volume of moving objects. However, the existing range query processing algorithms are almost centralized based on one single machine, which are hard to address the challenge due to the limited memory and computing resources. To address this issue, we propose a distributed search solution for processing concurrent range queries over moving objects in this work. Firstly, a Distributed Dynamic Index (DDI) that consists of a global grid index and local dynamic M-ary tree indexes was proposed to maintain the moving objects and support the search algorithm. Next, a Distributed Range Query Algorithm (DRQA) was designed based on DDI, which introduces an incremental search strategy to monitor the range queries as objects evolve; during the process, it further designs a computation sharing paradigm for processing multiple concurrent queries by making full use of their common computation to decrease the search cost. Finally, three object datasets with different distributions were simulated on a New York road network and three baseline methods were introduced to more sufficiently evaluate the performance of our proposal. Compared with state-of-the-art method, the initial query cost of the DRQA algorithm reduces by 22.7% and the incremental query cost drops by 15.2%, which certifies the superiority of our method over existing approaches.

Keywords: Continuous range query · Moving objects · DDI (Distributed Dynamic Index) · DRQA (Distributed Range Query Algorithm) · Location-based services

1 Introduction

At present, location-based services are increasingly used in daily life. Continuous range query over a large volume of moving objects is essential to many location-based services. The car-hailing service needs to instantly find cabs within a

Supported by the Open Fund of Key Laboratory of Urban Land Resources Monitoring and Simulation, Ministry of Natural Resources.

certain range when a user submits a request. Beside, it also need to monitor the nearby cabs when the user is moving, where the user and cabs can be regarded as a query point and moving objects respectively, then the task is an essential continuous range query over moving objects. Given a set O of moving objects, a query point q_i and its query range qr_i, our goal is to search moving objects covered by qr_i as the initial result of q_i and continuously update the query result of q_i as objects move.

Continuous range queries over moving objects have been extensively studied [5, 6, 25, 32], but most of them are centralized and cannot be used to handle extensive concurrent queries over a large volume of moving objects because of the limitation of memory and computing resources. Hence, this work aims to address this issue in a distributed search principle designed based on a cluster of servers.

However, the existing index structures used for processing range queries are usually R-Tree or the grid index structure, and both of them have their own flaws when deployed in a distributed environment. In particular, if we deploy a R-tree [18, 21, 35] in a cluster of servers, where each server keeps a part of nodes in the R-tree. As nodes in R-tree continuously merge or split, which are expensive in a distributed environment as these nodes lie in multiple different servers. The grid index structure [4, 12, 14, 16, 28, 33, 34, 38] is easy to be deployed on a cluster of servers. However, when the algorithm based on grid index processes cells partially intersecting with the query range, it needs to scan all moving objects in each of these cells to detect which objects are covered by the query range, which will incur a great query cost when processing a large number of cells intersecting with query ranges. In this paper, the query range qr_i of query q_i can be any polynomial shape. For simplicity, we assume that the query range is a circle.

There are some existing works [2, 10, 20, 27, 36] that adopt the distributed paradigm to process range queries. In the distributed paradigm, they treat each mobile device as a moving object, and the mobile devices and the data center constitute a distributed computing environment. As such, they can distribute the range query overhead to the mobile devices. However, the distributed paradigm requires the mobile devices to be powerful. However, not all mobile devices have enough computing resources, so the application of this approaches is limited. Moreover, frequent message transportation between mobile devices will cause considerable communication costs, which cannot be ignored and even dominate the total costs of these approaches.

In order to address above issues, we propose a distributed dynamic index (DDI for short), which is composed of a grid index and dynamic M-ary tree indexes. The entire query area is divided into $n \times n$ cells with equal sizes, and each cell records the moving objects it contains. Each cell is independent and can be deployed to different servers. To reinforce the pruning capability of the grid index, we construct a dynamic M-ary tree for each cell. The "dynamic" means the depth of the M-ary tree can be dynamically adjusted to adapt the density of moving objects in different regions. When constructing the M-tree, each cell is regarded as a root node. Beside, m child nodes are added to the root when the number of objects in the cell is greater than α. The moving objects in the cell are stored in the leaf nodes of the M-ary tree. When a leaf node contains more than α objects, m child nodes will be added into this leaf node and the lead node becomes a non-leaf node. The operation will proceed in this way until no leaf node contains more than α objects. If a set of leaf nodes with the same parent node have less than β objects, their parents will inherit their objects and the leaf nodes will be removed from the M-ary tree. DDI can improve the pruning power for processing range queries. As to each cell intersecting with the query range, we can explore its M-ary tree to identify the nodes that are completely covered by the query range and their objects have no need to be scanned.

Since each cell in the DDI is independent of each other, the whole index structure is easy to be deployed to distributed computing environments with Master-Worker architecture. Based on the DDI, this paper further proposes a Distributed Range Query Algorithm (DRQA for short). The algorithm decomposes each range query into sub-queries on multiple cells, which can be conducted by multiple servers in parallel to improve the query efficiency. When the range query continuously move, the DRQA incrementally computes the latest result at the current moment using the previous results of the query as much as possible. In addition, each server adopts a shared computing mechanism, which shares the computing results when processing multiple concurrent queries involve the same query region.

Main contributions can be summarized as follows:

1. We propose DDI that can be easily deployed in distributed computing environments and can dynamically adjust the index granularity of each cell according to the distribution density of moving objects. Moreover, DDI can help the search algorithm to reduce the traversal of unnecessary moving objects and provide greater pruning capability.
2. We propose DRQA, a Distributed Range Query Algorithm for processing extensive concurrent range queries over a large volume of moving objects. To efficiently monitor the results of continuous range queries, an incremental search is introduced to avoid the overhaul computation in each snapshot.
3. We deploy the proposed algorithm on Storm, a distributed computing platform for streaming data, and introduce three baseline methods into our experiments. Extensive experiments are conducted to verify the superiority of our proposal over the existing solutions.

The rest of the paper is organized as follows. Section 2 briefly discusses the related work about processing range queries. Section 3 gives some related definitions. Section 4 presents DDI index structure and DRQA algorithm is discussed in Sect. 5. The experimental results are reported in Sect. 6. Finally, the paper is summarized in Sect. 7.

2   Related Work

Range query over moving objects has been widely studied as a fundamental problem in the field of location-based services. In the following, we will introduce the moving object index structure, query scenarios and computational models based on the existing work.

The grid index is widely used for moving object queries [4,12,15,19,22,24, 28,33,34,37]. Kalashnikov et al. [12] proposed that the query performance based on the grid index is superior compared with other index structures. A sorting-based optimization method was also proposed to improve the cache hit rate. Dong et al. [28] and Tianyang Dong et al. [4] established a moving object grid index, which can know the road network according to the orientation to determine moving objects to move to the query point. Zhongbin Xue et al. [33] proposed a memory-based high-throughput moving object range query algorithm, which can execute multiple queries at a time. Yu et al. [34] proposed a grid-based stretchable algorithm. The algorithm not only indexes moving objects efficiently, but also improves query performance and robustness when moving objects are densely distributed. Shen et al. [24] proposed a grid-based index structure. It expands resident areas for monitoring continuous range queries in moving or common computing environments. Zhang et al. [37] presented an efficient grid-based SPatial inteRpolation function (SPRIG) for processing the range query and the kNN query.

In order to solve the above problem, the papers [3,7–9,17] introduced the concept of 'safety zone'. The 'safety zone' is a query movement area. It is calculated based on the distance of the nearest moving object inside or outside the query range boundary to the query boundary. In this region, the movement of the query point does not cause any change in the query result. Haidar et al. [8,9] studied a static approximate distance search algorithm, which can quickly determine the approximate range of the upper or lower bound of the 'safety zone'. Then the queries located in the specified safety zone are not reduplicate counted.

With the increasing popularity of indoor location services, the study of distance-aware queries for indoor moving objects has attracted attention from scholars [1,13,23,29,30,39] in the past few years. Wang et al. [29] defined and classified moving object relationships with uncertain indoor distances. Shao et al [23] pointed out that the features of the indoor space are underutilized by existing index structures and query algorithms. Therefore, they are proposed two new index structures with full consideration of indoor characteristics. They are Indoor Partitioning Tree (IP-Tree) and Vivid Indoor Partitioning Tree (VIP-Tree) respectively. Sultan et al. [1] proposed the C-tree index structure based on the grid index. C-tree can efficiently serve the indoor spatial query, the topological query, the abutting query and the density-based query.

Most of the above algorithms are centralized algorithms, limited by the computational capacity of the single node. Therefore, centralized algorithms are difficult to cope with large volume of concurrent queries. Silvestri et al. [26] used a parallel algorithm based on the mixed use of the CPU and GPU to handle large volume of moving object range queries. In addition, several researchers have studied distributed search algorithms for moving object range queries. Among them, the idea of edge computing for range queries are adopted in paper [2,10,36]. Such algorithms usually require mobile terminals with strong computing power, which limits the applicability of such algorithms. In contrast, the idea of distributed computing based on server clusters are adopted in paper [11,31,35]. Jun Feng et al. [11] proposed a static range query algorithm. The algorithm recursively traverses the road segments adjacent to the query point to update the moving objects on the road segments within the query range. However, the creation of multiple index tables imposes a huge additional load on the system when the algorithm handles large-scale concurrent queries.

To address the above problem, Jiangfeng Xu et al. [31] proposed a multidimensional index framework New-grid. This framework uses a linearization technique based on Hilbert curves to solve this problem, and points out that the grid index has good scalability in a distributed environment. However, these algorithms still need to traverse all the moving objects in the candidate cells when dealing with candidate cells that intersect with range queries. Yu et al. [35] proposed a hybrid distributed index structure based on a grid index and R-tree to solve the problem. The problem of the index structure is that the R-tree corresponding to each cell is constantly updated from the bottom up when the position of moving objects changes. It needs to be maintained frequently, resulting in costly index maintenance. In this paper, sharing computation results for multiple concurrent range queries involving the same region can effectively improve query efficiency.

3   Preliminaries

Definition 1 (Continuous range query). *A continuous range query q_i is represented by a triple $\{t_{q_i}^s, t_{q_i}^e, sq_i\}$, where $t_{q_i}^s$ is the start time of q_i, and $t_{q_i}^e$ is the end time of q_i, and qr_i is the query range of q_i.*

Definition 2 (Cell). *The search area is divided into equal-sized cells. Each cell ce_i uses three lists MOL_i, FCL_i and PCL_i to record respectively the moving objects contained in cell ce_i, the query point whose query range qr_i completely covers cell ce_i and the query point whose query range qr_i partially covers ce_i.*

Definition 3 (Candidate cell). *For a range query q_i, ce_i is a candidate cell of q_i if the cell ce_i completely or partially covered by qr_i. $ce_k \subseteq sq_i$ means that ce_k is completely covered by qr_i. $ce_k \subset sq_i$ means that ce_k is partially covered by qr_i.*

4   Distributed Index Structure

In this section, we first discuss the structure of Distributed Dynamic Index (DDI for short) in Sect. 4.1, and then introduce the construction of DDI in Sect. 4.2. In Sect. 4.3, we study the maintenance of DDI as object evolve.

4.1   Structure of DDI

We propose a distributed dynamic index (DDI for short), which consists of a grid index and dynamic M-ary trees.

Grid Index. First, the whole search area is divided into equal-sized cells. Each cell ce_i maintains three lists MOL_i, FCL_i, and PCL_i, which respectively record the moving objects contained in cell ce_i, the query point whose query range qr_i completely covers cell ce_i, and the query point whose query range qr_i partially covers ce_i. We will build a dynamic M-ary tree T_i for the cell ce_i when the number of moving objects in cell ce_i exceeds the threshold α.

Dynamic M-ary Tree. Firstly, each leaf node ln_f of the M-ary tree maintains a moving objects list QL_f, which records IDs of these moving objects covered by the leaf node. Each non-leaf node tn_i in the M-ary tree maintains a query list QL_i, which records query IDs that the query range qr_i can fully cover the node tn_i. Each leaf node ln_f also maintains a query list QL_i, which records the query IDs whose query scope completely covers the leaf node or partially intersects with the leaf node. As objects move, T_i can dynamically adjust the depth of the M-ary tree according to the distribution density of moving objects. Specifically, if the number of moving objects in a leaf node of T_i is equal to or greater than the specified threshold, the leaf node will be recursively split until the number of moving objects in each leaf node is less than α. If a set of leaf nodes with the same parent node have less than β objects, their parents will inherit their objects and the leaf nodes will be removed from the M-ary tree.

The purpose of introducing the dynamic M-ary tree index structure into the grid index is to avoid traversing all moving objects in a cell when dealing with a range query that partially intersects with the cell. Specifically, if the cell ce_i contains a large volume of moving objects and partially intersects with the query range qr_i, searching for the moving objects belonging to cell ce_i and covered by qr_i needs to traverse all the moving objects in the cell, which wastes a lot of computational resources. After the dynamic M-ary tree is introduced into each cell, the query algorithm can get accurate query results only by traversing partial nodes of the M-ary tree, which effectively reduces the computational cost.

In DDI, each cell is an independent index unit. Each cell can be deployed to any server of a distributed cluster. Each sever can maintain any number of grid indexes according to its own ability.

4.2   Construction of DDI

Building DDI is to insert moving objects and continuous range queries into different cells as well as their corresponding M-ary trees.

Object Insertion. Firstly, we search the current cell ce_j where mo_i is located. Then we add mo_i into the moving object list MOL_j of the cell ce_j. Finally, we insert mo_i into the M-ary tree T_i corresponds to ce_j. In the procedure of inserting the M-ary tree, we scan down layer by layer from the root node of T_i to determine if the leaf node ln_f covers $mo_i(x_i, y_i)$. Then mo_i is added to the moving object list NL_f of ln_f. If the number of moving objects in the leaf node ln_f reaches α, the leaf node ln_f is split into m new leaf nodes, and all moving objects in ln_f are inserted into the corresponding new leaf nodes.

Continuous Range Query Insertion. Firstly, we search for cells associated with the range query q_i. For the cell ce_j that is completely covered by the query range qr_i, q_i is directly added into the query list FCL_j of cell ce_j. For the cell ce_j that is partially covered by the query range qr_i, q_i is added into the query list PCL_j of cell ce_j. Next, we perform a top-to-bottom hierarchical traversal of the M-ary tree T_l in this cell to find a M-ary tree node tn_i that is completely covered by qr_i. q_i is added into the query list QL_i of node tn_i. And then we stop processing the child node of tn_i. If a node tn_j in the M-ary tree T_l partially intersects with the query range qr_i, we further traverse the child nodes of node tn_j until the leaf nodes. According to the insertion principle of q_i, only leaf nodes may partially intersect with qr_i among all nodes recorded in the M-ary tree T_l. Therefore, all moving objects in the node area are covered by qr_i if a non-leaf node of T_l records q_i.

4.3 Maintenance of DDI

With the location of moving objects and range query points changing, the DDI needs to be maintained in real time. In the following, we discuss the maintenance of moving objects and the maintenance of range queries respectively.

Maintenance of Moving Objects. We suppose the moving object mo_j moves from (x_j, y_j) to (x'_j, y'_j). For the cells and corresponding M-ary trees related with (x_j, y_j) and (x'_j, y'_j), the following processing should be done:

1. If (x_j, y_j) and (x'_j, y'_j) belong to the same cell ce_o, mo_j is removed from the leaf node containing (x_j, y_j). Meanwhile, mo_j is added into the leaf node containing (x'_j, y'_j), and the corresponding M-ary tree T_o of ce_o is updated.
2. If (x_j, y_j) and (x'_j, y'_j) belong to two different cells ce_o and ce_n respectively, mo_j will be deleted from MOL_o and leaf nodes containing (x_j, y_j), and the corresponding M-ary tree T_o of ce_o will be updated. Meanwhile, we add mo_j into MOL_n and the leaf node containing (x'_j, y'_j), and update the M-ary tree T_n corresponding to ce_n.

It should be noted that when updating the M-ary trees corresponding to cells in the above process, it needs to be handled according to the following conditions:

1. If the sum of the moving objects of the leaf node containing (x_j, y_j) and its brother nodes is less than the threshold β due to the movement of mo_j, all the moving objects of the leaf node in this group are saved by their parent node. Then the group of leaf nodes should be deleted, and their parent node becomes a new leaf node.
2. If the number of moving objects in the leaf node containing (x'_j, y'_j) reaches the threshold α due to the movement of mo_j, the leaf node should be recursively split until the number of moving objects in each leaf node is less than the threshold α.

Maintenance of Range Query. Suppose the range query area qr_i becomes qr'_i after the query point q_i is moved. At this point, the query list in the cells related to qr_i and qr'_i needs to be processed according to the following.

If qr_i covers ce_i and qr'_i does not intersect with ce_i, q_i should be removed from the list FCL_i of ce_i. If qr_i covers ce_i and qr'_i intersect with ce_i, q_i should be removed from FCL_i and inserted into the list PCL_i of ce_i. If qr_i intersect with ce_i and qr'_i does not intersect with ce_i, q_i should be removed from the list PCL_i of ce_i. If qr_i does not intersect with ce_i and qr'_i covers ce_i, q_i should be inserted into the list FCL_i of ce_i. If qr_i intersects with ce_i and qr'_i covers ce_i, q_i should be removed from PCL_i and inserted into the list FCL_i of ce_i. If qr_i does not intersect with ce_i and qr'_i intersects with ce_i, q_i should be inserted into the list PCL_i of ce_i.

The maintenance process of cell ce_i above only maintains the root node of T'_v, while the maintenance of a M-ary tree T_v requires top-down judging whether the query range can cover each node. And the range query is reinserted to maintain the query list QL_i.

Moreover, DDI is deployed in a distributed computing environment of a Master-Worker paradigm, which consists of an EntranceWorker server, multiple IndexWorker servers and multiple QueryWorker servers.

5   Distributed Range Query Algorithm

In this section, we first describe Distributed Range Query Algorithm (DRQA for short) for moving object range queries, then further introduce the shared computing optimization strategy for concurrent queries, and finally describe the distributed incremental query algorithm in the case of moving object locations and range query locations continuous changes.

5.1   DRQA Overview

Distributed Range Query Algorithm (DRQA for short) for moving object range queries is proposed based on DDI. For the query q_i, the EntranceWorker server first determines the candidate cell set GR_i of query q_i according to GGI, and sends the query q_i and sets GR_i to the QueryWorker. Thereafter, the Query-Worker maintains query q_i. Then, the EntranceWorker server notifies multiple IndexWorkers which maintain candidate cells to search the moving objects covered by the query range qr_i of q_i in their respective cells in parallel. In this search process, if a candidate cell is covered by qr_i, all the moving objects in the cell will be the query result of q_i. Otherwise, the M-ary tree corresponding to the candidate cell is traversed from top to bottom, so that we can quickly find the region intersecting with qr_i and get the moving objects belonging to q_i in the cell. Each IndexWorker sends the query results to the QueryWorker after it gets the moving objects that belonging to q_i in the candidate cells under its responsibility by computing. Whenever QueryWorker receives partial query results sent by a server, it judges whether the results of all candidate cells have been received according to set GR_i. If all the query results have been received, the final query result of q_i are returned.

5.2   Computation Sharing Mechanism

Transmission cost optimization. As we all know, the network transmission cost for the same scale data in a distributed environment is much greater than the CPU. When an IndexWorker gets the query results of different queries, it needs to send the query results to QueryWorkers that maintain these queries. At this time, the more the number of QueryWorkers, the greater the network transmission cost. To solve this problem, the strategy adopted in this paper is to route multiple range queries with more overlapping query ranges to the same QueryWorker for processing. That is to say, the IndexWorker that handles these range queries needs to send the query results to the same QueryWorker. Specifically, for the two range queries q_i and q_j, the EntranceWorker calculates the candidate cell sets of q_i and q_j as GR_i and GR_j respectively based on GGI. Then the EntranceWorker calculates the Jaccard similarity $\delta = |G_i \cap G_j| / |G_i \cup G_j|$ of sets GR_i and GR_j. If δ is greater than or equal to the specified threshold, q_i and q_j are sent to the same QueryWorker for processing. Otherwise, q_i and q_j are sent to different QueryWorkers for processing.

Suppose the query range qr_i of query q_i partially intersects with cell ce_j. When traversing the M-ary tree T_j corresponding to cell ce_j to calculate the query result of q_i, we find a non-leaf node of T_j is completely covered by the query range qr_i. In order to get moving objects belonging to that non-leaf node, we still need to continue traversing down until the leaf node. Because the same cell is likely to partially intersect with multiple range queries, these range queries require multiple traversals of the same M-ary tree. This not only requires a lot of repeated calculations but also consumes a lot of time. To solve this problem, we introduce a Bipartite Graph Index (BGI for short) in each cell.

BGI consists of the query set Q_s, the M-ary tree node set N_s and the set O_s of moving objects corresponding to the M-ary tree node. When querying the moving objects contained in qr_i, we traverse the root node of the M-ary tree T_j corresponding to cell ce_j. If a node tn_k of T_j is completely covered by qr_i, and the query q_j is recorded in the query list QL_k of node tn_k, we find q_j in the set Q_s of BGI. Then we find tn_k among the nodes corresponding to q_j in the set N_s according to q_j. Then we look for tn_k in the set N_s corresponding to q_j. At this point, the set O_s of moving objects of tn_k is determined. We don't need to continue traversing the child nodes of tn_k. Otherwise, we continue traversing the child nodes of tn_k to obtain the set O_s of moving objects of tn_k. Thereafter, if the query range of a query covers node tn_k, we can get the moving objects of tn_k directly from the N_s set of BGI.

5.3   Distributed Incremental Search Algorithm

For continuous range queries for which the initial results have been obtained, this paper needs to update their query results every Δt according to the position changes of moving objects and query points until the query fails. Therefore, this paper proposes an incremental query strategy to update the query results incrementally on the basis of making full use of the existing results. The incremental query strategy is discussed as follows.

The moving object position changes while the query point is fixed. After Δt, moving objects whose positions have changed report their previous positions and current positions to the EntranceWorker. Based on GGI, EntranceWorker determines a cell set G, which records the cells that moving objects need to be updated. Then EntranceWorker notifies corresponding IndexWorkers to update moving objects in set G. If a moving object is located in the same cell ce_m before or after the move, there is no impact on queries in list FCL_m. Only queries in PCL_m need to be updated. While updating queries in list PCL_m, multiple queries in list PCL_m can be updated simultaneously based on BGI in cell ce_m. That is to say, when the position of moving objects change while the query point is fixed, the query results of query points in the query set Q_s are updated according to the query list QL_i of tn_i if the moving object set of any node tn_i in the set N_s in BGI changes.

The position of the moving object is fixed while the position of the query point changes. We assume that the query range changes from qr_i to qr_i' after the query q_i is moved. When q_i reaches the EntranceWorker, it calculates the candidate cell sets GR_l and GR_c of q_i at the previous moment and the current moment according to qr_i and qr_i' respectively. If cell ce_k belongs to GR_l but not to GR_c, the IndexWorker (IW_k for short) maintaining ce_k notifies the QueryWorker (QW_i for short) responsible for q_i to remove the moving objects belonging to ce_k from the query result of q_i at the previous moment. If cell ce_k belongs to GR_c but not belongs to GR_l, IW_k informs QW_i to add the moving object belonging to ce_k to the query result of q_i at the previous moment. If cell ce_k belongs to both GR_l and GR_c, ce_k is processed according to the following rules.

If $(sq_i \subseteq c_k)\,\&\&\,(sq_i' \subseteq c_k)$ and the query range of q_i always covers cell ce_k, the query results don't need to be updated. If $(sq_i \subset c_k)\,\&\&\,(sq_i' \subseteq c_k)$, q_i is removed from PCL_k and inserted into FCL_k. IW_k calculates the moving objects in region $(c_k - (c_k \cap sq_i))$ according to the M-ary tree T_k. Then IW_k sends these moving objects to QW_i, which adds these moving objects to query result of q_i. If $(sq_i \subseteq c_k)\,\&\&\,(sq_i' \subset c_k)$, q_i is removed from FCL_k and inserted into PCL_k. IW_k calculates the moving objects in region $(c_k - (c_k \cap sq_i'))$ according to the M-ary tree T_k. Then IW_k sends these moving objects to QW_i, which removes these moving objects from the query result of q_i. If $(sq_i \subset c_k)\,\&\&\,(sq_i' \subset c_k)$, IW_k calculates the moving object sets O_d and O_a in region $(sq_i - (sq_i \cap sq_i'))$ and $(sq_i' - (sq_i \cap sq_i'))$ according to the M-ary tree T_k. Then IW_k informs QW_i to remove moving objects in set O_d from the query result of q_i, and adds moving objects in set O_a to the query result of q_i.

6   Experiments

In this paper, the DDI is evaluated by data sets with different moving objects distribution. Three moving object data sets are simulated based on New York road network: uniform distribution (UD) data set, gaussian distribution (GD) data set and Zipf data set. To simulate these data sets, the first is to regard the two-dimensional space which covers every road network as a 1×1 square area, and divide into 100×100 cells with the same size. The second is to calculate the number of moving objects in each cell according to the probability density distribution function. Finally, let the moving objects in each cell move at speed V_0 on the corresponding local road network.

This paper introduces three distributed algorithms as baseline methods to compare and evaluate the performance of DRQA. The first baseline algorithm naive search (NS) does not use any indexes, and each server contains all moving objects, and each query is randomly assigned to all servers. The second baseline algorithm grid index (GI) is to build a distributed grid index for moving objects. A given query is allocated to the corresponding servers based on the distributed grid index. Multiple servers compute the results of a given query in parallel. The third baseline algorithm DHI [35] is a hybrid index composed of global grid and R-tree structure proposed by Yu et al. Based on the distributed grid index, R-tree is established with the initial position of moving objects as leaf nodes, and the index granularity is adjusted by setting the size of leaf nodes.

The experimental server cluster consists of 20 Elastic Cloud Server(ECS) rented by Ali Cloud. Each server has 4 cores and 16G memory.

6.1 Performance of DDI

In this section, we will evaluate the building cost, maintenance cost, and throughput of DDI.

Construction Cost Evaluation. This group of experiments tests the effect of different bifurcation values of m on the DDI construction time, and the experimental results are shown in Fig. 1(a). From the experimental results, it can be seen that the DDI construction time decreases and then increases with the increase of m. When $m = 6$, the DDI construction time is the least. The reasons are as follows. When $m < 6$, although fewer child nodes need to be built for each split, more tree nodes need to be split. When $m > 6$, although fewer tree nodes need to be split, more child nodes need to be created for each split as m increases, so the DDI construction time increases.

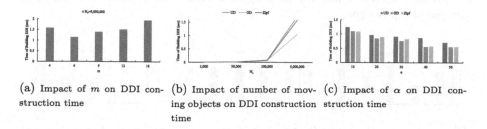

(a) Impact of m on DDI construction time

(b) Impact of number of moving objects on DDI construction time

(c) Impact of α on DDI construction time

Fig. 1. Impacts of different parameters on index building time

In this group of experiments, moving objects were put into Q_o at one time, and the time of constructing DDI for these moving objects was counted. As shown in Fig. 1(b), the DDI construction time and the number of moving objects basically increase in the same proportion. In addition, the time required to process moving objects in the GD data set is slightly lower. This is because the number of cells that need to build a M-ary tree is reduced, so the construction time decreases.

The parameter α directly affects the DDI construction time. Experimental results are shown in Fig. 1(c), regardless of which distribution the moving objects conform to, the construction cost of DDI decreases significantly as α increases. The reason is that α is directly related to the number of levels of the M-ary tree. The larger parameter α, the less likely the M-ary tree will split child nodes. Thus the number of layers of the M-ary tree is smaller, which makes the construction cost of DDI smaller.

6.2 Query Performance

This group of experiments tests the effect of different bifurcation values m on the query time, and the experimental results are shown in Fig. 2(a). From the experimental results, it can be seen that the query time decreases and then increases with the increase of m. The best result is achieved when $m = 6$. The reason is as follows. When the bifurcation value m is too small, although there are fewer child nodes to be traversed in each down layer, the number of layers to be traversed is more. Conversely, when the bifurcation value of m is too large, although the number of levels to be traversed decreases, the number of child nodes to be traversed increases at each next level, resulting in the increase of query time.

In this section, we test the query time of the same group of queries under different α, and the experimental results are shown in Fig. 2(b). The results show that with the increase of the α, the query time decreases and then increases, and the optimal effect is achieved when the α is set to 20. When the α is too small, the M-ary tree index granularity generally decreases, and the traversal cost is relatively large, resulting in the increase of in the overall query cost. On the contrary, when the threshold α is too large, the M-ary tree index granularity generally increases and the pruning effectiveness decreases, resulting in the increase of query time.

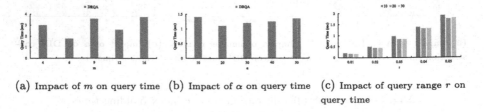

(a) Impact of m on query time   (b) Impact of α on query time   (c) Impact of query range r on query time

Fig. 2. Influence of different parameters on query time

In this group of experiments, the DDI index with a size of 100×100 was first established (the size of each cell was defined as 0.01×0.01) and the relationship between DRQA performance and query range was evaluated. The results are shown in Fig. 2(c) that the size of the query range has a certain influence on the performance of DRQA. The larger the query radius r of a query point, the greater the number of candidate query cells involved. Even though DRQA can use multiple servers to conduct parallel queries on the moving objects of candidate cells, with the increase of the number of candidate cells, the number of servers to be processed by the system also increases correspondingly. As all the servers need to communicate with QueryWorker, the query time of DRQA increases.

6.3 Comparison with Baselines

In this group of experiments, different numbers of range queries were set to test the query time of the four algorithms. The experimental results are shown in Fig. 3(a). The results show that the performance of DRQA is always better than NS, GI and DHI. This is because all servers use brute force search mode when NS processes each query, which causes its query time to increase linearly with the number of continuous range queries. GI needs to detect more moving objects than DRQA due to lack of M-ary tree index support when processing the same set of contiguous range queries. During query, DHI fails to consider the queries with a high query area overlap rate and may allocate these queries to different servers, resulting in extra computing overhead. DRQA not only considers the optimization of transmission cost, but also adopts BGI structure to eliminate the need to traverse the bottom of the M-ary tree for multiple range queries.

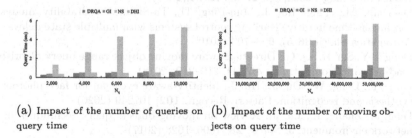

(a) Impact of the number of queries on query time

(b) Impact of the number of moving objects on query time

Fig. 3. Performance comparison of initial query time of multiple algorithms

In this group of experiments, different numbers of moving objects are taken as variables to test the change of query time of the four algorithms. In this group of experiments, 10,000 continuous range queries were input to Q_q at one time. The processing time of all queries by the four algorithms is shown in Fig. 3(b). As the number of queries increases, NS query time increases linearly, while GI, DRQA, and DHI performance are almost unaffected. This is because NS needs to scan all the moving objects to process each query, whereas GI, DRQA, and DHI can effectively prune the search space so that even if the number of moving objects increases dramatically, only a limited number of moving objects need to be processed. The reason why the performance of DRQA and DHI is significantly better than GI is that DRQA and DHI introduce M-ary tree index and R-tree index respectively, which further improve the index efficiency and can effectively process large volume of moving object range queries.

7   Conclusion

This paper proposes a distributed index structure to support continuous range queries over moving objects. The index structure has efficient pruning ability, low maintenance cost, and is easy to be deployed to a cluster of servers. Based on the index structure, we further propose a distributed incremental continuous query algorithm, which introduces the incremental search strategy and a computation sharing mechanism to enhance the efficiency of processing continuous range queries. In the future, we plan to study the distributed processing of range queries over moving objects with road network constraints.

References

1. Alamri, S., Taniar, D., Nguyen, K., Alamri, A.: C-tree: efficient cell-based indexing of indoor mobile objects. J. Ambient Intell. Humanized Comput. **11**(7), 2841–2857 (2020)
2. Cai, Y., Hua, K.A., Cao, G.: Processing range-monitoring queries on heterogeneous mobile objects. In: IEEE International Conference on Mobile Data Management, 2004. Proceedings. 2004, pp. 27–38. IEEE (2004)
3. De-Yuan, M., Ying-Min, J., Jun-Ping, D., Fa-Shan, Y.: Stability analysis of continuous-time iterative learning control systems with multiple state delays. Acta Automatica Sinica **36**(5), 696–703 (2010)
4. Dong T Y, S.Y.H., Q, C.: Direction-aware moving object range query algorithm in road network. Comput. Sci. **45**(11), 210–219 (2018)
5. Fang, Y., Deng, W., Du, J., Hu, J.: Identity-aware cyclegan for face photo-sketch synthesis and recognition. Pattern Recogn. **102**, 107249 (2020)
6. Feng, J., Zhang, L., Lu, J.: Review on moving objects query techniques in road network environment. J. Softw. **28**, 1606–1628 (2017)
7. Fu, X., Miao, X., Xu, J., Gao, Y.: Continuous range-based skyline queries in road networks. World Wide Web **20**(6), 1443–1467 (2017). https://doi.org/10.1007/s11280-017-0444-2
8. Haidar, A.K., Taniar, D., Betts, J., Alamri, S.: On finding safe regions for moving range queries. Math. Comput. Model. **58**(5–6), 1449–1458 (2013)
9. Haidar, A.K., Taniar, D., Safar, M.: Approximate algorithms for static and continuous range queries in mobile navigation. Computing **95**(10–11), 949–976 (2013)
10. Hu, H., Xu, J., Lee, D.L.: A generic framework for monitoring continuous spatial queries over moving objects. In: Proceedings of the 2005 ACM SIGMOD International Conference on Management of Data, pp. 479–490 (2005)

11. Feng, J., Li, D., Lu, J., Zhang, L.: Spatio-temporal index method for moving objects in road network based on HBASE. Comput. Appl. **38**(6), 1575–1583 (2018)
12. Kalashnikov, D., Prabhakar, S., Hambrusch, S., Aref, W.: Efficient evaluation of continuous range queries on moving objects. In: Hameurlain, A., Cicchetti, R., Traunmüller, R. (eds.) DEXA 2002. LNCS, vol. 2453, pp. 731–740. Springer, Heidelberg (2002). https://doi.org/10.1007/3-540-46146-9_72
13. Li, W., Xiao, X., Liu, J., Wu, H., Wang, H., Du, J.: Leveraging graph to improve abstractive multi-document summarization. arXiv preprint arXiv:2005.10043 (2020)
14. Li, W., Jia, Y., Du, J.: Distributed consensus extended kalman filter: a variance-constrained approach. IET Control Theor. Appl. **11**(3), 382–389 (2017)
15. Li, W., Jia, Y., Du, J.: Distributed extended kalman filter with nonlinear consensus estimate. J. Franklin Inst. **354**(17), 7983–7995 (2017)
16. Li, W., Jia, Y., Du, J.: Resilient filtering for nonlinear complex networks with multiplicative noise. IEEE Trans. Autom. Control **64**(6), 2522–2528 (2018)
17. Li, W., Jia, Y., Du, J., Zhang, J.: Brief paper-distributed consensus filtering for jump markov linear systems. IET Control Theor. Appl. **7**(12), 1659–1664 (2013)
18. Liang, Z., Du, J., Li, C.: Abstractive social media text summarization using selective reinforced seq2seq attention model. Neurocomputing **410**, 432–440 (2020)
19. Meng, D., Jia, Y., Du, J.: Robust iterative learning protocols for finite-time consensus of multi-agent systems with interval uncertain topologies. Int. J. Syst. Sci. **46**(5), 857–871 (2015)
20. Meng, D., Jia, Y., Du, J.: Consensus seeking via iterative learning for multi-agent systems with switching topologies and communication time-delays. Int. J. Robust Nonlinear Control **26**(17), 3772–3790 (2016)
21. Na, T., Zhanhao, Z., Jingjing, L., Yong, T., Xiaoping, Y.: Temporal-spatial phase point moving object data indexing: Pm-tree. Soft Comput. **44**(3), 579–593 (2021)
22. Ouyang, D., Wen, D., Qin, L., Chang, L., Zhang, Y., Lin, X.: Progressive top-k nearest neighbors search in large road networks. In: Proceedings of the 2020 ACM SIGMOD International Conference on Management of Data, pp. 1781–1795 (2020)
23. Shao, Z., Cheema, M.A., Taniar, D., Lu, H.: Vip-tree: an effective index for indoor spatial queries. Proc. VLDB Endowment **10**(4), 325–336 (2016)
24. Shen, J.H., Lu, C.T., Chen, M.Y., Yen, N.Y.: Grid-based indexing with expansion of resident domains for monitoring moving objects. J. Supercomput. **76**(3), 1482–1501 (2020)
25. Shi, C., et al.: Deep collaborative filtering with multi-aspect information in heterogeneous networks. IEEE Trans. Knowl. Data Eng. **33**(4), 1413–1425 (2019)
26. Silvestri, C., Lettich, F., Orlando, S., Jensen, C.S.: GPU-based computing of repeated range queries over moving objects. In: 2014 22nd Euromicro International Conference on Parallel, Distributed, and Network-Based Processing, pp. 640–647. IEEE (2014)
27. Sun, B., Du, J., Gao, T.: Study on the improvement of k-nearest-neighbor algorithm. In: 2009 International Conference on Artificial Intelligence and Computational Intelligence, vol. 4, pp. 390–393. IEEE (2009)
28. Tianyang, D., Lulu, Y., Qiang, C., Bin, C., Jing, F.: Direction-aware KNN queries for moving objects in a road network. World Wide Web **22**(4), 1765–1797 (2019)
29. Wang, Z.J., et al.: Sme: explicit & implicit constrained-space probabilistic threshold range queries for moving objects. GeoInformatica **20**(1), 19–58 (2016)
30. Wei, X., Du, J., Liang, M., Ye, L.: Boosting deep attribute learning via support vector regression for fast moving crowd counting. Pattern Recogn. Lett. **119**, 12–23 (2019)

31. Xu, J., Tan, Y.: Optimization of multidimensional index query mechanism based on HBASE. J. Comput. Appl. **40**(2), 571–577 (2020)

32. Xue, Z., Du, J., Du, D., Lyu, S.: Deep low-rank subspace ensemble for multi-view clustering. Inf. Sci. **482**, 210–227 (2019)

33. Xue Z. B, Z.H., S, W.: Throughput oriented range query algorithm for moving objects in dual stream mode. J. Softw. **26**(10), 2631–2643 (2015)

34. Yu, X., Pu, K.Q., Koudas, N.: Monitoring k-nearest neighbor queries over moving objects. In: 21st International Conference on Data Engineering (ICDE'05), pp. 631–642. IEEE (2005)

35. Yu, Z., Xhafa, F., Chen, Y., Ma, K.: A distributed hybrid index for processing continuous range queries over moving objects. Soft Comput. **23**(9), 3191–3205 (2019)

36. Zhang, D., Yang, D., Wang, Y., Tan, K.-L., Cao, J., Shen, H.T.: Distributed shortest path query processing on dynamic road networks. The VLDB J. **26**(3), 399–419 (2017). https://doi.org/10.1007/s00778-017-0457-6

37. Zhang, S., Ray, S., Lu, R., Zheng, Y.: Sprig: a learned spatial index for range and KNN queries. In: 17th International Symposium on Spatial and Temporal Databases, pp. 96–105 (2021)

38. Zhao, L., Jia, Y., Yu, J., Du, J.: H∞ sliding mode based scaled consensus control for linear multi-agent systems with disturbances. Appl. Math. Comput. **292**, 375–389 (2017)

39. Zhou, Y.T., Tang X.L., H.P.: Comparative analysis of indoor positioning technology. Eng. Technol. Res. **1**(3), 162–164 (2019)

Scaled Consensus of Switched Multi-Agent Systems with Controller Failure and Time-Varying Delay

Yaping Sun and Xinsong Yang

College of Electronics and Information Engineering, Sichuan University,
Chengdu 610065, People's Republic of China
xinsongyang@scu.edu.cn

Abstract This paper investigates the global exponential scaled consensus almost surely (GESC a.s.) of switched multi-agent systems (SMASs) with controller failure and time-varying delay, in which the SMASs contain both switching topologies and switching dynamics. To begin with, failure parameters which can depict the influences of unconnected networks and invalid controller, are introduced to design scaled consensus algorithms. Significantly, the algorithms are distributed and switched. Then based on Lyapunov function-based technology, scaled consensus criteria are obtained to guarantee GESC a.s. of delayed SMASs. These criteria mean that for the subsystems with unconnected network or invalid controller, the active time within any time interval can be very small or big. Finally, two numerical simulations are given to demonstrate the effectiveness of our results.

Keywords: Controller failure · Delay · Dwell time · Scaled consensus · Switched multi-agents system · Transition probability

1 Introduction

Although the multi-agent systems have been studied for decades, it still is the one of research hot-spots currently due to the fact that it can be widely applied in real life, such as multi-unmanned aerial vehicle system [1], multi-unmanned ground vehicle system [2], multi-unmanned surface vessel system [3], and so on.

SMASs have aroused discussion and concern among scholars because almost all of real MASs have switching characteristics, such as switching topologies or switching dynamics. In SMASs, one main focus of achieving consensus is

Supported by the National Natural Science Foundation of China (NSFC) under Grant No. 61673078, the Central guiding local science and technology development special project of Sichuan under Grant No 2021ZYD0015, the Fundamental Research Funds for Central Universities under Grant No. 2022SCU12009, the Sichuan Province Natural Science Foundation of China (NSFSC) under Grant Nos. 2022NSFSC0541 and 2022NSFSC0875, and the second batch of new engineering research and practice projects of the Ministry of Education of China under Grant No E-DZYQ20201427.

L. Zhang et al. (Eds.): CINT 2022, CCIS 1714, pp. 419–430, 2022.
https://doi.org/10.1007/978-981-19-8915-5_36

how to depict the switching characteristics of topologies or dynamics. Existing description methods can be divided into two categories. One is the arbitrary switching [4]; another one is the restricted switching [5]. Restricted switching, such as dwell time (DT) switching, has been widely studied because the condition that every closed-loop subsystem must be stable, is not necessary for restricted switching. Some results which considered consensus of SMASs with DT switching have been published in [6–9], but all the DT switching in these results have not considered the transition probability (TP) that widely exists in real systems. Recently, a TP-based and mode-dependent average DT (MDADT) switching is proposed in [11,12]. However, the two works are interested in the synchronization of switched complex network rather than the consensus of SMASs; and they focus on the switching topologies rather than the switching dynamics. In addition, the results in [11,12] cannot be directly extended to the consensus of SMASs because the control algorithm and analytical methods used in [11,12] cannot deal with the difficulties induced by distributional characteristics of multi-agent systems directly. This motivates us to study the consensus of SMASs via TP-based MDADT switching.

Moreover, agents' states reach a equilibrium rather than a common value in some real-world networks, such as compartmental mass-action systems and closed queueing networks [13]. Based on this phenomenon, some works which considered scaled consensus of SMASs are published in [14–17]. However, to the best of the author's knowledge, almost all of the existing results on scaled consensus of SMASs are interested in low-order systems and switching topologies rather than generalized linear SMASs and switching dynamics. And the results in [14–17] cannot be directly extended to the consensus of generalized linear SMASs with both switching dynamics and switching topologies because the control algorithms and analytical methods used in [14–17] cannot deal with the difficulties induced by generalized linear SMASs and switching dynamics directly. Therefore it is necessary to introduce some new methods and algorithms to solve the scaled consensus problems of generalized linear SMASs with both switching dynamics and switching topologies.

Furthermore, due to external perturbations and damaged devices, controller failure often happens on controllers. And for real SMASs, time-varying delay is inescapable due to limited information-acquisition speeds. Therefore controller failure and time-varying delay need to be considered in SMASs.

To sum up, this paper studies a generalized linear SMAS with switching topologies and switching dynamics. By introducing the TP-based MDADT switching and constructing a Lyapunov functional, scaled consensus conditions which can achieve the GESC a.s. of generalized linear SMAS with controller failure and time-varying delay, are obtained. The main contributions are as follows.

1) It is first attempt to design distributed and switched algorithms to achieve the GESC a.s. of generalized linear SMASs with controller failure and time-varying delay, in which the linear SMASs contain both switching topologies and switching dynamics. Moreover, the specific expressions of gain matrices are constructed; the scaled consensus criteria are derived.

2) Compared with the works in [11,12] which consider the TP-based MDADT switching, this paper focuses on the scaled consensus of SMASs; and both the switching dynamics and switching topologies are considered. Moreover, a distributed consensus algorithm and some new analytical techniques are introduced to solve this paper's problems which cannot be directly solved by the control algorithms and analytical methods used in [11,12].

3) Compared with the works in [14–17] which studied scaled consensus problems of SMASs, in this paper, generalized linear SMASs and switching dynamics are considered; the controller failure and time-varying delay are overcame. Moreover, for unconnected networks and invalid controllers, the active time within any time interval can be very small or big.

Notations: $\mathbb{R}^m$ denotes the set of m-dimensional Euclidean vector space. $\mathbb{R}^{m \times n}$ is the set of $m \times n$ real matrix space. $\text{sym}\,[M] = M^T + M$. M^+ denotes the generalized inverse of matrix M. $M < 0$ ($M > 0$) means that M is a symmetric negative (positive) definite matrix. $\mathbf{E}(\cdot)$ is the notation of mathematical expectation. $\mathbb{N}^+$ denotes the set of positive integers. Moreover, in order to increase the readability of the paper, the abbreviations are summarized as follows (Table 1).

Table 1. Full name and abbreviation.

Abbreviation	Full name
GESC a.s.	Global exponential scaled consensus almost surely
SMASs	Switched multi-agent systems
DT	Dwell time
TP	Transition probability
MDADT	Mode-dependent average DT

This paper's structure is outlined as follows. The problem description and some important definitions, assumptions, and lemmas are introduced in Sect. 2. In Sect. 3, the scaled consensus conditions for SMASs are derived. In Sect. 4, the results are verified by giving the numerical simulations. Finally, Sect. 5 concludes this paper.

2   Preliminaries

Firstly, consider an undirected graph $G = (\mathbb{V}, \mathbb{E})$ with a nonempty finite node set $\mathbb{V} = \{1, 2, \cdots, N\}$ and a nonempty finite edge set $\mathbb{E} = \{(i, j) |$ if nodes i and j can communication with each other$\}$. The adjacency matrix of graph G is described as $\mathbb{G} = [g_{ij}]_{N \times N}$, where $g_{ij} = 1$ if and only if $(i, j) \in \mathbb{E}$, otherwise $g_{ij} = 0$. The Laplacian matrix of graph G is described as $L = [l_{ij}]_{N \times N}$, where $l_{ij, i \neq j} = -g_{ij}$ and $l_{ii} = \sum_{j=1, j \neq i}^{N} g_{ij}$. For an undirected and connected graph, it holds $0 = \lambda_1 < \lambda_2 \leq \cdots \leq \lambda_i \leq \cdots \leq \lambda_N$, in which λ_i with $i = 1, \ldots, N$ are eigenvalues of Laplace matrix.

Secondly, consider SMASs with time-varying delay as follows.

$$
\begin{cases}
\dot{x}_i(t) & = A_{\sigma(t)}x_i(t) + B_{\sigma(t)}u_i^{\sigma(t)}(t) + D_{\sigma(t)}x_i(t - \tau(t)), \\
x_i(r) & = \hat{\alpha}_i(r) \in \mathbb{R}^{n_x}, r \in [-\tau_{\max}, 0],
\end{cases}
\tag{1}
$$

where $x_i(t) \in \mathbb{R}^{n_x}$ and $u_i(t) \in \mathbb{R}^{n_u}$ are state vector and input of agent i, respectively; $\tau_{\min} \leq \tau(t) \leq \tau_{\max}$; $\dot{\tau}(t) \leq \hat{\tau}$; $\hat{\alpha}_i(r) \in \mathbb{R}^{n_x}$ is the initial value; $\sigma(t) : \mathbb{N}^+ \rightarrow \{1, 2, \ldots, q\} = \mathbb{M}_q$ is a switching signal. Let $\{t_k, k \in \mathbb{N}^+\}$ be a time sequence satisfying $0 = t_0 < t_1 < \cdots < t_k < \cdots < \lim_{k\to\infty} t_k = +\infty$. $\sigma(t) = m$ when $t \in [t_{k-1}, t_k)$. $S_m(k) = t_k - t_{k-1}$ is the DT of the mth mode for the kth visiting of $\sigma(t)$.

Thirdly, consider a scaled consensus algorithm with controller failure as follow.

$$
u_i^{\sigma(t)}(t) = -\eta_{\sigma(t)}K_{\sigma(t)}^i \sum_{j=1, j\neq i}^{N} g_{ij}^{\sigma(t)}\left(x_i(t) - \frac{\phi_j}{\phi_i}x_j(t)\right),
\tag{2}
$$

where $\eta_{\sigma(t)} \in \{0, 1\}$ are failure parameters; $K_{\sigma(t)}^i$ are gain matrices of agent i to be designed; ϕ_i and ϕ_j are scale values of agents i and j, respectively.

The aim of this article is to achieve GESC a.s. defined as follows.

Definition 1. *A SMAS is said to achieve the GESC a.s., if and only if, for $\forall$ $\hat{\alpha}(r) \in \mathbb{R}^{n_x}, r \in [-\tau_{\max}, 0]$,*

$$
\limsup_{t\to\infty}\left(\ln \boldsymbol{E}\frac{\|\phi_i x_i(t) - \phi_j x_j(t)\|}{t}\right) < 0 \text{ almost surely.}
$$

Definition 2 [11]. *For any $m, \tilde{m} \in \mathbb{M}_q$ with $m \neq \tilde{m}$, $\sigma(t)$ switches from the mth mode to the $\tilde{m}$th mode with TP*

$$
\text{Prob}\{\sigma(t_k) = \tilde{m} | \sigma(t_{k-1}) = m\} = p_{m\tilde{m}},
\tag{3}
$$

where $0 \leq p_{m\tilde{m}} < 1$ with $p_{mm} = 0$; $P = (p_{m\tilde{m}})_{q\times q}$ is an irreducible matrix with $\sum_{\tilde{m}=1}^{f} p_{m\tilde{m}} = 1$; P is called a TP matrix.

Before moving on, some assumptions and lemmas are needed.

Assumption 1. *$\boldsymbol{E}(S_m(k)) = h_m$, $\boldsymbol{E}(S_{\tilde{m}}(k)) = h_{\tilde{m}}$, where $S_m(k)$ and $S_{\tilde{m}}(k)$ are independent positive random variables; h_m and $h_{\tilde{m}}$ are positive constants.*

Assumption 2. *For any m, the system matrix B is a full row or column rank matrix.*

Lemma 1 [10]. *Let $\pi = (\pi_1, \pi_2, \ldots, \pi_q)$. For $\forall m \in \mathbb{M}_q$, when*

$$
\pi_m > 0, \sum_{m=1}^{q} \pi_m = 1, \pi P = \pi,
\tag{4}
$$

then π is the unique stationary distribution of the irreducible matrix P.

Lemma 2 [12]. *Let $\sigma(t)$ be a switching signal given in Assumption 1 and π be the stationary distribution of P. Then, for $\forall m \in \mathbb{R}$, there holds*

$$\lim_{t \to \infty} \frac{T_m(t)}{t} = \bar{\pi}_m, \quad \text{a.s.,}$$

where $\bar{\pi}_m = \pi_m h_m / (\sum_{\tilde{m}=1}^{q} \pi_{\tilde{m}} h_{\tilde{m}})$, $T_m(t)$ is the total time for $\sigma(t) = m$ over the interval $[0, t]$.

Remark 1. Significantly, $\eta_{\sigma(t)} = 1$ if and only if the controllers are intact; the undirected networks are connected, otherwise $\eta_{\sigma(t)} = 0$.

Remark 2. The TP-based MDADT switching [11,12] introduced in this paper contains both TP and DT, which is more practically for real system. Moreover, MDADT switching and Markov switching are special cases of TP-based MDADT switching. Under the switching, for any mode, the active time within any time interval can be very small or big, in which the modes can be stable or unstable. Moreover, $S_m(k) = t_k - t_{k-1}$ is also described as the active time of mode m if $\sigma(t) = m$ for $t \in [t_{k-1}, t_k)$.

Remark 3. $r \in [-\tau_{\max}, 0]$ is common for any delay system. "$\sigma(t) = m$ when $t \in [t_{k-1}, t_k)$" is an assumption without loss of generality, in other words, $t_1, \ldots,$ $t_{k-1}, t_k, \ldots$ are relatively random and unpredictable. Moreover, the parameter m in $S_m(k) = t_k - t_{k-1}$ and $\sigma(t) = m$ denotes the mode m.

3   Main Results

This section solves GESC a.s. problems of switched MASs via a Lyapunov-like method. The results show that controller failure and time-varying delay in controllers are overcame; the active time within any time interval can be very big or small; GESC a.s. problems of SMASs via intermittent control are special cases.

Before moving on, some settings are helpful.

Combining SMAS (1) and scaled consensus algorithm (2), a closed-loop system can be obtained when $\sigma(t) = m$ for $t \in [t_{k-1}, t_k)$.

$$\dot{x}_i(t) = A_m x_i(t) + D_m x_i(t - \tau(t)) - \eta_m B_m K_m^i \sum_{j=1, j \neq i}^{N} g_{ij}^m \left(x_i(t) - \frac{\phi_j}{\phi_i} x_j(t) \right).$$

$$(5)$$

Let $X(t) = [x_1^T(t), \ldots, x_N^T(t)]$, $K_m = \text{diag}\{K_m^1, \ldots, K_m^N\}$, and $E(t) = (\mathbb{M}\Phi \otimes I)X(t)$, where $\Phi = \text{diag}[\phi_1, \ldots, \phi_N]$, $\mathbb{M} = I_N - \frac{1}{N}\mathbf{1}_N \mathbf{1}_N^T$. It holds

$$\dot{E}(t) = (I \otimes A_m - \eta_m (L_m \otimes B_m) K_m) E(t) + (I \otimes D_m) E(t - \tau(t)). \quad (6)$$

Significantly, $E = 0$ if and only if $\phi_1 x_1 = \phi_2 x_2 = \cdots = \phi_N x_N$.

Then the main results are stated as follows. Let $K_m^1 = \cdots = K_m^i = \cdots = K_m^N = \widetilde{K}_m$.

Theorem 1. *Suppose that Assumptions 1 and 2 hold. For given scalars $a_m \neq 0$, if there are matrices, $\mathbb{P}_{m,f} = \text{diag}\{\widetilde{\mathbb{P}}_{m,f}, \ldots, \widetilde{\mathbb{P}}_{m,f}\} > 0$, $f = 1, 2$, $\widetilde{\mathbb{Y}}_m$, such that for any $m \in \mathbb{M}_q$,*

$$\widetilde{\mathbb{J}}_m < 0, \quad \sum_{m=1}^{q} a_m \bar{\pi}_m > 0, \tag{7}$$

then the GESC a.s. of SMAS (1) with controller (2) together with gain matrices $\widetilde{K}_m = B_m^+ \widetilde{\mathbb{P}}_{m,1}^{-1} \widetilde{\mathbb{Y}}_m$ is achieved, where

$$\widetilde{\mathbb{J}}_m = \begin{bmatrix} \widetilde{\Phi}_m & (I \otimes \widetilde{\mathbb{P}}_{m,1} D_m) \\ (I \otimes D_m^T \widetilde{\mathbb{P}}_{m,1}) & (\hat{\tau} - 1)\mathbb{P}_{m,2} \end{bmatrix}, \tag{8}$$

$\widetilde{\Phi}_m = \text{sym}\left[I \otimes (\widetilde{\mathbb{P}}_{m,1} A_m - \eta_m \mu_m \widetilde{\mathbb{P}}_{m,1} B_m B_m^+ \widetilde{\mathbb{P}}_{m,1}^{-1} \widetilde{\mathbb{Y}}_m\right] + a_m \mathbb{P}_{m,1} + \mathbb{P}_{m,2}$; $\mu_m = \lambda_2$ and $a_m > 0$ when $\eta_m = 1$; $\mu_m = 0$ and $a_m < 0$ when $\eta_m = 0$.

Proof. Firstly, consider the following Lyapunov functional:

$$V(m,t) = \sum_{d=1}^{2} V_d(m,t), \tag{9}$$

where

$$V_1(m,t) = E^T(t)\mathbb{P}_{m,1} E(t),$$
$$V_2(m,t) = \int_{t-\tau(t)}^{t} e^{a_m(\alpha-t)} E^T(\alpha)\mathbb{P}_{m,2} E(\alpha). \tag{10}$$

Secondly, differentiating (9) along the trajectories of error system (6) holds

$$\mathbf{E}\{\mathcal{L}V(m,t)\} = \sum_{d=1}^{2} \mathbf{E}\{\mathcal{L}V_d(m,t)\}, \tag{11}$$

where

$$\begin{aligned} \mathbf{E}\{\mathcal{L}V_1(m,t)\} = &- a_m \mathbf{E}\{V_1(m,t)\} + a_m E^T(t)\mathbb{P}_{m,1} E(t) + 2E^T(t)\mathbb{P}_{m,1}\dot{E}(t) \\ = &- a_m \mathbf{E}\{V_1(m,t)\} + a_m E^T(t)\mathbb{P}_{m,1} E(t) \\ &+ 2E^T(t)\mathbb{P}_{m,1}[(I \otimes A_m - \eta_m (L_m \otimes B_m) K_m) E(t) \\ &+ (I \otimes D_m) E(t - \tau(t))], \end{aligned} \tag{12}$$

$$\begin{aligned} \mathbf{E}\{\mathcal{L}V_2(m,t)\} \leq &- a_m \mathbf{E}\{V_2(m,t)\} + E^T(t)\mathbb{P}_{m,2} E(t) \\ &- (1 - \hat{\tau})e^{-a_m \mu} E^T(t - \tau(t))\mathbb{P}_{m,2} E(t - \tau(t)). \end{aligned} \tag{13}$$

Because $\mathbb{P}_{m,f} = \text{diag}\{\widetilde{\mathbb{P}}_{m,f}, \ldots, \widetilde{\mathbb{P}}_{m,f}\}$ and $\widetilde{K}_m = B_m^+ \widetilde{\mathbb{P}}_{m,1}^{-1} \widetilde{\mathbb{Y}}_m$, $\mathbf{E}\{\mathcal{L}V_1(m,t)\}$ in (12) can be rewritten as

$$\begin{aligned} \mathbf{E}\{\mathcal{L}V_1(m,t)\} = &- a_m \mathbf{E}\{V_1(m,t)\} + a_m E^T(t)\mathbb{P}_{m,1} E(t) \\ &+ 2E^T(t)\left(I \otimes \widetilde{\mathbb{P}}_{m,1} A_m - \eta_m L_m \otimes \widetilde{\mathbb{P}}_{m,1} B_m B_m^+ \widetilde{\mathbb{P}}_{m,1}^{-1} \widetilde{\mathbb{Y}}_m\right) E(t) \\ &+ 2E^T(t)\left(I \otimes \widetilde{\mathbb{P}}_{m,1} D_m\right) E(t - \tau(t)). \end{aligned} \tag{14}$$

Based on the characteristics of Laplacian matrix, when $\eta_m = 1$, $\mathbf{E}\{\mathcal{L}V_1(m,t)\}$ in (14) can be estimated as

$$\mathbf{E}\{\mathcal{L}V_1(m,t)\} \leq - a_m\mathbf{E}\{V_1(m,t)\} + a_m E^T(t)\mathbb{P}_{m,1}E(t)$$
$$+ 2E^T(t)I \otimes \left(\widetilde{\mathbb{P}}_{m,1}A_m - \eta_m\lambda_2\widetilde{\mathbb{P}}_{m,1}B_m B_m^+\widetilde{\mathbb{P}}_{m,1}^{-1}\widetilde{\mathbb{Y}}_m\right)E(t)$$
$$+ 2E^T(t)\left(I \otimes \widetilde{\mathbb{P}}_{m,1}D_m\right)E(t-\tau(t)).$$
$$(15)$$

Thirdly, let $\xi(t) = [E(t), E(t-\tau(t))]^T$. Based on (13) and (15), $\mathbf{E}\{\mathcal{L}V_1(m,t)\}$ can be estimated as

$$\mathbf{E}\{\mathcal{L}V(m,t)\} \leq - a_m\mathbf{E}\{V(m,t)\} + \xi^T(t)\widetilde{\mathbb{J}}^m\xi(t). \tag{16}$$

With the help of condition (7), it holds

$$\mathbf{E}\{\mathcal{L}V(m,t)\} \leq - a_m\mathbf{E}\{V(m,t)\}, \tag{17}$$

which means

$$\frac{d(\ln\mathbf{E}\{V(\sigma(t),t)\})}{dt} \leq -a_{\sigma(t)},$$
$$\frac{\ln\mathbf{E}\{V(\sigma(t),t)\}}{t} \leq \underbrace{\frac{\ln\mathbf{E}\{V(\sigma(0),0)\}}{t} - \frac{1}{t}\int_0^t a_{\sigma(s)}ds}_{\text{Termi}}. \tag{18}$$

Then Termi implies that

$$\underbrace{\limsup_{t\to\infty}\frac{\ln\mathbf{E}\{V(\sigma(t),t)\}}{t}}_{\text{Termii}} \leq \underbrace{-\limsup_{t\to\infty}\frac{1}{t}\int_0^t a_{\sigma(s)}ds}_{\text{Termiii}}. \tag{19}$$

Based on Lemma 2, Termiii can be rewritten as

$$\text{Termiii} = - \sum_{m=1}^q a_m\limsup_{t\to\infty}\frac{T_m(t)}{t} = - \sum_{m=1}^q a_m\bar{\pi}_m, \quad \text{a.s.} \tag{20}$$

Combining condition (7) with (20) and (18), it holds

$$\text{Termii} \leq - \sum_{m=1}^q a_m\bar{\pi}_m < 0, \text{a.s.}, \tag{21}$$

which implies

$$\limsup_{t\to\infty}\frac{\ln\mathbf{E}\{\|E(t)\|\}}{t} \leq \frac{1}{\hat{\lambda}}\limsup_{t\to\infty}\frac{\ln\mathbf{E}\{V_1(\sigma(t),t)\}}{t}$$
$$\leq \frac{1}{\hat{\lambda}}\limsup_{t\to\infty}\frac{\ln\mathbf{E}\{V(\sigma(t),t)\}}{t} < 0, \text{a.s.},$$

where $\hat{\lambda} = 2\times\min\{\lambda_{\min}(\mathbb{P}_{m,1}), m \in \mathbb{M}_q\}$.

According to Definition 1, the GESC a.s. of SMAS (1) with controller (2) is achieved. The proof is completed. ∎

Next result shows that the GESC a.s. of MAS via intermittent control is a special case of the Theorem 1. Before moving on, some settings are useful.

Let $\mathbb{M}_2 = \{1, 2\}$, $\eta_1 = 1$, $\eta_2 = 0$, $A_1 = A_2 = A$, $B_1 = B_2 = B$, $D_1 = D_2 = D$, SMAS (1) with controllers (2) becomes

$$
\begin{cases}
\dot{x}_i(t) = Ax_i(t) + Dx_i(t - \tau(t)) - BK \sum_{j=1, j \neq i}^{N} g_{ij} \left(x_i(t) - \frac{\phi_j}{\phi_i} x_j(t) \right), \\
\hspace{5cm} t \in [t_{2k}, t_{2k+1}), \hspace{1cm} (22) \\
\dot{x}_i(t) = Ax_i(t) + Dx_i(t - \tau(t)), \, t \in [t_{2k+1}, t_{2k+2}).
\end{cases}
$$

Assumption 1 means that $\mathbf{E}(t_{2k+1} - t_{2k}) = h_1$, $\mathbf{E}(t_{2k+2} - t_{2k+1}) = h_2$, where h_1 denotes average control width; h_2 denotes average rest width.

Then the results about GESC a.s. of MAS (22) via intermittent control are as follows.

Corollary 1. *Suppose that Assumptions 1 and 2 hold. Consider an undirected and connected graph. For given scalars $\hat{a}_1 > 0$ and $\hat{a}_2 < 0$, if there are matrices,* $\hat{\mathbb{P}}_{m,f} = \mathrm{diag}\{\tilde{\hat{\mathbb{P}}}_{m,f}, \ldots, \tilde{\hat{\mathbb{P}}}_{m,f}\} > 0$, $f = 1, 2$, $\tilde{\hat{\mathbb{Y}}}_1$, *such that for any $m \in \mathbb{M}_2$,*

$$
\tilde{\hat{\mathbb{J}}}_1 < 0, \, \tilde{\hat{\mathbb{J}}}_2 < 0, \, \hat{a}_1 \bar{\pi}_1 + \hat{a}_2 \bar{\pi}_2 > 0, \hspace{1cm} (23)
$$

then the GESC a.s. of intermittent control MAS (22) with gain matrices $K = B^+ \tilde{\hat{\mathbb{P}}}_{1,1}^{-1} \tilde{\hat{\mathbb{Y}}}_1$ is achieved, where

$$
\tilde{\hat{\mathbb{J}}}_m = \begin{bmatrix} \hat{\Phi}_m & (I \otimes \tilde{\hat{\mathbb{P}}}_{m,1} D) \\ (I \otimes D^T \tilde{\hat{\mathbb{P}}}_{m,1}) & (\hat{\tau} - 1) \hat{\mathbb{P}}_{m,2} \end{bmatrix}, \hspace{1cm} (24)
$$

$$
\hat{\Phi}_1 = \mathrm{sym} \left[I \otimes (\tilde{\hat{\mathbb{P}}}_{1,1} A - \lambda_2 \tilde{\hat{\mathbb{P}}}_{1,1} B B^+ \tilde{\hat{\mathbb{P}}}_{1,1}^{-1} \tilde{\hat{\mathbb{Y}}}_1) \right] + a_1 \hat{\mathbb{P}}_{1,1} + \hat{\mathbb{P}}_{1,2}, \quad \hat{\Phi}_2 = \mathrm{sym} \left[I \otimes \tilde{\hat{\mathbb{P}}}_{2,1} A \right] + a_2 \hat{\mathbb{P}}_{2,1} + \hat{\mathbb{P}}_{2,2}.
$$

Proof. For the intermittent control MAS (22), let

$$
P = \begin{bmatrix} 0 & 1 \\ 1 & 0 \end{bmatrix} \hspace{1cm} (25)
$$

be TP matrix. Lemma 1 implies that $\pi = (0.5, 0.5)$ is the unique stationary distribution of TP matrix (25). Then the following proof is similar to that in the proof of Theorem (1). The proof is completed. ∎

4   Numerical Examples

Two examples are given to show the effectiveness of Theorem 1 and Corollary 1.

4.1   Example 1

Firstly, consider a SMAS (1) that contains three agents, in which the system matrices and Laplacian matrices with three modes ($\sigma = 1, 2, 3$) are selected as follows.

Mode 1:

$$A_1 = \begin{bmatrix} 0.2 & 0.4 \\ 0.8 & -0.6 \end{bmatrix}, D_1 = \begin{bmatrix} 0.08 & 0.16 \\ 0.32 & -0.24 \end{bmatrix}, B_1 = \begin{bmatrix} 1 \\ 0 \end{bmatrix}, L_1 = \begin{bmatrix} 2 & -1 & -1 \\ -1 & 2 & -1 \\ -1 & -1 & 2 \end{bmatrix}.$$

(26)

Mode 2:

$$A_2 = \begin{bmatrix} -1.2 & 0.2 \\ 0.5 & 0.9 \end{bmatrix}, D_2 = \begin{bmatrix} -0.48 & 0.08 \\ 0.20 & 0.36 \end{bmatrix}, B_2 = \begin{bmatrix} 0 \\ 1 \end{bmatrix}, L_2 = \begin{bmatrix} 1 & -1 & 0 \\ -1 & 2 & -1 \\ 0 & -1 & 1 \end{bmatrix}.$$

(27)

Mode 3:

$$A_3 = \begin{bmatrix} -0.9 & -0.5 \\ 0.3 & 0.4 \end{bmatrix}, D_3 = \begin{bmatrix} -0.36 & -0.20 \\ 0.12 & 0.16 \end{bmatrix}, B_3 = \begin{bmatrix} 1 & 0 \end{bmatrix}^T, L_3 = \mathbf{0}_{3 \times 3}.$$

(28)

Secondly, let $\eta_1 = \eta_2 = 1$, $\eta_3 = 0$, $\tau(t) = 0.15 + 0.05 \sin(10t)$, and

$$P = \begin{bmatrix} 0 & 0.89 & 0.11 \\ 0.92 & 0 & 0.08 \\ 0.54 & 0.46 & 0 \end{bmatrix}, \quad \pi = \begin{bmatrix} 0.4620 \\ 0.4511 \\ 0.0869 \end{bmatrix}^T.$$

(29)

Thirdly, taking $a_1 = 10$, $a_2 = 3.8$, $a_3 = -2.5$, $h_1 = 0.9\,\text{s}$, $h_2 = 0.8\,\text{s}$, $h_3 = 0.1\,\text{s}$, and solving the condition (7), the following gain matrices can be obtained.

$$\widetilde{K}_1 = \begin{bmatrix} 2.4641 & 0.1942 \end{bmatrix}, \widetilde{K}_2 = \begin{bmatrix} 0.3607 & 6.5381 \end{bmatrix}.$$

(30)

Combining the above settings and taking $r \in [-0.2, 0]$, the time step $\Delta t = 0.0001$, the scale values $\phi_1 = 0.5$, $\phi_2 = 1$, and $\phi_3 = 2$, the scaled state responses and switching signals presented in Fig. 1(a), and the evolutions of scaled consensus algorithms presented in Fig. 1(b), are obtained.

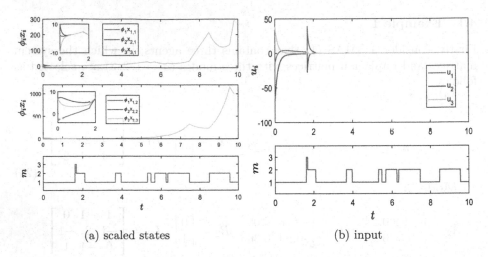

(a) scaled states   (b) input

Fig. 1. Convergence behaviors of the SMASs (1) with controllers (2).

Obviously, Fig. 1 shows that the scaled consensus of MAS (1) with controllers (2) is achieved, which verifies Theorem 1 perfectly.

4.2   Example 2

Firstly, for the SMAS (22), let $A = A_1$, $B = B_1$, $D = D_1$, $L = L_1$, where A_1, B_1, D_1, L_1 are selected from (26).

Secondly, let

$$P = \begin{bmatrix} 0 & 1 \\ 1 & 0 \end{bmatrix}, \quad \pi = \begin{bmatrix} 0.5 \\ 0.5 \end{bmatrix}^T. \tag{31}$$

Thirdly, taking $\tau(t) = 0.15 + 0.05\sin(10t)$, $a_1 = 10$, $a_2 = -2.5$, $h_1 = 2\,\mathrm{s}$, $h_2 = 2\,\mathrm{s}$, and solving the condition (23), the following gain matrix is obtained.

$$\widetilde{K}_1 = \begin{bmatrix} 2.4658 & 0.1944 \end{bmatrix}. \tag{32}$$

Similarly, combining the above settings and taking $r \in [-0.2, 0]$, the time step $\Delta t = 0.0001$, the scale values $\phi_1 = 0.5$, $\phi_2 = 1$, and $\phi_3 = 2$, the scaled state responses and switching signals presented in Fig. 2(a), and the evolutions of scaled consensus algorithms presented in Fig. 2(b), are obtained.

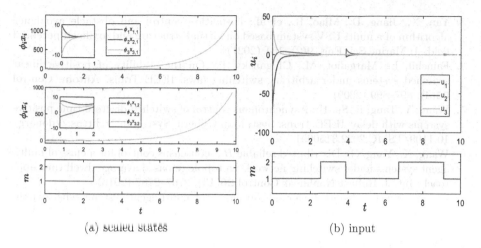

(a) scaled states

(b) input

Fig. 2. Convergence behaviors of the SMASs (22) with intermittent controllers.

Obviously, Fig. 2 shows that the scaled consensus of intermittent control MAS (22) is achieved, which verifies Corollary 1 perfectly.

5   Conclusions

In this paper, the GESC a.s. of SMASs with controller failure and time-varying delay is studied via distributed consensus control scheme. Firstly, switched and scaled consensus algorithms which focus on the influences of controller failure and unconnected networks, are proposed. Secondly, with the help of Lyapunov function-based method, scaled consensus conditions are obtained to guarantee the GESC a.s. of SMASs. Thirdly, Corollary 1 obtained in this paper shows that the GESC a.s. of MAS (1) via intermittent control is a special case of the Theorem 1. Finally, two examples are given to show the effectiveness of Theorem 1 and Corollary 1, respectively. In the future, we will focus on fixed time GESC a.s. of SMASs.

Acknowledgements. We would like to take this opportunity to thank the conference committee of CINT'22 for the insightful comments and constructive suggestions, which have helped us in improving the quality and presentation of the paper.

References

1. Shakeri, R., Al-Garadi, M., Badawy, A., et al.: Design challenges of multi-UAV systems in cyber-physical applications: a comprehensive survey and future directions. IEEE Commun. Surv. Tutor. **21**(4), 3340–3385 (2019)
2. Jing, L., Sreenatha, A., Matthew, G., et al.: Modified continuous ant colony optimisation for multiple unmanned ground vehicle path planning. Expert Syst. Appl. **196**, 116605 (2022)

3. Yan, X., Jiang, D., Miao, R., et al.: Formation control and obstacle avoidance algorithm of a multi-USV system based on virtual structure and artificial potential field. J. Marine Sci. Eng. **9**(2), 161 (2021)

4. Fainshil, L., Margaliot, M., Chigansky, P.: On the stability of positive linear switched systems under arbitrary switching laws. IEEE Trans. Autom. Control **54**(4), 897–899 (2009)

5. Wang, Y. Tang, R. Su, H.: Asynchronous control of switched discrete-time positive systems with delay. IEEE Trans. Syst. Man Cybern. Syst. (2022) .https://doi.org/10.1109/TSMC.2022.3150091

6. Wang, X., Yang, G.: Distributed reliable H_∞ consensus control for a class of multi-agent systems under switching networks: a topology-based average dwell time approach. Int. J. Robust Nonlinear Control **26**(13), 2767–2787 (2016)

7. Cui, Y., Xu, L.: Bounded average consensus for multi-agent systems with switching topologies by event-triggered persistent dwell time control. J. Franklin Inst. **356**(16), 9095–9121 (2019)

8. Cao, X., Li, Y.: Positive consensus for multi-agent systems with average dwell time switching. J. Franklin Inst. **358**(16), 8308–8329 (2021)

9. Xie, D., Shi, L., Jiang, F.: Second-order group consensus for linear multi-agent systems with average dwell time switching. Trans. Inst. Meas. Control **41**(2), 484–493 (2019)

10. Anderson, W.: Continuous-Time Markov Chains. Springer, Heidelberg (1991). https://doi.org/10.1007/978-1-4612-3038-0

11. Yang, X., Li, X., Lu, J., et al.: Synchronization of time-delayed complex networks with switching topology via hybrid actuator fault and impulsive effects control. IEEE Trans. Cybern. **50**(9), 4043–4052 (2020)

12. Yang, X., Liu, X., Cao, J., et al.: Synchronization of coupled time-delay neural networks with mode-dependent average dwell time switching. IEEE Trans. Neural Netw. Learn. Syst. **31**(12), 5483–5496 (2020)

13. Roy, S.: Scaled consensus. Automatica **51**, 259–262 (2015)

14. Meng, D., Jia, Y.: Scaled consensus problems on switching networks. IEEE Trans. Autom. Control **61**(6), 1664–1669 (2016)

15. Guo, X., Liang, J., Lu, J.: Scaled consensus problem for multi-agent systems with semi-Markov switching topologies: A view from the probability. J. Franklin Inst. **358**(6), 3150–3166 (2021)

16. Chen, L., Gao, Y., Bai, L., et al.: Scaled consensus control of heterogeneous multi-agent systems with switching topologies. Neurocomputing **408**, 13–20 (2020)

17. Li, M., Deng, F., Ren, H.: Scaled consensus of multi-agent systems with switching topologies and communication noises. Nonlinear Anal.: Hybrid Syst. **6**, 100839 (2020)

Resilient Event-Triggered Distributed Resource Allocation for Multi-agent Systems Under DoS Attacks

Xin Cai[1,2,3], Feng Xiao[1,2(✉)], and Bo Wei[2]

[1] State Key Laboratory of Alternate Electrical Power System with Renewable Energy Sources, North China Electric Power University, Beijing 102206, China
fengxiao@ncepu.edu.cn
[2] School of Control and Computer Engineering, North China Electric Power University, Beijing 102206, China
bowei@ncepu.edu.cn
[3] School of Electrical Engineering, Xinjiang University, Urumqi 830047, China
xincai@xju.edu.cn

Abstract. This paper presents a resilient event-triggered distributed algorithm for resource allocation of multi-agent systems under denial-of-service (DoS) attacks. A class of time-sequence-based and aperiodic DoS attacks exists in communication networks. A resilient event-triggered communication scheme is designed to determine when agents communicate with neighbors on the network in the presence of DoS attacks. An explicit condition in terms of the frequency and duration of DoS attacks is obtained to ensure the convergence of the designed resilient algorithm to the optimal allocation. Simulation results are given to validate the proposed method.

Keywords: Distributed resource allocation · DoS attacks · Event-triggered communication · Networked systems

1 Introduction

Distributed resource allocation is a class of optimization problems solved by a network of agents, who compute optimal allocation by local interactions. In recent decades, a large number of distributed algorithms has been designed to solve the resource allocation problem in many engineering scenarios, such as the economic dispatch in smart grids [1], power allocation in communication networks [2], and coverage control of wireless sensor networks [3].

Based on the primal-dual theory, a center-free algorithm was firstly proposed in [4]. To implement resource allocation algorithms in a distributed manner,

This work was supported in part by the National Natural Science Foundation of China (NSFC, Grant Nos. 61873074, 61903140), in part by the Beijing Natural Science Foundation (Grant No. 4222053) and in part by the Fundamental Research Funds for the Central Universities, China (Grant No. 2020MS019).

the coordination of Lagrange multipliers by virtue of consensus protocols was designed for the estimation of optimal Lagrange multipliers [1]. In addition to smooth cost functions [1,5], nonsmooth functions were considered in distributed resource allocation problems [6,7]. Considering the applications of engineering scenarios, the distributed resource allocation problem in multi-agent systems with various dynamics was studied, such as disturbed single-integrator systems [7,8], double-integrator systems [9,10], high-order systems [11] and nonlinear systems [12]. It is known that the design and the implementation of distributed resource allocation algorithms depend on communication networks among agents. The related distributed algorithms have been proposed for agents communicating on undirected graphs, weight-balanced or unbalanced directed graphs [1,5,13–15]. Moreover, fixed and time-varying communication delays were considered in distributed continuous-time resource allocation algorithms [16,17]. Additionally, in consideration of limited communication resources and massive transmitted data, many distributed algorithms with discrete-time communication were designed to alleviate network loads and to preserve systems' performance. Static event-triggered schemes were proposed for single/double-integrator agents to execute the designed algorithm with broadcast information [18,19]. Quantization schemes combined with an event-triggered communication strategy were designed to reduce both the communication frequency and the amount of transmission data [20]. Note that secure and reliable communication networks play an important role to guarantee the convergence of the above-mentioned distributed resource allocation algorithms. In recent years, the effects of cyber attacks on physical systems have attracted more and more attentions. However, most of distributed resource allocation algorithms was designed on reliable and secure networks. Recently, only a few work has focused on the design of resilient distributed algorithms on unreliable networks. In the case of communication networks under Byzantine attacks, resilient distributed algorithms based on primal-dual dynamics were proposed in [21]. The stability of a distributed resource allocation algorithm under denial-of-service (DoS) attacks was analyzed in [22]. Unprotected networked systems are vulnerable to cyber attacks and could become unstable and deviate from the optimal allocation. Furthermore, the above-mentioned distributed event-triggered algorithms were designed on reliable networks and may fail to converge to the optimal allocation under cyber attacks.

This paper focuses on a class of cyber attacks called DoS attacks, which can affect the availability of communication links among agents. To the best of our knowledge, there is few work on the design of resilient event-triggered communication schemes in distributed resource allocation algorithms for multi-agent systems under DoS attacks, which motivates us to present this work. The main contributions of this paper are summarized as follows.

(1) Compared with the existing distributed resource allocation algorithms designed for multi-agent systems on secure networks [1,5,13–15], this paper develops a resilient distributed resource allocation algorithm for multi-agent

systems under unreliable communication networks with DoS attacks. A class of time-sequence-based DoS attacks occurs aperiodically in the multi-agent system.

(2) Different from the distributed event-triggered algorithms proposed on reliable networks [18–20], a hybrid coordination framework is designed on the event-triggered broadcasting scheme for the system under DoS attacks. With the designed algorithm, the optimal allocation can be obtained to provide resilience against a class of DoS attacks that the frequency and duration of attacks satisfy certain conditions.

The organization of this paper is given as follows. In Sect. 2, the considered problem is formulated. In Sect. 3, a resilient event-triggered communication scheme is proposed and the convergence of the designed algorithm is analyzed. In Sect. 4, a simulation example is presented. The conclusions are stated in Sect. 5.

Notations: $\mathbb{R}$ and $\mathbb{R}^n$ denote the set of real numbers and the n-dimensional Euclidean space, respectively. $\mathbb{N}$ and $\mathbb{N}_0$ denote the sets of integers and non-negative integers, respectively. Given a vector $x \in \mathbb{R}^n$, $\|x\|$ is the Euclidean norm. $\otimes$ denotes the Kronecker product. A^T and $\|A\|$ are the transpose and the spectral norm of matrix A, respectively. Denote $\mathrm{col}(x_1, \ldots, x_n) = [x_1^T, \ldots, x_n^T]^T$. Given matrices $A_1, \ldots, A_n$, $\mathrm{blk}\{A_1, \cdots, A_n\}$ denotes the block diagonal matrix with A_i on the diagonal. I_n is the $n \times n$ identity matrix. $\mathbf{0}$ denotes a zero matrix with an appropriate dimension. 1_n and 0_n are the n-dimensional column vectors consisting of all 1s and 0s, respectively.

2   Problem Formulation

2.1   Resource Allocation Problem

In this paper, we consider a multi-agent system composed of N agents who are indexed in the set $\mathcal{V} = \{1, \ldots, N\}$ and cooperatively solve the following resource allocation problem.

$$
\begin{aligned}
&\min_{x_i \in \mathbb{R}^p, i \in \mathcal{V}} f(x) = \sum_{i=1}^N f_i(x_i) \\
&\text{s.t.} \ \sum_{i=1}^N x_i = \sum_{i=1}^N d_i.
\end{aligned} \tag{1}
$$

In (1), $x = \mathrm{col}(x_1, \ldots, x_N)$ denotes the resource allocation vector with initial condition $x(0)$ satisfying that $\sum_{i=1}^N x_i(0) = \sum_{i=1}^N d_i$. The quantity $\sum_{i=1}^N d_i \in \mathbb{R}^p$ is the available resource shared among agents. $f_i(x_i) : \mathbb{R}^p \to \mathbb{R}$ is the cost function of agent i. The following assumptions are given to facilitate the subsequent analysis.

Assumption 1. The cost function $f_i(x_i)$ is θ_i-strongly convex and sufficient smooth, i.e., $(x_i - x_i')^T (\nabla f_i(x_i) - \nabla f_i(x_i')) \geq \theta_i \|x_i - x_i'\|^2$, $\forall x_i, x_i' \in \mathbb{R}^p$. It's gradient $\nabla f_i(x_i)$ is l_i-Lipschitz continuous, i.e., $\|\nabla f_i(x_i) - \nabla f_i(x_i')\| \leq l_i \|x_i - x_i'\|$, $\forall x_i, x_i' \in \mathbb{R}^p$.

Assumption 2. The problem (1) has an optimal solution x^*.

2.2 Distributed Resource Allocation Algorithm with Discrete-Time Communication

For agent i, define $\{t_{k_i}^i\}_{k_i=0}^\infty$ as a sequence of times when agent i communicates with its neighbors. Inspired by [1], a distributed resource allocation algorithm with discrete-time communication is designed by

$$\dot{x}_i = -\nabla f_i(x_i) + \lambda_i, \tag{2a}$$

$$\dot{\lambda}_i = -\alpha \sum_{j \in \mathcal{N}_i} (\hat{\lambda}_i - \hat{\lambda}_j) - z_i - x_i + d_i, \tag{2b}$$

$$\dot{z}_i = \alpha \sum_{j \in \mathcal{N}_i} (\hat{\lambda}_i - \hat{\lambda}_j). \tag{2c}$$

In (2), $\nabla f_i(x_i)$ is the gradient of cost function f_i with respect to x_i, λ_i is the estimation of the Lagrange multiplier related to the equality constraint, z_i is an auxiliary state which facilitates λ_i to reach to the optimal Lagrange multiplier $\bar{\lambda} \in \mathbb{R}^p$. In addition, $\hat{\lambda}_i = \lambda_i(t_{k_i}^i)$ is the latest broadcast information of agent i. For $t \in [t_{k_i}^i, t_{k_i+1}^i)$, $\hat{\lambda}_i$ remains unchanged.

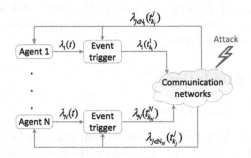

Fig. 1. A multi-agent system under DoS attakcs.

2.3 DoS Attack Model

The designed algorithm (2) may be executed in an insecure or unreliable communication network which may suffer from cyber attacks. Here, we consider the communication network subject to DoS attacks; that is, an attacker jams communication channels to prevent neighboring agents from sending and receiving data. This case is depicted in Fig. 1. Define $\{h_n\}_{n \in \mathbb{N}_0}$ as the sequence of DoS attacks. Assume that a DoS attack is lunched at time h_n and is sustained to $h_n + \triangle_n$. The n-th DoS attack time-interval is $H_n = [h_n, h_n + \triangle_n)$ with $h_{n+1} > h_n + \triangle_n$, which indicates that the attacker needs to sleep to supply its energy for the next attack after terminating one attack. Thus, for given $t \geq 0$, the set of time intervals, where communication is denied, is described by

$\Xi(0,t) = \cup H_n \cap [0,t], n \in \mathbb{N}$. Then, in the interval $[0,t]$, the set of time intervals where communication is allowed is $\Theta(0,t) = [0,t] \setminus \Xi(0,t)$. In addition, $|\Xi(0,t)|$ denotes the total length of the DoS attack within the interval $[0,t]$. $|\Theta(0,t)|$ denotes the total length of communication being available within $[0,t]$.

Definition 1. (DoS Frequency, [23]). *Let $\mathcal{N}(0,t)$ denote the number of DoS attacks occurring within the time interval $[0,t]$. There exist $\gamma > 0$ and τ_D satisfying*

$$\mathcal{N}(0,t) \leq \gamma + \frac{t}{\tau_D}, \ \forall t \geq 0. \tag{3}$$

Definition 2. (DoS Duration, [23]). *There exist $\zeta > 0$ and $T > 0$ satisfying*

$$|\Xi(0,t)| \leq \zeta + \frac{t}{T}, \ \forall t \geq 0. \tag{4}$$

This paper aims to design a resilient event-triggered communication scheme for the distributed algorithm (2) such that agents can cooperatively find the optimal resource allocation of problem (1) on the network in the presence of DoS attacks.

3   Main Results

3.1   Resilient Event-Triggered Communication Scheme

Inspired by the event-triggered scheme proposed in [24], a resilient event-triggering rule is proposed for agent i, $(i \in \{1, \dots, N\})$.

$$t_{k_i+1}^i = \begin{cases} t_{k_i}^i + \triangle_*, & \text{if } k_i \in \mathcal{F} \\ t_{k_i}^i + \triangle_{k_i}^i, & \text{otherwise,} \end{cases} \tag{5}$$

where $\triangle_*$ is a predefined period. $\mathcal{F}$ denotes the set of integers related to communication attempts occurring in the presence of DoS attacks, that is, $\mathcal{F} = \{(i, k_i) \in \mathcal{V} \times \mathbb{N} | t_{k_i}^i \in \cup_{n \in \mathbb{N}} H_n\}$. $\triangle_{k_i}^i = \max\{\tau_{k_i}^i, b_i\}$ with a positive constant b_i and $\tau_{k_i}^i$ determined by

$$\tau_{k_i}^i = \inf\{t > t_{k_i}^i | \|\hat{\lambda}_i - \lambda_i\|^2 \geq \beta_i \sum_{j \in \mathcal{N}_i} \|\hat{\lambda}_i - \hat{\lambda}_j\|^2\}, \tag{6}$$

where $\beta_i > 0$, and $b_i \leq \frac{1}{\nu}(\ln(1+\alpha\varrho_N/\nu) - \ln(1/(1+\sqrt{c}) + \alpha\varrho_N/\nu))$ with α defined in (2), $c = \frac{2\eta_2 \varrho_N^2(L)}{N(1-s_{max})}$, $s_{max} = \max\{\frac{4\varrho_N^2 \beta_i^2}{8d_i + (a\alpha - 2)^2 \|L\|}\}$, $\nu = \alpha\varrho_N + \frac{a+1}{2\theta} + \frac{2\alpha\varrho_2\theta - a - 1}{a\theta}$, and $\eta_2 < 1 - \beta_i$.

Remark 1. Note that the accurate estimations of Lagrange multipliers depend on the successful information transmission over the communication network. When the communication network is secure, the Lagrange multipliers are updated along

(2b)-(2c) with event-triggered communication rule (6). When the network suffers from DoS attacks, unlike [18–20], the designed algorithm fails since the estimations of Lagrange multipliers become incorrect by the failure of receiving neighboring agents' information. In such a case that the communication network is denied by the DoS attacks, the interactive terms in (2b)-(2c) are set to zero until the next successful transmission.

3.2   Convergence of Distributed Algorithm

Assumption 3. The communication graph is undirected and connected.

Let $e_i = \hat{\lambda}_i - \lambda_i$. Denote $e = \mathrm{col}(e_1,\ldots,e_N)$, $x = \mathrm{col}(x_1,\ldots,x_N)$, $\nabla f(x) = \mathrm{col}(\nabla f_1(x_1),\ldots,\nabla f_N(x_N))$, $\lambda = \mathrm{col}(\lambda_1,\ldots,\lambda_N)$, $z = \mathrm{col}(z_1,\ldots,z_N)$, and $d = \mathrm{col}(d_1,\ldots,d_N)$. The compact form of the designed algorithm (2) can be written by

$$\dot{x} = -\nabla f(x) + \lambda,$$
$$\dot{\lambda} = -\alpha(L \otimes I_p)(e+\lambda) - z - x + d, \qquad (7)$$
$$\dot{z} = \alpha(L \otimes I_p)(e+\lambda).$$

Theorem 1. *Suppose that Assumptions 1-3 hold. The designed resource allocation algorithm (2) with the event-triggered communication scheme (5) can converge to the optimal allocation of problem (1), provided that*

1) $\beta_i = \frac{2}{8d_i+(a\alpha-2)^2\|L\|}$ *in* (6) *with* $a > \max\{2, \frac{1}{2\theta} - 1\}$ *and* $\alpha > \frac{2+a^2+\|L\|}{2\varrho_2 a} + \frac{1}{a}$;

2) $\frac{1}{T} + \frac{\triangle_*}{\tau_D} < \frac{\alpha_1}{\alpha_1+\alpha_2}$ *with* $\alpha_1 = 2\min\{(a+1)\theta - \frac{1}{2}, (a\alpha-1)\varrho_2 - \frac{a^2}{2} - 1 - \frac{\|L\|}{2}, \frac{1}{4} - \frac{1}{2a}\}/(a+1)$ *and* $\alpha_2 = 2\varrho_{max}(P)$, $P = \begin{bmatrix} -(a+1)\theta & 0 & -\frac{1}{2} \\ 0 & 0 & -\frac{a+1}{2} \\ -\frac{1}{2} & -\frac{a+1}{2} & -1 \end{bmatrix}$.

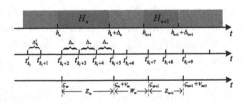

Fig. 2. Diagram for some DoS attack intervals and event instants for agent i.

Proof. The analysis of the designed resilient event-triggered distributed resource allocation algorithm has three steps.

Step 1 (Partition of time intervals): Define $\bar{\Theta}(0,t)$ as the union of sub-intervals of $[0,t]$ over which the inequality $\|\hat{\lambda}_i - \lambda_i\|^2 \leq \beta_i \sum_{j\in\mathcal{N}_i} \|\hat{\lambda}_i - \hat{\lambda}_j\|^2$ holds. $\bar{\Xi}(0,t)$ is the union of sub-intervals of $[0,t]$ over which the inequality

$\|\hat{\lambda}_i - \lambda_i\|^2 \le \beta_i \sum_{j \in \mathcal{N}_i} \|\hat{\lambda}_i - \hat{\lambda}_j\|^2$ needs not to hold. Specifically, there are two sequences of non-negative real numbers $\{\zeta_m\}_{m \in \mathbb{N}_0}$, $\{\nu_m\}_{m \in \mathbb{N}_0}$ such that $\bar{\Xi}(0, t) := \cup_{m \in \mathbb{N}_0} Z_m \cap [0, t]$ and $\bar{\Theta}(0, t) := \cup_{m \in \mathbb{N}_0} W_{m-1} \cap [0, t]$, where, $Z_m := \{\zeta_m\} \cup [\zeta_m, \zeta_m + \nu_m)$, $W_m := \{\zeta_m + \nu_m\} \cup [\zeta_m + \nu_m, \zeta_{m+1})$, and $\zeta_{-1} = \nu_{-1} := 0$. Figure 2 shows the partition of time intervals. In the following, the definitions of ζ_m and ν_m for $m \in \mathbb{N}_0$ are given. We firstly define $\bar{\Xi}_n = [h_n, h_n + \bar{\triangle}_n + \triangle_*]$ as the n-th time interval during which $\|\hat{\lambda}_i - \lambda_i\|^2 \le \beta_i \sum_{j \in \mathcal{N}_i} \|\hat{\lambda}_i - \hat{\lambda}_j\|^2$ does not necessarily hold. $\triangle_*$ is the predefined period in (5). $\bar{\triangle}_n$ is given by

$$\bar{\triangle}_n = \begin{cases} \triangle_n, & \text{if } \mathcal{F} = \emptyset \\ \max_{i \in \mathcal{V}} \{t_{k_i}^i | k_i \in \mathcal{F}\} - h_n, & \text{otherwise.} \end{cases}$$

Thus, ζ_m is defined by $\zeta_0 = h_0$ and $\zeta_{m+1} = \inf\{h_n | h_n \ge \zeta_m, h_n \ge h_{n-1} + \bar{\triangle}_n + \triangle_*\}$. ν_m is given by $\nu_m = \sum_{n \in \mathbb{N}_0, \zeta_m \le h_n < \zeta_{m+1}} |\bar{\Xi}(0, t) \backslash \bar{\Xi}(0, t)|$.

Step 2 (Convergence analysis): The convergence of the designed algorithm with the resilient event-triggered communication scheme is analyzed in the following two parts.

1) Consider the time interval $\bar{\Theta}(0, t)$. Let (x^*, λ^*, z^*) be the equilibrium of system (7).

Consider a Lyapunov candidate function $V = \frac{a+1}{2}\|x - x^*\|^2 + \frac{a}{2}\|\lambda - \lambda^*\|^2 + \frac{1}{2}\|\lambda - \lambda^* + z - z^*\|^2$ with $a > 0$. The derivative of V along solutions of (7) is given by

$$\begin{aligned} \dot{V} = &-(a+1)(x - x^*)^T(\nabla f(x) - \nabla f(x^*)) - (a\alpha - 1)(\lambda - \lambda^*)^T(L \otimes I_p)(\lambda - \lambda^*) \\ &- (a\alpha - 2)(\lambda - \lambda^*)^T(L \otimes I_p)e - (a+1)(\lambda - \lambda^*)^T(z - z^*) - \|z - z^*\|^2 \quad (8) \\ &- (z - z^*)^T(x - x^*) + s, \end{aligned}$$

where $s = -(\lambda - \lambda^*)^T(L \otimes I_p)(\lambda - \lambda^*) - 2(\lambda - \lambda^*)^T(L \otimes I_p)e = -\hat{\lambda}^T(L \otimes I_p)\hat{\lambda} + e^T(L \otimes I_p)e$. Under Assumption 1, we have that

$$-(a+1)(x - x^*)^T(\nabla f(x) - \nabla f(x^*)) \le -(a+1)\theta\|x - x^*\|^2, \quad (9)$$

where $\theta = \min\{\theta_1, \ldots, \theta_N\}$. Under Assumption 3, it yields that

$$-(a\alpha - 1)(\lambda - \lambda^*)^T(L \otimes I_p)(\lambda - \lambda^*) \le -(a\alpha - 1)\varrho_2\|\lambda - \lambda^*\|^2, \quad (10)$$

where ϱ_2 is the second smallest eigenvalue of Laplacian L of graph $\mathcal{G}$.

It follows from Young's inequality that

$$-(a+1)(\lambda - \lambda^*)^T(z - z^*) \le \frac{a^2 + 2}{2}\|\lambda - \lambda^*\|^2 + (\frac{1}{2a} + \frac{1}{4})\|z - z^*\|^2, \quad (11)$$

$$-(z - z^*)^T(x - x^*) \le \frac{1}{2}\|z - z^*\|^2 + \frac{1}{2}\|x - x^*\|^2, \quad (12)$$

and

$$(a\alpha - 2)(\lambda - \lambda^*)^T(L \otimes I_p)e \le \frac{\|L\|}{2}\|\lambda - \lambda^*\|^2 + \frac{(a\alpha - 2)^2\|L\|}{2}\|e\|^2. \quad (13)$$

Substituting (9)-(13) into (8) yields that

$$\dot{V} \le -((a+1)\theta - \frac{1}{2})\|x - x^*\|^2 - ((a\alpha - 1)\varrho_2 - \frac{a^2}{2} - 1 - \frac{\|L\|}{2})\|\lambda - \lambda^*\|^2$$

$$- (\frac{1}{4} - \frac{1}{2a})\|z - z^*\|^2 - \frac{1}{2}\sum_{i=1}^{N}\sum_{j\in\mathcal{N}_i}\|\hat{\lambda}_i - \hat{\lambda}_j\|^2 + \frac{1}{2}\sum_{i=1}^{N}(4d_i + \frac{(a\alpha - 2)^2\|L\|}{2})\|e_i\|^2.$$

$$(14)$$

For an event interval $[t_{k_i}^i, t_{k_i+1}^i)$ of agent i, it follows from the event-triggered rule (5) that $-\sum_{j\in\mathcal{N}_i}\|\hat{\lambda}_i - \hat{\lambda}_j\|^2 + (4d_i + \frac{(a\alpha - 2)^2\|L\|}{2})\|e_i\|^2 \le 0$. If $a > \max\{2, \frac{1}{2\theta} - 1\}$ and $\alpha > \frac{2 + a^2 + \|L\|}{2\varrho_2 a} + \frac{1}{a}$, $\dot{V} \le \alpha_1 V$ with $\alpha_1 = 2\min\{(a+1)\theta - \frac{1}{2}, (a\alpha - 1)\varrho_2 - \frac{a^2}{2} - 1 - \frac{\|L\|}{2}, \frac{1}{4} - \frac{1}{2a}\}/(a+1)$.

2) Consider the time interval $\bar{\Xi}(0, t)$, when the communication network is unavailable. For agent i, it cannot transmit or receive information. The compact form of the designed algorithm (2) becomes that

$$\begin{aligned} \dot{x} &= -\nabla f(x) + \lambda, \\ \dot{\lambda} &= -z - x + d, \\ \dot{z} &= 0. \end{aligned} \tag{15}$$

The derivative of V along solutions of (15) is given by

$$\begin{aligned} \dot{V} &= -(a+1)(x - x^*)^T(\nabla f(x) - \nabla f(x^*)) - \|z - z^*\|^2 \\ &\quad - (a+1)(\lambda - \lambda^*)^T(z - z^*) - (z - z^*)^T(x - x^*) \\ &\le -(a+1)\theta\|x - x^*\|^2 - \|z - z^*\|^2 - (a+1)(\lambda - \lambda^*)^T(z - z^*) - (z - z^*)^T(x - x^*) \\ &\le \alpha_2 V, \end{aligned}$$

where $\alpha_2 = 2\varrho_{max}(P)$ with $P = \begin{bmatrix} -(a+1)\theta & 0 & -\frac{1}{2} \\ 0 & 0 & -\frac{a+1}{2} \\ -\frac{1}{2} & -\frac{a+1}{2} & -1 \end{bmatrix}$.

3) According to the definitions of $\bar{\Xi}(0, t)$ and $\bar{\Theta}(0, t)$, it is derived that $V(t) \le e^{\alpha_2|\bar{\Xi}(0,t)|}e^{-\alpha_1|\bar{\Theta}(0,t)|}V(0)$. Since $t \ge 0$, $|\bar{\Theta}(0, t)| = t - |\bar{\Xi}(0, t)|$ and $|\bar{\Xi}(0, t)| \le |\Xi(0, t)| + (1 + n(0, t))\triangle_*$ with the number of DoS attacks $n(0, t)$. Thus, we have that

$$\begin{aligned} -\alpha_1|\bar{\Theta}(0, t)| + \alpha_2|\bar{\Xi}(0, t)| &= -\alpha_1 t + (\alpha_1 + \alpha_2)|\bar{\Xi}(0, t)| \\ &\le -\alpha_1 t + (\alpha_1 + \alpha_2)(|\Xi(0, t)| + (1 + n(0, t))\triangle_*) \\ &\le -\alpha_1 t + (\alpha_1 + \alpha_2)(\zeta + \frac{t}{T} + (1 + \gamma + \frac{t}{\tau_D})\triangle_*), \end{aligned}$$

where the second inequality comes from the frequency and duration constraints of DoS attacks in (3) and (4). It further yields that $V(t) \le e^{(-\alpha_1 + \frac{\alpha_1 + \alpha_2}{T} + \frac{(\alpha_1 + \alpha_2)\triangle_*}{\tau_D})t}e^{(\alpha_1 + \alpha_2)(\zeta + (1 + \gamma)\triangle_*)}V(0)$. If $-\alpha_1 + \frac{\alpha_1 + \alpha_2}{T} + \frac{(\alpha_1 + \alpha_2)\triangle_*}{\tau_D} < 0$, which derives that $\frac{1}{T} + \frac{\triangle_*}{\tau_D} < \frac{\alpha_1}{\alpha_1 + \alpha_2}$, $V(t)$ is a decreasing function. It indicates that the proposed resilient event-triggered rule (5) can guarantee that the designed distributed resource allocation algorithm (2) can converge to the optimal resource allocation x^* under DoS attacks.

Step 3 (Minimal inter-event interval): Similar to [24], when the communication network is available, the inter-event time of agent i is specified by $\tau^i_{k_i}$ or b_i based on (5). Denote $Q_1(t)$ and $Q_2(t)$ as the agent sets where the latest inter-event times are specified by $\{\tau^i_{k_i}\}_{i \in \mathcal{V}}$ and $\{b_i\}_{i \in \mathcal{V}}$, respectively. Then, $Q_1(t) \cup Q_2(t) = \{1, \ldots, N\}$ and $Q_1(t) \cap Q_2(t) = \emptyset$. To ensure $\|\hat{\lambda}_i - \lambda_i\|^2 \le \beta_i \sum_{j \in \mathcal{N}_i} \|\hat{\lambda}_i - \hat{\lambda}_j\|^2$ during $t \in [t^i_{k_i}, t^i_{k_i+1})$ for agent i, $(i \in \mathcal{N})$, we choose that for $\eta_1 + \eta_2 = \eta < 1$

$$\sum_{i \in Q_1(t)} \|\hat{\lambda}_i - \lambda_i\|^2 \le \eta_1 \sum_{i \in Q_1(t)} \sum_{j \in \mathcal{N}_i} \|\hat{\lambda}_i - \hat{\lambda}_j\|^2 \le \eta_1 \sum_{i=1}^{N} \sum_{j \in \mathcal{N}_i} \|\hat{\lambda}_i - \hat{\lambda}_j\|^2 \quad (16)$$

$$\sum_{i \in Q_2(t)} \|\hat{\lambda}_i - \lambda_i\|^2 \le \eta_2 \sum_{i \in Q_2(t)} \sum_{j \in \mathcal{N}_i} \|\hat{\lambda}_i - \hat{\lambda}_j\|^2 \le \eta_2 \sum_{i=1}^{N} \sum_{j \in \mathcal{N}_i} \|\hat{\lambda}_i - \hat{\lambda}_j\|^2. \quad (17)$$

A sufficient condition for (16) is $\eta_1 \ge \beta_i$. A sufficient condition for (17) is $\|\hat{\lambda}_i - \lambda_i\|^2 \le (\eta_2/N) \sum_{i=1}^{N} \sum_{j \in \mathcal{N}_i} \beta_i \|\hat{\lambda}_i - \hat{\lambda}_j\|^2 \le \frac{2\eta_2 \varrho_N^2(L)}{N(1-s_{max})} \|\lambda - \lambda^*\|^2$ with $s_{max} = \max\{\frac{4\varrho_N^2 \beta_i^2}{8d_i+(a\alpha-2)^2\|L\|}\}$. Let $c = \frac{2\eta_2 \varrho_N^2(L)}{N(1-s_{max})}$. If b_i is a lower bound for the evolution time of $\|\hat{\lambda}_i - \lambda_i\|/\|\lambda - \lambda^*\|$ from 0 to $\sqrt{c}$, for agent i in $Q_2(t)$, $t_{k_i+1} = t_{k_i} + b_i$ is sufficient to ensure (17). Denote $e_i = \hat{\lambda}_i - \lambda_i$.

$$\frac{d}{dt} \frac{\|e_i\|}{\|\lambda\|} = \frac{e_i^T \dot{e}_i}{\|e_i\|\|\lambda\|} - \frac{\|e_i\|\lambda^T \dot{\lambda}}{\|\lambda\|^3} \le (1 + \frac{\|e\|}{\|\lambda\|})(\frac{\alpha \varrho_N \|e\|}{\|\lambda\|} + \alpha\varrho_N + \frac{\|z\|}{\|\lambda\|} + \frac{\|x\|}{\|\lambda\|})$$

According to the above analysis, $\frac{\|z\|}{\|\lambda\|} + \frac{\|x\|}{\|\lambda\|}$ is bounded. It is further derived that $\alpha\varrho_N + \frac{\|z\|}{\|\lambda\|} + \frac{\|x\|}{\|\lambda\|} < \alpha\varrho_N + \frac{a+1}{2\theta} + \frac{2\alpha\varrho_2\theta - a - 1}{a\theta}$. Let $\nu = \alpha\varrho_N + \frac{a+1}{2\theta} + \frac{2\alpha\varrho_2\theta - a - 1}{a\theta}$. Then, $\frac{d}{dt} \frac{\|e_i\|}{\|\lambda\|} \le \alpha\varrho_N(1 + \frac{\|e\|}{\|\lambda\|})^2 + \nu(1 + \frac{\|e\|}{\|\lambda\|})$. By Comparison Lemma, it yields that $b_i \le \frac{1}{\nu}(\ln(1 + \alpha\varrho_N/\nu) - \ln(1/(1 + \sqrt{c}) + \alpha\varrho_N/\nu))$. ∎

4   Simulations

In this section, we give an example of the economic dispatch problem of a power system with four generators to illustrate the obtained results. The communication graphs among the four generators is a line. For agent i, the cost function is described by $J_i(x_i, x_{-i}) = a_i + b_i x_i + c_i x_i^2, \forall i \in \mathcal{I}$. The parameters in cost functions are given by $[a_1, \ldots, a_4]^T = [0.5, 1.5, 3.0, 1.0]^T$, $[b_1, \ldots, b_4]^T = [3, 4, 5, 2]^T$ and $[c_1, \ldots, c_4]^T = [2, 1, 0.5, 1.5]^T$. The total demand of this power system is $d = 145$, which is allocated by $[d_1, \ldots, d_4]^T = [30, 40, 40, 35]^T$. It is calculated that the optimal allocation is $x^* = [17.65, 34.85, 68.70, 23.8]^T$. In the designed algorithm (2), select parameter $\alpha = 2$. The initial conditions are

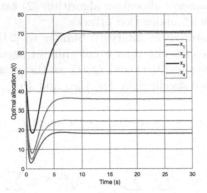

Fig. 3. Optimal resource allocation obtained by algorithm (2) with resilient event-triggered communication scheme (5) under DoS attacks.

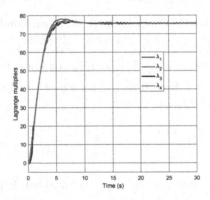

Fig. 4. Regulation of Lagrangian multipliers.

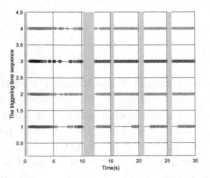

Fig. 5. Triggering instants of the four agents.

$x(0) = [40, 35, 45, 40]^T$, $v(0) = [0, 0, 0, 0]^T$, $\lambda = [0, 0, 0, 0]^T$, and $z = [0, 0, 0, 0]^T$. For the designed resilient event-triggered communication scheme (5), parameters are chosen by $[\beta_1, \ldots, \beta_4]^T = [0.6, 0.5, 0.5, 0.3]^T$, $b_1 = \cdots = b_4 = 0.05$, and $\triangle_* = 0.1$. Figure 3 shows that the outputs of the four generators converge the optimal allocation. Figure 4 shows that Lagrange multiplier λ_i converges to the consensus value. Moreover, the event-triggered instants of the four agents are depicted in Fig. 5, in which gray domains indicate the communication network subject to DoS attacks.

5   Conclusion

This paper studied a resilient event-triggered communication scheme for a multi-agent system under DoS attacks to solve the distributed resource allocation problem. Under certain conditions, the designed resilient event-triggered communication scheme ensured that agents achieved the optimal allocation and were resilient to DoS attacks. The convergence of the designed algorithm was obtained by analyzing the stability of a switched system. Furthermore, the designed resilient event-triggered scheme was free of Zeno behavior.

References

1. Yi, P., Hong, Y., Liu, F.: Initialization-free distributed algorithms for optimal resource allocation with feasibility constraints and application to economic dispatch of power systems. Automatica **74**, 259–1269 (2016)
2. Halabian, H.: Distributed resource allocation optimization in 5G virtualized networks. IEEE J. Sel. Areas Commun. **37**(3), 627–642 (2019)
3. Cortés, J., Martínez, T.K.S., Bullo, F.: Coverage control for mobile sensing networks. IEEE Trans. Autom. Control **20**(2), 243–255 (2004)
4. Ho, Y., Servi, L., Suri, R.: A class of center-free resource allocation algorithms. IFAC Proc. Vol. **13**(6), 475–482 (1980)
5. Liang, S., Zeng, X., Hong, Y.: Distributed sub-optimal resource allocation over weight-balanced graph via singular perturbation. Automatica **95**, 222–228 (2018)
6. Deng, Z., Nian, X., Hu, C.: Distributed algorithm design for nonsmooth resource allocation probelms. IEEE Trans. Cybern. **50**(7), 3208–3217 (2020)
7. Zhu, Y., Wen, G., Yu, W., Yu, X.: Nonsmooth resource allocation of multiagent systems with disturbances: a proximal approach. IEEE Trans. Control Netw. Syst. **8**(3), 1454–1464 (2021)
8. Feng, Z., Hu, G., Cassandras, C.: Finite-time distributed convex optimization for continuous-time multiagent systems with disturbance rejection. IEEE Trans. Control Netw. Syst. **7**(2), 686–698 (2020)
9. Li, S., Nian, X., Deng, Z.: Distributed resource allocation of second-order multiagent systems with exogenous disturbances. Int. J. Robust Nonlinear Control **30**(3), 1298–1310 (2020)
10. Deng, Z.: Distributed algorithm design for resource allocation problems of second-order multiagent systems over weight-balanced digraphs. IEEE Trans. Syst. Man Cybern. Syst. **51**(6), 3512–3521 (2021)

11. Deng, Z.: Distributed algorithm design for resource allocation problems of high-order multi-agent systems. IEEE Trans. Control Netw. Syst. **8**(1), 177–186 (2021)

12. Li, S., Nian, X., Deng, Z., Chen, Z., Meng, Q.: Distributed resource allocation of second-order nonlinear multiagent systems. Int. J. Robust Nonlinear Control **31**, 5330–5342 (2021)

13. Zhu, Y., Ren, W., Yu, W., Wen, G.: Distributed resource allocation over directed graphs via continuous-time algorithms. IEEE Trans. Syst. Man Cybern. Syst. **51**(2), 1097–1106 (2021)

14. Zhang, J., You, K., Cai, K.: Distributed dual gradient tracking for resource allocation in unbalanced networks. IEEE Trans. Signal Process. **68**, 2186–2188 (2020)

15. Chen, G., Li, Z.: Distributed optimal resource allocation over strongly connected digraphs: A surplus-based approach. Autotmatica **125**, 109459 (2021)

16. Li, K., Liu, Q., Zeng, Z.: Distributed optimization based on multi-agent system for resource allocation with communication time-delay. IET Control Theory Appl. **14**(4), 549–557 (2020)

17. Wang, X., Hong, Y., Sun, X., Liu, K.: Distributed optimization for resource allocation problems under large delays. IEEE Trans. Industr. Electron. **66**(12), 9448–9457 (2019)

18. Shi, X., Wang, Y., Song, S., Yan, G.: Distributed optimization for resource allocation with event-triggered communication over general directed topology. Int. J. Syst. Sci. **49**(6), 1119–1130 (2018)

19. Deng, Z., Wang, L.: Distributed event-triggered algorithm for optimal resource allocation of second-order multi-agent systems. IET Control Theory App. **14**, 1937–1946 (2020)

20. Li, K., Liu, Q., Zeng, Z.: Quantized event-triggered communication based multi-agent system for distributed resource allocation optimization. Inf. Sci. **577**, 336–352 (2021)

21. Turan, B., Uribe, C., Wai, H., Alizadeh, M.: Resilient primal-dual optimization algorithms for distributed resource allocation. IEEE Trans. Control Netw. Syst. **8**(1), 282–294 (2021)

22. Shao, G., Wang, R., Wang, X., Liu, K.: Distributed algorithm for resource allocation problems under persistent attacks. J. Franklin Inst. **357**, 6241–6256 (2020)

23. Persis, C., Tesi, P.: Input-to-state stabilizing control under denial- of-service. IEEE Trans. Autom. Control **60**(11), 2930–2944 (2015)

24. Fan, Y., Liu, L., Feng, G., Wang, Y.: Self-triggered consensus for multi-agent systems with Zeno-free triggers. IEEE Trans. Autom. Control **60**(10), 2779–2784 (2015)

A Method and Implementation of Automatic Requirement Tracking and Verification for Complex Products Based on X Language

Yuteng Zhang[1,2(✉)], Pengfei Gu[1,2], Zhen Chen[1,2], and Lin Zhang[1,2]

[1] Beihang University, Beijing 100191, People's Republic of China
zhangyutengbh@163.com, johnlin9999@163.com
[2] Engineering Research Center of Complex Product Advanced Manufacturing System, Ministry of Education, Beijing 100191, People's Republic of China

Abstract. Requirements modeling is often the first step in the development of complex products related to the fields of aviation, aerospace, and shipping. Requirements changes are made throughout the entire lifecycle of complex product development, making it critical to effectively track, manage, and quickly validate requirements. Existing requirements modeling, tracking and verification for complex products often require the collaboration of system-level modeling language SysML and physical-level modeling languages Modelica and Matlab/Simulink, which makes it difficult to track requirements and design products and maintain consistency. To address this problem, this paper proposes a requirement automatic verification method and system based on X language. It can realize the automatic derivation, tracing and verification of the relationship between requirements and design artifacts. First, rules for mining the implicit requirement relationships are defined, a requirement relationship tracking method is proposed based on the rules, and the vertical tracking relationship between requirements and design artifacts is established. Then, the relevant design artifacts are modeled and simulated using X language to verify the target requirements. Based on the above method, a requirement tracking system is developed, which can effectively support the tracking and verification of requirement relationships. Finally, this paper verifies the feasibility and advantages of this automatic requirement verification method and system by using a traffic model as an example.

Keywords: Complex products · X language · Requirements tracing · Requirements verification

1 Research Background

Complex products [1] are a category of products with complex product composition, complex customer requirements, complex product technology, complex project management, and complex manufacturing processes, such as automobiles, aircraft, spacecraft, etc. As the project size of complex products continues to get larger and more complex, the projects also face higher development costs and possible risks of failure.

© The Author(s), under exclusive license to Springer Nature Singapore Pte Ltd. 2022
L. Zhang et al. (Eds.): CINT 2022, CCIS 1714, pp. 443–455, 2022.
https://doi.org/10.1007/978-981-19-8915-5_38

The development of complex products is an iterative and continuous improvement process. Traditional systems engineering has been inconvenient in solving a series of problems of complex product development [2]. Therefore, it is necessary to use advanced systems engineering methods and combine them with perfect requirements development and management processes to solve a series of problems of resources, technology, software, and management in the process of complex product development. Currently, the mainstream systems engineering approach is Model-Based Systems Engineering (MBSE) formally proposed by INCOSE in 2007 [3]. The core idea of MBSE is to support the whole life cycle of a system from conceptual design, analysis, and verification to development through a unified, formalized, and standardized model. The core idea of MBSE is to support all phases of the life cycle of a system from conceptual design, analysis, and verification to development through a unified, formal, and standardized model, enabling the exchange of information between engineers from the traditional document-and physical model-driven R&D model to a model-driven R&D model [4].

Requirements modeling is the first step in complex product development, and requirements change throughout the entire lifecycle of complex product development. Therefore, it is critical for complex products to effectively track, manage, and quickly validate requirements.

Currently, the mainstream modeling language for implementing MBSE is SysML, a standard modeling language for systems engineering proposed by the Object Management Organization in 2001 based on the extension of the Unified Modeling Language UML [5]. However, since the SysML model itself is not executable, it can only perform logical verification of system architecture design and cannot realize modeling simulation of physical performance, thus, it is difficult to realize the verification of requirements. To address the above problems, related scholars have proposed solutions.

The literature [6] proposed a method to extend the SysML model through the mechanism of configuration files and use model transformation techniques to automate the generation from the extended SysML model to the tracking model. The literature [7] implemented a joint simulation of SysML functional architecture models and simulink physical models for multiple subsystems of the civil aircraft takeoff process based on FMI, enabling fast and effective requirements tracking and verification. Schamai, W. [8, 9] presented the first detailed approach for design and simulation integration by extending UML to achieve mapping to Modelica. Shuhua, Z. et al. 2018 [10] implemented a mapping from SysML to Modelica based on ATL and defined an M-Design extension package for converting metamodels, but did not support bidirectional conversion between models. In summary, although the current requirement tracking and verification methods [15, 17, 18] can solve the requirement tracking and verification of some models to some extent, it is difficult to achieve a complete mapping between requirements to simulation models due to the differences between existing system modeling languages and physical modeling languages.

In this paper, M&S-based systems engineering (MSBSE) is used to solve the critical problem of tracing and verifying requirement relationships. The MBSE can make the whole development process easy to trace and easy to maintain; achieve the one-time manufacturing success required for the development of complex products. In this paper, the X language [11] is chosen as the modeling language to model the system, which is an object-oriented language that enables the description of multi-featured, multi-granular models. Each category has two modeling forms, graphical and textual, which correspond one-to-one and can be converted to each other. Based on the unified feature of system modeling and physical modeling of X language, the requirements in the requirements graph established by X language can be directly traced to the corresponding simulation-ready physical modeling design artifacts without the need of mapping between system modeling language and physical modeling language. The continuous change for requirements can be managed effectively.

The main points and contributions of this paper are as follows.

(1) An automated requirements tracing algorithm based on X language is developed to mine implicit requirements relationships and automatically generate a requirements tracing model that describes the relationship between a target requirement and its upstream and downstream design artifacts.

(2) An automatic requirement verification method based on X language is proposed. The method uses a requirement auto-tracking algorithm to track the design artifacts corresponding to the target requirements, and uses X language to model and simulate the design artifacts. The model simulation results are used to verify that the requirements are satisfied.

(3) Based on the above requirement tracking and verification methods, an automatic requirement tracking and verification system based on X language was developed to integrate the above functions.

This paper is structured as follows: Sect. 2 introduces the X language and the requirements tracking algorithm developed based on it; Sect. 3 gives a methodology for simulation and verification of requirements using the X language; Sect. 4 verifies the feasibility of the above methodology through a traffic model and presents the system developed based on it; Sect. 5 concludes the whole paper and gives an outlook on future work.

2 Demand Tracking Algorithm Development Based on X Language

This chapter provides an introduction to the X language and leads to a methodology for requirements information tracking using the X language. Requirements traceability is considered to be very important in the development of complex products. In traditional methods of requirements tracing and verification, model transformation and automatic generation of code are indispensable. For example, the system modeling language is extended by specific configuration files. However, due to the differences between existing system modeling languages and physical modeling languages, it is difficult to implement the mapping between common design models and simulation models. Therefore, in this paper, X language is selected as the modeling language to model the system.

2.1 Introduction to X Language and Overview of Requirement Capture Methods

X language is a new generation of integrated modeling and simulation language for complex systems supporting MBSE. Its design goal is to provide a language that realizes integrated modeling and simulation of the whole process of complex systems (requirements, design, verification, etc.), multiple domains (mechanical, electrical, hydraulic, control, etc.), multiple granularities (parts, components, devices, subsystems, systems and even systems), and multiple characteristics (continuous, discrete, hybrid, etc.) [12].

Based on the unified system modeling and physical modeling features of the X language, the requirements in the requirements diagram created using the X language can be directly traced to the corresponding simulation-ready physical model modules without the need for mapping between the system modeling language and the physical modeling language.

An overview of the requirements tracking information capture method is given below. First of all X language requirements diagrams can be drawn using the X language development software XLab. Once the X language requirements diagram is drawn using XLab, XLab then performs a graphical transformation of the X language requirements diagram and exports an xl format file. The xl file is traversed and the requirement relationship information is located. Finally, the requirement relationship information is converted into program readable form and stored.

2.2 Demand Tracking Algorithm Development

In the requirements diagram of the X language, the relationships between requirements contain the following main types.

1. Derive relationship: if requirement R1 is derived from requirement R2, then requirement R2 is the basis and prerequisite for the implementation of requirement R1, and changes to requirement R2 will have an impact on requirement R1 [13]; for derive relationship, if requirement R1 is derived from requirement R2, then requirement R2 is the basis and prerequisite for the implementation of requirement R1. R1 can be satisfied only when R2 is satisfied. In the above example of R1 and R2, R1 is designated as upstream of R2 in the generated directed graph. The derivation relation possesses the following properties: first, the derivation relation is anti-self-reflexive and there is no dependence of the demand on itself; second, the derivation relation is antisymmetric and the demands do not depend on each other; and third, the derivation relation is transferable.

2. Decompose relationship: describes a local and overall relationship, a complex requirement can be decomposed into a number of simple requirements. For the decompose relationship, if R2 and R3 decompose R1, R1 can only be satisfied when R2 and R3 are satisfied. Taking the above example of R1, R2, R3, in the generated directed graph, R1 is designated as upstream of R2 and R3.

3. Refine relationship: refinement denotes a refinement or concretization that describes a tracing relationship between requirements with different levels of detail. If requirement R1 is a refinement of request R2, then requirement R1 is born in requirement R2 and adds more implementation details to R2. For the refinement relation, if requirement R1 is a refinement of the request R2, then requirement R1 is born in requirement R2 and is supplemented with more implementation details on top of R2. Take the above example of R1 and R2, and designate R1 as downstream of R2.

Through the above relationships between the three requirements, the requirements will form a network that can be stored in the form of a directed graph [16]. For better requirements analysis, in addition to the original relationships between requirements, it is also necessary to mine the requirements relationships that were not originally shown in the requirements graph, i.e., to mine the implicit requirements relationships in the requirements graph.

In order to build a demand tracking model, the demand relationships need to be connected in the form of paths. Therefore, a network of demand relationships can be obtained by creating a directed graph. When building a directed graph, not only the direction of demand relationships but also the type of demand relationships need to be established.

After establishing few rules, the implied demand relationship can be obtained from the original demand relationship. To implement the above rules, a new tracing algorithm needs to be built. The exact process of the requirement tracking algorithm is shown in Fig. 1.

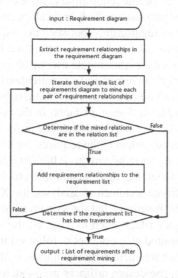

Fig. 1. Schematic diagram of the demand tracking algorithm

The requirement tracking model has the following pattern: a target requirement is selected, and if the target requirement is to be satisfied, all downstream requirements of the target requirement need to be satisfied. Therefore, to satisfy the target demand, it is sufficient to identify all paths containing the target demand and satisfy the most downstream demand in that class of paths to satisfy the target demand.

In order to visualize the demand tracking results, it is necessary to graphically represent the demand tracking results or in the form of a demand matrix. Therefore, the above algorithm is modified to include the DOT language for graphical representation of the requirement tracking model. To use the DOT language in Python, the python-graphviz module can be called. In python-graphviz module, Digraph is used to generate the graph,

Digraph.attr is used to set the style of the graph, Digraph.node is used to generate the nodes and Digraph.edge is used to connect the nodes. By the above method, the graphical representation of the requirement tracking model can be achieved.

3 X Language Based Requirements Validation

The requirements auto-tracking algorithm mentioned in the previous chapter can be used to mine implicit requirements relationships and automatically generate requirements tracking models. In this chapter, an X language based approach to requirements validation is presented. It also provides an introduction to the text modeling approach for the X language.

3.1 An X Language Based Approach to Requirements Validation

The first step in the X language based approach to requirements validation is to perform a requirements analysis of the specific requirements to be validated. The requirements to be validated are decomposed into more underlying and specific requirements through the inclusion, essence, and export relationships between the requirements, and the original and decomposed requirements relationships are represented in an X language requirements graph. Using an automatic requirements tracing algorithm, the implicit relationships in the requirements graph are mined and a requirements tracing model is automatically generated. The model can describe the relationship between the target requirement and its upstream and downstream design artifacts. In the requirement tracking model, the most downstream node is the design artifact. The most downstream node of all the paths containing the target requirement in the requirement trace model is the design artifact to be built to verify the target requirement. After obtaining the design artifacts that need to be built to verify, a functional architecture analysis is performed on the system. When performing the functional architecture analysis, the X language activity diagram can be used to determine the functions that the system needs to have and the functions and attributes that the design artifacts need to have. At the end of the functional architecture analysis, a top-down modeling concept is followed to establish the composition of the design artifacts and the interaction between them within the entire system based on coupled classes. Finally, the design artifacts are modeled. Using X language state machine diagrams to determine the functional and state transformations of the design artifacts, the structure and behavior logic of each subsystem are built and transformed into X language text models based on the above analysis. Once the text models of all subsystems are constructed, simulations can be performed. The simulation results of the models can be used to verify that the requirements are met. Figure 2 shows the complete process of the X language based requirements verification method.

3.2 X Language Text Model Building Rules

In order to simulate design artifacts using the X language, an X language text model needs to be created. This section describes the rules for building the X language text model.

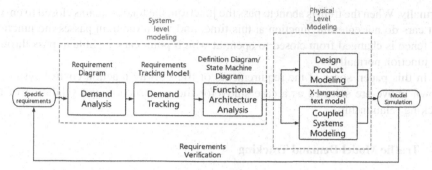

Fig. 2. X language based approach to requirements verification

In X language, for entities with different behaviors (continuous, discrete, hybrid) and entities with intelligent behaviors, four restricted classes (continuous class, discrete class, intelligent body class and coupling class) and three auxiliary modeling classes (record class, connector class and function class) are defined on the basis of the base class to enable the modeling description of complex systems with multiple domains, granularities and features.

After using X language for requirement modeling and functional modeling at the system level, the system-level logical architecture model and physical-level model can be completed based on the above specific classes provided by X language. The physical modeling of specific design artifacts is first performed in X language, and then based on DEVS theory, the system-level logical architecture model and physical-level model integration are achieved by building coupling classes based on the event port interaction mechanism to form a complete full-system simulation model. Therefore, the above rules enable the creation of a simulation-ready X language text model. In addition, the X language is capable of achieving graph-text transformation, i.e., the graphs of the X language can be automatically transformed into text models under the premise that the state machine graphs, definition graphs, and other graphs mentioned in the previous section are correctly built. Therefore, the graph-text transformation of X language can effectively reduce the errors that may occur in text modeling.

4   Traffic Model Case Studies

Based on the above approach of using X language for requirements tracking and verification, an automatic requirements verification system is developed in this paper. In this chapter, the functionality of this system will be demonstrated by a traffic model example of an intersection control system at a railroad and highway crossing.

The case for analysis in this chapter is as follows: a junction where a road and a railway cross, and trains and cars need to pass through it with certain rules, and only if both trains and cars pass through the junction according to specific rules, it is guaranteed that no accidents will occur. The rules are as follows: a fence exists at the intersection of the railroad and the highway, and the fence remains open normally when the train is not passing the intersection, at which point the cars can pass through the intersection normally. When the train is about to pass the junction, the fence remains closed to ensure that cars do not enter the junction at this time, and when the train passes the junction, the fence is changed from closed to open, at which point cars are able to pass through the junction normally.

In this paper, some of the requirements of the railway junction control system as shown above are selected as a case study for the construction and validation of the tracking relationship.

4.1 Traffic Model Demand Tracking

Based on the preliminary security analysis, we can first obtain two security requirements for the scenario: Req1 for "no train-car collision at the intersection" and Req2 for "no fence locking the car inside the intersection". Based on the approach described above, the two security requirements are modeled by means of a requirement graph in X language. In the requirements graph, the relationship between the requirements needs to be included so that the requirements can be tracked. And at the same time, in order to refine the above two system-level security requirements, the requirements need to be refined or refined in the following scheme: the Req1 can be decomposed into block-level security requirements Req3 and Req4, and Req2 can be decomposed into block-level security requirements Req3 and Req8; Req4 derives two security-related functional requirements Req5 and Req6; Req3 derives Req4 derives two security-related functional requirements Req5 and Req6; Req3 derives one security-related functional requirement Req7; Req8 derives two security-related functional requirements Req5 and Req9; Block Train has a direct "Satisfy" tracing relationship with security-related requirement Req6; Block Fence has a There is a direct "Satisfy" tracking relationship between block Fence and security-related requirements Req5 and Req9; there is a direct "Satisfy" tracking relationship between block Car and security-related requirement Req7 [14].

The requirements diagram created using XLab is shown in Fig. 3. In the requirements diagram, the relationships between requirements and the specific content of the requirements are shown [20].

Req1 can be selected as the target requirement by entering the model name (railway control system) and the target requirement name (Req1) in the requirement validation system.

After demand tracing the relationship between Req1 and other demands after mining can be obtained [19]: Req1 is decomposed by Req3 and Req4, and Req5, Req6 and Req7 are dependent on Req1. Representing the demand tracing model in graphical form gives the form of Fig. 4.

The red box in the figure represents the target requirement, which in the figure is Req1; the green box represents the modules related to the target requirement, which in the figure are Fence, Train and Car, and the rest are all requirements related to Req1, which in the figure are Req3, Req4, Req5, Req6 and Req7. In the requirement tracking model, to make the target requirement be satisfied, all the requirements downstream of the target requirement need to be satisfied. Therefore, Req3, Req4, Req5, Req6, and Req7 need to be satisfied in the demand tracking model with Req1 as the target demand.

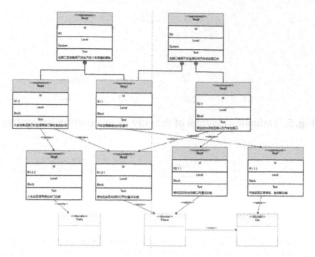

Fig. 3. XLab mapping of railway control system requirements

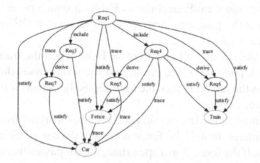

Fig. 4. Graphical demand tracking model (Color figure online)

4.2 Modeling of Traffic Systems at Railroad Crossings

After tracing the requirements, the modules (design artifacts) on which the target requirements depend are known, and therefore, the system consisting of the dependent modules is simulated in XLab. X language coupling classes are described at the graphical modeling level by definition diagrams and connection diagrams. In particular, the definition diagram (Fig. 5) describes the subsystems involved in the overall railway junction control system; the connection diagram (Fig. 6) describes the interactions between the subsystem information. The stakeholder (stakeholder) in the connection diagram is used to determine the train state and car state (train state and car state at the same time is considered as a train and car collision in the railway track).

4.3 Subsystem Modeling

Taking the validation requirement Req1 as an example, each of the three subsystems in this scenario has the following functionality.

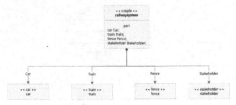

Fig. 5. Definition diagram of the railway junction control system

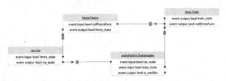

Fig. 6. Railroad junction control system connection diagram

The fence accepts the train signal and when the train is about to arrive at the junction, the fence receives the signal callFenceFunc = False, at which point the fence is closed. When the train leaves the junction, then the fence receives callFenceFunc = True, at which point the fence opens.

The train sends the signal callFenceFunc = False when the train is about to reach the junction, at which point the fence closes and the train passes through the junction. When the train leaves the junction, then the train sends the signal callFenceFunc = True, at which point the fence opens.

The car passes through the intersection and receives a signal from the fence. When the car reaches the intersection, if the fence is closed, the car waits in front of the fence until the fence opens. If the fence is in a open state, the car passes through the intersection normally.

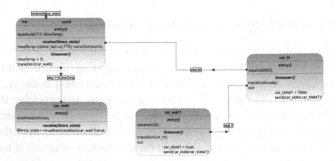

Fig. 7. Partial state machine diagram for car, fence, and train models

A train is set to arrive at the junction every 1000 s and it takes 60 s to drive through the junction; a car is set to enter the junction every 330 s and it takes 10 s to drive through the junction. The simulation starts at time 0 s and the states of the car and the train are detected. If the train and car are not inside the intersection at the same time for a period (e.g., 24 h), Req1 is considered to be satisfied, and if there is a state in which the train and car are inside the intersection at the same time, the train and car collision is considered to have occurred.

The structure and behavior description of each subsystem is implemented here based on discrete classes of the X language. In this case, the definition diagram describes the parameters and the input and output situations in each design artifact, and the state machine diagram describes the state and behavior logic of each design artifact. The partial state machine diagrams (Fig. 7) and definition diagrams (Fig. 8) for the three design artifacts of the car, train, and fence are shown below.

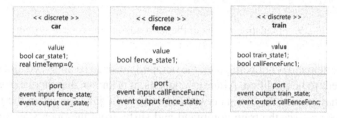

Fig. 8. Diagram defining the car, fence, and train models

4.4 Model Simulation and Requirements Verification

After building the graphical model of each subsystem, the graphical model can be automatically transformed into a text model in X language. After converting the X language text model into the corresponding C++ model using the X language interpreter, the model is simulated. The simulation time was adjusted to 24 h, i.e., the simulation was automatically stopped when the simulation time reached 24 h. If a collision between a train and a car occurs within 24 h of the simulation time (i.e., the train and car states are True at the same time), the requirement is considered to be unmet at this point. If the car and train do not collide within 24 h, the demand is not considered to be satisfied, and several data for the train and car should be modified, such as the interval between each train, the time when the train passes the intersection, etc., to make the model more realistic. Or, if the simulation time is lengthened to ensure that no accidents occur over an extended period, the demand analysis can be found to be reasonable.

To facilitate the model simulation, in this case, the time between the passing of trains and cars at the intersection is shortened and the frequency of the passing of trains and cars is increased to examine what might happen when trains and cars arrive at similar times.

Since in the system, the stakeholder is used to determine whether the train and the car enter the intersection at the same time, it is only necessary to determine whether the is_conflict signal in the stakeholder is True.

Figure 9 shows the visualization of the simulation record, when both CAR and TRAIN are true, the is_conflict indicator, which is used as a judgment of whether the train and the car collided, also becomes true, i.e., the train and the car are judged to have collided with each other.

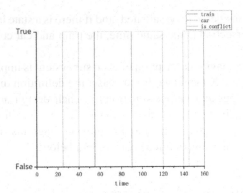

Fig. 9. Simulation results of the railroad junction control system

Since the demand is not being met, the demand needs to be analyzed and the demand or model needs to be modified. After the analysis, it is known that there exists a moment when a car has entered the entrance without exiting the junction when the train arrives and the fence receives the train command and shifts from the open state to the closed state. The car is shut into the junction and a collision with the train occurs. Therefore, the requirement Req4 can be modified to "The intersection fence system should be called to close the intersection 60 s before the train approaches the intersection", which can avoid the collision between the train and the car in the above analysis. After the modification of Req4, the functions of each subsystem should be modified and the modified railroad junction control system model should be simulated according to the above process to verify whether the requirements are satisfied.

5 Conclude

In this paper, we propose an requirement automatic auto-tracking and verification method based on X language, and combine it with the X language modeling and simulation software XLab to realize the complete process from requirement tracking to requirement simulation verification for railway junction control systems, which solves the shortcomings of the current mainstream requirement verification methods. This paper proposes an automatic requirements verification method based on X language that enables the automatic derivation, tracing and verification of the relationships between requirements and requirements, and requirements and design artifacts. First, rules for mining the implicit requirement relationships are defined, a requirement relationship tracking method is proposed based on the rules, and the vertical tracking relationship between requirements and design artifacts is established. Then, an X language based requirement automatic verification method is used to model and simulate the relevant design artifacts to verify the target requirements. Finally, integrates the above algorithms and methods by developing a system that can effectively support the tracing and verification of requirement relationships based on the above methods.

In this paper, this automatic requirement verification method has been validated using only discrete systems, and the next step may be to consider requirement modeling and simulation verification for continuous systems to validate and optimize the method.

References

1. Peng, W., et al.: Research on co-simulation modeling technology of virtual prototype of complex products. J. Syst. Simul. **16**(2), 274–277 (2004)
2. Xu, Z.: Research and Development of Complex product Requirement Modeling and Tracking System for MBSE. MS thesis. Zhejiang University (2017)
3. INCOSE. systems engineering vision 2020. INCOSE, Seattle (2007)
4. Pengfei, G., et al.: An integrated method of civil aircraft co-design and simulation for Takeoff scenarios based on X language. J. Syst. Simul. **34**(5), 929 (2022)
5. Friedenthal, S., Moore, A., Steiner, R.: OMG systems modeling language (OMG SysML) tutorial. INCOSE Intl. Symp. **9**, 65–67 (2006)
6. Liumeng, D., et al.: Extended SysML supports automatic generation of requirements tracing models. Comput. Sci. Explor. **13**(6), 950–960 (2019)
7. Liangyu, Z., et al.: Simulation of Takeoff scene of Civil Aircraft Based on MBSE. J. Syst. Simul. **33**(10), 2499 (2021)
8. Schamai, W.: Modelica modeling language (ModelicaML): A UML profile for Modelica. Linköping University Electronic Press, Linköping (2009)
9. Schamai, W., et al.: Execution of umlstate machines using modelica. In: 3rd International Workshop on Equation-Based Object-Oriented Modeling Languages and Tools; Oslo; Norway; October 3. No. 047. Linköping University Electronic Press (2010)
10. Shuhua, Z., et al.: System design and simulation integration of complex electromechanical products based on SysML and Modelica. J. Comput. Aid. Des. Comput. Graph. **30**(4), 728–738 (2018)
11. Zhang, L., et al.: X language: an integrated intelligent modeling and simulation language for complex products. In: 2021 Annual Modeling and Simulation Conference (ANNSIM). IEEE (2021)
12. Lin, Z., et al.: Architecture engineering based on modeling and simulation. J. Syst. Simul. **34**(2), 179 (2022)
13. Chen, G.: Research on requirement tracing method based on predicate logic. MS thesis. Nanjing University of Aeronautics and Astronautics (2016)
14. Deng, L.: Research on security requirement tracing and verification method based on SysML. MS thesis. Nanjing University of Aeronautics and Astronautics (2019)
15. Xinguang, L., Jihong, L.: SysML based system design-simulation model visualization transformation. J. Comput. Aid. Des. Comput. Graph. **28**(11), 1973–1981 (2016)
16. Fei, W., et al.: A requirement tracing method for security-critical embedded systems. Chin. J. Comput. **41**(3), 652–669 (2018)
17. Casse, O.: SysML in Action with Cameo Systems Modeler. Elsevier (2017)
18. Cao, D.: Research on software security analysis method based on security requirement extension. MS thesis. Nanjing University of Aeronautics and Astronautics (2015)
19. Haidrar, S., et al.: REQDL: A requirements description language to support requirements traces generation. In: 2017 IEEE 25th International Requirements Engineering Conference Workshops (REW). IEEE (2017)
20. dos Santos Soares, M., Vrancken, J., Verbraeck, A.: User requirements modeling and analysis of software-intensive systems. J. Syst. Softw. **84**(2), 328–339 (2011)

Global Mittag-Leffler Stability of Fractional-Order Inertial Complex-Valued Neural Networks

Hualin Song, Cheng Hu[✉][iD], and Juan Yu

Xinjiang University, Urumqi 830017, People's Republic of China
hucheng@xju.edu.cn

Abstract. This paper mainly focuses on the global Mittag-Leffler (ML) stability for a class of fractional complex-valued inertial neural networks (CINNs) without applying reduction and separation method. By introducing a novel Lyapunov function and using the fractional calculus theory, some sufficient criteria are derived for global ML stability of fractional CINNs. The effectiveness of the theoretical results is verified at last via a numerical model.

Keywords: Fractional calculus · Complex variable · Inertial neural network · Mittag-leffler stability

1 Introduction

Neural networks (NNs) have been resoundingly applied in optimization algorithm, automatic control, signal processing technology as well as pattern recognition [1] because of their unique structure and information processing mode. In recent years, a variety of neural networks modeled by the first derivative have been widely concerned, such as Hopfield NNs [2], cellular NNs [3] and Cohen-Grossberg NNs [4]. It is worth noting that the working mechanisms of semicircular canals and synapses in certain organisms cannot be effectively modeled by neural networks with only the first-order derivative. In order to overcome this difficulty, the second derivative term related to voltage was introduced into Hopfield NNs by Babcock and Westervelt in 1987 to establish inertial neural networks, and the bifurcation and chaotic behaviors of inertial neural networks (INNs) were discussed [5].

Nowadays, dynamic analysis for various types of INNs has been deeply studied [6–9]. In [6], the stabilization and robust exponential stability of INNs were

This work was supported by the Key Project of Natural Science Foundation of Xinjiang (2021D01D10), by National Natural Science Foundation of China (61963033), by the Special Project for Local Science and Technology Development Guided by the Central Government (ZYYD2022A05), and by Xinjiang Key Laboratory of Applied Mathematics (XJDX1401).

studied respectively by reducing the second-order NNs into two the first-order NNs. Obviously, the reduced-order method not only increases the system dimension and computational complexity, but also loses the original inertia characteristics of NNs. Based on the above consideration, Li et al. and Han et al. studied the stability of INNs and the synchronization of Cohen-Grossberg INNs based on non-reduced order methods respectively by introducing a special class of Lyapnov functionals [8,9].

Due to the memory and heritability of fractional calculus, Arena et al. used fractional cells to replace traditional first-order cells to establish a fractional cellular neural network in 1998, which is more effective to describe the neurodynamic characteristics of human brain [10]. In addition, the fractional derivative can enrich the dynamic behavior of NNs by adding one degree of freedom. Nowadays, fractional NNs have been largely utilized to system parameter estimation, secure communication and medical imaging [11,12]. In view of the wide application of fractional NNs, some interesting reports on the stability of fractional-order INNs have emerged [13–15]. Ke and Liu et al. analyzed the stability of delayed fractional-order INNs by using integer and non-integer reduction-order methods respectively [13,14].

As we all know, complex-valued neurons have stronger information storage and processing capacity than real-valued neurons, which leads to a great advantage for complex-valued NNs to deal with symmetry detection and XOR problem [16]. As a result, CINNs have caused enormous concern in dynamical analysis and applications [17–19]. Li et al. analyzed adaptive synchronization of a class of fuzzy CINNs by separating complex-valued system into two real-valued NNs [18]. The separation method directly results in a doubling of system dimension and the computational complexity in theoretical discussion. On the other hand, the criteria derived by the separation method are given in the form of two subsystems, which are difficult to test in practice. As a result, Yu et al. introduced a special Lyapunov functional and used complex function theory to derive the exponential synchronization criteria for a class of CINNs without separation methods [19]. Nevertheless, there seems to be no results to discuss the stability of fractional-order INNs without using separation and reduction-order technique. Hence, it is significant to develop a new method to discuss the challenging problem.

Inspired by the above analysis, the global ML stability for a class of fractional-order CINNs is investigated without using separation and reduction-order means. The main contributions are listed as follows.

Firstly, in the absence of the separation method used in [18], the stability of fractional-order CINNs is directly discussed by using complex function theory and inequality techniques, which makes the stability conditions easier to verify in practice.

Secondly, by introducing the fractional derivative into the Lyapunov function, the reduction-order technique in [13–15] is successfully avoided, and the computational complexity of theoretical analysis and criteria is greatly reduced.

Notations: In this paper, $\mathbb{N} = \{1, 2, \ldots, n\}$, n-dimensional real vector space and n-dimensional complex vector space are denoted by $\mathbb{R}^n$ and $\mathbb{C}^n$, respectively. For any $z \in \mathbb{C}^n$, $z = Re(z) + \mathbf{i}Im(z)$, where $\mathbf{i} = \sqrt{-1}$, $Re(z)$ and $Im(z)$ are the real and imaginary parts of z, respectively, and $\|z\|_2 = \sqrt{z\bar{z}}$, in which $\bar{z}$ is the conjugate of z. For any $\dot{Z} = (\dot{z}_1, \dot{z}_2, \ldots, \dot{z}_n)^T \in \mathbb{C}^n$, $\|\dot{Z}\|_2 = \sqrt{\dot{Z}^H \dot{Z}}$, where $\dot{Z}^H$ is the conjugate transpose of $\dot{Z}$.

2 Problem Statement and Preliminaries

Definition 1 [20]. For a differentiable function $\varphi(t) : [0, +\infty) \to \mathbb{C}$, its Caputo fractional-order derivative with order $\alpha \in (0, 1)$ is defined by

$$_0^C D_t^\alpha \varphi(t) = \frac{1}{\Gamma(1-\alpha)} \int_0^t \frac{\varphi'(\tau)}{(t-\tau)^\alpha} d\tau.$$

Definition 2 [20]. The Mittag-Leffler function is defined by

$$E_{\mu,\nu}(\sigma) = \sum_{r=0}^\infty \frac{\sigma^r}{\Gamma(\mu r + \nu)},$$

in which $\mu > 0, \nu > 0, \sigma \in \mathbb{C}$. If $\nu = 1$,

$$E_\mu(\sigma) = \sum_{r=0}^\infty \frac{\sigma^r}{\Gamma(\mu r + 1)} = E_{\mu,1}(\sigma).$$

Lemma 1 [20]. Let $m(s) \in \mathbb{C}$ be a continuous and analytic function, then

$$_0^C D_s^\alpha [m(s)\overline{m(s)}] \leqslant [m(s)\overline{_0^C D_s^\alpha m(s)} + [_0^C D_s^\alpha m(s)]m(s),$$

where $0 < \alpha < 1$, $s \geqslant 0$.

Lemma 2 [20]. Considering a differentiable function $\varphi : [0, +\infty) \to \mathbb{C}$, the Laplace transform of $_0^C D_t^\alpha \varphi(t)$ is shown as

$$\mathcal{L}[_0^C D_t^\alpha \varphi(t)] = s^\alpha F(s) - s^{\alpha-n} \sum_{k=0}^{n-1} s^k \varphi^{n-k-1}(0),$$

in which $n = [\alpha] + 1$, $F(s)$ denotes Laplace transform of $\varphi(t)$. Especially, when $0 < \alpha < 1$, it has

$$\mathcal{L}[_0^C D_t^\alpha f(t)] = s^\alpha F(s) - s^{\alpha-1}\phi(0).$$

Lemma 3 [21]. For functions $m(t)$ and $r(t)$, if their Laplace transforms $M(s)$ and $R(s)$ exist,

$$\mathcal{L}[m(t) * r(t)] = M(s)R(s),$$

in which $*$ represents convolution. In particular, when $m(t) = t$,

$$\mathcal{L}[t * r(t)] = \frac{R(s)}{s^2}.$$

Consider a type of fractional-order CINNs described by

$$\,_0^C D_t^{2\alpha}\dot{p}_i(t) = -m_i\,\,_0^C D_t^{\alpha}\dot{p}_i(t) - b_i\dot{p}_i(t)$$

$$+ \sum_{j=1}^{n} h_{ij}g_j(\dot{p}_j(t)) + I_i(t), \quad i \in \mathbb{N}, \tag{1}$$

in which $\dot{p}_i(t) \in \mathbb{C}$ is the state variable of the ith neuron at time t, $m_i > 0$, $b_i > 0$, $h_{ij} \in \mathbb{C}$ is connection weight, $g_j(\dot{p}_j(t)) : \mathbb{C} \to \mathbb{C}$ represents the activation function of the jth neuron, $I_i(t) \in \mathbb{C}$ is the input from outside. In addition, the initial values of system (1) are given as $\dot{p}(0) = \dot{p}_0 = (\dot{p}_{10}, \dot{p}_{20}, \ldots, \dot{p}_{n0})^T \in \mathbb{C}^n$ with $\dot{p}_i(0) = \dot{p}_{i0}$, and $\,_0^C D_t^{\alpha}\dot{p}(0) = \mathfrak{p}_0 = (\mathfrak{p}_{10}, \mathfrak{p}_{20}, \ldots, \mathfrak{p}_{n0})^T \in \mathbb{C}^n$.

Definition 3 (Global Mittag-Leffler Stability). For model (1) and its any two solutions $\dot{p}(t) = (\dot{p}_1(t), \dot{p}_2(t), \ldots, \dot{p}_n(t))^T \in \mathbb{C}^n$ and $\dot{q}(t) = (\dot{q}_1(t), \dot{q}_2(t), \ldots, \dot{q}_n(t))^T \in \mathbb{C}^n$ with different initial states $\dot{p}_0$ and $\dot{q}_0$, if there have numbers $M > 0$, $\lambda > 0$ and $\beta > 0$, such that

$$\|\dot{p}(t) - \dot{q}(t)\| \leqslant \left(ME_\alpha(-\lambda t^\alpha)\right)^\beta, t \geqslant 0,$$

then the model (1) is called to be globally ML stable.

Assumption 1. For each $i \in \mathbb{N}$, there exists a number $G_i > 0$ such that for any $p_1, p_2 \in \mathbb{C}$,

$$\|g_i(p_1) - g_i(p_2)\| \leqslant G_i\|p_1 - p_2\|.$$

Assumption 2. There exist some nonzero numbers ρ_i, ω_i and a positive number $\gamma_i > 0$ such that

$$\Theta_i < 0, \quad \Xi_i^2 < \Lambda_i\Theta_i, \quad i \in \mathbb{N}, \tag{2}$$

or

$$\Theta_i \leqslant 0, \quad \Lambda_i < 0, \quad \Xi_i = 0, \quad i \in \mathbb{N}, \tag{3}$$

where

$$\Theta_i = 2(\rho_i\omega_i - \rho_i^2 m_i) + \sum_{j=1}^{n} \rho_i^2\|h_{ij}\|G_j,$$

$$\Lambda_i = -2\rho_i b_i\omega_i + \sum_{j=1}^{n}(|\rho_i\omega_i|\|h_{ij}\|G_j$$

$$+ \rho_j^2\|h_{ji}\|G_i + |\rho_j\omega_j|\|h_{ji}\|G_i),$$

$$\Xi_i = \gamma_i + \omega_i^2 - \omega_i\rho_i m_i - \rho_i^2 b_i.$$

Theorem 1. *Under Assumptions 1–2, the neural model (1) is globally ML stable.*

Proof. Let $\dot{p}(t) = (\dot{p}_1(t), \dot{p}_2(t), \ldots, \dot{p}_n(t))^T$ and $\dot{q}(t) = (\dot{q}_1(t), \dot{q}_2(t), \ldots, \dot{q}_n(t))^T$ be solutions of model (1) from different initial states $\dot{p}_0 = (\dot{p}_{10}, \dot{p}_{20}, \ldots, \dot{p}_{n0})^T$ with $_0^C D_t^\alpha \dot{p}_0 = \mathfrak{p}_0$ and $\dot{q}_0 = (\dot{q}_{10}, \dot{q}_{20}, \ldots, \dot{q}_{n0})^T$ with $_0^C D_t^\alpha \dot{q}_0 = \mathfrak{q}_0$. Define $\epsilon(t) = \dot{p}(t) - \dot{q}(t) = (\epsilon_1(t), \epsilon_2(t), \ldots, \epsilon_n(t))^T$, in which $\epsilon_i(t) = \dot{p}_i(t) - \dot{q}_i(t)$. According to (1), the error model is written as

$$_0^C D_t^{2\alpha} \epsilon_i(t) = -m_i \, _0^C D_t^\alpha \epsilon_i(t) - b_i \epsilon_i(t) + \sum_{j=1}^n h_{ij} \hat{g}_j(\epsilon_j(t)), \quad i \in \mathbb{N}, \qquad (4)$$

where $\hat{g}_j(\epsilon_j(t)) = g_j(\dot{p}_j(t)) - g_j(\dot{q}_j(t))$.

Construct a Lyapunov function as follows

$$V(t) = \sum_{i=1}^n \gamma_i(\epsilon_i(t)\overline{\epsilon_i(t)}) + \sum_{i=1}^n \left(\rho_i \, _0^C D_t^\alpha \epsilon_i(t) + \omega_i \epsilon_i(t)\right)\overline{\left(\rho_i \, _0^C D_t^\alpha \epsilon_i(t) + \omega_i \epsilon_i(t)\right)}.$$

According to Lemma 1,

$$_0^C D_t^\alpha V(t) \leqslant \sum_{i=1}^n \gamma_i\left(\epsilon_i(t)\overline{_0^C D_t^\alpha \epsilon_i(t)} + \overline{\epsilon_i(t)}\,_0^C D_t^\alpha \epsilon_i(t)\right)$$

$$+ \sum_{i=1}^n \Big[\left(\rho_i \, _0^C D_t^\alpha \epsilon_i(t) + \omega_i \epsilon_i(t)\right)\overline{\left(\rho_i \, _0^C D_t^{2\alpha} \epsilon_i(t) + \omega_i \, _0^C D_t^\alpha \epsilon_i(t)\right)}$$

$$+ \overline{\left(\rho_i \, _0^C D_t^\alpha \epsilon_i(t) + \omega_i \epsilon_i(t)\right)}\left(\rho_i \, _0^C D_t^{2\alpha} \epsilon_i(t) + \omega_i \, _0^C D_t^\alpha \epsilon_i(t)\right)\Big]. \qquad (5)$$

By using Assumption 1, it has

$$_0^C D_t^\alpha V(t) \leq \sum_{i=1}^n 2(\rho_i \omega_i - \rho_i^2 m_i)\overline{_0^C D_t^\alpha \epsilon_i(t)}\,_0^C D_t^\alpha \epsilon_i(t)$$

$$+ \sum_{i=1}^n \left[\gamma_i + \omega_i^2 - \omega_i \rho_i m_i - \rho_i^2 b_i\right]\left(\overline{\epsilon_i(t)}\,_0^C D_t^\alpha \epsilon_i(t) + \epsilon_i(t)\overline{_0^C D_t^\alpha \epsilon_i(t)}\right)$$

$$- \sum_{i=1}^n 2\rho_i b_i \omega_i \overline{\epsilon_i(t)}\epsilon_i(t) + 2\rho_i Re\left(\sum_{j=1}^n h_{ij}\hat{g}_j(\epsilon_j(t))\left[\rho_i \overline{_0^C D_t^\alpha \epsilon_i(t)} + \omega_i \overline{\epsilon_i(t)}\right]\right)$$

$$\leq \sum_{i=1}^n 2(\rho_i \omega_i - \rho_i^2 m_i)\overline{_0^C D_t^\alpha \epsilon_i(t)}\,_0^C D_t^\alpha \epsilon_i(t)$$

$$+ \sum_{i=1}^n \left[\gamma_i + \omega_i^2 - \omega_i \rho_i m_i - \rho_i^2 b_i\right]\left(\overline{\epsilon_i(t)}\,_0^C D_t^\alpha \epsilon_i(t) + \epsilon_i(t)\overline{_0^C D_t^\alpha \epsilon_i(t)}\right)$$

$$- \sum_{i=1}^n 2\rho_i b_i \omega_i \overline{\epsilon_i(t)}\epsilon_i(t)$$

$$+ \sum_{i=1}^n \sum_{j=1}^n \rho_i^2 \|h_{ij}\| G_j\left(\overline{\epsilon_j(t)}\epsilon_j(t) + \overline{_0^C D_t^\alpha \epsilon_i(t)}\,_0^C D_t^\alpha \epsilon_i(t)\right)$$

$$+ \sum_{i=1}^{n} |\rho_i \omega_i| \sum_{j=1}^{n} \|h_{ij}\| G_j \left(\overline{\epsilon_j(t)} \epsilon_j(t) + \overline{\epsilon_i(t)} \epsilon_i(t) \right)$$

$$= \sum_{i=1}^{n} \left[2(\rho_i \omega_i - \rho_i^2 m_i) + \sum_{j=1}^{n} \rho_i^2 \|h_{ij}\| G_j \right] \overline{{}_0^C D_t^\alpha \epsilon_i(t)} \, {}_0^C D_t^\alpha \epsilon_i(t)$$

$$+ \sum_{i=1}^{n} \left[-2\rho_i b_i \omega_i + \sum_{j=1}^{n} |\rho_i \omega_i| \|h_{ij}\| G_j \right] \overline{\epsilon_i(t)} \epsilon_i(t)$$

$$+ \sum_{i=1}^{n} \sum_{j=1}^{n} \left[\rho_i^2 \|h_{ij}\| G_j + |\rho_i \omega_i| \|h_{ij}\| G_j \right] \overline{\epsilon_j(t)} \epsilon_j(t)$$

$$+ \sum_{i=1}^{n} (\gamma_i + \omega_i^2 - \omega_i \rho_i m_i - \rho_i^2 b_i) \left(\overline{\epsilon_i(t)} {}_0^C D_t^\alpha \epsilon_i(t) + \epsilon_i(t) \overline{{}_0^C D_t^\alpha \epsilon_i(t)} \right)$$

$$= \sum_{i=1}^{n} \left[2(\rho_i \omega_i - \rho_i^2 m_i) + \sum_{j=1}^{n} \rho_i^2 \|h_{ij}\| G_j \right] \overline{D_t^\beta \epsilon_i(t)} \, {}_0^C D_t^\alpha \epsilon_i(t)$$

$$+ \sum_{i=1}^{n} \left[-2\rho_i b_i \omega_i + \sum_{j=1}^{n} (|\rho_i \omega_i| \|h_{ij}\| G_j + \rho_j^2 \|h_{ji}\| G_i + |\rho_j \omega_j| \|h_{ji}\| G_i) \right] \overline{\epsilon_i(t)} \epsilon_i(t)$$

$$+ \sum_{i=1}^{n} \left[\gamma_i + \omega_i^2 - \omega_i \rho_i m_i - \rho_i^2 b_i \right] \left(\overline{\epsilon_i(t)} {}_0^C D_t^\alpha \epsilon_i(t) + \epsilon_i(t) \overline{{}_0^C D_t^\alpha \epsilon_i(t)} \right)$$

$$= \sum_{i=1}^{n} \Theta_i \overline{{}_0^C D_t^\alpha \epsilon_i(t)} \, {}_0^C D_t^\alpha \epsilon_i(t) + \sum_{i=1}^{n} \Lambda_i \overline{\epsilon_i(t)} \epsilon_i(t)$$

$$+ \sum_{i=1}^{n} \Xi_i \left(\overline{\epsilon_i(t)} {}_0^C D_t^\alpha \epsilon_i(t) + \epsilon_i(t) \overline{{}_0^C D_t^\alpha \epsilon_i(t)} \right). \tag{6}$$

From (2) and (6), if $\Theta_i < 0$ for each $i \in \mathbb{N}$,

$$\begin{aligned}
{}_0^C D_t^\alpha V(t) &\leq \sum_{i=1}^{n} \left[\Theta_i \left({}_0^C D_t^\alpha \epsilon_i(t) + \frac{\Xi_i}{\Theta_i} \epsilon_i(t) \right) \overline{\left({}_0^C D_t^\alpha \epsilon_i(t) + \frac{\Xi_i}{\Theta_i} \epsilon_i(t) \right)} \right. \\
&\qquad \left. + \left(\Lambda_i - \frac{\Xi_i^2}{\Theta_i} \right) \overline{\epsilon_i(t)} \epsilon_i(t) \right], \\
&\leq \sum_{i=1}^{n} \left(\Lambda_i - \frac{\Xi_i^2}{\Theta_i} \right) \overline{\epsilon_i(t)} \epsilon_i(t) \\
&\leq -A\epsilon(t)^H \epsilon(t), \tag{7}
\end{aligned}$$

where $A = \min\limits_{i \in \mathbb{N}} \{ \frac{\Xi_i^2}{\Theta_i} - \Lambda_i \} > 0$. From (7), there obviously has a nonnegative function $\ell(t)$ satisfying

$$\begin{aligned}
{}_0^C D_t^\alpha V(t) + \ell(t) = -A\epsilon(t)^H \epsilon(t). \tag{8}
\end{aligned}$$

Furthermore,

$$V(t) = \sum_{i=1}^{n} \gamma_i \epsilon_i(t)\overline{\epsilon_i(t)}$$

$$+ \sum_{i=1}^{n} (\rho_{i0}\,{}^C_{}D_t^\alpha \epsilon_i(t))$$

$$+ \omega_i \epsilon_i(t)) \left(\overline{\rho_{i0}\,{}^C_{}D_t^\alpha \epsilon_i(t) + \omega_i \epsilon_i(t)} \right)$$

$$\geqslant \sum_{i=1}^{n} \gamma_i \overline{\epsilon_i(t)} \epsilon_i(t)$$

$$\geqslant \underline{\gamma}\epsilon(t)^H \epsilon(t),$$

where $\underline{\gamma} = \min_{i \in \mathbb{N}}\{\gamma_i\}$, then there has a non-negative function $w(t) \geqslant 0$ satisfying

$$V(t) = \underline{\gamma}\epsilon(t)^H \epsilon(t) + t * w(t). \tag{9}$$

Taking Laplace transforms to (8) and (9), from Lemmas 2 and 3, one has

$$s^\alpha V(s) - s^{\alpha-1}V(0) + L(s) = -AE(s), \tag{10}$$

$$V(s) - \frac{W(s)}{s^2} = \underline{\gamma}E(s), \tag{11}$$

in which $V(s), L(s), W(s), E(s)$ are the Laplace transforms of $V(t), \ell(t), w(t),$ $\epsilon(t)^H \epsilon(t)$ respectively. Thus, it's not hard to get from (10) and (11),

$$\underline{\gamma}E(s) = \frac{s^{\alpha-1}}{s^\alpha + H}V(0)$$

$$- \frac{1}{s^\alpha + H}L(s) - \frac{s^{\alpha-2}}{s^\alpha + H}W(s), \tag{12}$$

where $H = \dfrac{A}{\underline{\gamma}}$. Taking the Laplace inverse transform for (12),

$$\underline{\gamma}\epsilon(t)^H \epsilon(t) = V(0)E_\alpha(-Ht^\alpha)$$

$$- t^{\alpha-1}E_{\alpha,\alpha}(-Ht^\alpha) * \ell(t)$$

$$- tE_{\alpha,2}(-Ht^\alpha) * w(t), \quad t \geq 0,$$

which implies that

$$\| \epsilon(t) \| = [\epsilon(t)^H \epsilon(t)]^{\frac{1}{2}} \leqslant \left[\frac{V(0)}{\underline{\gamma}} E_\alpha(-Ht^\alpha) \right]^{\frac{1}{2}}. \tag{13}$$

On the other hand, if $\Theta_i \leqslant 0$ for all $i \in \mathbb{N}$, according to (3) and (6), one can get

$$_0^C D_t^\alpha V(t) \leqslant \sum_{i=1}^n \Lambda_i \overline{\epsilon_i(t)} \epsilon_i(t)$$

$$\leqslant -B \sum_{i=1}^n \overline{\epsilon_i(t)} \epsilon_i(t),$$

where $B = \min_{i \in \mathbb{N}} \{-\Lambda_i\}$. Similar to the analysis of (9)-(13), one has

$$\| \epsilon(t) \| \leqslant \left[\frac{V(0)}{\gamma} E_\alpha(-\frac{B}{\gamma} t^\alpha) \right]^{\frac{1}{2}}. \tag{14}$$

Therofore, combining (13) and (14), system (1) is globally ML stable.

Remark 1. By introducing the fractional derivative $_0^C D_t^\alpha \epsilon_i(t)$ into Lyapunov function and using complex-variable function theory, the reduction-order method and separation method in [13–15, 18] are successfully avoided. Our methods not only reduce the computational complexity of theoretical analysis, but also ensure that the stability criteria can be applied directly to the second-order system.

Remark 2. It is not difficult to find that $\Xi_i = 0$ when $\gamma_i = -\omega_i^2 + \omega_i \rho_i m_i + \rho_i^2 b_i > 0$. Based on this, Assumption 2 is equivalent to the following statement and the following stability result will be obtained.

Assumption 3. For each $i \in \mathbb{N}$, there have nonzero numbers ρ_i, ω_i such that

$$-\omega_i^2 + \omega_i \rho_i m_i + \rho_i^2 b_i > 0, \ \Theta_i \leqslant 0, \ \Lambda_i < 0.$$

Corollary 1. Based on Assumptions 1 and 3, the model (1) is globally ML stable.

3   Numerical Verification

Consider the following fractional-order CINN with two neurons

$$_0^C D_t^{2\alpha} \dot{p}_i(t) = -m_i {}_0^C D_t^\alpha \dot{p}_i(t) - b_i \dot{p}_i(t)$$

$$+ \sum_{j=1}^2 h_{ij} g_j(\dot{p}_j(t)) + I_i(t), \quad i = 1, 2, \tag{15}$$

in which $\alpha = 0.9$, $m_1 = m_2 = 2$, $b_1 = b_2 = 4$,

$$I(t) = \left(5 \sin(8t) + \mathbf{i} 6 \cos(7t), 9 \cos(6t) + \mathbf{i} 8 \sin(8t)\right)^T,$$

$$g(t) = (\tanh(Re(p_1(t))) + \mathbf{i} \sin(Re(p_1(t))),$$
$$\tanh(Re(p_2(t))) + \mathbf{i} \sin(Re(p_2(t))))^T,$$

$$H = (h_{ij})_{2\times 2} = \begin{pmatrix} 0.1 + 0.1\mathbf{i} & -0.3 + 0.1\mathbf{i} \\ -0.1 - 0.1\mathbf{i} & 0.5 + 0.1\mathbf{i} \end{pmatrix}.$$

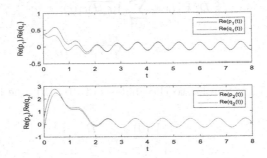

Fig. 1. Dynamic evolution of the real part of system (15).

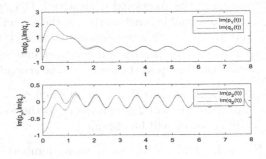

Fig. 2. Dynamic evolution of the imaginary part of system (15).

For $i = 1, 2$, select $\rho_i = \omega_i = 1$, $\gamma_i = \rho_i^2(m_i + b_i - 1)$. By simple calculating, $G_1 = G_2 = 1$, $\Theta_1 = -1.5424$, $\Theta_2 = -1.3487$, $\Lambda_1 = -7.1515 < 0$, $\Lambda_2 = -5.6964 < 0$, $\Xi_1 = \Xi_2 = 0$. Obviously, Assumptions 1 and 2 are satisfied. Therefore, system (15) is globally ML stable by means of Theorem 1.

Choosing two solutions of system (15) $p(t) = (p_1(t), p_2(t))^T$ and $q(t) = (q_1(t), q_2(t))^T$ from different initial values which are randomly chosen on $[-1, 1] + \mathbf{i}[-1, 1]$. The dynamical evolutions of $p(t)$ and $q(t)$ over time are shown in Figs. 1-2.

4   Conclusion

The ML stability for complex-valued INNs with fractional order has been investigated in this paper. To cut the computational complexity caused by the separation method and the reduction-order technique in theoretical discussion, complex function theory has been utilized and a new Lyapunov functional including the fractional derivative of neuron variables has been established. The obtained results have been confirmed via providing a numerical example with numerical simulations.

References

1. Goloboff, P.: Character optimization and calculation of tree lengths. Cladist. Int. J. Willi Hennig Soc. **9**(4), 433–436 (2010)
2. Massini, G.: Hopfield neural network. Int. J. Adhes. **33**(2), 481–488 (1998)
3. Chua, L., Yang, L.: Cellular neural networks: theory. IEEE Trans. Circuits Syst. I **35**(10), 1257–1272 (1988)
4. Cohen, M., Grossberg, S.: Absolute stability and global pattern formation and pattern memory storage by competitive neural networks. IEEE Trans. Syst. Man Cybern. **13**(5), 815–821 (1983)
5. Babcock, K., Westervelt, R.: Dynamics of simple electronic neural networks. Physica D **28**(3), 305–316 (1987)
6. Sheng, Y., Huang, T., Zeng, Z.: Exponential stabilization of inertial memristive neural networks with multiple time delays. IEEE Trans. Cybern. **51**(?), 570–582 (2021)
7. Chen, S., Jiang, H., Lu, B.: Pinning bipartite synchronization for inertial coupled delayed neural networks with signed digraph via non-reduced order method. Neural Netw. **129**, 392–402 (2020)
8. Li, X., Li, X., Hu, C.: Some new results on stability and synchronization for delayed inertial neural networks based on non-reduced order method. Neural Netw. **96**, 91–100 (2017)
9. Han, S., Hu, C., Yu, J., Jiang, H., Wen, S.: Stabilization of inertial Cohen-Grossberg neural networks with generalized delays: a direct analysis approach. Chaos Solitons Fractals **142**, 110432 (2020)
10. Arena, P., Caponetto, R., Fortuna, L.: Bifuration and chaos in noninteger order cellular neural networks. Int. J. Bifurc. Chaos **8**(7), 1527–1537 (1998)
11. Yang, Y., Hu, C., Yu, J.: Event-triggered quasi-synchronization of fractional-order reaction diffusion networks with disturbance. J. Xinjiang Univ. (Nat. Sci. Edn. Chin. English) **39**(2), 134–143 (2022)
12. Arshan, B., Ayrulu, B.: Fractional Fourier transform pre-processing for neural networks and its application to object recognition. Neural Netw. **15**(1), 131–140 (2002)
13. Ke, L.: Mittag-Leffler stability and asymptotic ω-periodicity of fractional-order inertial neural networks with time-delays. Neurocomputing **465**, 53–62 (2021)
14. Liu, Y., Sun, Y., Liu, L.: Stability analysis and synchronization control of fractional-order inertial neural networks with time-varying delay. IEEE Access **10**, 56081–56093 (2022)
15. Gu, Y., Wang, H., Yu, Y.: Stability and synchronization for Riemann-Liouville fractional-order time-delayed inertial neural networks. Neurocomputing **340**(7), 270–280 (2019)
16. Amin, M., Murase, K.: Single-layered complex-valued neural network for real-valued classification problems. Neurocomputing **72**(4), 945–955 (2009)
17. Hui, J., Yu, J.: Exponential synchronization of complex-valued inertial neural networks based on a periodically intermittent control. J. Xinjiang Univ. (Nat. Sci. Edn. Chin. English) **39**(2), 151–160 (2022)
18. Li, X., Huang, T.: Adaptive synchronization for fuzzy inertial complex-valued neural networks with state-dependent coefficients and mixed delays. Fuzzy Sets Syst. **411**(15), 174–189 (2021)

19. Yu, J., Hu, C., Jiang, H., Wang, L.: Exponential and adaptive synchronization of inertial complex-valued neural networks: a non-reduced order and non-separation approach. Neural Netw. **124**, 50–59 (2020)
20. Yang, S., Hu, C., Yu, J., Jiang, H.: Quasi-projective synchronization of fractional-order complex-valued recurrent neural networks. Neural Netw. **104**, 104–113 (2018)
21. Podlubny, I.: Fractional Differential Equations. Academic Press, New York (1999)

Distributed Fixed-Time Consensus and Optimization for Second-Order Multi-Agent Systems

Xuli Cao, Cheng Hu$^{(\boxtimes)}$ ⓘ, Juan Yu, and Haijun Jiang

Xinjiang University, Urumqi 830017, People's Republic of China
hucheng@xju.edu.cn

Abstract. This article mainly studies the distributed fixed-time (FT) consensus and optimization of second-order multi-agent systems (SOMASs). Firstly, a power-law algorithm is developed by virtue of the gradients of local cost functions and agent neighbor information. Under the algorithm, it is proved that all agents' velocities approach to zero, while the position state of each agent achieves consensus within a fixed time. In addition, it is further revealed that the problem of unconstrained convex optimization can be solved by this algorithm. An example is provided at last to illustrate the derived results.

Keywords: Distributed optimization · Second-order multi-agent systems · Fixed-time consensus

1 Introduction

The problem of consensus of multi-agent systems (MASs) has been extensively explored for many years, because of its successful application in practice, such as swarming [1], multi-mobile robots [2], tactical missile system [3] and so on. Consensus indicates that various agents reach a consistent state through information exchange in a complex network communication environment. In 1974, Degroot et al. proposed a centralized consensus protocol for MASs by means of the weighted average technique [4]. However, due to the complexity of communication environment, the difference of agent performance and the limitation of central processing unit, the centralized control is not suitable for MASs with large actuators and sensors. Therefore, the distributed protocol design has become a hot topic in MASs [5–7]. By proposed distributed control, Zhao et al. investigated the consensus of MASs with nonlinear dynamics and a leader based on directed communication [5]. The distributed mean square asymptotic

This work was supported by National Natural Science Foundation of China (61963033), by the Key Project of Natural Science Foundation of Xinjiang (2021D01D10), by the Special Project for Local Science and Technology Development Guided by the Central Government (ZYYD2022A05) and by Xinjiang Key Laboratory of Applied Mathematics (XJDX1401).

L. Zhang et al. (Eds.): CINT 2022, CCIS 1714, pp. 467–478, 2022.
https://doi.org/10.1007/978-981-19-8915-5_40

consensus and leader-following asymptotic consensus of SOMASs were discussed respectively in [6,7].

Note that in practical MASs such as multi-mobile robot systems, a finite time (FNT) needs to be required to ascertain the consensus of robots. Therefore, with the development of the theory of FNT stability, the distinguished results for distributed FNT consensus of MASs are emerged. Meng et al. and He et al. studied the FNT consensus of linear MASs and nonlinear SOMASs respectively [8,9]. However, the settling time of FNT consensus relies on the initial values of agents, which greatly affects the application of FNT consensus. Therefore, FT stability was proposed by Polyakov [10], and subsequently promoted in [11,12]. Consequently, FT consensus of MASs has become the mainstream in control field [13–15]. In [14], FT tracking consensus of SOMASs with directed topology was studied by designing a leader-based state observer and a distributed strategy. Based on the current researches, how to propose a new distributed algorithm to improve the estimation accuracy of consensus time is very necessary and urgent.

In addition to consensus problem, the distributed optimization based on multi-agents is also a hot topic in recent decades. For instance, Ning et al. discussed the distributed optimization of MASs with connected single-integrator dynamics, and further revealed that the FT state consensus is reached and the global cost function is minimized via an edge-based FT protocol [16]. To solve FT optimization of MASs based on equality constraints, a distributed algorithm was developed in [17]. Note that these results were derived in the framework of the first-order MASs, but most of practical applications are required to be described by the second-order or even higher-order systems. Therefore, the problem of distributed FT consensus and optimization for SOMASs is interesting and urgent topic. Nevertheless, the related results are very few and it is meaningful to be discussed for the challenging problem.

In this article, inspired by the above statements, the distributed FT consensus and optimization will be discussed for SOMASs. The main work can be summarized below.

Firstly, in view of FT stability theory proposed in [11], a distributed control protocol with faster convergence rate is developed. Based on this consensus protocol, the FT consensus criteria for SOMASs are established, and a more precise estimate for ST is obtained.

Additionally, by introducing gradients of local cost functions into the distributed control protocol, it is ensured that all agents' velocities approach to zero and the positions of all agents achieve FT consensus, and the problem of unconstrained convex optimization is distributively solved.

The remainder of this article is arranged below. Some important preliminaries are provided in Sect. 2. The distributed FT consensus and optimisation are investigated in Sect. 3. An illustrative example is given in Sect. 4 to test the theoretical results. A summary is made at last.

Notations: $R = (-\infty, +\infty)$, R^m is the m-dimensional Euclidean space. For any vector $x \in R^m$ (or matrix $B \in R^{m \times n}$), $x^T (B^T)$ represents its transpose. I_n is the $n \times n$ identity matrix, 0_m is the m-dimensional vector with 0 elements.

$\nabla g(\mathcal{Y})$ is the gradient of function $g(\mathcal{Y})$. For $\mathcal{Z} = (\mathcal{Z}_1, \ldots, \mathcal{Z}_m)^T \in R^m$, $\|\mathcal{Z}\|_1 = \sum_{i=1}^{m} |\mathcal{Z}_i|$, $\|\mathcal{Z}\|_2 = \sqrt{\sum_{i=1}^{m} \mathcal{Z}_i^2}$, $\text{sign}(\mathcal{Z}) = (\text{sign}(\mathcal{Z}_1), \ldots, \text{sign}(\mathcal{Z}_m))^T$ and $\text{sig}^p(\mathcal{Z}) = (\text{sig}^p(\mathcal{Z}_1), \ldots, \text{sig}^p(\mathcal{Z}_m))^T$, where $\text{sig}^p(\mathcal{Z}_i) = \text{sign}(\mathcal{Z}_i)|\mathcal{Z}_i|^p$, $i = 1, 2, \ldots, m$, $p > 0$ and $\text{sign}(\cdot)$ is the standard sign function. $\otimes$ represents the Kronecker product.

2 Preliminaries

2.1 Graph Theory

Graph $\mathcal{G}$ is denoted as $(\mathcal{I}, \mathcal{W}, \mathcal{B})$, in which $\mathcal{I} = \{1, 2, \ldots, n\}$ is the vertex set, $\mathcal{W} \subseteq \mathcal{I} \times \mathcal{I}$ is the undirected edge set, and $\mathcal{B} = [a_{ij}]_{n \times n}$ is the adjacency matrix, where $a_{ij} = 1$ if $(i, j) \subset \mathcal{W}$, otherwise, $a_{ij} = 0$. The Laplacian matrix $L = \mathcal{C} - \mathcal{B}$, here $\mathcal{C} = \text{diag}\{\mathcal{C}_1, \mathcal{C}_2, \ldots, \mathcal{C}_N\}$, $\mathcal{C}_i = \sum_{q=1}^{N} a_{iq}$. $\mathcal{N}_i = \{j \in \mathcal{I} | a_{ij} = 1\}$ and $[\mathcal{N}_i]$ represent the neighbor node set of node i and the number of neighbor nodes of node i in $\mathcal{G}$, respectively. In this paper, the case that the graph $\mathcal{G}$ contains self-loops or multiple edges is excluded.

2.2 Problem Formulation

Consider a SOMAS composed of n agents which is characterized by

$$\begin{cases} \ddot{\mathcal{Y}}_i(t) = \text{sign}(\mathcal{U}_i(t))(\|\mathcal{U}_i(t)\|_1^{k_1} + \|\mathcal{U}_i(t)\|_1^{k_2} + c_3), \\ \dot{\mathcal{U}}_i(t) = w_i(t), \quad i \in \mathcal{I}, \end{cases} \tag{1}$$

in which $\mathcal{Y}_i(t) \in R^m$ and $\mathcal{U}_i(t) \in R^m$ are the position vector and velocity vector of the agent i, $w_i(t)$ denotes a control protocol, power parameters $0 < k_1 < 1$, $k_2 > 1$, and $c_3 > 0$.

In the following discussion, a distributed algorithm will be developed based on local information of each agent, such that each agent reaches consensus in a fixed time and further the state of each agent cooperatively reaches the optimal state to solve the following optimization problem

$$\min_{\mathcal{Y} \in R^m} \quad g(\mathcal{Y}) = \sum_{i \in \mathcal{I}} g_i(\mathcal{Y}), \tag{2}$$

where $g(\mathcal{Y})$ is differentiable and convex called the global objective function and $g_i(\mathcal{Y})$ is convex and twice continuously differentiable called the objective function of the ith agent.

Definition 1. *The MAS (1) is called to realize FT consensus provided that there exist a FT $\hat{T}_{\max} > 0$, which does not rely on the initial state but on control parameters, and a number $\hat{T}(\hat{\chi}(0)) \geq 0$ called the settling time such that*

$$\lim_{t \to \hat{T}(\hat{\chi}(0))} \|\hat{\chi}(t)\| = 0, \quad \hat{\chi}(t) = 0_{mn}, \quad \forall \ t \geq \hat{T}(\hat{\chi}(0))$$

and $\hat{T}(\hat{\chi}(0)) \leq \hat{T}_{\max}$ for any $\hat{\chi}(0) \in R^{mn}$, where $\hat{\chi}(t) = (\hat{\chi}_1^T(t), \ldots, \hat{\chi}_n^T(t))^T$ and $\hat{\chi}_i(t) = \mathcal{Y}_i(t) - \bar{\mathcal{Y}}(t)$ with $\bar{\mathcal{Y}}(t) = \dfrac{1}{n} \sum_{j=1}^{n} \mathcal{Y}_j(t)$ and $i \in \mathcal{I}$.

Lemma 1 *[18]. Let $\zeta_i \geq 0$ for $i \in \mathcal{I}$, and $\iota > 1$, $0 \leq r \leq 1$, then,*

$$\sum_{i \in \mathcal{I}} \zeta_i^r \geq \left(\sum_{i \in \mathcal{I}} \zeta_i \right)^r, \quad \sum_{i \in \mathcal{I}} \zeta_i^\iota > n^{1-\iota} \left(\sum_{i \in \mathcal{I}} \zeta_i \right)^\iota.$$

Lemma 2 *[19]. Graph $\mathcal{G}$ is undirected and connected, then all eigenvalues of its Laplacian matrix $\mathcal{L}$ satisfy*

$$\lambda_N(\mathcal{L}) \geq \cdots \geq \lambda_2(\mathcal{L}) \geq \lambda_1(\mathcal{L}) = 0.$$

Moreover, for a positive semi-definite matrix $\Omega \in R^{m \times m}$ and a column vector $Y = (y_1^T, y_2^T, \ldots, y_N^T)^T \in R^{Nm}$ meeting $1_N^T Y = 0$,

$$Y^T(\mathcal{L} \otimes \Omega)Y \geq \lambda_2(\mathcal{L}) Y^T(I_n \otimes \Omega)Y.$$

For a positive definite function $V(Y(t)) : R^m \to R$ which is also radially unbounded, the following result is introduced.

Lemma 3 *[11,12]. If there have two positive numbers α_1 and α_2 such that*

$$\frac{d}{dt} V(Y(t)) \leq -\alpha_1 V^{\mathcal{X}}(Y(t)) - \alpha_2 V^{\varrho}(Y(t)), Y(t) \in R^m \backslash \{0_m\},$$

in which $0 \leq \mathcal{X} < 1$, $\varrho > 1$, then $Y(t) = 0_m$ for $t \geq \check{T}(Y(0))$, here $\check{T}(Y(0))$ is evaluated as

$$\check{T}(Y(0)) \leq \check{T} \triangleq \frac{\pi}{(\varrho - \mathcal{X})\alpha_1} \left(\frac{\alpha_1}{\alpha_2} \right)^{\frac{1-\mathcal{X}}{\varrho - \mathcal{X}}} \csc(\frac{1-\mathcal{X}}{\varrho - \mathcal{X}} \pi).$$

Assumption 1. The set $Y_i = \{o \in R^m | \nabla g_i(o) = 0_m\}$ is non-empty bounded for any $i \in \mathcal{I}$.

Remark 1. Note that the local objective function is generally convex but not strictly convex in the article. Thus, the set Y_i may be unbounded. In [20], an important example was provided to show the problem.

Lemma 4 *[21]. Under Assumption 1, there has a number $\varpi > 0$, such that $\|\mathcal{Y}_i\|_2 \leq \varpi$ for any $i \in \mathcal{I}$.*

Lemma 5 *[22]. For a differentiable and convex function $g(\mathcal{Y})$, it can reach its minimum value if and only if $\nabla g(\mathcal{Y}) = 0_m$.*

Assumption 2. The undirected graph $\mathcal{G}$ is connected.

Assumption 3. For any $i \in \mathcal{I}$, the gradient of local objective function g_i satisfies

$$\nabla g_i(\mathcal{Y}(t)) = p\mathcal{Y}(t) + \xi_i(\mathcal{Y}(t)),$$

where $p \geq 0$ and $\|\xi_i(x)\|_2 \leq \xi_0$, $\xi_0 > 0$.

3 Main Results

In the section, it will be proved that the optimization problem (2) is solved by the following steps. The first step is to realize consensus of position state of each agent and ensure the convergence of the velocity of each agent in a FT. The second step is to make all agents' positions approach to the optimal value.

Denote

$$T_1 = \frac{\pi}{\alpha_1 \lambda_2(\mathcal{L})(k_4 - k_3)} \csc\left(\frac{1-k_3}{k_4 - k_3}\pi\right) \times \left(\frac{\alpha_1}{\alpha_2(mNn)^{\frac{1-k_4}{2}}}\right)^{\frac{1-k_3}{k_4-k_3}},$$

and

$$T_2 = \frac{\pi}{k_2 \; k_1} \csc\left(\frac{1-k_1}{k_2 - k_1}\pi\right).$$

The FT algorithm here is designed as

$$
\begin{aligned}
w_i(t) = &- \alpha_1 \sum_{j \in \mathcal{N}_i} \mathrm{sig}^{k_3}\left[(\mathcal{Y}_i(t) + \mathcal{U}_i(t)) - (\mathcal{Y}_j(t) + \mathcal{U}_j(t))\right] \\
&- \alpha_2 \sum_{j \in \mathcal{N}_i} \mathrm{sig}^{k_4}\left[(\mathcal{Y}_i(t) + \mathcal{U}_i(t)) - (\mathcal{Y}_j(t) + \mathcal{U}_j(t))\right] \\
&- c_1 \sum_{j \in \mathcal{N}_i} \mathrm{sign}\left[(\mathcal{Y}_i(t) + \mathcal{U}_i(t)) - (\mathcal{Y}_j(t) + \mathcal{U}_j(t))\right] \\
&- \mathrm{sign}(\mathcal{U}_i(t))\left(\|\mathcal{U}_i(t)\|_1^{k_1} + \|\mathcal{U}_i(t)\|_1^{k_2} + c_3\right) \\
&- c_2 \nabla g_i(\mathcal{Y}_i(t) + \mathcal{U}_i(t)), i \in \mathcal{I},
\end{aligned}
\tag{3}
$$

where control gains $\alpha_1, \alpha_2 > 0$, $c_1, c_2 > 0$, power parameters $0 < k_3 < 1$, and $k_4 > 1$.

Remark 2. In algorithm (3), the first three terms are to realize FT consensus, while the fourth term is to make the velocity state converge to zero, and the last term, as a gradient term, is for the realization of optimization based on the local information.

Theorem 1. *Based on Assumptions 1-3, if $c_2 \leq \min\{\dfrac{c_1}{2n\xi_0}, \dfrac{c_3}{p\varpi + \xi_0}\}$, then the position states of all agents achieve consensus in the time $T_1 + T_2$ and the global cost function (2) is minimized asymptotically by algorithm (3).*

Proof. For $i \in \mathcal{I}$, define $\mathcal{S}_i(t) = \mathcal{Y}_i(t) + \mathcal{U}_i(t)$, then,

$$
\left\{
\begin{aligned}
\dot{\mathcal{Y}}_i(t) =\ & \mathrm{sign}(\mathcal{S}_i(t) - \mathcal{Y}_i(t))\left(\|\mathcal{S}_i(t) - \mathcal{Y}_i(t)\|_1^{k_1} + \|\mathcal{S}_i(t) - \mathcal{Y}_i(t)\|_1^{k_2} + c_3\right), \\
\dot{\mathcal{S}}_i(t) =\ & -\alpha_1 \sum_{j \in \mathcal{N}_i} \mathrm{sig}^{k_3}(\mathcal{S}_i(t) - \mathcal{S}_j(t)) - \alpha_2 \sum_{j \in \mathcal{N}_i} \mathrm{sig}^{k_4}(\mathcal{S}_i(t) - \mathcal{S}_j(t)) \\
& - c_1 \sum_{j \in \mathcal{N}_i} \mathrm{sign}(\mathcal{S}_i(t) - \mathcal{S}_j(t)) - c_2 \nabla g_i(\mathcal{S}_i(t)).
\end{aligned}
\right.
\tag{4}
$$

Denote $\chi(t) = (\chi_1^T(t), \chi_2^T(t), \ldots, \chi_n^T(t))^T$ and

$$
\begin{cases}
\chi_i(t) = \mathcal{S}_i(t) - \bar{\mathcal{S}}(t), \\
\bar{\mathcal{S}}(t) = \dfrac{1}{n} \sum_{j \in \mathcal{I}} \mathcal{S}_j(t).
\end{cases}
\tag{5}
$$

Choosing the following Lyapunov candidate function

$$
V_1(t) = \frac{1}{2} \sum_{i \in \mathcal{I}} \chi_i^T(t) \chi_i(t),
$$

and calculating the first-order derivative for time, one has

$$
\begin{aligned}
\dot{V}_1(t) = & - \alpha_1 \sum_{i \in \mathcal{I}} \sum_{j \in \mathcal{N}_i} \chi_i^T(t) \mathrm{sig}^{k_3}(\mathcal{S}_i(t) - \mathcal{S}_j(t)) \\
& - c_2 p \sum_{i \in \mathcal{I}} \chi_i^T(t) \mathcal{S}_i(t) - c_2 \sum_{i \in \mathcal{I}} \chi_i^T(t) \xi_i(\mathcal{S}_i(t)) \\
& - \alpha_2 \sum_{i \in \mathcal{I}} \sum_{j \in \mathcal{N}_i} \chi_i^T(t) \mathrm{sig}^{k_4}(\mathcal{S}_i(t) - \mathcal{S}_j(t)) \\
& - c_1 \sum_{i \in \mathcal{I}} \sum_{j \in \mathcal{N}_i} \chi_i^T(t) \mathrm{sign}(\mathcal{S}_i(t) - \mathcal{S}_j(t)) - \frac{1}{n} \sum_{i \in \mathcal{I}} \chi_i^T(t) \sum_{j \in \mathcal{I}} \dot{\mathcal{S}}_j(t).
\end{aligned}
\tag{6}
$$

Note that $\sum_{i \in \mathcal{I}} \chi_i^T(t) = 0_m^T$, then

$$
-\frac{1}{n} \sum_{i \in \mathcal{I}} \chi_i^T(t) \sum_{j \in \mathcal{I}} \dot{\mathcal{S}}_j(t) = 0,
\tag{7}
$$

and

$$
-c_2 p \sum_{i \in \mathcal{I}} \chi_i^T(t) \mathcal{S}_i(t) = -c_2 p \sum_{i \in \mathcal{I}} \chi_i^T(t)(\chi_i(t) + \frac{1}{n} \sum_{i \in \mathcal{I}} \mathcal{S}_j(t)) = -c_2 p \sum_{i \in \mathcal{I}} \|\chi_i(t)\|_2^2.
\tag{8}
$$

By means of Lemma 1,

$$
\begin{aligned}
& - \alpha_1 \sum_{i \in \mathcal{I}} \sum_{j \in \mathcal{N}_i} \chi_i^T(t) \mathrm{sig}^{k_3}(\mathcal{S}_i(t) - \mathcal{S}_j(t)) \\
= & - \frac{\alpha_1}{2} \sum_{i \in \mathcal{I}} \sum_{j \in \mathcal{N}_i} (\chi_i(t) - \chi_j(t))^T \mathrm{sig}^{k_3}(\chi_i(t) - \chi_j(t)) \\
\leq & - \frac{\alpha_1}{2} \sum_{i \in \mathcal{I}} \sum_{j \in \mathcal{N}_i} \|\chi_i(t) - \chi_j(t)\|_2^{k_3+1} \\
\leq & - \frac{\alpha_2}{2} \left(\sum_{i \in \mathcal{I}} \sum_{j \in \mathcal{N}_i} \|\chi_i(t) - \chi_j(t)\|_2^2 \right)^{\frac{k_3+1}{2}}.
\end{aligned}
\tag{9}
$$

Similarly,

$$-\alpha_2 \sum_{i\in\mathcal{I}}\sum_{j\in\mathcal{N}_i} \chi_i^T(t)\text{sig}^{k_4}(\mathcal{S}_i(t)-\mathcal{S}_j(t))$$

$$=-\frac{\alpha_2}{2}\sum_{i\in\mathcal{I}}\sum_{j\in\mathcal{N}_i}(\chi_i(t)-\chi_j(t))^T\text{sig}^{k_4}(\chi_i(t)-\chi_j(t))$$

$$\leq-\frac{\alpha_2}{2}m^{\frac{1-k_4}{2}}\sum_{i\in\mathcal{I}}\sum_{j\in\mathcal{N}_i}\|\chi_i(t)-\chi_j(t)\|_2^{k_4+1}$$

$$\leq-\frac{\alpha_2}{2}m^{\frac{1-k_4}{2}}\sum_{i\in\mathcal{I}}[\mathcal{N}_i]^{\frac{1-k_4}{2}}\Big(\sum_{j\in\mathcal{N}_i}\|\chi_i(t)-\chi_j(t)\|_2^2\Big)^{\frac{k_4+1}{2}}$$

$$\leq-\frac{\alpha_2}{2}(mNn)^{\frac{1-k_4}{2}}\Big(\sum_{i\in\mathcal{I}}\sum_{j\in\mathcal{N}_i}\|\chi_i(t)-\chi_j(t)\|_2^2\Big)^{\frac{k_4+1}{2}}, \tag{10}$$

where $N=max\{[\mathcal{N}_i],\ i\in\mathcal{I}\}$. Moreover,

$$-c_1\sum_{i\in\mathcal{I}}\sum_{j\in\mathcal{N}_i}\chi_i^T(t)\text{sign}(\mathcal{S}_i(t)-\mathcal{S}_j(t))=-\frac{c_1}{2}\sum_{i\in\mathcal{I}}\sum_{j\in\mathcal{N}_i}\|\chi_i(t)-\chi_j(t)\|_1. \tag{11}$$

Since the communication topology is connected, one has

$$\|\chi_i(t)\|_2\leq\frac{1}{n}\sum_{i\in\mathcal{I}}\|\mathcal{S}_i(t)-\mathcal{S}_j(t)\|_2$$

$$\leq\sum_{i\in\mathcal{I}}\sum_{j\in\mathcal{N}_i}\|\mathcal{S}_i(t)-\mathcal{S}_j(t)\|_2$$

$$\leq\sum_{i\in\mathcal{I}}\sum_{j\in\mathcal{N}_i}\|\chi_i(t)-\chi_j(t)\|_1. \tag{12}$$

Furthermore,

$$-c_2\sum_{i\in\mathcal{I}}\chi_i^T(t)\xi_i(\mathcal{S}_i(t))\leq c_2\sum_{i\in\mathcal{I}}\|\chi_i(t)\|_2\|\xi_i(\mathcal{S}_i(t))\|_2 \tag{13}$$

$$\leq nc_2\xi_0\sum_{i\in\mathcal{I}}\sum_{j\in\mathcal{N}_i}\|\chi_i(t)-\chi_j(t)\|_1.$$

From Lemma 2,

$$\sum_{i\in\mathcal{I}}\sum_{j\in\mathcal{N}_i}\|\chi_i(t)-\chi_j(t)\|_2^2=2\chi^T(t)(\mathcal{L}\otimes I_m)\chi(t)\geq 2\lambda_2(\mathcal{L})\chi^T(t)\chi(t). \tag{14}$$

Combining with (7)-(14),

$$\dot{V}_1(t) \le -\frac{\alpha_2}{2}\Big(\sum_{i\in\mathcal{I}}\sum_{j\in\mathcal{N}_i}\|\chi_i(t)-\chi_j(t)\|_2^2\Big)^{\frac{k_3+1}{2}} - \frac{c_1}{2}\sum_{i\in\mathcal{I}}\sum_{j\in\mathcal{N}_i}\|\chi_i(t)-\chi_j(t)\|_1$$

$$-\frac{\alpha_2}{2}\Big(mNn\Big)^{\frac{1-k_4}{2}}\Big(\sum_{i\in\mathcal{I}}\sum_{j\in\mathcal{N}_i}\|\chi_i(t)-\chi_j(t)\|_2^2\Big)^{\frac{k_4+1}{2}}$$

$$-c_2p\sum_{i\in\mathcal{I}}\|\chi_i(t)\|_2^2 + nc_2\xi_0\sum_{i\in\mathcal{I}}\sum_{j\in\mathcal{N}_i}\|\chi_i(t)-\chi_j(t)\|_1$$

$$\le -\frac{\alpha_1}{2}(4\lambda_2(\mathcal{L}))^{\frac{k_3+1}{2}}V_1^{\frac{k_3+1}{2}}(t)$$

$$-\frac{\alpha_2}{2}(mNn)^{\frac{1-k_4}{2}}(4\lambda_2(\mathcal{L}))^{\frac{k_4+1}{2}}V_1^{\frac{k_4+1}{2}}(t). \tag{15}$$

From Lemma 3, $\lim_{t\to T_1}\mathcal{S}_i(t) = \bar{\mathcal{S}}(t)$ and $\mathcal{S}_i(t) = \bar{\mathcal{S}}(t)$ for $t \ge T_1$.

Making use of the symmetry of undirected graph, one gets

$$\dot{\bar{\mathcal{S}}}(t) = \frac{1}{n}\sum_{i\in\mathcal{I}}\dot{\mathcal{S}}_i(t) = -\frac{c_2}{n}\sum_{i\in\mathcal{I}}\nabla g_i(\bar{\mathcal{S}}). \tag{16}$$

In addition,

$$\frac{d}{dt}\sum_{i\in\mathcal{I}}g_i(\bar{\mathcal{S}}) = -\frac{c_2}{n}\Big(\sum_{i\in\mathcal{I}}\nabla g_i(\bar{\mathcal{S}})\Big)^T\sum_{i\in\mathcal{I}}\nabla g_i(\bar{\mathcal{S}}). \tag{17}$$

From Assumption 3, $\sum_{i\in\mathcal{I}}g_i(\mathcal{S})$ is bounded. According to the analysis in [16], $\lim_{t\to+\infty}\|\sum_{i\in\mathcal{I}}\nabla g_i(\bar{\mathcal{S}})\|_2^2 = 0$, i.e.,

$$\lim_{t\to+\infty}\sum_{i\in\mathcal{I}}\nabla g_i(\bar{\mathcal{S}}) = 0_m. \tag{18}$$

Next, it will be proved that $\lim_{t\to T_2}\mathcal{U}_i(t) = 0_m$. When $t \ge T_1$,

$$\dot{\mathcal{U}}_i(t) = -\text{sign}(\mathcal{U}_i(t))(\|\mathcal{U}_i(t)\|_1^{k_1} + \|\mathcal{U}_i(t)\|_1^{k_2} + c_3) - c_2\nabla g_i(\mathcal{S}_i). \tag{19}$$

Taking $V_2(t) = \|\mathcal{U}_i(t)\|_1$, then,

$$\dot{V}_2(t) \le -\|\mathcal{U}_i(t)\|_1^{k_1} - \|\mathcal{U}_i(t)\|_1^{k_2} - c_3$$
$$-c_2p\|\mathcal{U}_i(t)\|_1 + c_2p\|\mathcal{Y}_i(t)\|_2 + c_2\xi_0$$
$$\le -\|\mathcal{U}_i(t)\|_1^{k_1} - \|\mathcal{U}_i(t)\|_1^{k_2} - (c_3 - c_2p\varpi - c_2\xi_0)$$
$$\le -V_2^{k_1}(t) - V_2^{k_2}(t). \tag{20}$$

By Lemma 3, $\lim_{t\to T_2}\mathcal{U}_i(t) = 0_m$ and $\mathcal{U}_i(t) = 0_m$ for $t \ge T_2$. Thus,

$$\lim_{t\to T_1+T_2}(\mathcal{Y}_i(t) - \bar{\mathcal{Y}}(t)) = \lim_{t\to T_1+T_2}(\mathcal{S}_i(t) - \bar{\mathcal{S}}(t)) = 0_m,$$

$$\mathcal{Y}_i(t) = \bar{\mathcal{Y}}(t), t \geq T_1 + T_2.$$

Therefore, the state of each agent achieves consensus in the FT $T_1 + T_2$.

Finally, it will be proved that the global cast function is minimized by algorithm (3). When $t > T_1 + T_2$, one has $\mathcal{Y}_i = \mathcal{S}_i = \bar{\mathcal{S}} = \bar{\mathcal{Y}}$. Thus, it can be concluded from (19) that $\nabla g(\bar{\mathcal{Y}}) = \sum_{i \in \mathcal{I}} \nabla g_i(\bar{\mathcal{Y}}) = \sum_{i \in \mathcal{I}} \nabla g_i(\bar{\mathcal{S}}) = 0_m$, for $t \to +\infty$. By Lemma 4, the global cost function $g(\mathcal{Y})$ can be minimized as $t \to +\infty$.   □

Remark 3. In the present result [21], the optimization of SOMASs has been studied, in which both consensus and optimization of agents are achieved asymptotically. Different from this work, the FT consensus and optimization are studied in our paper by applying a power-law protocol, in which the consensus is realized in a fixed time which just depended on control parameters.

4   Numerical Verification

Consider a multi-agent model composed of six nodes, and the communication structure is given in Fig. 1. The local objective function is the following form

$$g_i(\mathcal{Y}) = \frac{1}{18}(\mathcal{Y}_1 - i)^2 + \frac{1}{18}(\mathcal{Y}_2 + i)^2, i \in \{1, 2, 3, 4, 5, 6\},$$

where $\mathcal{Y} = (\mathcal{Y}_1, \mathcal{Y}_2)^T$. Then, the global objective function is written as

$$g(\mathcal{Y}) = \sum_{i \in \mathcal{I}} \left(\frac{1}{18}(\mathcal{Y}_1 - i)^2 + \frac{1}{18}(\mathcal{Y}_2 + i)^2 \right).$$

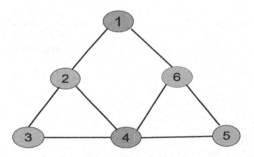

Fig. 1. The topology of system (1).

Obviously, Assumption 3 is met with $p = 0.12$ and $\xi_0 = 3.3$. By calculating, the smallest non-zero eigenvalue of Laplacian matrix is $\lambda_2 = 1.382$, and the optimal point of position state is $\mathcal{Y}^* = (3.5, -3.5)^T$, thus the minimum value of function $g(\mathcal{Y})$ is 1.94. The initial states of the agents are given as $(5, -6)^T$, $(-4, 3)^T$, $(3, -3)^T$, $(-1, 2)^T$, $(2, -5)^T$, $(-2, 4)^T$.

In the protocol (4), select $\alpha_1 = 4, \alpha_2 = 3, c_1 = 78, c_3 = 6.5, k_1 = 0.05, k_2 = 2.5, k_3 = 0.2, k_4 = 3.5, \varpi = 6, \dfrac{c_1}{2n\xi_0} = 1.89, \dfrac{c_3}{p\varpi + \xi_0} = 1.61, c_2 = 1.61$. Clearly,

$$c_2 \leq \min\{\frac{c_1}{2n\xi_0}, \frac{c_3}{p\varpi + \xi_0}\} = 1.61,$$

then all conditions of Theorem 1 are met, and so the consensus is realized and the optimization is solved. The numerical results are presented in Figs. 2-4, where the position trajectories are shown in Fig. 2, and Fig. 3 indicates that the velocities of the agents converge to zero. Besides, the trajectory of the global objective function with the time is displayed in Fig. 4.

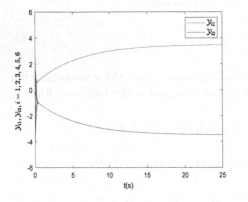

Fig. 2. The position state trajectories.   **Fig. 3.** The velocity state trajectories.

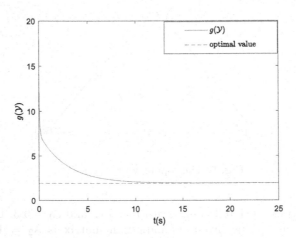

Fig. 4. The trajectories of global objective function with the protocol (4).

5 Conclusion

In the article, the distributed consensus and optimization for a type of SOMASs has been studied by developing a FT consensus strategy. By means of Lyapunov method and FT stability, some criteria have been derived. The acquired results showed that the agents' position states can achieve consensus in a FT under the proposed protocol, and further converge to the optimal value progressively.

References

1. Chu, T., Wang, L., Chen, T., Mu, S.: Complex emergent dynamics of anisotropic swarms: convergence vs oscillation. Chaos Solitons Fractals **30**(4), 875–885 (2006)
2. Jadbabaie, A., Jie, L., Morse, A.: Coordination of groups of mobile autonomous agents using nearest neighbor rules. IEEE Trans. Autom. Control **48**(6), 988–1001 (2003)
3. Fang, H., Shang, C., Chen, J.: An optimization-based shared control framework with applications in multi-robot systems. Science China Inf. Sci. **61**(1), 261–263 (2018)
4. DeGroot, M.: Reaching a consensus. J. Am. Stat. Assoc. **69**(345), 118–121 (1974)
5. Zhao, J., Cui, H., Li, Z.: Distributed reset control for leader-following consensus of nonlinear multi-agent systems. Int. J. Control Autom. Syst. **20**, 983–991 (2022)
6. Zou, W., Xiang, Z., Ahn, C.: Mean-square leader-following consensus of second-order nonlinear multiagent systems with noises and unmodeled dynamics. IEEE Trans. Syst. Man Cybern. Syst. **49**(12), 2478–2486 (2019)
7. Zhao, G., Cui, H.: A novel reset control approach to leader-following consensus of second-order nonlinear multi-agent systems. J. Franklin Inst. **358**(18), 9678–9697 (2021)
8. Meng, D., Jia, Y., Du, J.: Finite-time consensus for multiagent systems with cooperative and antagonistic interactions. IEEE Trans. Neural Netw. Learn. Syst. **27**(4), 762–770 (2016)
9. He, X., Hao, Y., Wang, Q.: Leaderless finite-time consensus for second-order Lipschitz nonlinear multi-agent systems with settling time estimation. Physica A **514**, 280–289 (2019)
10. Polyakov, A.: Nonlinear feedback design for fixed-time stabilization of linear control systems. IEEE Trans. Autom. Control **57**(8), 2106–2110 (2012)
11. Hu, C., He, H., Jiang, H.: Fixed/preassigned-time synchronization of complex networks via improving fixed-time stability. IEEE Trans. Cybern. **51**(6), 2882–2892 (2021)
12. Feng, L., Hu, C., Yu, J.: Fixed-time synchronization of coupled memristive complex-valued neural networks. J. Xinjiang Univ. **38**(2), 129–143 (2021)
13. Ni, J., Liu, L., Liu, C., Liu, J.: Fixed-time leader-following consensus for second-order multiagent systems with input delay. IEEE Trans. Industr. Electron. **64**(11), 8635–8646 (2017)
14. Ni, J., Tang, Y., Shi, P.: A new fixed-time consensus tracking approach for second-order multiagent systems under directed communication topology. IEEE Trans. Syst. Man Cybern. Syst. **51**(4), 2488–2500 (2021)
15. Liu, Y., Zhang, F., Huang, P., Lu, Y.: Fixed-time consensus tracking for second-order multiagent systems under disturbance. IEEE Trans. Syst. Man Cybern. Syst. **51**(8), 4883–4894 (2021)

16. Ning, B., Han, Q., Zuo, Z.: Distributed optimization for multiagent systems: an edge-based fixed-time consensus approach. IEEE Trans. Cybern. **49**(1), 122–132 (2019)
17. Yu, Z., Yu, S., Jiang, H., Mei, X.: Distributed fixed-time optimization for multi-agent systems over a directed network. Nonlinear Dyn. **103**(1), 775–789 (2021). https://doi.org/10.1007/s11071-020-06116-1
18. Hardy, G., Littlewood, J., Polya, G.: Inequalities. Cambridge University Press, Cambridge (1952)
19. Qin, J., Gao, H., Zheng, W.: Exponential synchronization of complex networks of linear systems and nonlinear oscillators: a unified analysis. IEEE Trans. Neural Netw. Learn. Syst. **26**(3), 510–521 (2015)
20. Lin, P., Ren, W., Farrell, J.: Distributed continuous-time optimization: nonuniform gradient gains, finite-time convergence, and convex constraint set. IEEE Trans. Autom. Control **62**(5), 2239–2253 (2017)
21. Mo, L., Liu, X., Cao, X., Yu, Y.: Distributed second-order continuous-time optimization via adaptive algorithm with nonuniform gradient gains. J. Syst. Sci. Complex. **33**, 1914–1932 (2020)
22. Boyd, S., Vandenberghe, L.: Convex Optimization. Cambridge University Press, New York (2004)

Emergency Evacuation Route Planning of Cruise Ship Based on Intelligent Optimization Algorithm

Cheng Peng[1($\boxtimes$)], Song Yu[1], and Lianyi Zhang[2]

[1] School of Automation Science and Electrical Engineering, Beihang University, Beijing 100191, People's Republic of China
pengc@buaa.edu.cn

[2] Beijing Simulation Center, Beijing Institute of Electronic System Engineering, Beijng 100854, People's Republic of China

Abstract. When an emergency such as fire happens on a cruise ship, it is of great significance to quickly plan out a reasonable and effective emergency escape route to ensure the life safety of passengers. First, to achieve the safe evacuation of passengers in an emergency, a three-deck diagram is constructed as the simulation evacuation place, which is modeled by the combination of undirected graph and data set. Secondly, combined with the characteristics of passenger ship personnel composition, the comprehensive evaluation index of route is established, the planning principle of combining global static path planning with local dynamic path planning was formulated, and the path planning algorithm is realized by using Dijkstra algorithm and A* algorithm. Finally, taking an emergency such as fire as an example, considering the influence of the changes of situation information such as fire diffusion, passenger flow density and path cost on the result of path planning, the simulation experiment is carried out in a deck fire scene, and the evacuation situation under the conditions of delay time and fire location is analyzed and compared, It provides a reference for the formulation of reasonable emergency evacuation strategies and key prevention areas.

Keywords: Emergency evacuation · Path planning · Fire scenarios · Intelligent Optimization algorithm

1 Introduction

When people are facing sudden disasters, the main cause of casualties is often not the first-time injury caused by the disaster, but the secondary injury caused by untimely escape. [1] However, affected by the emergency, tourists in cruises often generate great tension and lack professional escape skills, reducing the chance for successful escape. Therefore, if safe and efficient escape paths can be planned through technical means, tourists can escape from the accident orderly and safely, saving their lives successfully.

With the continuous developing of path planning technology, it plays an increasingly important role in crowd evacuation in emergencies. Many scholars have focused on the study of personnel evacuation under emergency in a building [2]. Kang et al. [1] adopted an improved Dijkstra path planning algorithm based on binary sorting tree and adjacency table, by marking hot points, exit points, optimal escape points and other means, to avoid the escape crowd congestion and meet the escape demands under mine disaster. Yang et al. [3] integrated the heuristic function of the two-way search mechanism and the proportional coefficient guidance factor into the traditional ant colony algorithm (ACA) to optimize the convergence speed of algorithm, which obtained the feasible path planning results. Qiao et al. [4] proposed an improved ACA by defining path probability, path feasible probability and path selection probability as the path planning parameters to avoid local area congestion and increase the evacuation efficiency by 10.88%. Hasan et al. [5]. Proposed a new emergency escape algorithm suitable for large areas, which adopts the method of maximizing the capacity of the evacuation network to improve the overall use efficiency of the path. Taking the nuclear leak as the background, Kim et al. [6] and others used Pathfinder software to model the evacuation path of surrounding residents, and simulated and solved the time required for surrounding residents to evacuate in different scenarios. Morten Goodwin et al. [7] proposed a new improved ant colony algorithm. Combining with fire dynamics simulation software, it can give a near optimal escape plan for people who cannot escape in time without fully understanding the dangerous scenes.

However, most of the current crowd evacuation studies are difficult to simulate special emergencies, ignoring the abnormal behavior of people facing emergencies and the dynamic changes of scenes. These limitations have caused many difficulties to test whether the current model is authentic and referential.

In order to realize the safe evacuation path planning of cruises in emergency, this paper designs an emergency evacuation method based on Dijkstra algorithm and a* algorithm by modeling the passenger ship network and dynamically updating the evacuation scene. The main contributions of this paper are as follows:

- We establish a new modeling method using undirected graph and data structure to reflect the spatial structure and attribute parameters of passenger ships through analyzing the functional space division and path of passenger ships and determining the distribution of internal cabin facilities and the available path attribute parameter information.
- We propose a path planning method with updating crowd density and fire diffusion information based on A* algorithm and Dijkstra algorithm, with designed planning principles, data storage structure and evaluation indicators which are suitable for the actual situation of cruise.
- We design 3 typical fire scenarios for experimental simulation to test the performance of our method in evacuating tourists under emergency, through which we obtain the evacuation strategies to improve the evacuation efficiency.

The rest of the paper is organized as follows: we describe our modeling method and objective function in Sect. 2. We propose our path planning in Sect. 3. Section 4 presents three fire scenarios to illustrate the effectiveness of our algorithm. Finally, we conclude our paper in Sect. 5.

2 Problem Statement

In this section, we establish our simulation road network model combing with the data files supporting path planning method design in the need of evacuation. And The final objective function is made as maximizing the evacuation efficiency to ensure the safety of tourists.

2.1 Model Statement

When modeling the cruise for emergency evacuation, we usually don't consider the specific structure or detailed functions of facilities, but focus on the overall area, personnel distribution and evacuation level which will affect the attributes of evacuation. Therefore, this paper abstracts the various areas where people may be distributed into nodes, ignoring the actual area occupied by various facilities on deck and using data documents to store these information.

In order to facilitate data reading and updating, it is necessary to build a relatively independent data structure to store information of the road network. Raster data structures such as rasterization method and quadtree method are discarded because of their low efficiency. Therefore, we adopt the vector data structure to describe the whole space, where the coordinate space is continuous and the geographical entities are described by points, lines and surfaces. The complex map data is stored by implicit relationship, which occupies less storage space than the grid map.

As the basic structure of the map and the basic unit of data storage, nodes should include the following information as far as possible: node coordinates, content, area and label. Besides nodes, path is another important element in building the hull model. The path reflects the connection relationship and traffic conditions between nodes. Because there can be no headless and tailless path, the starting point and ending point of the path must be the existing nodes. Similar to node information, path information required in emergency planning is also stored in data documents. The path information that needs for planning stored in the data file is as follows: path start and end points, path spatial attributes, path classification, path width, path length, etc.

According to the above modeling procedure, the undirected graph established for the three decks is shown in Fig. 1. The stair connection between floors is simplified into a line connection. At the same time, the data file containing cruise information stores in data file.

2.2 Objective Function

In this part, to cope with the cruise emergency escape planning, a multi-objective comprehensive objective function is constructed combined with common optimization indicators such as the shortest path, the shortest time, the lowest congestion, etc. The detailed information of variables is shown in Table 3.

Our optimization objective function consists of 4 components: evacuation time, evacuation distance, path congestion and path turns number. Each objective could be computed as follows:

$$U_1 = \min \sum_{i \in V} \sum_{\substack{j \in V \\ i \neq j}} (t_{ij} + \Delta t_{ij}) \tag{1}$$

$$U_2 = \min \sum_{i \in V} \sum_{\substack{j \in V \\ i \neq j}} (L_{ij} + \Delta L_{ij}) \tag{2}$$

$$U_3 = \min \sum_{i \in V} \sum_{\substack{j \in V \\ i \neq j}} (K_{ij}) \tag{3}$$

$$U_4 = \min \sum_{i \in V} \sum_{\substack{j \in V \\ i \neq j}} \sum_{\substack{k \in V \\ i \neq j \neq k}} \varphi(\theta_{ij,jk}) \tag{4}$$

where

$$\varphi(\theta_{ij,jk}) = \begin{cases} 0, \ \theta_{ij,jk} > \varepsilon \\ 1, \ \theta_{ij,jk} \leq \varepsilon \end{cases} \tag{5}$$

In this paper, we establish the final objective function based on entropy - revised G1 combination weighting [8] by assigning different weights to different sub-objectives. Combining the sub-objective importance ranking and expert target scoring data, we obtained the entropy importance ratio and weight of each sub-objective in Table 2. And the final objective function is:

$$C = \sum_{i=1}^{4} \omega_i U_i \tag{6}$$

where $\sum_{i=1}^{4} \omega_i = 1$.

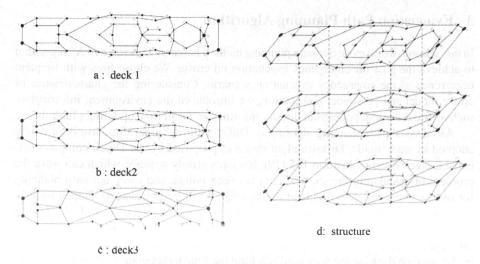

a : deck 1

b : deck2

d: structure

c : deck3

Fig. 1. Cruise deck map

Table 1. Variable definition

Variable	Definition
t_{ij}	The time cost from i to j in normal situation
Δt_{ij}	The extra time cost from i to j in emergency situation
V	Path node set
L_{ij}	The length from i to j in normal situation
ΔL_{ij}	The extra length from i to j in emergency situation
K_{ij}	The crowding degree from i to j
ε	Path angle threshold
$\theta_{ij,jk}$	The angle form path$_{ij}$ to path$_{jk}$

Table 2. Sub objective weight parameters

	Time	Distance	Crowd density	Turn numbers
ej	0.999343	0.996471	0.995673	0.991056
rk	—	1.002882	1.000801	1.004659
ωi	0.250931	0.25021	0.250009	0.24885

3 Evacuation Path Planning Algorithm

In this section, we propose our path planning method based on Dijkstra and A* algorithm to achieve the goal for emergency evacuation on cruise. We chose fires with frequent occurrence as the emergency evacuation scenario. Considering the characteristics of cruise model and personnel distribution, we introduced the environment information, such as fire diffusion, pedestrian density information for in time updating (Table 1).

As classical path planning algorithms, Dijkstra and A* algorithm have been wildly adopted in many fields. Dijkstra algorithm was proposed by the Dutch computer scientist Edsger·Wybe·Dijkstra in 1959 [9]. It adopts greedy strategy, which can solve the problem of calculating the shortest path between points, and carry out path planning for unstructured static environment on the map. A* algorithm was developed by P E. Hart. N. J. Nilsson and B Raphael [10]. Combining the characteristics of greedy best first search algorithm and Dijkstra algorithm, A* algorithm uses the distance estimation function as a heuristic function to sort all the nodes in the path, and finds the best point as the node on the planned path until reaching the final target node.

During evacuation planning, it is necessary to observe the current situation and predict the future situation of environment, for adjusting the previous planning results to obtain the optimal results under dynamic conditions. In this paper, we first consider the impact of fire diffusion and the impact of pedestrian density on each path to update the path cost in time. According to our established model, we only consider the effects of fire on nodes and paths. To be specific, When the fire affects a certain path, set the path as impassable; when the fire affects a certain node, setting the node and all paths connected to the node impassable. According to the research results of Liu Yi et al. [11], the diffusion speed of fire in this paper is taken as $v_k = 0.137$ m/s. The fire diffusion influence updating strategy is shown in **Strategy 1.**

While emergency evacuation, the crowd density of the paths and nodes often greatly affects the efficiency. Therefore, it is necessary to obtain the crowd density of each route and exit to adjust the planned path in time. The crowd density updating strategy is shown in **Strategy 2.**

Strategy 1 fire diffusion influence updating

Input: The current simulation Time t_0 ; Fire diffusion speed V_k; The current map information;

Output: Disabled node set N_{dis}; Disabled path set P_{dis};

1: Calculate the current influence range of fire;

2: For node n_I and path p_j in map:

3: if n_I in the current influence range of fire:

4:     put n_i in N_{dis}

5: End If

6: if p_j in the current influence range of fire:

7:     put p_j in P_{dis}

8: End If

9: End For

10: Return N_{dis} and P_{dis} ;

Strategy 2 crowd density updating

Input: The current simulation Time t; Tourists speed V_e; The current crowd density, The current map information, simulation interval Δt;

Output: The current crowd density, The new planning start;

1: For crowd$_i$ in each node:

2:   Calculate the distance of crowd$_i$ D_i in this interval

3:   If corwd$_i$ reach next node:

4:     update crowd density and start point

5:   End If

10: End For

In addition to the updating of fire diffusion and crowd density, this paper also updates the path cost in real time through the objective function established in Sect. 2.2 during planning, so as to obtain the most efficient path. The proposed evacuation path planning method is shown in **Algorithm 1**.

4   Simulation and Experiment

In this section, the evacuation path planning in emergency is experimented by simulating the scene of fire accidents and personnel distribution based on the deck model and data set established in previous text, adopting the method introduced in Sect. 3, and the evacuation effect is evaluated and analyzed.

Algorithm 1 emergency evacuation planning

Input: The initial map information; The fire location; The initial crowd density,s imulation total time t, simulation interval Δt

Output: planning path

1: Initialize parameters;

2: While $t_0 < t$ and $t_0 > t_{delay}$:

3:   update fire diffusion influence **with strategy 1**

4:   plan paths with Dijkstra or A* algorithm

5:   update crowd density with **strategy 2**

6:   update path cost with objective function

7:   $t_0 = t_0 + \Delta t$

8 : End While

4.1 Evacuation of the Whole Cruise Under Emergency

The experiment scenario is set as follows: the fire occurs in the daytime, and there are many tourists outside the cabin. The crowd is scattered without obvious aggregation. The fire occurs in the middle of deck 1, with coordinates of (140, 25), which is the red point in Fig. 2. At this time, the specific personnel distribution in the cabin is shown in Fig. 3, the evacuation information is shown in Table 3.

After planning, the change curves of the number of evacuees at each exit in each deck layer with time is shown in the Fig. 4 a to c below, the change of the total number of successful evacuations with time is shown in Fig. 4 (d).

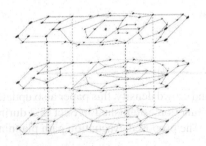

Fig. 2. Fire occurrence position

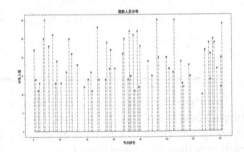

Fig. 3. Distribution of evacuee

According to the planning result, the total number of tourists in this case is 1141, and the evacuation is completed within 100 s. The number of evacuees changes rapidly in 40–60 s. Therefore, the congestion is serious during this period, and a small number of tourists take a long time in waiting. Therefore, tourists with a long evacuation distance

Table 3. Evacuation initial information

Deck	Exit node	Evacuee number	Distribution node number
1	7, 11, 35, 42	384	21
2	60, 64, 81, 90	382	20
3	109, 110, 128, 131	358	19

could be given higher evacuation priority to avoid crowded sections and reduce waiting time.

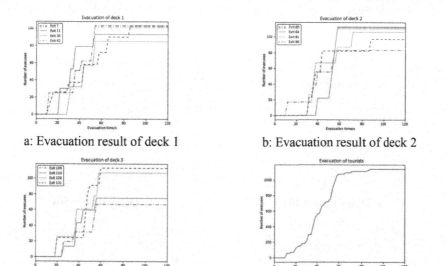

a: Evacuation result of deck 1   b: Evacuation result of deck 2

c: Evacuation result of deck 3   d: Time distribution of evacuation

Fig. 4. Evacuation results of the whole ship

4.2 Evacuation with Uncertain Delay Time

During fire evacuation, there will be a delay for the start of evacuation due to the perception and reaction of personnel. The other experimental conditions are the same as those in the previous section. Since the fire occurs on deck 1, we only consider the evacuation of deck 1 under different delay time as 10 s, 20 s, 30 s, 40 s, 50 s, 60 s and 90 s.

According to the experimental results, when the delay time is less than 30s, the evacuation results are not affected. The evacuation results of deck 1 obtained under other conditions are plotted in Fig. 5.

According to the planning results, as delay time increasing, exit 42 nearest to the fire occurrence point is the most affected. Tourists at nodes 21, 33 and 29 are unable to plan an available path due to the impact of the fire, and the number of successful evacuations continues to decrease. Therefore, planning the optimal paths is not the whole content of safe evacuation, improving the perception of disasters and accelerating the response of people to evacuation also counting.

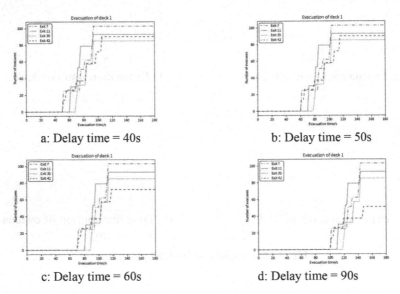

a: Delay time = 40s　　　　　b: Delay time = 50s

c: Delay time = 60s　　　　　d: Delay time = 90s

Fig. 5. Evacuation results under different delay time

4.3   Evacuation with Different Fire Location

Due to the uneven distribution of tourists and cabin structures, the occurrence location of fire will have a great impact on the evacuation results. In this experiment, we set the fire occurrence point on deck 1 with coordinate (180, 50) nearing exit 35 as shown in Fig. 6. Other simulation conditions are the same as experiment 1. The evacuation result is shown in Fig. 7.

According to the result, comparing with experiment 1, the number of evacuees at exit 35 is greatly reduced, and the evacuation is planned to other exits, such as exit 42. This leads to a great increase of evacuation time and reduced evacuation efficiency. Therefore, some areas, including escape exits, should be the key disaster prevention areas needing special attention.

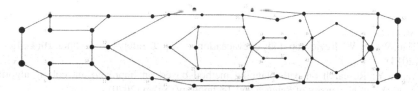

Fig. 6. Fire occurrence location

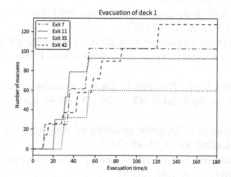

Fig. 7. Evacuation results with different fire location

5 Conclusion

In this paper, we proposed a modeling method which adopted undirected graph to reflect spatial structure and data file to store attribute information of the cruise. By updating fire diffusion crowd density and path cost information in time, we designed the evacuation algorithm based on A* and Dijkstra algorithm. The experiment results reflect that most tourists took about 40–60 s to evacuate and the change of delay time and fire area will greatly affect the evacuation efficiency. Based on this, the evacuation strategies of reducing the fire observation time, improving the reaction ability of tourists and paying extra attention to key areas are given.

References

1. Kang, N.: Research on Emergency Path Planing of Coal Mine Based on Improved Dijkstra Algorithm. Xi'an University of science and technology, Xi'an (2020)
2. Tian, W., Lv, W.: Review on study of evacuation in ship. J. Safety Sci. Technol. **10**(4), 133–138 (2014)
3. Yang, Y.: Research on path planning method based on improved ant colony algorithm. Xi'an:Xi'an University of Science and Technology, Xi'an (2020)
4. Qiao, Y.: Simulation study on passenger evacuation in cruise ships. In: Academic proceedings of Beijing Shipbuilding Engineering Society from 2018 to 2019. Beijing Shipbuilding Engineering Society, Beijing (2020)
5. Hasan, H., Van, P.: Large-Scale Zone-Based Evacuation Planning: Models, Algorithms, and Evaluation Networks (02), pp. 13-17 (2020)
6. Kim, J., et al.: Emergency evacuation simulation for a radiation disaster: a case study of a residential school near nuclear power plants in Korea. Rad. Protect. Dosim. **189**(3), 323–326 (2020)
7. Goodwin, M., Granmo, O.-C., Radianti, J.: Escape planning in realistic fire scenarios with ant colony optimisation. Appl. Intell. **42**(1), 24–35 (2014). https://doi.org/10.1007/s10489-014-0538-9
8. Wu, X., Wang, P., Zhang, T.: Dynamic planning of passenger ship evacuation path under sudden fire. China Martime Saf. **9**, 45–48 (2017)
9. Liu, Y., Shen, F.: Route selection model in indoor evacuation under real effect of fire spread. J. Control Decis. **33**(09), 1598–1604 (2018)
10. Dijkstra, E.W.: A note on two problems in connexion with graphs. Numer. Math. **1**, 269–271 (1959)
11. Wang, C., Wang, L., Qin, J., et al.: Path planning of automated guided vehicles based on improved A-Star algorithm. In: 2015 IEEE International Conference on Information and Automation. IEEE, 2071-2076 (2015)

Model Library System Based on Multi-Domain Simulation Model Integration Interface

Shuo Feng[1], Yuanjun Laili[1]([✉])(iD), Lin Zhang[1], and Lianyi Zhang[2,3]

[1] Beihang University, Beijing 100191, People's Republic of China
{forsure,lailiyuanjun,zhanglin}@buaa.edu.cn
[2] Beijing Simulation Center, Beijing 100854, People's Republic of China
lyzhang117@163.com
[3] Beijing Institute of Electronic System Engineering, Beijing 100854,
People's Republic of China

Abstract. Modeling and simulation has been applied to power, military, aerospace and many other fields. In view of the complex characteristics of complex systems, the support of model base system is essential. However, most of the existing simulation model library systems are aimed at a single field or a single simulation environment, and some can be aimed at multiple domains, but the scope is limited. In this paper, we build a model library system based on multi-domain simulation model integration interface, it describes the model in a uniform format, creates a model instance by model mapping, realizes the call of multi-domain models, and provides unified storage of models.

Keywords: Model integration · Model mapping · Multi-domain · Model library · Simulation

1 Introduction

Modeling and simulation has become an important method to solve the design, analysis, verification and decision-making of complex equipment and systems [8]. However, complex products have the characteristics of complex structure, complex component relation and complex mechanism, which involve strong coupling of multi-domain knowledge. Therefore, the process of model construction for complex systems often needs to be developed from bottom to top. Researchers in different fields build models of subsystems, and then build complex systems by model combination.

In order to realize efficient modeling and simulation, researchers propose model-based System Engineering, System of Systems [1] and other concepts and technical Systems. On this basis, the Model Engineering technology system is formed, which is driven by model and gradually moves from static model

This work is supported by the National Key Research and Development Program of China (Grant No. 2018YFB1701600).

management to dynamic model reconstruction and intelligent model generation through complex equipment modeling technology, system engineering technology and artificial intelligence technology.

According to the model engineering system, the model library system is a powerful tool to support the modeling and simulation of complex system. It can reuse, integrate and combine existing multi-domain models quickly. Most of the existing model library system, are aimed at a single domain. For example, paper [9] built a model library for liquid food precess lines by modelica, paper [6] built a model library for non-linear thermo-fluid dynamic systems by matlab/simulink. Some can realize the interaction between two types of models, but there is less attention to the construction of libraries for both types of models, for example, paper [11] realized the co-simulation of ANSYS and ADAMS.

Therefore, in order to make the process of complex system modeling and simulation more efficient, it is a very important step to establish a model library system that supports multi-domain model integration and management.

2   Background

A complex system is usually composed of several subsystems, most of which come from different fields, such as mechanics, control, electricity, etc. To a complex integrated system modeling and simulation, must use modular form, separate different subsystem modeling, then process combination simulation. Because the subsystems are comming from different fields, their modeling and simulation have to use its own modeling simulation software, to handle the more complex scenarios or get more accurate simulation results.

2.1   Software Platform Integration

Different sub-models from different domain use different modeling software. Taking a modeling and simulation software as the base, through its interface with various modeling and simulation software, the information transmission modes of each other are constructed, and then the integration of multiple information transmission modes of this form is achieved to obtain a simulation model of complex system.

A typical case of this method is Simulink, because it provides a module library containing a variety of models, it can cover control, electricity and other fields of multi-domain simulation, but it still faces professional problems or special scenes, its function is limited. Therefore, it provides s-function module and other modules that can package other software models, so as to obtain stronger description ability for specific scenes or fields.

Paper [10] mentioned a method to integrate CFD through S-function in Simulink, and carried out the simulation algorithm of photovoltaic pump system through this method. In paper [4], a method of S-funzation of hardware language VHDL and Verilog was proposed to realize the integration of professional circuit control through Simulink.

In addition, s-function can be used for integration of more types of simulation models. Finally, a complex system simulation can be realized through the combined modeling of Simulink's own modules and multiple S-Function modules.

2.2 Function Mock-up Interface

A simulation model integration method independent of a software platform is that an interface standard named FMI(Function Mock-up Interface). It realizes the unified call of multi-domain models by setting up a set of model description specifications and model packages.

FMI does not specify a specific software platform. Its model information is stored in the form of XML language, and model files are stored in the form of dynamic link library(dll), which has high generality and portability. Model Exchange and Co-simulation are also provided [3] to solve different problems.

The model in this form is also convenient to use. First, the model information in the corresponding XML file is read, which provides the function name, variable and function index of the model. Then, the model can be called through the standard library of FMI, including instance creation, data input and reading, and single step simulation.

In paper [5], the author used the FMI method to realize the multi-body simulation and control of the dynamic system. In paper [2], the industrial automation co-simulation was realized with Modelica simulation software.

In addition, FMI can even interact with Simulink.

As time goes on, the number of modeling and simulation software that can support the FMI specification increases. It is very convenient to build a complex simulation model, and the number of models can be supported from small to large, while ensuring that all subsystems of a complex system are built by the FMI specification.

2.3 Comparison of Integration Methods

First is universal, a complex system of wide field coverage, the modeling and simulation of it may need a lot of modeling and simulation software. In order to solve the problem of different fields, one can build a complex simulation model through the software platform, such as by simulink, but there is still a lot of software can't be integrated in it, and model libraries cannot be built within the software platform. The same is true of FMI, though a model library is easy to build because of the unified model form, it can only integrate the model types it supports.

On the feasibility of integration, when the builder of complex system is an independent modeling and simulation practitioner, he cannot build the interface between a certain software platform and other modeling and simulation software, because the process is limited to the developer of these modeling and simulation software. FMI provides the simulation model in the form of a specification, model with other type can be integrated by the specification. For models that don't provide such integration tool, practitioners of modeling and simulational are unable to step in. When a submodel of a complex system does not support FMI, the integration process cannot be performed.

In engineering practice, if a complex system in a project itself cannot take simulink and other modeling and simulation software as the base, it won't be integrated in this way. And a model integrated by FMI can not reproduce its original function, and the support version of different modeling simulation software for FMI is different, in the process of integrating multi-domain model by FMI, if the version is different between different models, the integration process will face certain difficulties.

3   Model Library System Construction

3.1   Model Information

For a complex system, its submodel may come from different domain, so they are different in data interaction and operation mode. In order to manage them uniformly, their information must be described in a certain form, so that it can cover the unique information of different models being standardized and simple enough. It can also be fully described when there is the possibility of adding other types of models later on.

In order to manage the model, call the model and make it easy to use, the model library system should establish an database to store the model related information.

At the model management level, the model name should be recorded, and the model code name should be recorded as the unique index of the model at the information retrieval level. Models should be classified according to field and the modeling and simulation software of it, so as to facilitate retrieval and management by class mode. The model file address should be recorded and corresponding to the actual address to facilitate the updating of the model.

At the model calling level, the model address should be recorded so that the model itself can be obtained. The format and indexs of inputs, outputs and parameters should be recorded, so that the interface can read and recognize, so as to realize model calling. The model class should be recorded so that the integration interface can recognize the class and use the corresponding solver.

At the user level, the model name, function and field classification should be recorded to facilitate users to find the required model. The meaning of all inputs, outputs, and parameters should be recorded so that users can better understand the model function and use the model.

3.2   Model Information Description Format

According to the necessary model information, this paper proposes a model information description format, as shown in Table 1, which can meet the requirements of model management, model calling and user operation.

Table 1. Model information description format

code_name	Unique index of a model
model_name	Can be repeated
model_function	For users
from_library	for Categorical retrieval
model_address	Load a model when simulating
input_type	Input data type
input_format	Variable names
input_meaning	Explain input function
output_type	Output data type
output_format	Variable names
output_meaning	Explain output function
parameter_type	Parameter data type
parameter_format	Variable names
parameter_meaning	Explain parameter function

By using database to manage multi-domain models, it is neccessary to consider the difference of the number of their inputs, outputs, and parameters. But the column number of a database is fixed, so this paper put the input, output and parameter information of a model in stacked arrangement, using an ";" to seperate different items.

3.3 Multi-Domain Model Integration Interface

Before designing model interfaces, the interface forms should be designed according to the characteristics of models in different fields. For submodels of complex system, it is neccessary to interact with other parts, so as to achieve a complex model, so the simulation model must have internal parameters and can interact with other models by input and output interfaces. And models need to use simulation solver, and the logic of different solvers is also different.

According to the function, models can be divided into parameter type and data stream type. The parameter type models are used to describe phenomena under certain initial conditions, such as models of COMSOL and NETLOGO. The data stream type models are used to process information, such as FMU models.

According to the simulation solver, models can be divided into independent solver type and no solver type, and independent solver type must be simulated by its own solver and no solver type can be simulated directly. Models simulated by independent solver have higher efficiency and accuracy, and more complete functions (Fig. 1).

3.4 Integrated Interface Architecture

By analyzing the characteristics of the simulation model, the model integration interface can be designed by the following structure according to the model information type and the model library.

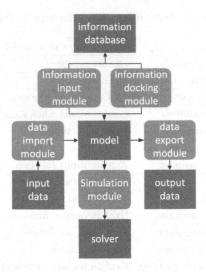

Fig. 1. Integrated interface architecture

1. Information input module. The model database realizes the combination of model retrieval and use by storing model information in the information database, and facilitates management. However, in the initial state, the model information does not exist in the information database, so the information input module is needed to insert model information into the database, so as to make the model retrieval possible.

2. Information docking module. In the process of using the model library, people should first visit the information library to obtain the necessary information of the model, and then find the model file to carry out the simulation behavior. Therefore, it needs the information docking module to obtain the information of the corresponding model through the model database, and provide the available interface of the corresponding type of model to realize the simulation.

3. Data import module. Because models in different fields have great differences in operation logic and data types, data import modules are required to transform input data into formats that can be recognized by models and provide them to models.

4. Simulation module. Different models may use different solvers. When using the model, the simulation process is carried out according to the way of single-step simulation or simulation process setting. If the model is running on an independent solver, the solver needs to be configured according to the model type to provide the corresponding solution to make the model run.

5. Data export module. Simulation models produce different information, such as model attribute lists, running results of a simulation, model attribute values, and so on. These information must be obtained in different ways from model running result variables, model files, model database, or model description files.

4 Model Library System Construction Experiment

According to the model library structure mentioned in Sect. 3, a model library system based on multi-domain simulation model integration interface is constructed according to the actual needs of the engineering practice. The system contains thousands of models, including models in electricity, magnetism, gas, control, fluid, mechanical, thermal, sociological analysis and other fields. It covers five kinds of modeling and simulation software, including MATLAB, Simulink, Comsol, Netlogo and Modelica, and stores the models and designs their integrated interface.

4.1 Integrated Interface

Information Input Module. This module gets all information of a model, and then record them in the model Information database. After select one model, depending on the type of it, the module will automatically read all information that is neccessary to call the model, and the information can also be altered by users.

Information Docking Module. By associating the model database with model file information, model file is obtained through model data, and the model information is presented to the user, with the information of the startup model reserved for simulation.

The module flow is as follows:

---

flow 1. Information Docking Module

Require: model name $name\_model$

Ensure: model information data table $infor\_list$, model input sequence $input\_list$, output sequence $output\_list$, parameter sequence $para\_list$, List of functions called by model $function\_list = \{function_1, ..., funtion_k\}$

1: search with $name\_model$ as index, and obtain model information data table $infor\_list$ through traversing the information database

2: take the content of $infor_7$, $infor_8$, and $infor_9$ as input, obtain the input sequence $input\_list$ through data form conversion

3: take $infor_{10}$, $infor_{11}$, and $infor_{12}$ as input, through data form conversion, Obtain the output sequence $output\_list$

4: take $infor_{13}$, $infor_{14}$, $infor_{15}$ as input, and obtain the parameter sequence $para\_list$ through data form conversion

5: use the model type represented by $infor_5$ as the index to search the list of classified interface functions and obtain $function\_list$ of the called functions of this model

---

Data Import Module. In order to deal with the characteristics of models with different input types, the data import module will process the input data accordingly. When it is the data stream input, the module will input data or variables into the model in two ways: step or simulation process; When it is input as a parameter, the module will provide the function of obtaining the parameter list, obtaining the parameter value and modifying the specified parameter.

The module flow is as follows:

---

flow 2. Data Import Module

Require: data file *input_data_file*, data variable *input_data*
Ensure: data conforming to the input format of the model *input_data_t*
1: **if** input is a file **then**
2:　　call the data read function to get data *input_data* from the file
3:　　**if** model uses independent solver **then**
4:　　　　input is stored in the workspace of the corresponding solver to obtain the corresponding real input variable *input_data_r*
5:　　**else**
6:　　　　input is saved to the current workspace
7:　　**end if**
8: **end if**
9: **if** input is parameters **then**
10:　　call *parameter_alter* to modify parameters as required
11:　　call the *save_model* function
12: **else**
13:　　call *form_converse* to obtain the input data *input_data_t* that meets the input requirements of the model
14: **end if**
15: **return** *input_data_t*

Simulation Module. Different models have different solvers, so their running modes are different. For the model that can be run in the programming language environment, the module provides single-step simulation function, and can also obtain the simulation results for a period of time through the combination of single-step simulation advance. For the model running under the corresponding other solvers, the module is responsible for setting the initial simulation conditions of the model in the original environment, inputting data and obtaining the simulation results of a certain time.

The module flow is as follows:

Data Export Module. The module obtains corresponding information from model file, model running process, corresponding database and model description file, such as parameter list, simulation result, current parameter value and default parameter value, etc. The current parameter value and simulation result must be obtained from the current running model. Parameter lists can be obtained from description files, and default parameter values can be obtained from model files that have never been run.

---

flow 3. Simulation Module

Require: model instance $model\_instance$, model information table $information\_list = \{infor_1, infor_2, ..., infor_15\}$, input data conforming to the requirements of the model $input\_data\_t$

Ensure: none

1: **if** model runs on independent solver **then**
2:     sets initial conditions for model execution $solution_i$
3:     $solution_i$ execution
4: **else**
5:     **while** the simulation deadline is not reached **do**
6:         execute single-step simulation function $simulate\_step$
7:         temporary storage of single-step simulation results
8:     **end while**
9: **end if**

The module flow is as follows:

---

flow 4. Data Export Module

Require: model instance $model\_instance$, model description file $description\_file$, model information table $information\_list=\{infor_1, infor_2, ..., infor_18\}$

Ensure: the desired result $data\_output$

1: **if** model runs on independent solver **then**
2:     get the model output $data\_output\_r$ in its solver workspace
3:     read $data\_output\_r$ and convert it to the model output $data\_output$ in the current workspace
4: **else**
5:     get the model output $data\_output$ in the current workspace
6: **end if**
7: **return** $data\_output$

---

5   Conclusion

This paper proposes a model library system construction method based on multi-domain simulation model integration interface, and carries out practical construction according to this method, and constructs simulation model integration interface including MATLAB, Simulink, COMSOL, Netlogo and Modelica. Based on these models, a model library system containing multi-domain models is constructed, and a multi-function model library system from model retrieval to model invocation is realized.

The method in this paper provides a solution for the integration of multi-domain models. Compared with the existing method, it has better improvement in universality and extensibility, and is the only option for independent modelers.

On the basis of this method, more models can be added to enrich model resources. Or build more types of model integration interfaces to provide broader support.

The practical cases mentioned in this paper do not provide specific solutions in the co-simulation. Users can use this method to attempt to introduce HLA/rti method [7].

References

1. Baudoin, C.R.: The evolution and ecosystem of the unified modeling language. In: Present and Ulterior Software Engineering, pp. 37–45. Springer, Cham (2017). https://doi.org/10.1007/978-3-319-67425-4_3
2. Cabral, J., Wenger, M., Zoitl, A.: Enable co-simulation for industrial automation by an FMU exporter for IEC 61499 models. In: IEEE International Conference on Emerging Technologies and Factory Automation, ETFA, vol. 2018-September, pp. 449–455. Fortiss Gmbh, Forschungs Institut des Freistaats Bayern für Softwareintensive Systeme und Services (2018)
3. Cech, M., Konigsmarkova, J., Reitinger, J., Balda, P.: Novel tools for model-based control system design based on FMI/FMU standard with application in energetics. In: 2017 21st International Conference on Process Control (PC), Process Control (PC), pp. 416–421 (2017)
4. Centomo, S., Lora, M., Portaluri, A., Stefanni, F., Fummi, F.: Automatic integration of HDL IPs in Simulink using FMI and S-function interfaces. In: Große, D., Vinco, S., Patel, H. (eds.) Languages, Design Methods, and Tools for Electronic System Design. LNEE, vol. 530, pp. 1–23. Springer, Cham (2019). https://doi.org/10.1007/978-3-030-02215-0_1
5. Chapuis, F., et al.: Multibody simulation and control of kinematic systems with FMI/FMU, pp. 262–264 (02 2019)
6. Jan, J.A., Sulc, B.: Object oriented own-built model library of non-linear thermo-fluid dynamic systems in MATLAB/Simulink. In: MATLAB 2001, Prague, Czech Republic, August 2001
7. Ji, H., Zhai, X., Song, X., Liu, X., Liang, Y., Jia, Z.: HLA-based federation development framework supporting model reuse. In: Li, L., Hasegawa, K., Tanaka, S. (eds.) AsiaSim 2018. CCIS, vol. 946, pp. 72–81. Springer, Singapore (2018). https://doi.org/10.1007/978-981-13-2853-4_6
8. Loper, M.L., Register, A.: Introduction to Modeling and Simulation. Modeling and Simulation in the Systems Engineering Life Cycle, May 2015
9. Skoglund, T., Dejmek, P.: A model library for dynamic simulation of liquid food process lines, pp. 5–12 (2006)
10. Xianfang, W., Heyu, Y., Minggao, T., Houlin, L.: Dynamic simulation of inner flow in a photovoltaic pump based on Simulink and CFD. Water Supply 21(8), 4442–4456 (2021)
11. Zhang, Y.D., Wang, Y.T., Wang, M.N., Jiang, J.G.: Co-simulation of flexible body based on ANSYS and Adams. Xitong Fangzhen Xuebao / J. Syst. Simul. 20(17), 4501–4504 (2008)

Multi-Agent Path Finding Algorithm of Merged Node Rule and Bounded Focal Search

Chaoen Tan[1], Xiaoqiang Ji[2(✉)], Weike Li[4], Hongmin Wang[1], Jianmin Zhang[1], Lanhui Fu[1], Huifeng Guan[1], Jiaming Zhong[1], Huanzhao Huang[1], Nannan Li[5], and Fuqin Deng[1,2,3(✉)]

[1] School of Intelligent Manufacturing, Wuyi University, Jiangmen 529000, China
dengfuqin@cuhk.edu.cn
[2] The Shenzhen Institute of Artificial Intelligence and Robotics for Society, The Chinese University of Hong Kong, Shenzhen 518000, China
jixiaoqiang@cuhk.edu.cn
[3] Irobotix Robotics Limited, 518000 Shenzhen, China
[4] LTD, Research and Development Center, CETC Potevio Science & Technology Co, Guangzhou 510220, China
[5] University of Science and Technology, Macau 999078, China

Abstract. The complexity of the problem of Conflict-Based Search (CBS) in the Multi-Agent Path Finding(MAPF) is a major issue that affects the scalability of the system. In order to address this issue, we proposed Rule and Bounded Conflict-Based Search (RBCBS), which uses rules of child node selection and bounded focus search. First, to reduce the number of nodes to be searched, the selection rules of RBCBS are formulated to ensure that the number of nodes is limited. Second, the lower bound of the path planning cost is determined using the bounded focused search method by combining the suboptimal factors to generate the interval range of the focused search, ensuring that the cost of the new node selection priority on the final path planning is close to the optimal value. The simulation studies reveal that, when compared to standard algorithms like CBS, ICBS, the proposed RBCBS decreases the number of nodes examined and the runtime, enhances the algorithm's scalability and allows the multi-agent to find collision-free pathways rapidly.

Keywords: Conflict-based search · Multi-agent · Path finding · Rules

This work was supported by National Key R&D Program of China (2020YFB1313300), the Basic and Applied Basic Research Foundation of Guangdong under Grant (2019A1515111119), Wuyi University-Hong Kong-Macao Joint Research and Development Fund (2021WGALH18), Innovative Program for Graduate Education (503170060259) from the Wuyi University, Shenzhen Peacock Plan of Shenzhen Science and Technology Program (KQTD2016113010470345), the special projects in key fields of Guangdong Provincial Department of Education (2019KZDZX1025), Shenzhen Science and Technology Program (Grant NO. RCBS20210706092219050), Guangdong Basic and Applied Basic Research Foundation (Grant No. 2022A1515110411), Shenzhen Institute of Artificial Intelligence and Robotics for Society (AC0122201001, AC01202101103)

© The Author(s), under exclusive license to Springer Nature Singapore Pte Ltd. 2022
L. Zhang et al. (Eds.): CINT 2022, CCIS 1714, pp. 501–509, 2022.
https://doi.org/10.1007/978-981-19-8915-5_43

1   Introduction

With the advancement of social technology, the level of intelligent warehousing and logistics and e-commerce is booming, and the MAPF problem [1] for warehousing and logistics is receiving increasing attention; at the same time, with the increase in the variety of goods and scales, resulting in increasingly severe congestion in the warehouse environment. The traditional MAPF algorithms for warehouse logistics can no longer meet modern industrial production's demands.

Therefore, in order to increase the efficiency of intelligent warehousing and logistics systems, more technical changes are necessary to the existing MAPF algorithms for warehousing and logistics. Furthermore, MAPF has a wide range of real-world applications, including traffic optimization [2], urban logistics [3], and automated parking [4]. Unfortunately, the MAPF has been identified to be an NP-hard problem [5].

Sharon [6] first proposed the CBS algorithm for solving conflicts between multi-agent paths in 2015. The CBS is a two-level path planning optimal algorithm, which resolves conflicts by adding constraints at the High-Level (HL) and planning paths consistent with these constraints at the Lower-Level (LL) using A* [7]. The CBS has gained more and more attention from scholars because of its optimality and can be used to solve MAPF scenarios of different scales. Boyarski proposed ICBS [8] algorithm which combines CBS and Bypass [9] methods in 2015. The method of Bypass is optimizing the search space of the constraint tree (CT) to reduce the runtime of CBS.

However, MAPF algorithms such as CBS and ICBS that satisfy the optimality under the current constraints are poorly scalable, and the performance of these algorithms degrades significantly as the number of agents increases. Moreover, there are problems with the strategy of selecting node extensions at the HL of CBS: CBS does not consider the type of node conflicts, and there is a possibility that extending nodes at the HL may result in more conflicts.

This study presents the RBCBS algorithm that combines node expansion rules with limited focus search [10] to overcome the drawbacks of the CBS. First, explicit child node selection rules are formulated according to different conflict types during the process of HL search and the process is guided by heuristic functions to reduce the possibility of conflicts. Second, RBCBS will ensure that the final path cost is close to the optimal value by inputting a suboptimal factor.

2   Related Word

2.1   Multi-Agent Path Finding

MAPF can be described as path planning for m agents $\{a_1, a_2, a_3, ...a_m\}$: without any conflicts, in a known or unknown map.

The following conditions are required to construct the model in this paper. (1) Rasterized map. The grid map has the advantage of being simple to understand and effective in representing irregularly shaped objects. (2) Temporal discretization. By reducing continuous time to each equal time step in discrete space, the location of the agent at different time steps and the moments of conflict can be better recorded, which helps to resolve conflicts and count path costs. (3) Direction of movement. The agents can move along the current position in four directions: up, down, left and right. (4) Paths constraint. The agents' start from the starting points and pass through different neighbors grids to reach their target endpoints. (5) Grid constraint. At the same moment, the same grid and its edges can only be occupied or traveled by one agent, otherwise, conflicts arise. (6) The total path cost is the sum of the path lengths of all agents [11].

For example, as shown in Fig. 1: In a 4 * 4 grid map with a time step of 0, the red and blue agents stand at their respective starting points A1 and D1. The red agent needs to reach the D4 target and the blue agent needs to reach the A4 target. After using the A* algorithm, the red agent's path is {A1, B1, B2, B3, C3, D3, D4} and cost is 7, the blue agent's path is {D1, C1, C2, C3, B3, A3, A4} and cost is 7, and the total cost of the paths is 14. However, they will both pass through the common edge of grid B3 and C3 at the same time in step 4, and a conflict will occur. In this case, resolving the conflict and generating a conflict-free path to the target location is necessary. This will be described in detail in Sect. 2.2.

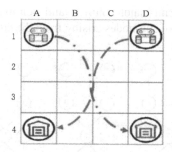

Fig. 1. MAPF example.

2.2 Conflict-Based Search (CBS)

The CBS is a mainstream two-level MAPF algorithm. The central idea of CBS is to plan a path independently for each agent, then create branches for resolving conflicts between agents' paths, and try to resolve conflicts on the branches until there are no conflicts between agents paths.

CBS consists of a LL and HL algorithm. On the LL, A* is used to plan paths for all agents individually that each satisfies the constraints. On the HL, CBS performs an optimal search on CT, where each node N of the CT contains a set of constraints used to coordinate the paths of the agents to avoid conflicts and a path scheme for each agent. Conflict is denoted as (a_i, a_j, v, t), implying that the agents a_i and a_j are in conflict at moment t and position v. The constraint is denoted as $Con\{a_j, v, t\}$, indicating that the agent a_i can not pass position v at moment t.

As described in the previous example in Sect. 2.1: Two agents will conflict at time step 4, so a constraint can be added for each of the two conflicting agent or individually added. For example, the red agent cannot pass through C3 at time step 4, as indicated by: $Con\{redagent, C3, 4\}$. Then, A* is then called to replan the path with constraints for the red agent in LL: {A1, B1, B2, B3, B4, C4, D4}. Finally, the path cost value of red agent and total path cost value are updated.

2.3 Improved Conflict-Based Search (ICBS)

The ICBS is a modification of the CBS algorithm, its main contribution is to alleviate the problems of CBS in selecting conflict nodes. ICBS classifies conflict nodes into major, semi-major, non-major conflicts (as detailed in Subsect. 3.1 of this paper) and then gives a higher priority to resolving the major conflict.

3   Rule and Bounded CBS (RBCBS)

3.1   Classification of Conflict Types

To speed up the search, RBCBS subdivides conflicts into the following three types (Fig. 2): major conflicts, semi-major conflicts and non-major conflicts, based on the total cost of resolving the two sub-nodes arising from the conflicts that occur in the CT.

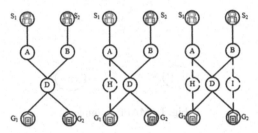

Fig. 2. Kinds of conflict: major (left), semi-major (middle), non-major(right).

Major conflicts occur when the cost of child nodes exceeds the cost of the parent node. Semi-major conflict occurs when the expense of merely one child node exceeds the parent's cost. Non-major conflict exists when neither child's cost is more than the parent's cost. RBCBS will give priority to nodes with major conflicts.

3.2   Bounded Focus Search

The RBCBS is solved by specifying a focusing constant such that the total path cost of the target node N solved by the algorithm is less than the product of ω and the minimum of total path cost C'.

RBCBS has two types of node lists: the OPEN list and the FOCAL list. The OPEN list is used to store all nodes to be traversed, while the FOCAL list is a sub-list of the OPEN list. The focusing search is implemented by the functions f_1 and f_2, denoted (f_1, f_2). f_1 stores the focus list of all nodes N in the OPEN list that satisfy $f_1(n) \leq \omega \cdot f_{1_{min}}$ ($f_{1_{min}}$ is the smallest value of f in the focus list), and f_2 is used to select the node in the focus list for expansion.

For CT node n, assume that:

$$LL(n) = \sum_{i=1}^{m} f_{min}(i). \tag{1}$$

For each generated CT node n, the RBCBS LL search returns two values to the HL search: N. cost and LL(n), such that:

$$LL = min(LL(n)|n \in OPEN). \tag{2}$$

For CT node n, assume that:

$$LL(n) = \sum_{i=1}^{m} f_{min}(i). \tag{3}$$

where OPEN is the open list of HL search CT nodes. Thus, LL is the minimum of total path cost C′ of the entire path planning solution problem. Focus search list FOCAL in RDCBS denoted as:

$$FOCAL = \{n|n \in OPEN, n.cost \le LL \cdot \omega\}. \tag{4}$$

Since LL is the minimum of total path cost C′ of the entire path planning solution problem, the total path cost of all nodes in the focused list is no greater than the product of the constant ω and the optimal solution C′. Therefore, if RBCBS can find a solution result for path planning that satisfies the current constraint, it can ensure that its total cost is at most ωC′. The pseudo-code for the RBCBS algorithm is shown below.

Algorithm 1: RBCBS High Level

Input: MAPF Instance, Suboptimal factor ω
Output: Paths without Conflict
1:N.Constraints = Ø
2:N.Solution = Paths
3:N.Cost = SIC(N.Solution)//Single Instance Cost
4:Insert N into OPEN
5:if OPEN =empty
6: **return** false
7:Calculate the LowLevel//According Suboptimal factor and the min R.cost
8:FOCAL ← The nodes which N.cost<LowLevel from OPEN
9:**while** FOCAL != empty
10: N←best node from FOCAL//According to the f₂
11: **if** P has nothing Conflict **then**
12:    **return** N.Solution //N is the goal node
13: C ← Conflict: (a_i, a_j, v, t) in N
14: **for** agent a_i in C **do**
15:    ChildrenNode ← new node //splitting
16:    ChildrenNode.Constraints ←N.Constraints+(a_i, s, t)
17:    Update ChildrenNode.Solution by invoking low-level（a_i)
18:    ChildrenNode.cost=SIC(ChildrenNode.solution)
19:    Insert ChildrenNode to OPEN
20:**return** to step 5

Pseudocode lines 1–4 initialize the root node's constraints, solutions, and path costs, and insert the root node into the OPEN list. The planning fails when the OPEN list is empty and the final solution is still not found. Lines 6–7 calculate the lower bound of the optimal path and generate the FOCAL list. Lines 9–13 enter the node selection loop, combine the node selection rules, select the conflicting nodes from FOCAL to expand the children, and call the LL algorithm to plan the list of path solutions that satisfy the constraints. Lines 14–19 update the path cost, inserts the child nodes into the OPEN list and continue the cycle until a conflict-free path is generated.

4   Experimental Results

The experiments are conducted on a computer configured with Intel i9-9900K CPU, the experimental platform is built on Ubuntu 18.04 and the program is written in C++.

To prevent memory overflow of the computer, the upper limit of experiment time for each group in this chapter is set to 5 min. The success rate referred to is the ratio of the number of instances that successfully plan a path for the given agents to the number of all tested instances. The formula for the success rate is:

$$Accuracy = \frac{Success}{Total}. \tag{5}$$

4.1   Different Focus Constants on RBCBS

Different focusing constants can have different degrees of impact on the success rate in different storage environments. To verify this conclusion, RBCBS performance was respectively tested in grid maps of 8 * 8, 14 agents with 20% obstacles and 32 * 32, 40 agents with 30% obstacles. As shown in Fig. 3, the success rates all increased as the focus constant increased until the success rates all stabilised at 100%. Only when the success rate is stable at 100%, the technical indicators are more meaningful for comparison. Therefore, the focus constant of 1.2 was taken for RBCBS in all subsequent experiments.

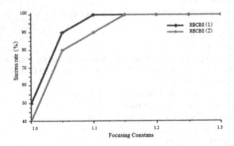

Fig. 3. Effect of different focusing constants on RBCBS.

4.2   Comparison to CBS, ICBS

To compare the capability of the RBCBS, ICBS and CBS, comparison experiments were made in different environments. The total path length, runtime, number of search nodes in HL and LL, and success rate are used as the comparison metrics for the experiments.

As shown in Table 1, RBCBS produces longer path lengths than ICBS and CBS solvers, but in the runtime metric, RBCBS is less than ICBS and CBS. This is because RBCBS improves the efficiency of path planning by sacrificing some solution quality. But, the path length generated by RBCBS is not greater than the product of the path length generated by CBS or ICBS and the input focus constant. On the other hand, since both ICBS and CBS are optimal algorithms satisfying existing constraints, except that the ICBS prioritises the nodes with major conflicts when resolving conflicts, the total path lengths of the agent solved by these two algorithms are equal.

Table 1. Total path length and time cost for agents in a different environment, $\omega = 1.2$

Environment			Path length			Runtime(ms)		
Sizes	Agents	Ostacles(%)	RBCBS	ICBS	CBS	RBCBS	ICBS	CBS
8 * 8	6	10%	53	50	50	14	28	36
	11	20%	63	59	59	1285	3053	8436
	14	20%	104	95	95	3575	7785	24643
32 * 32	20	20%	519	507	507	157	436	716
	30	30%	735	715	715	928	1885	5164
	40	30%	947	861	861	3679	5681	11342

To further explain why the total path cost of agents becomes longer in RBCBS, the runtime of the agents becomes smaller. We do the same environment as Table 1. In Table 2, since RBCBS only extends the nodes that satisfy Eq. 4, the number of HL or LL search nodes generated by RBCBS are both smaller than ICBS and CBS. Also, RBCBS will reduce the number of nodes to be searched by node selection rules, just like ICBS, which is why ICBS has a lower number of search nodes than CBS.

Table 2. Total search nodes in HL and LL for agents in a different environment, $\omega = 1.2$

Environment			Total of search nodes in HL				Total of search nodes in LL	
Sizes	Agents	Ostacles(%)	RBCBS	ICBS	CBS	RBCBS	ICBS	CBS
8 * 8	6	10%	1	2	4	36	53	87
	11	20%	10	35	279	484	2642	6973
	14	20%	35	167	1156	2375	5241	16214
32 * 32	20	20%	8	62	130	34272	96218	156917
	30	30%	114	226	486	739991	127585	381132
	40	30%	386	721	1328	311893	533964	821132

4.3 Scalability Experiments with RBCBS

To demonstrate the scalability of RBCBS, the experimental is set to the lak303d and den312 [12] atlases disclosed by Sturtevant et al. In Fig. 4, the success rate of RBCBS remains higher than ICBS and CBS when the amounts of agents rise. Within a fixed time, RBCBS sacrifices small solution quality, and reduces the number of HL and LL node searches, thus enabling more agents can be plan paths successfully as possible. Therefore, RBCBS is more scalable than ICBS and CBS.

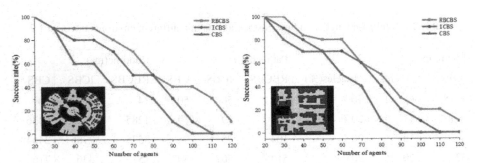

Fig. 4. RBCBS, ICBS, CBS in lak303d (left), den312 (right) map performance.

5 Conclusions

The RBCBS is proposed in this paper, which solves the problem of decreasing algorithm's efficiency due to the random selection of conflicting nodes that exists at the HL of CBS, and combines the idea of bounded search, which improves the speed of solving the CBS. Compared with CBS and its modified version ICBS in experiments, the RBCBS is not only quicker and scalability, but also guarantees the lower bound of the solution quality.

Like CBS and ICBS, RBCBS is not able to solve the problem about Iterative-Deepening [13]. Therefore, in the future, we will focus on how RBCBS can run for a long time.

References

1. Stern, R., et al.: Multi-agent pathfinding: definitions, variants, and benchmarks. In: Twelfth Annual Symposium on Combinatorial Search (2019)
2. Smierzchalski, R.: Evolutionary trajectory planning of ships in navigation traffic areas. J. Mar. Sci. Technol. **4**(1), 1–6 (1999)
3. Xidias, E., Zacharia, P., Nearchou, A.: Intelligent fleet management of autonomous vehicles for city logistics. Appl. Intell. **52**, 1–19 (2022). https://doi.org/10.1007/s10489-022-03535-y
4. Nimmo, M., Heß, F., Sommer, N.: Safety and security concept for an automated parking service. ATZ Worldwide **122**(12), 26–31 (2020)

5. Yu, J., LaValle, S.M.: Structure and intractability of optimal multi-robot path planning on graphs. In: Twenty-Seventh AAAI Conference on Artificial Intelligence (2013)
6. Sharon, G., Stern, R., Felner, A., Sturtevant, N.R.: Conflict-based search for optimal multi-agent pathfinding. Artif. Intell. **219**, 40–66 (2015)
7. Hart, P.E., Nilsson, N.J., Raphael, B.: A formal basis for the heuristic determination of minimum cost paths. IEEE Trans. Syst. Sci. Cybern. **4**(2), 100–107 (1968)
8. Boyarski, E., et al.: Icbs: Improved conflict-based search algorithm for multi-agent pathfinding. In: Twenty-Fourth International Joint Conference on Artificial Intelligence (2015)
9. Boyrasky, E., Felner, A., Sharon, G., Stern, R.: Don't split, try to work it out:Bypassing conflicts in multi-agent pathfinding. In: Proceedings of the International Conference on Automated Planning and Scheduling, vol. 25, pp. 47–51 (2015)
10. Barer, M., Sharon, G., Stern, R., Felner, A.: Suboptimal variants of the conflict-based search algorithm for the multi-agent pathfinding problem. In: Seventh Annual Symposium on Combinatorial Search (2014)
11. Li, J., Ruml, W., Koenig, S.: Eecbs: A bounded-suboptimal search for multi-agent path finding. In: Proceedings of the AAAI Conference on Artificial Intelligence, vol. 35, pp. 12353–12362 (2021)
12. Sturtevant, N.R.: Benchmarks for grid-based pathfinding. IEEE Trans. Comput. Intell. AI Games **4**(2), 144–148 (2012)
13. Boyarski, E., et al.: Iterative-deepening conflict-based search. In: Proceedings of the Twenty-Ninth International Conference on International Joint Conferences on Artificial Intelligence, pp. 4084–4090 (2021)

Dynamic Scheduling Method of Multi-objective Job Shop Based on Reinforcement Learning

Zhenwei Zhang[1]([✉]), Lihong Qiao[2], and Zhicheng Huang[2]

[1] Beijing Institute of Radio Measurement, Beijing 100039, China
rotos@163.com

[2] School of Mechanical Engineering and Automation, Beihang University, Beijing 100191, China

Abstract. Aiming at the dynamic scheduling problem in workshop production, we propose a multi-objective scheduling method. By analyzing the actual dynamic scheduling problem, a mathematical model is constructed. Then the dynamic interference factors in the actual production environment are classified, and the interference intensity and its parameters are designed. On this basis, a dynamic scheduling oriented process model is established by using reinforcement learning and scheduling rules, and the design of its state space, state action value table and reward function is introduced. Finally, the model is trained and we analyze the simulation results of different methods. The results show that the dynamic scheduling method based on reinforcement learning has good performance under different periods and disturbance intensity, which shows this method is effective and feasible for dynamic scheduling problem.

Keywords: Reinforcement learning · Dynamic disturbance · Dynamic scheduling · Scheduling rules · Multi-objective

1 Introduction

Due to the complexity of the actual production process, uncertain factors such as equipment downtime, urgent orders, repairing due to quality problems, time adjustment and other factors are difficult to avoid. Job shop scheduling is often shown as complex dynamic scheduling, which needs to adjust the job plan at any time according to the changes of production conditions. For the dynamic scheduling problem, the traditional methods are simplifying the problem, ignoring the disturbance and uncertainty, and transforming the complex problem into a static scheduling problem. These methods need to be redesigned according to the current new state, and models are needed to readjusted according to the changes in the production environment. Since the disturbance of the system state is not considered in traditional methods, the actual production needs cannot be met. In addition, for large-scale production workshops, the order tasks

This work is supported by the National Key Research and Development Program of China under Grant 2018YFB1701800.

are complex and a great number of resources are involved, which will geometrically increase the difficulty of scheduling problems. For these large-scale and more complex scheduling problems, traditional methods are not easy to be applied. Therefore, it is of great significance to study the dynamic scheduling problem for actual production.

Scheduling rule is a priority allocation rule, which has the characteristics of low time complexity and high robustness, and is applicable to solve dynamic scheduling problems. In recent years, scheduling rules are often used to solve job shop scheduling problems. Durasevic et al. [1] studied the applicability of different scheduling rules, and found out the scheduling standards suitable for each scheduling rule by testing nine standards and four job types. Kuck et al. [2] proposed an optimization method based on adaptive simulation to select appropriate scheduling rules for production control in the case of equipment failure in complex manufacturing systems. Zhang et al. [3] proposed a semantic-based scheduling rule selection system, which associated scheduling rules with optimization objectives through semantic similarity and semantic expressions, and realized the generation of scheduling rule combinations for a given production target. Rolf et al. [4] presented a method of scheduling rule allocation in solving the hybrid flow shop problem with sequence-related setup times. Lee et al. [5] proposed a sequential search method to set appropriate weight sets for scheduling rules, and used decision trees and hierarchical clustering to improve search efficiency. Braune et al. [6] proposed a tree based scheduling priority rule generation method, which realized the decision-making of job allocation and machine sequencing through single tree and multiple.

Reinforcement learning algorithm is a kind of method that does not rely on samples. Compared with traditional intelligent algorithm, it has higher efficiency and generalization ability. Q-learning (QL) is one of the main methods of reinforcement learning. It is a model-free learning method, which can avoid the huge amount of computation of large-scale scheduling, and is applicable to dynamic scheduling problems. At present, there are more and more researches on reinforcement learning for scheduling problems. Bouazza et al. [7] selected reasonable equipment and process routes for the dynamic scheduling by improving the state-action value table of the reinforcement learning algorithm. Shahrabi et al. [8] used QL algorithm to find the appropriate parameters for problem with equipment failure and dynamic arrival of workpieces. Shiue et al. [9] studied the problem of real-time scheduling (TRS) and proposed a real-time scheduling system using a multiple scheduling rules (MDR) mechanism to ensure that the knowledge base (KB) can respond to changes in the workshop environment in real time. Wang [10] proposed an adaptive scheduling strategy, which avoided the blind search problem of the traditional method through dynamic greedy search, and realized the weighted iteration of Q function by defining state error, which improved the speed and accuracy of the learning algorithm. Qu et al. [11] proposed a multi-agent method for the scheduling of production system covering multiple types of products, equipment and labor, which could adaptively update production plans in real time. Chen et al. [12] proposed a method for flexible job shop scheduling, which took genetic algorithm as the key and intelligently adjusted its parameters based on reinforcement learning. Kardos et al. [13] proposed a new method to select machines according to real-time information, so as to reduce the delay time of the workpiece in production.

The current research on dynamic scheduling problems is mostly based on specific workshop scenarios, and the scheduling scheme is only suitable for special environments, which is not universal. By analyzing the above research, this paper proposes a multi-objective dynamic scheduling method based on QL. Through QL technology, the optimal scheduling strategy under dynamic disturbance is obtained, and the real-time matching between the scheduling strategy and the production environment is realized.

2 Description of Dynamic Scheduling Problem

Job shop dynamic scheduling is a complex optimization problem, which can be described as: n workpieces $Q = \{Q_1, Q_2, ..., Q_n\}$ are processed on m equipment $M = \{M_1, M_2, ..., M_n\}$. Each workpiece Q_i has its corresponding process route and process, and each process corresponds to an optional equipment set. At the same time, it is necessary to consider the disturbance factors in actual production, such as equipment failure, urgent orders, etc. The goal of scheduling is to select the appropriate processing equipment for the workpiece under various constraints and dynamic disturbances, to determine the processing sequence of the workpiece and its working time, and to continuously improve the scheduling index through optimization to meet the expected index requirements.

For the universality of the problem, the dynamic scheduling problem in this paper is based on the several conditions:

- The workpieces arrive dynamically, and the arrival times of the workpieces are random, regardless of the delivery time of the material. The processing time of the operation includes the preparation time.
- Each process of the workpiece corresponds to an optional equipment set, and only one of the equipment can be selected to complete the process.
- The process cannot be stopped halfway after it starts.
- Each equipment can only be used for the processing of one workpiece at the same time, and other workpieces are not allowed to preempt after the processing starts.
- Each workpiece has a definite process route, and the processing is carried out in the order specified in the process route. The next process can only be carried out after its previous process.
- The processing time of an operation has nothing to do with the process route.

To define the dynamic scheduling problem, the definitions of relevant parameters are shown in Table 1:

For the dynamic scheduling problem, the constraints can be described as follows:

$$TQ_{sij} + X_{ijk} \times TQ_{ijk} \leq TQ_{eij} \tag{1}$$

$$TQ_{eij} \leq TQ_{si(j+1)} \tag{2}$$

$$TQ_{eiL_i} \leq C_{max} \tag{3}$$

Table 1. Parameter definition of dynamic scheduling problem

Symbol	Represention
Q_i	Workpiece i, $i = 1,2,...n$;
Q_{ij}	The jth process of workpiece i, $j = 1,2,...L_i$
M_k	The kth equipment, $k = 1,...,m$
K_{ij}	Optional equipment set of Q_{ij}
H_{ij}	Number of equipment in the optional equipment set of Q_{ij}
TQ_{ijk}	Time of the jth process of P_i on equipment k
TQ_{sij}	The start time of Qij
TQ_{eij}	The end time of Q_{ij}
T_{ei}	Delivery time requirements of workpiece i
t_i	Actual completion time of workpiece i
G_i	Arrival time of workpiece i
C_{max}	Maximum makespan
T_a	Total operation amount of all workpieces
X_{ijk}	1, Q_{ij} processing on equipment k 0, Q_{ij} is not processed on device k
Y_{ijkhr}	1, Q_{ij} is processed before O_{hr} 0, Q_{ij} is not processed before O_{hr}
inf	Positive infinity

$$TQ_{sij} + TQ_{ijk} \leq TQ_{shr} + \inf \cdot (1 - Y_{ijkhr}) \tag{4}$$

$$TQ_{eij} \leq TQ_{si(j+1)} + \inf \cdot (1 - Y_{ikhr(j+1)}) \tag{5}$$

$$\sum_{k=1}^{H_{ij}} X_{ijk} = 1 \tag{6}$$

$$\sum_{i=1}^{n} \sum_{k=1}^{L_i} Y_{ijkhr} = X_{hrk} \tag{7}$$

$$\sum_{h=1}^{n} \sum_{r=1}^{L_h} Y_{ijkhr} = X_{ijk} \tag{8}$$

In the above constraints, Eqs. 1 and 2 represent the production route constraints of the workpiece; Eq. 3 represents the constraint of the completion time of the process; Eqs. 4 and 5 indicate that a piece of equipment can only be used for one process at the same time; Eq. 6 represents the exclusive constraint of a process; Eqs. 7 and 8 represent the usability constraints of the equipment.

The goal of defining dynamic scheduling is to facilitate the evaluation of the effect of scheduling. Common scheduling performance evaluation includes production efficiency, such as maximum makespan; Stability of production process, such as deviation index; Economic indicators, such as production cost, total processing energy consumption and so on. This paper uses the synthesis of multiple indicators as the evaluation indicators.

$$f_1 = \min(\max(C_i)) \tag{9}$$

$$f_2 = \min(\frac{1}{n}\sum_{i=1}^{n}(C_i - G_i)) \tag{10}$$

$$f_3 = \min(\max_{i=1}^{n}(\max(C_i - T_{ei}))) \tag{11}$$

Equation 9 represents the maximum makespan requirement, Eq. 10 represents the index of average flow time, and Eq. 11 represents the index of delayed delivery time. We construct the final scheduling performance index by synthesizing the above indicators, as shown in formula 12, and f is the objective function of comprehensive optimization.

$$f = \min F(f_1, f_2, f_3) \tag{12}$$

3 Dynamic Disturbance and Scheduling Rules

3.1 Analysis of Dynamic Disturbance Factors

The dynamic disturbance factors in actual production can be divided into indirect disturbance and direct disturbance according to their performance characteristics. Indirect disturbances, such as processing time deviation, poor material turnover, and equipment efficiency decline, etc., will affect the execution of scheduling only when these factors accumulate to a certain extent. Direct disturbance will significantly interfere with the scheduling and cause the adjustment of the plan. Direct disturbance can be divided into two types. One is related to resources, such as equipment failure, operation interruption, personnel absence, material shortage or delay, etc. The other is related to the workpiece, such as emergency order insertion, random arrival of workpiece, task cancellation, delivery date adjustment, working hours change, workpiece repair, etc. Common dynamic disturbance factors are shown in Table 2.

This paper mainly studies the direct disturbance, focusing on four typical disturbance factors: the dynamic arrival of the workpiece, urgent order, equipment maintenance and workpiece repair. In the actual production process, the workpiece arrives randomly. In this paper, the arrival time of the workpiece is set so that they are uniformly distributed. For urgent order, it can be set by proportion R_1 and advance its delivery date. The equipment is not available if it is under the maintenance period, and the disturbance can be set by the maintenance time proportion R_2. For the quality problems in actual production, it is achieved by setting a certain number of workpieces with a proportion of F for rework. Considering the difference of disturbance degree in actual production, this paper reflects it through different disturbance intensity.

Table 2. Classification of dynamic disturbance factors

General category	Subclass	Disturbance factor	Impact on production
Direct disturbance	Workpiece related	Random arrival of workpiece	Plan deviation
		Order change	Production adjustment
		Delivery date adjustment	Change the number of batch tasks
		Work hours change	Plan ahead or behind schedule
		Workpiece rework	Increase in production tasks
		Urgent order insertion	Subsequent task rescheduling
		Process change	Workpiece process route change
	Resource related	Equipment failure	Reduction in the number of equipment
		Operating disturbance	Postponement of related tasks
		Personnel absenteeism	Increased manpower load
		Material shortage	Delay of material waiting task
Indirect disturbance	Resource related	Poor material turnover	Continuous accumulation will disrupt the original production progress
		Equipment performance degradation	Deviation accumulation will affect the production schedule
	Time dependent	Processing time deviation	The accumulation of time error will affect the implementation of the plan

3.2 Scheduling Rules

The scheduling rules are to calculate the priority of the workpiece according to the selection of processing time, process quantity, delivery period, etc., and select workpiece to be processed for idle equipment.

For dynamic scheduling problems, the evaluation method based on scheduling rules can be used. This method is relatively easy to implement in the actual production environment. It belongs to an efficient closed-loop control method, so it can be used for real-time job shop scheduling. In the process of scheduling, we need to consider the selection of equipment and the allocation of jobs. This paper analyzes the scheduling rules for these two types of problems, studies the performance differences of different scheduling rules under dynamic disturbance, and finally selects the rules with excellent performance. Common scheduling rules are shown in Table 3.

Table 3. Typical scheduling rules

Rule	Description
FIFO	Give priority to the workpiece that arrives first
SPT	The workpiece with the Minimum processing time is selected
LPT	The workpiece with the Maximum processing time is selected
EDD	The workpiece with the earliest delivery date is selected
MST	The workpiece with the least delay time is selected
MOR	Give priority to the workpiece with the most remaining operations
LOR	Give priority to the workpiece with the least remaining process
LRM	Give priority to the workpiece with the most remaining processing time
SRM	The workpiece with the least remaining processing time is selected

4 Dynamic Scheduling Problem Solving Based on Reinforcement Learning

4.1 State Space Definition

The job shop scheduling process is transformed through the state space to express the system environment of reinforcement learning. The definition of state needs to reflect the features and process of the scheduling environment, and it needs to be able to express different scenarios. In this paper, according to the state of the equipment and the workpiece. The state space is defined by means of feature vectors. The state space includes 5 features, which are shown as follows.

$$s_{k,1} = n_k / n \tag{13}$$

$$s_{k,2} = T_k^a / T^a \tag{14}$$

$$s_{k,3} = \sum_{j=1}^{L_i} TQ_{ijk} \Bigg/ \sum\sum TQ_{ij} \tag{15}$$

$$s_{k,4} = \sum_{h=j+1}^{L_i} TQ_{ih} \Bigg/ \sum_{j=1}^{L_i} TQ_{ij} \tag{16}$$

$$s_{k,5} = n_k^d \Big/ n \tag{17}$$

The above equations describe the current state of the system, where n_k represents the number of workpieces processed by the equipment k at the current moment; T_k^a indicates the number of processing operations of equipment k; n_k^d indicates the number of delayed workpieces processed by equipment k. Equation 13 reflects the distribution of processed workpieces on each equipment; Eq. 14 reflects the distribution of processes on the equipment; Eq. 15 reflects the proportion of processing time of the equipment; Eq. 16 reflects the proportion of remaining time of work in process; Eq. 17 reflects the distribution state of delayed workpieces.

The state values constitute a vector $[s11, s12, \ldots, s15, s21, s22, \ldots, s25, s31, \ldots, sm5]$. The state vector can be transformed into a state value located in a certain numerical interval (such as $[0,100]$) by using neural network, and the state value can be used as a criterion to distinguish the state of the scheduling environment.

4.2 Q-value Table

The action space of QL can be expressed as the scheduling behavior in the current state. This paper selects seven typical scheduling rules as the action space of QL. According to the aforementioned priority rules, the $Q(s, a)$ table can be established by combining the state values. In this paper, 11 states are used to construct the $Q(s, a)$ table, as shown in Table 4.

Table 4. $Q(s, a)$ table

State	Range	Scheduling rule						
		FIFO	SPT	LPT	EDD	MST	LRM	SRM
0	$T_v = 0$	0	0	0	0	0	0	0
1	$0 \le T_v \le 10$	$Q(1,1)$	$Q(1,2)$	$Q(1,3)$	$Q(1,4)$	$Q(1,5)$	$Q(1,6)$	$Q(1,7)$
2	$10 < T_v \le 20$	$Q(2,1)$	$Q(2,2)$	$Q(2,3)$	$Q(2,4)$	$Q(2,5)$	$Q(2,6)$	$Q(2,7)$
3	$20 < T_v \le 30$	$Q(3,1)$	$Q(3,2)$	$Q(3,3)$	$Q(3,4)$	$Q(3,5)$	$Q(3,6)$	$Q(3,7)$
4	$30 < T_v \le 40$	$Q(4,1)$	$Q(4,2)$	$Q(4,3)$	$Q(4,4)$	$Q(4,5)$	$Q(4,6)$	$Q(4,7)$
5	$40 < T_v \le 50$	$Q(5,1)$	$Q(5,2)$	$Q(5,3)$	$Q(5,4)$	$Q(5,5)$	$Q(5,6)$	$Q(5,7)$
6	$50 < T_v \le 60$	$Q(6,1)$	$Q(6,2)$	$Q(6,3)$	$Q(6,4)$	$Q(6,5)$	$Q(6,6)$	$Q(6,7)$
7	$60 < T_v \le 70$	$Q(7,1)$	$Q(7,2)$	$Q(7,3)$	$Q(7,4)$	$Q(7,5)$	$Q(7,6)$	$Q(7,7)$
8	$70 < T_v \le 80$	$Q(8,1)$	$Q(8,2)$	$Q(8,3)$	$Q(8,4)$	$Q(8,5)$	$Q(8,6)$	$Q(8,7)$
9	$80 < T_v \le 90$	$Q(9,1)$	$Q(9,2)$	$Q(9,3)$	$Q(9,4)$	$Q(9,5)$	$Q(9,6)$	$Q(9,7)$
10	$90 < T_v \le 100$	$Q(10,1)$	$Q(10,2)$	$Q(10,3)$	$Q(10,4)$	$Q(10,5)$	$Q(10,6)$	$Q(10,7)$

For state 0, that is, the scheduling action has not yet started. This state is empty and is also the initial state, so its value is 0.

4.3 Design of Reward Function

For the reward function R, its construction needs to consider the performance indicators of the scheduling system, and the function needs to reflect the impact of action selection on the scheduling results. Therefore, the design of R needs to reflect not only the immediate reward of the action, but also the cumulative impact on the production cycle, and it should also be suitable for scheduling problems of all sizes. For the production efficiency indicators related to time, because these indicators are related to the utilization of equipment, it can be considered to take the working state of equipment as a reward and punishment function, and the equipment state can be defined as follows.

$$\delta_i(t) = \begin{cases} -1, & \text{Equipment } i \text{ is idle at time } t \\ 0, & \text{Equipment } i \text{ is in working state at time } t \end{cases}$$

The reward and punishment function are as follows.

$$r_k = \frac{1}{m} \sum_{i=1}^{m} \int_{\tau=t_{k-1}}^{t_k} \delta_i(\tau) \tag{18}$$

In Eq. 18, m is the number of devices, and r_k represents the reward when it transitions from s_{k-1} to s_k. The absolute value of r_k is the same as the average time that each device is idle when the two states are transferred. It can be seen that the production cycle is negatively correlated with the cumulative return.

$$R_a = \sum_{k=1}^{K} r_k = \frac{1}{m} \sum_{k=1}^{K} \sum_{i=1}^{m} \int_{\tau=t_{k-1}}^{t_k} \delta_i(\tau) = \frac{1}{m} \sum_{i=1}^{m} \int_{\tau=0}^{c_{\max}} \delta_i(\tau)$$

$$= -\frac{1}{m} \sum_{k=1}^{m} \left(C_{\max} - \sum_{i=1}^{n} \sum_{j=1}^{L_i} TQ_{ijk} \right) = \frac{1}{m} \sum_{k=1}^{m} \sum_{i=1}^{n} \sum_{j=1}^{L_i} TQ_{ijk} - C_{\max} \tag{19}$$

In Eq. 19, R_a represents the cumulative return. It can be seen that the smaller the C_{max}, the greater the cumulative return R_a.

5 Case Study

To verify the effectiveness of the method, we carry out simulation analysis through MATLAB. The QL algorithm parameters settings: $\alpha = 0.05$, $\beta = 0.9$, $\varepsilon = 0.15$. The initial state-action reward value is zero. For the experimental data, the number of processes of a single workpiece is between 1 and 4, the total number of equipment is 10, the process processing time is between 10 and 25, and the workpiece cache is 100. The processing time, the time interval of arrival, and the required completion time data all meet the normal distribution. The dynamic disturbance parameter settings are shown in Table 5. The training data of QL is randomly generated by the system, with a total of 100000 pieces of workpiece data (the unit of time-related data is hour). In the test phase, seven sets of workpiece data such as 300, 600, 1000, 1500, 2000, 2500 and 3000 are used

Table 5. Dynamic disturbance parameter setting

Parameter	Setting
Time interval from workpiece to random arrival	Mean 15
Date of delivery	Tight period: working hours of workpiece × 3
	Medium period: work hours of workpiece × 5
	Loose period: working hours of workpiece × 8
Disturbance intensity $S(\%)$	Strength 1: $S(R_1, R_2, F) = [2]$
	Strength 2: $S(R_1, R_2, F) = [4]$
	Strength 3: $S(R_1, R_2, F) = [6]$

Table 6. Performance comparison of different rules and QL

Rule number of workpieces	FIFO	SPT	LPT	EDD	MST	LRM	SRM	QL
300	4681	4827	4560	4644	4263	4580	5120	4525
600	8835	9030	8875	8864	8531	8826	9275	8690
1000	14680	14501	14732	14680	14237	14653	15023	14271
1500	23684	22561	22490	23661	21649	23598	24061	21701
2000	31553	29553	30642	31508	29009	30801	31609	28902
2500	36952	36025	36201	36891	35803	36538	37568	35355
3000	43725	42845	42339	43356	42647	43228	44187	42208

respectively, and a single scheduling rule and the QL lgorithm in this paper are used for scheduling.

Table 6 shows the makespan data obtained by different scheduling rules and the QL algorithm in this paper. It can be seen that the advantage of QL is not obvious when the number of workpieces is small, but with the increase of the number of workpieces, the performance advantage of QL scheduling becomes obvious. Through QL, the frequency of the system selects different rules in different delivery periods is shown in Table 7.

It can be seen that there are differences in the selection frequency of scheduling rules. The rule of MST, EDD and LPT are used more frequently under tight period, and MST, LPT, EDD and SPT are used more frequently under medium period, and MST and SPT are used more frequently under loose period. MST has the highest frequency of use under the three periods. These rules with higher frequency contribute the most to the solution of QL algorithm, while other rules are used less frequently and contribute less to the solution of the system.

Table 7. Selection frequency of dispatching rules

Rule period	FIFO	SPT	LPT	EDD	MST	LRM	SRM
Tight	2.7%	17.7%	20.9%	23.5%	29.5%	2.8%	2.9%
Medium	3.0%	18.2%	21.3%	19.6%	32.3%	3.0%	2.6%
Loose	2.4%	26.4%	13.1%	11.4%	38.1%	4.7%	3.9%

Table 8 analyzes the comparison of the time limit and completion of QL and MST under the three periods. It can be seen that QL has better effect in the actual time limit, the tardiness and the advance.

Table 8. Comparison of time limit and completion under three periods

Workpiece	Period	Method	Planned duration	Actual construction period		Delayed completion		Early completion	
			Mean value	Mean value	Mean square deviation	Mean value	Mean square deviation	Mean value	Mean square deviation
1000	Tight	QL	213	244.5	625.6	832.9	854.7	123.5	54.9
		MST	213	290.3	854.2	791.8	1542.7	100	62.2
	Medium	QL	391	196	431.3	550.8	697.3	206.3	122.1
		MST	391	297.8	906.7	1152.4	1764.6	162.4	104.6
	Loose	QL	568	170	314.4	514.3	502	285.4	189
		MST	568	307.7	910.9	1958.9	1908.2	351.6	136.4
2000	Tight	QL	183	267.5	946.2	855.8	1188.6	106.9	51.9
		MST	183	336.9	1100	711.2	1481.1	93.8	54
	Medium	QL	336	202.8	571.2	656.8	1020.3	180.8	95.3
		MST	336	334	1114.2	908.5	1842.3	138.8	96.2
	Loose	QL	488	174.4	464.9	712.4	865.9	251.2	156.4
		MST	488	319.4	1068.3	1525.1	2280.7	279.5	128.4

Figure 1 shows the tardiness of QL and MST under different workpiece cache, including tight period and medium period. It is obvious that the tardiness of two methods increase with the expansion of the cache capacity, and the tardiness of tight period is worse than that of medium period. In addition, the QL curve rises gently than MST in both periods. In the medium period, the MST curve quickly crosses the QL curve when the workpiece cache capacity reaches 70, and it crosses the QL curve when the capacity is only 30 in the tight period.

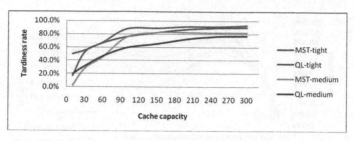

Fig. 1. Comparison of tardiness rate under different cache capacity

Figures 2, 3 and 4 shows the comparison between QL and MST in terms of the change of overdue rate with the number of workpieces under different disturbance intensity and different periods. It can be seen that under the three periods, the overdue rate of both methods increases with the increase of disturbance intensity. When the number of workpieces increases from 200 to 1000, the overdue rate of each period and disturbance intensity increases rapidly. The higher the disturbance intensity, the greater the slope of the curve. After the number of workpieces exceeds 1000, the overdue rate decreases slightly, but remains at a high level. During this period, the overdue rate of QL is generally lower than that of MST. After the number of workpieces exceeds 2000, the overdue rate of QL and MST gradually decreases and stabilizes, and it decreases faster using QL under tight period and high disturbance intensity. By comparison, it is obvious that QL has better effect under tight period and high disturbance intensity.

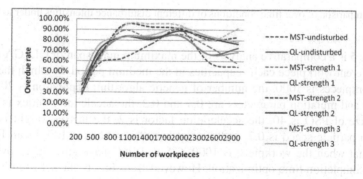

Fig. 2. Comparison of over time of different disturbance intensities under tight period

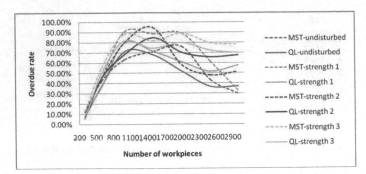

Fig. 3. Comparison of over time conditions of different disturbance intensities under medium period

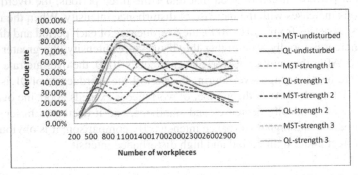

Fig. 4. Comparison of over time conditions of different disturbance intensities under loose period

Figure 5 is a comparative analysis of the maximum makespan of QL, GA and PSO under different workpiece cache capacities in the medium period, in which the number of the workpieces is 1000, the number of genetic algorithm population is 20, and the crossover and mutation parameters are 0.4 and 0.2, the acceleration index is 1.5. The particle size of PSO is 40, the acceleration factor is 2, the inertia weight is 0.5, the maximum particle speed is 0.7, and the number of iterations is 100. From Fig. 5 we can see that when the workpiece is 1000, GA and PSO have advantages over QL in terms of completion time optimization. However, from Fig. 6, the scheduling running time of GA and PSO is much higher than that of QL. When the workpiece cache is low, GA method is about 12 times the running time of QL. When the cache capacity is 80–150, the running time decreases slightly, and when the cache capacity is more than 150, it enters an upward trend. The performance of PSO is worse, and the running time increases sharply after the cache capacity exceeds 40. The running time of QL is always maintained at 2 s, which is only related to the number of workpieces and has nothing to do with the cache. It can be seen that QL is slightly weaker than GA and PSO in terms of completion time, but QL has a better time efficiency advantage in the case of large number of workpiece production and large workpiece cache.

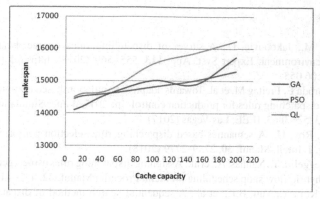

Fig. 5. Comparison of makespan of three algorithms

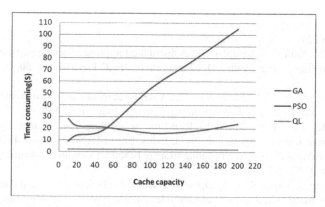

Fig. 6. Comparison of running time of three algorithms

6 Conclusion

This paper studies the dynamic scheduling problem based on reinforcement learning technology and scheduling rules. Typical production disturbances are classified and described through disturbance parameters, the dynamic scheduling problem and its optimization objectives can be consequently represented. On this basis, the state space, Q-value table and reward function of reinforcement learning scheduling are designed. The algorithm is carried out with simulation analysis by using the example data. Through the case study, the method proposed in this paper shows far superior to the traditional intelligent algorithm in time efficiency, and also has a good dynamic scheduling effect. This paper provides a new idea for large-scale job shop dynamic scheduling. For the selection of equipment, this paper adopts the method of man-hour priority, which still lacks the overall analysis of man-hour and load under the complete process route, and further in-depth research can be continued from this direction in the future.

References

1. Ðurasevic, M., Jakobovic, D.: A survey of dispatching rules for the dynamic unrelated machines environment. Expert Syst. App. **113**, 555–569 (2018). https://doi.org/10.1016/j.eswa.2018.06.053
2. Kuck M, Broda E, Freitag M, et al. Towards adaptive simulation-based optimization to select individual dispatching rules for production control. In: 2017 Winter Simulation Conference, WSC, pp. 3852–3863. IEEE, Las Vegas (2017)
3. Zhang, H., Roy, U.. A semantics based dispatching rule selection approach for job shop scheduling. J. Intell. Manuf. **30**, 2759–2779 (2018)
4. Rolf, B., Reggelin, T., Nahhas, A., et al.: Assigning dispatching rules using a genetic algorithm to solve a hybrid flow shop scheduling problem. Procedia Manuf. **42**, 442–449 (2020)
5. Lee, J.H., Kim, Y., Yun, B.K., et al.: A sequential search method of dispatching rules for scheduling of LCD manufacturing systems. IEEE Trans. Semicond. Manuf. **33**(4), 496–503 (2020)
6. Braune, R., Benda, F., Doerner, K.F., et al.: A genetic programming learning approach to generate dispatching rules for flexible shop scheduling problems. Int. J. Prod. Econ. **243**, 108342 (2022)
7. Bouazza, W., Sallez, Y., Beldjilali, B.: A distributed approach solving partially flexible job-shop scheduling problem with a Q-learning effect. IFAC Papersonline **50**(1), 15890–15895 (2017)
8. Shahrabi, J., Adibi, M.A., Mahootchi, M.: A reinforcement learning approach to parameter estimation in dynamic job shop scheduling. Comput. Indus. Eng. **110**(aug), 75–82 (2017)
9. Shiue, Y.R., Lee, K.C., Su, C.T.: Real-time scheduling for a smart factory using a reinforcement learning approach. Comput. Indus. Eng. **125**(Nov), 604–614 (2018)
10. Wang, Y.: Adaptive job shop scheduling strategy based on weighted Q-learning algorithm. J. Intell. Manuf. **31**, 417–432 (2018)
11. Qu, S., Wang, J., Govil, S., et al.: Optimized adaptive scheduling of a manufacturing process system with multi-skill workforce and multiple machine types: an ontology-based, multi-agent reinforcement learning approach. Procedia CIRP **57**, 55–60 (2016)
12. Chen, R., Yang, B., Li, S., et al.: A Self-Learning Genetic Algorithm based on Reinforcement Learning for Flexible Job-shop Scheduling Problem. Comput. Indus. Eng. **149**(1993), 106778 (2020)
13. Kardos, C., Laflamme, C., Gallina, V., et al.: Dynamic scheduling in a job-shop production system with reinforcement learning. Procedia CIRP **97**(1), 104–109 (2021)

A Runtime Verification Tool
for Distributed Simulation Systems

Lianyi Zhang[1,2]([✉]), Duzheng Qing[1,2], Han Zhang[1,2], Qingyun Wang[1,2],
and Yuanjun Laili[3]

[1] Science and Technology on Special System Simulation Laboratory,
Beijing Simulation Center, Beijing, China
[2] Beijing Institute of Electronic System Engineering, Beijing, China
lyzhang117@163.com
[3] Beihang University, Beijing, China

Abstract. Distributed simulation systems are complex systems that
may suffer from runtime uncertainty or runtime errors. The core of defect
detection in distributed simulation systems is to effectively traverse the
state space of communication between nodes in the system. In a distributed simulation system, simulation nodes communicate and exchange
data through event requests. Different event interaction sequences constitute different states of system behavior. Therefore, an efficient traversal
of the state space can be transformed into sequential control of event
requests in the system. This paper mainly studies the hybrid method
based on software testing and model checking to perform runtime verification of the temporal properties of distributed simulation systems.
We develop the runtime verification tool TempoRV. It monitors the distributed simulation system and responds immediately when the behavior
of the system violated certain temporal properties. Finally, to illustrate
the effectiveness of the proposed tool, we conduct a case study to show
that TempoRV provides an important guarantee for the temporal correctness of distributed simulation systems.

Keywords: Distributed simulation · Temporal properties · Runtime
verification

1 Introduction

Distributed simulation systems are complex systems and may have software
flaws. The core of defect detection is to effectively traverse the state space of
communication between nodes in the system. The nodes of a distributed system
communicate and exchange data through event requests, and different event
interaction sequences constitute different states of system behavior. Thus, an
efficient traversal of the state space can be translated into an examination of the
temporal nature of event requests in the system.

As the mainstream framework for distributed simulation, High-Level Architecture (HLA) [6] has been officially accepted as an IEEE standard. It is
mainly composed of four parts: Interface Specification (IFSpec), rules (Rules),

© The Author(s), under exclusive license to Springer Nature Singapore Pte Ltd. 2022
L. Zhang et al. (Eds.): CINT 2022, CCIS 1714, pp. 525–539, 2022.
https://doi.org/10.1007/978-981-19-8915-5_45

Object Model Template (OMT), Federation Development and Execution Process (FEDEP). The HLA simulation system is a distributed system software, and the services provided by multiple federates (Federate) through the Run Time Infrastructure (RTI) constitute a complete simulation system. Among them, the services provided by RTI include federal management, declaration management, object management, ownership management, time management, and communication management. The HLA simulation system has been developed rapidly, and HLA has a wide range of applications in many fields. Subsequently, the verification and verification of the HLA simulation system has also become a research hotspot.

From the perspective of engineering practice, the main methods of system verification can be divided into two categories: formal verification and dynamic testing methods. Dynamic testing methods, including a variety of testing methods, are to judge the correctness of its function by observing the execution of the system under a specific input or a certain system environment. The methods have many advantages, they can quickly and directly find system errors. However, these methods cannot cover all possible operating states of the system, and quantitative measurement methods are needed to judge the adequacy of the verification process in practice. Unlike dynamic testing methods, formal verification methods [16] can cover all possible operating states of the system. There are two main types of formal verification methods: model checking and theorem proving. Model checking is an effective verification method. It relies on the formal expression of the specification, describing the system with an abstract mathematical model, and describing properties with temporal logic. Temporal logic can express the operation of the system over time. The model checking method is an automatic verification method that has been applied in practical industrial fields. Model checking [14] is an important automatic verification technology, and the time series verification based on model checking is the process of judging whether a finite event string belongs to a given language. Therefore, many runtime verification algorithms are implemented using the model checking method of automata theory. The basic idea of model checking that use the state transition system M to represent the system behavior, and use the modal/sequential formula F to represent the nature of the system behavior. The question of "whether the system has a certain property" is transformed into the mathematical question "whether M satisfies F". For finite state systems, this problem is decidable by model checking methods. Compared with other formal verification methods, model checking has two significant advantages: one is that it can be automatically detected, and the other is that it can automatically generate counterexamples when the system does not satisfy the properties. SMV [4] is one of the earliest prototype systems implemented. McMillian developed a well-known symbolic model detection tool NuSMV [3] based on OBDD, which is used to verify network protocols, etc., and find previous potential errors in the protocol through detection and verification. Model checking techniques require a state space that enumerates the behavior of the system, and it suffers from the state explosion [5]. Based on the above reasons, the model checking method is often used to verify the correctness of system design, and there is still a certain gap to ensure the correctness of system implementation. In the existing related research work, there are some research on the federation performance of HLA simulation systems using formal verification [17], model checking [11], but no related research using effective technology. This paper will carry out research on the verification method of the distributed simulation system, and use the hybrid method of software testing and model checking to runtime verify the temporal properties of the distributed simulation system.

Runtime verification [2] is a hybrid technique of dynamic testing and model checking. Runtime verification monitors the software system in real-time and responds immediately when the behavior of the system violates certain system properties. Similar to model checking, runtime verification also uses formal temporal logic, such as LTL (linear temporal Logic), TLTL (timed linear temporal Logic), etc., to describe the temporal properties of system behavior. Among them, LTL has five temporal modal operators such as "next state (X)", "some state in the future (F)", "all states in the future (G)", "until a state occurs (U)" "Remain true before a certain state occurs (R)". In the program verification process, these five sequential operations are divided into three categories: the safety property "all state errors ϕ will not occur $(G\neg\phi)$", the liveness property "a future state ϕ will occur (F ϕ)", and the fairness property "If ϕ happens, ψ will happen (GF $\phi \to$ GFψ)".

The events and states of the systems that need to be monitored during runtime verification need to consider not only their timing characteristics but also their real-time characteristics and parametric characteristics. Runtime verification analyzes programs or traces generated by programs, and the resulting behavioral states are compared to the behavioral state of the complete system is greatly reduced so that its complexity can be handled by model checking. Runtime verification, on the one hand, avoids the problem of incomplete verification of test methods; on the other hand, runtime verification introduces formal methods, which are more flexible and extensible in describing properties and monitoring programs. The distributed simulation system will generate a large amount of simulation event data. To verify the time series events, it is necessary to obtain data through sampling. How to sample events correctly and efficiently, and how to reduce the impact of sampling activities on the behavior of the system are the main research content of this paper.

For the runtime verification of software systems, there are some solutions. Jass [1] is a tool for runtime verification of Java programs using annotation and code generation technology for runtime verification. JavaMop [8] inherits the architecture of MOP and can use sequential logic, such as CFG, LTL, etc., to describe the program specification, generate monitoring code, and compile the program monitoring code together with the program implementation code, and realize runtime verification. The MaC (Monitoring and Checking) [13] system provides a guarantee for the correct operation of the program. It separates the operation specification from the operational implementation. The operation specification adopts a higher-level formal description, has nothing to do with programming, and is flexible and extensible. sex. The aspect programming technology and code generation technology used by Jass and JavaMop, and the byte code insertion technology adopted by Java-MaC have currently commonly used runtime verification technologies. In addition, there are tools such as Java PathExplorer [10], which are also based on the above three technologies. Runtime verification is based on statistical theory and is suitable for quantitative analysis and verification of the system. Runtime verification can verify blackbox systems and infinite-state systems. As long as the system can be run, this method can be used to detect; More flexibility and scalability in monitoring.

Runtime verification analyzes the program or the traces produced by the program. To verify the system events, it is necessary to study how to collect and describe the key event information of the distributed simulation system to verify the correctness of temporal properties of the simulation system; how to describe the event timing properties, and perform runtime verification; how to design a runtime verification tool for the distributed simulation systems.

2   Tool Architecture and Functionality

2.1   Tool Architecture

This paper proposes the overall technical route and scheme by investigating and studying the following contents: First, fully investigate the existing runtime verification tools and methods, compare their technical principles and functions, and select an open source tool library that can effectively support the research objectives of this paper by comparing the simulator temporal verification requirements. Second, the description language of the verification property is studied, which is used to express the finite event string, while satisfying the expression requirements of the emulator's temporal events and the monitor's sequence receiving requirements. Thirdly, the method of generating monitors based on model checking of automata theory is studied. Fourth, monitor/judge whether the limited event string violates the given property specification. If it violates, the monitor will give a corresponding warning and stop the monitoring process, otherwise continue to monitor. Based on the above survey results and methodological research conclusions, the overall architecture of the tool is shown in Fig. 1.

2.2   Instrumentation

The runtime verification system consists of two parts: the monitored simulation system and the monitor module. The running events of the system are captured and stored in the event log, where each event is a variable assignment, variable output, or function call.

In this paper, AOP (Aspect-Oriented Programming) code instrumentation technology is used to capture system running events. AOP implements individual concerns in a loosely coupled manner and then combines these implementations

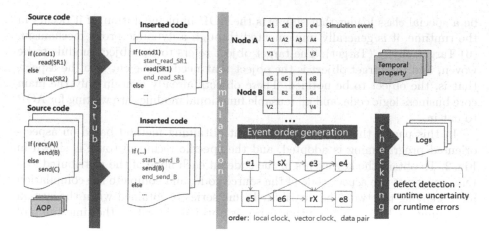

Fig. 1. Overall architecture and functionality

to build the final system. Systems built with it are loosely coupled. The relatively complete AOP tools mainly include AspectJ [12] on the java platform, while the current AOP tools on the C/C++ platform are mainly AspectC++ [9]. Use AspectC++ to "centrally" instrument logs for the system source code of the simulation platform without changing its source code structure. The important concepts of aspect-oriented programming include the following: (1) Aspect: Aspect refers to some code modules scattered in the system that can be reused, such as transaction processing module, logging module, authorization authentication modules, etc. (2) Joint Point: The joint point refers to the clear running node during the execution of the program. It is the node that can insert the aspect during the running process of the program and is generally the call of a method in the system. Common connection points include method invocation, exception throwing, field modification, etc. (3) Advice: Advice refers to the enhancement processing performed on a specific connection point. After the system intercepts the connection point, it is carried out according to the type of notification. Enhanced handling. Generally, notifications can be divided into five categories: before notification, post notification AfterReturning, exception notification AfterThrowing, final notification After, and surround notification. (4) PointCut: A pointcut is a connection point where enhanced processing can be inserted. When a connection point meets the execution requirements, the connection point will be processed by connection enhancement, and the connection point becomes a pointcut. (5) Weaving: The process of applying the aspect to the target object through the pointcut and causing the creation of the proxy object is called weaving. The process of applying the aspect to the target object to create a new proxy object. This process can occur in the compiler, class transfer period, and runtime. Different occurrence points have different implementations. If it occurs in the compiler, a special compiler that supports this AOP implementation is required. If it occurs in the class loading period, there needs to be a special class loader that supports the AOP implementation. If it occurs in the runtime, it is generally implemented through a dynamic proxy mechanism. (6) Target object (Target): The target object refers to the object module to be woven, and the target object is the object that needs to be cut into the aspect, that is, the object to be notified. These objects already contain only the main core business logic code, and all reusable functional modules are waiting for AOP to cut in.

In this paper, the system critical event obtaining method based on aspect-oriented programming is adopted, and the specific technical route is shown in Fig. 2. To obtain the key events in the code on each node of the distributed system, construct the aspect code of the source code, and complete the compilation after weaving the two. The distributed time series is obtained when the system is running, and the synthetic time series is obtained based on the timestamp of the event.

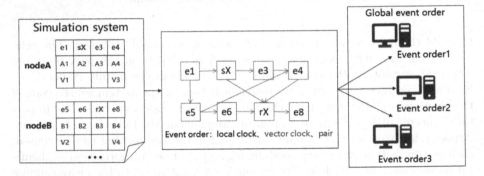

Fig. 2. Aspect-oriented programming-based method for obtaining key events in distributed systems

2.3   Temporal Property

In the simulation verification technology, the properties that the behavior of the simulation model should satisfy are generally described by the temporal property description language, and the monitor is also generated by the property description language. In this case, the simulation execution sequence, that is, whether the simulation trace is satisfied A given temporal property depends on the monitor execution sequence based on the current simulation behavior, as determined by monitor semantics. To more accurately describe the correctness of discrete-time simulation model behavior and event properties, this paper adopts linear temporal logic properties (LTL). The discrete behavioral properties of computer systems can be abstracted as LTL properties, so LTL is widely used in the modeling of computer systems. LTL uses the value of the semantic formula $\mu \models \phi$ to judge whether μ the execution sequence satisfies the given property

ϕ and the calculated value of the simulation trace μ is in $\{$ $\top$, $\bot$ $\}$. LTL is a temporal logic commonly used in model checking, using propositional logic operators "not" $\neg$, "and" $\wedge$, "or" $\vee$ condition "$\rightarrow$", and five temporal models. The state operators "ϕ is true when the next state occurs" ($X\phi$), "a certain state in the future ϕ is true" $F\phi$, "all future states ϕ is true" ($G\phi$), " until a certain state occurs ϕ remains true" $U\phi$, " ϕ remains true before a certain state occurs; if a certain state does not occur, ϕ remains true all the time" $R\phi$, expressing the temporal nature. For example, LTL describes the property G(request) $\rightarrow$ F(response), which means: that when the atomic proposition of the request is true, there will be a later instant (possibly simultaneously) in which the response is true.

2.4 Monitor Construction

The monitor module is constructed based on an automaton. After inverting the LTL properties, it is transformed into an automaton. Finally, it is checked whether the acceptance language of the system automaton is included in the accepted language of the property automaton. If so, the system has the properties described by the LTL formula; otherwise, it does not. Büchi is defined as follows:$A = (Q, \Sigma, \delta, q_0, F)$, where

1. Q is a finite set, and the elements in Q are called the states of A;
2. Σ is a finite set called the alphabet of A;
3. $\delta : Q \times \Sigma \rightarrow Q$ is called the state transition function of A;
4. q_0 belongs to Q and is the initial state of A;
5. $F \subseteq Q$ is the word acceptance condition.

Büchi automata must be infinite access to a certain acceptance state. In a Büchi automaton, there can be multiple accepting states, usually represented by double circles.

Limitations of Büchi automata in practical applications. Büchi automata are very suitable for monitoring system behavior, but due to the property of time in the operation of actual software systems, it is difficult to express the concept of "infinite word input" in a practical way. The way Büchi automata examine infinite word input is a theoretical model that cannot be directly applied to actual behavior monitoring. Therefore, this paper adopts Monitor automata in SPOT [7] library as the construction method of the monitor. A monitor is a special type of automaton, whose function is to read the time series generated when the system is running and complete the state transition according to the current time. The monitor detects an error when it cannot move, that is, the system has performed some action or reached a default state.

This monitor is used to check if yellow happens immediately after red. The monitor remains in its initial state until red becomes true. It can then wait in state 1 while red remains unchanged and yellow does not. When both red and yellow are false, return to the initial state. The only way this monitor can't run is if yellow becomes true in the second state, the monitor can't run. In this case, the violation should be reported.

Monitor automata and Büchi automata is that the former does not contain accepting states. The only sign that the Monitor has detected an error is that the automaton has stopped state transitions. The Monitor automaton is an optimization of the Büchi automaton, essentially transforming the Büchi automaton into a finite word-length automaton, which can accept all prefixes of the formula, and the monitor accepts every identified run.

In this paper, the Ltl2tgba tool in the SPOT tool set is used to automatically construct a Monitor-based monitor. The monitor construction tool automatically constructs the monitor automaton by parsing the LTL formula. The monitor is triggered by the characters of the execution sequence of the runtime system event. When the state cannot be correctly transited, it monitors that the execution of the running reduction system does not meet the requirements.

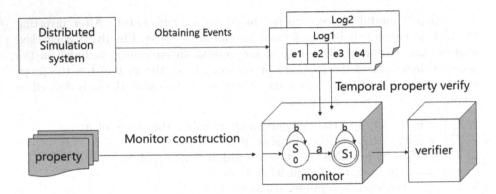

Fig. 3. Sequence property description and monitor construction method

2.5 Static Model Checking

This paper studies a monitor checking method based on static model checking. Its function is to read the time series generated when the system is running and complete the state transition according to the current time. The monitor detects an error when it cannot move, that is, the system has performed some action or reached a default state. Stop system operation or issue a warning at this time.

3   Tool Implementation

According to the requirement of runtime verification of simulation system, this work designs and implements the runtime verification tool TempoRV with temporal properties. The following mainly introduces the function realization of TempoRV and the operation method.

3.1   Tool Module

TempoRV software tool is shown in Fig. 4, including four main functional modules, namely, target property description module, event sequence obtaining module, monitor construction module, and temporal property verification module.

The target property description module expresses the time sequence properties that the user needs to verify with time sequence logic expressions and saves them in the XML configuration file. The properties concerned by the HLA distributed simulation system are divided into simulation application properties and simulation platform properties. Among them, the simulation application properties focus on the correctness of the temporal properties of the simulation application system, and the HLA simulation platform properties focus on the correctness of the temporal properties of the RTI time management module of the simulation running platform. All events with timestamps before the next point in time, and federation members cannot send new messages until the time advance is complete.

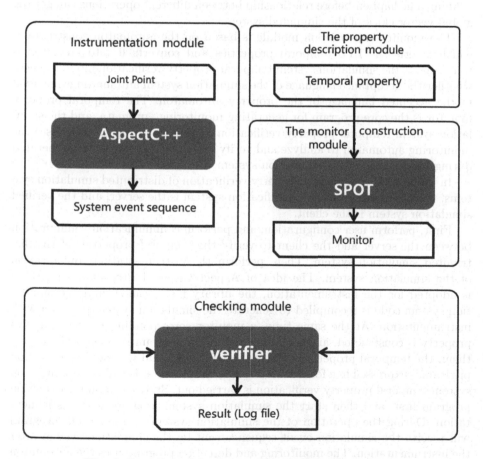

Fig. 4. Overall module design of TempoRV software tool

The event sequence obtaining module analyzes the source code of the simulation application and the simulation platform system locates the operation that generates the event and performs the instrumentation. During the simulation running process, the event request interception is adopted to identify and store the corresponding simulation event sequence. The information to be collected by instrumentation mainly includes the type of event, the prior time sequence relationship between events (on the same data transmission and reception), the local time when the event occurs, and the global vector time when the event occurs. Among them, the a priori temporal relationship between events needs to establish effective data annotation in the source code of the sender and receiver at the same time to establish a dual relationship; while the obtaining of the global vector time requires instrumentation to implement the vector clock protocol. The distributed simulation system is full of happen-before relationships. By analyzing the shared memory operation, thread creation operation, remote call creation operation, event en queue, and de queue operation, synchronization service update, and notification operation in the multi-thread simulation system, defining The happen-before relationship between different operations can get the global vector clock of the simulated system.

The monitor construction module is based on the automaton construction, which inverts the LTL temporal properties and converts it into an automaton. Finally, the simulation system temporal property verification module checks whether the acceptance language of the simulation system automaton is included in the accepted language of the property automaton. The temporal property monitor is the core program for generating monitoring automata, and the simulation system temporal property verification module is a program that uses the monitoring automaton to analyze and verify the simulation sequences generated during the running of the simulation system.

In the process of temporal property verification of distributed simulation systems, the distributed temporal verification system is the server, and the verified simulation system is the client.

First, perform user configuration, and perform communication configuration between the server and the client to verify the temporal properties of the distributed simulation system. Then, perform the instrumentation configuration of the simulation system. The idea of Aspect Oriented Programming (AOP) is adopted for the instrumentation, the library file is called, and the simulation system code is recompiled to generate the simulation system program with instrumentation. At the same time, a monitor corresponding to the temporal property is constructed, and a monitor detection program is generated. Among them, the temporal property is written in LTL logic, and the monitor detection program is expressed in a form similar to Büchi automata. Finally, the simulation system temporal property verification is carried out. Start the monitor detection program first, and then start the simulation system program with instrumentation. During the operation of the simulation system, the detection program will receive the simulation event sequence sent by the simulation system after the instrumentation. The monitoring and detection program uses the automaton checking algorithm to verify whether the simulation event sequence satisfies the temporal properties expressed by the automaton. Then continue to receive the next cycle of the simulation event sequence for verification, otherwise, send an error signal to the simulation system and generate an error log.

3.2 Application Process

In the process of temporal property verification of distributed simulation systems, the distributed temporal verification system is the server, and the verified simulation system is the client.

The first step is to write the user configuration file and to perform the communication configuration and log configuration of the server and the client for the time series property verification of the distributed simulation system. First, configure the server communication IP and port, and then set the log file. In this system, the log file is divided into a simulation event log file and a simulation temporal error log file. The simulation event log file records the simulation event sequence generated by instrumentation during the simulation process, which is a simulation event that needs attention in the simulation process; simulation error A file is a simulation event used to record an error in the simulation after the monitor finds an error.

The second step is to perform the instrumentation configuration of the simulation system, and the instrumentation adopts the idea of Aspect Oriented Programming (AOP). The simulation system uses the C++ language, so the AspectC++ library is used to generate the simulation event log. You need to call the aspect.hh file and write the .ah instrumentation file. First, call the aspect.hh file, the aspect.hh file the packed file. into the simulation system. Then, write the instrumentation statements in the .ah file. Set the instrumentation point and write the instrumentation function at the same time. Set the generated simulation event log format in the instrumentation function. Next, write the calling communication library in the instrumentation function, write the communication statement, and send the generated formatted simulation log to the monitor for detection. Finally, recompile the simulation system code, aspect.hh file and .ah file to generate the simulation system program with instrumentation.

The third step is to construct a monitor corresponding to the temporal property and generate a monitor detection program. Among them, the temporal property is written in LTL logic, and the monitor detection program is expressed in a form similar to Büchi automata. First, enter the LTL formula. In the configuration file, turn on the switch for inputting the formula and input the LTL formula. Then, call the automaton generation library to generate the monitor. The monitor is similar to the Büchi automaton, using the HOA format to represent the state and transition of the automaton, and at the same time, it can generate the automaton image file.

The fourth step is to carry out the verification of the temporal properties of the simulation system. Start the monitor detection program first, and then start the simulation system program with instrumentation. During the running process of the simulation system, the detection program will receive the simulation event sequence sent by the simulation system after the instrumentation, and the monitoring and detection program uses the automaton checking algorithm to verify whether the simulation event sequence meets the temporal properties expressed by the automaton. If so, it will continue to receive the next cycle of simulation event sequence for verification, and will display the words "Accept!" If an error is detected, the monitoring and detection program will display the error message on the terminal, generate a separate simulation error log file, and feedback the detected simulation error to the simulation system through a message, and the simulation system will respond accordingly.

4   Case Study

Digital simulators of The weapon system can run in the HLA distributed simulation platform. The weapon system digital simulators constitute command and control simulators, radar detection simulators, and launch vehicle simulators. The weapon system starts the combat process after being instructed by the target. The distributed simulator can obtain the initialization files issued by the simulation platform, complete the binding of the initialization parameters of the simulator, and can obtain the target scene data from the target simulator and the dynamic target scene simulator. In the simulation, the simulator sends key data generated in the process. The simulation platform supports the data recording and visual display and performs replays based on the recorded data. Here, is just a simple demonstration of the functions of the TempoRV tool. The simulation process and temporal verification properties do not reflect the true system, which will not be discussed here.

First, instrument the target system, that is, the digital simulator of the weapon system, and use the aspect-oriented programming tool AspectC++ to instrument the target system, to extract the simulation event information we are concerned about during the system running.

Then, you need to install the Zeromq [15] library in the target environment, and at the same time, put the aspect.hh file into the simulation system. Write instrumentation statements in the .ah file. Set the instrumentation point and write the instrumentation function at the same time. Set the generated simulation event log format in the instrumentation function. Next, write and call the communication library zeromq in the instrumentation function, write the communication statement, and send the generated formatted simulation log to the monitor for detection. Recompile the simulation system code, and aspect.hh file and .ah file to generate the simulation system program with instrumentation.

Next, we define the simulation timing constraints of our concern and generate the corresponding monitor detection program. Among them, the temporal property is written in LTL logic, and the monitor detection program is expressed in a form similar to Büchi automata.

1) Event2 can only be performed after the event Event1 is completed. Therefore, in the LTL language, the description is "G (Event $1 \rightarrow X$ Event2)". Run the program to generate the monitoring automaton.
2) Event3 can only be performed after Event2 is completed and Event2 will not be repeated. The above timing constraints are described in LTL language as "G (Event $2 \rightarrow X$ (Event3 $\wedge$! Event 2))" to run the program to generate a monitoring automaton.
3) Event4 can only be performed after the event Event3 is completed. Expressed in LTL language as "G (Event $3 \rightarrow X$ Event 4)" run the program to generate the monitoring automaton.
4) After Event5 is completed, Event1, Event2, Event3, and Event4 are no longer executed repeatedly. Expressed in LTL language as "G (Event $5 \rightarrow X$ (!Event 1 $\parallel$! Event 2 $\parallel$! Event 3 $\parallel$! Event 4))" Run the program to generate the monitoring automaton.

Synthesize the above automaton to generate a monitoring program. The synthesized monitoring automaton is shown in Fig. 5.

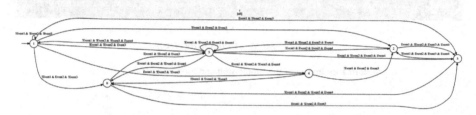

Fig. 5. Monitor automata of synthesizing property

Finally, temporal property verification of the simulation system is carried out. Start the monitor detection program first, and then start the simulation system program with instrumentation. During the running process of the simulation system, the detection program will receive the simulation event sequence sent by the simulation system after the instrumentation, and the monitoring and detection program uses the automaton checking algorithm to verify whether the simulation event sequence meets the timing properties expressed by the automaton. If it is satisfied, it will continue to receive the next cycle of simulation event sequence for verification, and will display the words "Accept!"

If an error is detected, the monitoring and detection program will display the error message on the terminal, generate a separate simulation error log file, and feedback the detected simulation error to the simulation system through a message, and the simulation system will respond accordingly.

The simulation runtime impact, shown in Fig. 8, after the running verification tool TempoRV is as follows.

After simple instrumentation, it has almost no effect on the operation of the simulation system under test, because the instrumentation does not bring a relatively large amount of calculation.

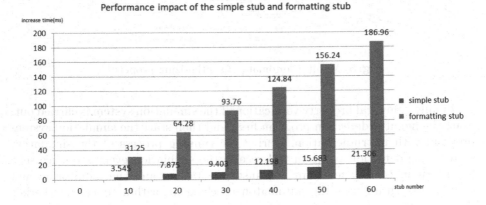

Fig. 6. Display of the checking process

Fig. 7. Display of checking error

Performance impact of the simple stub and formatting stub

Fig. 8. Impact of the stub on simulation time

5 Conclusion

This paper introduces a runtime verification tool TempoRV, which can guarantee
the temporal correctness of distributed simulation systems. This tool supports
the obtaining and synthesis of the simulation system event sequences, the system temporal formal description based on linear temporal logic, and temporal
property verification of the simulation system. It can effectively improve the
simulation system's temporal correctness and reliability. There is some work to

do with balancing detection cost and reliability. In general, there are impacts of instrumentation and global sequence synthesis on the runtime of the simulation system. With this, strategy optimization research can be carried out to improve the runtime verification method as a whole, so that it can optimally consider the cost-effectiveness of runtime verification.

References

1. Bartezko, D.: JASS-JAVA with assertions. ENTCS **55**(2), 103–117 (2001)
2. Bauer, A., Leucker, M., Schallhart, C.: Runtime verification for LTL and TLTL. ACM Trans. Softw. Eng. Methodol. **20**(4), 14 (2011)
3. Cimatti, A., Clarke, E., Giunchiglia, E., Giunchiglia, F., Pistore, M., Roveri, M., Sebastiani, R., Tacchella, A.: NuSMV 2: an opensource tool for symbolic model checking. In: Brinksma, E., Larsen, K.G. (eds.) CAV 2002. LNCS, vol. 2404, pp. 359–364. Springer, Heidelberg (2002). https://doi.org/10.1007/3-540-45657-0_29
4. Clarke, E.M.: Automatic verification of finite-state concurrent systems using temporal logic specifications. ACM Trans. Prog. Lang. Syst. **8**, 244–263 (1986)
5. Clarke, E.M.: Model checking – my 27-year quest to overcome the state explosion problem. In: Cervesato, I., Veith, H., Voronkov, A. (eds.) LPAR 2008. LNCS (LNAI), vol. 5330, pp. 182–182. Springer, Heidelberg (2008). https://doi.org/10.1007/978-3-540-89439-1_13
6. Dahmann, J.S., Fujimoto, R.M., Weatherly, R.M.: The Department of Defense High Level Architecture. The Department Of Defense High Level (1997)
7. Duret-Lutz, A.: Manipulating LTL formulas using spot 1.0. In: Van Hung, D., Ogawa, M. (eds.) ATVA 2013. LNCS, vol. 8172, pp. 442–445. Springer, Cham (2013). https://doi.org/10.1007/978-3-319-02444-8_31
8. Feng, C., Rosu, G.: JAVA-MOP: a monitoring oriented programming environment for java. In: Tools and Algorithms for the Construction and Analysis of Systems, 11th International Conference, TACAS 2005, Held as Part of the Joint European Conferences on Theory and Practice of Software, ETAPS 2005, Edinburgh, UK, 4–8 April 2005, Proceedings (2005)
9. Gal, A., Schrsder-Preikschat, W.: Aspectc++: An aspect-oriented extension to the c++ programming language. In: International Conference on Tools Pacific (2008)
10. Havelund, K., Rosu, G.: Monitoring java programs with java path explorer. Electron. Notes Theoret. Comput. Sci. **55**(2), 200–217 (2001)
11. He, X.: Simulation and verification in high-performance computing for cluster distributed doubly fed induction generators in the horizon of ecological marxism - sciencedirect. Energy Reports (2021)
12. Kiczales, G., Hilsdale, E., Hugunin, J., Kersten, M., Palm, J., Griswold, W.G.: an overview of AspectJ. In: Knudsen, J.L. (ed.) ECOOP 2001. LNCS, vol. 2072, pp. 327–354. Springer, Heidelberg (2001). https://doi.org/10.1007/3-540-45337-7_18
13. Kim, M.Z., Viswanathan, M., Kannan, S., Lee, I., Sokolsky, O.: JAVA-MAC̄: a run-time assurance approach for java programs. Formal Methods Syst. Des. **24**(2), 129–155 (2004)
14. Kurshan, R.P.: Model checking and abstraction. DBLP (2002)
15. Pu, F., Chen, J.: Distributed system based on zeromq. Electronic Test (2012)
16. Wing, J.M.: What is a formal method (1989)
17. Yang, H., Kang, F., Ma, Y., Cai, B.: A formal verification method for high level architecture (HLA) federation based on temporal logic. J. Northwestern Polytechnical University (2005)

Author Index